Ever seen a molecule from the inside? Grab your chance at Brussels' landmark Atomium (p89)

Maison Cauchie (p93) is one of Brussels' most beautiful Art Nouveau buildings

Check out the two distinct sides of Bruges' Heilig-Bloedbasiliek (p124)

Countryside

Paardevissers (horseback fishermen) trawl for shrimp in Oostduinkerke (p147)

The medieval castle (p283) in Vianden will bring tales of knights and princesses to life

Put on your hiking boots in Hautes Fagnes (p259)

Contents

The Authors 11

Getting Started 12

Itineraries 15

Belgium 19

Belgium Snapshot 21

History 22

The Culture 29

Environment 41

Mmmm...Beer 45

Food & Drink 52

Brussels 65

History	66
Orientation	66
Information	67
Sights	69
Activities	90
Walking Tour	92
Brussels for Children	93
Bizarre Brussels	94
Tours	95
Festivals & Events	95
Sleeping	97
Eating	101
Drinking	106
Entertainment	107
Shopping	112
Getting There & Away	115
Getting Around	116
AROUND BRUSSELS	117
Forêt de Soignes	117
Nationale Plantentuin van België	117

Western Flanders 119

Bruges	120
Damme	139

Ostend	140
Northeast Coast	145
Southwest Coast	147
Veurne	149
Around Veurne	150
Ypres	150
Around Ypres	153
Poperinge	156
Kortrijk	157
Oudenaarde	160
Ghent	160
St Martens-Latem	169

Eastern Flanders 170

Antwerp	171
Around Antwerp	199
Lier	199
Mechelen	201
Around Mechelen	204
Leuven	205
Around Leuven	209
Diest	209
Hasselt	210
Around Hasselt	212
Tongeren	213
Zoutleeuw	216

Hainaut & Brabant-Wallon 217

Tournai	218
Around Tournai	221
Mons	221
Around Mons	222
Nivelles	223
Waterloo	224
Villers-la-Ville	225
Charleroi	226
Botte de Hainaut	227

The Ardennes 229

Namur	231
Around Namur	235
Dinant	236
Around Dinant	237
Rochefort	238
Around Rochefort	239
Redu	240
Around Redu	240
St Hubert	240
Bouillon	241

Around Bouillon 243
Orval 243
Arlon 244
Bastogne 244
La Roche-en-Ardenne 245
Around La Roche 248
Durbuy 248
Around Durbuy 249
Liège 249
Spa 254
Stavelot 257
Coo 258
Malmédy 258
Hautes Fagnes 259
Verviers 261
Eupen 262

Luxembourg **265**

Luxembourg Snapshot **266**

Luxembourg City **268**
History 269
Orientation 269
Information 269
Sights 271
Activities 274

Walking Tour 275
Luxembourg City for Children 276
Tours 276
Festivals & Events 276
Sleeping 276
Eating 278
Drinking 279
Entertainment 279
Shopping 280
Getting There & Away 281
Getting Around 281

Around the Grand Duchy **282**
LUXEMBOURG ARDENNES 283
Vianden 283
Esch-sur-Sûre 285
Around Esch-sur-Sûre 286
Wiltz 286
Clervaux 287
GUTLAND 288
Vallée des Sept Châteaux 288
Ettelbrück 288
Diekirch 289
MÜLLERTHAL 290
Echternach 290
Around Echternach 292
Larochette 292

MOSELLE VALLEY 293
Remich 293
Around Remich 294
Ehnen 294
Wormeldange 294
Grevenmacher 294
THE SOUTHWEST 295
Esch-sur-Alzette 295
Around Esch-sur-Alzette 296

Directory **297**

Transport **314**

Health **326**

Language **329**

Glossary **337**

Behind the Scenes **339**

Index **343**

World Time Zones **350**

Map Legend **352**

Regional Map Contents

WESTERN FLANDERS (p121)
EASTERN FLANDERS (p172)
BRUSSELS (p70)
HAINAUT & BRABANT-WALLON (p218)
THE ARDENNES (p230)
AROUND THE GRAND DUCHY (p284)
LUXEMBOURG CITY (p270)

The Authors

LEANNE LOGAN

Leanne first tasted Belgium and Luxembourg as a kid in the '70s. Six months of diary writing while cooped up with her family in a campervan around Europe set life's direction. After university came newspapers then a long-awaited one-way ticket out of Australia. Years of exploring different cultures led naturally to Lonely Planet. And if that wasn't prize enough, day one of researching Belgium led her to Geert, a beer-guzzling, chip-loving chap from Antwerp. More than 15 years later, the pair still covers Belgium and Luxembourg, these days with two kids, Eleonor and Gwynevere, in tow. When not on the road, the family nestles down in Barkers Vale in beautiful northern New South Wales, Australia.

GEERT COLE

Geert was your atypical Belgian from the start. As a youngster he liked Brussels sprouts, as a teenager he hated fashion and as an adult he pulled the pin...travelling all over the world instead of building a little red-brick house. But years on the road led to a disturbing discovery – nowhere on earth is founded on beer, chips and chocolate except Belgium. So he returned to his stained-glass studio in home-town Antwerp and, as things would have it, met the love of his life, Leanne. Geert now divides his time between watching wallabies in Australia, the joys of fatherhood and Lonely Planet. The latter satisfies his fix for all things essentially Belgian.

Our Favourite Trip

We've road-tested more Belgian chocolates and beers than is fair in anyone's lifetime, but touring Belgium and Luxembourg as a family was our best trip ever. Travelling with kids reveals a whole new world. With or without munchkins, a week in Bruges (p120) was mandatory – there's so much to see and do within a steeple's fall of this medieval town. Lazy days at Ostend beach (p140) were followed by groovy Ghent (p160), surprising Mechelen (p201) and historic Brussels (p65): read canal rides, zoos, puppet shows and circuses. The Ardennes' calmness called us to La Roche-en-Ardenne (p245), good for kayaking and nearby caves. Luxembourg awaited with chairlifts (Vianden, p283), forest walks (Müllerthal, p290) and dreamy nights in medieval towers (Echternach, p291). Thumbs up to childhood revisited.

Getting Started

There's nothing quite like daydreaming about chocolate shops fit for royalty, linger-as-long-as-you-like *cafés*, and beer menus that simply go on and on and on. But to loose your head in the clouds and arrive in Belgium and Luxembourg with no preparation is inviting challenges. With a good plan, you'll know whether it's your French, German or Flemish that needs brushing up, whether you should you go by train or plane, and where to find discounted accommodation.

WHEN TO GO

There's a reason radio DJs in Belgium love the Beatles' 1969 classic 'Here Comes the Sun'. The weather here is fickle, and when the sun comes out everyone celebrates. To avoid major dampness coupled with biting cold, plan a visit for May to September (late spring to early autumn). For hiking and outdoor pursuits in the Ardennes and Luxembourg, these are certainly the months to go. The disadvantages of this time include considerable crowds at tourist sights in a few places and, depending on where you go, a scarcity of accommodation – Bruges is the most problematic in both these areas. Brussels, on the other hand, is quieter from mid-July to mid-September and, because of this, some hotels cut prices. Discounting is also common on weekends (p98).

See Climate Charts (p305) for more information.

The mild winter conditions from November to March usually mean grey, wet days with occasional light snow. Pack the right clothes and you can take advantage of uncrowded museums and plenty of cosy *cafés*.

As a weekend break Brussels, Antwerp, Bruges, Ghent, Ostend or Leuven are all perfect, and all easily accessible from London on the soon-to-be-even-faster Eurostar (see boxed text, p319) or from other neighbouring countries using the Thalys fast train network (see boxed text, p318). If you can tack on an extra day to your trip, choose Friday not Monday, as many museums in these cities close on Monday, and shops often take Monday mornings off.

You might want to time your trip for a local celebration – use the list on the next page as an initial guide. Both countries are big on festivals (p307), but the lion's share of events take place over summer.

DON'T LEAVE HOME WITHOUT...

- Photocopying important documents – leave one copy at home and take another with you.
- An umbrella – in an average summer it'll hardly dry off.
- An extra jumper for when summer temperatures plunge (p305).
- Your sweet tooth – it's praline paradise (p54).
- An airsick bag – it may be necessary after eating *filet américain* (p58).
- A small change purse to ward off zealous toilet sentinels (p311).
- Nerves of steel – you'll need them on the road (p323).
- A credit card for avant-garde fashions (p114; p197).
- Your favourite hangover cure (p45).
- A sense of humour – necessary when dried herrings are flapped in your face at carnival (p223).

TOP TENS

Festivals & Events
Choose from fun and festivities throughout the year. For more on festivals, see p307.

- Carnival, around February (p223)
- Brussels Jazz Marathon, May (p96)
- La Doudou, May/June (p222)
- KunstenFESTIVALdesArts, May (p96)
- Kroningsfeesten, July 2009 (p215)
- Couleur Café, June (p96)
- Luxembourg National Day, 23 June (p307)
- De Gentse Feesten, mid-July (p165)
- Ommegang, June to July (p96)
- Tapis des Fleurs, August (p97)

Paintings
From primitive passions to Rubens' nudes and surrealists at play, Belgium has a superb artistic heritage.

- *The Adoration of the Mystic Lamb,* Van Eyck (St Baafskathedraal, p161)
- *Secret Player,* Magritte (Musées Royaux des Beaux-Arts, p83)
- *Masks Fighting over a Hanged Man,* Ensor (Koninklijk Museum voor Schone Kunsten, p183)
- *Mystic Marriage of St Catherine,* Memling (Museum St Janshospitaal, p128)
- *The Descent from the Cross,* Rubens (Onze Lieve Vrouwekathedraal, p179)
- *Fall of Icarus,* Breugel the Elder (Musées Royaux des Beaux-Arts, p83)
- *Proverbs,* Breughel the Younger (Rockoxhuis, p180)
- *Sérénité,* Delvaux (Groeningemuseum, p127)
- *Portrait of Maarten Pepijn,* Van Dyck (Koninklijk Museum voor Schone Kunsten, p183)
- *The Three Nights,* Pierre Alechinsky (Groeningemuseum, p127)

Architectural gems
Belgium is full of architectural treasures, including glistening guildhalls, tranquil almshouses and Art Nouveau jewels.

- Grand Place (p69), Brussels
- Begijnhof (p128), Bruges
- Galeries St Hubert (p112), Brussels
- Musée Horta (p87), Brussels
- Cogels-Osylei (p184), Antwerp
- Old England Building (p83), Brussels
- Onze Lieve Vrouwekathedraal (p179), Antwerp
- Stadhuis (p124), Bruges
- Belfort (p124), Bruges
- Zuiderterras (p193), Antwerp

COSTS & MONEY

Belgium is, on average, slightly cheaper than Luxembourg, except for fuel and bulk purchases of cigarettes and alcohol. In both countries, accommodation and dining will burn the biggest hole in your pocket; though Belgium's exciting fashions, sublime chocolates and speciality beers can all seriously dent the credit card too. Public transport, on the other hand, is cheap – and that, coupled with the diminutive size of both countries, makes getting around a minor expense.

Those staying in hostels, doing a museum, filling up with fast fodder like *frites* (chips or fries) and baguettes and downing a good beer or two can expect to spend from €40 per day. Those opting for hotels with full amenities and midrange restaurants will pay from €120. B&Bs offer excellent value, as do those weekend discounts (p98).

Families can minimise expenses by staying at hostels, B&Bs or self-contained guesthouses (p299). Restaurants often have discounted children's meals, usually costing around €8. Also look out for the occasional restaurant offering complimentary children's meals. Keep in mind too that children under 12 travel for free on Belgian trains.

TRAVEL LITERATURE

Few foreigners have taken up the challenge of penning travel tales about Belgium…and only one man has tackled Luxembourg. Still, what's on offer is well worth reading.

A Tall Man in a Low Land (Harry Pearson) This tale of family travel in Belgium came out a decade ago and is still a hit among visitors. It's full of anecdotes of everyday life, and firmly shines the spotlight on the country's many idiosyncrasies.

Luxembourg & the Jenisch Connection (David Robinson) Fictional tale of an Englishman's holiday in Luxembourg that turns into a murder mystery. It's set during the record-breaking hot summer of 2003.

Neither Here nor There (Bill Bryson) The author's European sojourn took him via Belgium with the result that Brussels and the country as a whole receive detailed scrutiny in two fun-filled chapters.

The Factory of Facts (Luc Sante) Belgian-born but US-raised, Luc Sante returns at the age of 35 to explore the country he left behind. An interesting account of his thoughts and opinions on all things Belgian.

The Poisonwood Bible (Barbara Kingsolver) This excellent novel tells the tale of an American missionary family living in 1950s Belgian Congo.

INTERNET RESOURCES

The internet is a rich resource for travellers. Research your trip, hunt down bargain air fares, book hotels, check weather conditions or chat with locals and other travellers about the best places to visit (or avoid!).

Belgian Tourist Office (www.visitbelgium.com) The Belgian Tourist Office's excellent US site includes listings of events and general information on the country.

Belgium online in English (www.xpats.com) Belgium's international community provide lots of information, including local news in English and an entertainment agenda, to get travellers started.

Lonely Planet (www.lonelyplanet.com) Here you'll find succinct summaries on travelling to most places on earth, postcards from other travellers, the best beds to book and the Thorn Tree travel forum, where you can ask questions before you go or dispense advice when you get back.

Luxembourg Internet Directory (www.luxweb.lu) Good links to almost all Luxembourg-related websites.

Luxembourg National Tourist Office (www.ont.lu) Great for the local lowdown.

HOW MUCH?

Belgium

Midrange hotel double €70-140

Baguette sandwich €3

Kilo of pralines €30-58

Cinema ticket €6

Bike hire per day €10

Luxembourg

Midrange hotel double €70-140

Baguette sandwich €3.50

Bottle of sparkling wine €7-15

Cinema ticket €7

Bike hire per day €15-20

LONELY PLANET INDEX

Belgium

Litre of petrol €1.40

Litre of bottled water €0.80

Bottle of Trappist beer €3.50

Souvenir T-shirt €13

Street snack – frites €2.10

Luxembourg

Litre of petrol €1.15

Litre of bottled water €0.75

Bottle of Bofferding beer €2.50

Souvenir T-shirt €15

Street snack - croissant €1.80

Itineraries

CLASSIC ROUTES

FULL-ON FLANDERS
One Week / Brussels to Ostend

Brussels, Antwerp, Ghent, Bruges and Ostend. Five cities in as many days.
No way you say. But it can be *comfortably* done – thanks to proximity:
Antwerp is just 35 minutes from Brussels, Ghent 45 minutes from Antwerp,
and so on.

Start with two nights in **Brussels** (p65), Europe's capital. Sip the splendour
of the **Grand Place** (p69), one of the world's most beautiful squares, before
heading uptown to the Sablon's seductive **chocolate shops** (p113) and an Art
Nouveau jewel, the **Old England building** (p83). If you're only here for the beer,
look out (p107).

Next up is **Antwerp** (p171). This eclectic port city deserves two nights,
longer if you're into restaurants, *cafés* (pubs/bars) and designer fashions.
Follow on with **Ghent** (p160), an intimate medieval city that's recently awoken
to its inherent charms. Beautiful **Bruges** (p120) mustn't be missed. This
picture-postcard city is Belgium's most romantic getaway, though you may
need to time things to avoid the crowds. From here it's an easy day trip to
Ostend (p140), Belgium's best-known beach resort with superb seafood.

This grand tour of
Flanders' historic
art cities takes in
Belgium's best –
Brussels, Antwerp,
Ghent and Bruges –
with a side trip
to Ostend, should
you so desire. The
route is a neat
185km and, thanks
to these towns'
intimate proximity,
can be covered in
anywhere from a
week to a month.

THE ESSENTIALS   Two Weeks / Bruges to Vianden

Touring the length and, in parts, breadth of Belgium and Luxembourg is possible if you have a fortnight up your sleeve. Follow the one-week itinerary, but start in Bruges instead of Brussels, and add in **Ypres** (p150) and nearby **Poperinge** (p156). On the frontline in WWI, these little towns hold poignant reminders of life in this corner of Belgium nearly a century ago, and the terrible toll of war.

After Brussels, move onto the Ardennes, Belgium's southern reaches, a world away from the historic art cities to the north. **Namur** (p231) is the gateway and a good overnight stop in order to see the Gothic horde at the tiny **Trésor du Prieuré d'Oignies** (p232). From here head to either **La Roche-en-Ardenne** (p245) to explore smoked hams and little-visited centuries' old **limestone caves** (p248) at nearby Hotton; **Rochefort** (p238) for some easy biking; or **Bouillon** (p241) to combine creepy castles and kayaks. En route to Luxembourg, detour via the **Abbaye Notre Dame d'Orval** (p243) – the closest you'll get to the inside of a Trappist brewery.

Two days in **Luxembourg City** (p268) is ample time to explore the Grand Duchy's captivating capital. Take in **Place d'Armes** (p275), the new **Musée d'Art Moderne Grand-Duc Jean** (p273) and the beautiful **Chemin de la Corniche** (p275). Definitely book dinner at **Breedewee** (p278) – this Corniche eatery has unbeatable views.

Spend your last two days in **Echternach** (p290) and **Vianden** (p283), two small towns in the Grand Duchy's forested north. The latter is Luxembourg's most visited town, crowned by a hilltop castle. The former is steeped in Christian history and is a positively delightful little place to kick back. From Echternach there are fascinating walks in the weird world of the Müllerthal.

The essential two-week, 625km tour of Belgium and Luxembourg. Start with Bruges, Ostend and the battlefields of Ypres, before moving on to Ghent, Antwerp and Brussels. Explore castles and the serenity of the hilly Ardennes, then head to Luxembourg where the Grand Duchy's intimate capital and intriguing countryside await.

ROADS LESS TRAVELLED

CYCLING WESTERN FLANDERS   Two Weeks / Ghent to Ostend

This cycling tour takes in the oft-overlooked western corner of Flanders. It holds eclectic attractions – historic art towns, bizarre breweries, WWI reminders and the coast – all wonderfully accessible by bike. If you intend picking up wheels in Belgium, good bike outlets include Mobiel (p160), Fietsen Popelier (p130) and Biker (see p169). For general cycling information, see p300.

Start in **Ghent** (p160), a city with as many attractions as Antwerp or Bruges, and a fab range of B&Bs. After Ghent, head south on the LF30 Scheldedelta-route cycle route, following the Scheldt River to **Oudenaarde** (30km; p160), famed for its tapestries. Next day, continue south and take up a section of the **Flanders Cycle Route** (p301) to the effervescent town of **Kortrijk** (35km; p157). The next leg, Kortrijk to **Ypres** (47km; p150) follows the banks of the Leie River before arriving in Ypres with its WWI memorials and the **Ypres Salient** (p153). Ypres to **Diksmuide** (55km; p150) goes via the WWI and hops town of **Poperinge** (p156) and the monastery of **Westvleteren** (p150) with its famous but elusive **Trappist beer** (p47). **De Dolle Brouwers** (p50), a zany brewery at Esen, shouldn't be missed either. Diksmuide to **Veurne** (20km; p149) is an easy cycle, and in Veurne you can stay in a gorgeous hotel (see boxed text, p150). Veurne to **St Idesbald** (10km; p148) brings you to the coast via **De Panne** (p148) and the **Paul Delvaux Museum** (p148). Providing the North Sea winds are not gusting, St Idesbald to **Ostend** (30km; p140) is also a gentle cycle, and once in Ostend you can indulge in seafood delights – don't wimp on the *wollekes* (sea snails; p143).

Saddle up and hit the bike ways of Western Flanders in this 225km two-week cycle tour that takes in lesser-known as well as well-trodden parts of Belgium. From shy Ghent to the calm coast, this tour reveals old tapestry towns, poignant WWI sights, kooky breweries and surrealist art, together with some excellent places to stay.

TAILORED TRIPS

BELGIUM & LUXEMBOURG FOR KIDS

Belgium is dotted with fab theme parks, has excellent child-oriented museums, a sandy coastline that little kids love, plenty of cycling possibilities, easy nature excursions, annual fairs with attractions galore, circuses with live animals (they haven't fallen out of fashion here) and, on an everyday level, a load of high-quality playgrounds. For details on what's available, see p304.

One suggestion is to drop anchor for a week in **Bruges** (p120). Rent a self-contained guesthouse (p133) to keep expenses down, and hang up the car keys – there's so much to see and do that's easily accessible by train (kids under twelve are free). Within half an hour you'll be curling your toes in the sand at **Ostend** (p140). From Ostend catch the **Kusttram** (p145) north and get off at any beach stop along the way, or go south to a quintessential Belgian theme park, **Plopsaland** (p148) near De Panne. With good timing you may even catch the *paardevissers* (horsefishers) at **Oostduinkerke** (p147).

An alternative Belgian base for families travelling by car is **Ruttermolen** (p215), a self-contained B&B near Tongeren. From here, **Bokrijk Openluchtmuseum** (p212), **Plopsa Indoor** (p211) and **Het Land Van Ooit** (p214) are on the doorstep.

In the Grand Duchy, relax for a week in a medieval tower in **Echternach** (p291) and day-trip it to anywhere in Luxembourg.

WORLD HERITAGE SITES TOUR

Exploring Belgium and Luxembourg by World Heritage sites is a breeze.

Start with **Luxembourg City** (p268) – the entire ancient core of this dramatic city is on Unesco's hit list. Follow up with the 'Family of Man' exhibition in **Clervaux** (p287).

In Belgium, the charming town of **Diest** (p209) hosts the nation's most beautiful *begijnhof* (a cluster of cottages around a central garden; see p129). In **Kortrijk** (p159) it's even possible to overnight in one of these historic sites.

Brussels (p65) beckons with the amazing **Grand Place** (p69) and the **Musée Horta** (p87), the home of Art Nouveau master Victor Horta. **Bruges** (p120) is another must – this medieval city's whole historic centre is preserved. Next up there's **Ghent** (p160), whose belfry offers fab city views and, like many belfries in Belgium, has made the list.

But to really immerse yourself, take a look at a little corner of Wallonia. There's the Cathédrale Notre Dame in **Tournai** (p219), a huge Romanesque affair that is slowly being realigned after a freak storm a decade ago. In **Mons** (p221), an international committee recently voted to include the city's **La Doudou** (p222) festival on Unesco's list of intangible world heritage. Also proud of this status are the bizarre **Gilles** (p223) from nearby Binche. And not far away in the town of **Ath** (p222), giants are also listed.

Belgium

Belgium

Belgium Snapshot

At long last Belgium, it seems, has come of age. This little country recently celebrated its 175th anniversary of independence and, following several years of big, bold moves to shake off a mousy image, life is now on a pretty even keel. Sure, there are ups (tennis greats, p32) and downs (don't mention the Red Devils, p32, or national debt), but most Belgians are more than happy with their spot in the world, and wouldn't change it for quids (see p29).

On the moral freedom front, Belgium is a world leader. Much has been done recently to grant gays and lesbians equal rights to heterosexuals (see p308). Euthanasia was legalised in 2002, though recent proposals to broaden the laws to include adolescents and dementia sufferers are being fought by religious leaders.

Plenty of other subjects are hotly debated over a Duvel or two, not least the 2007 federal election, which may see Prime Minister Guy Verhofstadt returned for a third term. If the results of 2006's municipal elections are any indication, however, Verhofstadt's Vlaamse Liberalen en Democraten (VLD) party, plagued by infighting during the last few years, should be worried. So, too, should the Green parties, whose support has plummeted recently due to the major parties incorporating environmental issues into their own platforms.

Many are also discussing the future of ultraright-wing party, Vlaams Belang (VB). VB leader Filip Dewinter failed in his bid to become Antwerp's burgomaster during the municipal elections; for more, see p32.

The vexed question of separatism – should Flanders go it alone? – forever simmers under the surface (see p31). It reignited recently when a controversial manifesto setting out why Belgium should split in two was made public. Put together and endorsed by movers and shakers in Flanders, the manifesto was quickly quashed by King Albert during his 2006 New Year's speech. But his criticism of Flemish separatism went down badly in parts, and calls for the king to be stripped of most of his powers ensued.

This state of play is relatively new to Belgium's monarchy which, for the most part, enjoys broad public approval. Disenchantment grew in 2006, however, when heir to the throne Prince Philippe led a trade mission to South Africa, after which the Flemish press criticised his so-called ineffective conduct. For more on the monarchy, see p91.

On the street, security is once again a public issue following the stabbing in early 2006 of 17-year-old Joe Van Holsbeeck, who was killed for his MP3 player during peak-hour in Brussels' Central Station. Some 80,000 people marched through Brussels in memory of the young man and to put pressure on the government to curb street violence. The march was the biggest since the White March a decade earlier, when 300,000 people took to the streets to commemorate the victims of paedophile Marc Dutroux (who is serving a life sentence for the rape and murder of several young girls).

Other challenges facing Belgium, like many Western European countries, include an ageing population, affordability of social security, integration of migrant workers, the issue of asylum seekers and sustainable development.

FAST FACTS

Population: 10.5 million

Area: 30,278 sq km

Unemployment: Flanders 10%; Wallonia 18%; Brussels 21%

Inflation: 2.8%

GDP: US$350 billion

National debt: Belgium has one of the EU's highest debt levels – 94% of GDP in 2005

Minimum gross monthly salary: €1210

Beer consumption: 100L per head annually

Chocolate consumption: 16kg per head annually

Smoking: Banned in Belgian restaurants, but not in *cafés* (pubs/bars)

Sex: 58% of Belgians are satisfied with their sex life, up on the worldwide average of 44%

History

Belgium, Luxembourg and the Netherlands share a tangled history. The current borders of these three nations – known earlier as the Low Countries – were only realised in the 19th century. As such their pasts reflect some of the major historical events in Western Europe, and their fortunes and misfortunes have been largely shaped by Europe's ever-changing balance of power.

EARLY SETTLEMENTS

The Romans were the first of many to invade Belgium. In fact, the country's name even harks back to these times – Julius Caesar mentioned the Belgae during his conquest of Gaul, and when the nation needed a name following independence, the word 'Belgium' was born. Caesar's armies invaded in 57 BC and held Gallia Belgica for 500 years. There's little to show of their presence, except for the town of Tongeren in the province of Limburg. Built on an important trading route, Tongeren still has part of its original Roman rampart as well as an excellent Gallo-Roman Museum (p214).

In the 5th century, with the Roman Empire collapsing, Germanic Franks took regional control. This change in power was the basis of Belgium's current language division – the northern region became German speaking while the southern portion remained Latin based. The Frankish kings, known as the Merovingians, set up their short-lived kingdom in Tournai, a former Roman settlement, and from here they eventually controlled much of northern France. Tournai's early place in history ensured its survival, and today it remains one of Wallonia's most appealing towns (see p218).

For a resource index of articles, books and subjects on Belgian history, see http://vlib.iue .it/hist-belgium.

THE RISE OF FLANDERS

Parties of raiding Vikings forced the growth of feudal domains in the 9th and 10th centuries. While the kings of France and emperors of Germany had overall control, the real power was held by local counts who ruled over fiefdoms. Such was the case when Count Sigefroi built a castle on a high promontory in Luxembourg and laid the foundation stone of the Grand Duchy's present-day capital.

The counts of Flanders presided over one of the most powerful courts during feudal times. Baldwin the Iron Arm kicked it off by kidnapping and marrying the daughter of a French king and building a fortress in Ghent in AD 867. Over the next three centuries Baldwin's successors expanded the territory and influence of Flanders as far south as the Somme River in northern France.

As feudalism declined, the first towns rose. Flanders had been producing cloth since the 10th century, but its manufacture took off with the growth of cities like Ypres, Bruges and Ghent in the 12th and 13th centuries, which bloomed with the expansion of trade across northern Europe and further afield. Merchant ships from all over Europe docked in Bruges to trade Flemish cloth for cheese, wool, lead and tin; coal from England; pigs from Denmark; wine from Spain; silks and oriental spices from Venice and Genoa; and furs from as far away as Russia and Bulgaria. Cruise the canals in Bruges (p132) or Ghent (p165) to conjure up this bygone time.

57 BC	AD 1340
The Romans arrive, kicking off Belgium and Luxembourg's tumultuous history of invasions	Ghent grows to become the largest city in Europe after Paris

This flurry of activity bred a class of rich merchants who wanted increased political power. Meanwhile, craftsmen and traders joined forces to form groups known as guilds, setting standards for their craft and establishing a local trade monopoly. But it wasn't long before the aspirations of the burghers and weavers clashed with those of the local counts. The Flemish weavers relied on a steady supply of high-quality wool from England, and for this purpose they sided with the English during conflicts between England and France. The local counts, though, were vassals of the French king. The counts quelled demands for greater power by calling in the French army. This situation came to a head in 1302 in bloody confrontations known as the Brugse Metten (see p120) and, a few months later, the Battle of the Golden Spurs (see p159).

THE BURGUNDIAN EMPIRE

By the 14th century Ghent, Bruges, Ypres, Brussels, Leuven, Mechelen and Tournai were all prosperous towns. In fact, Ghent had grown to become the largest city in Europe after Paris by 1340. The city's sinister castle, Gravensteen (p163), was raised during this time and is still one of Ghent's chief sights.

The science of anatomy was founded in the 16th century by Brussels-born Andreas Vesalius, who wrote the first textbook on human anatomy.

The dukes of Burgundy ruled for less than a century, but the cultural changes that took place during this time were profound. The first of the dukes was Philip the Good (r 1419–67), who presided over a vast empire that included the Burgundian region of eastern France and the area covering most of modern-day Belgium and the Netherlands. The court had a palace in Dijon (France) but Philip ruled the kingdom from Brussels, earning the title Conditor Belgii (Belgium's founder).

Philip was the richest man in Europe; his court was the height of culture and fashion. In Brussels the magnificent Grand Place (p69) was constructed, flanked by elaborately decorated guildhalls – headquarters for increasingly wealthy merchant guilds. Belgium's first university was founded in Leuven and the arts, particularly painting and tapestry making, flourished. The court's wealth was legendary and is best seen today in the works of famous artists from that time, known as the Flemish Primitives (see boxed text, p125).

HAPSBURG RULE

Charles V was born in Ghent in 1500 and, at the ripe old age of 15, became Duke of Brabant and ruler of the Low Countries. The next year he became king of Spain and later of Naples, Sardinia, Sicily and the Spanish territories in the New World (ie Mexico, Peru and the Caribbean). He was crowned king of Germany and Holy Roman Emperor in 1519, thus becoming Europe's most powerful ruler.

Charles grew up in Mechelen and, after being crowned, initially ruled from Brussels, where he was advised by the great humanist Desiderius Erasmus. He spent much of his life travelling in far-flung parts of the empire and, later, ruling from Spain. His sister, Mary of Hungary, was responsible for the region for most of his reign, during which the Low Countries once again boomed.

But it wasn't all prosperous. The great Flemish cloth towns were in decline due to competition from cloth manufacturers in England and the silting of the Zwin, which connected Bruges to the North Sea. In addition Charles favoured up-and-coming Antwerp over the old cloth towns. His choice was fuelled by frustration with the rebellious burghers of Flanders; in 1540 the townsfolk of Ghent planned an uprising against taxes imposed on them to

15th century	**17th century**
Primitive passions flourish in the works of artists such as Jan Van Eyck and Hans Memling	Pieter Paul Rubens comes to the fore as northern Europe's greatest baroque artist

finance wars instigated by their absent leader, and Charles V personally suppressed these uprisings. In 1555, tired of continual revolts and a lifetime of war, Charles returned to Brussels and abdicated in favour of his son Philip II. By this time Antwerp had become the empire's greatest port.

RELIGIOUS REVOLT

During Charles' reign Protestantism swept much of Europe. This religious and political rethink of the world according to the Roman Catholic elite became known as the Reformation. It came about partly due to the advent of printing, which meant Bibles were no longer the treasure of the Church and the ruling classes alone. Theologians and humanists such as Martin Luther, the German leader of the Reformation, John Calvin, his French counterpart, and Erasmus offered interpretations on Scripture that were different to traditional religious thinking.

The Reformation met with severe repercussions in the Low Countries. In 1550 Charles ordered the Edict of Blood, which decreed the death penalty to those convicted of heresy. When his son Philip II came to the throne, the latter took a more zealous approach to the defence of Catholicism. Philip was born in Spain and ruled from there; he had little interest in the Low Countries and was largely unpopular. Determined to defend the Catholic faith, he quashed any resistance by implementing a string of anti-Protestant edicts and garrisoning towns in the Low Countries with Spanish mercenaries. In 1566 the Protestants revolted, running riot and ransacking churches in a wave of violence that has become known as the Iconoclastic Fury. Philip retaliated with a force of 10,000 troops led by the duke of Alva, who set up the Council of Blood, which handed out 8000 death sentences to those involved in the rioting.

In the turbulent years that followed – a period known as the Revolt of the Netherlands – the present-day borders of Belgium, Luxembourg and the Netherlands were roughly drawn. The Netherlands expelled the Spaniards, while Belgium and Luxembourg, known then as the Spanish Netherlands, stayed under southern rule.

THE SPANISH NETHERLANDS

Brussels was proclaimed capital of the Spanish Netherlands in 1585 and Protestants were forced to leave; thousands of tradespeople and anti-Spanish freethinkers moved north to the Netherlands.

In 1598 Philip II handed the Spanish Netherlands to his daughter Infanta Isabella and her husband, Archduke Albert of Austria. Their 40-year reign is most noted for its flamboyant court, which gave rise to new industries like lace making and diamond processing. In turn, this brief economic boom boosted cultural life in Brussels and Antwerp and brought to the fore great painters, such as Pieter Paul Rubens (see boxed text, p181). Rubens' studio in Antwerp can still be visited, and the city treasures many of his finest paintings.

Antwerp's time of glory was cut short by the Treaty of Westphalia, signed in 1648, which closed part of the Scheldt River to all non-Dutch ships. This act guaranteed the golden age of Amsterdam, the region's premier port, and caused Antwerp's collapse.

With many of its most skilled workers gone, much of the Spanish Netherlands sunk into poverty and life became an exercise in religious piety. During this Catholic Counter-Reformation, the newly formed Jesuit order

The Dutch Revolt by Geoffrey Parker documents this interesting period in Belgian history well. With Spanish rule in the 16th century nearing its end, this book looks at the fight between the southern rulers and the rebellious countries in the north.

1815	1830
Napoleon Bonaparte is defeated at the Battle of Waterloo near Brussels; Luxembourg is designated a Grand Duchy	An opera in Brussels sparks revolution and Belgium is born

prospered and multiplied. Elaborate baroque churches, such as St Carolus-Borromeuskerk (p180) in Antwerp, were built. Filled with magnificent statues, huge wooden pulpits and glorified paintings of Christ's suffering executed by artists such as Rubens, the churches were symbols of the Catholic Church's power and the magical redemption that awaited the faithful.

On an everyday level, life in the Spanish Netherlands worsened in the second half of the 17th century. French plans to dominate Europe meant war after war was fought in this buffer land. France's Louis XIV sent in his military engineer Vauban to fortify strongholds – the result can be seen today in mighty citadels such as that in Namur (p231). The fighting came to a head with the War of Spanish Succession (1701–13), which saw the Spanish Netherlands handed over to the Austrians.

AUSTRIAN & FRENCH OCCUPATION

The mighty Austrian Hapsburgs ruled from 1713 to 1794 and, overall, the century was a peaceful change to what had come before. Brussels was the base for central control but the Austrians allowed the country a large degree of independence, just as the Spanish had. The Enlightenment, a philosophical movement based on reason rather than the blind following of tradition, influenced the Austrians and they relaxed censorship and encouraged development.

After yet another battle in 1794, the French reclaimed the region and the following year absorbed it into France. French laws were ushered in, the Catholic Church was repressed (many churches were ransacked and monasteries closed) and conscription was introduced. The latter was widely unpopular and a passionate peasants' revolt in 1798 was cruelly put down.

In 1815 Napoleon Bonaparte, leader of the new French state, was defeated at the Battle of Waterloo near Brussels (see boxed text, p225). This resulted in the Congress of Vienna and the creation of the United Kingdom of the Netherlands, which incorporated the Netherlands, Belgium and Luxembourg.

THE UNITED KINGDOM OF THE NETHERLANDS

The United Kingdom of the Netherlands was created largely to preserve the balance of power in Europe and to create a buffer state should France have any northward ambitions. The fact that people of different religions and customs were being forced together was of little consequence. William of Orange-Nassau, crowned King William I in Brussels, was given the throne and he divided his time equally between Brussels and the new kingdom's twin capital, The Hague. But William made enemies quickly after refusing to give southern Belgium fair political representation and trying to impose Dutch as the national language. The latter angered not only the French-speaking Walloons in the south of Belgium but also Flemish speakers in the north who regarded their language as distinct from Dutch.

The inevitable Belgian revolution began during an opera performance in Brussels on 25 August 1830 (see boxed text, p110).

For a rundown on Belgian royalty and a great booklist, check out www .royalty.nu.

BELGIAN INDEPENDENCE

At the Conference of London in January 1831, the European powers recognised Belgian independence. The country was officially declared a neutral state and several years later was ceded the western portion of the Grand Duchy of Luxembourg.

1885	1914
King Léopold II personally acquires the Congo, to the gruesome fate of 10 million Africans	Belgium and Luxembourg are invaded by Germany; Ypres is wiped off the map

On 21 July 1831 Léopold of Saxe-Coburg Gotha, a dashing but melancholy 40-year-old widower and uncle of future British monarch Queen Victoria, became King Léopold I of Belgium. The country now celebrates his crowning as its annual 21 July National Day holiday. King Léopold oversaw the industrial revolution in Belgium where coal mines and iron-making factories took off in parts of Hainaut and Limburg provinces. The ensuing years saw the start of Flemish nationalism, with tension growing between Flemish and French speakers that would eventually lead to a language partition that divides the country to this day – see boxed text, (p31).

Léopold II (r 1865–1909) came to the throne on his father's death. He was committed to transforming the tiny country into a strong nation, both through colonial conquests and national development. He put great effort into bolstering Brussels, commissioning the construction of monumental buildings such as the Musées Royaux des Beaux-Arts (p83), home today to Belgium's finest art collection, and the daunting Palais de Justice (p85).

However, Léopold II had wider aspirations. In 1885, mainly through a series of dubious treaties and contracts, Léopold personally acquired a huge slice of central Africa – an area 70 times larger than Belgium. Over the next 25 years millions of Congolese died due to Léopold's rule, and in 1908 the king was stripped of his possession. Today his reputation is in tatters. For more on this dark chapter in Belgium's past, see Bizarre Brussels (p94). In 1909 Léopold II died and his death marked the end of the country's aspirations to grandeur. The Belgian state held on to the Congo until 1960.

The King Incorporated by British journalist Neal Ascherson deals with Belgium's heart of darkness: the appalling cruelty and savage exploitation of the Congo under the reign of Léopold II. It was written in 1963 but re-released in 1999.

WWI & WWII

Léopold II was succeeded by his 21-year-old nephew Albert I (r 1909–34), nicknamed the 'Soldier King' due to his popular actions during WWI. When war broke out in 1914, Germany violated Belgian neutrality and occupied the country. Albert moved his administration to the seaside town of De Panne, part of a small triangle of land that remained unoccupied throughout the war. From here he lead the Belgian army's efforts to man the northern end of the frontline, which separated the Allies and the strategic French coastal towns around Calais from the advancing German army. The former cloth town of Ypres (Ieper in Flemish) was reduced to rubble during the war, but was courageously rebuilt. The Ypres Salient (p153) holds many wartime reminders.

After the war the Treaty of Versailles abolished Belgium's neutral status and the country was given reparations from Germany, which included a chunk of land known today as the Eastern Cantons (see boxed text, p262), and the colonies of Burundi and Rwanda in central Africa. In 1934 Albert I died in a rock-climbing accident and was succeeded by his son, Léopold III (r 1934–51).

On 10 May 1940 the Germans launched a surprise air attack on the Netherlands, Belgium and Luxembourg and within eight days Belgium was occupied. Unlike his father, Léopold III put up little resistance and quickly surrendered to the Germans, leaving the Allies in a precarious state. The Belgian government opposed the king's decision and fled to London where it operated in exile throughout WWII. A strong resistance movement developed during Nazi occupation, but there was also collaboration from fascist elements of Belgian society and from within the Flemish movement. Belgium's Jewish population fared terribly during the war and the country's small Roma (gypsy) minority was all but wiped out (see boxed text, p203). Belgium and Luxembourg were

1919	1940
Jules Bordet, developer of the whooping cough vaccine, wins the Nobel Prize for Medicine for research into blood serum	Germany again invades both countries and they remain occupied throughout WWII

MAKING HISTORY

Belgium is a constitutional hereditary monarchy, led by a king or queen (succession was only opened to women in 1991) and a parliament. The parliament consists of the Senate and a Chamber of Representatives, which have responsibility for policies that affect the country as a whole, such as finance, defence and foreign affairs. In one famous example of how a monarch's personal convictions don't always complement parliamentary progress, King Baudouin abdicated for two days in 1990 to avoid giving his approval to a bill legalising abortion – during the 48 hours that he relinquished the throne, the Belgian parliament passed the bill. While this was seen by some Belgians as the admirable stance of a principled man, others saw it as a refusal by Baudouin to put the public's desire for change above his own conservative views.

liberated in September 1944, though many were still to lose their lives during the Battle of the Ardennes (see boxed text, p245).

POSTWAR BELGIUM

After WWII the country was caught up in a constitutional crisis over Léopold III's wartime actions. While some accused him of collaborating with the Germans, others said the early surrender saved the country. In 1951, under pressure from Walloon socialists, he abdicated in favour of his son Baudouin I (r 1951–93).

Although only 21 when he took the throne, Baudouin succeeded in bringing the nation together. His fair treatment of the Flemish and Walloons earned him respect from both sides, and many admired his famous stance on abortion (see boxed text, above). Proof came when he died suddenly in 1993 and the entire nation mourned. Childless, Baudouin was succeeded by his younger brother, the present King Albert II. Although initially reluctant to accept the throne, Albert's jovial disposition has made him a national success.

For a hyperlinked indepth profile of Belgium, see http://en.wikipedia .org/wiki/Belgium.

Like a phoenix rising from the ashes, Belgium emerged as a key player in international politics after WWII. In 1958 Brussels became the provisional seat of the European Commission and the Council of Ministers, the executive and decision-making bodies of today's EU (see boxed text, p87). In 1967 the North Atlantic Treaty Organisation (NATO) moved to Brussels from France a year after the French withdrew from NATO's military wing. A new NATO headquarters, being built on the northeastern outskirts of the capital, is expected to be finished in 2009.

While Brussels has been reborn as an important player in European affairs, the rest of the country's fortunes have been divided. The economy as a whole struggles with a huge public debt and high unemployment. Wallonia's economy rode on the back of the steel and iron-ore industries until their slump in the 1970s left this region floundering. Flanders, on the other hand, has surged ahead.

INTO THE 21ST CENTURY

Belgium kept a low profile on the international arena until the end of the 20th century, when it became best known for poisoned chickens and paedophiles (see p21). Sick of mismanagement and neglect, the nation turned to radical political reform and, in 1999, booted out the Christian Democrat party after 40 years in power.

1962	1967
The linguistic divide is drawn across Belgium, separating northern Flemish speakers and southern French-speaking Walloons	NATO moves to Brussels from France

For an overview of
Belgium's political scene,
including profiles of its
prime ministers, check
out www.premier.fgov.be
(in Flemish and French).

In came Liberal Prime Minister Guy Verhofstadt, who quickly sought to raise public morale by reinventing Belgium with robust foreign policies and new moral freedoms (see opposite). The country vocally sided with France and Germany against the US-led war in Iraq in 2003. Around the same time came a flood of lawsuits for war crimes against world leaders, including Israel's Ariel Sharon and former US president George Bush. They were made under Belgium's controversial universal competence law, which allows the judging of crimes against humanity no matter where they took place. Faced with potentially embarrassing diplomatic situations, the law was changed so that those charged had to live in Belgium. In 2005 a Brussels court sentenced two Rwandan half-brothers to prison under this law for their part in the 1994 Rwandan genocide.

Verhofstadt still leads the coalition government, which in 1999 saw a rather unusual grouping of Liberals, Socialists and Greens join forces to block the progress of the ultraright-wing Vlaams Blok (VB) and to stem rising racism (see p32). The Liberals and Socialists renewed their coalition in the national elections of 2003, though forecasts for the 2007 poll suggest the Liberals will have a tough time securing a third term.

1993	2005
Death of King Baudouin and succession to the throne of his younger brother, the present King Albert II	Belgium celebrates 175 years of independence

The Culture

THE NATIONAL PSYCHE

Outsiders looking in often consider Belgians somewhat bizarre. A pissing boy and a bowler hat are national symbols. Maybe too much surrealist art as kids is responsible – certainly their sense of humour can be odd. Liberalism and moral freedoms are big, as is a widespread fascination with the monarchy, and a love of both the traditional and the quirky. The latter two are best exemplified by folklore. Folkloric traditions are very strong here – see for yourself at one of the amazing array of weird and wonderful festivals that take place throughout the year.

In general Belgians are unrelentingly friendly, extremely polite and helpful, and pride themselves on their open intolerance of rudeness and other forms of nastiness. 'National' character, however, is elusive: Belgians think of themselves as Flemish or Walloon first, and Belgian second. The Flemish are considered arrogant by their southern counterparts; the Walloons are called feckless. And when talk of separation surfaces, it's always propelled from the Flemish side. It's true that Flanders is roaring along as the country's economic and artistic bastion, and many resent that this part of the country is financially propping up its poorer counterpart. Flemish nationalism is rising too, taking the already high level of casual racism up with it. Snob-value is minimal, except in arrogant Antwerp. Fab food, sublime chocolates and the best beers are accepted as part of daily life. Even so, Belgians complain a lot. About what? The weather, understandably so. Taxes, justifiable in one of Europe's most highly taxed nations. And dog mess on the streets. This, according to a 2005 poll, irritates Belgians more than anything else. So do all these woes add up to a desire for greener pastures? No way. Eight out of 10 Belgians are proud of their country and most have no wish to live anywhere else.

LIFESTYLE

If there's one thing that unites Belgian households, it's an obsession with neat and tidy. Life on the street may not be so manicured or presentable, but inside any home you can be sure there's a cupboard brimming with cleaning products and windows that sheen. Cleanliness comes second only to family life. Ties remain incredibly strong – it must be that brick in the stomach they're supposedly born with (according to this local saying, the Belgian desire to own their own home and stay close to kith and kin is so strong that they enter the world carrying their future home's first brick). After that, disparity rules. From royalty and aristocrats, to large sections of migrant communities living below poverty lines (see p33), household scenarios range widely. According to a UN index, Belgium is one of the world's most affluent countries, and is among the top 10 in living standards. You'll be hard pressed to believe that, however, when travelling through some regions and neighbourhoods.

Despite its strong Catholic past, civil liberties are now being championed. Belgium is a world leader in rights for gays (see p308), and in 2002 it became the second country (following the Netherlands) to legalise euthanasia. Recent proposals to extend this ruling are being contested (see p21).

Another social reform has also caused dissent. The government's proposal to limit access to early retirement and bring the earliest possible retirement age up from 57 to 60 by 2009 saw 100,000 workers take to the streets in protest in late 2005. Despite the demonstration, the government passed the reforms a month later, saying the measures were introduced to counteract the economic spectre of Belgium's ageing population.

Belgium is the second European country after the Netherlands to legally recognise same-sex unions. The first gay wedding took place in June 2003.

POPULATION

Belgium's population is basically split in two: the Flemish and the Walloons (see boxed text, opposite). Language is the dividing factor, made official in 1962 when an invisible line – or linguistic divide as it's called – was drawn across the country, cutting it almost equally in half.

To the north of the divide lies Flanders (Vlaanderen), whose Flemish speakers make up 60% of Belgium's population of 10.5 million. This is one of the most densely populated corners of Europe, with 400 people per square kilometre (compared with 240 in Britain and just 100 in France). It's heavily urbanised, with major cities sitting almost side by side in some areas.

South of the divide sits Wallonia (La Wallonie), where French-speaking Walloons make up most – but not all – of the remainder of the population. The remainder is a tiny German-speaking enclave in the far east in an area known as the Eastern Cantons (Ostkantons). Officially part of Wallonia, the Eastern Cantons flank the border with Germany around the towns of Eupen and St Vith and are home to 70,000 people (for more details, see p262). Wallonia is more rural than Flanders, though it too has large cities and plenty of heavy industry.

And then there's Brussels. Officially bilingual but predominantly French-speaking, it lies within Flanders but is governed separately. Brussels' population includes about 100 different nationalities among the foreign-born residents, and while many Belgian cities have large immigrant communities none are as multicultural as the capital. The mix includes many European nationalities as well as Moroccans, Turks and Africans. The African population is largely made up of immigrants from the former Belgian colony of Congo.

SPORT
Cycling

Cycling is the only sport in which the Belgians have sprouted a truly international hero, until the rise of tennis greats Kim and Justine that is (see boxed text, p32). Grocer's son Eddy Merckx is revered as one of the greatest natural cyclists ever, winning almost every classic cycling event, not to mention the Tour de France five times, during his domination of the sport from 1968 to 1975. Only in 2004 was Merckx's Tour de France record finally broken when Texan Lance Armstrong took out his sixth title. But even that hasn't detracted from Merckx's status as one of the best.

Bike helmets are not a legal requirement for cyclists and are generally ignored by adults.

Unlike Armstrong, Merckx won almost everything that was going, including the Giro and hour-records, in an era before aerodynamic bikes and helmets. He was known as the Cannibal (Kannibaal in Flemish), a nickname inadvertently started by the daughter of French cyclist Christian Raymond. One day in 1969, bemoaning the impossibility of ever beating Merckx, Raymond said: 'He's eating us all for breakfast.' 'Like a cannibal, Daddy?' his daughter replied. And so the name stuck. Merckx turned 60 in 2005, and these days busies himself making top-notch bicycles for the international arena.

Until recently, Belgium's days of cycling glory were long past but in 2005 Flemish cyclist Tom Boonen went some way to reviving the country's fortunes, winning not only the World Championship in Madrid but also, in the same season, Paris–Roubaix and the Tour of Flanders (or Ronde van Vlaanderen in Flemish). Other contemporary cyclists to watch out for include Leif Hoste and Rik Verbrugghe.

The domestic cycling season starts in full with the Ronde van Vlaanderen in early April, immediately followed by the equally demanding La Flèche Wallonne and Liège–Bastogne–Liège. The Grand Prix Eddy Merckx, held in Brussels in May, is the top event.

THE LINGUISTIC DIVIDE

A television station organises a prank broadcast announcing independence for Flanders, newspaper polls question the likelihood of a split, the king calls for regional harmony... Four decades after the linguistic divide was made – cutting Belgium almost equally in half between the Flemish and Walloon populations – this little country is still a divided land.

As a visitor, much of the tension created by this division will go unnoticed. The only peculiarity you're likely to encounter is on the road, when the sign you were following to 'Doornik', for example, suddenly disappears to be replaced by its French name, 'Tournai' (for details, see p320). In Flanders, people will readily communicate in whatever language is needed, be it English, French or Flemish. In Wallonia the story is slightly different, as the Walloons are less ready with Flemish or English.

The roots of Belgium's divisive language issue can be traced back to Roman times; however, it was the formation of the Belgian state in 1831 that crystallised it. The nation's first constitution was drawn up in French – the official language of the country at that time – by the ruling elite. A campaign for the Flemish language started, but it wasn't until 1898 that Flemish was recognised as a second language. Even then, it was another 30 years before it was used in schools and only in 1967 was the constitution finally published in Flemish.

In the 1950s and '60s, Flemish assertiveness grew as Flanders became the country's modern-day economic powerhouse. Soon after, Wallonia's steel and mining industries declined, leaving French-speaking Belgians in an impoverished region. Historical and economic tensions grew until, in 1962, it was decided to cut the country in half with an invisible line known as the linguistic divide. This division created the regions of Flanders, Wallonia and bilingual Brussels. Each region has its own government and autonomy, thanks to decentralisation of the national government during the 1980s and early '90s.

The establishment of regional governments was designed to appease the language communities and to a certain degree it has, but it has not thwarted the intercommunity squabbles or the 'them and us' mentality, particularly in some areas immediately around Brussels. The massive increase in bureaucracy generated by the additional tier of government is a burden for taxpayers, and many in Flanders resent the fact that their financially successful region is counterbalancing the country's less affluent south.

So what is the nation's future? Some parts of Flemish society call for independence but it is questionable whether the majority of Belgians would back such a move were it to be put to a vote. Those who think Belgium will stick together attribute this to the country's huge public debt, the question of what to do with Brussels, and the monarchy. The royal family, with its foreign origin, is linked to neither language community and is therefore a unifying force. In his 2006 New Year speech, King Albert II acknowledged the cultural and economic tensions between Belgium's regions but said separatism was an expensive and dangerous path.

The latest episode in the drama was played out in December 2006 when Francophone public broadcaster RTBF interrupted its normal programming with news that Flanders had declared independence. The fake news bulletin included footage of a reporter standing outside the Royal Palace in Brussels, claiming that King Albert had left the country. Only after half an hour did the programme makers admit that it was all a hoax. Although many in Belgium were displeased by this event, RTBF defended its actions, stating it intended to show the importance of the ongoing political debate on the future of Belgium.

Stay tuned!

Flemish
French
German
Bilingual

BELGIAN TENNIS DIVAS

If it wasn't for Justine Henin-Hardenne and Kim Clijsters, there'd be little to write of in the way of contemporary Belgian sporting icons. But in 2003 Belgium's tennis aces became the world's top two women's tennis players. Since then, the pair has continued to be highly competitive, despite a series of injuries and the rise of a host of Russian players.

It's odd that Belgium, a tiny country with just over 10 million people, could rear two outstanding female tennis players from different sides of the linguistic divide at the same time. Henin-Hardenne (b 1982) from Wallonia and Clijsters (b 1983) from Flanders climbed the ranks through separate tennis federations – one French-speaking, the other Flemish. They had different coaches and contrasting styles. But their rise was strangely parallel, both winning their first World Tennis Association (WTA) title in 1999 and entering the top ten in the same month.

Despite the similarities, there are plenty of contrasts. Henin-Hardenne's slight frame hides a cautious and at times withdrawn personality. She performs best on clay, and what she lacks in height and natural power, she makes up for with speed and accuracy. Clijsters, on the other hand, has a hefty physique and jovial nature, prefers hard-court tournaments and is quite at home in the public eye.

At the start of their rise, there were hopes that Belgium's tennis queens would somehow help unite this divided land. This hasn't happened of course. Instead the two have frequently stood in each other's way when it comes to winning a title (which may be a thing of the past if Clijsters retires in 2007, as announced). Despite that, however, they are two of the country's best-known names and in 2004 were awarded the Grand Cross Order of the Crown from King Albert, becoming the youngest recipients of the nation's top civil honour.

Football

Belgian football is going through one of its most humiliating periods in decades. The national team, the Red Devils, failed to even qualify for the 2006 World Cup in Germany – it was the first time since 1978 that Belgium didn't take part in football's biggest event, and fans countrywide mourned. This sad state of affairs came two years after Belgium failed to qualify for the 2004 European Championships in Portugal, and many felt it marked a nadir in the national side's fortunes. The fallout of all this has been the sacking of Red Devils former coach, Aimé Antheunis, and the appointment of new coach René Vandereycken, whom many hope can restore fortunes.

Belgium is probably best remembered in football terms for the tragedy at Heysel stadium during the European Cup final in Brussels in 1985. Thirty-nine people were killed (including 35 Juventus supporters) when Liverpool and Juventus fans clashed. English clubs were banned from European competitions for six years following that disaster and Heysel – the country's premier stadium – was in ruins. Ten years later it reopened under the new name Roi Baudouin (p111). These days it's the place to see the Red Devils' home games as well as a memorial, belatedly erected, to those who died at the Heysel disaster.

It's easy enough to get a ticket at the stadiums for any local football event – the country's best-known team on the domestic-league ladder is RSC Anderlecht (see p111).

MULTICULTURALISM

Belgium's main immigrant communities are Moroccan, Turkish and Congolese, although Brussels' multicultural population also includes many other European nationalities. The communes of Schaerbeek and St Josse in the capital are almost completely Turkish and North African in character. The relationship between these communities and the Bruxellois ranges from fearful distrust to cheerful cohabitation.

Economically, the picture for Belgium's migrant communities is quite grim. A 2006 study by universities in Antwerp and Liège found one in three people of Turkish or Moroccan descent were living in poverty in Belgium. And compared with European poverty standards, the findings were worse, with 60% of people of Turkish descent and 55% of Moroccan living below the €777 monthly threshold. This compares with 10% for native Belgians.

Many immigrants arrived in the 1960s to work in the mines. But four decades later, these communities have failed to integrate, and a high level of casual racism among Belgians towards immigrant families remains. Even second-generation immigrants with Belgian citizenship often don't feel at home in society here.

Up until early this decade, Belgians had not witnessed racist-related murders on their streets. But the killing of a Moroccan couple in Schaerbeek in 2002, followed six months later by the gunning down of a Moroccan school teacher in Antwerp, changed all that, sparking national debate about race, religion and culture. The issue resurfaced in 2006 following an apparently racist shooting in the heart of Antwerp in which a Malian nanny and a two-year-old white girl in her care were killed, and a woman of Turkish descent was seriously injured. A week later, Amnesty International released its annual report severely criticising Belgium on a number of points, particularly racism and discrimination. The report came just days before Antwerp's so-called White March, in which 18,000 people, clad in white, walked against racism. Peaceful demonstrations like this – usually to highlight justice or freedom issues – have found a place in Belgium ever since the first was held in the mid-1990s following the Dutroux paedophile scandal (see p21).

Most of the racial tension in recent times has surrounded Antwerp, which has 50,000 foreign residents (including 13,000 Moroccans), but this number doubles when second-generation immigrants are added. The suburb of Borgerhout in Antwerp is essentially Moroccan, with unemployment hovering at 35%.

Antwerp is the power base of Vlaams Belang, an ultraright-wing party with a blatantly anti-immigrant platform. Formerly Vlaams Blok, it changed its name and relaunched itself in 2004 after a court banned the party on the grounds of permanent incitement to segregation and racism. The party gained 30% of votes in local elections in 2000 but has since failed to make much further headway in Antwerp itself, though its support base in country areas is rising. At the 2006 municipal elections, Antwerp's Socialists overtook Vlaams Belang, powering ahead with a 16% swing to take 35% of the vote ahead of Vlaams Belang's 33%. Mayor Patrick Janssens was thrilled that he'd stopped Vlaams Belang leader Filip Dewinter from securing a majority in the city council.

Just before the elections, influential contemporary artist, Antwerp-born Luc Tuymans, joined forces with one of the country's best-known bands, Antwerp-based dEUS, to organise a festival to show that Antwerp is not synonymous with support for Vlaams Belang.

MEDIA

No big-name media barons or government domination here. Belgium's print media divides pretty evenly in content between the serious and the superficial and, on the political spectrum, between left and right. None make the sensationalist grade of tabloid journalism as seen in England. Due to the country's linguistic make-up, Belgium has several daily newspapers – *De Standaard* (Flemish), *Le Soir* (French) and *Grenzecho* (German) are the pick of the crop.

Until very recently, Belgium was far ahead of everyone in the TV stakes, thanks to the introduction of cheap access to analogue cable in the 1960s. About 95% of homes are hooked to this system, and can access 40-plus TV channels. This satisfaction with the status quo explains why Belgians are

The world's first newspaper, *Nieuwe Tydinghen*, was invented in Antwerp by Abraham Verhoeven in 1606.

not embracing the digital TV revolution. In 2005 only 3% of households subscribed digitally, compared to the European average of 25%, and nearly 50% in the US.

For more on Belgium's media, see boxed text, p298.

RELIGION

Christianity was established early in Belgium and today Catholicism reigns supreme. Roughly 75% of Belgium's population is Roman Catholic. Despite church attendance plummeting since the 1970s and '80s (only 3% of the Flemish population go to church weekly), traditions remain strong and religion influences many aspects of daily life, including politics and education.

Protestant, Jewish and Muslim communities also exist in Belgium. Antwerp is home to the country's largest Jewish community, based around the city's diamond district, a tight grid of streets immediately south of the main train station. Orthodox Jews from Eastern Europe arrived here in the late 19th century and immediately took control of the burgeoning diamond industry. It's still common in this quarter to see Orthodox Jewish men clad in black coats and fluffy hats and the whole district closes down on Saturday for Sabbath, the Jewish holy day.

Brussels and Antwerp also have sizable Muslim populations. Belgian Muslims number about 450,000, and come from various countries including Morocco, Turkey, Algeria and Pakistan. Some 380 mosques dot the country. For more information, see p32).

Belgium has many Christian-based festivals that date back centuries. It's well worth timing a visit to coincide with one of these events. Such festivals are a fabulous way of getting under the Belgian skin – you really see what makes these people tick and what they get excited about, and you'll probably come away with some odd sort of admiration for a country which has refused to lay down its love of folklore and religious tradition. These festivals tend to be extraordinarily lavish affairs in which the Belgians get right into some pretty odd behaviour (for examples see boxed text, p223).

Belgium also has an important place of pilgrimage, Scherpenheuvel (p210), near the Flemish town of Diest.

> Belgium's most bizarre carnival celebration takes place on Shrove Tuesday in Binche and involves masked men throwing oranges at the crowd. It's actually a serious affair, with rituals dating back hundreds of years, and recently received World Heritage listing.

ARTS

Fab artworks, architectural grandeur, dynamic dance, crazy comics… Belgium's art world is remarkably huge for such a small country. Enter Brussels' Grand Place or the stunning Galeries St Hubert and swoon under architectural beauties that have transcended time. One of the world's earliest-known oil paintings – a piece so rich it still feeds the senses – is holed up in Ghent. Comic characters enliven daily life, and dance demons take centre stage.

With a roll call like that, it's surprising that the Belgian state doesn't have a good reputation when it comes to preserving its artistic heritage. Sure, the big guns – works by Rubens, Breugel and Van Eyck – hold pride of place in top museums around the country. But as for cherishing later art forms and artists – such as Art Nouveau buildings and the homes and studios of artists such as Magritte and Ensor – the nation has definitely fallen short. Victor Horta's Maison du Peuple was demolished in 1965, Ensor's birthplace in Ostend has been torn down and Magritte's last home, inherited by the Belgian state in 1986, was immediately put up for public sale, contents included.

Visual Arts

Belgium's art heritage began in Bruges in the late Middle Ages with painters known as the Flemish Primitives. For more on these important artists, see p125.

Towards the end of the 15th century, Flemish art proceeded along two lines: some painters were influenced by Italian art while others developed an independent Flemish style. The port city of Antwerp was the region's art hub.

One Dutch painter worth mentioning at this time is Hieronymus Bosch (c 1450–1516). He worked mainly in the Netherlands but his style influenced Flemish artists and his works are prominent in museums in Flanders. In any case, the distinction between Dutch and Flemish painting actually dates from the late 16th century – prior to that Belgium and the Netherlands were simply known as the Low Countries and artists moved from one royal court or town to another. Bosch' paintings are nightmarish – scenes filled with gruesome beasts and devilish creatures devouring agonised humans and other such treats. It's easy to think Bosch suffered bad karma, but his paintings are generally thought to illustrate parables told in those days.

The greatest 16th-century Flemish painter was Pieter Breugel the Elder, who lived and worked in Brussels. The Musées Royaux des Beaux-Arts in the capital exhibits an excellent range of his works. For details on Breugel and his two painter sons, see boxed text, (p84).

Antwerp held its cultural high ground during the 17th century, mainly because of Flemish baroque painter Pieter Paul Rubens. The most famous of his altarpieces were painted for Onze Lieve Vrouwekathedraal (p179), Antwerp's delightful cathedral, and can still be seen there. For more on this prolific artist, see boxed text, p181.

Rubens' studio nurtured artists such as Antoon Van Dyck (1599–1641), who focused on religious and mythical subjects, as well as portraits of European aristocrats. In 1632 he was appointed court painter by Charles I of England and knighted. His contemporary Jacob Jordaens (1593–1678) was one of the few artists who did not go to Italy; he specialised in everyday Flemish life and merrymaking. Antwerp's Koninklijk Museum voor Schone Kunsten (p182) is the best place to catch works by both these artists.

The two big Belgian names in the 19th century were Constantin Meunier (p87), Belgium's most famous sculptor, and James Ensor (p142), a pioneer of expressionism.

Mechelen-born Rik Wouters (1882–1916) was one of the prime figures of Brabant Fauvism. His sun-drenched landscapes, light interiors and still-life canvases were a search for the vibration of light in pure colours.

One of the country's most pure expressionists was Frits Van den Berghe (1883–1939), who used primitive cubism and colours full of contrast and subtle tonal gradings. From 1904 two groups of painters, first symbolists and then expressionists, set up in the village of St-Martens-Latem near Ghent. Of the first group, Albert Servaes (1883–1952) was the best known; later came Gustave De Smet (1877–1943) and Constant Permeke (1886–1952). Permeke, the best known of the group, put out bold portraits of rural Flemish life that blended cubism, expressionism and social realism.

Surrealism, a movement that developed in Paris in the 1920s, used images from the subconscious to revolt against rationalism and to define a new way of perceiving reality. It found fertile ground in Belgium, where the perverse and bizarre often go hand in hand and where artists had grown up with the likes of Bosch and Breugel. Belgium's best-known surrealists were René Magritte (p90) and Paul Delvaux (p148).

Immediately following WWII, a group of artists that called itself La Jeune Peinture Belge (1945–48) produced mainly abstract work. Among the most prominent artists were Victor Sevranckx, Anne Bonnet and Louis Van Lint.

In 1948 an international group called CoBrA (an acronym standing for Copenhagen, Brussels and Amsterdam) was formed as a reaction against formalism in art and out of an interest in the iconography of children's painting

Introduced by Phillipe Robert-Jones, *History of Painting in Belgium* details the country's rich artistic heritage from the 14th century to contemporary works.

Michael Palmer's *From Ensor to Magritte: Belgian Art 1880–1940* is a large, soft-cover book with full-page colour reproductions of works by the major figures during this time. It covers some of the overlooked artists of that era.

and the primitive world of the mentally ill. The group sought to promote free artistic expression of the unconscious and used intense, expressive colours. Belgium's most famous member is Pierre Alechinsky (1927–), who has gained international prominence for his works (mainly in inks).

One of Belgium's best-known contemporary artists is Antwerp's avant-garde Panamarenko (1940–). Obsessed with space and flight, his bizarre sculptures fuse authentic and imaginary flying contraptions, and even his pseudonym – a bastardised abbreviation of 'Pan American Airlines Company' – harks to this theme. His works, including the enormous Aeromodeller, made in 1969, can be seen at Ghent's SMAK (p163), as well as at Ostend's PMMK (p142). Panamarenko retired in 2006.

Another name to catch is Jan Fabre (1958–), who made waves in international artistic circles recently by being the first contemporary artist chosen to have a solo exhibition at Paris' Louvre museum. He'll be showing there in 2008. Back in Belgium, you may also be able to see his work at Antwerp's Koninklijk Museum voor Schone Kunsten (p182).

Also worth tracking down are paintings by Antwerp-born Luc Tuymans (1958–), considered Belgium's most prominent living artist. His subjects range from major historical events, such as the Holocaust or the politics of the Belgian Congo, to the inconsequential and banal. He has the honour of being the first living Belgian artist to have works hung in London's Tate Modern.

To discover the Art Nouveau jewels of Brussels, visit www .brussels.artnouveau.be.

Architecture

Belgium is endowed with a fine legacy of architectural delights. Many of the country's earliest buildings, though largely restored in later centuries, are on Unesco's World Heritage List. These include mighty belfries such as the one in Bruges (p124), many Flemish *begijnhoven* (clusters of cottages around a central garden; p129) and, of course, Brussels' famous Grand Place (p69). For more, see the World Heritage Sites Tour, p18.

On the flip side, exciting modern architecture is only just starting to get a look in. The old rival cities of Antwerp and Bruges recently realised that modern can sit alongside ancient, and have embraced projects like the Concertgebouw (p137) in Bruges and, in Antwerp, the new Justitiepaleis (law courts; p184) and bOb Van Reeth's Zuiderterras (p193).

In recent times Brussels expertly brought new life to some of its landmark old buildings, such as the Old England building (p83) and the former Belgian radio and TV building, Flagey (on Place Flagey). But swathes of the city have also gone under the demolition ball to make way for the boring glass buildings that typify the EU quarter.

Churches are the lifeblood of Middle Ages architecture, and the ornate towers that dominate the skylines of many Belgian cities are this period's most enduring showpieces, built first in Romanesque style and then Gothic. Romanesque is characterised by columns and semicircular arches – a good example is the Collégiale Ste Gertrude (p223) in Nivelles, just south of Brussels. Gothic features the pointed arch, and the style is at its most impressive in Antwerp's monumental Cathedral of Our Lady (p179). During the 15th century, secular buildings were also built in the increasingly flamboyant Gothic style, such as Brussels' Hôtel de Ville (p79). Belgium's most stunning tribute to secular Gothic architecture is Leuven's town hall (p205).

Baroque was an artistic and architectural movement of the Counter-Reformation in the 16th and early 17th centuries, characterised by ornate and exuberant decoration. Flemish artists and architects of that time altered and made additions to baroque to come up with a homegrown style called Flemish Renaissance or Flemish baroque. Although it has Italian influences, it's a style unique to Flanders and is much flaunted in Antwerp. Indeed, the city is extremely proud of this heavy, distinct architecture; excellent examples are Rubens' house (p181) and St Carolus-Borromeuskerk (p180).

After the 1695 bombardment (p69) of Brussels, the guild houses on the Grand Place were rebuilt in Flemish baroque, though many retained Gothic features. Nearby is arguably the country's finest Flemish baroque church, Église St Jean Baptiste au Béguinage (p82). Incidentally, Brussels' famous little pisser, Manneken Pis (p80), also dates from this period.

For most of the 18th century, while Belgium was under Austrian rule, architecture took on a cold, rational, neoclassical style. It is best reflected in the cluster of stark white buildings surrounding Brussels' Place Royale (p82). The sombre Place des Martyrs (p81) is another good example. After Belgian independence in 1831, a number of extravagant buildings were constructed to enable Brussels to compete with the likes of Paris and London. One of the first buildings to be built was the gorgeous Galeries St Hubert (see boxed text, p112).

Throughout his reign, Léopold II (r 1865–1909) focused on urban development, realising that making Brussels more aesthetically appealing would boost its economic potential. He used the vast riches gained through scandalous exploitation of the Congo (see p96) to fund the construction of gigantic public buildings and elaborate town-planning schemes. Almost everything that's big or ruler-straight in Brussels is due to him, but it's an unloved style these days. His pride and glory was the Palais de Justice, Brussels' law courts (see p85).

An industrial boom in the late 19th century resulted in the construction of several glass and iron buildings in Brussels. Notable examples include the Halles de Schaerbeek (p88) built in 1901, and the massive, newly renovated complex known as Tour & Taxis (p89).

At the end of the 19th century, Art Nouveau hit Belgium. For details on this lavish style, see boxed text, p37.

The impassioned style of Art Nouveau cooled off with Art Deco, a movement that originated in the 1920s and developed into a major style in Western Europe and the USA in the 1930s. Victor Horta, the master of Belgium's Art Nouveau scene, abandoned curls and frills for the cleaner lines of Art Deco in his later works, which include Bozar (p110). The style's most intimate example is the Musée David et Alice Van Buuren (p88), one of Brussels' little gems.

Belgium's most unique post-WWII architectural structure is the newly revamped Atomium (p89), menacingly visible from the city centre on clear days. The EU's ill-fated but now reopened Berlaymont (see boxed text, p87) is another famous edifice.

Literature

Belgian poet and author Marguerite Yourcenar was the first woman elected (in 1980) to the male-dominated Académie Française.

Belgium's most famous and prolific novelist was Liège writer Georges Simenon (1903–89). For more on Simenon and his detective character Inspector Maigret, see boxed text, p253.

Hugo Claus is one of the few Flemish writers to succeed abroad. His best-known novel is *Het Verdriet van België* (The Sorrow of Belgium), published in 1983. It weaves a story of wartime Belgium seen through the eyes of a Flemish adolescent, though the underlying theme is Nazi collaboration during WWII.

Amélie Nothomb is one of few modern Belgian writers to have works translated into English. Her novels *The Stranger Next Door,* about strange events in the Belgian countryside, *Loving Sabotage,* set in 1970s Beijing, and *The Book of Proper Names,* which details a girl trying to emulate her mother, are easy to find.

Belgium's Francois Weyergans recently won France's prestigious Goncourt prize with his new work, *Trois Jours Chez Ma Mère* (Three Days at My Mother's). The story explores a mother-son relationship challenged by mental and physical problems.

Cinema

Belgium is almost too small to have a cinema industry. The scene is generally devoted to black humour and down-to-earth realism and, while well received in art-house circles, it's almost starving (Belgium is one of the least generous countries in Europe when it comes to film subsidies).

The biggest local names are brothers Luc and Jean-Pierre Dardenne who in 2005 won their second Golden Palm at Cannes, thereby joining a very select group of directors to have this double honour. Their most recent win was with *L'Enfant,* a harsh yet upbeat story about a petty crook coming to grips with fatherhood. This followed their 1999 win with *Rosetta,* another stark story, this time about a girl in search of a job and meaning to her life. For more on these films, see boxed text, p251.

Screen star Audrey Hepburn, known from *My Fair Lady,* was born in Brussels in 1929.

The country's biggest export to Hollywood is the 'Muscles from Brussels', actor Jean-Claude Van Damme. Van Damme's career took off in the late 1980s after he put on an impromptu martial arts display outside a posh restaurant for the head of a Hollywood studio. He has since earned millions from hit action movies such as *Universal Soldier* and *Timecop.*

THE 9TH ART

Belgium's so-called 9th art is the comic strip (*beeldverhalen* in Flemish, *bandes dessinées* in French). With colourful comic murals dotting the capital, specialist shops devoted exclusively to comics and their merchandising, and even a national centre in Brussels devoted to this art form, Belgium is proof that comics aren't just for kids.

It was Hergé (1907–83), the creator of Tintin, who set the ball rolling here. Hergé's real name was Georges Remi – his pseudonym comes from his reversed initials (RG) pronounced in French. In 1929 the first adventure, *Tintin au Pays des Soviets* (Tintin in the Land of the Soviets), was published. A further 22 books followed, all including the sanctimonious asexual roving reporter and his dog, Snowy, a pragmatic smart aleck with a penchant for booze. The series is still Belgium's top international seller, with close to 120 million copies sold in French and 90 million in other languages. Visitors arriving at Brussels' Gare du Midi in 2007 will come face to face with a large Tintin fresco especially created to celebrate Hergé's centennial, and the Belgian postal service will also issue commemorative stamps to celebrate the event.

The end of WWII saw a host of comic-strip authors emerge, including Antwerp artist Willy Vandersteen, who created the delightful Suske and Wiske (Bob and Bobette in English) in 1945. This is one of the nation's longest-running comic-book series and is the biggest domestic seller.

In 1946 Maurice De Bevère, better known as Morris, came up with Lucky Luke, a classic Western parody, and Edgar P Jacobs brought out the sci-fi exploits of Blake and Mortimer. The following year Marc Sleen invented Nero and in 1948 Pierre Culliford (aka Peyo) created the little blue characters known as the Smurfs *(Les Schtroumpf)*.

The next decade saw Belgium's comic authors move into the adult realm and this genre lives today. Well known are the works of Brussels artist François Schuiten and author Benoit Peeters, who teamed up to produce the highly regarded *Les Cités Obscures*. The best-known title from this intellectual series is *Brüsel*, the exaggerated story of an old city destroyed by the new (a thin disguise of Brussels and the EU). *De Kat* (The Cat) by Philippe Geluck is long-running and still going strong.

This bevy of comic-strip talent is easily admired in Brussels, where the Centre Belge de la Bande Dessinée (p81) showcases the nation's best, and where you can follow the Comic Strip Route – see boxed text, p82.

Festivals to catch include Anima or the International Festival of Fantastic Film, both in Brussels (p95), as well as Bruges' Cinema Novo Film Festival (p132) and Ghents' Filmfestival (p165).

Music

Jazz is right at home in Belgium. Adolphe Sax invented the saxophone and octogenarian Toots Thielemans still enthrals audiences with his legendary harmonica playing. To get right among the jazz scene don't miss Brussels' Jazz Marathon (p96).

In the 1950s Jacques Brel took the French-speaking world by storm and is still much-loved in his homeland (see p80).

www.tickets.com has online ticket bookings plus interesting links to venues.

Arno Hintjens is the godfather of Belgian rock. From early days as a bluesman, he created TC Matic in 1980 and went solo a few years later. He now weaves chanson, blues and funk. Love or loathe him, Helmut Lotti is also Belgian, not German, and pumps out crooners and the classics.

Belgium as a whole doesn't have a contemporary music scene, but Flanders does. The only groups to make it internationally come from the north and include the well-established K's Choice, the Antwerp-based dEUS, and Axelle Red, who plies her trade in French despite Flemish roots. Hooverphonic from St Niklaas near Ghent do trip-hop, while Praga Khan is heavy techno. Brothers David and Stephen Dewaele, also known as 2ManyDJs, are known internationally for their mixing skills, as well as being members of rock group Soulwax.

In the classical arena, opera has always been important – a performance in 1830 sparked Belgium's revolution (see boxed text, p110).

Theatre & Dance

The international site www.whatsonwhen.com gives good coverage of Belgium; it links every venue and event.

Belgium's dynamic contemporary dance scene centres on two companies – Rosas (p109) in Brussels and Charleroi/Danses (p226) in Charleroi. The country's drama scene is also inspiring. To combine the two, investigate Brussels' KunstenFESTIVALdesArts (p96). Most theatre and dance companies take a break during July and August. Antwerp is the realm of classical ballet – see the Koninklijk Ballet van Vlaanderen (p195).

Environment

There's no point beating around the bush – Belgium's environmental picture is not pretty. In a densely populated, tiny country that has been at the heart of European development and destruction for centuries, it's no wonder the environment is now highly degraded.

On top of that, national passions just don't include the environment. This is possibly understandable when you consider that today's Belgians were born into a country already chock-full of cities and towns, a country that's heavily industrialised, stripped of native vegetation and fast becoming an ecological desert. Unfortunately, Belgians are used to turning on the TV news or picking up the morning newspaper and coming face to face with headlines proclaiming the country to be the worst in Europe or the world in various environmental matters. When many Belgians think of nature, they look to France or Italy or, when allowed to throw the net wider, they dream of vast open spaces in places like Australia and parts of America; they don't associate nature and strong environmental policies with Belgium.

This dearth of grass-roots environmental consciousness means the already pitiful situation has improved little in recent decades. Way back in 1993 Belgium was dubbed the 'dirty child of Europe' by Greenpeace and, if recent reports are anything to go by, since then the country has not done anywhere near enough to clean itself up.

Greenpeace's Belgian site, www.greenpeace.be (in Flemish & French), has full international links.

THE LAND

Belgium is one of Europe's little countries. It's bordered by the Netherlands to the north, Germany and Luxembourg to the east, France to the south and a 66km North Sea coastline to the west. It's 240km at its widest from east to west and 193km from north to south. People have missed Belgium by dozing off in the car – when there are no traffic jams, you can cross it in 2½ hours.

The flat landscape of Flanders comprises the north of Belgium. It's topographically uninteresting; the only lumps or bumps to break the monotony of the horizon are grazing cattle and the slender steeples of village churches.

In stark contrast is the wonderfully hilly countryside of Wallonia's Ardennes region in Belgium's southeast corner. This area of rivers, wooded valleys, high plateaus and ancient caves is Belgium's most scenic region. Near the border with Germany, the Ardennes gives way to the Hautes Fagnes, a wild and untamed plateau of bogs and swamps that holds Belgium's highest point (694m).

Check out the highs and lows of Belgium's weather at www.meteo .be, the website of the Royal Meteorological Institute.

Belgium's North Sea coastline is monopolised by largely unattractive resort towns between which a few patches of windswept – and now highly prized – dunes have been spared from the developer's bulldozer. A few of these areas, such as Het Zwin and Zwin-Polder, both near Knokke-Heist, are now protected nature reserves, used each year by thousands of birds to breed and refuel while journeying between Europe and Africa.

The country is riddled with rivers, many of which have supported villages and towns for centuries. The largest is the Scheldt (Schelde in Flemish, Escaut in French), which enters Belgium from northern France and gradually widens as it passes through Flanders. By the time it gets to Antwerp it's a river to be reckoned with, and provides the city with its economic lifeline to the North Sea.

The Meuse River (Maas in Flemish) is the country's other great waterway. It originates near the northern French town of Charleville-Mézières and gently winds to Namur, where it's joined by the Sambre River. From here it flows east to Liège, Europe's third-largest inland port, en route becoming a heavily used waterway. When it crosses into the Netherlands just north of Liège, it's flanked by decaying industrial estates.

WILDLIFE
Animals

Before the last Ice Age, Belgium was home to mammoth and later to bears and bison; however, hunting and the destruction of habitat has meant that the only wild critters left today are deer, wild boars, foxes, badgers, squirrels and rabbits, and sightings of any (except rabbits) are rare. Hunting is still a beloved pastime among some Belgians and is largely based around the town of St Hubert in Wallonia. The season runs from 15 October to 15 January.

Birdlife has been similarly hammered by the destruction of habitat. Researchers of a bird atlas published in 2005 cited numbers of even common species such as sparrows, larks and partridges having fallen by almost 90% since the 1970s. Cuckoos, turtle doves and golden orioles have all but disappeared from the Forêt de Soignes (Zoniënwoud in Flemish; see Forêt de Soignes, p117) near Brussels, though it's still home to one of Europe's largest populations of sparrowhawks. For more on birdlife, see National Parks, below.

Storks are being successfully bred in Het Zwin reserve on the coast. The critically endangered black grouse *(Tetrao tetrix)* has found its last refuge in the Hautes Fagnes Nature Reserve, which has adopted it as the park's emblem. Protected in Belgium, these birds live in moorland habitats and, if you're lucky, can be spotted in bare branches of trees. The males are black and have a noticeable red bonnet.

Plants

The native forests that once covered much of Belgium have been destroyed by centuries of clearing, with the cleared land used for agriculture and pasturage. Today's forests – concentrated in the Ardennes – are largely coniferous monocultures used for logging and are unable to sustain the diversity of plant and animal species that once lived in this region. Other isolated patches of forest, mainly beech, birch and oak, are dotted around the countryside, such as the Forêt de Soignes, close to Brussels.

Belgium's National Botanic Garden (see Nationale Plantentuinvan België, p117) boasts one of the largest collections of plants in Europe, including many indigenous plants.

NATIONAL PARKS

Only two nationally protected areas exist – the Hautes Fagnes Nature Reserve (see boxed text, p260) east of Liège and the Nationaal Park Hoge Kempen (www.nationaalpark.be) in Limburg.

The Nationaal Park Hoge Kempen occupies 5700 hectares between the Limburg towns of Genk and Maasmechelen. It's Flanders' biggest uninterrupted area of forest and nature, consisting of heather fields, pine forest, lakes and hills that host rare plants and animals such as hawks, snakes, frogs and toads, insects and butterflies. A handful of walking trails crisscross the park, and there's also a recreation area known as Kattevennen near Genk.

The nature reserves of Het Zwin and the nearby Zwin-Polder, on the coast northeast of Bruges, protect a wetland ecosystem maintained by North Sea flooding. The area silted in the 16th century, transforming Bruges from a busy medieval port into a small provincial city. The reserves mix salt marshes, coastal dunes and freshwater wetlands, and provide sanctuary for numbers

Sidebars:

Although not your typical field guide, *Where to Watch Birds in Holland, Belgium & Northern France* by Arnoud Van Den Berg describes the best places in Flanders and Wallonia for watching and twitching.

About 400 species of flora exist in Belgium, and one in five is threatened.

The World Directory of Environmental Organizations, www.interenvironment.org, is a megadatabase that tells you who's doing what to protect the earth, the world over.

of bird and rare flora species, such as glasswort and seablite, which thrive on salty soil. For more on both reserves, see p146.

At the opposite end of the Belgian coast, abutting the border with France, is De Westhoek Vlaams Natuurreservaat (p148), a 340-hectare nature reserve and popular winter haven for migratory birds. Warblers, nightingales, the endangered crested lark and little ringed plover all live here, as do rare species of spiders and insects, toads and newts. The reserve is home to about a third of the wildflowers found in Flanders.

The Kalmthoutse Heide Nature Reserve, north of Antwerp on the Belgian–Dutch border, features important remnants of the area's original heath and dune landscape; its vegetation includes wet and dry heath as well as active and inactive sand dunes. Over 90% of the dragonfly species found in Belgium live here.

ENVIRONMENTAL ISSUES

Water and noise pollution, urbanisation and waste management are some of the most pressing environmental issues. Also on the agenda now is whether Belgium will continue with its nuclear phase-out plan (the country's seven reactors are due to be decommissioned between 2015 and 2025). Nuclear power provides two-thirds of the country's energy (Belgium is the lowest ranked country in Europe for use of renewable energy sources) and, despite the country struggling to meet its Kyoto Protocol targets, calls have been made to scrap the plan.

Belgium's high population density and its good standard of living have resulted in high energy consumption, the production of large quantities of waste, and intensive use of land for agriculture. About 25% of the country's surface area is cultivated; forest and pasture-land each make up an additional 20%. The remainder includes industry and urban living space, and a small area of wetlands.

A controversial UN report on water quality published back in 2003 firmly put Belgium last among 122 countries in terms of waste treatment, pollution control and quality of fresh water. Two more recent studies have not brightened the picture. A report from the Organisation for Economic Cooperation and Development (OECD) released in late 2006 said Belgium had the worst water in the industrialised world, with the highest concentrations of nitrates and pesticides. The OECD report stated that while Belgium had made an effort towards improving air and water quality, much still needed to be done, as the situation was worse now than a decade ago. Earlier in the same year, an American study by Yale and Columbia Universities ranked Belgium as Europe's biggest polluter, in 39th position worldwide. The study's report stated that things were also not looking good for flora and fauna biodiversity, with Belgium almost last in the rankings. Not only was there a lack of nature reserves, it said, but those that existed were too small and fragmented.

Belgium's largest rivers, the Scheldt and Meuse, are heavily polluted. In Brussels, untreated sewage went straight into the Senne River, just as it had done for centuries, right up until 2006 when new waste treatment plants finally came on line. Water taken from these rivers is treated, and tap water is drinkable, but there must be a reason why Belgians arrive at the supermarket cashier each week with trolleys brimming with bottled mineral water.

Belgium was a late-starter in recycling, beginning with selective household rubbish collection (paper, glass and compostable matter, each picked up individually) as late as 1998. Recycling and/or composting of household waste is in full swing.

Environmental groups have been around since the 1970s but the movement only gained recognition in the 1980s due to the rising power of the

Belgium has some of the smelliest farm fields in Europe. Liquid manures are commonly sprayed around Flanders' fields, and the region is constantly criticised for having the highest levels of ground-water nitrate pollution in the EU.

TRAVEL WIDELY, TREAD LIGHTLY, GIVE SUSTAINABLY – THE LONELY PLANET FOUNDATION

The Lonely Planet Foundation proudly supports nimble nonprofit institutions working for change in the world. Each year the foundation donates 5% of Lonely Planet company profits to projects selected by staff and authors. Our partners range from Kabissa, which provides small nonprofits across Africa with access to technology, to the Foundation for Developing Cambodian Orphans, which supports girls at risk of falling victim to sex traffickers.

Our nonprofit partners are linked by a grass-roots approach to the areas of health, education or sustainable tourism. Many – such as Louis Sarno who works with BaAka (Pygmy) children in the forested areas of Central African Republic – choose to focus on women and children as one of the most effective ways to support the whole community. Louis is determined to give options to children who are discriminated against by the majority Bantu population.

Sometimes foundation assistance is as simple as restoring a local ruin like the Minaret of Jam in Afghanistan; this incredible monument now draws intrepid tourists to the area and its restoration has greatly improved options for local people.

Just as travel is often about learning to see with new eyes, so many of the groups we work with aim to change the way people see themselves and the future for their children and communities.

two main green political parties, Groen! (renamed in 2003 from Agalev; in Flanders) and Ecolo (in Wallonia). Their 1999 electoral success, however, was torpedoed at the national election in 2003, and the downward trend has continued, with both parties polling poorly at communal elections in 2006.

Belgium needs better vision – and action – in relation to sustainable energy and air quality, and the government must put into place more fiscal measures to encourage ecologically sound practices. One of the chief stumbling blocks on environmental matters is the country's linguistic divide; until there's greater cooperation between the three regions – Flanders, Wallonia and Brussels – it's likely things will continue to stagnate.

Mmmm...Beer

Belgium may be tiny, but its beers are big and bold. No country in the world boasts a brewing tradition as rich and diverse. And nowhere will you find the quantity of quality beers as is offered by this little nation. Forget the stock-standard lagers of Jupiler, Maes and Stella Artois – these conventional beers mirror brands the world round. It's the Trappist beers made by monks, the golden nectars named after the devil himself, and the acquired taste of tangy lambics that get connoisseurs in a tizz.

The Belgian love of beer has nabbed both sexes and all ages. There's none of that beer-belly baggage that goes with beer drinking in Britain, the US or Australia. Here it's about sipping and appreciating flavours, not quaffing and nurturing hangovers. Unlike in many other countries, bottled beer is the preferred choice and, in *cafés* (pubs/bars) stocking several hundred brews, the lion's share will come bottled. Some beers even arrive in a champagne-style bottle with a caged cork. Presentation is all-important. Every beer has its own glass, uniquely embossed and specially shaped to enhance the taste and aroma. The Kwak glass looks like a science-lab escapee, and definitely takes some juggling. Some waiters pour beers, others leave that pleasure to you. There's an art to pouring Belgian beers and techniques differ from beer to beer. A tiny bowl of peanuts, cubed cheese or other savoury nibblies will also be offered. This seductive presentation and personal involvement is all part of the pleasure of beer drinking in Belgium.

It is St Arnold, the patron saint of brewers, who must be thanked for this bevy of beers. When plague broke out in the Middle Ages, St Arnold convinced locals to drink beer rather than water. As beer was boiled and water wasn't, this so-called 'cure' worked. Beer became an everyday drink – a 'liquid bread' to supplement an otherwise meagre diet. Honey and spices were added to enhance the flavour, as was *gruut*, a blend of herbs and flowers such as rosemary and myrtle. Coriander is another favoured spice, believed to protect against hangovers.

By the early 19th century, Belgium had more than 3000 breweries; however, WWI caused the collapse of half and, by 1946, only 775 remained. These days, about 100 breweries compete for the local market, though only a handful has taken on the international arena. This explains why, until the late 1980s, Belgian beer was one of Europe's best-kept secrets. Some of the quality beers – Chimay, Orval and Duvel for example – now commonly sit in off-licences worldwide, though mostly it's brews (such as Stella, Hoegaarden and Leffe) owned by Leuven-based InBev, the country's largest brewer and exporter, that dominate the market.

This chapter will unravel some of Belgium's beer mysteries, detail which breweries open their doors to curious travellers, and let you in on the dos and don'ts of Belgian beer. If you like beer, you'll love Belgium, and if you don't like beer, you soon might.

BEER CHECKLIST

Walk into a specialist beer *café* in Belgium, such as Brussels' Le Bier Circus (p107) or 't Brugs Beertje (p137) in Bruges, and you'll be handed a beer menu the size of a book. It's hard to define numbers – between 400 and 800 different beers are brewed in Belgium – ranging from deep-brown Trappist beers that come with a creamy white head and a kick to them, to thirst-quenching white beers that go down deliciously on hot summer days. Spontaneously fermented lambics sit alongside amber beers that hint at godly connections,

The *Good Beer Guide to Belgium & Holland* by Tim Webb is an excellent book, giving a bar-by-bar account of what to taste, where to taste it and which breweries welcome devotees.

www.belgianstyle .com is a US-oriented site but shows a love of Belgian beer, listing pubs, breweries and links.

and then there's a whole range of speciality beers produced for festive occasions or simply for the fun of creating.

Most *cafés*, of course, don't have every brew in stock, but your average pub will have no trouble coming up with 20 different beers and in specialist pubs you'll be looking at several hundred. With such choice, it's no wonder first-time visitors go gaga over the beer menu. Taking a stab in the dark or picking a beer by name is one solution; however, tasting by name is a tantalising if dangerous way to go – after sinking a Duchesse de Bourgogne, followed by a Guillotine and a Satan, you'll think you've got Delirium Tremens (whose logo appropriately features pink elephants); come the next morning you'll wish for Mort Subite (literally, Instant Death). Endeavour to resist the temptation to sample 10 different beers in the first night – Belgians generally stick to one or two types per night, and shine the next day.

No Belgian beer is exactly like the next – keep this in mind for acquired tastes like lambic, some of the artisanal brews, and even your first Trappist. The uninitiated have been known to make ghastly comments about their first Belgian beer. 'It's worse than medicine' was one Australian woman's reaction to one of the great Trappist ales. Harry Pearson, author of *A Tall Man in a Low Land,* also struck a brew he didn't much admire during his time touring Belgium: 'It came in a bottle with a witch on it and had a tannic edge so hard it felt like it was scraping the enamel off your teeth and using it to sandblast your tastebuds'. Our advice: start tasting and judge for yourself.

Trappist Beers

Belgium's most famous tipples are divine creations. Trappist beers – gold or dark in colour, smooth in taste and dangerously strong (from 6% to 12%

BELGIUM BY BREWERY

▦ Musée Bruxellois de la Gueuze (p90) – best intro to Brussels' strange lambic brews.

▦ De Dolle Brouwers (p50) – crazy brewers that defy categorisation.

▦ Brasserie à Vapeur (p51) – still blowing steam, and a great day out.

▦ Brouwerij De Halve Maan (p128) – Belgium's most accessible brewery.

---

alcohol by volume) – have been made for centuries by Trappist monks, members of the strict Cistercian order. In earlier times, when water was foul, monks were permitted to consume the regional beverage: those in France and Italy took to wine; in Belgium monks chose between buttermilk and beer. Only a handful of European abbeys have carried the brewing tradition into the 21st century, and Belgium has six – Westmalle, Westvleteren and Achel in Flanders, and Chimay, Orval, and Rochefort in Wallonia. Only Orval monastery (p243), except its brewing hall, is open to visitors.

Westmalle (www.trappistwestmalle.be; Antwerpsesteenweg 496, Westmalle; ☺ not open to visitors), northeast of Antwerp, is the oldest of the six-pack. Brewing started here in 1836 and these days it's well known for two beers: the deep-brown Double (7%), known as Dubbel in Flemish, and the gloriously bronze Triple (9%), one of Belgium's most popular drinks. The latter also has a devoted international following – during a recent beer competition organised by *The New York Times*, Westmalle Triple trumped the 25 contenders. Beer devotees will find **Café Trappisten** (☎ 03 312 05 02; Antwerpsesteenweg 487, Westmalle; ☺ 9am-midnight), a popular pit stop for thirsty cyclists on the main road near the abbey, is the closest drink they'll get to the abbey.

The Trappist beers hardest to come by are the trio produced by the **Abdij St Sixtus** (www.sintsixtus.be; ☺ not open to visitors) at **Westvleteren**, west of Ypres. These beers aren't even labelled – they come in dark bottles identified by the colour of their cap: the green cap (5.8%) is blond, light and refreshing while the blue cap (8%), known as 8, and the yellow cap (10.8%), or 12, are both dark, unfiltered, malty beers with vigorous flavours. Indeed, the latter was recently voted as the world's best beer by thousands of beer enthusiasts from 65 countries on www.ratebeer.com.

Westvleteren is the smallest of the Trappist breweries, producing just 500,000L annually, all of which sells out within days of being on the market. According to the monks, they have no plans to increase production, despite worldwide popularity. Very few ordinary *cafés* around Belgium stock Westvleteren beers – Oud Arsenaal (p193) in Antwerp is a notable exception.

The abbey is not open to visitors but you can visit the big, modern *café* **In de Vrede** (☎ 057 40 03 77; Donkerstraat 13, Westvleteren; ☺ 10am-8pm Sat-Thu), opposite the abbey, which also contains a small museum and beer shop. This place figures prominently on cycle routes in the area but there's no public transport passing by. At the shop you can buy six-packs (€8.70), but for larger purchases make an appointment with the abbey's beer master (☎ 057 40 10 57), then drive to Westvleteren to pick up the goodies. A crate costs €30 and, in order to make things fair, the monks limit purchases to two crates per car. The appointment system is new, introduced in 2006 to stem the queue of cars – it's not unknown for beer lovers from Italy to cross the Alps just for a crate or two, and in recent times police have been called in to handle traffic chaos.

Close to the Dutch border, in the province of Limburg, is the Benedictine abbey **De Achelse Kluis** (www.achelsekluis.org; De Kluis 1, Hamont-Achel; ☺ not open to visitors) in **Achel**. Monks from Westmalle founded this abbey in 1846 but it closed down during WWI. In 1999 another Westmalle monk, Brother Thomas, started

Many beers are best drunk at room temperature – ask for *van 't schap* (from the shelf) in Flemish or *tempéré* in French.

www.beerparadise.be is the site of the Confederation of Belgian Brewers.

Alcohol-free beers (*alcoholvrije bieren/bières sans alcool*) do exist in Belgium – try Tourtel, Jupiler NA or Groene Palm.

brewing three beers – 4, 5 and 6, named after their alcohol content. There's also now an Achel 8. The abbey's **pub** (☎ 011 80 07 69; ☺ 11am-6pm Tue-Sun) sells all the beers plus other local produce. To get there from Hasselt, take bus 18A.

The **Abbaye Notre Dame de Scourmont** (www.scourmont.com; Forges; not open to visitors), on a hillock near **Chimay** in the province of Hainaut in Wallonia, is the most famous Trappist monastery. In 1860 Chimay led the commercialisation of Trappist brews, and these days it's the one you're most likely to find in your local off-licence. Chimay's three main beers are identified by the colour of their caps and labels: Chimay red (7%) is bronze coloured and soft flavoured; Chimay white (8%) is golden with a fresh, slightly bitter taste; and Chimay blue (9%) is dark, fruity and aromatic. **Auberge de Poteaupré** (p228) is the abbey's official watering hole.

The colour of a beer usually depends on the temperature during the malting process – a pale malt makes light beers while well-roasted malt results in dark brews. The addition of sweeteners such as caramel and candy sugar also affect colour.

As locations go, the **Abbaye Notre Dame** (p243) at **Orval** boasts the most scenic monastic surroundings. Southeast of Bouillon, deep in the forests of the Ardennes and close to the French frontier, it is the only abbey open to visitors. Unlike all the other Trappist breweries, Orval produces just one beer – a beautiful deep-orange brew that undergoes a second fermentation, has a hoppy character, and is served in a solid, gold-rimmed glass.

Also in the Ardennes is the **Abbaye de St Rémy** (www.trappistes-rochefort.com in French; ☺ not open to visitors) at **Rochefort**. This abbey produces the strongest Trappist ale but its three brews are not as well known as those of Westmalle or Chimay. In ascending order of strength there's 6 (7.5%), a deep-amber beer with a spicy, fruity taste, 8 (9.5%), a poignantly dry brew with an assertive pallet, and 10 (11.3%), with a red-brown colour and full-on flavour.

Trappist beers should be poured slowly with the glass tilted – aim to have a full glass with a solid head. Many bartenders don't pour the last few millimetres of Trappist brews as the dregs cloud the beer, but it's perfectly fine to drink them.

White Beers

White beers – known as *witbier* in Flemish and *bière blanche* in French – are thirst-quenching wheat beers, drunk iced with a twist of lemon on summer afternoons. Typically pale and cloudy and served in a solid tumbler, the

---

TOP 10 BREWS

- Achel 6 – a relative newcomer to the Trappist scene, and richly flavoured.

- Bush Prestige – at 13% it's Belgium's strongest beer, produced by Dubuisson, a little brewery in Hainaut.

- Cantillon Gueuze – Brussels' lambic that's nectar to those in the know; others may need convincing.

- De Koninck – bowl up to a bar in Antwerp and order a *bolleke* of this much-loved ale.

- Duvel – a hallowed golden brew that stands in a class of its own. Loved on hot summer days as well as in the depth of winter. Deceptively strong, at 8.5% alcohol by volume.

- Karmeliet – strong amber abbey beer.

- Orval – Trappist brew deserving of its devoted following.

- Rochefort 10 – top-shelf Trappist that packs an 11.3% punch. If that's too strong, go for the 8 (9.5%).

- Westmalle Triple – all-time Trappist favourite, chocolate-brown and creamy, with a 9% kick.

- Westvleteren 12 – recently voted the 'world's best beer', but notoriously difficult to come by.

best-known and most popular is **Hoegaarden**, named after a Flemish village about 40km east of Brussels where this regional beer was revived by Pierre Celis in the 1960s. Celis thought the beer would be liked by older folk but it took off with young people and has been a hit ever since. That said, some connoisseurs have recently struck it off their list, claiming its flavour has gone downhill since beer giant InBev took over the brewery and subsequently moved it from Hoegaarden to a site near Liège.

If you're keen to try a white beer produced by a small local brewery, choose Brugs Tarwebier, produced by De Gouden Boom (The Golden Tree) in Bruges.

Lambics

The champagne of the beer world – that's lambic (*lambiek* in Flemish). Like real champagne, this unique beer takes up to three years to make and comes out sparkling at the end. On the way it spends a night of revelry with wild microorganisms in a cold attic, and later spontaneously ferments. Unlike champagne, lambics are not immediately likable – they're sharp and acidic and tend to contort the faces of novices.

Lambic is the traditional beer of Brussels and is best explored at the **Cantillon Brewery** (www.cantillon.be), also known as the Musée Bruxellois de la Gueuze (see p90). This brewery and museum is one of Belgium's most atmospheric breweries. Located on a faceless backstreet in dog-eared Anderlecht, it's utterly unpretentious – the outside is unrecognisable as a brewery and inside is full of dusty old barrels and pungent aromas. The Cantillon family has brewed lambic here for four generations and they know their stuff. Tours include the attic room where the wort (a cooked mixture of wheat, water, malt and hops) spends a night in a huge, shallow tub in order to meet up with lambic's essential ingredient, wild yeast. These microorganisms fly around in the grimy Anderlecht air and spark the beer's spontaneous fermentation.

Faro is a young lambic that's been sweetened with sugar or caramel and has a short shelf life; straight lambic has matured for longer, usually at least a year, and hasn't been tampered with sweeteners. Both are difficult to find in *cafés*. The most popular lambic is gueuze (pronounced 'gerze') – a sour, refreshing beer made from a mix of different-aged lambics. It's reminiscent of a hard-core cider and is readily available in many pubs. Then there are fruit lambics, made more palatable by adding real cherries, called *kriek,* or fresh *framboise* (raspberries). Make no mistake, they're still sour-tasting beers. Lambics are generally moderate alcohol beers (4% to 6%).

Easy to find are imitation fruit lambics. These beers are made using quick brewing methods, and fake sweeteners and flavourings are added for mass appeal. The results tend to be sickly sweet and nothing like the real thing.

Golden Ales & Abbey Beers

Golden ales comprise all the gleaming beers that have crept onto the market in recent years in an attempt to imitate one of Belgium's most beloved brews, **Duvel** (www.duvel.be). Duvel was invented immediately after WWI as a dark-coloured victory drink, and a passing comment that its taste 'comes from the devil' supplied the name. It was reinvented as a golden ale after WWII but it wasn't until 1970 that the present-day brew made its appearance. Duvel comes in a seductive undulating glass and has a dense, creamy, two-inch-thick head that slowly dissolves to reveal a strong, distinct flavour. It's produced by Duvel-Moortgat.

Another golden ale worth sizing is **Straffe Hendrik Blonde**, produced by De Halve Maan brewery (p128) in Bruges. This brewery does tours for individuals and groups but, as it's located in the heart of one of Belgium's most

---

One of the world's best beer writers, Michael Jackson waxes lyrical on all that Belgium has to offer in *The Great Beers of Belgium*. He goes into great detail to explain the different varieties of beer, their tastes and unique attributes.

A *gistje*, a foul-tasting yeast extract, is served in schnapps glasses in some pubs in Antwerp and downed by drinkers needing a shot of vitamin B. It's a brewing by-product and, not surprisingly, free.

TOP 10 BEER PUBS

▪ Beermania, Brussels (p113) – the place to start, or finish, any serious beer study.

▪ Bierhuis Kulminator, Antwerp (p193) – off the beaten route but well worth finding.

▪ Café Botteltje, Ostend (p144) – seaside pub with 280 beers and counting.

▪ De Garre, Bruges (p137) – well-hidden bar between Bruges' main squares.

▪ Herberg de Dulle Griet, Ghent (p168) – inside or outside, as the weather dictates.

▪ Het Waterhuis aan de Bierkant, Ghent (p168) – waterside location and a superb array of brews.

▪ Moeder Lambic, Brussels (p107) – grungy bar known worldwide for its extensive beer list.

▪ Oud Arsenaal, Antwerp (p193) – not a strict beer-specialist *café* (pub/bar), but can hold its own among the big guns.

▪ 't Brugs Beertje, Bruges (p137) – Belgium's most famous beer-specialist pub.

▪ Ter Posterie, Ypres (p153) – cellar *café* with a great summer courtyard.

touristy towns, the tours tend to be crowded and impersonal. Still, they're a good way to see inside a relatively small brewery, and if you're there outside summer the crowds will have thinned.

A plethora of **abbey beers** – Grimbergen, Maredsous and the ubiquitous Leffe, to name a few – compete in Belgium. Despite the divine title, these beers are not touched by the hand of God nor made in a monastery. The abbeys after which they're named have sold their labels to the big boys such as InBev and Moortgat. Abbey beers tend to be strong amber ales with substantial flavour. Karmeliet is a relative newcomer to this group, and well worth trying.

www.beermania.be is the site of a Brussels beer shop that organises exports worldwide.

Vlaams Rood & Oud Bruin

Vlaams Rood, or Flemish Red beers, are produced in the province of West-Vlaanderen and are best represented by Rodenbach brewery in Roeselare. Rodenbach Grand Cru is a Belgian classic and takes up to 20 months to mature in huge wooden barrels.

Oud Bruin, or Old Brown, beers originate from around Oudenaarde and nearby Zottegem in the province of Oost-Vlaanderen and are made by blending young and old beers that undergo a secondary fermentation in the bottle. They're a sourish beer with a nutty character and usually come in at around 5% alcohol per volume – the breweries of Roman (established in 1545) at Mater, and Liefmans (since 1679) at Oudenaarde are two of the best known. Neither brewery is open for visits, though *cafés* in Oudenaarde (p160) stock plenty of local brews.

Brussels' Grand Place is the setting for the Belgian Beer Weekend (www.belgianbeerweekend.be), a beer-tasting event showcasing new and time-honoured brews held annually in early September. Some 48 brewers were represented in 2006.

Speciality Brews

A plethora of small-production artisanal breweries in Belgium produce special beers that can't be categorised. They'll pull out a new one especially for Christmas, or try new variations of age-old recipes simply for the fun of brewing. In Wallonia they're often referred to as '*saisons*', or 'seasonal' beers, which tend to be light-flavoured but hoppy and are best imbibed on hot days to quench the thirst. These speciality brews explain why it's impossible to pin down the number of beers produced in Belgium – it's as fluid as the product being created.

De Dolle Brouwers (☎ 051 50 27 81; www.dedollebrouwers.be; Roeselarestraat 12B, Esen; ⏰ café 2-7pm Sat & Sun, tour 3pm Sun) is the nation's wackiest brewery. Its name – 'The Crazy Brewers' – says it all. Located about 3km east of Diksmuide in the province of West-Vlaanderen, it's well worth a stop if you're prepared to

BEER ON THE HOP

Belgium's most popular beers can be bought in any old supermarket but for the greatest diversity you'll need to head to a specialist beer shop.

- Beermania, Brussels (p113)
- Bottle Shop, Bruges (p138)
- De Biertempel, Brussels (p113)
- Den Dorstvlegel, Antwerp (p196)
- Ter Posterie, Ypres (p153)

get off the beaten track. The brewery opens its doors on weekends and offers a free tour. Four beers – each with kooky labels – are produced. The best known is Oerbier, while Dulle Teve (Mad Bitch) has one of the nation's more descriptive names. All are available for tasting in the brewery's little *café*.

Brasserie à Vapeur (☎ 069 66 20 47; www.vapeur.com; Rue du Maréchal 1, Pipaix; admission incl a beer €5; ⏰ 9am-noon Sun Mar-Oct & last Sat of each month), as its name foretells, is a steam-operated brewery, unique in Belgium. It's located in a snoozy village in the province of Hainaut, about 15km east of Tournai off the road to Ath. The current owner, Louis Dits, bought the place in the mid-1980s and has painstakingly restored it to its 18th-century origins. The beers – *saisons* and one called Cochonne (or Little Bastard) – have a strong hops flavour and some are quite spicy. Unquestionably, the best time to visit is the last Saturday of each month when Louis fires up the kettles at 9am to brew a new batch. Visitors can watch the whole process. At noon, sit down to a feast – including dishes made with the brews and unlimited beer – for €20. Book in advance if you plan to stay for lunch. To get there from Tournai, take the train or bus to Leuze and then another bus back to Pipaix (30 minutes all up).

While you're in the neighbourhood, another local brewery worth discovering is **Brasserie Dubuisson** (☎ 069 67 22 21; www.br-dubuisson.com; Chaussée de Mons 28, Pipaix; admission €5; ⏰ tour 3pm Sat), maker of Bush Prestige (13%) – Belgium's strongest beer. Others in the range include the bitter-sweet Amber (12%), the strong Blonde (10.5%), and a light ale (7%).

Antwerp extols the virtues of Belgian beers with the Bierpassie Weekend (www.beerpassion.com) in late June.

According to its label, Bush, one of the country's strongest beers (13% alcohol by volume), is produced by 'passion passed on for eight generations'.

Food & Drink

Belgians love their food…and foodies love Belgium. The country's cuisine is highly regarded throughout Europe – some say it's second only to French while in other people's eyes it's equal. Belgians are reputed to dine out, on average, more than any other people in the world. This national pastime crosses all age boundaries and is cherished by both sexes. It's as common to find octogenarians languishing over a beer at the end of a five-course lunch as it is to see minimalist restaurants filled night after night by the designer set. Discussing the merits of a particular restaurant or a new dish occupies Belgians for hours. And you can be sure every Belgian can run off their top-10 places to eat.

The Belgo Cookbook by Denis Blais and André Plisnier, the creators of a London-based Belgian restaurant, is a zany, in-your-face cookbook with advice on good tunes to play while cooking guinea fowl in raspberry beer, among other things.

Qualitywise, there's rarely reason to complain. Beautifully presented food using fresh ingredients and timeless recipes are paramount to the dining experience. From chic restaurants to casual brasseries, quality is the yardstick. Naturally, this high standard involves seasonal appreciation. Belgians count the days until spears of spring asparagus appear; they know by heart which months mean mussels; they eagerly await autumn's tasty game dishes, and year-round they warm up on soup.

Meat and seafood are abundantly consumed and although there are traditional regional dishes – such as Ghent's famous *waterzooi* (a cream-based chicken stew) – the most popular dishes have crossed local boundaries. And it's not all local fare. The Belgian palate is broad; Italian, Japanese, Irish, Greek, Turkish, North African, Portuguese and Asian cuisines all thrive here.

STAPLES & SPECIALITIES

Breakfast in Belgium mirrors the nation's cultural divide – folks in Flanders sit down to a hearty meal of cold meats, sliced cheese, bread, butter, chocolate, jam and coffee, while those in Wallonia content themselves with a coffee, croissant and bit of baguette (continental breakfast). This difference may go unseen, as visitors staying in hotels or B&Bs generally receive the full kit and caboodle, no matter whether in Antwerp or Liège; however, if your survival depends on a solid start to the day, quiz your accommodation host about their style of breakfast as some hotels still do just the continental version.

Lunch and dinner hold almost equal importance, and if you want to get into a particular Brussels restaurant at *midi* (noon), you'd be wise to book. If you're looking for a bargain, take advantage of lunchtime when many restaurants offer a *dagschotel/plat du jour* (dish of the day). Also watch for a 'menu of the day' (*dagmenu* in Flemish or *menu du jour* in French). These menus comprise three courses (but sometimes expand to seven), and work out cheaper than selecting individual courses à la carte.

A cute exposé on chocolate making and its history can be found at www.users.skynet .be/chocolat/uk

Belgians are great soup eaters and this timeless food is seeing a huge revival, with modern soup kitchens popping up in the trendiest cities. Game, including pheasant and boar, is an autumn speciality from the Ardennes, often accompanied by wild mushrooms and sauces made from forest berries. The Ardennes is also famed for its cured hams and pâté. Horse, rabbit, hare and guinea fowl are typical offerings throughout Belgium as is offal, including kidneys, brains, tripe and liver. Some chefs now incorporate Belgium's incredible range of beers into sauces to reveal unique flavours.

Steak is cooked in a way slightly unfamiliar to most English-speaking visitors. *Saignant* (rare) is a euphemism for dripping with blood; *à point* (medium) is what Anglophones would consider rare, and *bien cuit* is the closest thing you'll get to well done.

Vegetarians and vegans should keep in mind that salads, though popular entrées, often contain some form of cheese or meat, such as the ever-popular *salade de Liège* with potatoes, bacon and beans (see p56).

DRINKS
Nonalcoholic Drinks
Bottled mineral water, such as the Belgian manufactured Spa, is preferred over tap water. In a restaurant, you'll automatically be given costly mineral water – brace yourself for a contemptuous look should you summon ordinary *kraantjeswater/de l'eau du robinet* (tap water).

Coffee is generally strong and aromatic and served espresso-style. In Wallonia you can order *café au lait* (coffee with steamed milk). In Flanders coffee is usually accompanied by a tub of evaporated milk. Cappuccino-lovers beware: Belgians often replace the much-loved froth with artificial whipped cream.

Tea, including herbal varieties, is widely available.

Alcoholic Drinks
In Belgium, beer rules – and deservedly so. The quality is excellent and the variety incomparable (see p45). Prices match quality, with a 250mL lager costing from €1.60 to €2.50, and a 330mL Trappist beer going for between €2.80 and €4.50, depending on the *café* (pub/bar).

Wine – everything from French to international – is the standard accompaniment when dining; there's no such thing as bring your own (BYO). Belgium has a tiny home-grown wine industry that started in the 1970s. There are three appellations: Hageland, based around the villages of Rillaar and Zoutleeuw east of Leuven; Haspengouw, in the eastern part of Limburg province; and Côtes de Sambre et Meuse in Wallonia. The wines are predominantly white, rose and sparkling, and most are Germanic in style. They're not all that easy to find, though slowly more and more restaurants and wine bars are stocking these home-grown products.

To wash it all down, there's *jenever/genièvre* (gin). Like beer, it's hard to ascertain how many *jenevers* are made in Belgium – figures range from 150 to 270. There are two categories: *jonge* (young) and *oude* (old). These names are a misnomer as age is not what determines the category, rather it's the ingredients and techniques used. Age does decide quality: the best *jenevers* have matured in wooden barrels for at least eight years. Old *jenever* is typically pale yellow, has a smooth taste and contains 35% to 40% alcohol per volume. Other types include sweetened fruit *jenevers* and *pékèt*, a lighter *jenever* made in Wallonia.

Jenever is often sold in big earthenware bottles that are best stored at room temperature. When ordering at a bar in Flanders, ask for a *witteke* (literally, a 'little white one') – it should come in a tall shot-glass cooled in a bed of ice. Expect to pay anywhere from €2.50 to €3.50 depending on quality. For more, see boxed text, (p55).

CELEBRATIONS
You only need look back at a Middle Ages painting by Breugel to see the importance of food and drink to the Belgian psyche and the high place it's awarded in festivals and celebrations. No gathering here goes without food, and this starts right at the very beginning. On the arrival of each child, elaborately presented *suikerbonen* (sugar-coated almonds) are given to relatives and friends by proud new parents. Weddings, of course, are gourmet affairs, with entire afternoons and evenings taken over to drinking and feasting. Funerals also end in a reunion, with family and friends saying final farewells over coffee and cake. Birthdays, Christmas and Easter are always reason enough for families to come together for a five-course meal. Specialities of

Godiva (www.godiva
.com) is one of the most
famous names in Belgian
chocolate, although it's
no longer Belgian owned.

BELGIAN CHOCOLATE

Chocoholics beware! Nowhere in the world will test your self-control as much as Belgium. The Belgians have been quietly making the world's finest chocolate for well over a century, and locals simply regard good chocolate as an everyday part of life. Every Belgian city of any size has divine chocolate shops but in Brussels the choice is staggering.

Filled chocolates, or pralines (pronounced 'prah-*leens*'), are the nation's forte. Prices match quality and reputation – in the better establishments you'll be paying for the white gloves they wear to hand-pick each praline. Count on anywhere between €30 and €58 per kilogram, and savour the moment each praline is popped into a special little box, known as a *ballotin*.

Belgium's first chocolate shop, Neuhaus (p113) in Brussels' Galeries St Hubert, opened in 1857 and still exists. Neuhaus' grandson is credited with inventing the praline – in 1912 he filled an empty chocolate shell with sweet substances, and so a Belgian institution was born.

But not everything to do with chocolate is sweet. Arguments have raged in recent times over the EU's definition of chocolate. Belgian chocolate traditionally mixes cocoa paste, sugar and cocoa butter in varying proportions. Dark chocolate uses the most cocoa, milk chocolate mixes in milk, and white chocolate is made by extracting only the butter from the cocoa. Pure cocoa butter is the fundamental ingredient, and it was the EU's decision to allow cheaper vegetable fats to replace 5% of the cocoa butter that had Belgian manufacturers up in arms.

Five percent more or less may seem incidental to novices, but there's no denying the taste or smoothness of Belgian chocolate. Stirring the chocolate, or 'conching' as it's known in the industry, is what defines smoothness – grainy chocolate just hasn't been conched enough. And if you never thought your average block of chocolate was grainy before, you'll think differently after trying Belgian chocolate.

The Players

From local bakeries and supermarket delis, to chain stores and top-notch *chocolateries* (chocolate shops), hundreds of chocolate producers vie for the domestic market, though only a handful have gone international, such as the elephant-emblazoned Côte d'Or, the US-owned Godiva, and the seashell-shaped Guylian.

Domestically, the praline scene divides neatly into popular chains and national stars. Leonidas is the most ubiquitous of the chain shops. Next up is Neuhaus and Corné, both good mid-range producers. Galler has made a name for itself by experimenting with flavours and making the results accessible in a range of chocolate bars. Top of the ladder is a host of independent *chocolateries* such as Burie and Del Rey in Antwerp (see p196) and Mary's or Pierre Marcolini in Brussels (p113). In a short space of time, Marcolini has taken Belgium and key international cities by storm, dishing up the country's – and possibly the world's – most expensive pralines (€58 per kilo) in innovative boxes that break the *ballotin* mould.

Shopping List

Entering a Belgian chocolate shop involves a shift of consciousness. Row upon row of assorted pralines await, all lounging in air-conditioned comfort and attended by glove-clad assistants. The smell is sweet but spiced, the atmosphere calm and seductive. Lined up at the counter are the *ballotins*, ranging from 125g, 250g, 375g, 500g and 750g to 1kg jumbo packs. Many shops have prepackaged boxes, but that takes the fun out of buying. Ask the assistant to cover the full spectrum or to go heavy on a particular type if you've got a preference. Some terms include:

- *Crème fraîche* – praline filling made from fresh whipped cream.
- *Ganache* – blend of chocolate, fresh cream and extra cocoa butter flavoured with coffee, cinnamon or liqueurs.
- *Gianduja* – blend of milk chocolate and hazelnut paste.
- *Praliné* – mix of chocolate and finely ground toffee or nuts.
- *Praliné nougatine* – ditto but uses larger pieces of nuts or toffee to provide the crunch.

these times include *speculaas* (cinnamon-flavoured biscuits), traditionally given on December 6, the day Sinterklaas (St Nicholas) supposedly arrives by boat from Spain, riding a white horse and accompanied by his (now politically correct) offsider Piet (formerly, the Zwarte Piet, or Black Peter). These days *speculaas* are devoured at any time, and there are even shops specialising in them (see p113). On Easter Sunday, many kids eagerly await not only the Easter Bunny but also the Klokken van Rome (Bells of Rome), which apparently fly all the way from Rome and drop small chocolate eggs from the sky when they arrive in Belgium. And if you're the sort who likes turning simple ol' Sunday mornings into a special time of relaxation, Belgium's fabulous. Just wander down to the local bakery and join the locals choosing *koffiekoeken* (coffee cakes) from Sunday's vast array.

WHERE TO EAT & DRINK

Belgium's dining scene reflects the nation's love of food. Any place, any time, you'll find honest food being served at much-loved eateries. This love affair explains why so many restaurants can sit side by side in a city the size of Antwerp, and not only survive but thrive.

Restaurants command the lion's share of the dining scene and generally open for lunch and dinner, but some open for dinner only (for standard opening hours see p303). Brasseries and bistros tend to open from 11am to midnight. They're the type of place you come to for a drink and end up staying to eat. The food is usually either traditional Belgian fare, with sound portions and good quality, or a Belgian-world mix. Unlike restaurants, brasserie kitchens don't close, making them a great place to catch a late-night bite or to dine outside standard restaurant hours.

Tearooms open for breakfast and shut by about 6pm. They usually offer sandwiches, light meals and nonalcoholic drinks, served in convivial surroundings.

> Browse menus and book a table on www.resto.be, which lists almost 10,000 restaurants in Belgium.

Quick Eats

The Belgians swear they invented *frieten/frites* – chips or fries – and judging by the availability, it's a claim few would contest. The popularity of this snack cannot be understated. Every Belgian village has at least one *frituur/friture* (chip shop) where *frites* are served in a paper cone or dish, smothered until unrecognisable with large blobs of thick mayonnaise (or flavoured sauces) and eaten with a small wooden fork in a futile attempt to keep your fingers clean.

> What does a Belgian, when returning from space, most desire? According to cosmonaut Frank De Winne, nothing less than *frites!* He's gotta be Belgian.

THE ORIGINAL GIN

Jenever/genièvre (ye-*nai*-ver) is the precursor of modern-day gin. Traditionally made from grain spirit, grasses and juniper berries, it's been distilled in Belgium since the Middle Ages when it was drunk medicinally. Later it spread to Britain where the taste was adapted and the name changed to 'gin'. Today there are about 70 distilleries scattered around Belgium, but the big names are Filliers, St-Pol and Smeets.

Limburg is a good place for serious study and sampling (remember, it's sip not slam). The Limburg capital, Hasselt, boasts the Nationaal Jenevermuseum (p211) and it puts on the Hasseltse Jeneverfeesten (p211) in October.

On a daily level, the following trio are specialist *jenever cafés*:

- De Vagant, Antwerp (p193)
- 't Dreupelkot, Ghent (p168)
- La Maison du Pékèt, Liège (p253)

ABC OF BELGIAN CAFÉS

Belgium's *café* (pub/bar) scene is one of its idiosyncratic delights. All *cafés* serve alcohol and are open from around 10am. There's no official closing time – these linger-as-long-as-you-like pubs stay open until the last person leaves. On sunny days the populace emerges to soak up the sun and a drink at pavement *cafés* or, as the Flemish put it, *een terrasje doen* (doing a terrace). A few local terms include:

- Bar – mostly associated with *jenever* (gin) and other strong drinks; no food. See La Maison du Pékèt (p253).
- Brasserie – spacious modern eateries, often with a terrace, and staying open from lunch 'til late. Great for casual dining or a drink at any time. See Café Belga (p107).
- *Bruin café* – 'brown *café*'; a small, old-fashioned pub noted for its décor: wood panelling, mirrored walls and globe lights. Mostly drinking only. Also called a *bruine kroeg*. See Oud Arsenaal (p193).
- *Eetcafé* – literally 'eating *café*'. Flemish name for a *café* serving a decent range of beers plus a limited number of meals. Also called *eetkroeg* or *estaminet*. See Lokkedize (p135).
- Grand *café* – old-world establishments adored by elderly *mesdames* but attracting an eclectic clientele. Good for a drink or meal at any time. See Falstaff (p106) or Le Cirio (p106).
- *Herberg* – old Flemish title for a tavern. These places tend to be larger than ordinary *cafés*, and dish up drinks and sometimes meals. See Herberg Vlissinghe (p137).

A *belegd broodje/sandwich garni* is half a baguette filled with one of an array of prepared fillings – from *thon mayonnaise* (tuna with mayonnaise) to *poulet samouraï* (spiced chicken). Such sandwiches are immensely popular snack foods and cost around €2.50 or €3.50. Panos is a good national outlet. Stuffed *pitas* (pitta breads, also called gyros) are also popular snacks. On the coast, steaming bowls of *wollekes* (sea snails) are dished up from sidewalk stalls.

For something sweet, there's always a *wafel/gaufre* (waffle). Cooked as you wait and served piping hot from street vendors, they're a national favourite. And don't worry if someone suggests smothering them in *slagroom* – it's the Flemish word for whipped cream.

VEGETARIANS & VEGANS

Fear not: Belgium may be carnivore kingdom but vegetarians are catered for, albeit reluctantly at times. Vegans, on the other hand, will go hungry almost everywhere. The scene pretty much divides neatly into mainstream bistros and restaurants offering one or two vegetarian options (it may be nothing more exciting than a cheese omelette), health-food shops that have tacked on some form of eatery, and full-blown veggie restaurants where the clientele demand smoke-free surroundings untainted by meat. The latter have only surfaced in the past decade or so; prior to that vegetarians were

---

BELGIUM'S TOP FIVE EATERIES

- Taverne du Passage, Brussels (p102)
- Le Pain Quotidien/Het Dagelijks Brood (p103)
- Kaffee Pergola, Bruges (p135)
- Walrus, Antwerp (p191)
- Bouchon, Hasselt (p212)

considered somewhat of an enigma to this heavily meat-based society and restaurants were predominantly hidden behind or above health-food shops. The exception to all this is Lombardia (p191), a hypercool Antwerp eatery that's been telling meat eaters where to stuff it for decades. We've listed vegetarian options throughout the guide.

EATING WITH KIDS

Dining out with the kids is quite normal in Belgium. Local kids eat out at top-end establishments, but they're expected to behave perfectly. Highchairs for toddlers are often available but ring ahead if you want to be sure. Restaurants in Belgium became smoke-free in 2007, but bear in mind that *cafés* (often good for a snack) were exempt from this ruling and are still generally full of smoke – not the healthiest of environments for kids to hang out in. A great place to eat with kids is Lunch Garden, a chain of family-friendly, self-service restaurants – we've mentioned a couple in this guide. Midrange restaurants will often list children's meals on their menus. For jars of organic baby food, check out the Hipp Bio range sold in Delhaize supermarkets.

As far as snacking goes, indulging in chocolates, *frites* or waffles is sure to be a winner. For more general information on travelling with little ones, see p303.

HABITS & CUSTOMS

You're in for the duration when dining in Belgium. The national passion for eating means you'll find leisurely breakfasts followed by long lunches and topped by decadent dinners. It's common for Belgians, even at home, to have two- or three-course dinners, with soup being the standard starter. Considering the amount of time the average Belgian spends at the table, it's remarkable they aren't as fat as butter. Belgians take good food – along with great chocolate and beer – as part of everyday life. It's appreciated often, but not overdone.

· Smoking in restaurants was banned in Belgium in January 2007. The exception is restaurants that provide a special 'smoking room' – here blazing up is allowed only before meals are served and during dessert. Due to this development, nonsmoking symbols are not included in reviews throughout the Belgian chapters of this guide.

Fast food in the form of international chains has only belatedly found a foothold. The country's indigenous alternatives – *frituren/frituries* and the hamburger chain Quick – have been strong enough to keep big guns such as McDonald's to a minimum.

French-English Dictionary of Good Eating & Drinking, by Christian de Fouloy, aims to take some of the guesswork out of deciphering the many French menus you'll come across in Belgium and Luxembourg.

DOS & DON'TS

- Feel free to take your children to restaurants of all persuasions. Belgian children are educated at an early age into fine dining and generally behave perfectly. Don't let yours run riot.

- If you're invited to someone's home for dinner, it's usual to bring a gift – chocolates, flowers or a bottle of wine are standard accompaniments.

- Belgians sit down to eat, and expect it to be a social occasion, whether at home or not. Even in ubiquitous sandwich bars such as Panos, seating is provided; stuffing your face on the hoof is just not done. About the only thing you'll see Belgians munching as they window shop are piping hot waffles in winter and ice creams in summer.

- Traditionally, the rule of thumb is to eat mussels only during months with an 'r' in their name. But modern cultivation techniques have extended the season, and locals now tuck in from July. Don't eat any that haven't opened properly once they've been cooked. And don't worry about a fork – use an empty mussel shell to prise the others out.

TRAVEL YOUR TASTEBUDS

- *Bloedworst* – black pudding; blood sausage made from leftover pig. The meat is mixed with pig's blood, fat and bread and is made into sausages. It's traditionally served with *appelmoes* (apple sauce).
- *Breugel Kop* – the name translates to Breugel's Head, though how the great artist would take to being compared to chunks of beef and tongue set in gelatine is anyone's guess.
- *Cervelle de veau/agneau* – brain, either veal or sheep, was big on Belgian plates until mad cow disease made it lose its lustre.
- *Croque monsieur* – the essential grilled ham and cheese sandwich.
- *Filet américain* – deceptive name for this most adventurous of Belgian dishes. What sounds like a succulent American steak is actually a blob of minced beef served raw. Has been blamed for giving people worms, though it's still found on many menus around the country and is traditionally served with a pile of chips.
- *Fondue au fromage* – no swirling pot of melted cheese and chunks of bread here. This dish comprises deep-fried croquettes made with a cheesy/creamy filling.
- *Konijn met pruimen* – the Flemish favourite. Rabbit cooked until tender in a sauce spiked with prunes.
- *Mechelse asperges* – spring asparagus from Mechelen; a firm favourite.
- *Mosselen/moules* – considered by many to be Belgium's national dish: mussels cooked in white wine, or other less traditional sauces, served in steaming cauldrons and accompanied by a bowl of *frites* (chips or fries). Most mussels served in Belgium are grown in the Netherlands, but the first home-grown bivalves are expected to arrive on Belgian plates in 2007.
- *Paardefilet/steack de cheval* – no matter how you write it, this is horse in no uncertain terms.
- *Paling in 't groen/anguilles-au-vert* – eel in spinach sauce. Not the most visually appetising of dishes, nor is it moreish after the fourth chunk; try it as an entree.
- *Stoemp* – Grandma's kitchen come to the city. Princely portions of mashed potatoes are tarted up with toppings such as a *spiegelei* (fried egg) or a fat sausage.
- *Truffels/truffes* – Truffles; subterranean fungi that's a highly prized seasonal delicacy (autumn and winter).
- *Truite à l'Ardennaise* – Ardennes trout poached in a wine sauce and served sprinkled with almonds.
- *Waterzooi* – cream-based stew originating in Ghent where it was traditionally made with chicken. These days you'll find regional variations such as *Oostendse Waterzooi,* Ostend's fish version.

EAT YOUR WORDS

Want to be able to recognise horse from herring? Bacon from brains? Get behind the cuisine scene by getting to know the languages – both of them. For Flemish pronunciation guidelines see p330; for French see p333.

Useful Phrases
FLEMISH
A table for two, please.
    Een tafel voor twee, alstublief.   ən *taa*·fəl voar tway als·tu·*bleeft*
Do you have a menu in English?
    Hebt U de kaart in het Engels?   hept u də kaart in hət *eng*·əls
What's the speciality here?
    Wat is hier de specialiteit?   wat is heer də spay·sya·lee·*tayt*
I'd like the dish of the day.
    Ik had graag de dagschotel.   ik hat khraakh də *dakh*·skhoa·təl

I'd like the set menu.
　Ik neem het dagmenu.　　　　　　ik naym hət *dakh*·mə·nu
I'm a vegetarian.
　Ik ben vegetariër.　　　　　　ik ben vay·khay·*taa*·ree·yər
I'd like to order the…
　Ik zou graag… willen bestellen.　　ik zow khraakh… *wi*·lə bə·*ste*·lən
The bill, please.
　De rekening alstublief.　　　　　də *ray*·kə·ning als·tu·*bleeft*

FRENCH
A table for two, please.
　Une table pour deux, s'il vous plaît.　ewn ta·bler poor der seel voo play
Do you have a menu in English?
　Est-ce que vous avez la carte en anglais?　es·ker voo za·vay la kart on ong·lay
What's the speciality here?
　Quelle est la spécialité ici?　　　kel ay ler spay·sya·lee·tay ees·ee
I'd like the dish of the day.
　Je voudrais avoir le plat du jour.　zher voo·dray a·vwar ler pla doo zhoor
I'd like the set menu.
　Je prends le menu.　　　　　　zher pron ler mer·new
I'm a vegetarian.
　Je suis végétarien/végétarienne (m/f).　zher swee vay·zhay·ta·ryun/vay·zhay·ta·ryen
I'd like to order the…
　Je voudrais commander…　　　zher voo·dray ko·mon·day
The bill, please.
　La note, s'il vous plaît.　　　　la not seel voo play

Food Glossary
FLEMISH
Basics

avondmaal	*aa*·vont·maal	dinner
frituur	free·*tur*	chip shop
gevogelte	khə·*voa*·khəl·tə	poultry
groente	*khroon*·tə	vegetable
kruidenier	krəy·də·*neer*	grocery store
middagmaal	*mi*·dakh·maal	lunch
nagerecht	*naa*·khə·rekht	dessert
ontbijt	ont·*bayt*	breakfast
vis	vis	fish
vlees	vlays	meat
wild	wilt	game

Starters, Soups & Snacks

belegd broodje	bə·*lekht broa*·tye	filled sandwich
boterham	*boa*·tər·ham	slice of bread (with filling)
frieten	free·*tən*	chips/French fries
koude voorgerechten	*kow*·də *voar*·khə·rekh·tən	cold starters
pide	*pee*·də	Turkish pizza
snee brood	snay broat	slice of bread (no filling)
soep	soop	soup
warme voorgerechten	*war*·mə *voar*·khə·rekh·tən	warm starters

Meat

bloedworst	*blood*·worst	black pudding
eend	aynt	duck

everzwijn	*ay·vər·zwayn*	boar
fazant	fa·*zant*	pheasant
hammetje	*ha·mə·*tye	ham on the bone
hersenen	*her·*sə·nən	brains
hert	hert	venison
hesp	hesp	ham
kalfsvlees	*kalfs·*vlays	veal
kalkoen	kal·*koon*	turkey
kip	kip	chicken
konijn	ko·*nayn*	rabbit
lam	lam	lamb
lever	*lay·*vər	liver
paard	paart	horse
parelhoen	*paa·*rəl·hoon	guinea fowl
ribstuk	*rip·*stək	rib steak
rund	rənd	beef
schaap	skhaap	mutton
slak	slak	snail
spek	spek	bacon
tong	tong	tongue
varkensvlees	*var·*kəns·vlays	pork
vleeswaren	*vlays·*waa·rən	cooked/prepared meats
worst	worst	sausage

Fish & Seafood

ansjovis	an·*shoa·*vis	anchovy
baars	baars	bream
forel	foa·*rel*	trout
garnaal	khar·*naal*	shrimp
haring	*haa·*ring	herring
inktvis	*ingt·*vis	squid
kabeljauw	ka·bəl·*jow*	cod
krab	krap	crab
kreeft	krayft	lobster
maatjes	*maa·*tyəs	herring fillets
oester	*oos·*tər	oyster
paling	*paa·*ling	eel
rivierkreeft	ree·*veer·*krayft	crayfish
roodbaars	*roat·*baars	red mullet
St Jacobsschelp	sint·*yaa·*kop·skhelp	scallop
steurgarnaal	*steur·*khar·naal	prawn
tong	tong	sole
tonijn	to·*nayn*	tuna
zalm	zalm	salmon
zeebaars	*zay·*baars	sea bream

Vegetables

aardappel	*aart·*a·pəl	potato
ajuin	a·*yəyn*	onion
artisjok	ar·tee·*shok*	artichoke
asperge	as·*per·*zhə	asparagus
aubergine	oa·bər·*zhee·*nə	eggplant
boon	boan	bean
champignon	sham·pee·*nyon*	mushroom
courgette	koor·*zhet*	zucchini

erwtjes	erw·tyəs	peas
groene paprika	khroo·nə pap·raa·ka	green pepper (capsicum)
komkommer	kom·kom·ər	cucumber
kool	koal	cabbage
look	loak	garlic
maïs	ma·yees	sweet corn
olijf	o·layf	olive
peterselie	pay·tər·say·lee	parsley
pompoen	pom·poon	pumpkin
prei	pray	leek
rode paprika	roa·də pap·ree·ka	red pepper (capsicum)
selder	sel·dər	celery
spinazie	spee·naa·zee	spinach
spruitjes	sprəy·tyes	Brussels sprouts
witloof	wit·loaf	chicory
wortel	wor·təl	carrot

Desserts

cake	kayk	cake
koek	kook	biscuit
roomijs	roam·ays	ice cream
taart	taart	tart (pie)
wafel	waa·fəl	waffle

Drinks

bier	beer	beer
jenever	zhə·nay·vər	Belgian gin
lambiek	lam·beek	Brussels beer
wijn	wayn	wine

Miscellaneous

azijn	a·zayn	vinegar
boter	boa·tər	butter
brood	broat	bread
ei	ay	egg
geitenkaas	khay·tən·kaas	goat's cheese
kaas	kaas	cheese
konfituur	kon·fee·tur	jam
melk	melk	milk
pannenkoek	pa·nə·kook	pancake
peper	pay·pər	pepper
rijst	rayst	rice
speculaas	spay·ku·laas	cinnamon-flavoured biscuit
suiker	səy·kər	sugar
zout	zowt	salt
water	waa·tər	water

Cooking Methods

gebakken	khə·ba·kən	baked
gegratineerd	khə·khra·tee·nayrt	browned on top with cheese
gegrild	khə·khrilt	grilled
gegrild aan 't spit	khə·khrilt aant spit	spit-roasted
gepaneerd	khə·pa·nayrt	coated in breadcrumbs
gesauteerd	khə·soa·tayrt	sautéed
gestoomd	khə·stoamt	steamed

gerookt	khə-*roakt*	smoked
geroosterd	khə-*roas*-tərt	roasted
gevuld	khə-*vəlt*	stuffed
op het houtvuur bereid	op hət *howt*-vur bə-*rayt*	cooked in a wood stove

FRENCH
Basics

déjeuner	day-zher-nay	lunch
dessert	day-sair	dessert
dîner	dee-nay	dinner
épicerie	ay-pee-say-ree	grocery store
friture	free-tewr	chip shop
gibier	zhee-byay	game
légume	lay-gewm	vegetable
petit déjeuner	per-tee day-zher-nay	breakfast
poisson	pwa-son	fish
viande	vyond	meat
volaille	vo-lai	poultry

Starters, Soups & Snacks

croque monsieur	krok mer-syer	grilled ham and cheese sandwich
entrées chaudes	on-tray shod	warm starters
entrées froides	on-tray fwad	cold starters
frites	freet	chips/French fries
potage	po-tazh	soup
sandwich garni	son-dweesh gar-nay	filled sandwich
tartine	tar-teen	slice of bread

Meat

agneau	a-nyo	lamb
bœuf	berf	beef
boudin noir	boo-dun-nwar	black pudding
brochette	bro-shet	kebab
canard	ka-nar	duck
cerf	ser	venison
cervelle	sair-vel	brains
charcuterie	shar-kew-tree	cooked/prepared meats
cheval	sher-val	horse
dinde	dund	turkey
entrecôte	on-trer-kot	rib steak
escargot	es-kar-go	snail
faisan	fay-zon	pheasant
foie	fwa	liver
jambon	zhom-bon	ham
jambonneau	zhom-bon-no	ham on the bone
langue	long	tongue
lapin	la-pun	rabbit
marcassin	mar-ka-sun	boar
mouton	moo-ton	mutton
pintade	pun-tad	guinea fowl
porc	por	pork
poulet	poo-lay	chicken
saucisson	so-see-son	sausage
veau	vo	veal

Fish & Seafood

anchois	on·shwa	anchovy
anguille	ong·gee·yer	eel
brème	brem	bream
cabillaud	ka·bee·yo	cod
calmar	kal·mar	squid
coquille St Jacques	ko·kee·yer sun·zhak	scallop
crevette	krer·vet	shrimp
dorade	do·rad	sea bream
hareng	a·rong	herring
homard	om·ar	lobster
huître	wee·trer	oyster
langouste	long·goost	crayfish
raie	ray	ray
rouget	roo·zhay	red mullet
saumon	so·mon	salmon
scampi	skom·pee	prawn
thon	ton	tuna
truite	trweet	trout

Vegetables

ail	ai	garlic
artichaut	ar·tee·sho	artichoke
asperge	a·spairzh	asparagus
aubergine	o·bair·zheen	eggplant
champignon	shom·pee·nyon	mushroom
chicon	shee·kon	chicory
chou	shoo	cabbage
choux de Bruxelles	shoo der brew·sel	Brussels sprouts
citrouille	see·troo·yer	pumpkin
concombre	kong·kombr	cucumber
courgette	koor·zhet	zucchini
échalote	ay·sha·lot	shallot
épinards	ay·pee·nar	spinach
haricot	a·ree·ko	bean
maïs	ma·ees	sweet corn
oignon	on·yon	onion
persil	pair·sil	parsley
petit pois	pay·tee pwa	peas
poireau	pwa·ro	leek
poivron rouge/vert	pwav·ron roozh/vair	red/green pepper (capsicum)
pomme de terre	pom der tair	potato
truffe	trewf	truffle

Desserts

couque	kook	biscuit
gâteau	ga·to	cake
gaufre	go·fref	waffle
tarte	tart	tart (pie)
glace	glas	ice cream

Drinks

bière	bee·yair	beer
genièvre	zhay·nyevr	Belgian gin

| *lambic* | lom·bik | Brussels beer |
| *vin* | vun | wine |

Miscellaneous

beurre	bur	butter
confiture	kon·fee·tewr	jam
crêpe	krep	pancake
eau	o	water
fromage	fro·mazh	cheese
fromage de chèvre	fro·mazh der she·vrer	goat's cheese
œuf	erf	egg
lait	lay	milk
pain	pun	bread
poivre	pwa·vrer	pepper
riz	ree	rice
sel	sel	salt
sucre	sew·krer	sugar
vinaigre	vee·nay·grer	vinegar

Cooking Methods

à la broche	a la brosh	spit-roasted
à la vapeur	a la va·per	steamed
au feu de bois	o fer der bwa	cooked over a wood stove
au four	o foor	baked
farci	far·see	stuffed
fumé	foo·may	smoked
gratiné	gra·tee·nay	browned on top with cheese
grillé	gree·yay	grilled
pané	pa·nay	coated in breadcrumbs
rôti	ro·tee	roasted
sauté	so·tay	sautéed

Brussels

If ever a city could claim split personality, it's Brussels. French versus Flemish, historic versus hip, bizarre versus boring. Full of contrasts, contradictions and intrigue, this is a multicultural equation that goes much deeper than just red tape and Eurocrats. An historic heirloom is closer to the mark. And in an age where so much is already discovered, Belgium's capital seduces as one of Western Europe's unknowns.

Brussels is a city of fine food, *café* culture, Art Nouveau architecture and the surreal. Pull up a chair and join laissez-faire locals who value the city's casual atmosphere. Watch money go down on swish Ave Louise or buy dried caterpillars just blocks away in Matonge, the capital's African quarter. Some of the world's most enduring images of surrealist art were created in the nondescript northern suburb of Jette. And the architecture ranges from monumental edifices such as the Grand Place to organic Art Nouveau façades and the EU's real-life Gotham City.

Constant among all this is the quality of everyday life – the shopping's great, the restaurants fab, the chocolate shops sublime and the pub scene extraordinary. For a long time Brussels didn't go out of its way to impress, but its stint as Cultural Capital of Europe in 2000 saw the city dusted and polished in a flurry that brought renewed life to historic buildings and decaying streets. A new spirit, just short of cockiness, emerged, flaming outside interest and inner-city regeneration. Nearly a decade on, Brussels is looking better than ever.

HIGHLIGHTS

- **Kick Back** The Grand Place on a summer's evening (p69)
- **Jewel in the Crown** The capital's Art Nouveau gems (p92 & p93)
- **Art History** Old masters and surrealists at the Musées Royaux des Beaux-Arts (p83)
- **Popping Beers** Strange brews at the Musée Bruxellois de la Gueuze (p90)
- **Bizarre Booty** Koninklijk Museum voor Midden-Afrika (p94)
- **Musical Views** Panoramas, instruments and Art Nouveau all wrapped up in the Musée des Instruments de Musique (p83)
- **Parades & Pageants** A festival for all seasons (p95)
- **Fashion Feast** Capitalising on fashion (p114)
- **Diner's Delight** From ancient *cafés* to minimalist marvels (p101)
- **Drinking Scene** Pubs by the thousands…and no two alike (p106)

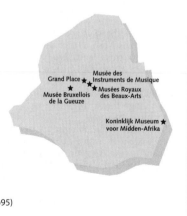

Grand Place · Musée des Instruments de Musique · Musée Bruxellois de la Gueuze · Musées Royaux des Beaux-Arts · Koninklijk Museum voor Midden-Afrika

POPULATION: 999,900	LANGUAGES: FRENCH & FLEMISH

HISTORY

Legend has it that St Géry, Bishop of Cambrai and Arras, built a chapel on one of the islands in the swampy Senne (Zenne) River in AD 695, although the name Bruocsella (from *bruoc*, marsh or swamp, and *sella*, dwelling) wasn't recorded until 966. In 979 Charles, Duke of Lorraine, built a fort on the St Géry island and moved from Cambrai to Bruocsella. A settlement developed and, protected by several defensive ramparts and gates, it evolved into an administrative and commercial hub. By 1100 Brussels had its first fortified wall.

In 1229 Henri I, Duke of Brabant, published the first Brussels charter, which guaranteed protection for citizens and private property, and established punishments for crimes. The dukes of Brabant controlled the region on and off for the next two centuries and their fortunes were aligned through marriage to the dukes of Burgundy. In 1482, upon the death of Mary of Burgundy, the Hapsburgs came to power. Emperor Charles V used Brussels as the capital of his vast kingdom and the city flourished under his patronage.

Charles V's successor, Philip II, ruled from Spain. Philip's fanatical Catholicism lead to the Protestant's Iconoclastic Fury (see p24), which Philip quashed through the Spanish Inquisition. Among the thousands given death sentences at this time were Counts Egmont and Hoorn, vocal protesters against Spanish rule. They were executed on Brussels' Grand Place in front of the Maison du Roi.

In 1695 Louis XIV's French army under Marshal De Villeroy bombarded Brussels for two days in retaliation for Dutch and English attacks on French Channel ports. They destroyed 4000 houses and much of the Grand Place, although this was restored to its full glory within five years.

Austrian rule in the 18th century fostered urban development, with the construction of squares such as Place Royale and completion of the royal palace at Laeken (1784). Many of the Upper Town's architectural gems were built during this time.

The French Revolution inspired similar sentiments in Brussels and the Austrians were eventually forced out by the French. They held power until 1815 when Napoleon was defeated at the Battle of Waterloo (p225) and Belgium and Luxembourg were incorporated into the newly formed United Kingdom of the Netherlands. This setup didn't last long;

THE BRUSSELS REGION

Brussels comprises 19 *communes*, collectively known as the Brussels Region (Brussels Gewest in Flemish, Région de Bruxelles in French). This region is the only area in Belgium to be officially bilingual and the *communes* often (but not always) have two names – thus you'll see signs for the *commune* of Elsene (as it's known in Flemish) and Ixelles (its French name). The same goes for the names of streets, train stations, public buildings, you name it. We've used French place/street names throughout this chapter.

Brussels residents revolted in 1830 (see boxed text, p110) and Belgium became an independent state with Brussels, at that time home to 100,000, as its capital.

The city grew enormously in both population and stature during the next century due largely to the expansionist policy of King Léopold II (see p96).

After WWII, Brussels developed unchecked, first becoming the headquarters of NATO and later the EU (p87). But it was its stint as Cultural Capital of Europe in 2000 that gave the city the push it needed. Neglected buildings and neighbourhoods were spruced up and a shift of consciousness gave birth to new spirit. This spirit was radically expressed in the 2001 local elections when the Bruxellois ousted the long-standing Liberals for a red-green coalition. While things have since mellowed politically, with the Socialists alone taking poll position in the 2006 election, culturally Brussels is still riding a high.

ORIENTATION

Most of Brussels is surrounded by the Ring, a motorway which provides easy central access. Another ring – the Petit (Small) Ring – encases the historic centre in a pentagon of boulevards that allows rapid transit.

Central Brussels is divided into two main areas – the Lower and Upper Towns. The **Lower Town** (Map p74) comprises the medieval core based around the imposing Grand Place, a former market square. This area is best explored on foot, its cobbled streets leading to popular quarters such as **Ilôt Sacré**, **Ste Catherine**, **St Géry** and, to the south, the **Marolles** (Map pp76–7), an old working-class neighbourhood where some locals still speak Bruxellois, the city's old dialect. Unbeknown to most visitors, the Senne River, on which the city grew up, still runs through this area but was covered over in the late 19th century for health reasons (cholera outbreaks and the like).

The **Upper Town** (Map pp72–3 & Map p74) has a vastly different atmosphere. It rises to the east and southeast of the Grand Place and was traditionally home of Belgium's French-speaking elite. Thus you'll find wide boulevards flanking monumental buildings such as the Palais Royal and the Palais de Justice, as well as the Belgian parliament and government headquarters, and some major museums and chic shopping precincts based around the Sablon and Ave Louise areas.

There's plenty to see within the Petit Ring, but Brussels extends much further. The modern **EU quarter** (Map p86) – signposted Europese Instellingen/Institutions Européennes – lies to the east and borders the vibrant **Ixelles** (Map pp76–7), which straddles Ave Louise. Ixelles and its neighbour, **St Gilles** (Map pp76–7), are known for their many Art Nouveau buildings, although the latter also has a down-at-heel quarter not far from Gare du Midi, the city's main international train station. Brussels' 30,000-strong Portuguese community is based around Place Flagey where the first immigrants settled in the 1960s. The renovated Flagey building, now an entertainment complex, has seriously boosted the area's nightlife. Also in Ixelles is **Matonge**, a lively quarter home to the capital's African community, and given its unofficial name from a square in the Congolese capital Kinshasa. South of Ixelles, the affluent commune of **Uccle** (Map pp70–1) flanks the Bois de la Cambre, a popular park that eventually joins the Forêt de Soignes.

North of the old city centre is a business district built around Blvd Émile Jacqmain and resembling a miniature Manhattan. Immediately west of here in **Molenbeek** (Map pp70–1) is the city's modern-day port, based along the Canal de Charleroi, which links Brussels with Charleroi to the south and Antwerp to the north. Until recently, this area of industrial decay held little appeal for visitors, but new urban developments like Tour & Taxis (p89) have put it on the map.

Further north, the canal separates the run-down immigrant neighbourhoods of **Schaerbeek** (Map pp70–1) and **St Josse** (Map pp72–3) from the affluent *commune* (suburb) of **Laeken** and the **Domaine Royal** (Map pp70–1), the main residence of Belgium's royal family. Just northwest of here is Heysel, site of the infamous 1985 soccer stadium disaster and home to the Atomium, a space-age leftover from the 1958 World Fair.

Last, northwest of the centre are the little-visited communes of **Jette** (Map pp70–1) and **Koekelberg** (Map pp70–1), and to the southwest is **Anderlecht** (Map pp70–1), best known for its soccer team but also boasting an interesting museum and a not-to-be-missed eatery (see boxed text, p105).

Brussels has three main train stations: Gare du Nord, Gare Centrale and Gare du Midi. For details, see p115.

INFORMATION
Bookshops
Anticyclone des Açores (Map p74; ☎ 02 217 52 46; Rue du Fossé aux Loups 34) Travel specialist.

Évasions 1 (Map p74; ☎ 02 502 49 56; Rue du Midi 89; ☑ 9.30am-6pm) Buys and sells all sorts of books. Expect floor-to-ceiling stacks.

FNAC (Map pp72-3; ☎ 02 209 22 11; City 2 shopping centre, Rue Neuve; ☑ 10am-7pm Mon-Sat) Department store with extensive literary selection, English-language books, travel guides and maps.

La Librairie de Rome (Map pp76-7; ☎ 02 511 79 37; Rue Jean Stas 16a; ☑ 8am-8pm Sun-Tue, to 9pm Wed-Sat) For international magazines and newspapers.

Nicola's Bookshop (Map pp76-7; ☎ 02 513 94 00; 106 Rue de Stassart; ☑ 11am-7pm Mon-Sat) Small English-language bookshop specialising in world literature.

Pêle Mêle (Map pp72-3; ☎ 02 548 78 00; Blvd Maurice Lemonnier 55) Cavernous secondhand bookshop.

Sterling Books (Map p74; ☎ 02 223 62 23; Rue du Fossé aux Loups 38; ☑ 10am-7pm Mon-Sat, noon-6.30pm Sun) Comfy sofas, a kids' play area and helpful staff make this English-language bookshop a welcome respite.

Waterstones (Map p74; ☎ 02 219 27 08; Blvd Adolphe Max 71-75; ☑ 9am-7pm Mon-Sat, 11.30am-6pm Sun) Brussels' biggest English-language bookshop.

Emergency
Ambulance/Fire (☎ 100)
Police (☎ 101)

Internet Access
BXL (Map p74; ☎ 02 502 99 80; Place de la Vieille Halle aux Blés 46; ☑ noon-midnight; per hr €2) Groovy *café*/bar with an internet alcove.

Concepts Telecom (Map pp76-7; Gare du Midi; ☑ 9am-8.30pm Mon-Fri, 10am-7.30pm Sat; per hr €4) Inside the main international train station.

BRUSSELS IN...

Two Days

Order a *petit noir* on the **Grand Place** (opposite), Brussels' gorgeous central square, before exploring nearby cobbled streets and the **Galeries St Hubert** (p112). Head to the Upper Town to take in old and modern masters at the **Musées Royaux des Beaux-Arts** (p83) before viewing the cityscape from the **Old England building** (p83). Ogle **chocolate shops** (p113) on the swish Place du Grand Sablon, followed by Art Nouveau at the **Musée Horta** (p87). At night head to **Rue des Bouchers** (p80), Brussels' famous restaurant street, before pub crawling around the **Lower Town** (p106).

Head out of the centre on day two to either the **Koninklijk Museum voor Midden-Afrika** (p94), one of Belgium's more bizarre outings, or the **Musée Bruxellois de la Gueuze** (p90) for strange Brussels brews. Chill out in the afternoon with some shopping (p112) – first the **Rue Antoine Dansaert** quarter, then **Ave Louise**. Dine at one of many restaurants in or around Ixelles' **Rue St Boniface** (p104), and finish up with a drink at **Place Flagey** (p107), one of the city's trendiest locales.

Four Days

Follow the two-day itinerary, then on your third day add a surrealist trip to the **Musée Magritte** (p89) or an Art Deco day at the **Musée David et Alice van Buuren** (p88). On day four delve into the city's comic-strip culture – choose either the **Centre Belge de la Bande Dessinée** (p81) or trace the **Murals of Brussels** (p82) walk. There's no shortage of restaurants and pubs to finish up in.

Laundry

Salon Lavoir de la Chapelle (Map pp72-3; Rue Haute; 8am-6pm Mon-Fri) Old-fashioned, full-service laundrette.
Was-Salon Lavoir (Map pp72-3; Rue de Laeken 145; 7am-10pm) Self-service laundrette.

Left Luggage

Brussels National Airport Luggage lockers on Level 0 of the terminal.
Train stations Luggage lockers (€2.60 to €3.60 per 24 hours depending on the size of the locker, with a maximum of 72 hours) or left-luggage offices (€2.50 per article per day; open 5am or 6am to 9pm).

Libraries

Centre Belge de la Bande Dessinée (Map pp72-3; 02 219 19 80; Rue des Sables 20; noon-5pm Tue-Thu, noon-6pm Fri & Sun, 10am-6pm Sat) Specialised comic-strip library. Small admission charge (€2) to access the reading room or study section.

Medical Services

Helpline (02 648 40 14) Twenty-four-hour assistance line run by Community Help Service. Can provide a list of English-speaking doctors, dentists and other health professionals.
Hôpital St Pierre (Map pp76-7; 02 535 31 11, emergency 02 535 40 51; cnr Rue Haute & Rue de l'Abricotier; 24hr) Central hospital offering emergency assistance.

Money

ATMs and exchange facilities are found on and around the Grand Place, at Gare du Midi and Brussels National Airport.

Post

Post office Main post office (Map p74; Blvd Anspach 1; 8am-6pm Mon-Fri, 10.30am-4.30pm Sat); Gare du Midi (Map pp76-7; Ave Fonsny 1E; 7am-7pm Mon-Fri, 10am-3pm Sat); City 2 shopping centre (Map pp72-3; Rue Neuve; 9.30am-6.30pm Mon-Fri, 10am-1pm Sat)

Tourist Information

Belgian Tourist Information Centre (Map p74; 02 504 03 90; www.visitflanders.com, www.belgique-tourisme.net; Rue du Marché aux Herbes 63; 9am-6pm Mon-Fri, 9am-1pm & 2-6pm Sat & Sun, to 1pm Sun Jan & Feb) Supplies national tourist information (as opposed to information on Brussels itself).

DISCOUNT CARDS

The **Brussels Card** (€30) is valid for three consecutive days and offers free entry to nearly all museums, free public transport and discounts in various restaurants, bars and shops. It's available at all participating museums, the tourist offices in Brussels, public transport agencies and some hotels.

WHAT STREET IS THIS?

First-time visitors to Brussels are often flabbergasted by its peculiarly long street names. Blue-and-white street-corner plaques proclaim titles like 'Petite Rue de la Violette Korte Violetstraat' or 'Place de la Vieille Halle aux Blés Oud Korenhuis'. It's tricky recalling what street a great *café* is on when it's almost impossible to get your tongue around the name.

Street names become manageable when you remember it's two names in one – the French followed by the Flemish. Thus Petite Rue de la Violette is the French name followed by Korte Violetstraat, the Flemish. Note also that, in French, *rue* (street) comes at the start of the name whereas in Flemish *straat* is tacked on to the end.

Move on to Brussels' working-class Marolles and street names become even more vexed as three languages are used – French, Flemish and Bruxellois (the city's old dialect). Try wrapping your tongue around Rue Haute Hoogstraat Op d'Huugstroet (ie High Street).

Brussels International (Map p74; ☎ 02 513 89 40; www.brusselsinternational.be; Grand Place; ♥ 9am-6pm Easter-Oct, 9am-6pm Mon-Sat, 10am-2pm Sun Nov-Dec, 9am-6pm Mon-Sat Jan-Easter) The city of Brussels' tourist office, located inside the town hall and usually crammed. Sells a couple of discount booklets or cards, such as the Brussels Card (see boxed text, opposite).

Brussels International – Tourism (Map pp76-7; Gare du Midi; ♥ 8am-8pm Sat-Thu, to 9pm Fri May-Sep, 8am-5pm Mon-Thu, 8am-8pm Fri, 9am-6pm Sat, 9am-2pm Sun Apr-Oct) For visitors arriving by Eurostar or Thalys.

Espace Wallonie-Bruxelles (Map pp70-1; ☎ 02 725 52 75; arrivals hall Brussels National Airport; ♥ 8am-9pm;) Gives information on Brussels and Wallonia. For information on Flanders, you'll have to visit the Belgian Tourist Information Centre (opposite).

Travel Agencies

Airstop/Taxistop (Map p74; ☎ 070 22 22 92; www.taxistop.be; Rue du Fossé aux Loups 28) A travel agency that matches long-distance travellers and drivers headed for the same destination for a reasonable fee. Offers cheap charter flights and car transport (€3 per km) to other European cities.

Connections (Map p74; ☎ 02 550 01 30; www.connections.be; Rue du Midi 19) All-round travel agent.

SIGHTS
Grand Place

For one of Europe's finest urban views, head straight to Brussels' magnificent central square, **Grand Place** (Map p74; metro Gare Centrale or premetro Bourse). It boasts the country's best baroque guildhalls, the beautiful Hôtel de Ville (Town Hall), museums, pavement *cafés*, chocolate shops and intimate cellar restaurants – a combination that lures visitors in droves. Hidden at the very core of the old town, it's revealed as you enter from one of six narrow side alleys (Rue des Harengs is the best) – a discreet positioning that adds charm.

The square dates from the 12th century and rose on a site that was once marshland. By the early 15th century, Brussels was booming through the cloth trade and the patronage of the dukes of Burgundy. A prosperous market covered not only the Grand Place but also neighbouring streets, such as the beguilingly named Rue au Beurre (Butter St) and Rue des Bouchers (Butchers' St). The city's increasingly wealthy merchant guilds established headquarters – guildhalls – on the square. The construction of the Hôtel de Ville sealed the Grand Place's role as the hub of commercial, political and civic life. Medieval tournaments and public executions took place before high-spirited crowds.

In 1695 much of central Brussels, including the Grand Place, was bombarded for 36 hours under the orders of Louis XIV of France. The attack was designed to distract the allied forces of England and the Spanish Netherlands, with whom the French king was at war. Most of the guildhalls, as well as thousands of houses and many churches, were destroyed. Miraculously, the Hôtel de Ville survived the bombing, but nearly all the other buildings that you see on the Grand Place today are 17th-century replacements.

The Grand Place takes on different auras depending on the time of day and the season. In the morning the superb guildhalls at the southern end glint in the sun; at dusk the azure sky makes a vivid backdrop to the illuminated buildings. For three days in August (even years only), a carpet of flowers covers the whole square. At any time of the day or night, you'll find people milling about here, simply gazing up and absorbing its beauty.

(Continued on page 79)

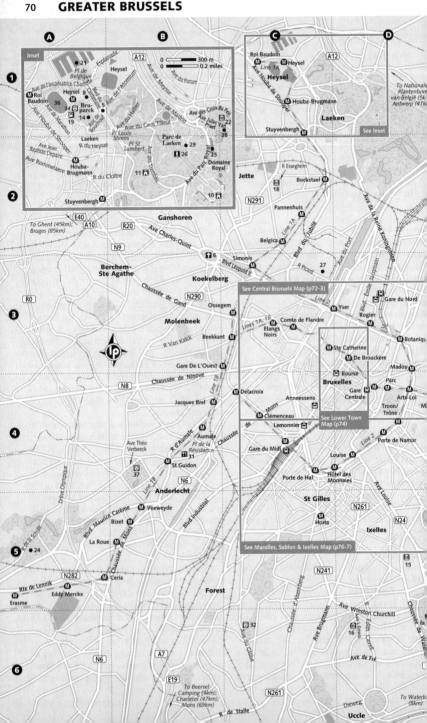

Inset

A12

0 ——————— 300 m
0 ——————— 0.2 miles

Pl de Belgique
Esplanade
Heysel
Ave de l'impératrice Charlotte
Roi Baudoin
36
34
19
14
Heysel
8
Bru-parck
5
Ave de l'Atomium
Ave du Forum
Ave de Meysse
Ave du Haller
Ave de Bouchat
Ave de Madrid

Laeken
R du Heysel
Ave Jean Baptiste Depaire
Ave de Marathon
Ave Houba-de-Strooper
Ave Rommelaere
Houba-Brugmann

Pl Louis Steens
Pl St Lambert
Ave du Gros Tilleul

Ave des Trembles
Ave Jules Van Praet
Ave des Croix du Feu
12
28
25
29
26
Parc de Laeken
Domaine Royal
Ave du Parc Royal

11
10

Stuyvenbergh
R du Cloître

Roi Baudoin
Heysel
A12
Ave Houba de Strooper
Heysel
Houba-Brugmann
Laeken
Stuyvenbergh
See Inset

To Nationale Plantentuin van België (5k Antwerp (41k

R Esseghem
Jette
R Esseghem
Bockstael
18
Pannenhuis
Ave de la Reine Konings

Ganshoren
To Ghent (45km); Bruges (85km);
E40
A10
R20
Ave Charles-Quint
N291

N9
6
Simonis
Blvd Léopold II
Belgica
Blvd du Jubilé
Ave du Port

Berchem-Ste Agathe
Koekelberg
R Picard
27

R0
Chaussée de Gand
N290
Ossegem

Molenbeek
R Van Kalck
Beekkant
Line 1A, 1B

See Central Brussels Map (p72-3)
Line 2
Yser
Gare du Nord
Rogier
Blvd Émile Jacqmain
Comte de Flandre
Etangs Noirs
Ste Catherine
Botaniqu
De Brouckère
Madou
Bourse
Bruxelles
Parc
Gare Centrale
Arts-Loi
Troon/Trône

N8
Chaussée de Ninove
Gare De L'Ouest
Line 1B
Delacroix
Mons
Anneessens
See Lower Town Map (p74)
Jacques Brel
Clémenceau
Lemonnier

Ave Théo Verbeeck
R d'Aumale
Pl de la Résistance
Aumale
31
St Guidon
N6
Line 1B
Gare du Midi
Louise
Porte de Namur
Porte de Hal
Hôtel des Monnaies
Line 2

Anderlecht
37
Veeweyde
Blvd Maurice Carême
Bizet
La Roue
Chaussée de Mons
Blvd Industriel
St Gilles
N261
Horta
Ixelles
N24

24
Ceria
N282
Rte de Lennik
Eddy Merckx
Erasme
Drève Olympique
Côte de Scheut

Forest
See Marolles, Sablon & Ixelles Map (p76-7)
N241
15

32
Chaussée d'Alsemberg
Ave Winston Churchill
16
Ave Edith Cavell
Ave Brugmann

N6
A7
E19
To Beersel Camping (4km); Charleroi (47km); Mons (69km)
N261
R de Stalle
Diewe
Uccle
To Waterloo (8km)
Ave de Fré
Chaussée de Water

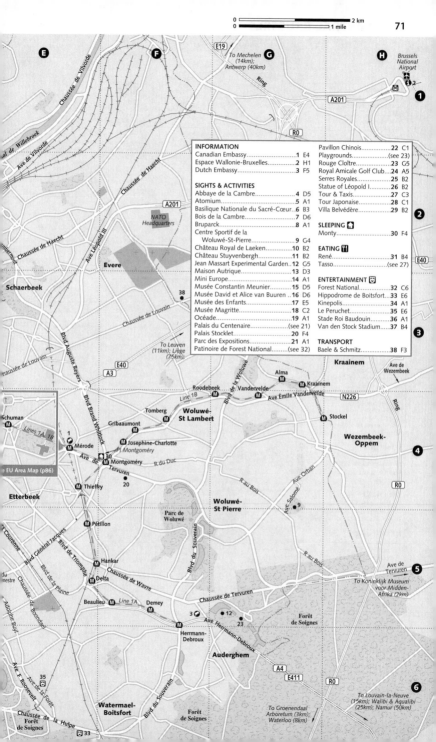

0 — 2 km
0 — 1 mile

INFORMATION
Canadian Embassy...............................**1** E4
Espace Wallonie-Bruxelles................**2** H1
Dutch Embassy....................................**3** F5

SIGHTS & ACTIVITIES
Abbaye de la Cambre.........................**4** D5
Atomium...**5** A1
Basilique Nationale du Sacré-Cœur.**6** B3
Bois de la Cambre..............................**7** D6
Bruparck...**8** A1
Centre Sportif de la
  Woluwé-St-Pierre.............................**9** G4
Château Royal de Laeken.................**10** B2
Château Stuyvenbergh.....................**11** B2
Jean Massart Experimental Garden..**12** G5
Maison Autrique.................................**13** D3
Mini Europe...**14** A1
Musée Constantin Meunier..............**15** D5
Musée David et Alice van Buuren....**16** D6
Musée des Enfants.............................**17** E5
Musée Magritte...................................**18** C2
Océade...**19** A1
Palais du Centenaire.....................(see 21)
Palais Stocklet...................................**20** F4
Parc des Expositions.........................**21** A1
Patinoire de Forest National........(see 32)

Pavillon Chinois.................................**22** C1
Playgrounds....................................(see 23)
Rouge Cloître......................................**23** G5
Royal Amicale Golf Club...................**24** A5
Serres Royales....................................**25** B2
Statue de Léopold I............................**26** B2
Tour & Taxis..**27** C3
Tour Japonaise...................................**28** C1
Villa Belvédère...................................**29** B2

SLEEPING 🛏
Monty..**30** F4

EATING 🍴
René...**31** B4
Tasso...(see 27)

ENTERTAINMENT 🎭
Forest National...................................**32** C6
Hippodrome de Boitsfort...................**33** E6
Kinepolis..**34** A1
Le Peruchet..**35** E6
Stade Roi Baudouin...........................**36** A1
Van den Stock Stadium.....................**37** B4

TRANSPORT
Baele & Schmitz..................................**38** F3

INFORMATION
Amazone.....................................**1** H3
Australian Embassy.....................**2** H6
FNAC..(see 47)
French Embassy...........................**3** H5
Pêle Mêle....................................**4** C6
Post Office..................................(see 47)
Salon Lavoir de la Chapelle.........**5** E6
USA Embassy...............................**6** H5
Was-Salon Lavoir........................**7** E3

SIGHTS & ACTIVITIES
Cathédrale des Sts Michel & Gudule.**8** F5
Centre Belge de la Bande Dessinée..**9** F4
Cercle Royal de Billiard.............**10** C6
Colonne du Congrès...................**11** G4
Crosly Super Bowling.................**12** E6
Flanders Gate Squash Club.........**13** C3
Godefroid de Bouillon Statue......**14** F6
Grand Magasin Waucquez..........(see 9)
Halles de Schaerbeek................**15** H1
Le Botanique............................**16** G3
Musée BELvue...........................**17** F6
Musée Bruxellois de la Gueuze....**18** B6
Musée d'Art Ancien..................(see 21)
Musée d'Art Moderne...............(see 21)
Musée des Instruments de Musique.**19** F6
Musée du Jouet.........................**20** G3
Musées Royaux des Beaux-Arts....**21** F6
Old England Building.................(see 19)
Palais Royal..............................**22** G6
Playground...............................**23** G5

SLEEPING 🏠
2Go4......................................**24** E3
Art Hotel Siru..........................**25** F2
B&B Phileas Fogg.....................**26** H3
Centre Vincent van Gogh..........**27** H3
Hooy Kaye Lodge.....................**28** D2
Hôtel Astoria...........................**29** G4
Hôtel du Congrès......................**30** G4
Hôtel George V.........................**31** C5
Jacques Brel............................**32** G3
Les Auberges de Jeunesse..........(see 32)
Sleep Well...............................**33** F3

EATING 🍴
Comme Chez Soi.......................**34** D6
In 't Spinnekopke.....................**35** C4
Metin......................................**36** H2
Super GB.................................(see 47)

DRINKING 🍷
De Ultieme Hallucinatie.............**37** H2
La Fleur en Papier Doré.............**38** D6
Le Bier Circus..........................**39** G4

ENTERTAINMENT 🎬
Bozar.....................................**40** F6
Cirque Royal............................**41** G4
Dirty Dancing@Mirano..............**42** H4
Kaaitheater.............................**43** D1
Koninklijke Vlaamse Schouwburg..**44** E2
Musée du Cinéma.....................**45** F6
Théâtre National......................**46** E3

SHOPPING 🛍
City 2 Shopping Centre.............**47** F3
DoD.......................................**48** H4
Galerie Ravenstein...................**49** F5
Mary's...................................**50** G4

TRANSPORT
Eurolines................................**51** F1
Touring Club de Belgique...........**52** H5

See Lower Town Map (p74)

See Marolles, Sablon & Ixelles Map (p76-7)

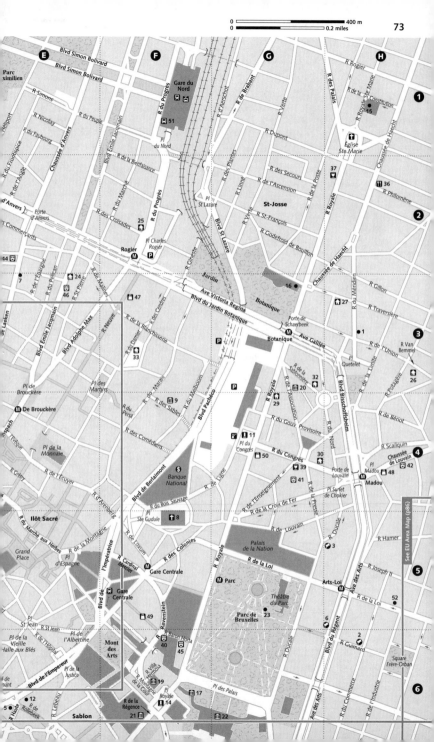

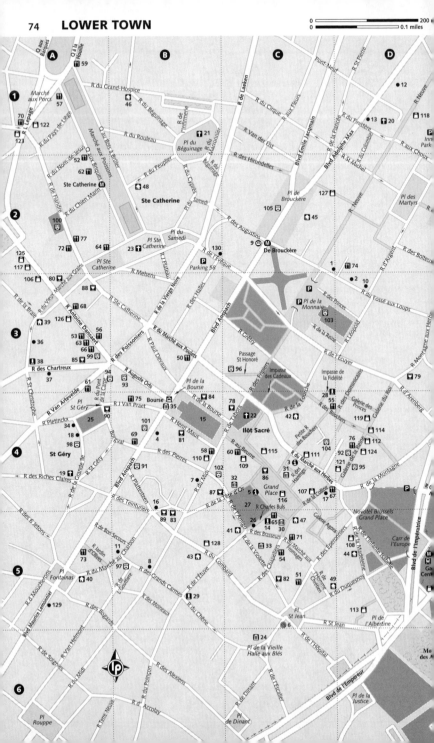

INFORMATION
Accessible Travel Info Point........(see 3)
Airstop/Taxistop.............................1 C2
Anticyclone des Açores................ 2 D3
Belgian Tourist Information
Centre.......................................3 C4
Brüsel..4 B4
Brussels International....................5 C4
BXL...6 C5
Connections....................................7 B4
Évasions 1......................................8 B5
Post Office......................................9 C2
Sterling Books............................ 10 D3
Tels Quels....................................11 B5
Waterstones................................12 D1

SIGHTS & ACTIVITIES
ARAU...13 D1
Art Nouveau Plaque................. 14 C5
Bourse..15 B4
Broussaille Mural........................16 B4
Brussels City Tours.....................17 C4
Clock repair shop..................(see 37)
Courtyard Entrance................... 18 A4
Église Notre Dame des Riches
Claires..................................... 19 A4
Église Notre Dame du Finistère...20 D1
Église St Jean Baptiste au
Béguinage...............................21 B1
Église St Nicolas........................22 C4
Église Ste Catherine...................23 B2
Fondation Jacques Brel..............24 C6
Halles St Géry.............................25 A4
Horse Drawn Carriage...............26 C5
Hôtel de Ville..............................27 C4
Jeanneke Pis...............................28 C4
Manneken Pis..............................29 B5
Musée de la Brasserie 30 C5
Musée de la Ville de Bruxelles.... 31 C4
Musée du Cacao et du Chocolat..32 C4
Musée du Costume et de la
Dentelle...................................33 C5
Nero Mural...................................34 A4
Scientastic Museum....................35 B4
Stained-Glass Windows..............36 A3
Statue Everard 't Serclaes..........(see 14)
Tower..37 A3
Zinneke..38 A3

SLEEPING 🛏
Atlas...39 A3
Downtown-BXL............................40 A5
Hôtel Amigo.................................41 C5
Hôtel Arlequin.............................42 C4

Hôtel La Légende.......................43 B5
Hôtel Le Dixseptième.................44 D5
Hôtel Métropole..........................45 C2
Hôtel Noga...................................46 B1
Hôtel Saint Michel.......................47 C5
Hôtel Welcome............................48 B2
Royal Winsor Hotel....................49 C5

EATING 🍴
AD Delhaize.................................50 B3
Al Barmaki...................................51 C5
Bij den Boer.................................52 A2
Bonsoir Clara...............................53 A3
Brasserie de la Roue d'Or..........54 C5
Chez Léon....................................55 C4
Comocomo...................................56 A3
Comus & Gastera........................57 A1
Fritland...58 B4
GB Express...................................59 A1
GB Express...................................60 C4
Gourmet d'Asie...........................61 A3
Jacques...62 A2
Kasbah..63 A3
La Belle Maraîchère....................64 A2
La Maison du Cygne...................65 C5
Le Pain Quotidien/Het
Dagelijks Brood......................66 A3
Panos..67 C4
Pataya...68 A3
Petite Beuxer...............................69 B4
Picnik..70 A1
Pita Places...................................71 C5
Pré Salé..72 A2
Rugantino....................................73 A5
Samourai......................................74 D2
Shamrock.....................................75 B4
Taverne du Passage....................76 D4
Viva M'Boma...............................77 A2

DRINKING 🍷
À la Bécasse................................78 C4
À la Mort Subite.........................79 D3
De Markten...................................80 A3
Falstaff..81 B4
Goupil le Fol................................82 C5
Le Belgica....................................83 B5
Le Cirio...84 B4
Le Greenwich...............................85 A3
Le Roy d'Espagne........................86 C4
L'Homo Erectus...........................87 B4
Monk...88 A3
Rainbow House.............................89 B5
Toone......................................(see 104)
Zebra..90 A4

ENTERTAINMENT 🎭
Actor's Studio..........................(see 42)
Ancienne Belgique.....................91 B4
Arenberg Galeries......................92 D4
Beursschouwburg.......................93 B3
Beursschouwburg Café............(see 93)
Bizon..94 A3
Brussels on Stage........................95 D4
Caroline Music............................96 C3
Chez Maman................................97 B5
Dr Vinyl..98 A4
L'Archiduc....................................99 A3
Maison la Bellone....................100 A2
Pathé Palace.............................101 B4
The Music Village......................102 B4
Théâtre du Vaudeville.............(see 95)
Théâtre Royal de la
Monnaie/Koninklijke
Muntschouwburg.................103 C3
Théâtre Royal de Toone..........104 C4
UGC De Brouckère
Cinema...................................105 C2

SHOPPING 🛍
Annemie Verbeke.....................106 A3
Boutique Tintin.........................107 C4
Corné Port Royal......................108 D5
Dandoy......................................109 C4
Darakan.....................................110 B4
De Biertempel...........................111 C4
Delvaux.....................................112 D4
Galerie Bortier..........................113 D5
Galeries St Hubert....................114 D4
Galler...115 C4
Grand Place Flower
Market...................................116 C4
Idiz Bogam................................117 A2
Inno..118 D1
Kaat Tilley.................................119 D4
La Maison de la BD..................120 D5
Manufacture Belge de
Dentelles................................121 D4
Marina Yee................................122 A1
Martin Margiela.........................123 A1
Neuhaus.....................................124 D4
Nicolas Woit..............................125 A2
Olivier Strelli.............................126 A3
Passage du Nord.......................127 C2
Planète Chocolat......................128 B5
Stijl.......................................(see 117)

TRANSPORT
Hertz..129 A5
STIB/MIVB Office......................130 B2

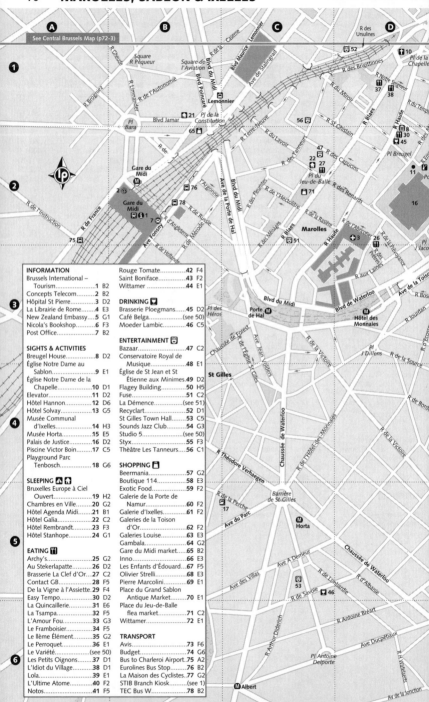

See Central Brussels Map (p72-3)

INFORMATION
Brussels International –
Tourism...................1 B2
Concepts Telecom..........2 B2
Hôpital St Pierre...........3 D2
La Librairie de Rome.......4 E3
New Zealand Embassy.....5 G1
Nicola's Bookshop.........6 F3
Post Office................7 B2

SIGHTS & ACTIVITIES
Breugel House...............8 D2
Église Notre Dame au
Sablon.....................9 E1
Église Notre Dame de la
Chapelle................10 D1
Elevator...................11 D2
Hôtel Hannon..............12 D6
Hôtel Solvay...............13 G5
Musée Communal
d'Ixelles..................14 H3
Musée Horta...............15 E5
Palais de Justice...........16 D2
Piscine Victor Boin........17 C5
Playground Parc
Tenbosch.................18 G6

SLEEPING
Bruxelles Europe à Ciel
Ouvert...................19 H2
Chambres en Ville........20 G2
Hôtel Agenda Midi........21 B1
Hôtel Galia................22 C2
Hôtel Rembrandt..........23 F3
Hôtel Stanhope...........24 G1

EATING
Archy's...................25 G2
Au Stekerlapatte.........26 D2
Brasserie La Clef d'Or....27 C2
Contact GB................28 F5
De la Vigne à l'Assiette...29 F4
Easy Tempo...............30 D2
La Quincaillerie...........31 E6
La Tsampa.................32 F5
L'Amour Fou..............33 G3
Le Framboisier...........34 F5
Le llème Élément.........35 G2
Le Perroquet.............36 E1
Le Variété................(see 50)
Les Petits Oignons........37 D1
L'Idiot du Village.........38 D1
Lola......................39 E1
L'Ultime Atome...........40 F2
Notos....................41 F5

Rouge Tomate............42 F4
Saint Boniface............43 F2
Wittamer..................44 E1

DRINKING
Brasserie Ploegmans......45 D2
Café Belga.................(see 50)
Moeder Lambic..........46 C5

ENTERTAINMENT
Bazaar....................47 C2
Conservatoire Royal de
Musique.................48 E1
Église de St Jean et St
Étienne aux Minimes....49 D2
Flagey Building............50 H5
Fuse......................51 C2
La Démence...............(see 51)
Recyclart..................52 D1
St Gilles Town Hall........53 C5
Sounds Jazz Club..........54 G3
Studio 5...................(see 50)
Styx......................55 F3
Théâtre Les Tanneurs......56 C1

SHOPPING
Beermania.................57 G2
Boutique 114..............58 E3
Exotic Food...............59 F2
Galerie de la Porte de
Namur...................60 F2
Galerie d'Ixelles..........61 F2
Galeries de la Toison
d'Or.....................62 F2
Galeries Louise............63 E3
Gambala..................64 G2
Gare du Midi market......65 B2
Inno......................66 E3
Les Enfants d'Édouard....67 F5
Olivier Strelli.............68 E3
Pierre Marcolini..........69 E1
Place du Grand Sablon
Antique Market.........70 E1
Place du Jeu-de-Balle
flea market..............71 C2
Wittamer..................72 E1

TRANSPORT
Avis.......................73 F6
Budget....................74 G6
Bus to Charleroi Airport..75 A2
Eurolines Bus Stop........76 B2
La Maison des Cyclistes...77 G2
STIB Branch Kiosk.........(see 1)
TEC Bus W................78 B2

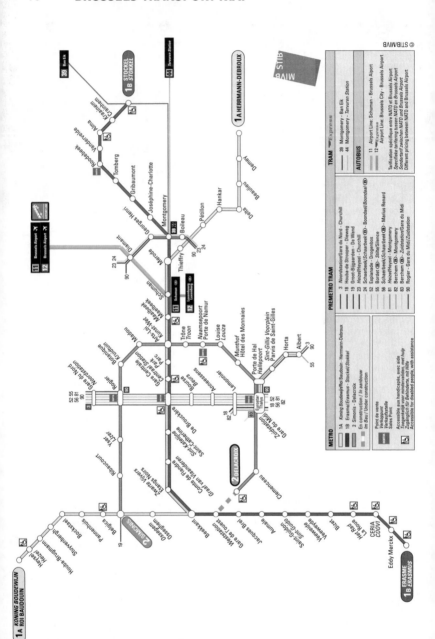

© STIB/MIVB

METRO

1A Koning Boudewijn/Roi Baudouin - Herrmann-Debroux
1B Erasmus/Erasme - Stockel/Stokkel
2 Simonis - Delacroix

En construction / In aanbouw
Im Bau / Under construction

Point de vente
Verkoopspunt
Verkaufsstelle
Sales Point

Accessible aux handicapés, avec aide
Toegankelijk voor mindervaliden, met hulp
Zugänglich für Behinderte, mit Hilfe
Accessible for disabled people, with assistance

PREMETRO TRAM

3 Noordstation/Gare du Nord - Churchill
18 Houba-de Strooper - Dieweg
19 Groot-Bijgaarden - De Wand
23 Heizel/Heysel - Churchill
24 Schaerbeek/Schaarbeek ⑤ - Boondael/Boondaal ⑥
52 Esplanade - Drogenbos
55 Bordet ⑤ - Stila/Silence
56 Schaerbeek/Schaarbeek ⑤ - Marius Renard
81 Heizel/Heysel - Montgomery
82 Berchem ⑤ - Montgomery
83 Berchem ⑤ - Zuidstation/Gare du Midi/Zuidstation
90 Rogier - Gare du Midi/Zuidstation

TRAM ⇒ Express

39 Montgomery - Ban Eik
44 Montgomery - Tervuren Station

AUTOBUS

11 Airport Line: Schuman - Brussels Airport
12 Airport Line: Brussels City - Brussels Airport

Tarification spécifique entre NATO et Brussels Airport
Specifieke tarifering tussen NATO en Brussels Airport
Sondertarif zwischen NATO und Brussels Airport
Different pricing between NATO and Brussels Airport

(Continued from page 69)

HÔTEL DE VILLE

The splendid Gothic-style **Hôtel de Ville** (Map p74) was the only building on the Grand Place to escape the 1695 French bombardment – ironic considering it was the target. It's a superb structure, with a creamy façade covered with stone reliefs of nobility and gargoyles, and an intricate 96m-high tower topped by a gilded statue of St Michel, the city's patron saint. The building is not symmetrical; the left-hand side was begun in 1402 but the right wing wasn't added until 1444 and is, due to space constraints, shorter. **Guided tours** (tours €3; 3.30pm Tue & Wed Apr-Sep, 45 min) are possible; inquire at Brussels International (p69).

GUILDHALLS

The splendour of the Grand Place is due largely to its antique frame of guildhalls. Each merchant guild erected its own building, which is named (there were no street numbers back then) and adorned with gilded statues and elaborate symbols related to its trade. When the guildhalls were obliterated in the 1695 bombardment, the guilds rallied and rebuilt their headquarters in under five years, using stone (rather than partial timber as before) for the façades and adding fanciful baroque touches to the gables.

Some of the highlights:

Maison du Roi (King's House) Opposite the Hôtel de Ville, this dark, brooding building was never home to royalty, despite the name. These days it houses the Musée de la Ville de Bruxelles (right).

No 1: Maison des Boulangers (Bakers' House) Le Roy d'Espagne (p106), one of the square's most popular *cafés*, occupies this building, which belonged to the bakers' guild. The gilded bronze bust above the door represents their patron, St Aubert.

No 2: La Brouette (The Wheelbarrow) Faint gold wheelbarrows can still be seen above the door of this house, which was home to the grease-makers. The statue of St Gilles was added in 1912.

No 4: Le Sac (The Bag) This incredibly ornate building was the headquarters of the cabinet-makers.

No 5: La Louve (The She-Wolf) The archers' guild topped their building with a golden phoenix rising from the ashes to signify the rebirth of the Grand Place after the bombardment.

No 6: Le Cornet (The Horn) The boatmen's guild is easily identified by the stern-shaped gable.

No 7: Le Renard (The Fox) This house served the haberdashers.

No 8: L'Étoile (The Star) Across Rue Charles Buls from the Hôtel de Ville, this is the smallest building on the square. Everard 't Serclaes (see below), the city's hero and modern-day good luck charm, died here.

No 9: Le Cygne (The Swan) Adorned with a huge swan and built in classical style, this house originally served the butchers' guild. Nowadays it's home to the square's finest restaurant.

No 10: L'Arbre d'Or (The Golden Tree) Hops plants climbing columns hint at this building's former and current role as the brewers' headquarters.

Nos 26 & 27: Le Pigeon This guildhall belonged to the city's artists. Later, Victor Hugo lived here during his exile from France in 1852.

MUSÉE DE LA VILLE DE BRUXELLES

The **Brussels City Museum** (Map p74; 02 279 43 50; www.brucity.be; Maison du Roi, Grand Place; adult/concession €3/2.50; 10am-5pm Tue-Sun) provides an historical overview of the city through old maps, architectural relics, paintings and, displayed on the ground floor, Pieter Breugel the Elder's *Cortège de Noces* (Wedding Procession) of 1567. One room on the 3rd floor is devoted to the worldly wardrobe of Manneken Pis, though only a fraction of his 700-odd garments are displayed.

MUSÉE DE LA BRASSERIE

The **Brewery Museum** (Map p74; 02 511 49 87; www.beerparadise.be; Grand Place 10; admission €4; 10am-5pm daily Easter-Nov, noon-5pm Sat & Sun Dec-Easter) occupies the basement of the brewers' guildhall, L'Arbre d'Or. The small museum aims to enlighten visitors on the modern world of brewing but, in two words, don't bother. If you want to see a real brewery, head to the Musée Bruxellois de la Gueuze (p90).

South of Grand Place

RUE CHARLES BULS

Leading off the southern side of Grand Place is **Rue Charles Buls** (Map p74; metro Gare Centrale). It paves the way to Manneken Pis and, not surprisingly, is lined with lace and trinket shops. At the start of the street, in a small arcaded gallery, you'll find an 1899 gilded Art Nouveau plaque dedicated to the city by its appreciative artists. Next to it is a reclining statue of Everard 't Serclaes, a 14th-century hero who defended the city – rub his gleaming torso for good luck.

MUSÉE DU COSTUME ET DE LA DENTELLE

A stone's throw from the Grand Place, the **Costume and Lace Museum** (Map p74; 02 213 44 50; Rue de la Violette 12; metro Gare Centrale; admission €3;

⏰ 10am-12.30pm & 1.30-5pm Mon, Tue, Thu & Fri, 2-5pm Sat & Sun) is Belgium's second-best lace exhibition (top honours goes to the Nationaal Vlas, Kant en Linnenmuseum in Kortrijk, p158). Read about Belgium's place in lace history in the boxed text, p138). Notice the sombre black attire once worn by women *en promenade* (out walking in public) and the more colourful lace gowns for women *en visite* (visiting someone's home). Note also the antique underwear, including an old *bustehouder* (bra). Pick up the English-language booklet before setting off.

MANNEKEN PIS

A national symbol and known throughout the world, **Manneken Pis** (Map p74; cnr Rue de l'Étuve & Rue du Chêne; metro Gare Centrale or premetro Bourse), a little boy cheerfully taking a leak into a pool, never fails to disappoint visitors despite its diminutive size. It's three blocks from the Grand Place.

The present-day bronze Manneken Pis was sculpted by Jerôme Duquesnoy in 1619, but a stone version – named Little Julian – stood here from the mid-14th century. The statue's origins are lost in legend: some say he's modelled on a boy who extinguished a fire, others say he was a nobleman's son. Whatever, the people of Brussels have adopted him as the symbol of their indomitable and irreverent spirit, and on occasion dress him up in one of his 700-odd costumes. Kitsch? Well, there's more – his little 'sister', Jeanneke Pis (opposite), squats in an alley on the north side of Grand Place, and Zinneke (p82), a mongrel dog with cocked leg, stands in St Géry.

FONDATION JACQUES BREL

The **Jacques Brel Foundation** (Map p74; ☎ 02 511 10 20; www.jacquesbrel.be; Place de la Vieille Halle aux Blés 11; metro Gare Centrale; adult/concession €5/3.50; ⏰ 10.30am-5pm Tue-Sat) is an archive centre and museum dedicated to Brussels' raspy-voiced singer Jacques Brel (1929–78).

Brel rose to stardom in Paris in the 1950s for his passionate songs that have transcended a generation. The legendary *chansonnier* was a transient troubadour who performed with intensity. According to a member of the Fondation Jacques Brel: 'He sang like a boxer and usually lost a kilo during each performance'. Love, freedom, the spirit of revolt and the hypocrisy of the bourgeoisie were his passions. His career started in 1952 in La Rose Noire, a Brussels cabaret. The following year he headed to Paris and mixed with songwrit-

ers and singers such as Édith Piaf. His first record was cut in 1955 and within two years he was an idol.

In the early 1960s Brel toured the USA and USSR and became known as the singer from France. He never denied his Belgian status – his songs often hark back to his flat, bleak homeland – but he cherished France, so much so that his first daughter is named France. He died of lung cancer in 1978 and is buried on one of the Marquesas Islands in French Polynesia, near Paul Gauguin, the French painter.

MUSÉE DU CACAO ET DU CHOCOLAT

The **Museum of Cocoa and Chocolate** (Map p74; ☎ 02 514 20 48; Rue de la Tête d'Or 9; premetro Bourse; adult/concession/child €5/4/free; ⏰ 10am-4.30pm daily Jul & Aug, 10am-4.30pm Tue-Sun Sep-Jun) is for chocolate diehards. The admission cost entitles you to one chocolate-dipped biscuit, a wander through some mediocre exhibits and taste-testing at a praline-making demonstration.

North of Grand Place

BOURSE

The **Belgian Stock Exchange** (Map p74; Place de la Bourse; premetro Bourse) occupies a grandiose neoclassical edifice from 1873. The cream façade is festooned with friezes and sculptures of exotic fruits, reclining nudes, lunging horses and a multitude of allegorical figures. One of the statues is by Rodin.

ÉGLISE ST NICOLAS

The **Church of St Nicolas** (Map p74; Rue au Beurre 1; premetro Bourse; ⏰ 8am-6.30pm Mon-Fri, 9am-6pm Sat, 9am-7.30pm Sun) is a pint-sized edifice encrusted with shops and easily overlooked. Appropriately enough, it's dedicated to the patron saint of merchants. Almost as old as Brussels itself, it has been heavily restored through the centuries. The dark and sombre interior is noted for the unusual angle at which its three aisles were built.

GALERIES ST HUBERT

For details on Galeries St Hubert, see boxed text, p112.

RUE DES BOUCHERS

Leading off Galeries St Hubert in a lively little quarter known as **Îlot Sacré** is the famous **Rue des Bouchers** (Map p74; metro Gare Centrale or premetro Bourse). Whether you decide to eat at one of the many seafood restaurants here or not, this pedestrianised cobbled street is a spectacle not to be missed. Both sides of the street are packed with tables for dining throughout the year – overhead heaters keep frostbite at bay in winter. Waiters entice diners with iced displays of marine delicacies and the odd novelty (expect dancing plastic fish). Many of the restaurants are not recommended but there are exceptions, including Chez Léon (p101).

JEANNEKE PIS

Manneken Pis' female counterpart is **Jeanneke Pis** (Map p74; Impasse de la Fidélité; metro Gare Centrale or premetro Bourse), just off Rue des Bouchers. This little girl, gleefully squatting, was erected in 1985 by Denis Adrien Debouvrie 'in honour of loyalty'. Loyalty to what we're not sure, but certainly there's no bond between her and the tourist office, whose official guidebook fails to acknowledge her existence.

CATHÉDRALE DES STS MICHEL & GUDULE

This twin-towered **cathedral** (Map pp72-3; www .cathedralestmichel.be; Place Sainte-Gudule; metro Gare Centrale; admission free, crypt €1; 8am-6pm), named after Brussels' male and female patron saints, sits gleaming on the hillside to the north of Gare Centrale. The out-of-the-way location between the Lower and Upper Towns means it is often overlooked by visitors. In addition, poor city planning has left it marooned like an ancient island in the midst of modern development.

Begun in 1226, the cathedral took some 300 years to build and consequently reveals a blend of styles – from Romanesque through all the stages of Gothic and right up to Renaissance. The interior is light and airy but almost bereft of decoration due to plundering, first by Protestants in the 17th century and later by the French army. Stained-glass windows flood the nave with light and the enormous wooden pulpit, sculpted by Antwerp artist Hendrik Verbruggen, is worth inspecting – note Adam and Eve being driven out of Eden by fearsome skeletons. In the crypt are the remains of an 11th-century Romanesque chapel.

CENTRE BELGE DE LA BANDE DESSINÉE

The **Belgian Comic Strip Centre** (Map pp72-3; 02 219 19 80; www.comicscenter.net in Flemish & French; Rue des Sables 20; metro Rogier; adult/concession €6.20/5; 10am-6pm Tue-Sun), about 800m northeast of the Grand Place, is not to be missed. Tour the country's rich, vibrant comic-strip culture, from its earliest beginnings to contemporary

favourites, all housed in a remarkable building, the **Grand Magasin Waucquez**. This former department store was created by Victor Horta in 1906 for the Waucquez family textile business. It's pure Art Nouveau: light, airy and full of glass and wrought iron. Despite standing empty for 16 years, it was spared from the demolition madness that stripped Brussels of many of its Art Nouveau showpieces.

For more on comics, see boxed texts, p39 and p82.

RUE NEUVE AREA

Rue Neuve (Map p74; premetro De Brouckère, metro Rogier) is a pedestrianised street that's wall-to-wall shoppers, especially on Saturday afternoons.

One of the few sights in this area is **Église Notre Dame du Finistère**, an 18th-century church that sits in vivid contrast to the modern mania around it. Nearby is the sombre **Place des Martyrs**, with its monument to the 467 who died in the 1830 revolution. Rejoin Rue du Neuve to meander through the **Passage du Nord**, an elegant 19th-century shopping arcade (see boxed text, p112).

Rue Neuve terminates at Place de la Monnaie, an ugly square that is home to Brussels' most prestigious cultural venue, the **Théâtre Royal de la Monnaie/Koninklijke Muntschouwburg** (see p110).

St Géry & Ste Catherine

Neighbouring **St Géry** (Map p74; premetro Bourse) and **Ste Catherine** (Map p74; metro Ste Catherine) are prime downtown real estate. Colourful, trendy and full of restaurants, *cafés*, bars and fashion shops, these quarters lend the city an invigorating air.

Start exploring at Place St Géry, an engaging square surrounded by popular *cafés* and dominated by **Halles St Géry**, a renovated meat market that now hosts exhibitions. From a public courtyard off Place St Géry (go through the black steel gates next to the bistro La Lion St Géry), there's a view of **Église Notre Dame des Riches Claires**, an intriguing asymmetrical church. Nearby is the **Nero** mural, one of the city's many comic-strip murals (see boxed text, p82).

Head up Rue du Pont de la Carpe to Rue des Chartreux. Pause for a drink at **Le Greenwich** (p106), or proceed to the **clock repair shop** at No 42 where (weekdays only) you can push open the black door to reveal part of a 12th-century sandstone **tower**, one of 50 such

---

MURALS OF BRUSSELS

Brussels' Comic Strip Route is a series of giant comic murals and colourful statues that enliven alleys and main thoroughfares throughout the old city centre. Moseying past some of the murals is a great way to explore less-visited neighbourhoods and discover the city's nooks and crannies. Set aside three hours to trace the 6km circuit (detailed in a free brochure available from Brussels International, p69). Alternatively, just pick out a few. One not to miss is **Broussaille** (Map p74; Rue du Marché au Charbon; premetro Bourse), by Frank Pé. Painted in 1991, it was the city's first, depicting a young couple arm-in-arm discovering Brussels. The strip is located in Brussels' gay nightlife hub and, in the original version, it was difficult to tell whether the couple was straight or not. Gay establishments used the mural to promote the quarter until 1999 when the mural was repainted and the black-haired figure was given a more feminine hairstyle, earrings and (slightly) bigger breasts.

---

defensive towers that once stretched for 4km around the old city centre.

First there was Manneken Pis, then Jeanneke Pis and now **Zinneke** (cnr Rue des Chartreux & Rue du Vieux Marché aux Grains), a statue of a dog with its leg cocked. Designed by Flemish sculptor Tom Frantzen, Zinneke exemplifies Brussels' irreverent spirit and has given rise to one of the city's zaniest festivals (see p96).

An Art Nouveau gem is concealed nearby on Rue du Vieux Marché aux Grains. Go through the black doors at number 36-40 to a small courtyard (this is private property but the owners do not mind if visitors peek inside – the doors are open 7am to 5pm weekdays) where two old **stained-glass windows** (Rue du Vieux Marché aux Grains 36-40) are visible. One features a young woman in a white gown standing before a pond, the other a Chinese lady.

Rue Antoine Dansaert is the ruler-straight border between Ste Catherine and St Géry. Once a quiet street where farmers from Flanders bought hardware, it's now home to avantgarde fashion shops (see p114).

Cross the street to reach the 19th-century **Église Ste Catherine** (Church of St Catherine; Map p74; Place Ste Catherine; metro Ste Catherine; 8.30am-5pm Mon-Sat, 8.30am-noon Sun), the nominal heart of this quarter. Take a look at the 15th-century black statue of the Virgin and Child; Protestants hurled it into the Senne in 1744, but locals found it floating on a chunk of turf and fished it out.

Nearby is the imposing façade of the **Église St Jean Baptiste au Béguinage** (Church of St Jean Baptiste au Béguinage; Map p74; Place du Béguinage; metro Ste Catherine; 10am-5pm Tue-Sat, 10am-8pm Sun). Deemed by many to be Belgium's most beautiful, the church dates from the 17th century and was designed by Luc Fayd'Herbe, a student of Rubens, which explains its strong Flemish baroque style.

Marolles

Between Grand Place and Gare du Midi, in the shadow of the huge Palais de Justice, lies the **Marolles** (Map pp76–7). Once resolutely working-class, this quarter is fast shedding its proletarian past, as intimate restaurants and antique and interior design shops set up along the main streets, Rue Haute and Rue Blaes. Tiny pockets, however, are still full of working-class kudos (see boxed text, opposite), and the quarter's best-known attraction, the **Place du Jeu-de-Balle flea market** (p115), is definitely worth a visit.

The **Église Notre Dame de la Chapelle** (Map pp76-7; Place de la Chapelle; metro Gare Centrale or premetro Anneessens; 9am-5pm Mon-Sat, 8am-7.30pm Sun) rises between the Marolles and the Sablon. Built in Romanesque Gothic style, it is Brussels' oldest church, founded in 1134. Inside, there's a chapel devoted to Pieter Breugel the Elder, who lived nearby.

The **Breugel House** (Map pp76-7; Rue Haute 132) occupies the house where Pieter Breugel the Elder lived and died (see boxed text, p84). The museum is only open by reservation – ask at Brussels International (p69).

A glass **elevator** connects the Marolles' Place Breugel with Place Poelaert in the Upper Town, offering a great way to move between the quarters plus a fab city view.

Place Royale

Brussels' Royal precinct is based around the busy **Place Royale** (Map pp72–3), immediately above Gare Centrale in the Upper Town. Use **Mont des Arts**'s open-air stairway, to reach here from Gare Centrale. At the centre of Place Royale stands a **statue of Godefroid de Bouillon**, an 11th-century crusader considered one of Belgium's ancient heroes. A new highlight in this area is the Magritte Museum, recently

BRUSSELS

BRUSSELS' DIALECT

In Bruxellois, the old dialect of Brussels, the word *architekt* is a first-degree insult. The word originated in the 19th century when architect Joseph Poelaert designed the massive Palais de Justice and, in so doing, forcibly evicted many inhabitants of the Marolles, one of the dialect's strongholds.

Bruxellois has its roots in both French and Flemish but, with few speakers left, the dialect is dying. The city's changing face is the reason behind the decline. The Marolles dates from the 17th century when workers moved here to be close to the Upper Town's building boom. It continued to be a bustling working-class quarter complete with factories set along the Senne River right up until the late 19th century when the river was covered. Many Marolles residents moved out and more have gone in recent times as the district is being bought up and gentrified. Only in the shops round Place du Jeu-de-Balle or at the counter of the few old pubs on Rue Haute are you likely to overhear some of the dialect's earthy expressions.

incorporated into the Musées Royaux des Beaux-Arts (below).

MUSÉE DES INSTRUMENTS DE MUSIQUE & OLD ENGLAND BUILDING

Brussels' **Musical Instrument Museum** (Map pp72-3; ☎ 02 545 01 30; www.mim.fgov.be; Rue Montagne de la Cour 2; metro Gare Centrale or Parc, tram 92, 93 or 94; adult/concession €5/3.50; ⏰ 9.30am-5pm Tue, Wed & Fri, 9.30am-8pm Thu, 10am-5pm Sat & Sun) is another must. It boasts one of the world's biggest collections of instruments, all displayed in the Old England building, a former department store and Art Nouveau showpiece built in 1899 by Paul Saintenoy. The building's black façade is a swirl of wrought iron and arched windows. Although empty for many years, it miraculously escaped demolition and early this century metamorphosed into this fab museum. Don't miss a drink at the roof-top *café* – the terrace gives a superb city panorama.

MUSÉES ROYAUX DES BEAUX-ARTS

The **Royal Museums of Fine Arts** (Map pp72-3; ☎ 02 508 32 11; www.fine-arts-museum.be; Rue de la Régence 3; metro Gare Centrale or Parc, tram 92, 93 or 94; adult/concession €6/3, 1-5pm 1st Wed of month free; ⏰ 9.30am-5pm Tue-Fri, 10am-5pm Sat & Sun) combines the Musée d'Art Ancien, the adjoining Musée d'Art Moderne and the brand new Magritte Museum. It's Belgium's premier collection of ancient and modern art, and is not to be missed. It's particularly well endowed with works by Pieter Breugel the Elder and Rubens, though Belgian surrealist René Magritte currently holds pride of place. Part of the Musée Moderne reopened in 2007 as a museum devoted exclusively to this famous artist. The museum has the world's largest Magritte collection – some 150 paintings and drawings, including his famous Secret Player.

To view the collections chronologically, start with the **Musée d'Art Ancien**. Begin with the Flemish Primitives (see boxed text, p125), including works by Rogier Van der Weyden, Dirk Bouts, Hans Memling and Gerard David. Move onto Quinten Matsijs, whose paintings demonstrate a turning point in Flemish art as traditional realistic scenes were superseded by the more flamboyant Renaissance style imported from Italy.

The Breugel family, in particular Pieter Breugel the Elder (see boxed text, p84), comes along next. The mysterious *Fall of Icarus* is one of his most famous works, although *De Volkstelling* (The Census at Bethlehem, painted in 1566) is more typical of his distinctive peasant scenes. *The Fall of the Rebel Angels* (1562) is characteristic of his gruesome religious allegories.

The champion of the 17th and 18th centuries is Rubens. Portraits and small, engaging sketches (such as *Studies of a Negro's Head*) contrast vividly with gigantic masterpieces, including the acclaimed *Ascent to Calvary* (c 1638). Jordaens, one of Rubens' contemporaries, is also well represented.

The **Musée d'Art Moderne** houses 19th- and 20th-century art and occupies a subterranean gallery that meanders for six levels below ground. Due to the opening of the new Magritte Museum here, some of the collection has been moved to the Dexia Art Centre in Rue de l'Écuyer. Whether here or there, earlier highlights to look out for include sculptures by Constantin Meunier, Ensor's macabre fighting skeletons, and many paintings by Paul Delvaux. Other national artists include Léon Spilliaert and Rik Wouters, both of whom belonged to the Fauve group of painters. The international scene is much less extensive but

THE BREUGEL FAMILY

The Breugels dominated Flemish art in the latter half of the tumultuous 16th century and early into the next. The family comprised Pieter Breugel the Elder and his sons Pieter the Younger and Jan. Art circles debate the spelling of their names (with or without and 'h', and so on) but, no matter how it's written, Breugel the Elder (c 1525–67) was undeniably the family's master. His work ranged from powerful landscapes to satirical allegories likened to those of Hieronymus Bosch. But it's for his quirky scenes of contemporary peasant life, woven around portentous religious events and myths, that he's best remembered. Many of his works were painted in a house on Rue Haute (Map pp76–7) in Brussels where he spent much of his life.

Breugel's first son, Pieter the Younger (1564–1638), largely copied his father's style but later earned the nickname 'Hell Breughel' for his preoccupation with scenes of damnation. Jan Breughel (1568–1625) spent most of his artistic life in Antwerp and was a colleague of Rubens. His sensitive paintings of landscapes and flowers led to his sobriquet, 'Velvet'.

The best place to see works by Breugel the Elder is Vienna's Kunsthistorisches Museum. In Belgium, content yourself with the excellent collection of family works in Brussels' Musées Royaux des Beaux-Arts (p83).

look out for Francis Bacon's delightful *Le Pape aux Hiboux* (Pope with Owls).

North of Place Royale
PALAIS ROYAL & MUSÉE BELVUE
Overlooking the southern end of Parc de Bruxelles is the **Royal Palace** (Map pp72-3; ☎ 02 551 20 20; www.monarchy.be; Place des Palais; metro Parc, tram 92, 93 or 94; admission free; ☷ 10.30am-4.30pm Tue-Sun late Jul-early Sep). This 19th-century palace is a low, cream-toned building that commands little attention these days as it's no longer the royal residence. Since the death of Queen Astrid, wife of Léopold III, Belgium's monarchs have lived at Laeken (p88), although this palace is still their 'official' abode. The Palais Royal is open to visitors for a limited time in summer (usually late July to early September), when a largely Belgian crowd comes to gawk at its most controversial feature, a ceiling lined with green wings taken from millions of moths (where else but bizarre Belgium!). For more on the royal family, see boxed text, p91.

Attached to the palace's western end is the new **Musée BELvue** (Map pp72-3; ☎ 02 545 08 00; www.belvue.be; Place des Palais 7; metro Parc, tram 92, 93 or 94; adult/child €3/2; ☷ 10am-6pm Tue-Sun Jun-Sep, until 5pm Oct-May). An English-language audio-guide takes you through Belgium's history from independence. The museum's brochure claims 'there will be few secrets left about Belgium's past' following a visit here. Well, one subject that's still skirted is the genocide in the Congo during King Léopold II's rule (see p96). Just one out of 958 exhibits touches this subject – a newspaper clipping from the *New York American*, published 10 December 1904, showing Congolese men and children with chopped off hands, and an article expressing outrage at the goings on.

PARC DE BRUXELLES
Brussels is well endowed with outlying forests and parklands, but in the inner city it's a different story. The largest central patch of greenery is the **Parc de Bruxelles** (Map pp72-3; metro Parc, tram 92, 93 or 94), an old, formal park flanked by the Palais Royal and the Palais de la Nation. Laid out under the dukes of Brabant, it's dotted with classical statues and framed by trees with mercilessly trellised branches. Lunchtime office workers, joggers and families with kids love it in summer.

COLONNE DU CONGRÈS
The **Congress Column** (Map pp72-3; Place du Congrès; metro Botanique or Madou, tram 92, 93 or 94) was erected in 1850 to commemorate the National Congress of 1831, which proclaimed the Belgian constitution. It was designed by Joseph Poelaert (better known for his massive Palais de Justice, opposite) and soars 25m high to be crowned by a statue of Léopold I. At its base burns the eternal flame, homage to the Belgians who died during the two world wars. Although the square is at a good elevation, the view from here is drab.

South of Place Royale
ÉGLISE NOTRE DAME AU SABLON
Flamboyant Gothic is the style of this large but gloomy **church** (Map pp76-7; Rue de la Régence 3b;

tram 92, 93 or 94; ⓧ 9am-6.30pm Mon-Fri, 10am-7pm Sat & Sun), located at the top end of the Sablon. It began as a chapel, built by the archers' guild in the 13th century, but was enlarged in the 15th century when pilgrims descended in droves to pay homage to a statue of the Madonna reputed to have healing powers. The statue has long since gone and the inside is now best noted for its 11 impressive stained-glass windows and the chapel of the local Tour et Taxis family, who founded Belgium's postal service.

PLACE DU PETIT SABLON
About 200m uphill from Place du Grand Sablon, this charming little **garden** (Map pp76-7; tram 92, 93 or 94) is framed by 48 bronze statuettes depicting the medieval guilds. At its heart is a monument to Counts Egmont and Hoorn, who were beheaded on the Grand Place in 1568 for defying Spanish rule.

PALAIS DE JUSTICE
Larger than St Peter's in Rome, this colossal **law court** (Map pp76-7; ☎ 02 508 64 10; Place Poelaert; metro Louise; admission free; ⓧ 8am-5pm Mon-Fri) was one of Léopold II's most stupendous projects. It was purposely sited on a hill above the working-class Marolles as a symbol of law and order. Its design, intended to evoke the temples of the Egyptian Pharaohs, is equally intimidating. The building was created by the architect Joseph Poelaert, who died during its construction in 1879; legend has it he was struck by illness brought on by witchcraft attributed to the many Marolles residents evicted to make way for the building.

The nearby **viewing platform** offers a vista of northern Brussels, and here too is the glass **elevator** that connects Place Poelaert with the Marolles' Place Breugel.

EU Quarter
The **EU district** (Map p86) is bordered by the Petit Ring to the west and Parc du Cinquantenaire to the east. By and large it's not an area for idle wandering but it does offer interesting sights, including museums, the Berlaymont and European Parliament buildings and Art Nouveau houses.

EU BUILDINGS
The most famous building is the four-winged **Berlaymont** (Map p86; Rue de la Loi 200; metro Schuman). Built in 1967, it was the European Commis-

sion's headquarters until 1991 when leaking asbestos forced its evacuation. It finally reopened in 2006, and is once again the area's landmark sight. New information panels dotted around the building give insight into the history of this neighbourhood and Brussels' international role, and are well worth browsing if you're in the area.

The distinctive domed **European Parliament** (Map p86; Rue Wiertz 43) sits next to Parc Léopold. Opened in 1998 by King Albert II, it's all steel and blue glass and is nicknamed 'Caprice des Dieux' (Whim of the Gods) after a French cheese. The European Parliament is the EU's legislative branch; elections are held every five years (next in 2010). It is the only EU institution that meets and debates in public. It's possible to sit in on a parliamentary session in the huge debating chamber (the hemicycle), or to tour the hemicycle when parliament's not meeting. Free **tours** (ⓧ tours 10am & 3pm Mon-Thu, 10am Fri), using multilingual headphones, start at the **visitor's centre** (Map p86; ☎ 02 284 34 57; Rue Wiertz 43), attached to the Paul-Henri Spaak section of the parliament.

The easiest way to get to the European Parliament from central Brussels is with bus 38 (direction Homborch; departs from next to Gare Centrale) to the stop De Meeus on Rue du Luxembourg (Map pp76-7). From this street there's a good view of the parliament's blue dome. Also visible are the remains of **Gare du Luxembourg** (Map p86; Place du Luxembourg), until recently the oldest train station in Belgium. Despite avid opposition, all but the façade of the old ticket hall has been demolished. Pass next to the façade and cross the concrete walkway to arrive at the Paul-Henri Spaak entrance (directly in front of you – go through the covered passageway); the visitor's centre is down to the left.

MUSÉE DES SCIENCES NATURELLES
The excellent **Museum of Natural Sciences** (Map p86; ☎ 02 627 42 38; www.naturalsciences.be; Rue Vautier 29; metro Trône or Maelbeek, bus 34 or 80; adult/concession €4/3; ⓧ 9.30am-4.45pm Tue-Fri, 10am-6pm Sat & Sun) is undergoing renovation and expansion until late 2007. But even with some rooms closed, there's plenty to see. The museum's stars are the fossilised skeletons of nine iguanodons – two-legged, 10m-high dinosaurs that lived 135 million years ago – found in a coal mine in Bernissart, a village near Mons in Hainaut province, in 1878.

MUSÉE ANTOINE WIERTZ

Down the road from the Musée des Sciences Naturelles is the **Musée Antoine Wiertz** (Map p86; ☎ 02 648 17 18; Rue Vautier 62; metro Trône or Maelbeek, bus 34 or 80; admission free; ☺ 10am-noon & 1-5pm Tue-Fri, plus alternate weekends) – if you're into the shocking or nasty, it may appeal. Antoine Wiertz (1806–65) was a 19th-century Brussels artist bent on painting giant religious canvases depicting hell and other frenzied subjects. The building was Wiertz's home and studio and was also once the residence of the noted Flemish writer Hendrik Conscience.

PARC DU CINQUANTENAIRE

Parc du Cinquantenaire (Map p86; metro Schuman or Mérode) was built during Léopold II's reign. It's best known for its cluster of museums – art, history, military and motor vehicles – and the massive **Arcade du Cinquantenaire**, a triumphal arch built in 1880 to celebrate 50 years of Belgian independence. In summer, this area is put to good use with a popular drive-in cinema (p108).

Musées Royaux d'Art et d'Histoire (Map p86; ☎ 02 741 72 11; www.kmkg-mrah.be in Flemish & French; Parc du Cinquantenaire 10; metro Mérode; adult/concession €4/3, 1-5pm 1st Wed of month free; ☺ 9.30am-5pm Tue-Fri, 10am-5pm Sat & Sun) is chock-full of antiquities from around the world. All labelling is in French and Flemish but there is an English-language audio-guide.

Musée Royale de l'Armée et d'Histoire Militaire (Map p86; ☎ 02 737 78 11; www.klm-mra.be; Parc du Cinquantenaire

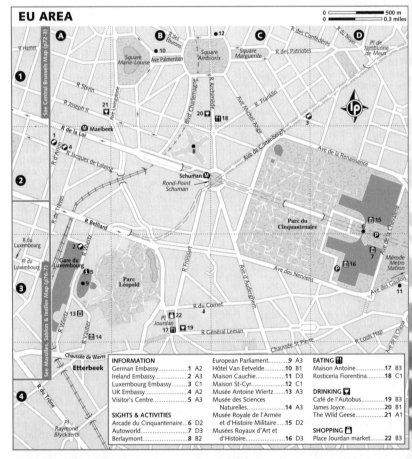

EU AREA

0 — 500 m
0 — 0.3 miles

INFORMATION
German Embassy................1 A2
Ireland Embassy................2 A3
Luxembourg Embassy................3 C1
UK Embassy................4 A2
Visitor's Centre................5 A3

SIGHTS & ACTIVITIES
Arcade du Cinquantenaire....6 D2
Autoworld................7 D3
Berlaymont................8 B2

European Parliament................9 A3
Hôtel Van Eetvelde................10 B1
Maison Cauchie................11 D3
Maison St-Cyr................12 C1
Musée Antoine Wiertz................13 A3
Musée des Sciences
  Naturelles................14 A3
Musée Royale de l'Armée
  et d'Histoire Militaire......15 D2
Musées Royaux d'Art et
  d'Histoire................16 D3

EATING
Maison Antoine................17 B3
Rosticeria Fiorentina................18 C1

DRINKING
Café de l'Autobus................19 B3
James Joyce................20 B1
The Wild Geese................21 A1

SHOPPING
Place Jourdan market................22 B3

3; metro Mérode; admission free; 9am-noon & 1-4.30pm Tue-Sun) boasts a staggering collection of all things military dating back to Belgian independence. Take the elevator to the top floor, where an outside balcony affords good city views.

As its name foretells, **Autoworld** (Map p86; 02 736 41 65; www.autoworld.be; Parc du Cinquantenaire 11; metro Mérode; adult/concession €6/4.70; 10am-6pm Apr-Sep, 10am-5pm Oct-Mar) is one of Europe's biggest ensembles of vintage cars and other wheeled contraptions.

ART NOUVEAU HOUSES

The EU area is a treasure trove of Art Nouveau. For details on Maison St-Cyr, Hôtel Van Eetvelde and Maison Cauchie, the three most famous buildings, see 'Brussels' Art Nouveau Top 10' (p93).

Ixelles & St Gilles
MUSÉE HORTA

A superb introduction to the late-19th-century Art Nouveau movement is the **Musée Horta** (Map pp76-7; 02 543 04 90; www.hortamuseum.be; Rue Américaine 25; tram 91 or 92; admission €5; 2-5.30pm Tue-Sun). It occupies two adjoining houses in St Gilles that Horta designed and built between 1898 and 1901 and is where he lived until 1919 (for more information, see boxed text, p88).

From the outside, the most noticeable thing is usually the queue of people waiting to get in. In typical Horta style it's the inside that tells the story. There are airy rooms radiating from an iron-laced staircase, mirrored walls, glorious timber panelling, intimate stained-glass inlays and even curly door handles.

Unfortunately, the splendour dims somewhat when it's too crowded – time your visit for a weekday. For details on other Art Nouveau treasures in this district, follow our walking tour (p92) and see boxed text, p93.

MUSÉE CONSTANTIN MEUNIER

The southern part of Ixelles is home to the intimate **Musée Constantin Meunier** (Map pp70-1; 02 648 44 49; Rue de l'Abbaye 59; tram 93 or 94; admission free; 10am-noon & 1-5pm Tue-Fri, plus alternate weekends). Constantin Meunier (1831–1905), a Brussels-born artist, is best known for his emotive sculptures fed by social realism. Larger-than-life bronzes depict working-class themes – muscular miners from Hainaut, dockworkers from Antwerp and men reaping fields. The museum occupies the town house where he lived and worked during his last years.

MUSÉE COMMUNAL D'IXELLES

The **Ixelles Museum** (Map pp76-7; 02 515 64 22; www.musee-ixelles.be in French; Rue Van Volsem 71; tram 81 or 82;

THE EU IN BRUSSELS

The capital of Europe – that's Brussels' boast, thanks to the EU. The EU, an economic and political union, is made up of 25 countries stretching from the Arctic Circle to the Mediterranean Sea. Ten new members – mainly Eastern European countries – joined in 2004, and negotiations are underway to admit Turkey. In 2007 the EU celebrated 50 years since the formation of the Treaty of Rome and the start of European institutions in Brussels.

As the capital of this union, Brussels has fared well. More and more multinationals and foreign companies are based here, and parts of the city are full of Eurocrats, lobbyists and journalists, all bent on working, manipulating, watching or reporting the political goings-on. The knock-on effect for service industries has been huge.

But there's also plenty of Eurosceptics who lament the EU's excesses (the European Parliament building cost US$1.6 billion but its debating chamber is used for just a few weeks each year), and complain about high civil servant salaries and the bureaucracy size. There are also those who resent the demolition of Quartier Léopold, a residential suburb with distinctive town houses, that was wiped out to make way for the EU's real-life Gotham City.

The EU area (Map p86) lies east of central Brussels. The two main thoroughfares – Rue de la Loi and Rue Belliard – house ugly office blocks and bellow with traffic. As a visitor, there's not a great deal to see though there are landmarks to seek (p85).

Everywhere in Brussels – on car licence plates, T-shirts and umbrellas – you'll see a dark-blue flag featuring a circle of 12 five-pointed gold stars. It's the EU flag, originally designed for the Council of Europe in the 1950s and adopted by the European Commission in 1985.

For more on the EU, check out www.europa.eu.int.

HORTA'S CREATIONS

Of all the buildings Victor Horta (1861–1947) created in the short flowering of Art Nouveau, the Maison du Peuple (1896–99) was his most famous. It was designed to be an entertainment venue – a project based on socialist principles. Horta, like many of the architects of the Art Nouveau movement, was committed to creating works for the people rather than the bourgeoisie, although works for the latter paid his bread and butter.

The Maison du Peuple was built on Place Vandervelde, on a slope just below the Sablon. It was a daring glass-vaulted building full of Horta trademarks, particularly his love of creating transparent places in which light was free to play. But, like many buildings of its genre, it was eventually abandoned and in 1965, amid international criticism, torn down. Leftovers from the original have been used to construct the Grand Café Horta (p193) in Antwerp.

After the Maison, Horta turned his talent to his own house at Rue Américaine (now the Musée Horta, p87), and then to the Grand Magasin Waucquez (now the Centre Belge de la Bande Dessinée, p81). His exile in England and the USA during WWI marked a transition in styles – gone was the sensuous Art Nouveau and in its place stood the clean-cut functionalism of Art Deco. From 1922 to 1928 Horta designed the bold but severe Palais des Beaux-Arts – an innovative multipurpose entertainment centre that is still used today (see Bozar, p110). His last major work was the arguably ugly Gare Centrale.

adult/concession €6.20/5; ⏰ 1-6.30pm Tue-Fri, 10am-5pm Sat & Sun) has a small but engaging collection of modern Belgian and French art. It covers most of the movements of the 19th and 20th centuries and features works by Magritte and Delvaux.

BOIS DE LA CAMBRE

This **forest** (Map pp70-1; tram 93 or 94), at the end of Ave Louise, separates Ixelles and Uccle and is named after the Abbaye de la Cambre, a former 12th-century convent. The park was established in 1862 and joins the much larger Forêt de Soignes (p117). It's immensely popular with couples, cyclists and families on weekends, and has lawns, *cafés*, a playground, roller-skating rink and artificial lake.

Uccle

The exquisite **Musée David et Alice van Buuren** (Map pp70-1; ☎ 02 343 48 51; www.museumvanbuuren .com; Ave L Errera 41; tram 23 or 90; adult/concession €10/5; ⏰ 2-5.30pm Wed-Mon) is located in the former house of Dutch banker David van Buuren, a wealthy collector and patron of the arts who built this Art Deco showpiece in 1928.

Five rooms are open to the public and are crammed with ancient paintings, including a version of the *Fall of Icarus* by Pieter Breugel the Elder, as well as more modern works such as *Peeling Potatoes* by Vincent van Gogh. Sublime furnishings, stained glass and carpets are dotted throughout and the meticulous staff ensure plastic shoe-coverings are donned before entering.

St Josse & Schaerbeek

LE BOTANIQUE

On the edge of St Josse, **Le Botanique** (Map pp72-3; ☎ 02 218 79 35; Rue Royale 236; metro Botanique) is the cultural centre of Brussels' French-speaking community. The impressive neoclassical glass building from 1826 originally housed the city's botanical garden. These days it supports a solid programme of theatre, exhibitions and concerts.

HALLES DE SCHAERBEEK

The **Halles de Schaerbeek** (Map pp72-3; ☎ 02 218 21 07; www.halles.be in Flemish & French; Rue Royale Ste Marie 22; tram 92 or 93), a former food market, is just past Église Ste Marie in southern Schaerbeek. Built in 1901, it's a great example of industrial architecture and has been restored as a performing arts venue.

Laeken

DOMAINE ROYAL & PARC DE LAEKEN

The Domaine Royal (Royal Estate; Map pp70–1) is home to Belgium's ruling family. King Albert II and Queen Paola live in the Villa Belvédère; former Queen Fabiola (widow of King Baudouin) inhabits the Château Stuyvenbergh; and the heir-apparent Prince Philippe and Princess Mathilde occupy the main building, the Château Royal de Laeken. All the chateaux are out of bounds to tourists, but you can visit the nearby Serres Royales, the Pavillon Chinois and the Tour Japonaise. For more on the royals, see boxed text, p91.

The enormous **Serres Royales** (Royal Greenhouses; Map pp70-1; ☎ 02 551 20 20; www.monarchy.be; Ave du Parc Royal 61; metro Bockstael then bus 53; admission €2; ☾ late Apr–early May) were built by Alphonse Balat (Horta's teacher) during Léopold II's reign. Fuchsias and all sorts of tropical species thrive inside, and Belgians queue en masse during the two weeks each year when the greenhouses are open to the public. Exact opening dates are available annually from January – check with Brussels International (p69).

Standing almost opposite each other on the edge of the Domaine Royal are the **Pavillon Chinois** and **Tour Japonaise** (Chinese Pavilion & Japanese Tower; Map pp70-1; ☎ 02 268 16 08; Ave Jules Van Praet 44; tram 23 or 52; admission €3, 1–4.45pm 1st Wed of month free; ☾ 10am–4.45pm Tue–Sun). Both are Léopold II leftovers, built after he saw similar at the 1890 Paris World Fair. The former is a gloriously glittering affair and houses an extensive collection of Chinese porcelain; the latter is used for temporary Japanese art exhibitions.

The **Parc de Laeken** starts opposite the Domaine Royal and stretches to the Atomium. Dotted with chestnut and magnolia trees, its focal point is Léopold I's statue, erected in 1880.

ATOMIUM & PARC DES EXPOSITIONS

The **Atomium** (Map pp70-1; ☎ 02 475 47 77; www .atomium.be; Square Atomium; metro Heysel; adult/concession/ child €9/6/free; ☾ 10am–5.30pm) is a space-age leftover from the 1958 World Fair. It was built by the powerful Belgian metal industry as a model of an iron molecule – enlarged 165 billion times. The 102m-high steel structure consists of nine balls linked by columns. When approached from central Brussels, it looms over houses in the nearby suburbs like an alien from a '60s Hollywood movie. Originally destined for demolition post-1958, it became a symbol of postwar progress and is now a city icon. Recent renovation saw it closed for a couple of years, but it reopened in 2006 with shiny new stainless steel spheres and updated displays inside. To get there head for Heysel metro station or, more scenically, take tram 81.

Up the road from the Atomium is **Parc des Expositions** (Map pp70-1; Place de Belgique), a trade fair complex built in the 1930s to commemorate a century of independence. The major building here is Palais du Centenaire, an Art Deco piece featuring terraced tiers capped by statues.

Jette, Koekelberg & Molenbeek
MUSÉE MAGRITTE

A completely anonymous, suburban yellow-brick house: that's the façade of the **Musée Magritte** (Map pp70-1; ☎ 02 428 26 26; www.magritte museum.be; Rue Esseghem 135; metro Simonis then tram 19; adult/concession €6/5; ☾ 10am–6pm Wed–Sun), and the façade that René Magritte, Belgium's most famous surrealist artist, showed the outside world. This museum in Jette occupies the house where Magritte and his wife Georgette lived from 1930 to 1954. Its appeal comes from its incredibly ordinary nature. It's odd to think the man responsible for some of the 20th century's most enduring images spent 24 years of his life in this bourgeois backstreet.

The museum opened in 1999 as the private initiative of a friend of the widow Magritte. With scandalously little support from the Belgian state, the curators assembled hundreds of original items – from Magritte's passport to paintings, photos, furniture and a pipe. Not everything's original – the piano in the salon is a copy – but there's more than enough to give an inkling into Magritte's private world. And fans will delight in discovering details of the house that Magritte faithfully reproduced in dozens of his famous paintings (many of which can be seen at the Musées Royaux des Beaux-Arts, p83). For more information, see boxed text, p90.

BASILIQUE NATIONALE DU SACRÉ-CŒUR

This mighty **basilica** (Map pp70-1; Parvis de la Basilique 1; metro Simonis then bus 87; admission free; ☾ 9am–5pm May–Sep, 10am–2pm Oct–Apr) sits at the end of ruler-straight Blvd Léopold II in Koekelberg. It's the world's fifth-largest church and is also arguably the city's most ghastly religious edifice, a discordant mix of neogothic and Art Deco with dull brown stonework, capped towers and a bulbous 90m-high dome (€3 to climb).

TOUR & TAXIS

The newly revamped **Tour & Taxis** complex (Map pp70-1; ☎ 02 420 60 69; www.tourtaxis.be; Rue Picard 3; metro Yser) is the first stage of a massive transformation of Brussels' unloved canal quarter. These old warehouses and customs depots, now prime examples of the city's industrial heritage, were built at the start of last century by the Tour et Taxis family, founders of Belgium's postal service. Abandoned in the 1980s, the complex is now being developed into a new waterfront neighbourhood.

MR MAGRITTE

René Magritte (1898–1967) was one of the world's most prominent surrealist painters, blending ordinary images with those that could be conjured up only from the subconscious. His most famous motif, the man in the bowler hat whose face is hidden from view, exemplified surrealism's main premise: a rebellion against European rationalism, which had deteriorated into the horrors of WWI. That same bowler hat is now one of Belgium's international icons.

Born in Lessines north of Mons, Magritte spent most of his working life in Brussels. His interest in surrealism was sparked in 1922 after seeing a reproduction of Giorgio de Chirico's painting *The Song of Love* (1914), featuring the unlikely combination of a classical bust and a rubber glove. For the next few years, Magritte became active in the Belgian surrealist movement and in 1926, with the support of a Brussels art gallery, he became a full-time painter. His paintings often confused space and time, as in *Time Transfixed* (1939) in which a steaming locomotive roars out of a living-room mantelpiece as if it is just leaving a tunnel.

In 1927 Magritte and his wife Georgette moved to Paris where he befriended several Parisian surrealists, including poets André Breton and Paul Élouard. The couple returned to Brussels three years later and moved into an ordinary house on an ordinary street in the ordinary Brussels suburb of Jette – Magritte's thoughts and paintings may have been surreal but he was at the same time conventional to the hilt. This house is now the Musée Magritte (p89). Magritte painted most of his famous works here – he set up his easel in the kitchen and painted wearing a three-piece business suit. The kitchen window offered a view of a postage-stamp garden and a brick wall; for Magritte it was a looking glass into another world.

The couple moved from Jette in 1954 to a villa in Schaerbeek. When Georgette died in 1987, the villa and all its furnishings were given to the Belgian state, which promptly offered it all up for public sale. It was a prime example of Belgium's indifference to its artistic heritage.

But amends are being made and, if you're keen to see a swathe of Magritte's artworks, check out the new Magritte Museum, which opened at the Musées Royaux des Beaux-Arts (p83) in 2007. Two *cafés* also offer nostalgic reminders: La Fleur en Papier Doré (p107) was a former surrealist haunt, and Le Greenwich (p106) was where Magritte hawked his paintings. Two excellent books to explore are *Magritte* by Suzi Gablik and *René Magritte* by AM Hammacher.

Exhibition centres, shops, restaurants and modern apartments are either on the drawing board, near completion or newly opened. Have a meal in the first restaurant to have opened here, Tasso (p106), to see what's going on.

Anderlecht

Anyone with even a vague interest in Belgian beers must not miss a visit to the excellent **Musée Bruxellois de la Gueuze** (Brussels Gueuze Museum; Map pp72–3; ☎ 02 521 49 28; www.cantillon .be; Rue Gheude 56; premetro Lemonnier; adult/concession €3.50/3; ☷ 9am-4pm Mon-Fri, 10am-4pm Sat). It's not so much a museum as a self-guided tour through the family-run Cantillon brewery, where the owners still proudly use traditional methods to make their strange lambic beers (p49). After a brief introduction, make your own way around the ancient complex before returning to sample a beer or two.

Seventy years ago, 50 family-run breweries in and around Brussels made lambics. Today Cantillon is Brussels' sole survivor, although a handful of other breweries still operate in Lembeek and Beersel southwest of the capital.

ACTIVITIES
Billiards

For a sedate billiard hall, go no further than **Cercle Royal de Billiard** (Map pp72–3; ☎ 02 511 10 08; 3rd fl, Palais du Midi, Rue Rogier Van der Weyden 3; premetro Lemonnier; ☷ 5pm-midnight Mon, 2pm-midnight Fri, 2-7pm Sat). Tables cost €3.50 per hour.

Bowling

The capital's largest bowling alley, housed in a '60s building on the edge of the Marolles, is **Crosly Super Bowling** (Map pp72–3; ☎ 02 512 08 74; Blvd de l'Empereur 36; metro Gare Centrale; ☷ 2pm-midnight Mon-Fri, 2pm-2am Sat, 10am-1pm Sun). There are 20 lanes and a bar.

Chess

For a spot of chess, head to **Le Greenwich** (see p106) or, for something less smoky, **De Ultieme Hallucinatie** (p107).

A ROYAL READ

Belgium's monarchy has hit headlines plenty of times during their 175-or-so years on the throne. Léopold I kicked things off when crowned the first king on 21 July 1831 – the country's annual national day holiday commemorates this event. All was relatively peaceful until his son, Léopold II became king and set about exploiting the Congo (see boxed text, p96). Crisis followed crisis after that, first with the death of the next monarch, King Albert, in a rock climbing accident in 1934, and then a year later with the death of his daughter-in-law, Queen Astrid (mother of the present monarch, King Albert) in a car crash on the shores of Lake Lucerne. Astrid's husband, King Léopold III, was at the wheel at the time.

Léopold III's cosy relationship with Hitler during WWII backfired after the war, and public hostility forced him into exile. In 1950 the majority of Belgians voted in a referendum against his return and so his eldest son Baudouin took the reins. Baudouin's reign largely restored the institution of the monarchy, and he's credited with holding the country together during some difficult times, including its move to a federal state. After his sudden death in 1993, his younger brother, Albert, took over.

While Baudouin had remained childless, King Albert and Italian-born Queen Paola ascended the throne with three grown-up children and more. In 1999 the existence of a fourth child to Albert became public. Delphine Boël, born in 1968, was the outcome of a long affair between the then-prince and Belgian Baroness Sybille de Selys-Longchamps. The king has never publicly acknowledged this daughter, though he has hinted that his marriage went through difficult times. During celebrations as part of the country's 175th anniversary in 2005, Boël, an artist, was barred from attending an official event. Angry at the palace's snub, her mother went public for the first time, accusing the king of discrimination against his daughter.

The royalty again made headlines in 2006 when Crown Prince Philippe was attacked by the Flemish media for his apparent lack-lustre performance during an African trade mission. On top of that, there are always those ready to question his ability to be king. Newspaper hints that King Albert might soon abdicate to make way for Philippe have failed to materialise. And as for the future of the royals? While there are occasional calls for the king's powers to be reduced, the monarchy's survival is generally not questioned as it's widely seen as an essential – if expensive (€12 million per year to Belgian taxpayers) – ingredient in keeping Belgium together.

On a glossy level, recent pickings have been rich with two royal weddings – the first was heir-apparent Prince Philippe to Princess Mathilde, followed by Prince Philippe's younger brother Prince Laurent's marriage to Princess Claire – and a string of blue-blood births.

Golf

If you fancy a game of golf, there are several courses to be found in and around Brussels. The **Royal Amicale Golf Club** (Map pp70-1; ☎ 02 521 16 87; Rue de la Scholle; metro Eddy Merckx) in Anderlecht has 18 holes. Green fees cost €35/50 during the week/weekend.

Ice Skating

The Marché aux Poissons (the square around Ste Catherine metro station) converts to a *patinage à glace* (ice-skating) rink in the last two weeks of December; Brussels International (p69) will have details.

The **Patinoire de Forest National** (Map pp70-1; ☎ 02 345 16 11; Ave du Globe 36; tram 18, bus 48; adult/child €5/4.50; ☺ 8.30am-4.30pm Mon-Thu, 8.30am-4.30pm & 8-11pm Fri, 10am-6pm Sat & Sun) has an indoor rink. Skate hire is €2.50.

Squash & Tennis

On the edge of St Géry is **Flanders Gate Squash Club** (Map pp72-3; ☎ 02 512 98 23; Blvd Barthélémy 17; metro Comte de Flandre; ☺ noon-2pm & 4.30-11pm Mon-Fri). It has six courts and members/nonmembers pay €5.50/8 per half-hour or €45/68 for a five-hour card.

Centre Sportif de la Woluwé-St-Pierre (Map pp70-1; ☎ 02 773 18 20; Ave Salomé 2; tram 39) is a huge sporting complex in Woluwé-St-Pierre with squash and tennis courts. Rates range from €4.50 to €6 per half-hour for squash and €11 per hour for tennis.

Swimming

Belgium isn't much of a swimming nation but those who are interested in unusual pools might want a dip at **Piscine Victor Boin** (Map pp76-7; ☎ 02 539 06 15; Rue de la Perche 38; premetro

Horta, tram 18 or 81; ⊙ 8am-7pm Mon, Tue, Thu & Fri, 2-7pm Wed, 9am-6pm Sat) in St Gilles. This covered Art Deco pool has a *bain turc* (Turkish bath) at the rear, which is reserved for women on Tuesday and Friday; it's reserved for men Monday, Thursday and Saturday. A single pool ticket costs €2.

WALKING TOUR

Brussels' brief flirt with Art Nouveau furnished the capital with a prized collection of buildings. This walking tour takes in Art Nouveau gems in the adjoining neighbourhoods of Ixelles and St Gilles (Map pp76–7). It covers famous works as well as buildings by lesser-known architects.

The walk takes about two hours, not including time spent inside the few buildings that are open to the public. If you intend visiting the Musée Horta as part of this tour, note that it is open afternoons only, and closed on Monday.

The tour begins at Place Flagey near the Étangs d'Ixelles (Ixelles Ponds); to get there take tram 81 or 82 from Gare du Midi. Walk along the pond's western side then deviate off to reach **Rue du Lac 6 (1)**, one of 11 houses in this area designed by Ernest De Lune. It has a fantastically tall stained-glass window and a lovely 2nd-floor balcony.

WALK FACTS

Start Place Flagey
Finish Hôtel Hannon
Distance 3.2km
Duration About 2 hours

Rejoin the lake, and follow it to two groups of houses designed by Ernest Blérot. The first two, at **Ave Général de Gaulle 38 and 39 (2)**, have excessive wrought-iron railings. The other pair, at **Rue Vilain XIV 9 and 11 (3)**, are noted for their sgraffito and are signed and dated (1902) by Blérot. Blérot's own home stood between these two groups until it was torn down in the 1960s. A prolific builder with a great imagination, Blérot designed 60 houses all up, each different from the next.

Continue up Rue Vilain XIV, turn right into Ave Louise, and follow it northwards to Horta's **Hôtel Solvay (4**; opposite). Cross Ave Louise to arrive at **Hôtel Tassel (5)** at Rue Paul-Émile Janson 6. Built in 1893, it was Horta's first true Art Nouveau house. Continue straight ahead to reach Albert Roosenboom's creation at **Rue Faider 83 (6)**. It has simple Art Nouveau tones, including a beautiful, gilded sgraffito design at the top. Roosenboom also signed this house.

Now wander past two houses by Paul Hankar. The first, the large **Maison Camberlaini (7**; Rue Defacqz 48) was being renovated at the time of writing. The second, **Maison Hankar (8**; Rue Defacqz 71) was his own studio, built in 1893. Turn left into Rue Amazone, then round the corner to find **Rue Africaine 92 (9)**, designed by De Lestrée in 1903. It has creamy tones, harmonious lines and a big circular window, a favoured feature of many Art Nouveau houses. From here it's a short walk to the **Musée Horta (10**; p87).

The final two houses on the walking tour are two (big) blocks south down Chaussée de Charleroi. The first of these abodes, **Les Hiboux**

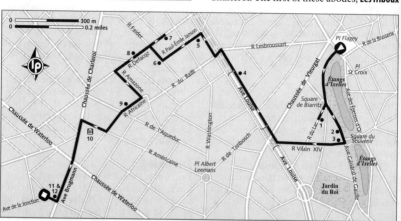

11; Ave Brugmann 55) has intimate owls adorning the façade. Right next door to it is one of the city's showpieces, Jules Brunfaut's **Hôtel Hannon (12**; below).

From here, walk back to the tram stop Ma Campagne at the intersection of Chaussée de Charleroi and Chaussée de Waterloo to take tram 92 (direction Ste Marie) back to town. Alternatively, stay onboard until the tram reaches De Ultieme Hallucinatie (p107) in Schaerbeek, and have a drink in one of the city's most famous Art Nouveau *cafés*.

BRUSSELS FOR CHILDREN

There's absolutely no reason for kids to utter the 'b'-word in Brussels. From puppets to parks and pools, this child-friendly city offers plenty.

Smack in town, the **Scientastic Museum** (Map p74; ☎ 02 732 13 36; www.scientastic.com; above premetro station Bourse; adult/concession €4.40/2.90; ⊙ 2-5.30pm Sat & Sun, daily during school holidays) has interactive science-related pursuits for youngsters aged six and up. Don't be put off by the grim setting when arriving in the *premetro* station's concourse – inside it's great.

BRUSSELS' ART NOUVEAU TOP 10

Art Nouveau is Brussels' architectural jewel. Plenty of buildings can be visited (see www.brussels artnouveau.be), but a handful is closed to the public except to those on ARAU tours (p95). The following (in alphabetical order) are Brussels' best:

- **De Ultieme Hallucinatie** (p107)

- **Falstaff** (p106)

- **Hôtel Hannon** (Map pp76-7; ☎ 02 538 42 20; Ave de la Jonction 1; tram 91 or 92; admission €2.50; ⊙ 11am-6pm Wed-Fri, 1-6pm Sat & Sun) This lovely building, with its stone frieze and stained glass, was designed in 1902 by Jules Brunfaut. It's now the Contretype photography gallery and is one of the few Art Nouveau buildings readily accessible to the public.

- **Hôtel Solvay** (Map pp76-7; Ave Louise 224; tram 93 or 94) Horta designed this in 1894 at the age of 33 and it's considered one of his masterpieces. It was commissioned by the Solvay family (soft-drink manufacturers), who gave him free rein in matters of design and budget. It's open only to ARAU tours; if you can't time that, the hints of Art Nouveau visible on the outside are worth a look.

- **Hôtel Van Eetvelde** (Map p86; Ave Palmerston 2-4; metro Schuman) While the outside of this building is unusual, the interior is another Horta masterpiece (1895–1901). It was commissioned by Baron Van Eetvelde, Minister for the Congo at that time and the country's highest-paid civil servant. Exotic timbers stud the interior, and there's a central glass dome infused with African-inspired plant motifs. Admission is limited to ARAU tours.

- **Maison Autrique** (Map pp70-1; ☎ 02 215 66 00; www.autrique.be; Chaussée de Haecht 266; tram 92 or 93; admission €5; ⊙ noon-6pm Wed-Sun) The Schaerbeek house that started it all. Horta's first building of note (1893) opened its doors to the public a couple of years ago. There's little luxury or extravagance, but many design elements hint at what's to come, and it's well worth viewing.

- **Maison Cauchie** (Map p86; ☎ 02 673 15 06; Rue des Francs 5; metro Mérode; admission €4; ⊙ 11am-1pm & 2-6pm 1st Sat & Sun of month) Built in 1905, this stunning house was the home of architect and painter Paul Cauchie (1875–1952), and its sgraffito façade, adorned with graceful female figures, is one of the most beautiful in Brussels. A petition saved the house from demolition in 1971 and since 1975 it has been a protected monument. Try timing a visit to meet the limited opening hours; if that's not possible, the façade alone definitely warrants a visit.

- **Maison St-Cyr** (Map p86; Square Ambiorix 11; metro Schuman) The haunting façade of this narrow building (up for sale in 2006 for €725,000) is an extravagance of knotted and twisted ironwork. It was built in 1903 for the painter Léonard St-Cyr by Gustave Strauven (1878–1919), who worked as an apprentice to Horta and also built Art Nouveau houses in Schaerbeek.

- **Musée Horta** (p87)

- **Old England Building** (p83)

Le Peruchet (Map pp70-1; ☎ 02 673 87 30; Ave de la Forêt 50, Ixelles; tram 32; admission €5.50; ☼ 3pm Wed, Sat & Sun, closed Jul & Aug) is one of several small private puppet theatres to survive in Brussels. It's aimed specifically at kids (as opposed to productions at Théâtre Royal de Toone, p111) in the two-to-eight age group. Occupying an old whitewashed stone farmhouse in the middle of modern Ixelles, the theatre is totally at odds with all around it, making it one of those Brussels experiences you won't forget. Go through thick curtains to discover a world of fables and fairytales, and an adjoining museum chock full of colourful characters. All productions are in French, but the set up is unique enough for kids of any language to enjoy.

Bruparck (Map pp70-1; ☎ 02 474 83 77; www.bruparck.com in Flemish & French; Blvd du Centenaire 20; metro Heysel) is a theme park located near the Atomium. It incorporates the **Océade** (☎ 02 478 43 20; over/under 1.3m €14/11.20; ☼ 10am-7pm Mon-Fri, 10am-9pm Sat & Sun), a subtropical water fun park that kids love, the giant **Kinepolis cinema** (p108), and **Mini Europe** (☎ 02 478 13 13; www.minieurope.com; adult/child €11.80/8.80; ☼ 9.30am-8pm). The latter displays miniature mock-ups of European highlights, like London's Big Ben and Venetian gondolas. Playgrounds, fairground rides and fast-food outlets are dotted throughout Brupark.

Hanging to see the latest blockbuster? Drop the kids off at **Les Samedis du Cinéma**, a supervised kid's screening (€1.50) organised every Saturday morning at 9am by the **UGC De Brouckère cinema** (p108), and join other parents catching an adult film.

Musée des Enfants (Children's Museum; Map pp70-1; ☎ 02 640 01 07; www.museedesenfants.be; Rue du Bourgmestre 15; tram 23 or 90; admission €6.70; ☼ 2.30-5pm Mon-Fri Jul, Wed & Sat May & Jun, Sun Sep-Apr) is basically a big old mansion that's morphed into an indoor playground. Kids (aged three to nine) can paint, plant a garden, explore a space capsule, bake biscuits and more. It's very popular, particularly on wet days.

Musée du Jouet (Map pp72-3; ☎ 02 219 61 68; www.museedujouet.be; Rue de l'Association 24; metro Botanique or Madou; adult/child €4.50/3.50; ☼ 10am-noon & 2-6pm) is a newly renovated museum that explores the toys of yesteryear. It's full of stuff, but it's not 'Hands off!'.

The most central **playground** is in Parc de Bruxelles (p84). Ixelles' small **Parc Tenbosch** (Map pp76-7; Chaussée de Vleurgat; tram 93 or 94) has a fenced, sandy, dog-free play area for toddlers. The Rouge Cloître in the **Forêt de Soignes** (p117)

offers a playground suitable for kids up to about 12.

Several travelling circuses set up during autumn and into winter. All use animals. The Italian family-run **Florilegio** (www.florilegio.com) concentrates on acrobatics, and raises its big top annually at the **Hippodrome de Boitsfort** (Map pp70-1; ☎ 02 533 10 80; Chaussée de la Hulpe 51-53; tram 94).

Walibi & Aqualibi (Map p218; ☎ 010 42 17 17; Rue Joseph Dachamps, Wavre; adult/child €30/25; ☼ 10am-11pm Apr-Oct) combines a theme park and water park located about 20km southeast of Brussels off the E411 to Namur. Roller coasters, wave makers and pools make this a big day out. Closing hours vary depending on the month, so phone for details.

Other attractions:

Atomium (p89) Kids love exploring this space-age leftover.

Autoworld (p87) For youngsters into cars.

Bois de la Cambre (p88) One of Brussels' favourite parks.

Centre Belge de la Bande Dessinée (p81) Comicstrip museum.

Crosly Super Bowling (p90) Bowling alley located in the heart of town.

Koninklijk Museum voor Midden-Afrika (below) Africa museum.

Musée des Instruments de Musique (p83) Offers kids a playful approach to music.

Musée des Sciences Naturelles (p85) Great for rainy afternoons. Lots of interactive displays.

Baby-sitting organisations in Brussels:

Gezinsbond (☎ 02 507 89 66) Family-oriented organisation with centres throughout Flanders. Baby-sitters charge €2.50/3 per hour in the day/evening, or €15 for overnight service (see also p303).

ULB Job Service (☎ 02 650 21 71) Run by students at the Université Libre de Bruxelles. They will baby-sit at hotels or B&Bs, and charge €4 to €5.50 per hour (€8 after midnight). Book at least a day ahead.

BIZARRE BRUSSELS

The **Koninklijk Museum voor Midden-Afrika** (Royal Museum of Central Africa; ☎ 02 769 52 11; www.africamuseum.be; Leuvensesteenweg 13, Tervuren; tram 44; adult/concession €4/3; ☼ 10am-5pm Tue-Fri, 10am-6pm Sat & Sun) is one of Belgium's most haunting sights. It's an easy half-day excursion from Brussels that won't be readily forgotten. Located on the edge of Tervuren, a Flemish-speaking town 14km east of Brussels, this museum houses the world's most impressive array of artefacts from Africa, much of which was plundered during King Léopold II's exploitation of the Congo in the 19th century (see p96).

Start by jumping on tram 44 from its terminus at Montgoméry metro station. This old yellow tram runs all the way to Tervuren along a beautiful tree-lined track next to the wide Ave de Tervuren, passing opulent embassy villas, the ponds at Parc de Woluwé and, later, through the northern reaches of the leafy Forêt des Soignes. Sit on the right and keep a sharp eye out to view the **Palais Stocklet** (Map pp70–1; Ave de Tervuren 281; not open to the public). This radical geometric building was designed by Josef Hoffman between 1906–11 and it's claimed to be the world's most complete example of Art Nouveau. Twenty minutes later tram 44 trundles to its Tervuren terminus, from where it's a few minutes walk down the main drag to Léopold's extravagance.

The museum houses a staggering collection of stuffed animals, bottled creatures and dead insects, not to mention an enormous 22m-long *pirogue* (canoe) crafted by the Lengola people, a Gallery of Remembrance commemorating the 1508 Belgians who never returned from the dark continent, plus masks, tools and woven baskets. It's formidable booty, and what's displayed is only a fraction of what's still locked in the museum's vaults.

But the permanent exhibition has long been regarded as an imperialistic showpiece, mirroring views from decades ago when it was established, but way off centre with current thinking. What happened in the Congo is simply not addressed. A new sign in the Gallery of Remembrance acknowledges 'there is no mention of the Congolese victims' and that 'the viewpoint is exclusively European'. But that's it. Since the beginning of this decade, museum director Guido Gryseels has been overhauling exhibits in preparation for the museum's 2010 centennial celebrations. It'll be interesting to see then whether the facts are faced.

Inside the museum, a small café serves meals (€7 to €15), snacks and drinks including African beer. Fanning out before the museum entrance is the pleasant **Park van Tervuren**, where walking paths meander past manicured lawns and into the forest.

TOURS

Atelier de Recherche et d'Action Urbaine (ARAU; Map p74; 02 219 33 45; www.arau.org; Blvd Adolphe Max 55; metro De Brouckère), a heritage conservation group, was set up in 1969 by locals concerned at the destruction taking place around their ears. In 1975 it began running tours of the city's

architectural gems, and today offers a variety of theme tours to Art Nouveau buildings, Art Deco houses, the EU quarter, the Grand Place area and the Marolles. They're highly recommended, especially if you're keen to get into some of the private Art Nouveau showpieces (p93). There are usually only one or two tours per theme per month, so you may have to plan your visit. The cost is €15 for bus tours and €10 for walking tours (2½ hours). The Art Nouveau bus tours (three hours) are held at 10am on the second and forth Sunday of the month (May to mid-September). Most tours depart from Place de Brouckère, and some tours are conducted in English. Brussels International (p69) has full details of ARAU's seasonal programme and will book tours.

Brussels City Tours (Map p74; 02 513 77 44; www.brussels-city-tours.com; Rue de la Colline 8) is the main bus-tour company, with 2¾-hour tours of all the major sights costing adult/concession/child €25/23/12.50. It also runs the cheaper **Visit Brussels Line** (adult/concession/child €16.50/14.5/8; 10am-5pm daily Jul & Aug, 10am-3pm Sun-Fri Sep-Jun), hop-on hop-off double-decker buses that stop at 13 places including the Atomium, Place Royale and the EU's Rond Point Schuman. These buses leave Gare Centrale every half-hour. Tickets can be bought on the bus.

Horse-drawn carriages (Map p74; per carriage €18; 20 min) do circuits of the Lower Town starting from Rue Charles Buls, near Grand Place.

Cycle tours are offered by La Maison des Cyclistes (p116) and Centre Vincent van Gogh (p98).

FESTIVALS & EVENTS

JANUARY & FEBRUARY

Foire des Antiquaires/Antiekbeurs The revamped Tour & Taxis (p89) customs depot is the new venue for this annual 10-day antique fair held in late January, which offers the best from antique dealers in Belgium and neighbouring countries.

Anima Brussels Animation Festival (www.awn.com) Twelve-day festival in late February premieres feature-length films and about 100 shorts produced in Belgium and elsewhere.

MARCH & APRIL

Ars Musica (www.arsmusica.be) Respected festival of contemporary classical music from mid-March to early April. Attracts a showcase of musicians to various venues.

Serres Royales (www.monarchy.be) The royal greenhouses (p89) at the Domaine Royal in Laeken are open to the public for 10 days from the end of April.

LÉOPOLD II & THE CONGO

In 1885, Belgium's King Léopold II personally acquired the Congo in Africa, an area almost 100 times the size of his homeland. Between then and 1908, when the Belgian state stripped the king of his possession, it is estimated up to 10 million Africans died because of starvation, overwork or murder carried out in Léopold's quest for rubber (tyres were developed in the mid-1890s), ivory and other commodities.

Congo army manuals from that time describe women and children kept hostage to force men to fulfil rubber quotas. To keep account of ammunition, troops had to bring back the severed right hand of those killed. While all this was going on, Léopold set up philanthropic fronts to 'protest' the slave trade.

A BBC TV documentary *White King, Red Rubber, Black Dead,* aired in Belgium in 2004, shone this period of history squarely into Belgian faces – and some didn't like what they saw. Outspoken foreign minister Louis Michel retaliated, saying it was biased and didn't take into account the social context of that time. Belgium's new history museum, BELvue (p84), which opened in 2005 to celebrate 175 years since independence, also doesn't acknowledge what happened.

It will be impossible to know for sure the number of people who died. On Léopold's orders, the Congo archives were destroyed. According to Adam Hochschild in his book *King Léopold's Ghost,* the furnaces in the Congo offices in Brussels burnt for over a week. But what is sure is that the booty from this barbarity was enormous. Brussels' landmarks – such as the Arcade du Cinquantenaire (p86) – were built on these proceeds. So too was the Koninklijk Museum voor Midden Afrika, set up as homage to Léopold. But two years before its completion in 1910, the Belgian government stripped the king of his personal fiefdom due to international criticism of the atrocities committed under his rule. He died the following year, and today his reputation is in tatters.

Brussels International Festival of Fantastic Film (www.bifff.org) *The* most popular get-together for European fans of cult fantasy, thriller and sci-fi movies. Runs for two weeks mid-March.

Artbrussels (www.artbrussels.be) Annual four-day contemporary art fair held in mid-April.

Les Nuits Botanique (www.botanique.be in Flemish & French) A week of rock, electro and pop in Le Botanique (p88) from late April.

MAY & JUNE

Zinneke Parade (www.zinneke.org) Biennial one-day multicultural parade in May (even years) that's designed to bridge social divides and to expose Brussels' zanier side. Unlike many of the capital's traditional events, this one has only been going since 2000 and is thoroughly contemporary.

Brussels 20km Run (www.20kmdebruxelles.be) Annual competition held in the streets of the capital on the last Sunday in May, attracting about 20,000 runners. Starts and ends at Parc du Cinquantenaire (p86).

Brussels Jazz Marathon (www.brusselsjazzmarathon .be) Three days of free, nonstop jazz concerts on stages all over the city. Big names sit alongside local newcomers, and special buses shuttle punters from one venue to the next. Last weekend of May.

Concours Musical International Reine Élisabeth de Belgique (www.concours-reine-elisabeth.be) The Queen Elisabeth International Music Competition is one of Belgium's most prestigious classical music events. It began half a century ago and was inspired by the nation's former Queen Elisabeth, who was a violinist. Young talent from around the world is drawn to a month-long competition in May in three rotating categories (violin, piano and song).

KunstenFESTIVALdesArts (www.kunstenfestivaldesarts .be) Big names – both local and international – in the worlds of music, dance, theatre and opera are showcased over the last three weeks in May. This is one of the few festivals where Brussels' French- and Flemish-speaking communities meet.

Couleur Café (www.couleurcafé.be) World-music event staged over three days during the last weekend in June. Huge marquees are set up at the newly revamped Tour & Taxis complex (p89).

Ommegang (www.ommegang.be) This medieval-style procession takes place in late June or early July. Ommegang (a 'walk around' in Flemish) dates back to the 14th century, when celebrations were held following the arrival in Brussels of a statue of the Virgin Mary brought by boat from Antwerp. By the 16th century the procession was presided over by royalty and was held to honour Charles V. It is now one of the capital's most famous events. The procession starts at the Place du Grand Sablon and ends in a dance at the illuminated Grand Place. Tickets for the finale need to be bought well in advance.

GAY & LESBIAN BRUSSELS

Brussels' gay and lesbian communities are small but thriving. The quarter is smack in the city centre, concentrated around Rue du Marché au Charbon, Rue des Pierres and Rue de la Fourche (all on Map p74).

Tels Quels (Map p74; ☎ 02 512 32 34; www.telsquels.be in French; Rue du Marché au Charbon 81; prémetro Anneessens; ◷ from 5pm Sun-Tue, Thu & Fri, from 2pm Wed & Sat) The main French-speaking gay/lesbian group in Belgium. It's home to a popular *café* and information centre, a good starting point for finding out what's on. It also runs a telephone helpline, Telégal (☎ 02 502 07 00; 8pm to midnight). *Tels Quels Magazine*, a monthly French-language magazine (€2.65), lists gay bars, restaurants and activities in Brussels and Wallonia.

Rainbow House (Map p74; ☎ 02 503 59 90; www.rainbowhouse.be in Flemish & French; Rue du Marché au Charbon 42; ◷ 6.30-10.30pm Wed-Sat) This bar/information centre is the newest kid on the block for gays, lesbians and bisexuals.

Le Belgica (Map p74; www.lebelgica.be; Rue du Marché au Charbon 32; prémetro Bourse; ◷ 10pm-3am Thu-Sat, 7pm-3am Sun) Despite the unassuming façade, this is one of the city's oldest gay pubs. Attracts an international set and is a must when visiting the capital.

La Démence (Map pp76-7; ☎ 02 511 97 89; www.lademence.be in French; Rue Blaes 208) Once a month, Fuse (p111) becomes a huge gay rave that attracts men from all over Belgium and from neighbouring countries. Check the website for dates.

L'Homo Erectus (Map p74; ☎ 02 514 74 93; Rue des Pierres 57; ◷ from noon Mon-Fri, from 4pm Sat & Sun) You'll easily recognise this place as soon as you see the evolution of man from ape graphically depicted on the front window. User-friendly opening hours mean it's one of the capital's most popular bars – relatively quiet during the day but crammed at night.

Chez Maman (Map p74; ☎ 02 502 86 96; www.chezmaman.be in French; Rue des Grands Carmes 12; ◷ from 10pm Thu-Sun) The capital's most beloved transvestite show.

Petite Boxeur (Map p74; ☎ 02 511 40 00; Borgval 3; mains €13-19.50; ◷ dinner Tue-Sat) Tiny candlelit restaurant that's great for a meal before a night out – the kitchen stays open 'til 12.30am and the cuisine is modern Belgian. Reservations essential Friday and Saturday.

Darakan (Map p74; ☎ 02 512 20 76; Rue du Midi 9) Tiny gay bookshop.

For gay-friendly accommodation in the heart of town, see **Downtown-BXL** (p98).

The **Festival du Film Gay & Lesbien de Bruxelles** (www.fglb.org in French) runs for 10 days in late January and is firmly established. **Belgian Gay & Lesbian Pride** (www.blgp.be) is held in Brussels on the first Saturday in May and the march ends with an all-night party.

JULY & AUGUST

Foire du Midi This huge, annual funfair is almost as old as Belgium itself – its 125th anniversary was celebrated in 2005. It runs from mid-July to mid-August on Blvd du Midi near Gare du Midi (Map pp76–7).

Meyboom (www.meyboom.be) The raising of the Maypole is a folkloric event held annually on 9 August. A procession of 'giants' winds down from the Sablon to the Grand Place where they plant a maypole.

Tapis des Fleurs (www.flowercarpet.be) Brussels' famous Floral Carpet takes over the Grand Place for five days in mid-August every two years in even years.

Ivo Van Damme Memorial (www.sport.be/memorial vandamme) This meet attracts a good serving of international athletes and is held in late August or early September at the Roi Baudouin stadium (p111) at Heysel. It's named after local athlete Ivo Van Damme (1954–76), whose promising career (two silver Olympic medals in 800m and 1500m in Montreal) was ended in a fatal car accident.

SEPTEMBER–DECEMBER

Belgian Beer Weekend (www.visitbelgium.com/beer .htm) Brussels' Grand Place comes alive in early September with beer stalls where visitors can sample many of the nation's brews.

Comics Festival (www.comicsfestivalbelgium.com) St Gilles town hall (Map pp76–7) is the venue for this annual industry shindig held over a weekend in early October. Rub shoulders with the artists and writers behind some of Belgium's best-known comic characters.

Designers' Trail (see boxed text, p114)

Marché de Noël The Grand Place is the setting for a Christmas craft market held over a week in early December and featuring stalls from many EU countries.

SLEEPING

Start hunting around the Grand Place, an area rich with accommodation to suit all budgets. Breakfast is included in all prices, unless otherwise stated. Most of Brussels' B&B accommodation is organised via **Bed & Brussels** (☎ 02 646 07 37; www.bnb-brussels.be).

Budget

Beersel Camping (☎ 02 331 05 61; campingbeersel@pandora.be; Steenweg op Ukkel 75, Beersel; adult/tent/car €3/2/1.50; ☺ year-round) Small ground south of the Brussels region in Beersel. Tram 55 (direction Uccle) stops 3km away, from where you take bus UB (direction Halle) to Beersel.

Bruxelles Europe à Ciel Ouvert (Map pp76-7; ☎ 02 640 79 67; Chaussée de Wavre 203; bus 34 or 80; ☺ Jul & Aug) This summer-only camp site is for campers with tents (no caravans or campervans) who want to be relatively central.

Centre Vincent van Gogh (Map pp72-3; ☎ 02 217 01 58; www.chab.be; Rue Traversière 8; metro Botanique; dm/s/d/q €13.50/28/42/66, bed sheets €4; ☒ 🖳) Forget this place if you've succumbed to middle-age spread – Brussels' most groovy hostel is strictly for 17-to-35ers. Run by a young, fun crew, it has laid-back vibes, a garden courtyard, bar and adjoining conservatory, laundry, kitchen and internet (€1 for 15 minutes). Rooms are clean but basic (some doubles have private bathrooms for no extra cost – ask when you book). In July and August, there are guided bike tours (€12, 3½ hours). ISIC cardholders get a 10% discount. It's located 1.2km uphill from Gare Centrale.

Sleep Well (Map pp72-3; ☎ 02 218 50 50; www.sleepwell.be; Rue du Damier 23; metro Rogier; hostel dm/s/d/tr €19/28/50/66, hotel s/d/tr €39/57/80; ☒ 🖳) Big, bright, modern place one block from Rue Neuve, Brussels' main shopping thoroughfare. The hotel section has rooms with private bathroom facilities and no daytime lockout. In the hostel section, bathroom facilities are shared and the rooms can't be accessed between 11am and 3pm. It's all very polished but a tad sterile.

Jacques Brel (Map pp72-3; ☎ 02 218 01 87; brussels.brel@laj.be; Rue de la Sablonnière 30; metro Madou; dm/s/d €17.60/33/50; ☒) One of three HI-affiliated hostels in Brussels. This one's old and presentable. It's a 1km uphill walk from Gare Centrale.

2GO4 (Map pp72-3; ☎ 02 219 30 19; www.2GO4.be; Blvd Émile Jacqmain 99; dm/s/d/q excl breakfast €21/43/59/99; ☒ 🖳) Brussels' newest hostel occupies a bright-red terrace house at the slightly sleazy end of town. The zany ground-floor furnishings calm down by the time you get upstairs. Two features to note include a chunk of old Atomium sheeting hanging above reception, and a small kitchen.

Midrange

Downtown-BXL (Map p74; ☎ 0475 29 07 21; www.downtownbxl.com; Rue du Marché au Charbon 118-120; prémetro Anneessens; r €60) Brussels' most central B&B occupies the last house on the capital's gay drag, and is superbly located for those wanting to dance the night away. Gay-friendly owner Theo Linder has decked the rooms in simple but interesting décor (choose the 'Marilyn' room for a round bed), and blends modern with touches of the old (the original staircase is a hoot with luggage). The extended continental breakfast is a feast, but you won't leave hungry. All in all it's excellent value.

Hôtel Galia (Map pp76-7; ☎ 02 502 42 43; www.hotelgalia.com; Place du Jeu-de-Balle 15; metro Porte de Hal, prémetro Lemonnier; s/d/tr €60/65/70; ☒) The only frills in this well-maintained little place are the comic-strip embellishments. Overlooking Brussels' well-known bric-a-brac market square, it has well-sized clean rooms (tiny bathrooms) and is handy to nightlife.

Hôtel Rembrandt (Map pp76-7; ☎ 02 512 71 39; www.hotel-rembrandt.be; Rue de la Concorde 42; metro Louise; s €45-65, d €70-90, ste from €75) Fantastic-value hotel.

WEEKEND DEALS

By and large, Brussels' accommodation scene is aimed squarely at Eurocrats and business travellers. Hotels catering to these visitors have boomed in recent decades, resulting in an ongoing price war among hotels and some good deals for tourists. At the weekend, when all the EU visitors and business people have evacuated, many hotels around the city drop their rates dramatically. There's no hard and fast rule regarding days discounts are offered – some hotels go for Friday and Saturday nights, others Saturday and Sunday, and some all three. Some top-end hotels charge extra for breakfast on weekdays, but throw in great buffet spreads on weekends. You'll find details of weekday and weekend rates in the hotel listings in this chapter.

Note that some midrange and top-end establishments also drop their rates during the summer holiday months (roughly from mid-July to mid-September). Again, it's well worth searching the internet and inquiring about possible discounts at this time.

THE AUTHOR'S CHOICE

Hooy Kaye Lodge (Map pp72-3; ☎ 02 218 44 40; www.hooykayelodge.com; Quai aux Pierres de Taille 22; metro St Catherine or Yser; r €95-125) Corinne De Coninck is one of those B&B owners who loves what she does. And judging by her new B&B, it's not a passing fad. So leave behind the bright red-brick façade of this 17th-century merchant house to enter a calm and elegant B&B, where original authenticity is paramount. Unpolished steps and banisters lead up two or three flights to four rooms, each different in shape, size and layout. The common thread is tone – chocolate colours, antique furnishings, and ancient garments from Myanmar have been used throughout to adorn. Breakfast at a common table downstairs, then step outside onto a newly revamped street on the edge of bustling Ste Catherine. It's a fabulous address.

incongruously located near Ave Louise. All sorts of old ornaments, oil paintings and polished wooden furnishings adorn every available place. Outside it's just as twee, with a pale-pink façade and flower boxes. The rooms are crisp and well cared for, albeit a tad small. Note, reception closes at 9pm.

Hôtel George V (Map pp72-3; ☎ 02 513 50 93; www .george5.com; Rue 't Kint 23; prémetro Anneessens; s/d/t/q €64/75/86/97) This family-run hotel on the edge of St Géry has prices that are a snip for this funky part of town. The rooms are ordinary but clean and presentable.

Chambres en Ville (Map pp76-7; ☎ 02 512 92 90; www .chez.com/chambreenville in French; Rue de Londres 19; metro Trône; s/d €60/80, 1-night supplement per rm €15) With its ordinary façade on a poky backstreet just metres away from the EU's gleaming quarter, you'll arrive at this B&B and wonder what you're in for. Once inside, it's obvious. Run by quietly spoken graphic designer Philippe Guilmin, the town house has four large guest rooms, each individually named and subtly decorated. Choose from La Gustavienne, done out in the sober house-style of a Swedish king, or Le Levant, bathed in cinnamon and milk chocolate. Some rooms have double beds, others are twins. The wooden floors are scrubbed, the ceilings are high. It's lovely.

B&B Phileas Fogg (Map pp72-3; ☎ 02 217 83 38; www.phileasfogg.be; Rue Van Bemmel 6; metro Madou; s/d/tr/f €75/85/100/120; ✗) Exotic B&B in St Josse run by Karin Dhadamus, an exuberant mother, avid traveller and master of many languages. The four rooms are all different, decorated with artworks she's picked up on worldly travels, as well as local touches including a feather lamp designed in Antwerp. All rooms have private bathrooms, although two share a toilet. The Blue Room, with its kooky high basin, low futon bed, off-set bathroom and tiny terrace overlooking the garden, is a favourite.

Hôtel Welcome (Map p74; ☎ 02 219 95 46; www.hotel welcome.com; 1 Rue du Peuplier; metro St Catherine; s/d/ste €85/95/140; ✗) Incredibly friendly little theme hotel in Ste Catherine that's been around for years. Rooms reflect Brussels' cosmopolitan nature – overnight in Bora Bora, Congo or Japan, to name a few. The busy décor is a bit ugly but the concept's good. Rooms range in size from 'eco' singles to the Egyptian suite with a king-size bed and view over tree-lined Marché aux Poissons. The breakfast room (originally a horse stable) features a delightful wall mosaic. Babies and dogs are welcome.

Hôtel Agenda Midi (Map pp76-7; ☎ 02 520 00 10; www.hotel-agenda.com; Blvd Jamar 11; metro Gare du Midi; s/d/f €86/99/114) There's little to recommend the Gare du Midi area but, if you need to be close for travel reasons, this is the pick of the crop. Good biceps are needed to open the Fort Knox–style security gate. The modern rooms have rich earthy tones and kids are welcome.

Hôtel Saint Michel (Map p74; (☎ 02 513 64 79; www .hotelsaintmichel.be; Grand Place 11; metro Gare Centrale; s/d/tr €65/100/125, with view €113/133/156) Choice real estate this – the *only* hotel smack bang on Brussels' famous square. The royal entrance downgrades to ordinary rooms that are overpriced, but hey, outside your window is the Grand Place! Keep in mind that rooms at the front, though nicer, lighter and larger, are also much noisier, especially on summer nights when the square comes alive. Weekend discounts often available.

Hôtel Noga (Map p74; ☎ 02 218 67 63; www.noga hotel.com; Rue du Béguinage 38; metro Ste Catherine; s/d/tr/q €85/105/130/155; 🖳) Another Ste Catherine gem. This well-equipped little hotel started in 1958 and mixes modern and old décors in a self-assured feast for the eyes. Rich colour schemes and a nautical theme are used throughout, with plenty of statues and paintings, antique and kitsch. The rooms are spacious, and overall it offers excellent facilities for a hotel of

BRUSSELS

this price, with a bar, separate billiard room, lounge and even bike hire (€10/13 half-/full-day). It's also child and baby friendly.

Hôtel Arlequin (Map p74; ☎ 02 514 16 15; www .arlequin.be; Rue de la Fourche 17; prémetro Bourse; s/d/tr from €110/130/210) Well hidden on a backstreet not far from the Grand Place, this hotel's 7th-floor breakfast room – with lovely rooftop views – is its outstanding feature. The rooms are white-washed and presentable, though décorwise blasé. A word of warning: don't be seduced by weekend discounts if you need to sleep before 3am – the basement party space goes boom boom until the small hours.

Monty (Map pp70-1; ☎ 02 734 56 36; www.monty-hotel .be; Blvd Brand Whitlock 101; metro Montgomery; s/d €110/130, weekend €85; 🖳) Bills itself as a 'small design hotel' but feels more like a bordello. Must be something to do with the blood-red décor. If you're into designers and atypical décor, and want to be out of the centre (EU vicinity), it'll do.

Other recommendations:

Hôtel La Légende (Map p74; ☎ 02 512 82 90; www .hotellalegende.com; Rue du Lombard 35; metro Gare Centrale; s/d/tr/f from €80/90/130/140; 🗙) Well sited just two blocks from the Grand Place. The older (and cheaper) rooms are a tad small, but they're all modern and comfortable.

Hôtel du Congrès (Map pp72-3; ☎ 02 217 18 90; www.hotelducongres.be; Rue du Congrès 42; metro Madou; s/d €100/115; 🗙 🖳) Elegant hotel occupying four renovated town houses in the Upper Town towards Place Madou. Off-the-beaten-track location.

Atlas (Map p74; ☎ 02 502 60 06; www.atlas.be; Rue du Vieux Marché aux Grains 30; prémetro Bourse, metro Ste Catherine; s/d/tr/f €110/125/155/175; 🖳) Central hotel with kitchen; equipped, split-level duplex apartments good for families.

Top End

Hôtel Le Dixseptième (Map p74; ☎ 02 502 57 44; www .ledixseptieme.be; Rue de la Madeleine 25; metro Gare Centrale; s/d €120/200, ste €250-390; 🗙 🖳) Discreet doesn't begin to describe this exclusive hotel. Little more than a doorbell gives its location away, on an old street leading from the historic core to Gare Centrale. Ring the bell and wait for the door to open into this former 17th-century residence of the Spanish ambassador. The 24 rooms are sumptuously decorated and all unique. Each is named after a Belgian artist. The Breughel and Jordaens rooms are the most opulent in the hotel's ancient section; Magritte and Permeke are arguably the most special in the modern part (the studio rooms here come with kitchenette). In deliberate contrast to many of Brussels' top-enders, Le Dixseptième does not drop its rates on weekends. 'We're keeping it exclusive' is the motto.

Art Hotel Siru (Map pp72-3; ☎ 02 203 35 80; www .comforthotelsiru.com; Place Charles Rogier 1; metro Rogier; s/d €200/225, weekend s & d €110; 🖳) Close to the Gare du Nord railway station, this hotel is for those into modern Belgian art. Built in 1932 but done over in the 1990s, each of the 102 rooms features work by a contemporary Belgian artist – some pieces are mundane, others more nightmarish. Many of the rooms are small, and regular prices are grossly inflated; weekend deals are better value.

Hôtel Métropole (Map p74; ☎ 02 217 23 00, reservations 02 214 24 24; www.metropolehotel.com; Place de Brouckère 31; metro De Brouckère; s/d/ste €330/360/500, weekend from €115 🗙 🗷) Brussels' sumptuous, late-19th-century showpiece, owned by the Wielemans family since it opened in 1895. An opulent French Renaissance-style foyer with marble walls and coffered ceiling leads to an imperial reception hall backed by beautifully etched stained-glass windows. Unlike the lavish entrance, the elegant rooms are soberly furnished.

Hôtel Amigo (Map p74; ☎ 02 547 47 47; www.hotel amigo.com; Rue de l'Amigo 1-3; metro Gare Centrale; s/d weekday from €400/500, s/d weekend incl breakfast €215/280, ste from €700; 🗙 🗷 🖳 🖾) Full of history and

---

THE AUTHOR'S CHOICE

Royal Windsor Hôtel (Map p74; ☎ 02 505 55 55; www.warwickhotels.com; Rue Duquesnoy 5; r €345-440; ste from €900; 🗙 🗷 🖳) So fashion's your thing and you're here to shop. Why not take it a step further and really get to know some Belgian designers by sleeping with them – so to speak. Choose Nicolas Woit, Marina Yee or Kaat Tilley, for example, and ensconce yourself in a room fitted out by these well-known designers. The Royal Windsor has 12 so-called 'Fashion Rooms', ranging in décor from conventional to extreme or something in between.

The hotel itself is a bland, red-brick building, discreetly located on a quiet backstreet just a steeple's fall from the Grand Place. It looks like nothing from the outside. Inquire about weekend rates. Breakfast costs €25.

celebrities, this 18th-century-style hotel rates amongst Brussels' best. Built in the 1950s on the site of a former prison just behind the Grand Place, it was purchased by Rocco Forte Hotels a few years back and totally refurbished. The result is a splendid mix of old and contemporary. The public rooms feature antique furnishings, 18th-century tapestries and centuries' old paving stones. Head upstairs to find smooth rooms. Breakfast costs €28. One room is fitted for travellers with disabilities.

Other recommendations:

Hôtel Stanhope (Map pp76-7; ☎ 02 506 91 11; www .stanhope.be; Square du Meeûs 4; metro Trône; s/d weekday from €195/245, weekend incl breakfast from €120/140, ste €560; ✄ 🖵 ♿) This English-style hotel offers excellent value close to the EU quarter. Breakfast costs €25.

Hôtel Astoria (Map pp72-3; ☎ 02 227 05 05; www .sofitel.com; Rue Royale 103; metro Madou, tram 93 or 94; s/d weekday €240/340, weekend incl breakfast €125/135) Gearing up for its centennial celebration in 2009, the Astoria harks back to the exuberant era of Léopold II. Breakfast costs €25.

EATING

As the capital of a nation of foodies, Brussels is overly endowed with quality eateries. The city's cosmopolitan nature means there's no shortage of cuisines, be it Italian, Spanish, Turkish or Japanese. The essential Brussels experience, however, involves old-world restaurants where aproned waiters bustle across tiled floors and diners tuck into hearty Belgian cuisine in wood-panelled surroundings. Packed at both lunch and dinner, these places offer no-nonsense service where good food is the *raison d'être*. But don't make the mistake of thinking the scene's all yesteryear. Minimalism has swept Brussels, bringing exciting restaurants offering world cuisines and a certain snob value that was missing not long ago. For dining outside the normal times, brasseries and bistros await.

The cobbled streets around the Grand Place are the natural starting point, but it's well worth wandering further afield. Good for fish and seafood is Ste Catherine's fish-market area; go to the streets around Place St Géry for a small line-up of Asian eateries. The Marolles shelters the intimate and trendy, while Ixelles' Rue St Boniface offers a treat of cuisines.

Grand Place
BUDGET
Fritland (Map p74; ☎ 02 514 06 27; Rue Henri Maus 49; prémetro Bourse; ⏲ 11am-1am) Thirty years old and still *the* downtown place for a cone of chips.

Panos (Map p74; ☎ 02 513 14 43; Rue du Marché aux Herbes 85; metro Gare Centrale) Chain bakery and sandwich shop doing *belegd broodje/sandwich garni* (half a filled baguette), slices of quiche and pizza.

Rugantino (Map p74; ☎ 02 511 21 95; Blvd Anspach 184; prémetro Anneessens; mains €8-16.50; ⏲ lunch Mon-Fri, dinner Mon-Sat) Little slice of Italy on one of the capital's busiest boulevards. Simple menu, great food and loud voices emanating from the kitchen.

Chez Léon (Map p74; ☎ 02 513 04 26; Rue des Bouchers 18; metro Gare Centrale; mains €13-20; ⏲ noon-11pm) Long-time tourist favourite in the heart of Brussels' famous dining street, Rue des Bouchers. This rambling place occupies several gabled houses and offers fast service at any time of the day or night, substantial plates of mussels and chips, and free meals for kids under 12. You'll find branches all over Belgium, and worldwide.

Other recommendations:

Pita Pick from the swarm of places along Rue du Marché aux Fromages (Map p74; metro Gare Centrale). Most are open from lunchtime until 6am and serve basic pitas from €3.50, a *brochette* (kebab) for €7.50 and vegetarian pitas. Eat in or take away.

GB Express (Map p74; Rue au Beurre 25; prémetro Bourse; ⏲ 8am-10pm) Little supermarket near the Grand Place.

Super GB (Map pp72-3; Rue Neuve; metro Rogier) Big supermarket in the basement of the City 2 shopping centre.

AD Delhaize (Map p74; cnr Rue du Marché aux Poulets & Blvd Anspach; prémetro Bourse; ⏲ 9am-8pm) Supermarket.

MIDRANGE
Brasserie de la Roue d'Or (Map p74; ☎ 02 514 25 54; Rue des Chapeliers 26; metro Gare Centrale; mains €15-28; ⏲ noon-12.30am, closed Jul) The décor pays homage to the city's surrealist artists and the food is traditional and excellent – it's got locals well and truly hooked. Great for late-night dining.

Al Barmaki (Map p74; ☎ 02 513 08 34; Rue des Éperonniers 67; metro Gare Centrale; mains €18-28; ⏲ dinner Mon-Sat) Hidden on a quiet backstreet, Al Barmarki has long been considered one of Brussels' best Middle Eastern eateries. And now, after more than three decades of faithful service to uncompromisingly authentic Lebanese food, it's made the Michelin guide. Expect cool Moorish décor, brusque service and succulent skewered lamb kebabs. Great for vegetarians too.

TOP END
Samourai (Map p74; ☎ 02 217 56 39; Rue du Fossé aux Loups 28; metro De Brouckère; mains €25-38; ⏲ closed Sun lunch & Tue) Japanese restaurant tucked away inside a gallery on a busy downtown street.

BRUSSELS

THE AUTHOR'S CHOICE

Taverne du Passage (Map p74; ☎ 02 512 37 31; Galerie de la Reine 30; metro Gare Centrale; mains €15-20; ⏰ noon-midnight, closed Wed & Thu Jun & Jul) Consistently keen service and faithful Belgian meals are the pivotal points of this Brussels institution. Located in the sublime Galeries St Hubert, it has been around since 1928 and stepping through the draped doorway is like zapping away a century. An all-male middle-aged crew strut their stuff in slightly crumpled penguin uniforms, serving ample portions of Belgian classics such as *moules-frites* (mussels and chips) and *waterzooi* (cream-based chicken or fish stew). With some daring, this could be the place to try *filet américain* (raw minced beef). No matter how busy it gets, the blokes are unfailingly friendly. In summer, tables line up in the gallery outside, and kids are always welcome.

The food's as authentic as it gets, and is highly regarded by the busloads of Japanese who turn up here.

La Maison du Cygne (Map p74; ☎ 02 511 82 44; Rue Charles Buls 2; metro Gare Centrale; mains €37-65; ⏰ lunch Mon-Fri, dinner Mon-Sat; 🛇) This sophisticated restaurant occupies the 2nd-floor of an elaborate guildhall and offers a few tables with much-cherished views of the square. The French/Belgian cuisine changes with the season and is top-notch – the pigeon will even be carved at your table. For something less formal there's also the cheaper 1st-floor Ommegang brasserie.

St Géry & St Catherine

BUDGET

Picnik (Map p74; ☎ 02 217 34 84; Rue de Flandre 109; metro Ste Catherine; soup €2-3, daily special €8, 3-course menu €9.50; ⏰ 11.30am-4pm Mon-Fri) One of the new breed of snack bars gathering steam in Brussels. This one's firmly Flemish, totally vegetarian, mostly organic and, for its size, incredibly baby friendly. An out-of-the-way location that's worth finding.

Gourmet d'Asie (Map p74; ☎ 02 503 13 57; Rue Van Artevelde 14; prémetro Bourse; mains €7-13; ⏰ lunch & dinner, closed Tue) One of two tiny Vietnamese take-away restaurants sitting side-by-side on a busy St Géry street. Choose from a huge assortment of authentic dishes including the house speciality, pig's ear.

Shamrock (Map p74; ☎ 02 511 49 89; Rue Jules Van Praet 27; prémetro Bourse; mains €7-15; ⏰ lunch & dinner, closed Mon) Flashy neon lights and mediocre Asian cuisine is the trademark of this street. The exception is this oddly-named Indian restaurant (reincarnated from an Irish pub) where tandoori specialities are the go. Expect horrible décor and deliciously authentic food.

Pataya (Map p74; ☎ 02 513 30 57; Rue Antoine Dansaert 49; prémetro Bourse; mains €11-14; ⏰ lunch Tue-Fri, din-ner Tue-Sun) Absolutely nondescript little Thai restaurant that fills up early and keeps diners rolling in until late (closes 11.30pm). The red, yellow and green curries are superb, and vegetarians will find plenty to choose from.

Comocomo (Map p74; ☎ 02 503 03 30; Rue Antoine Dansaert 19; prémetro Bourse; 3/6/9 pintxos €8.50/14/19; ⏰ lunch & dinner) Park your backside on a black bar stool and watch colour-coded *pintxos* (the Basque version of tapas) snake past on an 80m-long conveyor belt at this relatively new arrival to Happening Street. Choose blue for fish, green for veggies, red for pork, and so on. It's all very hip, understandably so for this part of town.

Kasbah (Map p74; ☎ 02 502 40 26; Rue Antoine Dansaert 20; prémetro Bourse; mains €12-18; ⏰ lunch & dinner; 🛇) Next door to Bonsoir Clara, this dark and intimate Moroccan restaurant, with its tell-tale oranges in the window, is a feast for the senses. The friendly and flamboyant owner does couscous, lamb *brochettes* and *tajines* (spicy meat-based stews), all at excellent prices. Reservations for Friday and Saturday nights are necessary.

Viva M'Boma (Map p74; ☎ 02 512 15 93; Rue de Flandre 17; metro Ste Catherine; mains €12-18; ⏰ lunch & dinner Mon-Sat) Another cool, white-tiled Bruxellois bistro (an old butcher's shop) that has hit the spot with the food-crazy locals – must be the hand-cut *frites* (chips). Squeeze past the line-up ordering baguette sandwiches in the deli-style takeaway out front, and peer like Alice through the looking glass at a room full of foodies devouring hefty Belgian classics (including plenty of tripe). You may need a booking to join them in Wonderland.

Other recommendations:

Comus & Gasterea (Map p74; ☎ 02 223 43 66; Quai aux Briques 86; metro Ste Catherine; ⏰ 11am-6pm Mon-Fri, 2-6pm Sun) Modern ice-cream parlour where everything's homemade, including the cones.

THE AUTHOR'S CHOICE

Le Pain Quotidien/Het Dagelijks Brood (Map p74; ☎ 02 502 23 61; Rue Antoine Dansaert 16; prémetro Bourse; sandwiches €6-8, salads €10-13; ☯ 7.30am-7pm, to 6pm Sun) Spend any time in Belgium and you'll soon come across this local success story. Baker Alain Coumont started his first bakery and tearoom here on Rue Antoine Dansaert in 1990. Wholesome bread, sweet and savoury pies, salads, sandwiches, breakfast and lunch were (and still are) the staples. So what? The same as many other eateries, you might rightly say. But Le Pain Quotidien had one fundamental difference – a big wooden table sitting smack in the middle of its smoke-free surroundings. And it was that table that defined its success. Now with branches nation- and worldwide, Le Pain Quotidien's communal table is as popular as ever.

PS. It's not all wholesome – chocoholics should be warned that the *bombe au chocolat* (chocolate bomb) is a chocolate-mousse cake like no other.

GB Express (Map p74; Quai au Bois à Brûler 4; metro Ste Catherine; ☯ 7am-8.30pm) Little supermarket in Ste Catherine.

MIDRANGE

Jacques (Map p74; ☎ 02 513 27 62; Quai aux Briques 44; metro Ste Catherine; mains €15-25, mussels €22; ☯ lunch & dinner, closed Sun) It's rare to see Jacques anything but full. This down-to-earth restaurant, one of the city's oldest seafood establishments, has been around well over 60 years. It attracts an older, largely local crowd for lunch and a younger, more cosmopolitan set at night. For lobster ring a day in advance.

In 't Spinnekopke (Map pp72-3; ☎ 02 511 86 95; Place du Jardin aux Fleurs 1; prémetro Bourse; mains €15-25; ☯ lunch & dinner Mon-Fri, dinner Sat) This long-time favourite with its odd name (In the Spider's Head) occupies a 17th-century whitewashed cottage on a newly revamped square. Dine outside in summer, or cosy up inside in winter and enjoy Brussels' specialities (in particular the cod or the assortment of meats cooked in beer-based sauces).

Bij den Boer (Map p74; ☎ 02 512 61 22; Quai aux Briques 60; metro Ste Catherine; mains €15-28; ☯ lunch & dinner Mon-Sat) A longtime seafood favourite with a no-fuss interior and newly revamped blue-tiled façade. Real Brussels experience.

Pré Salé (Map p74; ☎ 02 513 43 23; Rue de Flandre 20; metro Ste Catherine; mains €16-18; ☯ lunch & dinner Wed-Sun, closed mid-Jun–mid-Jul; ☒) Local diner on a shabby backstreet that's become an institution with the locals. Looks a bit like a butcher's shop when you first enter – all white tiles, bright lights and big plates of spare ribs – but it's very infectious, particularly on Friday nights when you'll need to book a few weeks in advance to partake in the *soirée spectacle*, a vaudeville-style dinner show.

Bonsoir Clara (Map p74; ☎ 02 502 09 90; Rue Antoine Dansaert 18; prémetro Bourse; mains €17-25; ☯ lunch Mon-Fri, dinner daily) An enduring success story. The twin salons boast bold colours, subtle lighting and lots of metal and geometry. It struck a chord with locals years ago and continues to serve generous portions of modern European food, particularly Mediterranean flavours. Reserve in advance for weekend dinners.

TOP END

La Belle Maraîchère (Map p74; ☎ 02 512 97 59; Place Ste Catherine 11a; metro Ste Catherine; mains €26-48, 4-course menu €33; ☯ lunch & dinner Fri-Tue) This intimate family-run restaurant overlooking the church in Ste Catherine is well known for classic seafood dishes, nostalgic décor and crisp service. It's popular with businessmen at lunchtime, and a mixed clientele in the evenings.

Marolles

Brasserie La Clef d'Or (Map pp76-7; ☎ 02 511 97 62; Place du Jeu-de-Balle 1; metro Porte de Hal, prémetro Lemonnier; snacks €3.50-8; ☯ 5am-5pm Tue-Sun) Unassuming café that's been serving *soupe de la maison* (house soup) and a good *croque-monsieur* (grilled ham and cheese sandwich) to flea-market vendors for years. It's as unpretentious as they come. The unusual opening hours reflect the needs of the clientele.

Easy Tempo (Map pp76-7; ☎ 02 513 54 40; Rue Haute 146; metro Louise, bus 27; pizza €7-11; ☯ lunch Tue-Sun, dinner Tue-Sat) Suave pizza joint in an old *boulangerie* (bakery) with a gorgeous ceramic-tiled wall that's now a protected monument. An ultrafriendly crew skim along the counter, topping pizzas with marinated aubergine, sun-dried tomatoes and artichokes.

Au Stekerlapatte (Map pp76-7; ☎ 02 512 86 81; Rue des Prêtres 4; metro Hôtel des Monnaies; mains around €16;

dinner Tue-Sun;) The grungy façade hides a cavernous bistro where the approach is casual, the menu extensive and the portions large. Meat, fish and fowl – cooked in traditional Belgian ways – are the staples. Well hidden but definitely known.

Les Petits Oignons (Map pp76-7; 02 512 47 38; Rue Notre Seigneur 13; metro Louise/bus 27; mains €18-25, 3-course lunch menu €18, 4-course dinner menu €28; lunch & dinner Mon-Sat) Firm Marolles favourite, 'The Little Onions' has been wooing all manner of diners for years with an outdated '70s ambience, hefty servings of Belgian and French cuisine, friendly service and, depending on the weather, a tranquil garden setting outback or a blazing log fire inside.

L'Idiot du Village (Map pp76-7; 02 502 55 82; Rue Notre Seigneur 19; metro Louise, bus 27; mains €18-26; lunch & dinner Mon-Fri) An address for those in the know, this fabulous little restaurant (not signposted) is hidden away behind a graffiti-covered shutter on a side street off Rue Blaes. Step down from street level to enter a slightly surreal world designed to feed all the senses, not just the stomach. The cuisine is eclectic, and the atmosphere intimate. Bookings are essential.

Comme Chez Soi (Map pp72-3; 02 512 29 21; Pl Rouppe 23; prémetro Anneessens; mains €40-60, 4-course menu from €67; lunch & dinner Tue-Sat;) Ask any Bruxellois to name the city's finest restaurant and the answer, until very recently, was invariably CCS. For 27 straight years, this Brussels institution received three Michelin stars in the famed food guide, due largely to the innovative cuisine by master chef Pierre Wynants. The recent transition to new chef, Lionel Rigolet,

Wynants' son-in-law, saw the restaurant loose one star in 2006. A good bite out of your weekly wage can be sunk here on a main course alone, and reservations are still needed.

Sablon

Le Perroquet (Map pp76-7; 02 512 99 22; Rue Watteeu 31; metro Porte de Namur; light meals €8-10; noon-1am) Lovely Art Nouveau *café* that stands out as a cheap eatery in this affluent part of town. Salads and stuffed pitas, including vegetarian options, are the mainstay, and the kitchen stays open 'til 1am. Stained glass, marble-topped tables and dark wood panelling lend it a smooth atmosphere.

Wittamer (Map pp76-7; 02 512 37 42; Place du Grand Sablon 12-13; tram 92, 93 or 94; cakes €11, light meals €15-17; 9am-6pm Wed-Sun) Watching the Sablon's parade of fur coats, felt hats and well-fed poodles is best undertaken at this exclusive pâtisserie and tearoom. Terrace tables fan out towards the square in summer; in winter warm yourself in the 1st-floor tearoom.

Lola (Map pp76-7; 02 514 24 60; Place du Grand Sablon 33; tram 92, 93 or 94; mains €16-28; lunch & dinner Mon-Fri, noon-midnight Sat & Sun;) Lola's done its apprenticeship, and Brussels' designer set still loves it. Combines classic French and Italian cuisine with a modern minimalist interior and an atmosphere that simply pops and buzzes.

EU Quarter

Maison Antoine (Map p86; Place Jourdan; metro Schuman; 11.30am-1am, until 2am Fri & Sat) For decades, this little *friture* (chip shop) has attracted politicians, rock stars and locals alike for what used to be Brussels' best chips. In our opinion it's

---

THE AUTHOR'S CHOICE

Can't choose where or what to eat? Then head straight to Ixelles' **Rue St Boniface**. This intimate little street, lorded over by the local church, is crammed with indoor/outdoor eateries of all persuasions.

One of the originals and still an all-round favourite for a casual meal is **L'Ultime Atome** (Map pp76-7; 02 513 13 67; Rue St Boniface 14; metro Porte de Namur; mains €11-20; 11am-midnight). An eclectic crowd keeps this brasserie buzzing day and night (the kitchen is open nonstop from noon until midnight) and there's a wide range on offer including vegetarian fare and an inspiring beer menu.

Immediately opposite is **Le IIème Élément** (Map pp76-7; 02 502 00 28; Rue St Boniface 7; metro Porte de Namur; mains €10-20; lunch & dinner, closed Sat & lunch Sun), a modern minimalist Thai restaurant with a straightforward menu including soups.

Too trendy? Then try **Saint Boniface** (Map pp76-7; 02 511 53 66; Rue St Boniface 9; metro Porte de Namur; mains €15-22; lunch & dinner Mon-Fri). Turn off your phone to enter this old-world restaurant where checked tablecloths, oil lamps and authentic dishes from France's Périgord region (ie foie gras, duck and Puy lentils) are the norm.

no longer No 1, but still very much worth a detour if you're hungry and in the district.

Rosticeria Fiorentina (Map p86; ☎ 02 734 92 36; Rue Archimède 43; metro Schuman; pasta from €7.50, other mains €14-18; ☻ lunch & dinner, closed Sat) One of a handful of restaurants on this street catering squarely to Eurocrats. Hearty dishes served on paper tablecloths in family-style surroundings with Italian meals made by Mama.

Ixelles

L'Amour Fou (Map p76-7; ☎ 02 514 27 09; Chaussée d'Ixelles 185; bus 54 or 71; salads €9, pasta €9; ☻ 9am-2am) Head deep into Ixelles to find this simple bistro and long-time favoured late-night bite stop.

Archy's (Map pp76-7; ☎ 02 511 50 52; Rue Longue Vie 20; metro Porte de Namur; mains €10-12; ☻ lunch & dinner Mon-Fri, dinner Sun) Tiny Latin-American restaurant in Matonge, Brussels' African quarter, that's been serving up specialities from California to Peru for more than 15 years. Join diners at one of just four tables on the pedestrianised street, or head inside to meet Archy himself.

La Tsampa (Map p76-7; ☎ 02 647 03 67; Rue de Livourne 109; tram 93 or 94; daily special €12; ☻ noon-2pm & 7-9.30pm Mon-Fri, closed Aug) Brussels' oldest and least compromising vegetarian restaurant. Enter via the organic delicatessen.

Le Variété (Map p76-7; ☎ 02 647 04 36; Place Ste Croix 4; tram 81; mains €15-20; ☻ lunch & dinner) One of the trendiest restaurants in Brussels. It occupies part of the restored Flagey building and is a great place for dinner premovie at Studio 5. Specialises in spit-roasts but there's plenty of other modern European fare and vegetarians have innovative choices. It's open until midnight; reservations are essential most evenings.

Notos (Map p76-7; ☎ 02 513 29 59; Rue de Livourne 154; tram 93 or 94; mains €17-24; ☻ lunch Tue-Fri, dinner Tue-Sat) Certainly Belgium's best Greek restaurant and arguably the best in Europe outside

Greece. No plate-smashing or faded posters of sun-soaked isles at this subtle little place. Instead the refined ambience is backed up by superb *nouvelle* Greek *cuisine*. The limited menu remembers vegetarians.

Rouge Tomate (Map p76-7; ☎ 02 647 70 44; Ave Louise 190; tram 93 or 94; mains €19-28; ☻ lunch Mon-Fri, dinner Mon-Sat) Modern Mediterranean cuisine (with plenty for vegos) is served in two huge rooms on the ground floor of a 19th-century townhouse. In summer, a terrace shaded by old trees draws diners from afar. The décor's big but not busy, the overall tone's mellow but not insipid, and relaxed young staff keep it humming.

Other recommendations:

Le Framboisier (Map p76-7; ☎ 02 647 51 44; Rue du Bailli 35; tram 93 or 94; ☻ noon-11pm Tue-Sun) Imaginatively flavoured ice cream and sorbets made from Cantillon beers are the house specialities. Take away or, in summer, sit in the garden.

De la Vigne à l'Assiette (Map p76-7; ☎ 02 647 68 03; Rue de la Longue Haie 51; tram 93 or 94; mains €17-22, 2-course lunch menu €14, 3-/4-course dinner menu €21/35; ☻ lunch & dinner Tue-Fri, dinner Sat) Sommelier Eddy Dandrimont matches good French cuisine and wine at this little corner restaurant on a quiet backstreet uphill from Ave Louise.

La Quincaillerie (Map p76-7; ☎ 02 533 98 33; Rue du Page 45; tram 91 or 92; mains €17-27; ☻ lunch Mon-Fri, dinner daily) The gleaming brass interior gives a clue to this brasserie's former life as an ironmonger's shop. It woos with seafood specialities.

Contact GB (Map p76-7; Rue du Bailli 63; tram 93 or 94; ☻ 9am-7pm) Supermarket.

St Josse

Metin (Map pp72-3; ☎ 02 217 68 63; Chaussée de Haecht 94; bus 65; pide €4-7; ☻ 11am-11pm, closed Tue) One of many little Turkish restaurants strung along this street, this is a good spot for a bite after visiting nearby Maison Autrique (p93). They started in the mid '70s, about 15 years after the first Turkish immigrants moved in, and continue to draw plenty of local diners. Start with an *iskembe corba* (tripe soup), followed by a boat-shaped *pide* (Turkish pizza), and wash it down with a glass of *ayran* (buttermilk).

Molenbeek & Anderlecht

Tasso (Map pp70-1; ☎ 02 427 74 27; 86c Ave du Port, Molenbeek; metro Yser; mains from €17; 8am-midnight Mon-Fri, from 10am Sat & Sun) Tasso opened in 2006 as one of the first attractions in the new Tour & Taxis complex (p89). The setting is awesome, but also intimate, and the food is a pleasing world mix.

For a memorable dining experience in Anderlecht, see boxed text, p105.

DRINKING

It's seductively easy to drink until you drop in Brussels. Nearly every street in the city centre has at least one atmospheric pub, *café* or bar. The Grand Place area is thick with options, from showy Art Nouveau places to old brown *cafés* that have contentedly buzzed for decades. St Géry is the Lower Town's hip hub, although to really nudge this scene head into Ixelles. The EU quarter is big on English and Irish pubs, and for a slice of beer heaven go to St Gilles.

Grand Place

Le Roy d'Espagne (Map p74; ☎ 02 513 08 07; Grand Place 1; metro Gare Centrale) Sit and sip (pricey beers) the splendour of the Grand Place in this former guildhouse. And, yes, those are inflated dried pigs' bladders above your head.

Falstaff (Map p74; ☎ 02 511 87 89; Rue Henri Maus 17; prémetro Bourse) A century old and still popular with the fashionable young and eccentric old, this Art Nouveau *grand café*, designed by Horta-disciple Houbion, is an exotic world of mirrors, glass and fluidity. Ignore the location – this street has been screaming for attention for years.

À la Mort Subite (Map p74; ☎ 02 513 13 18; Rue Montagne aux Herbes Potagères 7; metro Gare Centrale;) A must. Long *café* with wood panelling, mirrored walls and brusque service. One of the country's many brews is named after it (the name means 'instant death' but the beer itself is not that strong). Nonsmokers can breathe relatively easily in the tiny nonsmoking section.

Goupil le Fol (Map p74; ☎ 02 511 13 96; Rue de la Violette 22; metro Gare Centrale; 9pm-5am) Bastion of French *chanteuse* and other crooners. You'll only hear the likes of Barbra Streisand, Édith

Piaf and Brussels' own Jacques Brel in this kooky little bar that's been around for years.

Le Cirio (Map p74; ☎ 02 512 13 95; Rue de la Bourse 18; prémetro Bourse) Stalwart sentinel of days gone by. This sumptuous *grand café* dates from 1886 and its opulent interior and aproned waiters attract coiffured mesdames with small dogs, and tourists galore. The house speciality is a half-and-half, a champagne/white wine mix (€2.75).

Fontainas Bar (Map p74; ☎ 02 503 31 12; Rue du Marché au Charbon 91; prémetro Anneessens) The grooviest kid on the nightlife block. Ripped black vinyl seats, '70s décor and cool sounds.

Thirty seconds from the Grand Place – at the end of easily missed alleys – are four old *cafés*. The best known is **Toone** (Map p74; noon-midnight) at the Théâtre Royal de Toone (p111). Another favourite of the four, **À la Bécasse** (Map p74; ☎ 02 511 00 06; Rue de Tabora 11; metro Gare Centrale), has one hall with long rows of tables and good-hearted revelry reminiscent of the days of Breugel. Go for a jug of draught lambic.

St Géry & Ste Catherine

Le Greenwich (Map p74; ☎ 02 511 41 67; Rue des Chartreux 7; prémetro Bourse) A den for chess-players or anyone who just likes hearing the pieces fall. This big, ancient *café* with wood panelling and mirrored walls is another Brussels must. Grandmasters such as Gary Kasparov and Anatoly Karpov have entered this hall, and even Magritte used to get thrashed here. The atmosphere is always thick with smoke and concentration, the lack of music makes it a pleasant spot to read the newspaper, and the beers are cheap.

De Markten (Map p74; ☎ 02 514 66 04; Rue du Vieux Marché aux Grains 5; metro Ste Catherine) Spacious modern *café* that's a popular Flemish pit stop for shoppers trawling the nearby Rue Dansaert boutiques. In fine weather, pull up a chair at one of its tables on the tree-lined square across the road.

Monk (Map p74; ☎ 02 503 08 80; Rue Ste Catherine 42; metro Ste Catherine) Contemporary-meets-old-brown-*café* in this 17th-century gabled house just metres from Place St Catherine. The two big rooms sport tiled floors, mirrored walls and brown tables and attract a hip clientele.

The coolest bars in Brussels have been established by local legend Fred Nicolay. The three on Place St Géry (Zebra, Mappa Mundo and Roi des Belges) were his first, and **Zebra** (Map p74; ☎ 02 511 09 01; Place St Géry 33; prémetro Bourse) is the original of the originals.

All three share the same traits – uncomfortable wooden garden chairs, lax service and the hippest of clientele.

Marolles

La Fleur en Papier Doré (Map pp72-3; ☎ 02 511 16 59; Rue des Alexiens 53; metro Anneessens) Another favourite of Magritte and his surrealist pals – the nicotine-stained walls of this tiny *café* are covered with their writings and scribbles. These days it draws a cross section of customers, from intellectuals to Eurocrats, young and old, dull or animated.

Brasserie Ploegmans (Map pp76-7; ☎ 02 514 28 84; Rue Haute 148; metro Louise, bus 27) An endangered species. This bar is the local of old folk from the Marolles and has plenty of working-class kudos. It's one of only a couple of remaining family-owned pubs on this street and is generally full of smoke, a rich assortment of characters and Brussels dialect.

EU Quarter

Café de l'Autobus (Map p86; ☎ 02 230 63 16; Place Jourdan; metro Schuman) Old-timers' bar opposite Maison Antoine (p104), the city's most famous *friture*. The owners don't mind if you demolish a cone of *frites* while downing a beer or two. On Sunday it's a breather for vendors from the Place Jourdan food market.

The Wild Geese (Map p86; ☎ 02 230 19 90; Ave Livingstone 2; metro Maelbeek) Within staggering distance of Maelbeek metro station, Brussels' biggest Irish pub heaves with Eurocrats and their underlings on weekdays, and is deserted on weekends. A jazz quartet play here on the last Tuesday of the month (from 9pm), and there's dancing from 11pm Thursday to Saturday.

James Joyce (Map p86; ☎ 02 230 98 94; Rue Archimède 34; metro Schuman) The first Irish pub in Brussels. Sometimes rowdy, but it does have quieter moments and there's occasional live music.

Ixelles & St Gilles

Café Belga (Map p76-7; ☎ 02 640 35 08; Place Flagey 18; tram 81; ☻ 8am-2am Sun-Thu, 8am-3am Fri & Sat) Hippest of hip brasserie in a corner of the renovated Flagey liner. Spacious, split-level, Art Deco–style interior and ample outdoor area. Grab a terrace table fronting the ponds, ignore the noise from the nearby interminable roadworks, then settle back.

Moeder Lambic (Map pp76-7; ☎ 02 539 14 19; Rue de Savoie 68; prémetro Horta; ☻ 4pm-4am) Home to the A to Z of Belgian beers. Dark, smoky brown *café* on a residential street and *the* place to sample every brew in the book. Chunky hand-hewn tables, tattered comic books and windows adorned with pink elephants and pissed monks make the décor. To be sure, it's at the top of every serious beer lover's crawl.

Two great brasseries for a drink in Ixelles are **L'Ultime Atome** (p104) and **L'Amour Fou** (p105).

Upper Town

Le Bier Circus (Map pp72-3; (☎ 02 218 00 34; Rue de l'Enseignement 89; metro Madou; ☻ noon-2.30pm Mon-Fri, 6pm-midnight daily) Serious beer buffs should make this one of their first ports o' call. Several hundred brews and staff who know their stuff make it an excellent place to start investigations. The décor's hardly fuel for the imagination, but that's the beer's job anyway. As Belgian pubs go, this one has very limited opening hours, reflecting its odd location in an unloved part of town.

Schaerbeek

De Ultieme Hallucinatie (Map pp72-3; ☎ 02 217 06 14; Rue Royale 31; metro Botanique, tram 92, 93 or 94; ☻ noon-2am Mon-Fri, 4pm-2am Sat) Famous Art Nouveau bar and restaurant to the north of town. Built in 1904 by Brussels architect Paul Hamesse, its painted, green façade hides a rich wrought-iron interior.

ENTERTAINMENT

The English-language magazine *Bulletin* has a 'What's On' guide with excellent coverage of cinema, contemporary and classical live music, theatre, dance, opera and the visual arts. Also check Wednesday's MAD supplement in *Le Soir*, the French-language monthly

Kiosque, and online at www.agenda.be (in Flemish and French).

Ticket agencies:

Brussels on Stage (Map p74; ☎ 02 512 57 45; www .arsene50.be in Flemish & French; Galerie de la Reine; metro Gare Centrale; ⏰ 12.30-5.30pm Tue-Sat) Last-minute discounted tickets for big shows are sold at this ticket service inside Galeries St Hubert.

Caroline Music (Map p74; ☎ 02 217 07 31; Passage St Honoré 20; prémetro Bourse) Music shop and ticket agency for contemporary live gigs, festivals and club nights.

FNAC (Map pp72-3; ☎ 02 275 11 15; City 2 shopping centre, Rue Neuve; metro Rogier; ⏰ 10am-7pm Mon-Sat, to 8pm Fri) Tickets for classical and contemporary events can be booked and bought here.

Cinemas

Film buffs will find Brussels a big draw, with everything from small art-house cinemas to multiplexes and even a Cinema Museum and drive-in (see below). Tickets range from €1 to €8. Some films are dubbed so to avoid watching your favourite actor lip-synching in French, check the coding on publicity boards or newspaper listings: 'VO' (original version), 'V fr' (French version), 'V angl' (English version) and 'st' (subtitles, called *sous-titrés* in French, *ondertiteld* in Flemish).

Actor's Studio (Map p74; ☎ 02 512 16 96; Petite Rue des Bouchers 16; prémetro Bourse; adult/child €6/5) Three-screen cinema with a handy location near the Grand Place. Intimate vibes, tiny bar and mixed programme of art-house flicks and mainstream reruns.

Arenberg Galeries (Map p74; ☎ 02 512 80 63; www .arenberg.be in Flemish & French; Galerie de la Reine 26; metro Gare Centrale) Remodelled Art Deco cinema located inside Galeries St Hubert. Foreign and

---

MOVIES UNDER THE ARCADE

With drive-in theatres a thing of the past, Brussels has re-invented the genre in the magnificent setting of **Arcade du Cinquantenaire** (p86) at Parc du Cinquantenaire. These highly successful summer-only drive-in screenings (all films in their original versions, with French and Flemish subtitles) are at 10.30pm (July) and 10pm (August) on Friday, Saturday and Sunday nights. Tune your car's radio to 97.7 Mhz or, for those without wheels, pull up a chair and don headphones (included in entry price). Tickets are cheap – €15 per car or €1 for pedestrians.

---

art films are the staples, and once a month there's a sneak preview. The latter is designed to gauge the audience's reaction to new films – viewers have no idea what's on offer and must rate it at the end. You can be lucky to score a hit although a lot are art-house films that will never see the light of day.

Kinepolis (Map pp70-1; ☎ 02 474 26 00; Blvd du Centenaire 1; metro Heysel; adult/concession/child €8/7/6; ♿) The multiplex that started the multiplexes rolling around the world. Some 24 screens (plus an IMAX theatre) with a capacity to seat 7000. Three auditoriums have wheelchair access.

Musée du Cinéma (Map pp72-3; ☎ 02 507 83 70; Rue Baron Horta 9; metro Gare Centrale; admission €2.50; ⏰ from 5pm) One to make cinema buffs swoon. Two auditoria: silent movies with live piano accompaniment are screened in one every night of the year; the other is devoted to classic talkies shown in their original language. Up to seven films per night are screened, and it's worth arriving early to browse the museum's old projectors and cinema memorabilia. This all happens in a side wing of Bozar, however it's expected to be closed until late 2007 for extensive renovations. On reopening, check the *Bulletin* for nightly screenings.

Studio 5 (Map pp76-7; ☎ 02 641 10 20; Place Ste Croix; tram 81; adult/under 26/child €6/4.20/3) Relatively new cinema and a hit with Brussels' movie-loving public. Part of the restored Flagey building near the Ixelles ponds, it has one auditorium with three screenings per night (last at 10.30pm) and a bimonthly programme based either on theme or director.

Styx (Map pp76-7; ☎ 02 512 21 02; Rue de l'Arbre Bénit 72; bus 54 or 71; admission €5) The façade forewarns that it's seen better days but this tiny two-screen Ixelles cinema is still a fab spot to catch repeats, with midnight sessions on Friday and Saturday in summer.

UGC De Brouckère (Map p74; ☎ 0900 10 440; Place de Brouckère 38; metro De Brouckère; adult/child €7.90/6) This 12-screen multiplex opposite the swish Hôtel Métropole is the capital's *grande dame* – sip on a beer and relax in armchairs while watching the latest Hollywood offerings.

Pathé Palace (Map p74; Blvd Anspach 85; metro Bourse) Belgium's best-known movie directors, the Dardenne brothers (see p38), plan to reopen this old downtown cinema as a new art-house venue. Brussels International (p69) will know if it's up and running.

DANCE

Brussels boasts an impressive array of innovative dance companies and wonderful venues, such as La Monnaie (p110), Bozar (p110) and Théâtre Les Tanneurs (p112). Oddly enough, there's no classical ballet here – for that you'll have to go to Antwerp (p195).

The queen of Brussels' scene is Anne Teresa De Keersmaeker, director of **Rosas** (www.rosas.be). This Flemish dance company strikes a winning balance between the traditional and the avant-garde. De Keersmaeker also launched **PARTS** (Performing Arts Research & Training Studios; www.rosas.be/parts), an internationally acclaimed contemporary dance school set up in conjunction with La Monnaie. Rosas' future was uncertain at the time of writing following its ousting from La Monnaie, its home for the past 15 years. In 2006, La Monnaie's new director Peter De Caluwé announced Rosas' residency would not be renewed at the end of 2007. De Caluwé said he wanted to break with the tradition of maintaining a house dance company, instead favouring one-off collaborations with Belgian and other choreographers. La Monnaie will retain some ties with Rosas, coproducing at least one show per year until 2010, and it will continue to subsidise PARTS. The loss of the residency is expected to hit Rosas hard financially. De Keersmaeker has said Rosas' permanent dancers may have to be cut in number almost by half, but she's ruled out a move abroad. Rosas now works in conjunction with other venues in Brussels, including the Kaaitheater (p112), and with foreign co-productions.

The other big name in the world of Belgian dance is **Charleroi/Danses** (p226). Performances are held at the company's home town of Charleroi, but also at its second home, **Raffinerie** (☎ 02 410 33 41; Rue de Manchester 21), in Molenbeek.

Others on the dance scene include the raw **Ultima Vez** (www.ultimavez.com), a company directed by controversial Wim Vandekeybus and big on stark, confrontational images, and **Michèle Noiret**, resident choreographer at Théâtre Les Tanneurs (p112), a tiny, much-loved theatre in the Marolles.

Live Music

ROCK

Ancienne Belgique (AB; Map p74; ☎ 02 548 24 00; www.abconcerts.be; Blvd Anspach 110; prémetro Bourse) AB is an excellent venue in the heart of the city. Its two auditoriums accommodate international and home-grown bands; one in two concerts here is Belgian.

Beursschouwburg (Map p74; ☎ 02 513 82 90; www.beursschouwburg.be in Flemish & French; Rue Auguste Orts 22; prémetro Bourse) This essential part of Brussels' live music scene is back after a few years of renovations. It showcases a diverse mix of contemporary music including rock, jazz, rap and disco.

Forest National (Map pp70-1; ☎ 02 340 22 11; www.forestnational.be in Flemish & French; Ave du Globe 36; tram 81) The city's temple for large international gigs and local favourites.

Also see **Le Botanique** (p88) and **Halles de Schaerbeek** (p88).

JAZZ & BLUES

L'Archiduc (Map p74; ☎ 02 512 06 52; Rue Antoine Dansaert 6; prémetro Bourse; ☺ 4pm-late) Exclusive Art Deco bar built in the 1930s and located on one of the city's hippest streets. Once for those in-the-know but now well and truly known. Saturday's concerts feature local line-ups (admission free) and Sundays bring in international talent (admission around €10).

The Music Village (Map p74; ☎ 02 513 13 45; Rue des Pierres 50; prémetro Bourse; ☺ from 7.30pm Wed-Sat) Brussels' most polished jazz venue is housed in two 17th-century buildings a few streets back from the Grand Place. Theoretically it's members-only (annual membership €10), but nonmembers can enter by adding €2 to the nightly cover charge (€7.50 to €24). Wine and dine from 7.30pm, with concerts beginning at 8.30pm. The musos are squeezed onto a small podium that's visible from everywhere. Bookings are wise.

Sounds Jazz Club (Map pp76-7; ☎ 02 512 92 50; Rue de la Tulipe 28; bus 54; admission free-€15; ☺ 8pm-4am Mon-Sat) Unassuming but immensely popular Ixelles venue with a small podium out back where local or visiting musicians play modern, big band or salsa six nights a week. You can grab a meal preconcert; acts start around 10pm.

Bizon (Map p74; ☎ 02 502 46 99; Rue du Pont de la Carpe 7; admission free; ☺ 6pm-late) Happening little grunge bar in St Géry where home-grown blues are belted out.

REVOLUTIONARY PERFORMANCE

An opera performance at the La Monnaie in Brussels on 25 August 1830 started a revolution. That night marked the Brussels premiere of a new opera, *La Mouette de Portici* (The Dumb Girl of Portici), by French composer Daniel-François-Esprit Auber. The story, which centres on a 1647 Naples uprising against the Spanish, features large crowd scenes and dramatic effects.

But the opera was nothing compared with the encore that followed on Brussels' streets. Patriotic cries such as 'Far better to die than to live a wretched life in slavery and shame!' and 'Away with the yoke before which we tremble, away with the foreigner who laughs at our torment!' incited an instant rebellion, with the mainly bourgeois audience pouring into the streets to join workers already demonstrating outside the theatre against their Dutch rulers.

Together they stormed the Palais de Justice, chased out the Dutch troops and in a glorious crowning moment raised the flag of Brabant over Brussels' Hôtel de Ville (City Hall).

Belgian independence was recognised at the Conference of London in January 1831 and Léopold of Saxe-Coburg Gotha became Belgium's first king.

OPERA & CLASSICAL

Classical music buffs will find Brussels offers high quality and ample choice – check the *Bulletin*'s 'What's On' supplement.

Théâtre Royal de la Monnaie/Koninklijke Muntschouwburg (Map p74; ☎ 02 229 13 72; Place de la Monnaie; metro De Brouckère) Brussels' premier venue, better known as La Monnaie to French-speakers or De Munt to the Flemish. The revolution of 1830 was sparked during an opera performance here (see boxed text, above). Contemporary dance (see p109) and opera are the draws, the latter having an eclectic programme of classic remakes and modern productions. The season runs from September to June. To find out what's on, pick up the free quarterly *La Monnaie/De Munt Magazine*.

Bozar (Map pp72-3; ☎ 02 507 82 15, bookings 02 507 82 00; Rue Ravenstein 23; metro Gare Centrale) Celebrated classical-music venue, recently given this snappy name after years as the Palais des Beaux Arts. Designed by Horta, it opened in 1928 and is home not only to the National Orchestra but also to the Philharmonic Society, which organises much of the capital's classical-music programme. The Henri Le Bœuf *salle* (hall) is considered to be one of the five best in the world for acoustic quality. Pick up the monthly *Bozar Magazine* to find out what's on.

Conservatoire Royal de Musique (Royal Music Conservatory; Map pp76-7; ☎ 02 511 04 27; Rue de la Régence 30; metro Louise) The city's other major classical music venue, although it's smaller than Bozar and hosts a more modest programme.

The **Concours Musical International Reine Élisabeth de Belgique** is one of the year's musical highlights – see p96 for details.

Many smaller venues worth noting:

Cathédrale des Sts Michel & Gudule (p81)

Cirque Royal (Map pp72-3; ☎ 02 218 20 15; www .cirque-royal.org in Flemish & French; Rue de l'Enseignement 81; metro Madou) Converted indoor circus is now a venue for dance, operetta and classical and contemporary music.

Église de St Jean et St Étienne aux Minimes (Map pp76-7; ☎ 02 511 93 84; Rue des Minimes 62; bus 27) Baroque church below the Palais de Justice is an immensely popular venue with a sizable programme.

Flagey (Map pp76-7; ☎ 02 641 10 10; www.flagey .be; Place Flagey; tram 81) Ixelles' flagship has several concerts halls, including the large Studio 4.

Maison La Bellone (Map p74; ☎ 02 513 33 33; www.bellone.be in French; Rue de Flandre 46; metro Ste Catherine) The glass-vaulted courtyard of this 18th-century stunner is used for occasional concerts.

Théâtre du Vaudeville (Map p74; ☎ 02 512 57 45; Galerie de la Reine 13-15; metro Gare Centrale) This venue, inside Galeries St Hubert, is used for everything from cabarets to concerts.

Nightclubs

Brussels boasts that it invented European techno, and it's all largely thanks to one DJ and his Marolles club, Fuse (opposite). But club culture also goes way beyond the capital's leafy borders. Antwerp, Ghent, Liège and even little Lier are all within reach, so clubbing does not mean holing up in the capital. Look out for flyers posted around town or check out what's on at music shops like **Dr Vinyl** (Map p74; ☎ 02 512 73 44; Rue de la Grande Île 1; ☷ noon-7pm Mon, Tue, Fri & Sat, noon-8pm Wed & Thu) or **Caroline Music** (p108). Online there's www.noctis.be (in French; funk, electro, house and clubs) or www.netevents.be (in Flemish and French; nightlife information).

Fuse (Map pp76-7; ☎ 02 511 97 89; www.fuse.be; Rue Blaes 208; metro Porte de Hal; admission €3-12; ☺ 11pm-7am Sat) The Marolles club that put Brussels firmly on the international circuit. It has been attracting international DJs for well over a decade and is still going strong. The man, DJ Pierre, still spins here. On any given Saturday night, Fuse crams up to 2000 movers onto its two dance floors for house and deep-house mixes. Once a month it also hosts La Démence (p97).

Recyclart (Map pp76-7; ☎ 02 502 57 34; www.recy clart.be; Gare de la Chapelle, Rue des Ursulines 25; prémetro Anneessens; admission free-€8) Located in the Marolles' disused Chapelle train station, Recyclart is an urban regeneration project based around club nights, a daytime *café* and workshops for unemployed youth. Club nights are listed on the website, and you can be sure what you'll hear is cutting edge. This is where Brussels' newest DJ talent is born, and the line-up is invariably inventive.

Beursschouwburg Café (Map p74; ☎ 02 513 82 90; www.beursschouwburg.be; Rue Auguste Orts 20-28; prémetro Bourse; admission free; ☺ 7.30pm-late Thu-Sun) Brussels' Flemish youth love the big bold bar at their newly renovated theatre/concert hall. While not strictly speaking a club, by the wee small hours when everyone's moving it serves the same purpose, and is handily located smack in the centre of town.

Dirty Dancing@Mirano (Map pp72-3; ☎ 02 227 39 48; www.dirtydancing.be; Chaussée de Louvain; metro Madou; before midnight €5, midnight-4am €10; ☺ 10.30pm-6am Sat) Brussels' hottest new club has captured the hearts of many. Dress up to gain entry to the Mirano Continental and get set for a night of almost anything – pop, electro, house and even live rock at midnight.

Bazaar (Map pp76-7; ☎ 02 511 26 00; Rue des Capucins 63; metro Porte de Hal; admission €8; ☺ 7.30pm-late Thu-Sat) Once you've eaten your fill in the extravagant upstairs restaurant, head to the basement club to catch rock, funk, soul and a little disco fever. The music won't necessarily set your feet or your imagination on fire, but you'll bump into plenty of other foreigners.

Sport

International attention rarely focuses on Brussels with its limited number of quality sporting venues. The national stadium, **Stade Roi Baudouin** (Map pp70-1; ☎ 02 479 36 54; Ave de Marathon 135; metro Heysel) in Heysel, is the main host, attracting cycling races, athletics meetings

and football matches. Brussels' most famous football team, RSC Anderlecht, plays at **Van den Stock Stadium** (Map pp70-1; ☎ 02 522 15 39; Ave Théo Verbeeck 2; metro St Guidon) in Anderlecht. For more information on football, see p32. For details about cycling events, see p30.

The Ivo Van Damme Memorial (p97) and Brussels 20km Run (see p96) are two of the capital's biggest athletic events.

For details on sporting activities, see the Activities section (p90).

Theatre

Brussels' bilingual status means theatre gets divided along language lines. Both the Flemish and French theatrical communities have operated somewhat in limbo in recent times, awaiting the opening of sparkling new venues that promise to boost the local scene. Most local productions are in French or Flemish; however, touring international productions supplement the scene for English-speaking audiences. The season runs from September to June.

Koninklijke Vlaamse Schouwburg (Map pp72-3; ☎ 02 210 11 12; www.kvs.be; Rue de Laeken 146; metro Yser) The Royal Flemish Theatre is better known by its acronym, KVS. The 2006 season saw it back in business in its beautifully restored neo-Renaissance building after five years in an old bottle factory. The theatre's original façade has been retained, but inside it's completely custom-made and, in bold Flemish style, it's captivating and confident. The KVS' new programming promises challenging, edge-of-your-seat theatre and dance, with the possibility of occasional English-language productions.

Théâtre National (Map pp72-3; ☎ 02 203 41 55; www .theatrenational.be in French; Blvd Émile Jacqmain 111-115; metro Rogier) The French-speaking community's flashy new showpiece is a modern glass affair. For the last couple of years, the company played in a converted downtown cinema complex but it has wooed its loyal audience to its new home here at the northern end of town.

Théâtre Royal de Toone (Map p74; ☎ 02 511 71 37; www.toone.be; Petite Rue des Bouchers 21; metro Gare Centrale; €10; ☺ 8.30pm Thu-Sat) Whether you understand Bruxellois dialect or not, don't miss a performance at this famous marionette theatre. Eight generations of the Toone family have been staging puppet productions of works such as *The Three Musketeers*, *Faust* and *Hamlet* here for well over a century. The plays are mainly staged for adults, although children enjoy the puppets and sets. Programmes are available from the *café* at the theatre.

Other theatres:

Kaaitheater (Map pp72-3; ☎ 02 201 59 59; www
.kaaitheater.be; Square Sainctelette 20; metro Yser) Bastion
of Flemish avant-garde theatre.

Théâtre Les Tanneurs (Map pp76-7; ☎ 02 512 17 84;
www.lestanneurs.be in French; Rue des Tanneurs 75; metro
Porte de Hal) Marolles theatre known for its dynamic
dance and drama.

SHOPPING

Brussels is home to Europe's first shopping arcade, the grand Galeries St Hubert (see boxed text, below). This gallery ensured the locals' early indoctrination into the art of shopping, and their love affair with browsing arm-inarm past boutiques and tailored stores has not waned.

The capital has long been a centre for commerce and trade. The medieval guilds set up shop in their elaborate houses on the Grand Place from where they controlled the trades and crafts. Brussels' river, the Senne, once brought trade to the city, though this ended abruptly in 1870 when the river was covered over. Until then, fishing boats moored in the heart of Ste Catherine and a daily fish market took over what is now the concrete area around the Ste Catherine metro station.

Brussels divides quite neatly into shopping districts. The Grand Place and streets shooting off from it are lined with tourist shops hawking chocolate, beer, lace and EU merchandise. Go to Galeries St Hubert if you're after the same sort of items but sold in a setting of complete grandeur. The Place St Géry quarter, in particular Rue Antoine Dansaert, is the nerve

---

GREAT GALERIES

The **Galeries St Hubert** (Map p74; Rue du Marché aux Herbes; metro Gare Centrale), just one block from the Grand Place, is the *grande dame* of Brussels' many shopping galleries. This gorgeous arcade was a European first, opened in 1847 in a gala event by King Léopold I, and immediately a draw for the fashionable elite. At the time it housed not only fancy shops and glistening window displays, but also *cafés*, restaurants and entertainment venues – much the same as today. It comprises three connecting sections: Galerie du Roi, Galerie de la Reine and the smaller Galerie des Princes at the side. The arcades contain an eclectic mix of fashion, chocolate, book and music shops, as well as a cinema, theatre, restaurants and *cafés*. They're all wrapped up in a fine neoclassical setting – the vaulted glass roof allows the light to pour in while marble columns, statues and gleaming ironwork add the embellishments.

Such was the success that other galleries soon followed. JP Cluysenaer, St Hubert's designer, went to work on **Galerie Bortier** (Map p74; Rue de la Madeleine; metro Gare Centrale). It opened in 1848 and, although much smaller and less flamboyant than the original, it follows a similar style and is well worth a look, particularly if you're into secondhand books. The cavernous but rundown **Galerie Ravenstein** (Map pp72-3; Rue Ravenstein; metro Gare Centrale) connects Gare Centrale with the Upper Town. **Passage du Nord** (Map p74; Rue Neuve; metro De Brouckère) is another glass-vaulted affair, connecting the Lower Town's brash shopping thoroughfare, Rue Neuve, to Place de Brouckère.

It wasn't long before *galeries* reached the Upper Town, where **Galeries Louise** (Map pp76-7; Ave Louise; metro Louise) and **Galeries de la Toison d'Or** (Map pp76-7; Ave de la Toison d'Or; metro Porte de Namur) still beckon with clothing and jewellery shops, though architectural splendour is nonexistent in these two networks.

The most interesting of the Upper Town arcades is the tiny **Galerie d'Ixelles** (Map pp76-7; Chaussée d'Ixelles; metro Porte de Namur) and its continuation, **Galerie de la Porte de Namur** (Map pp76-7). Although not far from Ave Louise, these two galleries are culturally a world away, located in the Matonge quarter, home to Brussels' Congolese community. Mainstays here include pint-sized shops selling African cloth, Kinshasa's latest CD imports and hairdressing salons with names like 'Dream Hair' or 'The New Image of Black Men'. To explore this scene further, head along Chaussée de Wavre where shops such as **Exotic Food** (Map pp76-7; Chaussée de Wavre 27; metro Porte de Namur) specialise in produce like Ngolo catfish from Guinea, little packages of leaf-wrapped cassava from Cameroon and even dried caterpillars. If you're into trying an African beer, stop off at **Gambela** (Map pp76-7; ☎ 02 502 00 14; Rue Longue Vie 7; metro Porte de Namur; ♥ 11am-8pm Mon-Sat), a local produce store where Primus, Tembo and Doppel beers line the shelves.

centre of design and urban cool – most of the city's avant-garde fashion shops are located here. The Sablon and the Marolles are for antiques and flea markets. Meanwhile, the Upper Town is home to Gucci, Chanel, Louis Vuitton and home-grown designers, all lined up along either Ave Louise or Blvd de Waterloo.

Markets are a great way to discover the city and shop at the same time. Some 30 operate; we've highlighted the best.

Antiques

The Sablon (Map pp76–7) is the area for antiques, followed by the Marolles. The Sablon's many private galleries resemble miniature museums, with ancient artefacts from around the world as well as contemporary art. Start with the chic shops on Place du Grand Sablon (site of a weekly antique market – see p115), then follow your nose along Rue des Minimes and surrounding streets like Rue Charles Hanssens and Rue Watteeu before descending (price tags drop accordingly) to the Marolles and the mix of retro/antiques/clothing shops that line Rue Haute and Rue Blaes. An antique bargain or two may also be possible among the jumble of stalls on Place du Jeu-de-Balle (see p115).

Beer

Beermania (Map pp76–7; ☎ 02 512 17 88; www.beermania .be; Chaussée de Wavre 174; bus 95 or 96; ⏰ 11am–9pm Mon-Sat Jan-Nov, daily Dec) Belgium's first specialist beer shop, now complete with a tasting *café*, is a great first or last stop. With some 400 brews to behold, it's an ideal place to get acquainted with key players and rare nectars. There's no menu or price list – just wander around and point to the one(s) you want. Most 330/250mL bottles cost €3/2.50. The exception is, of course, Westvleteren (p47) – if it's in stock, you'll be looking at a way overpriced €12. Before leaving Brussels, arrange a door-to-door delivery of your favourite brews to your home address, or buy a few bottles to plug up gaps in your suitcase. The shop also holds occasional beer-appreciation sessions.

De Biertempel (Map p74; ☎ 02 502 19 06; Rue du Marché aux Herbes 56; prémetro Bourse; ⏰ 9.30am-7pm) Handy location and stocks 550 Belgian brews plus matching glasses and all manner of beer paraphernalia.

Biscuits

Dandoy (Map p74; ☎ 02 511 03 26; Rue au Beurre 31; metro Bourse) Belgium's spicy *speculaas* biscuits are

sold en masse from this exquisite little shop close to the Grand Place. *Pain à la grecque*, long loaves loaded with sugar nuggets, are another house speciality. It's worth a look for the window display alone.

Chocolate

Corné Port Royal (Map p74; ☎ 02 512 43 14; Rue de la Madeleine 9; metro Gare Centrale; ⏰ 10am-8pm) First chocolate shop en route from Gare Central to the Grand Place and recommended if you can't hang out a minute longer. Friendly service, well priced (€35 per kg) and higher quality than bulk handlers such as Leonidas.

Galler (Map p74; ☎ 02 502 02 66; Rue au Beurre 44; ⏰ 10am-9.30pm) A step up from chain shops such as Godiva and Neuhaus and the one to choose if orange livery is your thing. A reputation for innovative flavours and a handy location just off the Grand Place.

Mary's (Map pp72-3; ☎ 02 217 45 00; Rue Royale 73; tram 92, 93 or 94; ⏰ 9.30am-6pm Mon-Sat) In some chocolate circles, it gets no better than this. Scrumptious pralines (filled chocolates) are sold from one exclusive boutique in the royal quarter of town. Supplies Belgium's royals, and George W has indulged here too.

Neuhaus (Map p74; ☎ 02 512 63 59; Galerie de la Reine 25; metro Gare Centrale) Stunning shop with stained-glass windows and sumptuous displays. Established in 1857 and is now a reasonably priced, national chain.

Pierre Marcolini (Map pp76-7; ☎ 02 514 12 06; Place du Grand Sablon 39; tram 92, 93 or 04) Belgium's most expensive pralines (€58 per kg) are made by this relative newcomer to the chocolate scene. In the past few years Marcolini has taken the country, and major cities worldwide, by storm. He also broke the *ballotin* (praline box) mould, instead using low, flat chocolate boxes designed by Delvaux (of national handbag fame).

Planète Chocolat (Map p74; ☎ 02 511 07 55; Rue du Lombard 24; premetro Bourse) Frank Duval is the force behind this innovative chocolate shop and tearoom where both the moulds and the chocolates are made on site. If you're after unusual shapes, head here. The tearoom, two doors along, does wicked hot chocolate drinks as well as a praline-making demonstration at 4pm each Saturday.

Wittamer (Map pp76-7; ☎ 02 512 37 42; Place du Grand Sablon 6; tram 92, 93 or 94) Another fabulous Sablon address. Sister establishment to the nearby posh pâtisserie, and long-time maker of excellent pralines.

Comic Books

Boutique Tintin (Map p74; ☎ 02 514 51 52; Rue de la Colline 13; 10am-6pm Mon-Sat, 11am-5pm Sun) Stocks every Tintin comic you've ever wanted and more.

Brüsel (Map p74; ☎ 02 502 35 52; Blvd Anspach 100; 10.30am-6.30pm Mon-Sat, noon-6.30pm Sun) Chic comic-book shop named after a book by one of Belgium's best-known contemporary comic artists, François Schuiten. Comics with English translations available.

Also recommended:

Centre Belge de la Bande Dessinée (p80) Comic specialist.

La Maison de la BD (Map p74; ☎ 02 502 94 68; Blvd de l'Impératrice 1; 10am-7pm Tue-Sun) Comic specialist.

Fashion

Annemie Verbeke (Map p74; ☎ 02 511 21 71; Rue Antoine Dansaert 64; premetro Bourse) Ypres-born designer with no formal training who has managed to juggle motherhood with a highly successful career designing women's clothing. Recently opened a new store in Antwerp, and is sold throughout Europe and in the US and Japan.

Kaat Tilley (Map p74; ☎ 02 514 07 63; Galerie du Roi 4; metro Gare Centrale) Women's wear – everyday, formal and bridal – and children's communion outfits are the staples of this Mechelen-born designer, with a flagship store in Paris. Located in Galeries St Hubert.

Idiz Bogam (Map p74; ☎ 02 512 10 32; Rue Antoine Dansaert 76; premetro Bourse) Cavernous store specialising in retro, vintage and global second-hand gear. Big on furs, hats and sequins, and with an unbeatable assortment of shoes.

Marina Yee (Map p74; ☎ 0496 33 58 70; Marché aux Porcs 3; metro Ste Catherine) New shop by the least known of the Antwerp Six (p197). Look for wisteria cladding at the revamped northern end of Ste Catherine.

Martin Margiela (Map p74; ☎ 02 223 75 20; Rue de Flandre 114; metro Ste Catherine) Belgian fashion icon and the unofficial seventh member of the Antwerp Six, Paris-based Margiela opened this whitewashed corner shop in Ste Catherine a few years ago. The little building is unmarked but easily recognised; ring the doorbell to gain entry. Collections include men's and women's clothes and accessories.

Nicolas Woit (Map p74; ☎ 02 503 48 32; Rue Antoine Dansaert 80; premetro Bourse) Woit opened here a decade ago and has flourished ever since. His trademark is handmade women's clothes using new and secondhand materials – retro fabrics and contemporary accessories.

Olivier Strelli Upper Town (Map pp76-7; ☎ 02 512 56 07; Ave Louise 72; metro Louise); Lower Town (Map p74; ☎ 02 512 09 42; Rue Antoine Dansaert 44; premetro Bourse) Known throughout the world for his men's and women's collections, Strelli is Belgium's most successful fashion label. Born in the Congo, he's a Jewish Belgian of Italian and Turkish roots who has been in the business for more than three decades. The Ave Louise boutique is his headquarters.

Stijl (Map p74; ☎ 02 512 03 13; Rue Antoine Dansaert 74; premetro Bourse) Home to top Belgian designers, including some of the Antwerp Six, it was this boutique that lead the pack into Rue Dansaert back in the mid '80s when the area was forlorn and forgotten. All the most up-to-the-minute designers are represented here including Xavier Delcour and Olivier Theyskens.

Other recommendations:

Boutique 114 (Map pp76-7; ☎ 02 512 40 27; Rue de Stassart 114; metro Louise) Just off Ave Louise; handles designer cast-offs.

Delvaux (Map p74; ☎ 02 512 71 98; Galerie de la Reine 31; metro Gare Centrale) Delvaux is a household name in leather handbags and accessories in Belgium. Located in Galeries St Hubert.

FASHION RIVAL

Antwerp may be the Belgian capital of avant-garde, but Brussels is closing the gap. With boutiques popping up everywhere and young designers from Brussels' fashion school, La Cambre, making it big in the last decade, the city is determined to come out of the big A's shadow. Brussels nominated 2006 as its Year of Fashion and Design, and it has established Modo Bruxellae (www.modobruxellae.be), the capital's fashion champion. Modo is behind the Designers' Trail, a biennial fashion event (even years) which sees fashion shows, boutiques and animations taking over the capital's designer heartland, the Rue Antoine Dansaert quarter, for a weekend in late October.

New names to look out for amongst the city's creative talent are Olivier Theyskens (who designs for Rochas), Laetitia Crahay (Chanel and Delvaux) and José Enrique Ona Selfa (Loewe). Former La Cambre student, Xavier Delcour, has his own label – his designs are available at Stijl (above).

DoD (Map pp72-3; ☎ 02 219 80 42; Chaussée de Louvain 16; metro Madou) Designer fashions (mainly French) at dirt cheap prices is the motto of this series of warehouse-like stores that occupy much of this street – Dod Men is here at No 16, with women, junior, shoes etc just down the road.

Inno Lower Town (Map p74; ☎ 02 211 21 11; Rue Neuve 111; metro Rogier); Upper Town (Map p76-7; ☎ 02 513 84 94; Ave Louise 12; metro Louise) Belgium's only home-grown department store.

Les Enfants d'Édouard (Map p76-7; ☎ 02 640 42 45; Ave Louise 175; tram 93 or 94) Swish boutique for men's and women's designer hand-me-downs and end-of-line stocks.

Lace

Manufacture Belge de Dentelles (Map p74; ☎ 02 511 44 77; Galerie de la Reine 6-8; metro Gare Centrale) Brussels' oldest lace shop – now located inside Galeries St Hubert but in existence since 1810. An excellent stock of antique lace and a staff with a love affair for true lace. Also see boxed text, p138.

Markets

Gare du Midi (Map pp76-7; metro Gare du Midi; ◷ 6am-1pm Sun) Brussels' biggest general market is held next to the railway lines and has a distinctly North African and Mediterranean feel. Bulbous cheeses, strings of sausages and vendors announcing their wares are all part of it. A rich and colourful affair.

Place du Jeu-de-Balle flea market (Map pp76-7; Place du Jeu-de-Balle; metro Porte de Hal, prémetro Lemonnier; ◷ 7am-2pm) The Marolles' famous secondhand market has been running almost every day since 1919. It's best at weekends (although prices are higher then). Genuine antiques are few but there's some great junk. Haggling is expected.

Other recommendations:

Grand Place (Map p74; metro Gare Centrale; ◷ mornings Mon, Wed & Fri) Small flower market.

Place du Grand Sablon (Map p76-7; tram 92, 93 or 94; ◷ 9am-6pm Sat, 9am-2pm Sun; tram 92, 93 or 94) Weekly antique market.

Place Jourdan (Map p86; metro Schuman; ◷ 7am-2pm Sun) Food and clothes at this little suburban market.

GETTING THERE & AWAY
Air

Brussels National Airport (Map pp70-1; ☎ 02 753 42 21, flight information 0900 70 000; www.brusselsairport.be; Zaventem), in times past referred to as Zaventem airport, is 14km northeast of Brussels. The compact terminal's Promenade floor (Level 4) includes shops and a cafeteria with a view of the runways. Level 3 is the departures hall, where you'll find an information desk and free airport maps. The arrivals hall is on Level 2. Facilities here include a post office, ATM, car-rental agencies and tourist information counters. On the next floor down is the bus terminus (Level 0) and luggage storage lockers. The train station is on the lowest floor (Level -1). For airlines servicing Brussels, see p314. For details on getting to/from the airport, see p116.

Bus

Eurolines (Map pp72-3; ☎ 02 274 13 50; www.eurolines .be; Rue du Progrès 80; metro Gare du Nord) has its office at Gare du Nord, and most buses depart from here (though some also stop at Ave Fonsny near Gare du Midi; Map pp76-7). For more information on Eurolines services, see p317.

Destinations from Brussels include Amsterdam (one-way/return €18/30, 3¾ hours, six daily), Frankfurt (€34/55, 5¼ hours, one daily), London (€38/60, 8½ hours, six daily) and Paris (€25/40, 3¾ hours, nine daily).

Car & Motorcycle

Major car-rental companies have downtown premises, as well as offices at Gare du Midi and Brussels National Airport. Rentals from both the airport and Gare du Midi cost considerably more due to additional taxes.

Avis (Map p76-7; ☎ 02 537 12 80; Rue Américaine 145)

Baele & Schmitz (Map pp70-1; ☎ 02 762 60 27; Chaussée de Louvain) Rents 600cc motorbikes (€75/450 per day/week). Hefty deposits are required.

Budget (Map pp76-7; ☎ 02 646 51 30; Ave Louise 327b)

Hertz (Map p74; ☎ 02 513 28 86; Blvd Maurice Lemonnier 8)

Train

Brussels' three main train stations are **Gare du Midi** (Map pp76-7; South Station), **Gare Centrale** (Map p74; Central Station), and **Gare du Nord** (Map pp72-3; North Station).

Gare du Midi is the main station for international connections: the Eurostar and Thalys fast trains stop here only. Most other international trains stop at both Gare du Nord and Gare du Midi, and some also stop at Gare Centrale. There are information offices at all three stations, open early morning to late evening. For all international and national inquiries call ☎ 02 555 25 55.

For information on train services between Belgium and neighbouring countries, including Eurostar and Thalys trains, see p316.

Brussels is well connected with other Belgian cities and Luxembourg City. Examples of connections include the following (prices are one-way second-class fares):

Destination	Fare (€)	Duration (min)	Frequency (per hr)
Antwerp	6	35	2
Bruges	11.80	60	2
Brussels National Airport	2.60	15	4
Charleroi	7.80	60	2
Ghent	7.40	40	2
Hasselt	10.70	75	2
Jemelle	14.10	100	1
Kortrijk	10.70	60	2
Leuven	4.30	20	1
Liège	12.40	65	2
Luxembourg City	28.60	180	1
Mechelen	3.70	15	2
Mons	7.80	45	2
Namur	7.40	60	2
Nivelles	4.70	40	1
Ostend	14.10	75	2
Tournai	10.70	60	2
Villers-la-Ville	5	60	1
Ypres	14.60	90	2

GETTING AROUND
To/From the Airport

The **Airport City Express** (☎ 02 528 28 28; one-way €2.80; ⏰ 5.30am-12.20am) train runs between Brussels National Airport and the city's three main train stations (Gare du Nord, Gare Centrale and Gare du Midi). It runs every 15 minutes and the trip takes 15 to 25 minutes (depending on your station).

A taxi between the airport and central Brussels costs around €30. Taxis wait outside the airport arrivals hall. Official taxis have a yellow and blue plaque near the numberplate.

Bicycle

Cycling in central Brussels is not for the faint-hearted: intolerant drivers, slippery cobblestones and tram tracks are all potential hazards. That said, there are some bike lanes (usually painted red and marked with white lines) and paths (separated from the traffic), but these are mostly on the outskirts of town where there's a bit more room. Closer to town, the busy EU thoroughfare Rue de la Loi now has a dedicated cycle lane.

For bike hire contact ProVélo's **La Maison des Cyclistes** (Map pp76-7; ☎ 02 502 73 55; www.provelo.be; Rue de Londres 15; metro Porte de Namur; per hr/half-day/full day/weekend/week €4/11/13/24/72; ⏰ 10am-6pm Tue-Fri, also Sat Apr-Oct). Children's bikes and child seats are available, and they also run guided bike tours (April to October).

Car & Motorcycle

Driving in Brussels has its thrills – see boxed text, p323. The slightest hiccup on either ring road brings traffic to a halt, and Friday afternoons are notoriously congested. For information on road rules, see p322.

Parking poses the usual problems. Signs saying *betalend parkeren/stationnement payant* mean that it's paid street parking (usually 9am to 7pm Monday to Saturday).

Two central car parks:
Inno Parking (Map p74; Rue du Damier)
Parking 58 (Map p74; Rue de l'Évêque) Check out the great view from the 10th floor.

Public Transport

Brussels' efficient public transport system is operated by **Société des Transports Intercommunaux de Bruxelles** (STIB in French, MIVB in Flemish) Main kiosk (Map p74; ☎ 02 515 20 00; Rue de l'Évêque 2; ⏰ 10am-6pm Mon-Sat); Branch kiosk (Map pp76-7; Gare du Midi; ⏰ 7.30-5.30 Mon-Sat, 8.30am-2pm Sun). Metro, trams, *premetro* (trams that go underground for part of their journey) and buses make up the network. Public transport runs from about 6am to midnight, after which a nightbus network operates.

TICKETS & PASSES

Tickets are valid for one hour and are sold at metro stations, STIB/MIVB kiosks, newsagents and on buses and trams. The pricing system is simple – a single-journey ticket costs €1.50, five-/10-journey tickets cost €6.50/10.50 and a one-day pass for unlimited travel is €4. Children under six travel for free.

Tickets must be validated before travel in machines located at the entrance to metro platforms or inside buses and trams. Tickets without validation (random checks are made) incur fines of €55.

The city tourist office, Brussels International (p69), sells one-day passes as well as the Brussels Card.

METRO

Brussels' metro system opened in 1965. Metro stations are marked by signs with a white 'M' on a blue background. There are three lines: Line 1A goes from Roi Baudouin station to Herrmann-Debroux; Line 1B runs from Erasme to Stockel; and Line 2 is a loop that joins Simonis with Delacroix, basically following the Petit Ring. There's a train roughly every 10 or 15 minutes.

Keep an eye out for artworks while in the metro and premetro stations. The following are highlights:

Bourse (Map p74) Paul Delvaux' *Nos vieux trams bruxellois* depicts old trams in the capital.

Horta (Map pp76-7) Relics from Horta's Maison du Peuple have been integrated into the station's foyer.

Porte de Hal (Map pp76-7) Comic-strip artist François Schuiten's wall compositions entitled *Le Passage Inconnu* (The Unknown Passage) merge old trams and futuristic vehicles in scenes mirrored in his best cartoons.

Stockel (Map pp70-1) Walls adorned with life-sized paintings of Tintin and pals.

TRAM, PREMETRO & BUS

There's no central transport hub for buses or trams which means working out where to jump on is akin to finding a needle in a haystack. Also, make sure you know in which direction you're heading. Many bus (and tram) routes start at one side of the city and finish on the other, it's possible to be on the right-numbered bus (or tram) but travelling in the wrong direction. Pick up the STIB/MIVB's free transport map to help find your way around.

Tram and bus stops have red-and-white signs. *Premetro* trams run mainly between Gare du Nord and Gare du Midi, travelling underneath the ruler-straight boulevard known consecutively as Adolphe Max/Anspach/Maurice Lemonnier.

Brussels' nightbus network expanded in 2007, with 20 nightbus lines now operating around the capital on Friday and Saturday nights until 3am. Most lines depart from Place de Brouckère, and single tickets cost €3.

Taxi

Taxis are metered, and cabbies have a reputation for aggressive driving and argumentative behaviour. Taxes and tips are officially included in the meter price so you should ignore requests for extra service charges.

Fares are calculated starting with a basic day/night rate of €2.40/4.30, plus €1.15/1.30 per kilometre within/outside the Brussels region. The waiting rate is €22 per hour. You'll find taxis near all three central train stations as well as outside Hôtel Amigo (Map p74), near the Grand Place (Map p74) and at Place Stéphanie (Map pp76–7) on Ave Louise. Alternatively, call **Taxis Bleus** (☎ 02 268 00 00) or **Taxis Verts** (☎ 02 349 49 49).

AROUND BRUSSELS

Just out of Brussels in the province of Brabant-Wallon are Waterloo (see p224), Nivelles (see p223) and Villers-la-Ville (see p225), all ideal day-trip destinations. For information on the Koninklijk Museum voor Midden-Afrika at Tervuren, see p94.

FORÊT DE SOIGNES

This forest (Map pp70–1) southeast of Brussels is the largest patch of green in the capital's vicinity. It was originally part of a much greater oak forest that was progressively cut down during the 16th and 17th centuries. The oldest trees here today are beech, planted in the 18th century under the Austrian rulers.

The park is one of Belgium's most important state-owned forests and is home to wild boar and deer. It is popular throughout the year but particularly so in summer when the old trams operated by Brussels' Musée du Transport Urbain trundle through. The park includes two arboreta – Tervuren and Groenendaal – as well as the **Jean Massart Experimental Garden** (Map pp70–1) and the **Rouge Cloître** (Map pp70–1), a 14th-century abbey. A series of good **playgrounds** (Map pp70–1) are located near the latter.

There are various public transport options to the forest, depending on which part you wish to access. If you just want to get to any patch of green, take bus 95 from the **Bourse** (Map p74) in central Brussels.

NATIONALE PLANTENTUIN VAN BELGIË

Belgium's **National Botanic Garden** (☎ 02 260 09 20; www.botanicgarden.be; Domein van Boechout, Meise; adult/concession €4/3; ☺ 9.30am-6.30pm Apr-Oct, 9.30am-5pm Nov-Mar) is a 93-hectare park located in the village of Meise, 12km north of downtown Brussels. It's based around two lakes and the Kasteel van Boechout (Boechout Castle), which Léopold II gave to his sister, Princess Charlotte, after her castle at Tervuren burnt down in 1879.

The park boasts 18,000 plant species including orchids, carnivorous plants and the famous giant Amazonian water lilies. They are housed in the spectacular Plantenpaleis (Plant Palace), a series of 13 connecting greenhouses built in 1966.

Other highlights are the outdoor medicinal garden and, nearby, a small but stunning greenhouse shaped like a king's crown that was built in 1864 by Balat (Horta's teacher and the architect responsible for the Serres Royales, p89). The 18th-century orangery has been converted into a *café* and shop.

To get to the park by car, take the A12 (direction Antwerp) to the Meise exit and follow the signs. By bus, take De Lijn bus 250 or 251 from Gare du Nord (Map pp72–3) to the Nationale Plantentuin van België stop.

Western Flanders

Belgian *chansonnier* Jacques Brel famously referred to this part of Belgium as *le plat pays* – the flat country. He sang about his reluctant love for all that it stood for, and about its bleakness. Indeed, on cold winter days the scene here can be downright dismal. Winds howl across flat fields and whip through villages, wrapping around church steeples and belfries – monuments that have survived the centuries to become resounding symbols of the region's rich historic past. Many are now World Heritage–listed.

Although the term 'Flanders' now covers all of northern Belgium, it was once associated with this western portion only. The great cities of Bruges, Ghent, Ypres and Kortrijk rose in medieval times on the wealth of cloth and international trade. Other towns – Oudenaarde, famed for its 15th-century tapestries, and Veurne, with its macabre medieval procession – followed. Nowadays Western Flanders is still full of atmospheric, albeit tourist-packed, towns.

Belgians adore their 66km coastline. Look past the unsightly coast-hugging high-rises to find wide, flat beaches. Relive the age-old tradition of shrimp fishing on horseback at Oost-duinkerke, or stroll arm-in-arm along broad promenades, passing rows of candy-coloured beach huts. Choose charming De Haan or bustling Ostend as your base; both are engaging towns snuggled into the few remaining coastal dunes.

Flanders' far western corner is where some of WWI's most dreadful battles were fought. The frontline town of Ypres draws visitors young and old from around the globe.

HIGHLIGHTS

- **Full-on Festivities** De Gentse Feesten (p165) in Ghent
- **Primitive Passions** Art at Bruges' Groeningemuseum (p125)
- **Salient Reminder** Flanders' WWI battle-fields near Ypres (p153)
- **Cycle City** On ya bike in and around Bruges (p130) or Kortrijk (p160)
- **Art Heaven** *The Adoration of the Mystic Lamb* in Ghent's cathedral (p161)
- **Beaut Brewery** De Dolle Brouwers (p50) near Diksmuide
- **Sublime Surrealism** Paul Delvaux's surprising St Idesbald home (p148)
- **Coastal Cruise** The Kusttram (Coast Tram; p145) reveals all

- PROVINCES: WEST-VLAANDEREN (WEST FLANDERS: CAPITAL BRUGES), OOST-VLAANDEREN (EAST FLANDERS: CAPITAL GHENT)
- LANGUAGE: FLEMISH

BRUGES

pop 117,000

Touristy, overcrowded and a tad fake. Preface any other city with these descriptions and it would be struck off the list. But not Bruges (Brugge in Flemish, Bruges in French). This Flemish city is Belgium's most popular destination and, despite being overrun much of the year, it's not to be missed.

Suspended in time centuries ago, Bruges is now one of Western Europe's most-visited medieval cities. Picturesque market squares, dreamy canals and old whitewashed almshouses all evoke a world long since gone. But its reputation as one of the most perfectly preserved cities is in part fabrication. Bruges has been renovated time and again to retain its medieval appearance. Whereas what you see reflects that of centuries ago, much of the architecture dates only from the 19th and 20th centuries.

To enjoy Bruges, timing is essential. Stay overnight or late on a midsummer evening, when the carillon chimes seep through the cobbled streets, and local boys (illegally) cast fishing rods into willow-lined canals. Visit in spring when daffodils carpet the tranquil *begijnhof* (a walled community once housing a Catholic order of women), or in winter when you can sometimes skate on the canals and have the town almost to yourself. At these times, Bruges readily reveals its age-old beauty. Alternatively, jump on a bike and cycle off for the day. By the time you return, most of the day-trippers will be well on their way.

History

In medieval times the sea flooded the area around present-day Bruges, carving out channels and waterways. Baldwin the Iron Arm, the first count of Flanders, built a castle as protection from Viking raids, and gradually a town grew up. Trade came via the nearby village of Damme and its waterway, the Zwin.

As in other Flemish cities, textiles were Bruges' ticket to prosperity. Much trade was connected to England's wool industry, the source of the finest grade of wool, and by the late 13th century Bruges was a major cloth-trading centre. When Philip the Fair, King of France, visited Bruges in 1301, his wife, Joanna of Navarre, was so surprised by the inhabitants' wealth and luxurious clothes that she purportedly claimed: 'I thought I alone was queen, but I see that I have 600 rivals here'.

But the city's increased wealth brought political tension and, after guildsmen refused to pay a new round of taxes in 1302, the army was sent in to garrison the town. Pieter De Coninck, Dean of the Guild of Weavers, and Jan Breydel, Dean of the Guild of Butchers, led a revolt against the 2000-strong army that would go down in Flanders' history books as the Brugse Metten (Bruges Matins). Early in the morning on 18 May, the guildsmen crept into town and murdered anyone who could not correctly pronounce the Flemish phrase '*schild en vriend*' (shield and friend). This revolt sparked a widespread rebellion and led to the Flemish victory against the French six weeks later at the Battle of the Golden Spurs near Kortrijk (see boxed text, p159). Independence was short-lived, though, and the French soon regained control.

In the 14th century Bruges became a key member of the Hanseatic League of Seventeen Cities, a powerful association of northern European trading cities, and the city reached its economic peak. Italian cities such as Genoa, Florence and Venice built trade houses here, and ships laden with exotic goods from all over Europe and further afield docked at the Minnewater, a small lake to the city's south.

Prosperity continued under the dukes of Burgundy, especially Philip the Good (r 1419–67), who arrived in 1430 to marry Isabella of Portugal. Bruges grew fat and by 1500 the population had ballooned to 200,000, doubling that of London. Flemish art blossomed and the city's artists – known as the Flemish Primitives (see boxed text, p125) – perfected paintings that are still vivid today.

During the 15th century the Zwin, the waterway linking Bruges to the sea, silted up. Despite attempts to build another canal, the city's economic lifeline was gone. When the headquarters of the Hanseatic League moved from Bruges to Antwerp at the end of the 15th century, many merchants followed, leaving abandoned houses, deserted streets and empty canals. Bruges, a former hub of Europe, slept for 400 years.

The city slowly emerged from its slumber in the early 19th century as tourists passed through en route to the Waterloo battlefield near Brussels. In 1892 Belgian writer and poet Georges Rodenbach published *Bruges-la-Morte* (Bruges the Dead), a novel that beguilingly described the town's forlorn air and alerted the well-heeled to its preserved charm. Curious, wealthy visitors brought

WESTERN FLANDERS

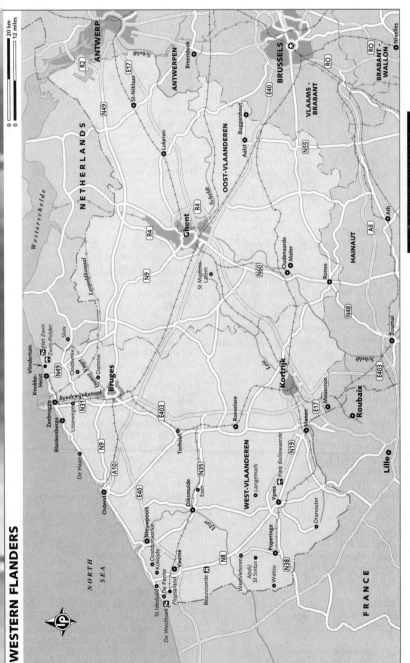

much-needed money into Bruges, and sealed its fate as a town frozen in time.

In 1907 the Boudewijnkanaal, a canal linking Bruges to the new port of Zeebrugge, was constructed. Although Zeebrugge suffered extensive damage during both world wars, Bruges escaped unscathed. As the capital of West-Vlaanderen province, it now lives largely off tourism, although it also has a manufacturing centre outside the city that produces glass, electrical goods and chemicals.

Bruges' stint as European City of Culture in 2002 proved that it's more than just a medieval showpiece. A daring red concert hall, the Concertgebouw, was built to celebrate the event, and contemporary came to the historic centre in the form of the Toyo Ito pavilion (p124).

Orientation

Bruges is neatly encased by an oval-shaped moat that follows the city's medieval fortifications; four of the nine gates built around 1300 still stand. At its heart are two squares, the Markt and the Burg. The city is an ambler's ultimate dream, its sights sprinkled within leisurely walking distance of its compact centre. The train station is about 1.5km south of the Markt; buses shuttle regularly between the two.

Information

BOOKSHOPS

De Reyghere (Map p126; ☎ 050 33 34 03; Markt 12) Good all-round bookshop with a separate travel section next door.

EMERGENCY

Ambulance/Fire (☎ 100)
Police (☎ 101)

INTERNET ACCESS

Bauhaus Cybercafé (Map p123; ☎ 050 34 10 93; Langestraat 137; per 15min €1.30; ☺ 10am-midnight) Town's hippest internet café, at the Bauhaus hostel.
Coffee Link (Map p126; ☎ 050 34 99 73; St Janshospitaal building, Mariastraat 38; per 15min/1hr €1.50/5; ☺ 11am-6pm Thu & Sat-Tue, 11am-3pm Fri) Atmospheric café with coffee, cakes and a bank of terminals.

LAUNDRY

Ipsomat (Map p123; Langestraat 151)
Wassalon (Map p126; Ezelstraat 51)

LEFT LUGGAGE

Train station lockers (per 24hr €2.60-3.60)

LIBRARY

Openbare Bibliotheek Biekorf (Map p126; ☎ 050 47 24 00; Biekorf Bldg, Kuipersstraat 3; ☺ closed Sun) Main public library.

MEDICAL SERVICES

Akademisch Ziekenhuis St Jan (☎ 050 45 21 11; Ruddershove 10) The city's main hospital, with a 24-hour emergency unit.
Apotheek Dryepondt (Map p126; ☎ 050 33 64 74; Wollestraat 7) Modern pharmacy housed in an antique façade.
Doctors on weekend duty (☎ 050 36 40 10)
Pharmacists on weekend duty (☎ 050 40 61 62)

MONEY

ATM Post office (Map p126, Markt 5); Fortis Bank (Map p126, Simon Stevinplein 3); Europabank (Map p126, Vlamingstraat 13)
Goffin Change (Map p126; ☎ 050 34 04 71; Steenstraat 2; ☺ 9am-6pm Mon-Sat, 11am-6pm Sun)
ING Bank (Map p126; ☎ 050 44 45 40; Markt 19; ☺ 9am-12.30pm & 1.30-4.15pm Mon-Fri, 9am-noon Sat) Handles cash, travellers cheques and credit card cash advances.

POST & FAX

Post office (Map p126; ☎ 050 33 14 11; Markt 5)
Varicopy (Map p126; ☎ 050 033 59 43; fax 050 34 61 92; Oude Burg 22a) For sending and receiving faxes.

TOURIST INFORMATION

In&Uit Brugge (Map p126; ☎ 050 44 86 86; www .brugge.be; 't Zand 34; ☺ 10am-6pm Fri-Wed, 10am-8pm Thu) Modern new tourist office and events booking service located in the Concertgebouw.
In&Uit Brugge branch (Map p123; ☺ 9.30am-12.30pm & 1-5pm Tue-Sat) Near the ticket counters.

TRAVEL AGENCIES

Airstop (Map p126; ☎ 070 23 31 88; Dweersstraat 2) Offers cheap charter flights.
Connections (Map p126; ☎ 050 34 10 11; St Jakobsstraat 30) All-round travel agent.
Reizen Wasteels (Map p126; ☎ 050 33 65 31; Geldmuntstraat 30a) Eurolines agent.

Sights

AROUND MARKT & BURG

Bruges' nerve centre is the historic Markt, a large open square flanked by medieval-style buildings and bustling with horse-drawn carriages, open-air restaurants and camera-clicking tourists. Standing tall at its centre is a **monument** (Map p126) to Pieter De Coninck

BRUGES

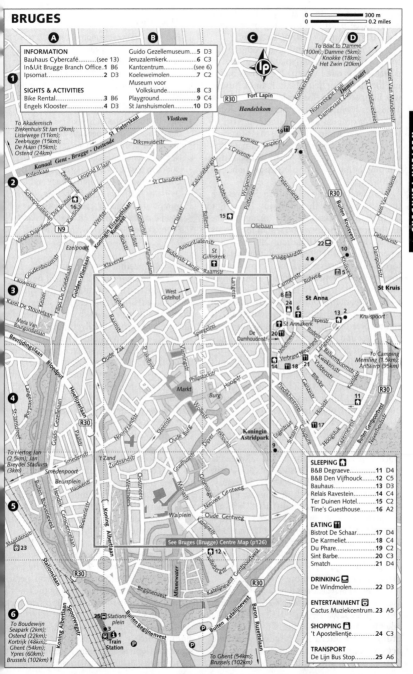

0 _____ 300 m
0 _____ 0.2 miles

INFORMATION
Bauhaus Cybercafé..........(see 13)
In&Uit Brugge Branch Office.**1** B6
Ipsomat.............................**2** D3

SIGHTS & ACTIVITIES
Bike Rental.......................**3** B6
Engels Klooster................**4** D3

Guido Gezellemuseum....**5** D3
Jeruzalemkerk................**6** C3
Kantcentrum.................(see 6)
Koeleweimolen...............**7** C2
Museum voor
    Volkskunde.................**8** C3
Playground....................**9** C4
St Janshuismolen..........**10** D3

WESTERN FLANDERS

SLEEPING 🛏
B&B Degraeve..............**11** D4
B&B Den Vijfhouck........**12** C5
Bauhaus.......................**13** D3
Relais Ravestein...........**14** C4
Ter Duinen Hotel..........**15** C2
Tine's Guesthouse........**16** A2

EATING 🍴
Bistrot De Schaar..........**17** D4
De Karmeliet................**18** C4
Du Phare......................**19** C2
Sint Barbe....................**20** C3
Smatch.........................**21** D4

DRINKING 🍺
De Windmolen..............**22** D3

ENTERTAINMENT 🎭
Cactus Muziekcentrum..**23** A5

SHOPPING 🛍
't Apostelientje............**24** C3

TRANSPORT
De Lijn Bus Stop...........**25** A6

and Jan Breydel, the leaders of the Brugse Metten (see p120), and lording over everything is the fabulous belfry (see below).

Most of the gabled guildhalls edging the Markt are not original. Notable at Markt 16 is **Craenenburg café** (Map p126); in this building the Hapsburg heir Maximilian of Austria was imprisoned by the leaders of the city in 1488 after attempting to restrict their privileges. When Maximilian later became emperor, he took revenge by directing trade to Antwerp.

The Markt's eastern side is dominated by the **Provinciaal Hof** (Map p126), a neogothic building home to the post office and a handy ATM.

Smaller but arguably more impressive than the Markt is the adjoining Burg. For more than five centuries the former palace on this majestic site was the seat of the counts of Flanders. The St Donatian Cathedral also stood here until 1799, when religious zealots tore it down. These days the Burg contains the city's most appealing cluster of buildings, plus the contemporary **Toyo Ito pavilion** (Map p126), a geometric bunker that sits in a pool of stagnant water opposite the city hall. To some it creates an image of lightness, progress, transience and evolution; to others it's simply a form that gets the cold shoulder.

Rising 83m above the Markt is Belgium's most famous **Belfort** (Belfry; Map p126; adult/child/concession €5/free/3; ⏰ 9.30am-5pm, last tickets sold 4.15pm). Built in the 13th century when Bruges was a bustling centre of trade, it's now on Unesco's World Heritage List (one of 32 Belgian belfries to be listed). The 366 steps to the top are an exhausting and usually squeezy climb but are well worth it, particularly in the afternoon when the view reveals the town's rustic roofs and warm tones. On the way up there's a barred treasury, a triumphal bell, the clock and, further up, the 18th-century *beiaard* (carillon). Its 47 bells are still played manually by **Aimé Lombaert** (⏰ 9-10pm Mon, Wed & Sat, 2.15-3pm Sun mid-Jun–Sep, 2.15-3pm Wed, Sat & Sun Oct–mid-Jun). The grand building from which the Belfort soars is the Hallen (Halls), a 13th-century (but frequently restored) former marketplace with a massive central courtyard.

The **Heilig-Bloedbasiliek** (Basilica of the Holy Blood; Map p126; Burg 5; ⏰ 9.30-11.50am & 2-5.50pm Apr-Sep, 10-11.50am & 2-3.50pm Thu-Tue, 10-11.50am Wed Oct-Mar) takes its name from the relic of Christ's blood brought here after the Crusades, sometime between 1150 and 1200. The church has two distinct and highly contrasting sections: the

sombre 12th-century lower chapel, built along pure Romanesque lines and almost devoid of decoration, and the much-renovated and lavishly embellished upper chapel, accessed by wide stairs near the lower chapel's entrance. In the upper chapel is the silver tabernacle containing the phial that holds a few drops of the holy blood. This relic is still venerated in one-hour services at 10am and 3pm every Friday. On Ascension Day it is paraded through the city in Bruges' biggest annual event, the Heilig-Bloedprocessie (see p132). Duck into the pint-sized **Museum of the Holy Blood** (adult/child €1.50/free) next door to see the jewel-coated reliquary that holds the phial during the procession.

Bruges boasts Belgium's oldest, and arguably most beautiful, **stadhuis** (city hall; Map p126; Burg 12). Built between 1376 and 1420, its exquisite turreted Gothic stone façade is decorated with replica statues of the counts and countesses of Flanders (the originals were torn down in 1792 by French soldiers). Inside, a few rooms are open to the public but the chief attraction is the 1st-floor **Gotische Zaal** (Gothic Hall; Map p126; adult/child/concession €2.50/free/1.50, admission includes entry to nearby Brugse Vrije; ⏰ 9.30am-5pm). The hall's polychromatic ceiling almost drips with medieval carvings, and murals depicting the town's history add to the room's magnificence. Pick up an audio-guide before setting off.

Just one exhibit – an immense 16th-century chimneypiece – draws visitors to the Renaissancezaal (Renaissance Hall) of the **Brugse Vrije** (Liberty of Bruges; Map p126; Burg 11a; adult/child/concession

€2.50/free/1.50, admission includes entry to nearby stadhuis; 9.30am-12.30pm & 1.30-5pm). This hall was the alderman's room of the palace of the Liberty of Bruges, a medieval administrative body. Completed in 1531, the chimney's upper section is a detailed oak carving depicting Emperor Charles V alongside an entourage of relatives; black marble and an alabaster frieze adorn the lower part. All in all it's pretty impressive, even without the men's overblown medieval codpieces.

Devoted to all things dark and delicious, **Choco-Story** (Map p126; ☎ 050 61 22 37; www.choco story.be; Wijnzakstraat 2; adult/child €6/4; 10am-5pm) is definitely Belgium's best chocolate museum. Wander past exhibits detailing everything from cocoa-growing to the virtues of hot chocolate, before sampling pralines made as you watch.

SOUTH OF MARKT
Groeningemuseum
Bruges' prized collection of art dating from the 14th to the 20th century is housed in the small **Groeningemuseum** (Map p126; Dijver 12; adult/child/concession €8/free/5; 9.30am-5pm Tue-Sun). Following a radical and quite controversial re-vamp a few years ago, the Flemish Primitives no longer hold pride of place and the artworks are now not presented in strict chronological order. If sequence is your thing, start in Room 2, then backtrack to Room 1 and from there proceed through the rest of the museum. Free English-language booklets and audio-guides are available at the entrance.

Room 1, entitled Municipal Patronage, concentrates on works from the 15th and 16th centuries, many of which were commissioned by the city of Bruges. The gruesome *Judgement of Cambyses* (1498) by Gerard David depicts the Persian king being led from his throne and flayed alive. Here too is *The Last Judgement*, a fantastically nightmarish work by Hieronymus Bosch. It's filled with fire and mayhem, men and nuns being boiled alive and strange creatures devouring everything in sight.

Room 2 presents the Flemish Primitives. Most notable are works by Jan Van Eyck, who is generally considered to be the first great master of this period (see boxed text, below). Van Eyck's masterpiece *Madonna with Canon George Van der Paele* (1436) is a radiant portrayal of the Madonna and the infant Jesus surrounded by

---

THE FLEMISH PRIMITIVES

The period of the Flemish Primitives was one of Belgium's most glorious artistic times. Artists were commissioned to record the lifestyles of the ruling class as well as religious works. Their work was characterised by the use of radiant colours and intricate detail, which brought texture and subjects to life. These artists and artworks greatly influenced the course of European art and, centuries later, still astonish viewers.

Jan Van Eyck (c 1390–1441) Widely credited as the artist who invented oil painting. This isn't strictly true – what Van Eyck did was use oil as a medium for mixing colours instead of using the traditional, less-resilient tempera (an egg-based substance). He lived in Bruges but worked both there and in Ghent. His most celebrated artwork is *The Adoration of the Mystic Lamb* (1426–32), painted for Ghent's cathedral (p161). It's one of the world's greatest art treasures and a must-see.

Rogier Van der Weyden (c 1400–64) Succeeded Van Eyck as court painter to Philip the Good, and followed the style of his predecessor, blending religious emotion with sharp realism. Van der Weyden became the town painter for Brussels and executed works for the Hôtel de Ville (Town Hall) there, though many were destroyed during 1695's French bombardment. One of his masterpieces, *De Kruisafneming* (The Descent of the Cross), now hangs in Madrid's Museo del Prado, but a few are on display in Bruges' Groeningemuseum (above).

Hans Memling (c 1440–94) Frankfurt-born Memling was one of the most acclaimed artists of his day. He carefully composed paintings and expertly used colour to faithfully recreate God's material world. Bruges is the place to see his works. His famous *Moreel Triptych* (1484), named after Willem Moreel, Bruges' mayor, was innovative in its use of true perspective and is displayed in the Groeningemuseum. A handful of other works can be seen at Bruges' Museum St Janshospitaal (p128).

Gerard David (c 1460–1523) Arrived in Bruges from the Netherlands in the 1480s and succeeded Memling as Bruges' premier painter. As events would have it, he became the last great artist of this era because Bruges' fortunes waned and Antwerp, the great port city to the northeast, became the focus of Belgium's next artistic period.

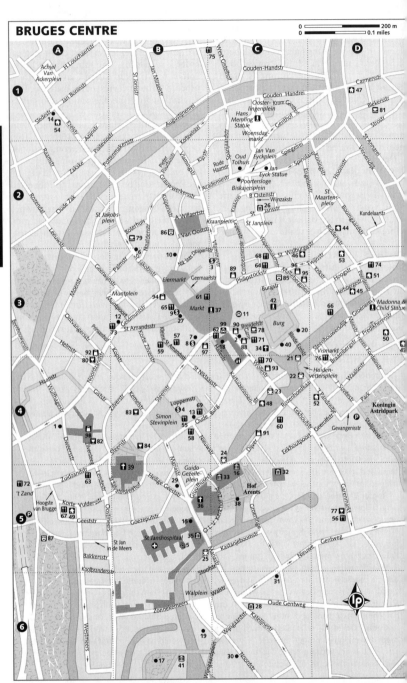

BRUGES CENTRE

three figures: the kneeling canon and, next to him, St George (his patron saint), while a richly clothed St Donatian looks on. The textures and detail are almost photographic – to viewers in the 15th century the portrait must have appeared incredible. Also in this room is Van Eyck's very honest portrait of his wife, Margaret. Here too is Hans Memling's *Moreel Triptych,* in which the serious central scene of brown-garbed saints is offset by fine detail such as the cheeky grin on a nearby child or the priest petting a deer.

Room 3 moves on to the Renaissance in Bruges, with several works by Jan Provoost and Pieter Pourbus. The latter is noted for his stern portraits. Rooms 4 to 8 explore baroque, neoclassicism and symbolism, as well as sculpture.

Room 9 is given over to Belgian modern art from early last century, and includes works by Henry Van de Velde, Jean Brusselmans and Rik

Wouters, as well as several dark pieces by Constant Permeke. Dominating the whole scene is the *Last Supper* (1929) by Gustave Van de Woestyne, one of the expressionists who set up at St Martens-Latem near Ghent early in the 20th century. Surrealism also gets a look in, with the movement's pivotal figure, René Magritte, represented by *L'Attentat* (The Assault; 1932). There's also Paul Delvaux's strange *Sérénité.*

Rooms 10 and 11 focus on more-recent modern art, with Pierre Alechinsky's *The Three Days* (1959) a highlight.

Other Sights

Occupying a stately 18th-century patrician house formerly owned by the Arents family, the **Arentshuis** (Map p126; Dijver 16; adult/child/ concession €2.50/free/1.50; ☉ 9.30am-5pm Tue-Sun) divides into two. The ground floor is reserved for temporary exhibitions while upstairs is given over to the powerful paintings and

INFORMATION
Airstop...1 A4
Apotheek Dryepondt...................2 C3
ATM Europabank........................3 C3
ATM Fortis Bank.........................4 B4
ATM.......................................(see 11)
Coffee Link..................................5 B5
Connections.................................6 B3
De Reyghere................................7 B3
Goffin Change.............................8 B3
In&Uit Brugge.......................(see 87)
ING Bank.....................................9 B3
Openbare Bibliotheek
    Biekorf....................................10 B3
Post Office..................................11 C3
Reizen Wasteels.........................12 B3
Varicopy.....................................13 B4
Wassalon....................................14 A1

SIGHTS & ACTIVITIES
Apotheek...................................15 B3
Arentshuis..................................16 C5
Begijnhof....................................17 B6
Belfort..18 C3
Brouwerij De Halve Maan.........19 B6
Brugse Vrije................................20 C3
Canal Cruises..............................21 C4
Canal Cruises..............................22 C4
Canal Cruises..............................23 C4
Canal Cruises..............................24 C4
Canal Cruises..............................25 B5
Choco-Story...............................26 C2
Craenenburg Café.......................27 B3
Diamantmuseum........................28 C6
Fietsen Popelier..........................29 B5
Godshuis De Vos........................30 C6
Godshuis St Jozef &
    De Meulenaere........................31 C6
Gotische Zaal.......................(see 40)
Groeningemuseum.....................32 C5
Gruuthuse..................................33 C5
Heilig-Bloedbasiliek...................34 C3

Museum of the Holy Blood.....(see 34)
Museum St Janshospitaal..........35 B5
Onze Lieve Vrouwekerk............36 B5
Pieter De Coninck & Jan
    Breydel Monument................37 C3
Provinciaal Hof......................(see 11)
St Bonifaciusbrug......................38 C5
St Salvatorskathedraal...............39 B5
Stadhuis.....................................40 C3
't Begijnhuisje............................41 B6
Toyo Ito Pavilion......................42 C3

SLEEPING 🛏
B&B Dieltiens............................43 D3
B&B Gheeraert...........................44 D2
B&B Huyze Hertsberge..............45 D3
B&B Setola.................................46 C3
Hotel Adornes............................47 D1
Hotel De Orangerie...................48 C4
Hotel Lybeer..............................49 A5
Huyze De Blokfluit.....................50 D3
Number 11.................................51 D3
Pand Hotel.................................52 D4
Ridderspoor................................53 D3
Snuffel.......................................54 A1

EATING 🍴
Bhavani......................................55 B4
Christophe..................................56 D5
De Belegde Boterham................57 B3
De Koetse..................................58 B4
De Stove....................................59 B3
Den Dyver.................................60 C4
Food & Flower Market...............61 B3
Frietkotjes..................................62 C3
GB Express.................................63 A5
Het Dagelijks Brood..................64 B3
Huyze Die Maene.......................65 B3
Kaffee Pergola...........................66 D3
Lokkedize..................................67 A5
Lotus...68 C3
Louis Delhaize............................69 B4

Mezzogiorno..............................70 C4
Opus Latino...............................71 C3
Produce Market.........................72 A5
Proxy/Delhaize...........................73 B3
Ryad..74 D3
Tom's Diner...............................75 C1
Vismarket..................................76 D4

DRINKING 🍷 🍺
Bolero..77 D5
De Garre....................................78 C3
De Republiek.............................79 B2
Est Wijnbar................................80 A4
Herberg Vlissinghe....................81 D1
Joey's Café.................................82 A4
't Brugs Beertje.........................83 B4
Top..84 B4

ENTERTAINMENT 🎭
Celtic Ireland.............................85 C3
Cinema Liberty...........................86 B2
Cinema Lumière....................(see 79)
Concertgebouw..........................87 A5

SHOPPING 🛍
B..(see 93)
Bottle Shop................................88 C3
Chocolatier Van Oost ....(see 88)
De Biertempel............................89 C3
Delvaux......................................90 C3
Dijver Antique Market...............91 C4
Galler....................................(see 97)
L'Héroïne...................................92 A3
Mille-Fleurs...............................93 C4
Olivier Strelli.............................94 B3
Rombaux...................................95 C3
Secondo.....................................96 C3
Tintin Shop................................97 B3
Zilverpand 98 A4

TRANSPORT
Taxi Rank...................................99 C3

etchings of Frank Brangwyn (1867–1956), a Bruges-born artist of British parentage. Industrial themes are his strong point, and the exhibition is well worth visiting if you're into sombre paintings of dockyards and the like.

The tree-lined square at the rear of the Arentshuis is **Hof Arents**, a tranquil respite from the busy Dijver. Sit and contemplate four sculptures by Rik Poot entitled *De Ruiters van de Apocalyps* (Riders of the Apocalypse) before exiting the square to discover a tranquil canal lined with timber houses – one of the most picturesque nooks in Bruges. The canal is backed by humped **St Bonifaciusbrug** (Map p126). Cross the bridge to find a tiny window at the back of the Gruuthuse museum – according to local belief, it's Europe's smallest Gothic window.

Applied and decorative arts are the themes of the **Gruuthuse** (Map p126; Dijver 17; adult/child/concession €6/free/4; 9.30am-5pm Tue-Sun). The museum takes its name from the flower and herb mixture – the *gruut* – traditionally used for brewing beer. Most of the exhibits are labelled in Flemish only. Still, it's well worth spending some time here for the superb local tapestries, furniture and sculptures.

The **Onze Lieve Vrouwekerk** (Church of Our Lady; Map p126; Mariastraat; adult/child/concession €2.50/free/1.50; 9.30am-5pm Mon-Sat, 1.30-5pm Sun) is a dark, sober building that dates from the 13th century and is most noted for its art treasures. Of these, the *Madonna and Child* by Michelangelo is the undisputed gem. This small marble statue (1504) was bought in Italy by a Bruges merchant and was the only work of art by Michelangelo to leave Italy in his lifetime. Although pilfered several times by occupying forces, the statue has always been returned. It's also possible to visit the tombs of Charles the Bold (Karel de Stoute) and his daughter, Mary of Burgundy.

The prestigious **Museum St Janshospitaal** (St John's Hospital Museum; Map p126; Mariastraat 38; adult/child/concession €8/free/5; 9.30am-5pm Tue-Sun) is housed in a restored chapel of a 12th-century hospital. It's home to six masterpieces by Hans Memling (see boxed text, p125), and works by lesser-known painters of that time. Memling is noted for the fine quality of the figures in his religious paintings, such as the central panel of the *Mystic Marriage of St Catherine* triptych (1479) that's presented here. Perhaps more enchanting is the reliquary of St Ursula. Shaped like a miniature wooden Gothic church, the reliquary's six painted panels depict the medieval tale of the beautiful St Ursula and the 11,000 virgins

who were massacred by the Huns in Germany while returning from a pilgrimage to Rome. The attention to detail is stunning.

Next to the museum is a restored 17th-century **apotheek** (pharmacy; Map p126), which originally belonged to the hospital. Feel free to wander in after visiting the museum.

The 13th-century **St Salvatorskathedraal** (St Saviour's Cathedral; Map p126; Steenstraat; 2-5.45pm Mon, 9am-noon & 2-5.45pm Tue-Fri, 9am-noon & 2-3.30pm Sat, 9-10am & 2-5pm Sun) is Bruges' oldest parish church. After years covered in scaffolding, the church's unusual 99m-high tower – incorporating turrets and spires with neo-Romanesque flair – is once again distinctly visible. Inside, the **Treasury** (adult/child €2.50/1.50; 2-5pm Sun-Fri) displays works by Dirk Bouts and Pourbus.

The slick **Diamantmuseum** (Diamond Museum; Map p126; 050 34 20 56; Katelijnestraat 43; admission €6; 10.30am-5.30pm) reveals Bruges' medieval role as the first diamond-polishing centre. It's home to the world's two smallest diamond sculptures – tiny profiles of the former King Baudouin and Queen Fabiola, each no more than 3mm in diameter. Even with a magnifying glass, it takes a sizable imagination to pick the resemblance. Diamond-polishing demonstrations are held at 12.15pm, and cost an extra €3.

Family brewery **Brouwerij De Halve Maan** (Map p126; 050 33 26 97; www.halvemaan.be; Walplein 26; admission €4.50; 11am-4pm Apr-Sep, 11am-3pm Oct-Mar), founded by Henri Maes in 1856, produces Straffe Hendrik (Strong Henry), a medium strong (7%) ale, and Straffe Hendrik Blonde, a golden ale. These beers took their names from the family's tradition of baptising the first-born son from each generation 'Henri'. Crowded guided tours (45 minutes; in Flemish, French and English all at once) wind their way up and down the brewing hall and through a museum to finish with a beer. Tours depart on the hour and can include as many as 50 people.

The serene **begijnhof** (Map p126; admission free; 9am-6.30pm) dates from the 13th century and was traditionally the home of Beguines (see boxed text, opposite). The modest but dignified whitewashed houses are these days home to some 50 single women of all ages. The large convent at the rear of the tree-lined square is inhabited by Benedictine nuns. In spring a carpet of daffodils covers the grass. All this quaintness makes it one of Bruges' top attractions – in summer loads of people wander around but, despite the numbers, it remains a tranquil haven and a 'must see'. Just

BEGIJNEN & BEGIJNHOVEN

Begijnhoven (*béguinage* in French) are clusters of small houses surrounded by a protective wall and built around a central garden and church. In a nutshell, they're a town within a town. They were built in the Low Countries in the 12th century by *Begijnen* (Beguines), a Catholic order of unmarried or widowed women. The order was established largely due to the gender imbalance caused by the Holy Land Crusades – large numbers of men embarked on these adventures but many never returned. With little prospect of marriage, some single women joined forces and set up religious communities that adhered to vows of obedience and chastity but not, unlike nuns, poverty. The women were often from wealthy families and devoted their time to caring for the elderly and sick, and to work such as making lace. Their communities were independent and the women earned their living from making textiles and from benefactors who would pay the Beguines to pray for them.

At the start of the 20th century there were about 1500 Beguines in Belgium but the order has now virtually died out. Flanders' many *begijnhoven*, however, still exist and are still lived in, these days by ordinary townsfolk. In 1998 Unesco added 14 of the country's 22 *begijnhoven* to its World Heritage List.

The best-preserved and most beautiful *begijnhoven* to visit are those in Diest (see St Katharina-begijnhof, p209), Lier (p200), Bruges (opposite) and Kortrijk (p157). The latter even offers overnight accommodation – see p159.

inside the main entrance is **'t Begijnhuisje** (Map p126; adult/student/senior €2/1/1.50; ☻ 10am-noon & 2-5pm Mon-Sat, 11am-noon & 2-5pm Sun). The *begijnhof* is a 10-minute walk south of the Markt – head down Steenstraat, crossing Simon Stevin-plein and walking down Mariastraat before turning into Wijngaardstraat, and you'll soon see the main entrance, across the humped bridge.

Known in English as the Lake of Love, the **Minnewater** (south of Walplein) harks back to Bruges' medieval heyday. This waterway was a dock from where ships as far afield as Russia came laden with cargoes of wool, wine, spices and silks and left loaded with Flemish cloth.

ST ANNA QUARTER

Most of the following sights are located in the St Anna quarter, or Verloren Hoek (Forgotten Corner) as it's nicknamed. This area is somewhat off the beaten track, and spreads out northeast of the Markt, east of St Anna-rei canal. It's largely a tranquil, residential quarter, dotted with churches, windmills and small museums.

The quarter's biggest attractions are the lace centre and adjacent church, occupying alms-houses in St Anna's heart. The **Kantcentrum** (Lace Centre; Map p123; www.kantcentrum.com; Peperstraat 3a; adult/child €2.50/1.50; ☻ 10am-noon & 2-6pm Mon-Fri, to 5pm Sat) is best known for its bobbin lace-making demonstrations – informal gatherings of 20 or so women who congregate (afternoons only) in a small room at the rear of the complex. It's

fascinating to watch, and a credit that these women are determinedly keeping the art form alive. The centre's lace museum displays a very modest collection of traditional lace.

The adjacent, onion-domed **Jeruzalemkerk** is more intriguing, built by the Adornes family in the 15th century as a replica of Jerusalem's Church of the Holy Sepulchre. It's a macabre monument. The dark, split-level church is dominated by a gruesome altarpiece (note the skulls and ladders) and the black-marble tomb of Anselm Adornes, whose heart was buried here after he was murdered in Scotland in 1483. To top it all off there's a replica of Christ's tomb, complete with imitation corpse.

The **Museum voor Volkskunde** (Folklore Museum; Map p123; Balstraat 43; adult/concession €3/2; ☻ 9.30am-5pm Tue-Sun) occupies a row of restored *godshuizen* (see boxed text, p130). Exhibits include an old Flemish kitchen, a hatter's shop and a 1930s-style *snoepwinkel* (sweet shop). One room has been converted into a café – De Zwarte Kat – serving drinks and snacks.

Flanders' best-known poet is celebrated at the **Guido Gezellemuseum** (Map p123; Rolweg 64; adult/concession €2/1; ☻ 9.30am-12.30pm & 1.30-5pm Tue-Sun). Gezelle became a cult figure among Flemish freethinkers in the early 20th century. He was born in 1830 in this house, which belonged to a noble family – his father was the gardener and Gezelle lived here until age 16, when he left to study at Roeselare (between Bruges and Kortrijk). The museum contains books and documents recalling his life and

---

GODSHUIZEN OF BRUGES

One of the delights of wandering around Bruges is the chance of coming across a complex of *godshuizen* (almshouses). These groups of terraced houses were built by merchant guilds for their members and by wealthy philanthropists for the poor and elderly. There are still 46 *godshuizen* in Bruges – the oldest date from the 14th century. The complexes are usually surrounded by a protective wall that encloses a central garden and chapel.

One of the town's cutest and most central *godshuizen* is **Godshuis De Vos** (Map p126; Noordstraat 2-8). It dates from 1713 but was restored in 1995. Another is **Godshuis St Jozef & De Meulenaere** (Map p126; Nieuwe Gentweg 8-32), which can be entered through large black doors. Two *godshuizen* have even been turned into museums – the Museum voor Volkskunde (p129) and the museum at the Kantcentrum (p129).

---

works, such as *The Evening and the Rose*, are sold at reception.

In the 13th century, Bruges' great walls were dotted with *molens* (windmills) where cereals were ground into flour. Four still stand on the eastern rampart and two can be visited: the 18th-century **St Janshuismolen** (Map p123; Kruisvest; adult/concession €2/1; ☺ 9.30am-12.30pm & 1.30-5pm Tue-Sun May-Aug, Sat & Sun Apr-Sep), and the nearby **Koeleweimolen** (Map p123; Kruisvest; ☺ 9.30am-12.30pm & 1.30-5pm Tue-Sun Jul & Aug). The sails are occasionally set in motion, and each houses a tiny museum.

The **Engels Klooster** (English Convent; Map p123; Carmersstraat 85; admission free; ☺ 2-3.30pm & 4.15-5.15pm Mon-Sat) was founded in 1629 by a community of canonesses (women who belong to a religious order but have not taken a vow) who fled England and, for many years, offered shelter to other Catholic exiles. One sister is on duty each day to give tours of the sumptuous baroque church. Just enter the courtyard, ring the bell and wait inside.

Activities

Saddle up – Bruges is ideal for cyclists. Either rent one and head off by yourself, or join a group (see p132). Stay around town – there's no better way to see a sizable swath of the city in a relatively short time – or head out along the Damse Vaart canal to Damme (30 minutes, 6km one way). Alternatively, the Riante Polder Route is a full-day excursion, clocking up 44km and taking in Damme and Knokke at the coast. Note that strong North Sea winds can make cycling impossible along the polders and the coast on windy days.

The Bruges tourist office has produced an English-language brochure for visiting cyclists entitled *5x on the Bike Around Bruges* (€1.50). It gives a map and good explanations of five possible routes ranging from 18km to 29km;

the Damme to Oostkerke route (23km) is picturesque.

Bike-rental outfits are abundant, and **Fietsen Popelier** (Map p126; ☎ 050 34 32 62; Mariastraat 26; normal bike per hr/half-/full day €3.50/7/10, tandem €8/15/22; ☺ 10am-6pm, to 8pm Jul & Aug) is recommended. Children's bikes (same prices as adults') are available, and baby/toddler seats and baskets are provided for free. Helmets can also be hired. No deposit required for bikes. The cycles here are in excellent condition, never more than six months old, with moulded seats, six gears and good suspension. Some regional cycling maps, including the Riante Polder Route, are sold.

It's also possible to rent bikes from the **train station** (Map p123; per half-/full day €6.50/9.50, deposit €12.50; ☺ 7am-8pm).

Walking Tour

The **Markt** (1; p122) is the natural starting point. After craning your neck here, sidestep the many horse-drawn carriages and jostle down Wollestraat, a shopping favourite, before crossing the canal to **Rozenhoedkaai** (2). This quay offers the city's best belfry shot – make a mental note to return later when it's stunningly illuminated against a dark evening sky.

Follow the canal to **Huidenvettersplein** (3), a charming square (lined with popular restaurants) that leads to the **Vismarkt** (4; p137), Bruges' morning fish market. Follow Steenhouwersdijk to the next bridge, where romantics might want to make a dinner booking at **Kaffee Pergola** (5; p135). Continue on **Groenerei** (6), a short but delightful promenade along a particularly pretty part of the city's canal system. At the corner of Groenerei and Peerdenstraat is a street-corner **statue** (7) of the Madonna and Child; such elevated statues are common in Flanders, although this one is unusual for its modern features.

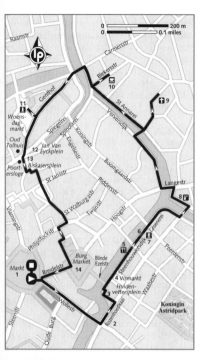

WALK FACTS

Start Markt
Finish Markt
Distance 2.8km
Duration About two hours

Groenerei peters out into a pedestrian walkway and curves sharply to a bridge. Cross the bridge and turn left, zigzagging your way past Predikherenrei's many terrace tables, to arrive at the confluence of two canals. Here there's a superb **view (8)** – at its best in the afternoon – of the city's turreted skyline.

The next part of the tour takes you off the beaten track to Bruges' less touristy quarters. Join Langestraat, cross the bridge, take the first right into Verversdijk and follow it to the first pedestrian bridge. Cross the canal to see **St Annakerk (9)**; this 15th-century church lends its name to the St Anna quarter that fans out east of here. Once across the canal, turn left and follow St Annarei to the next bridge, which marks the junction of two canals and offers a great view to the southwest of the

15th-century Poorterslodge (Burghers' Lodge). The city's wealthiest merchants once met in this slender-towered building. Opposite the Poortersloge is the Oud Tolhuis, where, until the 18th century, tolls were levied on goods being brought into the city.

Stop for a drink at Bruges' oldest *café* (pub), **Herberg Vlissinghe (10**; p137), or wander along Genthof to Woensdagmarkt to see a **statue of Hans Memling (11)**, erected in 1874. The Flemish Primitive artist is buried in St Gilliskerk, a few blocks further north. For a statue of the most famous artist of this genre, head to nearby **Jan Van Eyckplein (12)**. This square marks the end of a canal that was once crammed with boats en route to the Markt.

Head due south now through quiet residential backstreets, past the smell of warm chocolate emanating from **Choco-Story (13**; p125), to eventually join the **Burg (14**; p124). From here, navigate through the tourists swarming along Breidelstraat and you're back at the Markt.

Bruges for Children

Bruges is a great place to hang out with little kids, though you'll have to watch out for the open canals. Kids generally enjoy taking a **canal trip** (p132) or **horse-drawn carriage ride** (p132), or climbing the 366 steps up the **belfry** (p124). Taste-testing at **Choco-Story** (p125) or feeding the resident swans at the **Begijnhof** (p128) are also popular, as is the boat ride to **Damme** (p140). To let off steam, there's a popular **playground** (Map p123) at the southern end of Koningin Astridpark.

Cycling is fabulous for kids of various ages, and bikes can easily be hired (opposite). If your kids are young, the town centre is not the best place to safely cycle, and there are too many cobbles. Instead, make for the Minnewater, from where you can access the raised cycle path that circles the town. Head northeast on this path and you'll pass the windmills at Kruisvest. Continue north to reach the Noorweegse Kaai, the start of the Damse Vaart canal, which runs from Bruges to Damme (6km) and is flanked by a great cycling path. Alternatively, join a QuasiMundo tour (p132) – staff provide baby seats or 'third-wheels' (p304), and children under eight years go for free.

Boudewijn Seapark (☎ 050 40 84 08; www.boudewijn seapark.be; A Debaeckestraat 12, St Michiels; over/under 12yr €21/18, children under 1m free; ⏰ 10am-5pm Thu-Tue Apr-Jun, 10am-6pm Thu-Tue Jul & Aug, 10am-5pm Wed, Sat & Sun Sep) is a theme park with rides, a big playground, a mini-train, ice-skating in winter and a controversial dolphinarium (a US dolphin psychologist recently found the animals living under constant stress). It's about 2km south of Bruges, and can be reached on bus 7 or 17 from 't Zand or Biekorf.

Other regional theme parks are **Plopsaland** (p148) and **Earth Explorer** (p142).

Kids love the Belgian coast and it's within spitting distance of Bruges – 20 minutes by car to **De Haan** (p145), or 15 minutes by train to Ostend. If you choose the latter, remember there's a 1km walk from the train station to **Ostend beach** (p141), or simply jump on the **Kusttram** (Coast Tram; see boxed text, p145). With luck, you may even catch *paardevissers* (horseback fishermen) at Oostduinkerke (p147).

The **Gezinsbond** (☎ 0479 76 22 10; www.gezinsbond .be) has baby-sitters, but it's not as easy as just phoning and delivering (see p304).

Tours

BIKE TOURS

Cycle tours are big business in Bruges, and several companies offer three- to four-hour tours of the town and/or the surrounding countryside. **QuasiMundo** (☎ 050 33 07 75; www.quasimundo.com; under/ over 26yr €18/20, with own bike €14; ☺ mid-Mar–mid-Oct) is highly recommended. The guy who runs this company has been involved in cycle tourism for more than a decade. Three tours with English commentary are offered: a 2½-hour (8km) tour of Bruges; a four-hour (25km) cycle to the Dutch border and back via Damme; or tours of Bruges by night. Bookings are necessary.

CANAL TOURS

Taking a **canal tour** (adult/child €5.70/2.80; ☺ 10am-6pm Mar–mid-Nov) is a must. Yep, it's touristy, but what isn't in Bruges? Viewing the city from the water gives it a totally different feel than by foot. Cruise down Spiegelrei towards Jan Van Eyckplein and it's possible to imagine Venetian merchants entering the city centuries ago and meeting under the slender turret of the Poortersloge building up ahead. Boats depart roughly every 20 minutes from jetties south of the Burg, including Rozenhoedkaai and Dijver, and tours last 30 minutes. Expect queues in summer.

HORSE-DRAWN CARRIAGE RIDES

The clip-clop of hooves hitting cobblestones resounds constantly in the streets of Bruges. In summer, aim to jump on board between 6pm and 7pm – by this time day-trippers have left the city, locals are stirring dinner at home, and most tourists are taking a shower. Bruges' streets take on a semitranquil air at this time of day, and the gold-topped buildings shimmer in the late sun rays. All the carriages depart from the Markt, and their well-trodden route takes 35 minutes (including a pit stop at the Begijnhof). The cost is €30 (for five people).

MINIBUS TOURS

Quasimodo (☎ 0800 975 25; www.quasimodo.be; under/ over 26yr €40/50) is a small company that's been offering two excellent day trips for years. The Triple Treat tour explores Damme plus nearby castles and promises a waffle, beer and chocolate at various establishments around Bruges. The Flanders Fields tour takes in Ypres and its famous WWI battlefields. The price includes all admission charges and a picnic lunch. Reservations are necessary. Both trips (9am to 5pm) operate Tuesday to Sunday from April to October. The rest of the year there's a Triple Treat tour on Monday, Wednesday and Friday, and a Flander's Field tour on Tuesday, Thursday and Sunday. Tours don't run between mid-December and mid-February.

Sightseeing Line (☎ 050 35 80 24; www.citytour.be; adult/child €11.50/6.50; ☺ 10am-8pm Jul-Sep, 10am-6pm Apr-Jun & Oct, 10am-5pm Mar, Nov & Dec, 10am-4pm Jan & Feb) runs a don-your-multilingual-headphone, 50-minute minibus City Tour, leaving the Markt hourly.

Festivals & Events

Bruges Festival Musica Antiqua (www.musica-anti qua.com) Week-long music festival in early February.
Cinema Novo Film Festival (www.cinemanovo.be) Ten-day festival in mid-March that highlights Asian, African and Latin American films.
Heilig-Bloedprocessie (www.holyblood.com) The Holy Blood Procession is Bruges' most famous annual event. It's held at 3pm on Ascension Day (17 May 2007, 1 May 2008 and 21 May 2009) and celebrates the drops of Christ's blood that are kept in the town's basilica. The relic is paraded through town in an elaborate, medieval-style procession. Tickets for a grandstand/bench seat on the Markt cost €11/4.75 and are sold in In&Uit Brugge (see p122).
Cactus Festival (www.cactusmusic.be in Flemish) Two-day festival of world music held on the second weekend of July at the Minnewater.
Praalstoet van de Gouden Boom The Pageant of the Golden Tree has been held roughly every five years since 1958 (the next is 4pm on 25 and 26 August 2007). It celebrates the marriage of Charles the Bold (Karel de Stoute) to Margaret of York in 1468.

Sleeping

Bruges has a wealth of accommodation. All options are oppressively overbooked during the high season, which starts soon after Easter and lasts until October (sometimes longer). Most places don't charge more in the high season. The tourist office will book accommodation for free.

Like B&Bs, self-contained guesthouses and holiday flats are booming in Bruges. The tourist office's brochure *Logies* details many. Inquire about discounted rates in winter, and for stays of more than three nights.

BUDGET

Camping Memling (☎ 050 35 58 45; www.campingmemling.be; Veltemweg 109, St Kruis; camp sites per adult/child/tent/car €5/3/4/5; ☿ year-round) The quietest local camping ground, located in St Kruis, about 2.5km east of town. Take bus 11 from the train station to the Vossensteert stop and walk 400m back in the direction of Bruges.

Snuffel (Map p126; ☎ 050 33 31 33; www.snuffel.be; Ezelstraat 47-49; dm/d per person €14/18; ✗ ▣) Funky, unpretentious place that's been around for years and is the most 'alternative' hostel in Bruges. The rooms are basic but original, the staff is friendly, and there's a kitchen, bar and occasional live music. From the train station take bus 3 or 13 and get off at the first stop after the Markt.

Bauhaus (Map p123; ☎ 050 34 10 93; www.bauhaus.be; Langestraat 135; hostel dm/d/tr per person €15/17/19, hotel s/d €28/44, flats per person €25; ▣) This place just keeps growing. It started life as a bustling hostel and over the years has added a hotel section and, more recently, self-contained flats. It's one of the most popular hang-outs for young travellers, though the blue rooms hardly fuel the imagination. The double rooms in the hotel section have private shower cubicles; elsewhere there are communal bathrooms. The spacious apartments, located above the new reception

and internet café, are good value but have simple (almost makeshift) furnishings. Bauhaus has a bar and adjoining café that are lively and loud, and good cheap meals are available. Take bus 6 or 16 from the train station.

B&B Degraeve (Map p123; ☎ 050 34 57 11; www.stardekk.com/bedbreakfast; Kazernevest 32; s/d/tr €33/45/58) In a quiet, untouristed part of town and owned by a good-humoured woman, Marjan, who has filled the two spacious rooms with way-out décor. Expect religious trinkets, stuffed swans and a delicious homemade sweet apple wine. Breakfast is taken in your room, and the bathroom facilities are shared.

Hotel Lybeer (Map p126; ☎ 050 33 43 55; www.hotellybeer.com; Korte Vuldersstraat 31; s/d/tr/q with bathroom €38/55/72/90, s/d without bathroom €25/45; ☿ closed last fortnight Jun; ▣) Half a step up from your average hostel. Located in a typical Bruges terrace house that's 'just clean enough to be healthy, just dirty enough to be happy', according to a sign at reception. It's run-down in parts – peeling paintwork, scruffy carpet and cracked walls – but the rooms have colourful décor and a hotchpotch of furnishings. There's a bar and kitchen.

MIDRANGE

B&B Gheeraert (Map p126; ☎ 050 33 56 27; www.users.skynet.be/brugge-gheeraert; Riddersstraat 9; s/d/tr €55/60/80, €10 extra for 1-night stay; ✗ ▣) The three lofty rooms at this B&B are lovely. Occupying the top floor (up a steep spiral staircase) of a listed historic mansion just 300m from the Burg, the rooms are spacious, and have white décor and polished timber floors. The two nicest rooms, at the rear, look out over the garden. Breakfast is taken in the family's dining room, and there's also a small salon for guests to use. Children and babies (cot and highchair available) are welcome.

B&B Dieltiens (Map p126; ☎ 050 33 42 94; www.bedandbreakfastbruges.be; Waalsestraat 40; s/d/tr €55/65/85,

---

THE AUTHOR'S CHOICE

B&B Setola (Map p126; ☎ 050 33 49 77; www.bedandbreakfast-bruges.com; St Walburgastraat 12; s/d/tr/f €50/60/80/100, €10 extra for 1 night stay; ✗) If you want to stay right under the belfry, or thereabouts, don't go past this vibrant B&B. Located on a quiet backstreet a few minutes' walk from the Markt, it occupies a mansion dating from 1740 and has three spacious 2nd-floor guestrooms with cool, clean vibes. One room can even accommodate a family with two older kids (they'll need to climb a steep ladder to a mezzanine bed). A fabulous buffet breakfast tops it all off and Lut, the woman who runs this B&B, is as helpful and hospitable as they come. Children and babies (cot and highchair available) are genuinely welcome.

€10 extra for 1-night stay) This place is run by a very friendly couple, Annemie and Koen, who've welcomed visitors for well over a decade – and their hospitality still shines. Their classical-style home occupies a mansion that featured on the first map of Bruges, published in the 16th century. Lovingly restored, the house has three polished guestrooms, all with private facilities and TV, situated on the top (2nd) floor. Wooden floors, subtle warm tones and modern furnishings are the theme throughout.

Tine's Guesthouse (Map p123; ☎ 050 34 50 18; www
.tinesguesthouse.com; Zwaluwenstraat 11; s/d/f €55/65/124; ✗)
If you don't want the carillon within cooee, consider heading here. For service, you'll find no better. This B&B is run by the wonderfully effervescent Tine, whose mission in life is to spoil visitors – she'll happily pick you up from the train station and, as the B&B is located 1.5km north of the Markt, she provides free bikes. Oh, there's also a free packed lunch to follow the awesome breakfast. The two rooms – plus kitchen, lounge room and small patio – have fresh décor and are situated on the 1st floor of the house next door to Tine's. If you're travelling with kids, this place is ideal, and there's free street parking.

Huyze De Blokfluit (Map p126; ☎ 050 33 42 94; www
.bedandbreakfastbruges.be; Peerdenstraat 16; studio for 2
people €65, apt €75, per extra guest per night €10; ☐ ✗)
This cute 17th-century terrace house is divided into a small ground-floor studio and a slightly larger 1st-floor duplex apartment. Neither place is huge, but neither are the prices. Furnishings are simple but authentic and, as it's owned by the couple who operate B&B Dieltiens, attention to detail is paramount.

B&B Den Vijfhouck (Map p123; ☎ 050 34 44 02; www
.denvijfhouck.be; Sulferbergstraat 1; s/d €70/75, €10 extra for
1-night stay) One block south of the Begijnhof,

this beautiful little grey corner cottage is almost like a mini boutique hotel. Rooms are pristine and service is immaculate, and Janien, the woman who runs this place, is a joy.

Ridderspoor (Map p126; ☎ 050 34 90 11; www
.ridderspoor.be; Riddersstraat 9; studio for 2 people €75, apt €85,
per extra guest per night €10; ☐ ✗) This is a superb address in a neoclassical mansion in the heart of town. All the rooms are fully equipped with kitchen, washing machine and spacious living areas. Choose from the attic loft (two people) with its wonderful belfry view, or one of three larger apartments (four to six people).

Ter Duinen Hotel (Map p123; ☎ 050 33 04 37; www.ter
duinenhotel.be; Langerei 52; s/d from €98/105; ✗) A little hotel facing a canal, just over 1km north of the Markt. The neat rooms have a refined, romantic air and the staff is efficient and friendly. Prices depend on room size and location – front rooms with a canal view are dearer. The long breakfast room looks out onto a pretty paved courtyard.

Hotel Adornes (Map p126; ☎ 050 34 13 36; www
.adornes.be; St Annarei 26; s/d/f from €95/110/140; ✗ closed
Jan-15 Feb) Pleasant hotel with a rustic feel that occupies three old gabled houses in the often-overlooked St Anna quarter. The 20 rooms are all modern and there's a good buffet breakfast, complimentary parking, free bikes and a crackling open fire in the breakfast room. Rates as one of the friendliest and most helpful midrange hotels in Bruges. Baby cots are available (€10), and a child's bed costs €15.

B&B Huyze Hertsberge (Map p126; ☎ 050 33 35 42;
www.huyzehertsberge.be; Hertsbergestraat 8; d €120-145)
One of the city's newest B&B addresses, and a must for antique aficionados. Run by charming Caroline Van Langeraert, this mocha-toned townhouse on a quiet back lane in the city heart has been in Caroline's family for four generations. The four spacious rooms

---

THE AUTHOR'S CHOICE

Number 11 (Map p126; ☎ 050 33 06 75; www.number11.be; Peerdenstraat 11; d €115-140, ste €215) There's no mincing words – this is a stunner. The couple who run it, Annie and artist husband, Pavel, offer travellers the intimacy of a boutique hotel combined with the personal charm of a B&B. It's housed in a charcoal-coloured terrace house in the historic centre. The three rooms – 'Vanilla', 'Grey' and 'Chocolate' – bathe in individual charm but harmonise as a whole. Antique furnishings sit alongside Pavel's philosophical artworks, a claw-foot tub (the Vanilla room) reclines next to a modern vanity unit, a sunken bath (Chocolate) looks out over exposed attic beams. The ground-floor suite (a small self-contained apartment) opens onto the home's trim terrace garden. The breakfast room, with its communal dining table, shares this view. Guests have a salon for their exclusive use, which is overseen by the most kooky chandelier you'll ever see.

are each elegantly different from the next, and the pristine breakfast room has views to a tranquil canalside garden where guests are free to while away spare moments.

TOP END

Pand Hotel (Map p126; ☎ 050 34 06 66; www.pand hotel.com; 't Pandreitje 16; s/d/ste from €125/150/225; ✗ ✗ ➖) Boutique hotel, hidden away on a tree-lined backstreet just a few minutes' walk from the Markt and very much for lovers of luxury. A former 18th-century carriage house, it sports 26 rooms, each individual and loaded with antiques and *objets d'art* (the family who owns the hotel also runs an antique shop). The more expensive rooms have Jacuzzis, and the suites are draped in rich Ralph Lauren fabrics. Breakfast is served in a virginal white dining room.

Hotel De Orangerie (Map p126; ☎ 050 34 16 49; www.hotelorangerie.com; Kartuizerinnenstraat 10; s/d/t €170/195/250; ➖ ➘) Refined but friendly 20-room hotel that started out as a 15th-century convent and boasts a canalside position (close to the Markt) that's impossible to beat. The hotel's façade is one of the prettiest scenes in Bruges. Avoid room No 103 – it's something of an afterthought. Breakfast's available for €19.

Relais Ravestein (Map p123; ☎ 050 47 69 47; www.relais ravestein.be; Molenmeers 11; d from €248; ➖) Hip new canalside hotel that offers a beautiful marriage between classic grandeur and contemporary chic. Exposed beams in the bedrooms vie for attention with bubble baths and so-called 'tropical rain' showers (ie blast yourself with 36L of water per minute – lucky Belgium's not suffering from drought, yet).

Eating

From cosy *estaminets* (taverns) to first-class restaurants – Bruges has all bases covered.

CAFÉS & BRASSERIES

Huyze Die Maene (Map p126; ☎ 050 33 39 59; Markt 17; mains €10-14; ✦ lunch & dinner Wed-Mon) A classic brasserie in a prime position on the Markt. Great for a casual lunch or dinner. Limited Flemish cuisine is backed by friendly service.

Lokkedize (Map p126; ☎ 050 33 44 50; Korte Vulderstraat 33; dishes €10-14; ✦ from 6pm Tue-Sun) Good spot for a late-night bite. An open fire and moody music ensure return patronage. Meals are typically Mediterranean, such as meze or moussaka, and the kitchen stays open 'til midnight, sometimes later.

Du Phare (Map p123; ☎ 050 34 35 90; www.duphare.be; Sasplein 2; mains €11-18; ✦ 11.30am until late, closed Tue) Off-the-beaten-track tavern serving everything from kangaroo steaks to ostrich or carpaccio. The generous servings, great atmosphere and reasonable prices ensure its popularity in this unvisited quarter. Known also for its monthly live blues/jazz session (check the website for dates). Bus 4 stops out the front.

Mezzogiorno (Map p126; ☎ 050 33 42 29; Wollestraat 25/3; mains €14-16; ✦ noon-6pm, closed Wed) Contemporary Italian *café* that's proves Bruges is not all old hat. Head up the cement steps near design shop B and enter a world where modern décor and fresh food are paramount.

Opus Latino (Map p126; ☎ 050 33 97 46; Breidelstraat 24; mains €14-17; ✦ lunch & dinner, closed Wed) Hidden down a narrow cobbled alley on the busy link between the Markt and Burg, most tourists miss this funky brasserie – don't make the same mistake. Local demand is high for the few canalside tables. The cuisine is modern, and prices refreshingly low for this part of town.

RESTAURANTS

Lotus (Map p126; ☎ 050 33 10 78; Wapenmakerstraat 5; ✦ 11.45am-2pm Mon-Sat) Quaint lunchtime restaurant catering to those who love colourful healthy meals. The cuisine is vegetarian and the menu consists of two choices: a *kleine maaltijd* (small meal; €9.20), or a good-value *grote* (large) version (€10).

Sint Barbe (Map p123; ☎ 050 33 09 99; De Damhouderstraat 29; mains €10-17; ✦ lunch Thu-Tue, dinner Thu-Mon) Hidden away opposite St Anna church, this

---

THE AUTHOR'S CHOICE

Kaffee Pergola (Map p126; ☎ 050 44 76 50; Steenhouwersdijk; mains €20-23; ✦ closed dinner Tue & Wed) Follow the fairy lights to this most romantic of outdoor addresses, hidden among greenery beside a quiet and very picturesque stretch of canal right in the centre of Bruges. Book one of the four tables perched along the canal, and settle back to the sound of birdsong and the glow of fading light as evening mellows. A limited range of delicious Belgian specialities is offered, and the service is attentive. This place is owned and operated by the discreet top-end Hotel Die Swaene, located across the canal, and though relatively new is highly popular.

confident little restaurant offers a small selection of Belgian dishes, including meat, fish and vegetarian options. With modern décor, ultrafriendly staff and excellent prices, it's little wonder the locals have taken it to heart.

Ryad (Map p126; ☎ 050 33 13 55; Hoogstraat 32; mains €13-20; ☻ dinner) Bruges' dining scene has been boosted by the influx of many new cuisines in recent times. This intimate Moroccan haunt is one of note. Couscous and tagines are its forte, and the décor's deliciously dark.

Bhavani (Map p126; ☎ 050 33 90 25; Simon Stevinplein 5; mains €14-20; ☻ lunch & dinner, closed Wed) A simple Indian restaurant on a bustling tree-lined square off Bruges' main shopping street. As you'd expect, vegetarians and nonvegetarians are well catered for, and the food is authentic and moreish.

Bistrot De Schaar (Map p123; ☎ 050 33 59 79; Hooistraat 2; mains €15-21; ☻ lunch & dinner, closed Thu) An out-of-the-way, good-value restaurant located just below street level. In fine weather there's also a large terrace across the road next to the canal lock. The cuisine is a Mediterranean-Belgian mix and the char-grilled specialities are excellent.

Tom's Diner (Map p126; ☎ 050 33 33 82; West Gistelhof 23; mains around €17; ☻ 6.30pm-1am, closed Tue & Wed) To the north of town, a little way out of the tourist centre and all the better for it. This whitewashed gabled corner house has a rustic interior and serves stylish modern-Belgian food at very affordable prices.

De Koetse (Map p126; ☎ 050 33 76 80; Oude Burg 31; mains €17-36; ☻ lunch & dinner, closed Thu) Restaurants on the Markt dish up the ubiquitous mussels and *frites* (fries), but quality and ambience can be trite and lacking. If you want both good mussels and attentive service, follow the locals here. *Paling in 't groen* (eel in spinach sauce; €20), another Belgian speciality, also features.

Den Dyver (Map p126; ☎ 050 33 60 69; Dijver 5; dishes €18-27, 3-course menu incl beers €46; ☻ dinner, closed Tue) For an evening of Burgundian-style revelry and indulgence, head to this large, well-established restaurant located on the tree-lined Dijver. The cuisine is traditional Belgian, inventively spiced with beer-based sauces and marinades.

De Stove (Map p126; ☎ 050 33 78 35; Kleine St Amandsstraat 4; mains €18-28, menu with/without wine €58/42; ☻ lunch Sat-Tue, dinner Fri-Tue) A charming little restaurant tucked away on a pedestrianised lane close to the Markt. Despite the perennial rave reviews, it refuses to flaunt itself. The

eight tables are arranged around an old stove, the service is intimate and personable, and the food – largely fish specialities – is excellent.

Christophe (Map p126; ☎ 050 34 48 92; Garenmarkt 34; mains €20-30; ☻ 7pm-1am Thu-Mon) A cool late-night bistro with marble table-tops and a decent range of Flemish staples such as fresh Zeebrugge shrimps. Excellent late-nighter.

Hertog Jan (☎ 050 67 34 46; Torhoutsesteenweg 479; mains €48-50, menus from €70; ☻ lunch & dinner Tue-Sat) Hail a taxi to experience Hertog Jan. About 3.5km west of the centre, this suburban restaurant is the current talk of gourmet circles. Expect French cuisine such as Limousin lamb and Bresse dove, or sample the works with the *degustation* menu.

De Karmeliet (Map p123; ☎ 050 33 82 59; Langestraat 19; lunch menu €60, menu degustation €145; ☻ lunch & dinner; ☒) If Michelin stars are your quality assurance, then this is Bruges' top address. Not one but three twinkles means it has long been a firm favourite of food lovers throughout Belgium. Chef Geert Van Hecke's French *haute cuisine* is responsible for all the fuss. For weekends you'll need to book a week ahead.

QUICK EATS

Het Dagelijks Brood (Map p126; ☎ 050 33 60 50; Philipstockstraat 21; snacks €5-11; ☻ 7am-6pm, closed Tue) Part of a national bakery-tearoom chain (see p103), with just one big table where you can eat breakfast or feast on lunch staples such as salads, *boterhammen* (sandwiches) or savoury pies.

De Belegde Boterham (Map p126; ☎ 050 34 91 31; Kleine St Amandsstraat 5; ☻ noon-4pm, closed Sun) No-fuss tearoom tucked away in a pedestrianised alley close to the Markt. Firm local favourite, and the filled baguette sandwiches (€6.50) are delicious. Also serves salads (€10).

Frietkotjes (Map p126; Markt; ☻ 11am-11pm) Takeaway *frites* (from €2.50) and hot dogs (from €3) can be bought from the two green vans on the Markt. These little vans, by the way, are a gold mine for the local city council, paying €250,000 per year to be able to use this prime spot.

SELF-CATERING

Recommended supermarkets:

GB Express (Map p126; Zuidzandstraat 5)
Louis Delhaize (Map p126; Oude Burg 22)
Proxy/Delhaize (Map p126; Geldmuntstraat)
Smatch (Map p123; Langestraat 55; ☻ 8.30am-7.30pm Mon-Sat)

TO MARKET, TO MARKET

Soaking up Bruges at one of its weekly markets is a great way to do as locals do. Belgians love comparing produce at fruit and vegie stalls, complementing flower-sellers on their latest array or browsing bric-a-brac. You'll find little old ladies assessing the state of the charcuterie, young couples doing their weekly shop and gents politely inspecting antiques.

The **food and flower market** (Map p126; 7am-1pm Wed) on the Markt is the most picturesque. If you're here on a weekend, content yourself with the busy fresh **produce market** (Map p126; 8am-1pm Sat) on 't Zand, which is also a general goods market.

At the colonnaded **Vismarkt** (Fish Market; Map p126; Steenhouwersdijk; 8am-1pm Tue-Sat), fishmongers have been selling their North Sea produce for centuries. These days only a few vendors set up on the cold stone slabs, but it's still worth a wander. Join locals buying snacks such as *maatjes* (herring fillets). On weekends, the Vismarkt and nearby **Dijver** (Map p126; 10am-6pm Sat & Sun mid-Mar–mid-Nov) are taken over by antique and bric-a-brac stalls.

Drinking

De Republiek (Map p126; 050 34 02 29; St Jakobsstraat 36; from 11am) Local favourite and one of Bruges' most congenial pubs. A modern affair, located under the same roof as Cinema Lumière, and with a big, out-back terrace in summer. Meals are available (€9 to €13) and the kitchen is open 'til midnight. DJs take over on Friday and Saturday nights.

De Garre (Map p126; 050 34 10 29; Garre 1; noon-1am) Hidden in a narrow cul-de-sac between the Markt and the Burg, this tiny old *estaminet* is a beer-specialist pub – browse through the umpteen-page menu while trying to decide.

Joey's Café (Map p126; 050 34 12 64; Zilversteeg 4; from 11.30am Mon-Sat Oct-May, daily Jun-Sep) Lose the tourists at this muso's haunt, strangely located inside the Zilverpand shopping centre. The candle-lit atmosphere is dark and relaxing. Once in a blue moon the affable owners, Kristel and Stevie, organise live gigs.

Est Wijnbar (Map p126; 050 33 38 39; Noordzandstraat 34; from 5pm Thu-Mon) Tidy wine bar with a pleasant summer terrace and live music – jazz, blues, boogie or folk – every Sunday from 7.30pm.

Top (Map p126; St Salvatorskerkhof 5; from 9pm Tue-Sat, from 10pm Sun) A cool little bar that opens late and moves until morning. The décor's cool, stark and bland.

't Brugs Beertje (Map p126; 050 33 96 16; Kemelstraat 5; 4pm-1am, closed Tue & Wed) Probably Belgium's most famous beer pub. It's a tiny place situated on a poky backstreet, and offers around 200 national brews, listed by brewery.

Bolero (Map p126; 050 33 81 11; Garenmarkt 32; 10pm-4am, closed Tue & Wed) Bruges' only gay and lesbian bar.

De Windmolen (Map p123; 050 33 97 39, Carmersstraat 135; from 11am, closed Sat) Quaint corner *café* overlooking St Janshuismolen in St Anna. A fitting port o' call for a drink after visiting the windmills or nearby Guido Gezellemuseum.

Entertainment

Concertgebouw (Map p126; 050 47 69 99; www.concertgebouw.be; 't Zand 34) Contemporary comes to Bruges in the form of this concert hall, the newest building on the city's skyline. Opened in 2002 to celebrate Bruges' year-long stint as the European City of Culture, its minimal design incorporates the city's three famous towers and its colour perfectly melds with the city's rosy hues. It regularly stages theatre, classical music and dance.

Cactus Muziekcentrum (Map p123; 050 33 20 14; www.cactusmusic.be in Flemish; Magdalenastraat 27) The city's premier venue for contemporary and world music – either live or DJ. It's a little way out of the town centre, and small as live music venues go.

Celtic Ireland (Map p126; 050 34 45 02; Burg 8) Offers pints of draught Guinness and live music (rock, jazz or blues) on Friday and/or Saturday evenings from 10pm (every night in summer).

THE AUTHOR'S CHOICE

Herberg Vlissinghe (Map p126; 050 34 37 37; Blekerstraat 2; from 11am, closed Tue) Bruges' oldest *café*. Someone has been pouring beer here since 1515 – mind-blowing, really. Local legend has it that Rubens painted an imitation coin on the table here and then did a runner. Snacks are available.

LACED UP

Lace (*kant* in Flemish, *dentelle* in French) blossomed in Flanders in the 16th century. *Naaldkant* (needlepoint lace), which developed in Italy, was predominantly made in Brussels while *kloskant* (bobbin lace) is believed to have originated in Bruges. The latter requires thousands of painstaking and meticulous movements of bobbins and pins. Each lace-maker had her own patterns, which stayed in the family and were handed down through generations.

The bulk of lace sold in shops throughout Belgium these days is either handmade in Asia or machine-made in France. If you want handmade lace from Belgium you're going to have to hunt for it and state what you want. Even reputable shops generally do not advertise which of their stock is made outside Belgium.

Watch lace-makers at work at the **Kantcentrum** (p129), or take a stab at it yourself with **Caroline Flokman** (☎ 050 67 87 61; http://users.telenet.be/brugesprivatelacelessons), who gives half-day private lessons (€60) in her Bruges home.

In the mood for a movie? Grab your partner and head for either of these cinemas:

Cinema Liberty (Map p126; ☎ 050 33 20 11; Kuipersstraat 23) Mainstream movie offerings.

Cinema Lumière (Map p126; ☎ 050 34 34 65; St Jakobsstraat 36) Features two auditoriums, and shows foreign and mainstream films and an occasional classic.

Shopping

Steenstraat, the main shopping thoroughfare, is lined with a small collection of international chain stores. The nearby Geldmuntstraat and Noordzandstraat are home to boutiques. For details on the city's markets, see p137.

't Apostelientje (Map p123; ☎ 050 33 78 60; Balstraat 11; ⏰ 9.30am-5pm Mon-Sat, 10am-1pm Sun) It's not finding lace that's the problem in Bruges – it's avoiding it. About 80 lace shops operate in the city, many tucked away in nooks and crannies or concentrated along Wollestraat and Breidelstraat. This shop is well away from all of these and stocks about 70% antique lace. For more on lace, see boxed text, (above).

B (Map p126; ☎ 050 49 09 32; Wollestraat 31a) An outlet for all manner of Belgian designs – everything from clothes to household products and toys.

De Biertempel (Map p126; ☎ 050 34 37 30; Philipstockstraat 7) Beer specialist shop where you can even pick up a well-priced bottle of Westvleteren (€4.95).

Bottle Shop (Map p126; ☎ 050 34 99 80; Wollestraat 13; ⏰ 10am-7pm) Not your typical off-licence – this shop goes to town with copious quantities of beer, *jenever* (gin) and mineral waters, all displayed in slick surroundings.

Chocolatier Van Oost (Map p126; ☎ 050 33 14 54; Wollestraat 11) A small establishment with an excellent reputation for handmade pralines.

It's on a hectic shopping street, and is easily overlooked – allow the scent of warm chocolate to lead the way. Once inside, accustom yourself to the rich displays, then note the vats of molten chocolate being stirred out back.

L'Héroïne (Map p126; ☎ 050 33 56 57; Noordzandstraat 32; ⏰ Mon-Sat) Some of Belgium's top designers are represented in this discreet boutique on one of Bruges' main shopping streets.

Tintin Shop (Map p126; ☎ 050 33 42 92; Steenstraat 3; ⏰ daily) Stocks everything any Tintin buff could ever want, and more.

Other recommendations:

Delvaux (Map p126; ☎ 050 49 01 31; Breidelstraat 2) Home-grown handbags and other leather goods.

Galler (Map p126; ☎ 050 61 20 62; Steenstraat 5) One of Belgium's better chocolate chain shops.

Mille-Fleurs (Map p126; ☎ 050 34 54 54; Wollestraat 33) Specialises in Flemish tapestries.

Olivier Strelli (Map p126; ☎ 050 34 38 37; Eiermarkt 3) Prominent corner boutique given over to Belgium's best-known designer.

Rombaux (Map p126; ☎ 050 33 25 75; Mallebergplein 13) Fabulous music shop in an antique setting.

Secondo (Map p126; ☎ 050 33 07 88; Mallebergplein 3) Sells pre-loved Delvaux handbags, most in pretty good nick.

Zilverpand (Map p126) Shopping gallery between Steenstraat and Noordzandstraat.

Getting There & Away
BUS

Busabout buses pass through Bruges (for more information, see p318). They pick up and drop off at Snuffel (p133).

TRAIN

Bruges' **train station** (☎ information office 050 30 24 24) is about 1.5km south of the city centre.

There are trains every half-hour to Brussels (one way €11.60, one hour) and Ghent (€5.40, 20 minutes). Hourly trains go to Antwerp (€12.40, 70 minutes), De Panne (€7.40, one hour; change at Lichtervelde), Knokke (€3, 15 minutes), Kortrijk (€6.40, 40 minutes), Ostend (€3.30, 15 minutes) and Zeebrugge (€2.40, 10 minutes).

To get to Ypres (Ieper in Flemish; €10.10, two hours), take the train to Kortrijk; here you must wait 30 minutes for the hourly connection. Buy a B-Dagtrip ticket (see boxed text, p324) if you're planning a day trip. This ticket costs €11.40 and includes a return train fare, admission to four museums and a drink in a *café*.

Getting Around

A small network of buses operated by **De Lijn** (☎ 070 22 02 00; www.delijn.be in Flemish) covers destinations in and around Bruges. Most depart from De Lijn's information office (Map p123) on the square in front of the train station, and many stop at central locations such as 't Zand, Markt, Wollestraat and Biekorf on Kuipersstraat.

From the train station, buses 1, 3, 4, 11, 13, 14 and 16 head for the centre – take any bus marked 'Centrum'.

A single ticket bought at De Lijn's information office costs €1.20 (or €1.50 on the bus), a *dagpas* (day ticket) is €5 (or €6 on the bus) and a 10-journey *lijnkaart* (network card) is €8 (€10 on the bus). A *tweerittenkaart* (two rides) costs €2 and can be used either for one journey by two people, or for two rides by one person. Buses run from 5.30am until about 11pm. On Friday and Saturday, limited night-bus services run from the centre to the suburbs (and to Damme) until 2am.

CAR

A medieval city enmeshed by waterways is hardly an ideal place for four wheels. There are several big car parks in town but it's considerably cheaper to leave your car at the periphery. The best place is the covered car park next to the train station. Here you'll pay €0.50 per hour or just €2.50 for 24 hours, and you get a free return bus ticket to the centre for the car's driver and all passengers.

TAXI

Taxis wait on the Markt and at Stationsplein (in front of the train station). Otherwise phone ☎ 050 33 44 44 or ☎ 050 38 46 60.

DAMME

pop 10,900

Day-trippers prize the former fishing village of Damme, 6km northeast of Bruges. A long time ago, Damme nestled on the edge of the Zwin, a waterway connected to the sea. A canal was built between it and Bruges and, by the 13th century, Damme was the region's bustling port. But along with Bruges, its fate was sealed when the Zwin silted.

Information & Sights

Central to everything is the Gothic **stadhuis**, where Charles the Bold, one of the nation's 15th-century rulers, and Margaret of York wed in lavish style in 1468. Directly in front of the stadhuis is a **statue of Jacob Van Maerlant**, a 13th-century Flemish poet who lived and died in Damme. He's buried in **Onze Lieve Vrouwekerk** (Our Lady's Church; Kerkstraat). This church dates back to the 12th century and was vastly expanded in the village's heyday, only to be abandoned and partially torn down when things started to wane. In summer, climb the robust tower for good views.

Opposite the stadhuis, a restored patrician's house is home to the **tourist office** (☎ 050 28 86 10; www.vvvdamme.be in Flemish; Jacob Van Maerlantstraat 3; 9am-noon & 2-5pm Mon-Fri, from 10am Sat & Sun) and the **Uilenspiegel Museum** (☎ 050 28 86 10; www.vvvdamme.be/arrangementen.htm in Flemish; Jacob Van Maerlantstraat 3; adult/family €2.50/5; 9am-noon & 2-6pm Mon-Fri, from 10am Sat & Sun mid-Apr–mid-Oct, 9am-noon & 2-5pm Mon-Fri, 2-5pm Sat & Sun mid-Oct–mid-Apr). The latter recounts the stories of Uilenspiegel, a villain in German folklore but a jester and freedom fighter in Flemish literature.

Sleeping & Eating

B&B De Stamper (☎ /fax 050 50 01 97; Zuiddijk 12; r €95) Enter this rural retreat to timewarp centuries. Located 2km from Damme, this old farmhouse dates from 1647 – and the worn-down stairs to the bedrooms prove it. The rustic rooms have farmyard views and are close to a huge open kitchen where sizable dinners (€28) are prepared.

Eetcafé De Spieghel (☎ 050 37 11 30; Jacob van Maerlantstraat 10; tapas €2-5, mains around €18; Wed-Mon) Rustic split-level eatery next to the tourist office that serves snacks and typical Flemish fare.

Napoleon (☎ 050 35 32 99; Damse Vaart Zuid 4; mains €19-26, 3-course lunch menu €29; Thu-Mon) This small classical restaurant presents seasonal French cuisine using a creative market kitchen. It's situated next to the road, immediately across from the canal, and has a small outdoor terrace plus an intimate interior.

De Zuidkant (☎ 050 37 16 76; Jacob van Maerlantstraat 6; mains €20-25; ☒ closed Wed & Thu) Tucked behind the town hall, this designer restaurant is run by a young chef who blends Belgian, French and Mediterranean cuisines. His attention to detail is obvious by the thoughtfully presented meals.

Getting There & Away

A **barge** (one way adult/child €5.20/3.70, return €6.70/4.70; ☒ departures every 2hrs from 10am to 6pm Apr–mid-Oct), SW *Lamme Goedzak*, plies the Damse Vaart between Bruges and Damme. A one-way trip takes around 35 minutes. From Bruges it leaves from Noorweegse Kaai, a 45-minute walk from the Markt. Alternatively, take bus 4 from the Markt in the direction of 'St Jozef–Koolkerke'.

The cheapest way to get to Damme, other than walking, is by bus 43 (€1.80, 20 minutes, every two hours from 9.30am to 3.30pm, April to mid-October). It departs Bruges' train station and picks up at the Markt.

For information on cycling to Damme, see p131 and p132.

OSTEND

pop 68,200

Bustling Ostend (Oostende in Flemish, Ostende in French) was once one of Europe's most stylish seaside resorts. Royalty and the upper crust favoured this cosmopolitan retreat and Léopolds I and II both frequently spent time here, the latter leaving some typically grandiose monuments. Ostend was home to Ensor, Belgium's best-known 19th-century artist, and it was during a prolonged stay here that US singer Marvin Gaye wrote one of the greatest soul songs of all time, *Sexual Healing*.

While posters around town still hark back to its *belle époque*, the aristocratic lustre has long gone. These days Ostend is a down-to-earth fishing port waking from years of nostalgia and decline. No longer does it vainly proclaim itself the 'Queen of Belgian Beaches'; instead it has set its sights on youth and fun, enticing visitors with new museums and attractions, a hip image and shops that open every day.

History

From humble beginnings as an 11th-century fishing village, Ostend grew to be Belgium's most important Channel port, a position it lost only in the 19th century when Zeebrugge developed. During the Revolt of the Netherlands, the townsfolk bravely held out against the Spanish for three years, only to be taken in 1604 at the cost of thousands of lives.

The city suffered heavily during the two world wars and much of the original town was demolished by air strikes. Its post-war development favoured high-rise buildings draped along the beachfront – a trend mirrored in most of Belgium's coastal towns. The result is an ugly line of buildings that cast long shadows over the beach and provide ocean views for a select few. Thankfully, there's the wonderful promenade.

Orientation & Information

Ostend's relatively compact centre is crisscrossed by a grid of ruler-straight streets. Life centres on the recently renovated Kursaal casino on Monacoplein. The main shopping thoroughfare is the pedestrianised Kapellestraat.

ATM (Marie Joséplein 11)

Goffin Exchange (☎ 059 50 68 28; St Petrus & Paulusplein 19; ☒ 9.30am-6pm) Currency exchange bureau handy to the train station.

In&Uit Oostende (☎ 059 70 11 99; www.inenuit oostende.be; Monacoplein 2; ☒ 9am-7pm Mon-Sat & 10am-7pm Sun Jun-Aug, 10am-6pm Mon-Sat & 10am-5pm Sun Sep-May) Revamped tourist office, adjacent to the casino, about 1.25km from the train station (the 'Centrumbus' from the station stops nearby).

OK (☎ 059 29 50 53; Monacoplein; ☒ 11am-11pm) Free internet (when you dine) at this funky *café*.

Post office (☎ 059 56 47 20; Lijndraaiersstraat 60) Inconveniently located away from the town centre.

Sights & Activities

Ostend is primarily a seaside resort – it's the sea, and hope of sun, that brings droves of Belgians. But the town does have plenty of attractions, some which have been recently spruced up.

VISSERSKAAI QUARTER

Marking the entrance to the harbour is the **pier** – don't miss a walk along it but be rugged up against the wind. **Visserskaai** (Fishermen's Quay), the town's famed seafood quay-side, is nearby, as is the tiny **Noordzeeaquarium** (North Sea Aquarium; ☎ 059 50 08 76; Visserskaai; adult/child €2/1; ☒ 10am-12.30pm & 2-6pm Jun-Sep, 10am-noon & 2-5pm Apr-May, 10am-12.30pm & 2-6pm Sat & Sun Oct-Mar), housed in former seafood auction rooms.

Follow Visserskaai to the end and you'll see **St Petrus & Pauluskerk** (Sint Pietersstraat). This church holds the tomb of Queen Louise-Marie, the nation's first queen. From here it's a short walk to the old harbour, where two ships have been turned into small museums. The superbly preserved **Amandine** (☎ 059 23 43 01; Vindictievelaan 35-Z; adult/child €3/1.50; ☺ 10am-7pm Tue-Sun, 2-7pm Mon) was the last Ostend trawler to fish around Iceland. At the harbour's opposite end is the **Mercator** (☎ 059 70 56 54; www.zeilschip-mercator.be; Old Harbour; adult/child €4/2; ☺ 10am-5.30pm Jul & Aug, 10am-12.30pm & 2-4.30pm Apr-Jun & Sep, 10am-12.30pm & 2-4.30pm Oct-Mar), a 1932 sailing ship formerly used for Belgian navy training purposes.

OSTEND BEACH
The best beach is west of town near the Thermae Palace hotel. Walk there via the seafront

Albert I promenade, which converts into the **Koningsgalerijen** (Royal Galleries), a covered walkway built for Léopold II and marked by a first-rate colonial relic – an enormous **statue** of the monarch astride a horse amid fawning peasantry and Congolese.

If you're coming to Ostend for the day by public transport, it'll take about 15 minutes to walk from Ostend train station to the nearest beach at the northern end of Albert I promenade. Alternatively, jump straight off the train and onto the nearby Kusttram (see boxed text, p145) to find a more secluded spot on the outskirts of town or in the dunes further afield.

As in all Belgian coastal resorts, Ostend's broad promenade has its fair share of wheeled

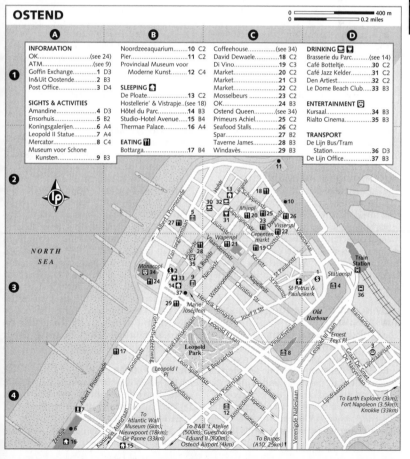

WESTERN FLANDERS

OSTEND

0		400 m	
0		0.2 miles	

INFORMATION
OK.................................(see 24)
ATM.................................(see 9)
Goffin Exchange.................1 D3
In&Uit Oostende................2 B3
Post Office.........................3 D4

SIGHTS & ACTIVITIES
Amandine.........................4 D3
Ensorhuis.........................5 B2
Koningsgalerijen................6 A4
Leopold II Statue...............7 A4
Mercator..........................8 C4
Museum voor Schone
    Kunsten.......................9 B3

Noordzeeaquarium.........10 C2
Pier..............................11 C2
Provinciaal Museum voor
    Moderne Kunst............12 C4

SLEEPING
De Ploate.......................13 C2
Hostellerie' & Vistrapje..(see 18)
Hôtel du Parc..................14 B3
Studio-Hotel Avenue........15 B4
Thermae Palace..............16 A4

EATING
Bottarga........................17 B4

Coffeehouse...............(see 34)
David Dewaele...............18 C2
Di Vino........................19 C3
Market.........................20 C2
Market.........................21 C2
Market.........................22 C2
Mosselbeurs 23 C2
OK...........................(see 34)
Ostend Queen...........(see 34)
Primeurs Achiel..............25 C2
Seafood Stalls................26 C2
Spar............................27 B2
Taverne James...............28 B3
Windavès.....................29 B3

DRINKING
Brasserie du Parc.........(see 14)
Café Bottleltje...............30 C2
Café Jazz Kelder.............31 C2
Den Artiest....................32 C2
Le Dome Beach Club.....33 B3

ENTERTAINMENT
Kursaal........................34 B3
Rialto Cinema................35 B3

TRANSPORT
De Lijn Bus/Tram
    Station....................36 D3
De Lijn Office................37 B3

NORTH SEA

Train Station

Leopold Park

Leopold I Pl

To Atlantic Wall Museum (6km);
Nieuwpoort (18km);
De Panne (33km)

To B&B 'L Atelier (500m); Guesthouse Eduard II (800m); Ostend Airport (4km)

To Bruges (A10, 25km)

To Earth Explorer (3km);
Fort Napoleon (3.5km);
Knokke (33km)

EERIE ENSOR

The **Ensorhuis** (Ensor's House; ☎ 059 80 53 35; Vlaanderenstraat 27; adult/concession €2/1; ☻ 10am-noon & 2-5pm, closed Tue) is where expressionist pioneer James Ensor lived and painted from 1875 to 1916. The ground floor was a souvenir shop owned by his aunt. When Ensor inherited it, he installed a studio upstairs and it was here that he painted his most riotous piece, *The Entry of Christ into Brussels*, in 1888.

Ensor (1860–1949) was in part rejected by the art world due to his coastal seclusion. He's best known for his macabre and sometimes quite savage images of skeletons, phantoms and garish masks. After a brief stint doing seascapes and portraits, he abandoned the traditional for clashing colours and carnivalesque scenes that often have a whiff of death and a distinctly unnerving effect. *The Entry of Christ into Brussels*, depicting a brilliantly colourful parade of sins, was shamefully sold off to the USA half a century ago, evidence of the low esteem in which Ensor was held by the Belgian state. Only in the last decade has effort been made to show national appreciation – a comprehensive retrospective was held in Brussels in 1999, the 50th anniversary of Ensor's death.

Ostend also made much ado about this anniversary, but it has still been criticised for allowing his birthplace on Langestraat to be demolished. The restoration of the Ensorhuis in 2001 went a little way to silence critics. There's not a great deal to see inside, and none of his original works are displayed – for those you'll need to head to Ostend's Museum voor Schone Kunsten (below) or, better still, the excellent collection at Antwerp's Koninklijk Museum voor Schone Kunsten (see p182). Instead, life-size reproductions of many of his most famous pieces adorn the walls here. Probably the most interesting object is the ground-floor cabinet filled with garish old masks that Ensor used as inspiration in many of his paintings. The piano, table and seat located in the salon are also original furnishings.

A good book to pick up to explore the artist's life is *Ensor* by Ulrike Becks-Malorny.

contraptions for kids – everything from mini ice-cream vans to flying horses are available for rental.

MUSEUM VOOR SCHONE KUNSTEN

The **Museum of Fine Arts** (☎ 059 80 53 35; Marie José-plein 11) should be open again by the time you read this, following relocation to an old post office building in the heart of town. The permanent collection features works by local lads such as James Ensor (see boxed text, above), and Leon Spilliaert. Spilliaert was born in Ostend in 1881, and was captivated by the seascapes around him.

PROVINCIAAL MUSEUM VOOR MODERNE KUNST (PMMK)

The **Provincial Museum of Modern Art** (☎ 059 50 81 18; www.pmmk.be in Flemish; Romestraat 11; adult/concession €5/4; ☻ 10am-6pm Tue-Sun), better known as PMMK, exhibits an enjoyable selection of modern Belgian paintings and sculptures. It's a good place to catch a work by recently retired Antwerp sculptor Panamarenko. His *Vliegende sigaar – Vliegende tijger* (Flying cigar – Flying tiger) stays true to his flights of fancy.

FORT NAPOLEON

Resting atop secluded dunes some 3.5km north of town, the impenetrable pentagon of **Fort Napoleon** (☎ 059 32 00 48; www.fortnapoleon.be in Flemish; Vuurtorenweg; adult/child/concession €4/free/3.50; ☻ 11am-1pm & 2-6pm Apr-Oct, 2-5pm Sat & Sun Nov-Mar) is Europe's only intact Napoleonic fortress. Started in 1812, it was built to fight off seafaring attackers, but the Brits never obliged. Its chequered history includes becoming a German headquarters in WWII and later a rendezvous point for 'bad boys and naughty girls', as the audio-guide says. Cross the 2.5m-thick walls, tour the dry moat and take in the rooftop before beating a retreat to the well-priced bistro located within the fort, or the high-style restaurant tacked onto the side. The Kusttram stop 'Duin en Zee' is about 500m away.

EARTH EXPLORER

Let the kids loose at **Earth Explorer** (☎ 059 70 59 59; www.earthexplorer.be; Fortstraat 128b; adult/child €12.50/10; ☻ 10am-6pm Feb–mid-Nov, Thu-Sun mid-Nov–Feb), a science-based theme park 3km north of town. The Kusttram stop 'Duin en Zee' is out the front.

ATLANTIC WALL MUSEUM
Also known as Domein Raversijde, this **open-air museum** (☎ 059 70 22 85; Nieuwpoortsesteenweg 636; adult/child €5/free; ☾ 2-5pm Mon-Fri, 10.30am-6pm Sat & Sun Apr–mid-Nov) tells the chilling tale of wartime occupation via kilometres of underground passageways and artillery – artillery that still menacingly faces to sea. Take the Kusttram southwest to the stop 'Domein Raversijde'.

Festivals & Events
Ostend's biggest annual event, the **Bal des Rats Morts** (Dead Rats Ball), is an exuberant costumed event held on the first Saturday in March.

Sleeping
Ostend groans under the weight of hotels (some close from December to March). Unless indicated otherwise, all of our recommendations are open year-round. Prices given are for the peak summer period (July and August) – it's well worth inquiring about discounts at other times of the year.

B&B 't Atelier (☎ 059 43 61 01; www.atelier-oostende .be; Velodroomstraat 43; s/d €55/70, weekend €75/90, penthouse per week/weekend €300/200, loft per week/weekend €325/200; ☾ Easter-Dec; ☒) A stone sculptor's home just a few minutes walk from the beach, with two 2nd-floor guestrooms plus a self-contained penthouse (with private terrace) and a 'loft' (odd name for a basement family apartment but the space works well). The mocha-coloured rooms are functional and sober, with artistic flourishes. The Kusttram stops at Koninginnelaan, two minutes' walk away. Greet, the woman who runs it, is vibrant.

Guesthouse Eduard II (☎ 059 43 03 08; www.oostende -bedandbreakfast.be; Eduard Decuyperstraat 11; s/d €60/76) This is an Art Deco house dating from 1933 that's been beautifully restored. A spiral staircase leads up to two 2nd-floor tasteful guestrooms with modern, minimal décor.

Hôtel du Parc (☎ 059 70 16 80; www.duparcoostende .com; Marie Joséplein 3; s/d/tr/f from €57/87/94/100) An Art Deco gem. This hotel is a classified monument and it has loads to recommend it. Located above a brasserie of the same name, it's smack bang in the middle of town and only 100m from the beach. An old-world atmosphere pervades until you reach the rooms, entirely renovated a few years back and still fresh and modern. If a little balcony matters, request a 1st-floor room at the front of the hotel.

Studio-Hotel Avenue (☎ 059 80 55 44; www.hotel avenue.be; Koninginnelaan 27; s/d/t/q €70/85/90/97) A nondescript sort of place, one block from the beach, that offers comfortable, self-contained rooms ideal for families. Rates don't include breakfast, and prices are considerably reduced outside summer holidays. The Kusttram stops at Koninginnelaan, 50m away.

Thermae Palace (☎ 059 80 66 44; www.thermaepalace .be; Koningin Astridlaan 7; d with/without sea view €195/170, ste from €220; ☒ ▯ �}) The city's top address, on the beachfront west of the centre. This palatial Art Deco building affords wonderful sea views. The rooms are stock-standard but the breakfast is worth writing about, a huge buffet strewn along a room that almost communes with the sea. The Kusttram (direction De Panne) stops at the hotel. Babies and children are welcome.

Other recommendations:

De Ploate (☎ 059 80 52 97; www.vjh.be; Langestraat 82; dm €16.60) Uninspiring hostel but well located in the heart of town.

Hostellerie 't Vistrapje (☎ 059 80 23 82; Visserskaai 37; s/d/t/q €45/70/87/109, apt €100) A long-established little hotel-restaurant recommended for both its food and its 2nd-floor apartment (sleeps four adults) with Visserskaai views.

Eating
Visserskaai is the place for seafood snacks. Every day – summer and winter from early morning to evening – colourful *kraampjes* (stalls) set up along the quay, and vendors sell prepared plates of cooked fish, seafood cocktails and, best of all, bowls of steaming hot *wollekes* (sea snails).

OK (☎ 059 29 50 53; Monacoplein; snacks €4-9; ☾ 11am-11pm) Finger food, burgers and sandwiches are the staples at this hip new *café* attached to the casino.

Di Vino (☎ 0473 87 12 97; Wittenonnenstraat 2; mains €12.50-16; ☾ lunch Thu-Sat, dinner Tue-Sun) Intimate wine bistro that's big with the locals. A small

---

THE AUTHOR'S CHOICE
Taverne James (☎ 059 70 52 45; Galerie James Ensor 34; ☾ 10am-8pm Fri-Wed) This Ostend institution is one of those experiences that's available nowhere else. Located in a small covered shopping gallery in the heart of town, this small wood-panelled *café* basks in its international reputation for excellent *garnaalkroketten* (deep-fried prawn croquettes). A plate of two croquettes will set you back €9.50. The tavern's been around since 1954 and, although twee, it drones with homespun and international visitors.

chalked-up menu offers staples like goat-cheese salad, lasagne and vegetarian dishes.

Bottarga (☎ 059 80 86 88; Albert I Promenade 64c; mains €14-20; ⊙ closed Mon Sep-Jun) This bistro brings modern to Ostend's beachfront. Splashy purple and orange décor, a choice of Belgian or Thai cuisines, and ultrafriendly staff make it stand out from the promenade pack.

Mosselbeurs (☎ 059 80 73 10; Dwarsstraat 10; mains from €17; ⊙ lunch & dinner, closed Mon) The place in Ostend to eat well-priced mussels – 1.3kg jumbo pots go for €17 to €19. Don't be put off by the building's tacky façade (plastered with fake mussels) – this place packs in diners thanks to fresh produce and efficient service.

Ostend Queen (☎ 059 29 50 55; Kursaal, Monacoplein; mains from €26; ⊙ lunch & dinner) Fishy business at its best. This relatively new seafood brasserie on the 1st floor of Kursaal casino received *Michelin Guide* accolades before even opening. Thanks to the subsequent controversy, tables have since been in high demand. If OQ doesn't fit the bill, stay downstairs for a steak or salad on the long seaside terrace at the casino's Coffeehouse (☎ 059 29 50 52).

David Dewaele (☎ 059 70 42 26; Visserskaai 39; mains €27-43; ⊙ lunch & dinner Tue-Sun) This inconspicuous little restaurant is nestled among the throng on Visserskaai, and is one of Ostend's best seafood haunts. Dewaele worked at De Karmeliet (p136), Bruges' top restaurant, and his cuisine is nothing short of inventive. However, the modest interior borders on boring.

Other recommendations:

Windavès (☎ 059 80 89 29; Koningsstraat 2; mains €15-20; ⊙ lunch Fri-Wed, dinner Fri-Tue) Colourful and spacious restaurant offering world cuisines plus plenty of imaginative vegetarian fare.

Food markets (⊙ 7am-2pm Thu) Vendors set up on Wapenplein, Groentenmarkt and Mijnplein.

Primeurs Achiel (Nieuwstraat 19; ⊙ 8.30am-1pm & 2.30-7.30pm Wed-Mon) Supermarket.

Spar (Van Iseghemlaan 49) Supermarket.

Drinking & Entertainment

More than ever before, nightlife in Ostend centres on Monacoplein, home to the revamped casino. In the streets leading off from it, particularly Langestraat and Van Iseghemlaan, you'll find a cinema, nightclubs and pubs.

Kursaal (☎ 059 70 51 11; www.kursaaloostende.be in Flemish; Monacoplein) Following a lengthy overhaul, Ostend's landmark beachfront casino is back in action, with all its early '50s features intact. Even if you're not into gaming (pass-

port needed to play), it's worth a wander – take a look at the statue of Marvin Gaye, go for a drink at the beachfront Coffeehouse (left), move onto the Liquid Healing nightclub, or check out who's performing in the concert hall.

Café Botteltje (☎ 059 70 09 28; Louisastraat 19; ⊙ 3pm-3am Tue-Sun) Bills itself as a 'delightful brown *café* with the biggest selection of beers and gins on the Belgian coast'. While it's more like a rambling English pub than a *gezellige bruine kroeg* (cosy, convivial brown *café*), it does have an excellent variety of beers (280 varieties), and is packed most summer evenings.

Den Artiest (☎ 059 80 88 89; Kapucijnenstraat 13; ⊙ from 5pm) Trendy split-level brasserie serving everything from fruit *jenevers* to house beer. Live music most Tuesdays from 9pm – expect local bands doing jazz or covers, and admission is free.

Other recommendations:

Café Jazz Kelder (☎ 0475 41 18 20; Langestraat 71; ⊙ 8pm Thu-Sun) Little cellar venue with live jazz.

Le Dome Beach Club (☎ 059 80 32 15; Langestraat 15; ⊙ from 10pm daily summer, Thu-Sun winter) Draws a young clubbing crowd.

Rialto Cinema (☎ 059 70 61 58; Langestraat 39) Eight-screen cinema.

Getting There & Around

Like other port towns in this part of the world, the Channel Tunnel impacted sharply on Ostend. Hoverspeed services came to an end and, for a few years, there were no ferry connections between here and the UK. There is now one sea link – **TransEuropa Ferries** (www.transeuropaferries.com; ☎ 059 34 02 60), but they're only for those travelling by car, motorcycle or mobile home (no foot passengers). For more details see p319.

Hourly trains run from Ostend to Bruges (€3.30, 15 minutes), Brussels (€14.10, 1¼ hours), Ghent (€7.80, 50 minutes) and Anterp (€15.20, 1½ hours). To Ypres (€12.90, otal journey 1¾ hours), take a train to Roese-ire (via Bruges), then the local bus to Ypres. or all train details contact Ostend **train station** ☎ 059 70 15 17).

De Lijn (☎ 070 22 02 20) operates regional buses nd trams. Buses are used on inland routes; the Kusttram (see boxed text, below) runs along ne coastline. Some useful bus services include nose to Veurne (bus 69, €2, 1¼ hours) and Piksmuide (bus 53, €2, 45 minutes). De Lijn has ticket/information office inside the bus/tram erminal next to the train station, plus a small iosk in the town centre at Marie Joséplein. To et from the train station into the town centre, ike a Kusttram (direction De Panne).

IORTHEAST COAST

The Belgian coast northeast of Ostend tretches for just 33km, from the discreet vil-ige of De Haan to the Zwin nature reserves on ne Dutch border. En route is the bland town f Blankenberge, the port of Zeebrugge and ne wealthy resort of Knokke, as well as small illages. All of the towns are easily reached by ne Kusttram (see boxed text, below).

e Haan
op 11,700

rim and proper De Haan (The Cock) nes-es among dunes 12km north of Ostend. It's elgium's most enchanting beach resort – *belle-époque* gem made up of winding av-nues, early 20th-century villas and a pretty rt Nouveau tram station. Legend has it that group of fishermen were saved from ship-reck by the crow of a rooster, hence its name. Pe Haan's most famous visitor was Albert instein, who lived here for a while after flee-ng Hitler's Germany in 1933.

The **main tourist office** (☎ 059 24 21 34; www .dehaan.be; Leopoldlaan 24; ◷ 9am-noon & 2-5pm) is in the *gemeentehuis* (town hall). Handier is the **branch tourist office** (☎ 059 24 21 35; Koninklijk Plein; ◷ 10am-noon & 2-5pm Apr-Oct, Sat & Sun only Nov-Mar) inside the town's tram station.

B&B Stella Maris (☎ 059 23 56 69; www.stellamaris .be; Memlinglaan 11; s/d €50/60) is a nondescript 19th-century brick house, just metres from the tram station. It turns into a woodcutter's dream upon entering – timber panelling, wooden floors and heavy furnishings throughout. Two of the three rooms share a bathroom.

La Tourelle (☎ 059 23 34 54; www.latourelle.be in Flemish & French; Vondellaan 4; s/d/t with bathroom €65/75/92, without bathroom €50/60/82, €3 extra for 1-night stay) occupies a pale, turreted mansion not far from the tram station. It's decorated in soft, romantic tones; room No 9 occupies the corner tower and is particularly lovely. Kids and babies welcome.

Romantik Manoir Carpe Diem (☎ 059 23 32 20; www.manoircarpediem.com; Prins Karellaan 12; s/d/f from €120/125/240, ste from €160; 🖳) is a connoisseur's hotel, situated on one of the highest dunes in De Haan, a few hundred metres from the beach. The whitewashed villa, with its distinct semicircular entrance, offers tranquillity and English-style charm – open log fires in the public areas and immaculate rooms.

Blankenberge & Zeebrugge

Nine kilometres northeast of De Haan is Blankenberge (population 18,000), an unre-markable seaside town full of high-rise apart-ments and summer crowds.

Just 4km further is Zeebrugge (population 4000), a former fishing village that has been dwarfed by the enormous artificial harbour that's been under construction here since 1895. The initial project was based around a

---

DE KUSTTRAM

Trams that trundle almost the length of Belgium's 66km coastline are known as **De Kusttram** (The Coast Tram; ☎ 070 22 02 20). They're operated by De Lijn and call in at all the seaside towns and villages between Knokke, to the northeast, and De Panne in the southwest. The trams are a superb means of getting around the area and also make enjoyable day trips from one coastal resort to another. They pass along the dunes and through the heart of Ostend – you can glimpse the landmark Kursaal casino and the harbour – and stop at the coast's most picturesque village, De Haan (above). Heading southwest, obvious attractions are the Paul Delvaux Museum (p148) and, for those travelling with kids, Plopsaland (see p148). There are 70 stops en route and it takes just over two hours to traverse the whole strip. Trams depart every 15 minutes from 5.30am to 11pm. A single ticket for a short/long journey costs €1.20/2, or you can purchase a one-/three-day ticket for €5/10, which allows unlimited travel on the tram and also on local De Lijn buses.

crescent-shaped mole, built out from the shore to safeguard incoming and outgoing ships. It was finished in 1907 and the harbour proved an economic success until WWI when Allied forces sunk blocking ships at its entrance in a bid to foil German submarine activity. One of the town's few sights is the **St George Memorial**, erected in honour of the sailors who died in this operation; it's at the base of the reconstructed mole. In WWII, the harbour was bombed by the Germans; it only reopened to sea traffic in 1957 after the mole was rebuilt and *Thetis*, the last of the WWI blocking ships, was removed.

Despite all the wartime operations, Zeebrugge is sadly best remembered for the *Herald of Free Enterprise* tragedy. In 1987 a car ferry en route to Dover from Zeebrugge sank immediately after departure, killing nearly 200 people on board. The ferry's bow doors had not been closed when the ferry set sail.

Like some other coastal towns, Zeebrugge is divided into two: Zeebrugge-Centrum (Centre) and Zeebrugge-Bad (Beach). It's at the latter you'll find the **tourist office** (☎ 050 54 50 42; Zeedijk; ⌚ 10am-1pm & 1.30-6pm Jul, Aug & school hols), in a little beachfront kiosk.

If you should happen to be in the area at lunchtime, head to the new **Channel 16** (☎ 050 60 16 16; Werfkaai 16; mains €18-40; ⌚ from 11am) near Zeebrugge-Centrum. This welcoming 1st-floor bistro is located in a semi-industrial area with views over the old fishing harbour.

For details on overnight ferries between here and England and Scotland, see p319. The ferry terminal is 3km from Zeebrugge train station, but there's no bus connection.

Knokke-Heist

pop 33,700

Welcome to northern Europe's St Tropez. Knokke-Heist is the collective title for five villages that line the northeastern end of the Belgian coast. The main town, Knokke, is the preferred summer destination for the nation's bourgeoisie. On first inspection it looks anything but elite, with monotonous high-rise apartments blocking views of the beach and sea. Dig a bit deeper to find the choicest slice of this conglomeration, Zoute, a village dotted with palatial white mansions, art galleries and swanky shops.

Knokke maintains its lead in the coastal resort stakes by offering a diverse calendar of annual events including a celebrity ball in March, a photographic festival in April and an International Cartoon Festival (in June or Jul that has been running since the early 1960s.

The **tourist office** (☎ 050 63 03 80; www.knokke-he .be; A Verweeplein 1; ⌚ 8.30am-12.30pm & 1.30-6pm) o cupies a room in the stadhuis, about 500 from the train and neighbouring tram statio When arriving in town, head straight dow Lippenslaan, the town's main street, and you' find it on the right.

Entertainment rests largely on **Casino Knokk** (☎ 050 63 05 05; www.casinoknokke.be in Flemish & Frenc Zeedijk-Albertstrand 509), home to a 72m-long mur entitled *Le Domaine Enchanté*, painted by Rer Magritte in 1953. Chances are you won't se this famous piece, as the complex is expecte to close for some time while a new 98m-hig tower is built on top of the existing 1930s ca sino. The tower, due for completion by 200 will include a hotel and apartments.

Hotel Villa Verdi (☎ 050 62 35 72; www.hotelvil verdi.be in Flemish; Elizabetlaan 8; s/d €100/130) occupie a typical whitewashed villa in Zoute. It ha perfectly placed rooms and is very reasonab priced for this affluent part of the coast.

Bartholomeus (☎ 050 51 75 76; Zeedijk 267; mains fro €25; ⌚ lunch & dinner Fri-Mon) is considered one c Belgium's best restaurants, and that for a self taught chef. The cuisine is, of course, fish basec and the tables have sea views (a rarity on th Belgian coast given either the rows of high-rise or candy-coloured beach cabins).

Knokke is easily reached by train fro Bruges (€3, 15 minutes), or by tram (€2, on hour) from Ostend.

Zwin Nature Reserves

The area northeast of Knokke is home to couple of nature reserves that have served a bird refuges for millennia. The best know is **Het Zwin** (☎ 050 60 70 86; www.zwin.be in Flemis & French; Graaf Leon Lippensdreef 8; adult/child €5.20/3.2 combined ticket incl the Vlindertuin €8.40/5.20; ⌚ 9am-7pr Easter-Sep, 9am-5pm Oct-Easter, closed Wed Nov-Mar), 5kr northeast of Knokke. It's a tranquil region o polders and mud flats, a vastly different land scape from that of medieval times when th Zwin, one of the world's busiest waterways connected Bruges with the sea.

The Zwin silted long ago and the area, a a whole, is now the largest salt marsh in Bel gium. Flanked by the North Sea, Het Zwi covers 150 hectares (an additional 25 hec tares stretch into the Netherlands) and is a important destination for migrating swans ducks and geese – some 20,000 reed gees flock here annually. Europe's largest owl, the *oehoe* (eagle owl), lives here, as do storks, the result of a highly successful breeding program that started in 1956. The salty landscape hides rare species of beetle and spider, as well as the *zwinnebloem* (sea lavender) that coats much of the area in purple in summer.

A third of the reserve is open to the public, and there are paths for hikers (rubber boots are essential for much of the year). Guided walks (€2 and usually in Flemish or French) are conducted at 10am every Thursday and Sunday.

The **Vlindertuin** (Butterfly Garden; ☎ 050 61 04 72; Bronlaan 14; adult/child €4.60/2.90, combined ticket incl the 'win €8.40/5.20; ☻ 10.30am-5.30pm Easter-Oct), halfway between Knokke and Het Zwin, is a popular side trip.

Bus 12 (€1.50, hourly) links Knokke train station with Het Zwin. Services are limited outside school holidays.

Little known by outsiders is another official reserve, **Zwin-Polder**, immediately northeast of Knokke. It was secured by the Flemish Community's nature division in 2002 following a lengthy legal battle with real-estate developers. Its 222 hectares plays host to some of the most rare birds in Europe, many of which can be seen during the bird-watching period from March to November.

SOUTHWEST COAST

Head southwest along the coast from Ostend and you enter the Westkust, another 33km stretch of coastal resorts, including Nieuwpoort, Oostduinkerke, Koksijde, St Idesbald and De Panne, that ends at the border with France. Once again, the Kusttram (see boxed text, p145) shuttles the full length of this coastline and is ideal for getting around.

Nieuwpoort
pop 10,600

Nieuwpoort holds a special place in Belgian history. It was here that the German advance during WWI was halted when local partisans opened the sluicegates on the Noordvaart canal, allowing the sea to flood the fields between the IJzer River and the train line and forcing the retreat of three German divisions. As a result, Nieuwpoort was put squarely on the front line, where it remained for the rest of the war. Just east of the town, at the bridge over the IJzer, you can see the sluicegates, together with a series of **memorials** to the hundreds who died here in WWI. A **statue of King**

Albert I marks the centre of the largest monument, a creamy-brick rotunda erected in 1938 and situated 300m from Nieuwpoort's port.

The town itself is largely uninteresting. It comprises two parts: the historic 12th-century fishing port of Nieuwpoort, situated on the IJzer and now also home to one of northern Europe's biggest marinas, and Nieuwpoort-Bad (also called Nieuwpoort-aan-Zee), the modern beachfront resort some 2km away.

Like Ostend, Nieuwpoort is a favoured seafood hunting ground for Belgian day-trippers. Fish shops, such as **Vishandel Gaëtane** (☎ 058 23 70 68; Kaai 35), line the main road opposite the port.

Continue along this road and you'll arrive at Nieuwpoort-Bad. Here is the beachfront **tourist office** (☎ 058 23 39 23; Hendrikaplein 11; ☻ 9.30am-12.30pm & 2-5pm) and a cache of hotels. The best address is the newly revamped hotel and restaurant **Cosmopolite** (☎ 058 23 33 66; www.cosmopolite.be; Albert I-laan 1; s/d/t from €72/107/132; ☒). Set back one block from the beach, its seaweed-green décor's a delight. The restaurant has mains for €17 to €25 and does a generous three-course seafood lunch menu for just €20.

Alternatively, **B&B New Largo** (☎ 058 23 80 28; www.newlargo.be; Victorlaan 6; d/tr €54/84), about 500m from the beach, offers five tidy pastel-toned rooms in a separate building next to the owner's whitewashed cottage. It feels like a mini-hotel, rather than a traditional B&B.

Oostduinkerke, Koksijde & St Idesbald
pop 20,900

It's 6km from Nieuwpoort-Bad to **Oostduinkerke**, where a handful of local men have preserved an age-old tradition of shrimp fishing on horseback. Half an hour before and an hour after low tide, the **paardevissers** (horseback fishermen) ride on stocky Brabant horses into the sea, dragging triangular nets as they trawl for shrimp. Until the start of the 20th century, horse fishing was still carried out along the Belgian coast, as well as in parts of the Netherlands, France and Britain. It died out after WWI, except in Oostduinkerke. These days it's done for tourists and tradition rather than to haul any great catch, and can be seen irregularly between April and June and again in September and October (when water temperatures are ideal for shrimps). Ask for the season's schedule at the Oostduinkerke **Dienst Toerisme** (Tourist Office; ☎ 058 53 21 21; Leopold II-laan 2, Oostduinkerke; ☻ 8am-noon & 1.15-5pm Mon-Thu, to 4.15pm Fri), located in the old town hall, 1.5km inland opposite a hard-to-miss horsefisher statue. For more about fishing, visit the newly renovated **Nationaal Visserijmuseum** (National Fishery Museum; ☎ 058 51 24 68; Pastoor Schmitzstraat 5, Oostduinkerke; adult/child €2/1.25; ☻ 10am-noon & 2-6pm Tue-Sun), behind the tourist office.

Oostduinkerke has one of the coast's few hostels. The new, low-set **De Peerdevisser** (☎ 058 51 26 49; www.vjh.be; Duinparklaan 41, Oostduinkerke; dm/d per person €16.60/29; ☐) is 1km inland from the main coastal road, set back in a leafy residential street. It caters to families, and even has a small playground.

Riding the Kusttram west, you'll be hard-pressed to pinpoint where Oostduinkerke ends and Koksijde and adjoining **St Idesbald** begin. There's nothing to see in Koksijde, but St Idesbald has a major attraction, the **Paul Delvaux Museum** (☎ 058 52 12 29; www.delvauxmuseum.com; Delvauxlaan 42; admission €5; ☻ 10.30am-5.30pm Tue-Sun Apr-Sep, Thu-Sun Oct-Dec). The museum occupies the house and studio of Paul Delvaux (1897–1994), one of Belgium's famous surrealist artists. Delvaux covered canvases with haunting images such as dreamy and erotic sleepwalkers in trams and stations, skeletons, moonlight, classical features and reclining nude women. The pretty whitewashed cottage and garden sitting smack in coastal suburbia come as a surprise considering Delvaux's penchant for out-of-the-ordinary scenes. The exhibition contains plenty of drawings, sketches and original paintings as well as memorabilia – family photos, letters, a toy train and the like. The museum is 1km from the Koksijde/St Idesbald tram stop. From the stop, walk along the main road (in the direction of De Panne) to the first main street on the left, from where the museum is signposted.

For somewhere to stay there's **B&B Certi Momenti** (☎ 058 51 89 05; www.certimomenti.be; Myriamweg 16, St Idesbald; d €65; ☒). This B&B occupies a whitewashed villa on a quiet backstreet about 200m from the main coastal road and not far from the Delvaux Museum. It has bold colours, thoughtful décor, and individual (but small) rooms – choose from Nameste, Déjà vu, or Stones & Things. The owners live in an annexe so there's plenty of privacy. The bathroom and toilet are communal.

Back on the main road, head to **Oh** (☎ 058 52 05 72; Koninklijke Baan 289, St Idesbald; menu €20, incl drinks €50; ☻ lunch Thu-Tue, dinner Thu-Mon) to sample Belgium's booming restaurant and lounge scene. Lie back among purple tassels and dine on a blend of Belgian, Italian and Asian dishes.

De Panne
pop 9900

The Kusttram ends its southwestward journey 4km past St Idesbald at De Panne. This busy resort started life as a fishing village set in a *panne* (hollow) among the dunes. Its most noted feature, an imposing beachfront **monument** to Léopold I, commemorates the spot where the king first set foot on Belgian territory in 1831.

Historically, De Panne is best known for the role it played in both world wars. It was part of a small patch of Belgian territory that remained unoccupied by the Germans during WWI, due to flooding around the IJzer (see Nieuwpoort, p147). King Albert I moved his home and the government here, where they remained until 1918. In WWII, the retreating British army reached the sand dunes between De Panne and Dunkerque (Dunkirk in English) in France from where they were famously evacuated in 1940.

De Panne's **tourist office** (☎ 058 42 18 18; www.depanne.be; Zeelaan 21; ☻ 8am-6pm Mon-Fri, 9am-noon & 1-6pm Sat & Sun Jul & Aug, 8am-noon & 1-5pm Mon-Fri, from 9am Sat & Sun Sep-Jun) is in the *gemeentehuis*, 1km inland from the closest tram stop.

For a walk in protected sand dunes along well-marked paths, head 2km west of De Panne to **De Westhoek Vlaams Natuurreservaat**, a nature reserve bordering the French frontier. This area is rich in migratory birds in winter, and on a summer's evening you might even hear a nightingale. Climb to the top of Belgium's highest dune, Hoge Blekker (33m), for an as-far-as-the-eye-can-see beach vista.

For kids young and old there's **Plopsaland** (☎ 058 42 02 02; www.plopsaland.be in Flemish; De Pannelaan 68, Adinkerke-De Panne; adult/under 1m/concession €23/free/22; ☻ 10am-5.30pm Apr-Jun, 10am-7pm Jul & Aug, 10am-5.30pm Wed, Sat & Sun Sep & Oct). This theme park is based around Belgian TV characters Samson and Gert, Plop the gnome and Wizzy and Woppy, to mention a few, and is one of the most visited attractions in the whole country. There's a plethora of rides, all free once you're inside. The Kusttram from De Panne stops nearby.

Hotels are abundant but all are old-fashioned and fussy. However, **Artevelde** (☎ 058 41 10 51; www.artevelde.info; Sloepenlaan 24; s/d €35/60; ☻ Easter-Sep), only 50m from the beach, is family run and family friendly. Rooms with a private bathroom are a tad more expensive.

For a breath of contemporary, dine at seductive **Venue** (☎ 058 41 13 70; Nieuwpoortlaan 56;

mains €18-25; ⊗ closed Wed). Located on the main coastal road, De Panne's newest restaurant offers a slinky setting and (once again) a marriage of Belgian, Asian and Italian cuisines.

While the Kusttram rattles along the main coastal road, those arriving by train are inconveniently deposited 2.5km inland from the beachfront – to get to the heart of things just jump on the Kusttram or hire a bike (€9.50 per day, with a €12.50 deposit) from De Panne train station.

VEURNE

pop 11,900

Veurne (Furnes in French) is a charming little town with an absorbing cluster of medieval buildings, all barely a five-minute drive from the coast. Unlike nearby Ypres and Diksmuide, Veurne remained relatively unscathed throughout both world wars (it was the Belgian army's headquarters in WWI), and its picture-postcard central square is now a day-tripper magnet. Accommodation is limited, but it's well worth an overnight trip, especially if you're travelling with young kids or looking for a romantic hideaway. In July it hosts the Penitents' Procession (see boxed text, below).

The **tourist office** (☎ 058 33 55 31; www.veurne.be in Flemish; Grote Markt 29; ⊗ 10am-noon & 1.30-5.30pm Apr-Sep, 10am-noon & 2-4pm Tue-Sun Oct-Mar) is in the town hall, in the heart of town.

Sights

Make a beeline for the **Grote Markt** with its cluster of interesting buildings. The Flemish Renaissance-style **stadhuis**, erected between 1596 and 1612, features a bluestone loggia extending from the original façade. Connected to the stadhuis is the **Gerechtshof**, a former court of justice, and its attached **belfort**, a lovely mustard-toned affair complete with tiers and a balcony. Brooding behind the World

Heritage–listed belfry is the massive bulk of **St Walburgakerk**. This church drew pilgrims from far and wide during the Middle Ages.

On the opposite side of the Grote Markt, at the start of Ooststraat, is the 15th-century **Spaans Paviljoen** (Spanish Pavilion), originally built as a town hall but converted into a garrison for Spanish officers during the Hapsburg rule. Opposite is the former **Vleeshuis**, a gabled butchers' hall from 1615 that now houses a library.

Rising from Appelmarkt, on the Grote Markt's southeast corner, is **St Niklaaskerk** (admission €1.50; ⊗ 10-11.45am & 2-5.15pm mid-Jun–mid-Sep). The church's bulky, detached tower affords good views.

Snowdrops raise their heads in February in the small **park** behind the stadhuis; here too is a **bust of Paul Delvaux**.

The **Bakkerijmuseum** (Bakery Museum; ☎ 058 31 38 97; Albert I-laan 2; adult/child €4/1; ⊗ 10am-5.30pm Mon-Fri, 1-5.30pm Sat & Sun Jul & Aug, 10am-noon & 1-5.30pm Mon-Thu Sep-Jun, 1-5.30pm Sat & Sun Apr-Jun & Sep, 1.30-5pm Sun Oct-Mar) is the only real highlight away from the Grote Markt.

Sleeping & Eating

De Loft (☎ 058 31 59 49; www.deloft.be; Oude Vestingstraat 36; s/d/tr/f €57/67/86/99; ⊗) Small hotel/tearoom/art gallery situated halfway between the train station and the Grote Markt. Not the most visually appealing place but it's a great option for families because it's very child-friendly (there are rooms with kitchenettes, and a secured play area). The beach and Plopsaland (see opposite) are also just a short drive away. From the train station, turn left into Statiestraat, cross the canal, turn right, and then veer left into Oude Vestingstraat.

Two good options for dining are ensconced in and around St Niklaas church. **Onder den Toren** (☎ 058 31 65 66; St Niklaaspleintje 1; mains €17-25; ⊗ dinner Wed-Mon) is a modern, split-level bar/

WESTERN FLANDERS

PENITENTS' PROCESSION

Veurne holds one of Belgium's most unusual gatherings – the *Boetprocessie,* better known in English as the Penitents' Procession. On the last Sunday in July, hundreds of anonymous people clad in dark-brown cowls solemnly carry enormous wooden crosses through the streets in a parade that dates back, in its current form, to 1644. The roots of the parade go back much further. In the 11th century, Count Robert II of Flanders was returning from a pilgrimage to Jerusalem when his ship was lost in a storm. He vowed that if he were saved, he would give the relic of the cross that he was carrying to the first church he saw. Veurne's St Walburgakerk was the recipient. In today's procession, many of the penitents go barefoot, a simple act that lends weight to this eerie evocation of long-past traditions.

THE AUTHOR'S CHOICE

't Kasteel en 't Koetshuys (☎ 058 31 53 72; www.kasteelenkoetshuys.be; Lindendreef 5; s/d with bathroom €90/100, without bathroom €70/80; ✕) The most delightful place to stay in Veurne (or in this whole corner of Flanders, for that matter). And it's also excellent value, to boot. The red-brick mansion dates from 1907 and has a half-dozen or so rooms, done out in pale blues, browns and caramels – a deliciously romantic combination. High ceilings, old marble fireplaces (not in use), linen sheets, bathrobes, small balconies and a caring welcome from the woman who runs it are the attractions. Breakfast and light meals (mains €12 to €20) – bistro-style cuisine using organic produce – are taken in a restored stable at the garden's rear (open 10am to 7pm). Children are welcome, and there's a baby cot. It's 300m from the town centre.

restaurant hidden under the church's tower (hence the name). Alternatively, there's **Le Petit Cabaret** (☎ 058 62 04 02; Appelmarkt 1; mains €25-27; ☯ lunch & dinner, closed Wed & lunch Sat), an intimate corner restaurant where sand or sawdust crunch under your feet.

The Grote Markt is lined with inexpensive *cafés* and brasseries. **Taverne Flandria** (☎ 058 31 11 74; Grote Markt 30; ☯ closed Wed evening & Thu), a down-to-earth pub with a drunken monk logo, is a good place to try some brews (sadly, the nearby Westvleteren beers aren't stocked). At **Brasserie Excelsior** (☎ 058 31 10 86; Grote Markt 31; snacks €8, mains €12-17; ☯ closed Mon evening & Tue) taste the town speciality, *potjesvlees*, a terrine made of chicken, veal and rabbit and served cold with slices of bread.

Other recommendations:

Spar (Zuidstraat 36) Supermarket on one of the main shopping streets.

Market (Grote Markt; ☯ 8am-12.30pm Wed) Weekly food market.

Getting There & Away

Veurne's attractive little **train station** (☎ 050 30 49 73), a protected monument, is 600m east of the Grote Markt – head straight up Ooststraat, the main shopping street. Trains leave half-hourly for De Panne (€1.60, seven minutes) or inland to Diksmuide (€2.50, 11 minutes) and Ghent (€10.10, 65 minutes).

AROUND VEURNE
Kasteel Beauvoorde

The Renaissance-style **Beauvoorde Castle** (☎ 058 29 92 29; Wulveringemstraat 10, Wulveringem; adult/child €4/free) is secreted away in the hamlet of Wulveringem, about 7km south of Veurne. Audio-guides are handed out for English-speaking visitors – good for delving into the life and times of Arthur Merghelynck, who owned and restored the castle from 1875. It's best to ring in advance

for opening hours because they're complicated. There's no public transport from Veurne.

Diksmuide
pop 15,500

Like Ypres, the town of Diksmuide, 10km southeast of Veurne, was obliterated during WWI due to its frontline position on the IJzer's eastern bank. Although painstakingly restored, its 20th-century gables just don't have the authenticity needed to make it a big pull.

About 1.5km from town is the **IJzertoren** (☎ 051 50 02 86; www.ijzertoren.org; IJzerdijk 49; adult/child/family €6/3/15; ☯ 10am-6pm Apr-Sep, to 5pm Jan-Mar & Oct-Dec), a colossal 84m-high cement tower that's long served as a Flemish nationalist symbol. The original tower, built in 1930 as a war memorial, was mysteriously blown up 16 years later. This 1950 replacement spans 22 floors and houses a new museum devoted to war-associated displays and Flemish emancipation.

In beer circles, the town of Diksmuide is best known for its speciality brewery, **De Dolle Brouwers** (p50).

Westvleteren

Another pilgrimage point for beer lovers is the **Abdij St Sixtus**, 4km from the village of Westvleteren, halfway between Veurne and Ypres. Monks at this abbey brew one of the country's famous Trappist beers (see West-vleteren, p47).

YPRES
pop 35,000

Only the hardest of hearts are unmoved by Ypres (Ieper in Flemish). In Belgium's southwest corner, Ypres and its surrounding area was the last bastion of Belgian territory unoccupied by the Germans in WWI. As such, the region was a barrier to a German advance towards the French coastal ports around Calais.

More than 300,000 Allied soldiers were killed here during four years of fighting that left the medieval town flattened. Convincingly rebuilt, the town and its surrounds, known as the Ypres Salient, are dotted with cemeteries and memorials.

Information

British Grenadier (☎ 057 21 46 57; Meensestraat 5; ◷ 9.30am-1pm, 2-6pm, 7.30-8.30pm) Bookshop specialising in all things WWI related, including war graves searches and tour bookings.

Commonwealth War Graves Commission (☎ 057 20 01 18; www.cwgc.org; Elverdingestraat 82; ◷ 8.30am-noon & 1.30-4.30pm Mon-Fri) Supplies detailed information on Commonwealth cemeteries and individual graves. This office covers all the cemeteries in northern Europe.

Internet (In het Klein Stadhuis, Grote Markt 32, Ypres; ◷ 11am-8pm, closed Sun in winter) There's one terminal here (free use when you purchase something).

Post office (Diksmuidsestraat 33)

Visitors centre (☎ 057 23 92 20; www.ieper.be; Lakenhalle, Grote Markt; ◷ 9am-6pm Mon-Fri, 10am-6pm Sat & Sun Apr-Sep, to 5pm Oct-Mar) Tourist office for Ypres and surrounds.

Sights

In medieval times, Ypres ranked alongside Bruges and Ghent as an important cloth town, and its postwar reconstruction holds true to its former prosperity.

The enormous **Lakenhalle** (cloth hall) with its 70m-high belfry dominates the Grote Markt. The original version was completed in

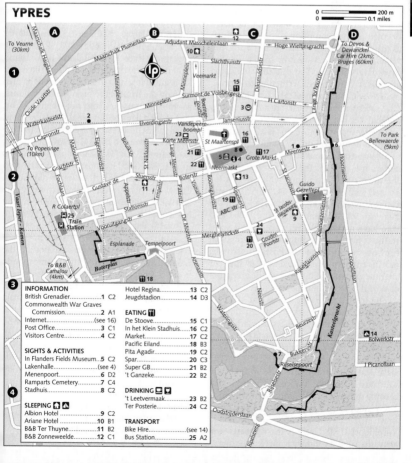

YPRES

0 ——————— 200 m
0 ——————— 0.1 miles

INFORMATION	
British Grenadier	**1** C2
Commonwealth War Graves Commission	**2** A1
Internet	(see 16)
Post Office	**3** C1
Visitors Centre	**4** C2

SIGHTS & ACTIVITIES	
In Flanders Fields Museum	**5** C2
Lakenhalle	(see 4)
Menenpoort	**6** D2
Ramparts Cemetery	**7** C4
Stadhuis	**8** C2

SLEEPING	
Albion Hotel	**9** C2
Ariane Hotel	**10** B1
B&B Ter Thuyne	**11** B2
B&B Zonneweelde	**12** C1
Hotel Regina	**13** C2
Jeugdstadion	**14** D3

EATING	
De Stoove	**15** C1
In het Klein Stadhuis	**16** C2
Market	**17** C2
Pacific Eiland	**18** B3
Pita Agadir	**19** C2
Spar	**20** C3
Super GB	**21** B2
't Ganzeke	**22** B2

DRINKING	
't Leetvertmaak	**23** B2
Ter Posterie	**24** C2

TRANSPORT	
Bike Hire	(see 14)
Bus Station	**25** A2

WESTERN FLANDERS

1304 beside the Ieperslee River, which is now underground. In those times, ships could sail in to the Lakenhalle to unload their cargoes of wool, which were stored on the 1st floor and sold from the halls at street level.

The Renaissance-style **stadhuis** is attached to the eastern end of the Lakenhalle. It's noted for the lovely arcade gallery that runs along the front and, inside, for a huge and impressive stained-glass window.

Stories have long been told about the WWI battlefields of Flanders. There were the tall red poppies that rose over the flat, flat fields, the soldiers who disappeared forever in the quagmire of battle, and the little town of Ypres that was wiped off the map. **In Flanders Fields Museum** (☎ 057 23 92 75; www.inflandersfields.be; Grote Markt 34; adult/child/family €7.50/3.50/18; ⏰ 10am-6pm Apr-Sep, 10am-5pm Tue-Sun Oct-Mar) tells such stories and more. Located on the Lakenhalle's 1st floor, it's devoted to the promotion of peace as much as the remembrance of war, and is a moving testament to the wartime horrors experienced by ordinary people. The museum is named after the famous poem written in the spring of 1915 by Canadian medical officer John Mc-Crae, who was posted near Ypres. Last tickets are sold one hour before closing time.

The **Menenpoort** (or Menin Gate, as this memorial is known in English) stands at the end of Meensestraat, about 300m from the visitors centre. It is perhaps the saddest reminder of the town's past. The huge white gate is inscribed with the names of 54,896 British and Commonwealth troops who were lost in the quagmire of the trenches during WWI and who have no graves. Every evening at 8pm, traffic is halted while buglers from the local fire brigade sound the Last Post. This simple, moving tradition was started in 1928, the year after the gate was built, and with the exception of WWII has continued ever since.

The town's southern half is flanked by a wide moat and steep stone ramparts that are topped by pleasant gardens and walking/cycling paths, know as **Vestingroute**. Pick up the tourist office's *Ramparts Route* brochure to explore these historic fortifications. The walk described in the brochure starts in the southeast at an old ammunition dump (accessible only with a city guide) and traces the entire ramparts (2.5km) to the Menin Gate. Between Leeuwentoren (Lion's Tower) and Rijselpoort (Lille Gate) is the **Ramparts Cemetery**, the closest military cemetery to town.

For details on the Salient as well as organised and self-guided tours of the area, see p156.

Festivals & Events
Kattenfestival Ypres' main folkloric event is the annual Festival of the Cats. Although cat-lovers around the world may be enraged by the idea, the festival has its roots in the 12th-century tradition of throwing live cats from the Lakenhalle's belfry. Cats, it was believed, personified evil spirits and this ritual, which continued until 1817, was their undoing. Today's version – which sees (toy) cats hurled on the second Sunday in May – was revived in the 1930s. The celebration has its climax every three years when the town hosts the Kattenstoet, a parade of giant cats – the next is May 2009.
Dranouter Folkfestival For information on this festival, see Dranouter, p156).

Sleeping
Ypres has a smattering of options in most price brackets.

B&B Ter Thuyne (☎ 057 36 00 42; www.terthuyne .be; Gustave de Stuersstraat 19; s/d €40/70; 🖵) Martine Eggermont runs this delightful B&B, found right in the heart of town. The three rooms are all comfortable and modern – the light blue room at the front is the pick. Wooden floors, warm contemporary (but not trendy) décor, and an excellent buffet breakfast (served on small tables downstairs) are key features.

B&B Camalou (☎ 057 20 43 42; www.camalou.com; Dikkebusseweg 331; s/d €55/70, discount per night for 2 nights or more €6; 🖵) Good for those with a car. Located 4km out of town with three lovely old rooms. The woman who runs it is a local tourist guide and will readily assist travellers. The B&B even has its own beer, brewed in nearby Watou.

Hotel Regina (☎ 057 21 88 88; www.hotelregina.be; Grote Markt 45; standard s/d €65/75, executive s/d €90/100) Located on the Markt and overlooking the Lakenhalle, this is Ypres' most atmospheric hotel. A complete makeover a few years back brought its 17 rooms into minimalist line. Service can be standoffish, but that's also part of the minimalist trend.

Ariane Hotel (☎ 057 21 82 18; www.ariane.be; Slachthuisstraat 58; s/d €85/110) A friendly, modern hotel in a quiet residential area just north of the Grote Markt. Wartime memorabilia dots the common rooms, and there is also a tidy restaurant.

Other recommendations:
Jeugdstadion (☎ 057 21 72 82; info@jeugdstadion .be; Bolwerkstraat 1; camp sites per adult/car €4.50/4.50; ⏰ mid-Mar–Oct) Camping ground and youth centre 900m southeast of the town centre.

&B Zonneweelde (☎ 057 20 27 23; Adjudant
Masscheleinlaan 18; s/d €25/48) Old-world and fastidiously
lean, with shared bathroom facilities and a hotchpotch
f furniture and décor. Room No 1 is the best. In summer,
here's a two-night minimum.

Albion Hotel (☎ 057 20 02 20; www.albionhotel.be; St
acobsstraat 28; s/d €80/98) Functional, unfussy (with not
ven a painting on the walls), modern hotel.

Eating & Drinking

't Ganzeke (☎ 057 20 00 09; Vandepeereboomplein 5; mains
€13-24; ⏱ Tue-Sun) Family-friendly, no-nonsense
brasserie good for a snack or light meal. On
Saturday it's a favourite with stallholders from
the nearby market, and the atmosphere is
particularly animated.

't Leetvermaak (☎ 057 21 63 85; Korte Meersstraat 2;
mains €18-23; ⏱ lunch Wed-Sun, dinner Tue-Sun) Smooth
new bistro – hidden on a quiet backstreet well
away from tourist tracks – that was instantly
loved by the locals. Sit at the counter or on
a big comfy chair and enjoy the jazz sounds
while awaiting excellent Belgian cuisine, including homemade *garnaalkroketjes* (shrimp
croquettes).

De Stoove (☎ 0479 22 92 33; Surmont de Volsberg-
estraat 12; mains under €20; ⏱ lunch Thu-Tue, dinner Thu-
Mon) There's a relaxed ambience at this stylish
fish restaurant, located just a few streets away
from the Lakenhalle. In season, it's good for
mussels.

Pacific Eiland (☎ 057 20 05 28; Eiland 2; mains €20-22;
⏱ lunch Wed-Mon, dinner Wed-Sun) Located on an
island in the middle of the ramparts, this place
is good for families (it includes a small playground and rowboats) and those discovering
the Vestingroute (see opposite). The décor's
unexceptional but the setting and classic Belgian cuisine are fine.

THE AUTHOR'S CHOICE

In het Klein Stadhuis (☎ 057 21 55 42; Grote
Markt 32; mains €14-19; ⏱ closed Sun winter; 🖳)
There's just something about this little *café/
brasserie* that makes it one of our perennial
favourites. Is it the location, tucked away in
a quaint guildhall next to the stadhuis? The
split-level design and unfailingly friendly
staff? The delicious and really good-value
meals (plus plenty for vegos and kids)? Or
simply the fact that it rates just as highly
among locals as it does tourists? Whatever,
it's a must for a casual meal.

Ter Posterie (☎ 057 20 05 80; Rijselsestraat 57;
⏱ 11.30am-2am Thu-Tue, shop 11am-7pm Thu-Tue) Beer
devotees head straight to this large cellar pub,
which stocks 170 national brews (and sells 250
types from the adjoining shop). Set back from
the street and has a garden terrace.

Other recommendations:

Market (Grote Markt; ⏱ Sat morning) Food and clothing
market.

Pita Agadir (☎ 057 20 12 91; Rijselsestraat 42;
⏱ 11.30am-2am & 5.30pm-2am, closed Tue) Pitta joint
that's been around for years and serves couscous (€13.25)
and pitta or kebab (€4).

Spar (Rijselsestraat 72) Supermarket.

Super GB (Vandepeereboomplein 15) Supermarket.

Getting There & Around

From Ypres **train station** (☎ 025 28 28 28) there
are hourly trains direct to Kortrijk (€4.30, 30
minutes) and Ghent (€9.50, one hour), and west
to nearby Poperinge (€1.90, eight minutes). For
Brussels (€14.60, 1½ hours), Bruges (€10.10, 1¼
hours), Antwerp (€16.30, two hours) and Ostend (€12.90, two hours), change in Kortrijk.

Regional buses leave from the bus station
to the left outside the train station.

Cars can be rented from **Devos & Dewanckel**
(☎ 057 20 13 35; Industrielaan 2; per day with unlimited
kms €50, deposit €500), about 2km north of the
Grote Markt.

As Ypres' wartime sights are spread over
a wide area, you'd need several days to do
the area justice by bike, and even then you'd
only be covering the tip of the iceberg. Note
also that this region is not as flat as much of
the rest of Flanders. The Ypres visitors centre
sells bike maps (€2) but the explanations are
in Flemish only. Bikes can be rented from
Jeugdstadion (see opposite) for €5 per day.

AROUND YPRES
Ypres Salient

The Ypres Salient was the site of some of
WWI's most fierce and bloody battles – for
more information, see boxed text, p154. The
Salient's wartime reminders are scattered over
a large area – it would take weeks to tour it
extensively. To see the sights in Ypres itself
plus just a handful of the outlying cemeteries
and memorials, you'll either need to take an
organised tour or allow a full day to get around
by car (see p154). Touring by bike is also possible (see Getting There & Around, above).
Those looking for specific graves should contact either the Commonwealth War Graves

AT THE CROSSROADS OF WAR

The Ypres Salient was formed by Allied attempts to push the invading German army away from its goal – the North Sea and its strategic French port towns. The geological formation of the Salient – a line of long, low ridges that ran for about 25km from Langemark north of Ypres to near Menen, close to the border with France – provided good vantage points. The armies fought battle after battle at the cost of hundreds of thousands of lives in a bid to hold the ridges. As one local tour operator, Salient Tours, describes it: 'The years of deadlocked trench warfare created a barren landscape of mud and despair…local villages such as Passendaele slowly descended into a merciless hell on earth'.

There were four key battles at Ypres. The first, in October and November 1914, basically set the lines of the Salient, with both sides digging in and gaining relatively little ground either way for the remainder of the war. The second battle in spring of the next year was a gas attack launched by the Germans around Langemark immediately to the north of Ypres. Gas was a tactic employed for the first time in WWI, and it had devastating effects not only on the advancing soldiers it targeted but also on the retreating army. In this case, French, Algerian and Canadian soldiers took the brunt of the German onslaught and counterattack. On 31 July 1917 British forces launched the third battle, which stretched over three months and is commonly remembered as the Battle of Passendaele, or the 'battle of the mud'. This horrific episode was fought in shocking weather in fields already torn to bits by shells. It cost the lives of thousands and thousands of soldiers, all for a few kilometres of ground. In April 1918 the Germans made their final assault and, although the Allied gains of the previous year were lost, the tide was about to turn. By November, the war was over.

These days, particularly in summer when the weather is good and life in this rural corner of Belgium seems to go on as it always has, it's initially hard to imagine the destruction and loss of life that took place. But the 170 cemeteries with row upon row of crosses soon hammer home the bloodshed. Should you be here on a cold day in winter when the lifeless fields are no more than muddy bogs and fog hangs inches from your face and drapes the graves of the dead, you'll have less difficulty conjuring up the scene of almost a century ago.

The Belgian army still diffuses large quantities of unexploded munitions from this area. Most of what's found is unearthed on farms, so it's unlikely you'll come across anything while doing the rounds of the sights. Much less common is the discovery of remains – in 2006, in a freshly ploughed field near the village of St Yvon, the remains of three British soldiers were found. One was even identified, thanks to the metal name tag he wore.

Commission or the British Grenadier (see Information, p151, for details of both).

The following publications are available either at the Ypres visitors centre or the British Grenadier.

In Flanders Fields Route booklet (€2.50) is an 82km itinerary complete with map and sight information. Allow two days by car for the whole itinerary; if you have just one day, concentrate on areas north and east of Ypres.

Another booklet is *Major & Mrs Holt's Concise Battlefield Guide to the Ypres Salient* by Toni and Valmai Holt (€4.85). It offers three- and four-hour itineraries plus plenty of historical information. This guide is designed to be used with the Holt's *Battle Map of the Ypres Salient* (€4.15), an essential extra if you want to track down some of the lesser-known sights.

For something more concise there's *The Great War in Flanders* (€1).

They Called It Passchendaele by Lyn MacDonald (€16) is an excellent oral history of more than 600 people involved in one of Ypres' major battles. *The Roses of No Man's Land* (€17.80) by the same author tells the unsung story of the medical teams who struggled to save the soldiers.

DRIVING TOUR

The following tour begins and ends in Ypres and winds through the Salient's northern and central sectors. It can be comfortably covered by car in a day and is outlined on the Salient Tour map (p155).

From central Ypres, head north on the N369 (direction Diksmuide) to the **Essex Farm Cemetery (1)**, on the right about 3km from town just past a motorway flyover. The wounded from the battlefields across the canal at the rear of this cemetery were brought to a first-aid bunker here, the remnants of which can be seen next to the cemetery. It was here, too, that Canadian doctor John McCrae wrote the famous poem *In Flanders Fields*.

From Essex Farm Cemetery, continue along the N369 for a couple of kilometres to a bridge across the canal near Boezinge. Turn right, cross the canal and continue toward Langemark, noticing on your left en route the **Carrefour des Roses (2)**, a simple but moving Breton stone calvary erected in memory of the French soldiers who died in 1915's first gas attack.

Continue for about 4km to the village of Langemark, then turn left at the crossroad and follow the road for 750m to the **Deutscher Soldatenfriedhof (3**; German Cemetery). This cemetery, with its rows of black headstones interspersed with mossy stone crosses, is the resting place of more than 44,000 German soldiers, many of them young students and cadets who fell in the first battle of Ypres. Behind the stone entrance gate is a massive common grave; as you pass through the gate, four statues by German sculptor Emil Krieger are visible as silhouettes.

Retrace your path to the crossroad at Langemark and continue straight on for nearly 2km to the crossroad marked by the **St Juliaan Memorial (4)**, also known as the Brooding Soldier. This soaring Canadian monument, erected in 1921, depicts a soldier with head bowed resting on the butt of his gun.

From the memorial, take the main road (direction Zonnebeke) to the third turn-off on the left (about 2.25km). This leads to a crossroad marked by a **New Zealand Memorial (5)**, a solitary column dedicated to those who died in the Battle of Broodseinde in October 1917.

Leaving the memorial behind you, turn right and follow the road about 1.25km to the turn-off to **Tyne Cot Cemetery (6)**. The largest British Commonwealth war cemetery in the world, it sits on a plateau with the towers of Ypres visible in the distance. The Northumberland infantrymen who tried taking this ridge gave the cemetery its name – they fancied that the German bunkers positioned on the hillside here looked like Tyneside cottages. One of these bunkers can partly still be seen, as it was incorporated into the white Cross of Sacrifice that stands as the cemetery's focal point. Before the cross are row upon row of

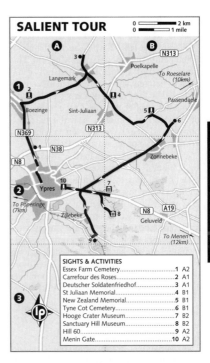

SALIENT TOUR

0 —— 2 km
0 —— 1 mile

SIGHTS & ACTIVITIES		
Essex Farm Cemetery	1	A2
Carrefour des Roses	2	A1
Deutscher Soldatenfriedhof	3	A1
St Juliaan Memorial	4	B1
New Zealand Memorial	5	B1
Tyne Cot Cemetery	6	B1
Hooge Crater Museum	7	B2
Sanctuary Hill Museum	8	B2
Hill 60	9	A2
Menin Gate	10	A2

pristine white headstones, lined up at regular intervals and each bearing a name, rank, serial number, date of birth, national emblem and, sometimes, an inscription chosen by a member of the family. Behind the cross is a cluster of graves of soldiers who were buried here during the last stage of the war – the random positioning of their graves stands in stark contrast to the orderly rows below. In all, 11,956 soldiers are buried at Tyne Cot. At the rear of the cemetery is a huge semicircular wall inscribed with the names of 34,857 soldiers who have no known grave and whose names were unable to fit on Ypres' Menin Gate.

From Tyne Cot head down through the village of Zonnebeke and join the road leading to Zillebeke. It's ruler-straight and eventually joins the N8, the road to Menen. Turn left here to proceed to two small museums where you can browse around (and even buy) some wartime memorabilia or have a drink and a snack.

On the left, about 1.5km along the Menen road (N8), is the **Hooge Crater Museum (7**; ☎ 057 46 84 46; Meenseweg 467; adult/child €3/1.50; ⏲ 10am-5pm Mar-Nov Tue-Sun). It features a polished WWI display.

The other option is the **Sanctuary Hill Museum** (8; ☎ 05 746 63 73; Canadalaan 26; admission €2; ☼ 10am-6pm) at Hill 62, whose turn-off is about 500m before the Hooge Crater Museum. This hotchpotch of a place is stuffed full of old photos, helmets, shoes, guns, grenades etc, all collected by the present owner's grandparents immediately after the war. At the back, some of the original trenches (and the relic of a bombarded tree) have been left to convey to visitors a little of the wartime scene.

Backtrack to the N8, then turn off to the last sight, **Hill 60 (9)** at Zillebeke. From central Zillebeke (1.5km from the N8), follow the signs for another 1.5km to arrive at this enclosed grassy area on the left. Hill 60 is nothing more than a few concrete bunkers, bomb holes pocking the landscape, and trenches that are obvious after all these years. A photo board near the roadside memorial shows what the hill looked like during wartime. Some people find that this site – more than any cemetery, museum or memorabilia collection – conveys the essence of war.

From Hill 60, backtrack to the N8, turn left, and return to Ypres via the **Menin Gate (10)**.

TOURS

Two companies offer very good bus tours and they're an excellent way to see well-known and some out-of-the-way sights. Bookings at least a day or two in advance are necessary. **Salient Tours** (☎ 057 21 46 57; www.salienttours.com; 2½-/4hr tour €20/25; ☼ Thu-Tue Mar-Nov) These highly personalised tours (just eight people) are run by an Englishman based in Ypres. Book at the British Grenadier (see p151). **Quasimodo** (p132).

Dranouter

Fiddlers three and more make their way to this village, 12km southwest of Ypres, on the first weekend in August for its famous folk music festival. For the rest of the year, be content with the town's **'t Folk Experience Museum** (☎ 057 44 69 33; www.folkdranouter.be; Dikkebusstraat 234; adult/child €6/4; ☼ 10am-6pm Mon-Sat). From Ypres, bus 71 (30 minutes) runs three times daily.

Park Bellewaerde

This kid's **theme park** (☎ 057 46 86 86; Meenseweg 497; adult/child €25/21.50; ☼ 10am-6pm Jun-Aug, 10am-5pm Easter hols & Wed-Sun May) is 5km from Ypres along the road to Menen (by bus, take direction Menen, from the train station). There's a multitude of attractions including a 4-D cinema, rides and animals.

POPERINGE

pop 19,400

During WWI the small town of Poperinge, 12km west of Ypres, acted as a posting station for soldiers heading to or from the Ypres Salient. To the English, this town of entertainment and prostitutes, out of the range of artillery fire, became a good-time destination known simply as 'Pops'. This endearing name gave no clue to its more sinister side as a place of execution for wartime deserters.

To the Belgian mind, Poperinge is associated with beer (plenty of small breweries operate in this area) and, more specifically, hops. The town has been the heart of Belgium's hops-growing region for centuries and even boasts a newly renovated hops museum. Poperinge also has the most unusual and finest accommodation option in this corner of Flanders (see boxed text, opposite).

You'll find the **tourist office** (☎ 057 34 66 76; www.poperinge.be; Grote Markt 1; ☼ 9am-noon & 1-5pm Apr–mid-Nov, closed Sun mid-Nov–Mar) in the stadhuis basement.

When exiting the tourist office, turn right and head 30m down the road to the town hall courtyard – step inside the courtyard to arrive at a most chilling sight. Gone is the hustle and bustle of modern life, replaced by a soundscape telling of the 1917 execution here of 17-year-old soldier Herbert Morris, and others, for desertion. The stone-walled **death cell** where they spent their last night is just metres from the original **shooting post**, now softened somewhat by a backdrop engraved with Rudyard Kipling's epitaph of war, *The Coward*. Brochures available in the cell explain in some detail the injustices of that time.

Talbot House paints a different wartime picture – for details see boxed text, opposite.

To find out all you ever wanted to know – and more – about hops there's the **Nationaal Hopmuseum** (☎ 057 34 66 76; Gasthuisstraat 71; adult/child €2.50/1; ☼ 2-6pm Jul-Sep, Sun only May & Jun), located in De Stadsschaal, a newly renovated 19th-century hops storehouse two blocks west from the tourist office.

The region's best overnighting and dining option is **Hotel Recour/Restaurant Pegasus** (☎ 057 33 57 25; www.pegasusrecour.be; Guido Gezellestraat 7; d/ste €150/325; breakfast €14,5-course menu €65; ☒ ☐), located in an 18th-century grey-stone mansion, previously home to a hops merchant, right in the heart of town. It's rustic refinement: just eight individually themed rooms, antiques, nostalgic colour combinations and king-sized four-poster beds.

Poperinge is one of the few places in the country where you can sample *hopscheuten* (hops shoots). These shoots, just centimetres long, are a regional delicacy. Up until recently, they were available only in April, but modern soil-heating techniques and tunnelled greenhouses mean they're now on menus from around New Year until April. **Café de la Paix** (☎ 057 33 95 78; Grote Markt 20) is good for the shoots, and for one of the region's best-known beers, Homelbier.

Poperinge sits at the end of the train line from Ypres (€1.90, eight minutes, hourly).

KORTRIJK
pop 74,000

The Texas of Flanders: that's Kortrijk (Courtrai in French). This effervescent town, just 7km from the French frontier, has a strong sense of identity and is powering ahead with buoyant industries (textiles and steel) and an increasingly modern centre. Although often overlooked by visitors on the go between Flanders' old cloth cities and the famous WWI battlefields, it's well worth an overnight stay.

Kortrijk was founded as a Roman settlement known as Cortoriacum and, along with other regional towns, became an important Middle Ages cloth-trading centre. The town was known for linen – its position on De Leie, a chalk-free river, allowed for good-quality flax production. In 1302 Kortrijk was the scene of the famous Battle of the Golden Spurs (see boxed text, p159), now brought to life in a new museum.

Orientation & Information

Kortrijk train station is 400m from the town hub, the Grote Markt.

The **tourist office** (☎ 056 27 78 40; www.kortrijk.be /toerisme; Begijnhofpark; ⏰ 9am-6pm Mon-Fri, 10am-5pm Sat & Sun Apr-Sep, 9am-5pm Mon-Fri, 10am-4pm Sat & Sun Oct-Mar) is newly housed in a purpose-built pavilion attached to the Groeningeabdij.

Free internet access is available at **Centrale Bibliotheek** (Central Library; ☎ 056 27 75 00; Leiestraat 30; ⏰ 9.30am-7pm Mon & Wed, 9.30am-12.30pm & 2-6.30pm Tue, Thu & Fri, 9.30am-noon Sat).

Sights

The new **Kortrijk 1302** (☎ 056 27 78 50; Begijnhofpark; adult/child €6/2.50; ⏰ 10am-6pm Tue-Sun Apr-Sep, to 5pm Oct-Mar) uses interactive multimedia to revisit the famous Battle of the Golden Spurs (see boxed text, p159). It's next to the tourist office and attached to the **Groeningeabdij** (Groeninge Abbey; ☎ 056 27 77 80; Houtmarkt; admission free; ⏰ 10am-noon & 2-5pm Tue-Sun), which details other aspects of Kortrijk's history. Applied and decorative arts – including fine examples of locally produced silver and damask (linen with a woven pattern) – are the highlights.

The **Grote Markt** was heavily bombed by the Allies in WWII, leaving few original buildings. At its core stands the turreted **belfort**, a lonely remnant of the medieval cloth hall that was bombed irreparably. A war memorial now marks the belfry's base. The **stadhuis** (Grote Markt; admission free; ⏰ 9am-5pm Mon-Fri) houses two 16th-century chimneypieces: one in the ground-floor Schepenzaal (Aldermen's Room), the other upstairs in the Raadszaal (Council Chamber).

A block east of the Grote Markt is **St Maartenskerk**, an oft-renovated church with a sturdy but decorative tower. Immediately north, a portal opens to Kortrijk's enclosed **Begijnhof** (see boxed text, p129). Flemish countess Joan of Constantinople founded this charming cluster of houses in 1242, though what you see today

WESTERN FLANDERS

THE AUTHOR'S CHOICE

For those wanting to get a real feel of the Great War, there's nothing quite like Poperinge's **Talbot House** (☎ 057 33 32 28; www.talbothouse.be; Gasthuisstraat 43; admission Ticket 1/Ticket 2 €5.50/8; ⏰ 9.30am-5.30pm, closed Mon). Little imagination is needed to conjure up the scene of yesterday, when soldiers used this house as a home away from home and to momentarily forget the realities of war. Reverend Philip 'Tubby' Clayton set up the Everyman's Club here in 1915 to offer a place of rest and retreat for anyone, regardless of rank. These days it offers simple accommodation (in either the original building or the garden house, single/double per person €25/23, breakfast €6) plus two new permanent exhibitions about life behind the lines and at the house itself. Families are welcome to stay – there's a kitchen for whipping up meals and even a baby cot and highchair. Note that you don't need to stay here to visit the exhibitions – Ticket 1 includes access to everything except the main house; Ticket 2 is the complete tour.

is just 300 years old. Narrow cobbled streets wind round the whitewashed cottages that feature dark green trim. Only modern intercom systems, attached to each doorway, detract from the old-world ambience. One house is a tiny museum, while another is a B&B (see B&B De Begijnhofkamers, opposite).

Continue north to **Onze Lieve Vrouwekerk** (Our Lady's Church), where the spurs from the French knights killed in the great battle were brought. Long since gone, the church's principal treasure now is Van Dyck's *Kruisoprichting* (Raising of the Cross). A short walk will bring you to the only reminders of the town's original stone walls, the twin-towered **Broeltorens**, squatting on either side of the Leie River.

The nearby **Broelmuseum** (☎ 056 27 77 80; Broelkaai 6; admission free; ☸ 10am-noon & 2-5pm Tue-Sun) occupies a classical mansion and houses sculptures, ceramics and paintings by local artists, including Roeland Savery, a 16th-century painter employed throughout Europe for his detailed landscapes.

The town's only other sight is outside the city centre but is well worth finding. The **Nationaal Vlas, Kant en Linnenmuseum** (National Flax, Lace & Linen Museum; ☎ 056 21 01 38; Etienne Sabbelaan 4; adult/child €3/1.75, or both sections €4.75/3; ☸ 9am-12.30pm & 1.30-6pm Tue-Fri, 2-6pm Sat & Sun Mar-Nov) is the country's finest lace museum. In short, it's Belgium's answer to London's Madame Tussaud's, with wax figures bringing to life dioramas that illustrate flax production and lace use throughout the cen-

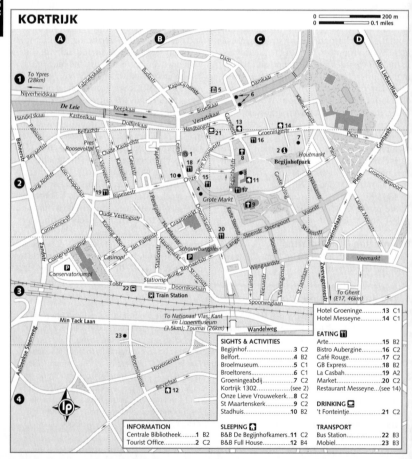

KORTRIJK

0 — 200 m
0 — 0.1 miles

SIGHTS & ACTIVITIES	
Begijnhof	3 C2
Belfort	4 B2
Broelmuseum	5 C1
Broeltorens	6 C1
Groeningeabdij	7 C2
Kortrijk 1302	(see 2)
Onze Lieve Vrouwekerk	8 C2
St Maartenskerk	9 C2
Stadhuis	10 B2

Hotel Groeninge	13 C1
Hotel Messeyne	14 C1

EATING 🍴	
Arte	15 B2
Bistro Aubergine	16 C2
Café Rouge	17 C2
GB Express	18 B2
La Casbah	19 A2
Market	20 C2
Restaurant Messeyne	(see 14)

DRINKING 🍷	
't Fonteintje	21 C2

INFORMATION	
Centrale Bibliotheek	1 B2
Tourist Office	2 C2

SLEEPING 🛏	
B&B De Begijnhofkamers	11 C2
B&B Full House	12 B4

TRANSPORT	
Bus Station	22 B3
Mobiel	23 B3

BATTLE OF THE GOLDEN SPURS

In medieval times, the folk of the Flemish cloth towns were known for their spirited opposition to French domination – the Battle of the Golden Spurs (*Guldensporenslag* in Flemish) is their most famous fight.

On 11 July 1302 a lightly armed force of weavers, peasants and guild members from Bruges, Ypres, Ghent and Kortrijk met outside Kortrijk to face the aristocratic army of Philip the Fair, King of France. Philip had sent well-equipped knights to seek retribution for the massacre at the Brugse Metten (see p120). As part of their tactics, the Flemish townsfolk disguised a boggy marsh with brushwood. Expecting little from their lowly foes, the knights on horseback failed to notice the trap and were quickly snared and slaughtered. For the first time, professional knights were defeated by an amateur infantry, and the event became a symbol of Flemish resistance and the subject of Flanders' first great novel, *De Leeuw van Vlaanderen* (The Lion of Flanders), written by Hendrik Conscience. These days Flanders celebrates a holiday on 11 July.

---

turies. Some famous Belgians, including Eddy Merckx, were used as models. The museum has two sections – the modern lace and linen museum and an adjoining flax section (the latter housed in a restored farm shed). It's about 3km south of the centre; take bus 3 (every 20 minutes) from the train station to the stop in front of the museum.

Sleeping

Kortrijk offers a selection of innovative, well-priced accommodation.

B&B Full House (☎ 056 21 00 59; www.full-house.be /en/index.php; Beverlaai 27; s/d €65/72 Sun-Thu, €72/78 Fri & Sat) Heaven for those with a sweet tooth. The three rooms, done in different colours and stunning in even the minutest detail, are based on the same theme: Belgian sweets. One is called Napoleon, another is Babelutte and the third is Chocotoff.

B&B De Begijnhofkamers (☎ 056 22 83 74; Begijnhof 23; s/d/t/q Sun-Thu €50/62/87/112, Fri & Sat €69/85/120/150) This is your chance to stay in a Flemish *begijnhof*. Two neat small rooms – pink Marcella and white Laura – are offered in this beautifully renovated cottage.

Hotel Groeninge (☎ 056 22 60 00; www.hotelgroeninge .be; Groeningestraat 1a; s/d €60/75) Yet another unusual address. This atmospheric hotel dates from 1895, with spacious rooms radiating from an impressive spiral staircase. Furnishings are a happy mix of modern and old. Baby cots are available.

Hotel Messeyne (☎ 056 21 21 66; www.messeyne.com; Groeningestraat 17; s/d €115/130; ▢) Kortrijk's newest hotel/restaurant is a dynamic duo. Originally a patrician's house, the owners have struck a winning chord by combining classic architectural features – beamed ceilings and original fire-

places – with modern accents. The restaurant (open lunch and dinner Monday to Friday and dinner Saturday) offers excellent traditional French/Belgian cuisine (mains €21 to €25).

Eating & Drinking

Arte (☎ 056 25 99 88; Grote Markt 3a; mains under €20; ♡ 11am-11pm, closed Mon) One of a line-up of pleasant *cafés*/restaurants on the Markt.

La Casbah (☎ 056 25 36 46; Rijselsestraat 42; mains €14-19; ♡ lunch & dinner, closed Wed) Ignore the gaudy wall murals at this corner Moroccan restaurant and concentrate instead on the flavoursome *lamsschenkel* (leg of lamb) couscous.

Café Rouge (☎ 056 25 86 03; St Maartenskerkhof 6a; mains €14-23; ♡ from 11am Tue-Sun) Fabulously located on a tree-lined pedestrianised square between the Begijnhof and St Maartenskerk, this modern bistro offers a large variety of cuisines and the town's most inviting terrace tables.

Bistro Aubergine (☎ 056 25 79 80; Groeningestraat 16; mains €17-26; ♡ closed lunch Sat & dinner Sun) Split-level bistro in a tastefully restored townhouse. The well-heeled clientele, particularly lunchtime businesspeople, dine on innovative Flemish cuisine spiked with local beers.

't Fonteintje (☎ 056 22 20 88; Handboogstraat 12; ♡ 11am-9pm Wed-Mon Sep-Jun, to 11pm Jul-Aug) One of Kortrijk's oldest *cafés* (dating from 1661), this atmospheric hideaway has modern art, smoke-stained walls and also the city's only riverside terrace. The latter's a great place for a drink or snack in summer.

Also recommended:

Restaurant Messeyne (see Hotel Messeyne, left).

Market (Grote Markt, Doorniksestraat & Schouwburgplein; ♡ 8am-noon Mon) Food and clothing market.

GB Express (Leiestraat 12) Supermarket.

Getting There & Around

Trains depart Kortrijk **station** (☎ 056 26 33 10) for Oudenaarde (€3.60, 20 minutes), Ghent (€5.70, 20 minutes), Ypres (€4.30, 30 minutes), Tournai (€4.30, 50 minutes), Bruges (€6.40, 50 minutes) and Brussels (€10.70, one hour).

De Lijn (☎ 059 56 53 53) runs local buses that depart from in front of the train station.

For bikes there's **Mobiel** (☎ 056 24 99 10; www .mobiel.be; Bloemistenstraat 2b; city bike hire half-/full day €7/9; 8.30am-noon & 1.30-6.30pm Mon-Fri, 10am-noon & 1.30-6pm Sat). This outfit offers Belgium's best range of rental bikes and accessories – everything from stock-standard *stadsfiets* (city bikes) to *ligfiets* (lying-down bikes) and even *riksjahs* (rickshaws). If you prefer something gratis, ask for a 'sponsored' bike (free for a half-day). Mobiel keeps a full complement of kids' bikes, and also has *aanhangfiets* ('third-wheels'; see p304) and *fietskar* (enclosed trailers that two small kids can sit in). Long-term bike rentals are particularly attractive – for example, a trekking bike costs €12 per day but just €60 for a month. Decent secondhand bikes are also for sale (€80 to €100). You'll need to show your passport to rent a bike.

OUDENAARDE
pop 28,000

The little Flemish town of Oudenaarde (Audenarde in French) is known around the world for its magnificent wall tapestries…and in beer circles for its brewing prowess (although none of the local breweries, such as Roman, Felix and Liefmans, are open to individual visitors).

Almost equidistant between Kortrijk and Ghent, the town drapes the Scheldt River (Oudenaarde means 'old landing place') and had firm access to the early cloth trade. But its fame was sealed when the local weavers switched to tapestry-making in the mid-16th century. Enormous wall tapestries filled with exquisite detail and luminous scenes of nature, nobility or religion were soon in demand by royalty in France and Spain; Oudenaarde grew fat and famous. However, the wars that swept this part of Europe in the next two centuries embroiled the small town, and by the end of the 18th century the tapestry industry had all but disappeared.

The best place to see a dozen of these works is the Clothmakers' Hall in the **stadhuis**, which also happens to be one of Flanders' most striking town halls. This late-Gothic structure imperially occupies the northern end of the Markt, Oudenaarde's main square, and is home to the impressive collection of genuine tapestries, plus the **tourist office** (☎ 055 31 72 51; www.oude naarde.be in Flemish; 9am-5.30pm Mon-Fri, 10am-5.30pm Sat & Sun Apr-Oct, 9am-4pm Mon-Fri, 2-5pm Sat Nov-Mar).

Should you decide to stay overnight, there's a smattering of hotels and restaurants. Dignified and stylish hotel/restaurant **Hostellerie La Pomme d'Or** (☎ 055 31 19 00; www.lapommedor.be; Markt 62; s/d €75/100, mains €15-25), across from the stadhuis, is the town's best locale. Not far off the Markt **Wine & Dine** (☎ 055 23 96 97; Hoogstraat 34; mains €14-20 closed Sun dinner & Mon) serves fine food, and the interior is trendy. **De Carillon** (☎ 055 31 14 09; Markt 49) is an endearing *café* in a stand-alone gable house at the base of St Walburgakerk. Terrace tables provide enjoyable views of the stadhuis, and it's a good spot to sample one of the regional brews (such as Ename Tripel, Liefmans Kriek and Oudenaards Bruin).

Oudenaarde is well placed as a day-trip destination from almost anywhere in this part of Flanders. There are frequent trains from Kortrijk (€3.60, 20 minutes) or Ghent (€3.70, 35 minutes), and Brussels, Bruges and Antwerp are all less than 1½ hours away. The train station is 1km from the Markt – turn right when leaving the station and head along Stationsstraat and Nederstraat.

GHENT
pop 229,300

Ghent is Flanders' unsung city. Sandwiched between Brussels, Bruges and Antwerp, this attractive medieval canal city has long been overlooked by visitors on the traditional art-town hop between Belgium's big three. But if you're the type who prefers exploring away from the tourist hordes, funky Ghent's definitely the go.

Known as Gent in Flemish and Gand in French, Ghent was medieval Europe's largest city outside Paris. Sitting on the junction of the Leie and Scheldt Rivers, it was the seat of the counts of Flanders who built a fearsome castle, Het Gravensteen, that's visible today. By the mid-14th century Ghent had become Europe's largest cloth producer, importing wool from England and employing thousands of people. The townsfolk were well known for their armed battles, civil liberties, and protests against the heavy taxes imposed on them.

Charles V, one of the most important rulers in European history, was born in Ghent in 1500. In 1540, when the townsfolk refused to pay taxes to fund Charles' military forays into France, he came down swiftly and heavily on the city, crushing the rebellion and abolishing the town's privileges. His actions gave the locals a nickname (see boxed text, p215).

These days, Ghent is the capital of the province of Oost-Vlaanderen and is Flander's biggest university town. Time your trip to coincide with the fabulous Gentse Feesten (see Festivals & Events, p165) to see the city at its liveliest.

Orientation

The Korenmarkt, the westernmost of Ghent's three central squares, is the city's centre. It's 2km from the main train station, St Pietersstation, but is regularly connected by trams 1, 10 and 11.

Halfway between the city centre and the train station is the university quarter, spread along St Pietersnieuwstraat.

Information

BOOKSHOPS
FNAC (☎ 09 223 40 80; Veldstraat 88) Department store with a strong bookshop.

INTERNET ACCESS
Coffeelounge (☎ 09 329 39 11; Botermarkt 6; per hr €2; 🕙 10am-7pm Wed-Mon) Atmospheric *café* with four computers.

LAUNDRY
Ipsowash (St Jacobsnieuwstraat 9) Self-service laundrette.

MEDICAL SERVICES
Apotheek Van Gansbeke (☎ 09 223 27 08; Korte Munt 6) Central pharmacy.

MONEY
ATM At the post office on Maria Hendrikaplein, close to the train station.
Europabank (☎ 09 221 00 31; St Pietersstation; 🕙 10am-12.30pm & 2-6.30pm Mon-Fri) Exchange agency located inside the train station.

POST
Main post office (Lange Kruisstraat 55) In the town centre.
Post office (Maria Hendrikaplein 69) Handy to the train station.

TOURIST INFORMATION
Tourist office (☎ 09 266 52 32; www.visitgent.be; Botermarkt 17; 🕙 9.30am-6.30pm Apr-Oct, to 4.30pm Nov-Mar) In the vaulted cellar underneath the belfry.

Use-it (www.use-it.be; St Pietersnieuwstraat 21; 🕙 1-6pm Mon-Fri) Tourist office for young travellers. Produces all manner of maps and guides aimed specifically at under 26ers.

TRAVEL AGENCIES
Connections (☎ 09 223 90 20; www.connections.be; Hoogpoort 28) All-round agency.

Sights & Activities

ST BAAFSKATHEDRAAL
Although **St Baaf's Cathedral** (☎ 09 269 20 45; St Baafsplein; 🕙 8.30am-6pm Apr-Oct, 9am Nov-Mar) is unimpressive from the outside, formidable queues form to see *De Aanbidding van het Lam Gods –* **The Adoration of the Mystic Lamb** (adult/child €3/1.50; 🕙 9.30am-4.30pm Mon-Sat & 1-4.30pm Sun Apr-Oct, 10.30am-3.30pm Mon-Sat & 1-3.30pm Sun Nov-Mar). This lavish representation of medieval religious thinking is one of the earliest-known oil paintings. Completed in 1432, it was painted as an altarpiece by Flemish Primitive artist Jan Van Eyck, and has 20 panels (originally the interior panels were displayed only on important religious occasions, but these days they're always open to view). The work represents an allegorical glorification of Christ's death: on the upper tier sits God the Father flanked by the Virgin and John the Baptist and on the outer panels are the nude Adam and Eve. The lower tier centres on the lamb, symbolising the sacrifice made by Christ, surrounded by all manner of religious figures and a landscape dotted with local church towers. The luminous colours and the rich, detailed crowd scenes are stunning.

The painting has had an illustrious history – the Calvinists nearly destroyed it; Austria's Emperor Joseph II was horrified by the nude Adam and Eve and had the panels replaced with clothed versions (the originals are now back in place); and the painting was marched off to Paris during the French Revolution and

DISCOUNT CARDS

Ghent's Museum Pass (€12.50) gives free entrance to the top museums and monuments, including all the sights listed below (except for canal cruises). It's valid for three days and can be bought from the tourist office and the museums. It's worth buying, especially if you intend visiting the Gravensteen and Stedelijk Museum voor Actuele Kunst (SMAK), the city's most expensive sights, plus a few cheaper attractions.

GHENT

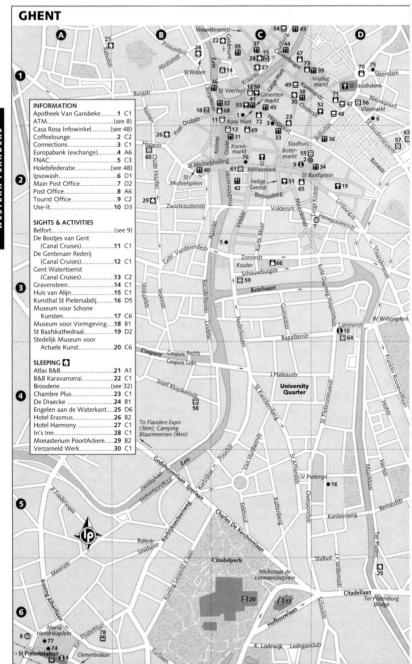

INFORMATION
Apotheek Van Gansbeke..........**1** C1
ATM...................................(see 8)
Casa Rosa Infowinkel...........(see 48)
Coffeelounge.......................**2** C2
Connections.........................**3** C1
Europabank (exchange)..........**4** A6
FNAC.................................**5** C3
Holebifederatie.................(see 48)
Ipsowash.............................**6** D1
Main Post Office..................**7** D2
Post Office..........................**8** A6
Tourist Office.......................**9** C2
Use-It...............................**10** D3

SIGHTS & ACTIVITIES
Belfort................................(see 9)
De Bootjes van Gent
 (Canal Cruises)................**11** C1
De Gentenaer Rederij
 (Canal Cruises)................**12** C1
Gent Watertoerist
 (Canal Cruises)................**13** C2
Gravensteen.......................**14** C1
Huis van Alijn.....................**15** C1
Kunsthal St Pietersabdij.......**16** D5
Museum voor Schone
 Kunsten.........................**17** C6
Museum voor Vormgeving....**18** B1
St Baafskathedraal...............**19** D2
Stedelijk Museum voor
 Actuele Kunst.................**20** C6

SLEEPING
Atlas B&B...........................**21** A1
B&B Karavanserai................**22** C1
Brooderie..........................(see 32)
Chambre Plus.....................**23** C1
De Draecke **24** B1
Engelen aan de Waterkant....**25** D6
Hotel Erasmus....................**26** B2
Hotel Harmony...................**27** C1
In's Inn.............................**28** C1
Monasterium PoortAckere....**29** B2
Verzameld Werk..................**30** C1

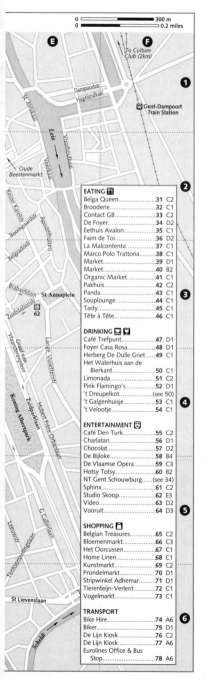

EATING 🍴		
Belga Queen	**31**	C2
Brooderie	**32**	C1
Contact GB	**33**	C2
De Foyer	**34**	D2
Eethuis Avalon	**35**	C1
Faim de Toi	**36**	D2
La Malcontenta	**37**	C1
Marco Polo Trattoria	**38**	C1
Market	**39**	D1
Market	**40**	B2
Organic Market	**41**	C1
Pakhuis	**42**	C2
Panda	**43**	C1
Souplounge	**44**	C1
Tasty	**45**	C1
Tête à Tête	**46**	C1

DRINKING 🍷 🍸		
Café Trefpunt	**47**	D1
Foyer Casa Rosa	**48**	C1
Herberg De Dulle Griet	**49**	C1
Het Waterhuis aan de		
Bierkant	**50**	C1
Limonada	**51**	D1
Pink Flamingo's	**52**	D1
't Dreupelkot	(see 50)	
't Galgenhuisje	**53**	C1
't Velootje	**54**	C1

ENTERTAINMENT 🎭		
Café Den Turk	**55**	C2
Charlatan	**56**	D1
Chocolat	**57**	D2
De Bijloke	**58**	B4
De Vlaamse Opera	**59**	C3
Hotsy Totsy	**60**	B2
NT Gent Schouwburg	(see 34)	
Sphinx	**61**	C2
Studio Skoop	**62**	E3
Video	**63**	D2
Vooruit	**64**	D3

SHOPPING 🛍		
Belgian Treasures	**65**	C2
Bloemenmarkt	**66**	C3
Het Oorcussen	**67**	C1
Home Linen	**68**	C1
Kunstmarkt	**69**	C2
Prondelmarkt	**70**	D1
Stripwinkel Adhemar	**71**	D1
Tierenteijn-Verlent	**72**	C1
Vogelmarkt	**73**	C1

TRANSPORT		
Bike Hire	**74**	A6
Biker	**75**	D1
De Lijn Kiosk	**76**	C2
De Lijn Kiosk	**77**	A6
Eurolines Office & Bus		
Stop	**78**	A6

was later stolen by the Germans who concealed it in an Austrian salt mine during WWII. The panel *De Rechtvaardige Rechters* (The Fair Judges), stolen in 1934, is still missing.

The church houses many other paintings, including the replacement panels of Adam and Eve, and Rubens' 1624 *St Bavo's Entrance into the Monastery of Ghent,* as well as beautiful stained-glass windows.

BELFORT
This 14th-century World Heritage–listed **belfry** (☎ 09 233 39 54; Botermarkt; adult/child €3/free; 🕙 10am-12.30pm & 2-5.30pm Easter–mid-Nov) rises from the old Lakenhalle (cloth hall); the entrance is around the back of the tourist office. As is to be expected, it affords spectacular views of the city – use the lift or the stairs.

MUSEUM VOOR VORMGEVING
The **Design Museum** (☎ 09 267 99 99; www.design.museum.gent.be; Jan Breydelstraat 5; adult/child/concession €2.50/free/1.20, 10am-1pm Sun free; 🕙 10am-6pm Tue-Sun) is one of Ghent's little-known gems. It comprises two sections: furnishings from the Renaissance to the 19th century adorn the front part of the building, whereas 20th-century art – everything from a Victor Horta–designed Art Nouveau wall cabinet to '70s psychedelic sofas – takes centre stage in the glass-covered rear wing.

GRAVENSTEEN
This fearsome 12th-century **castle** (☎ 09 225 93 06; St Veerleplein; adult/child/concession €6/1.50/2.50; 🕙 9am-6pm Apr-Sep, to 5pm Oct-Mar), located smack in the heart of the city, belonged to the counts of Flanders. It's the quintessential castle, with moat, turrets and arrow slits, and was built to protect the townsfolk as well as to intimidate them into law-abiding submission.

STEDELIJK MUSEUM VOOR ACTUELE KUNST (SMAK)
Ghent's highly regarded **Museum of Contemporary Art** (☎ 09 221 17 03; www.smak.be; Citadelpark; adult/child/concession €5/free/3.80, 10am-1pm Sun free; 🕙 10am-6pm Tue-Sun), better known by its acronym, SMAK, is located south of the city centre. It opened in the 1990s under the direction of Jan Hoet, one of Europe's most famous museum curators. It's a huge place and you'll need the map handed out at reception to find any of the big names. Look out for works by Karel Appel, Pierre Alechinsky and Panamarenko – three of Belgium's best-known modern artists – as

well as artworks by international celebrities such as Christo, Warhol and Hockney.

MUSEUM VOOR SCHONE KUNSTEN

Ghent's **Museum of Fine Arts** (☎ 09 240 07 00; www .mskgent.be; Citadelpark) is expected to reopen in 2007 following restoration. In the meantime, some of its collection is exhibited in St Baafskathedraal (p161) and at SMAK (p163). The museum has a good collection of Flemish Primitives and a couple of typically nightmarish works by Hieronymus Bosch – including one of Bosch's most famous pieces, *De Kruisdraging* (Bearing of the Cross), depicting Christ surrounded by hideous mocking characters.

KUNSTHAL ST PIETERSABDIJ

The **Art Centre of St Peter's Abbey** (☎ 09 243 97 30; www.gent.be/spa; St Pietersplein 9; adult/child €3/free; ⏱ 10am-6pm Tue-Sun Apr-Nov, last entry 4.30pm) is a venue for art and culture exhibitions in the setting of a former abbey. Well worth a look if something's on at the time of your visit.

HUIS VAN ALIJN

The **Alijn House** (☎ 09 269 23 50; www.huisvanalijn.be in Flemish; Kraanlei 65; admission free, puppet show €2.50; ⏱ 11am-5pm Tue-Sun) occupies a set of beautifully restored almshouses in the city's heart. The museum's theme focuses on life as it was at the start of the 20th century. It's all very quaint, even more so on Sundays when puppets (10am) take centre stage.

Walking Tour

Ghent's celebrated medieval core contains not one but three central squares separated by two imposing churches and a belfry. This trio of towers has long been the skyline's trademark, and viewing it is the essential start. Begin at the westernmost square, **Korenmarkt (1)**, then turn your back on the view until you're right in the centre of **St Michielsbrug (2)**, the nearby bridge over the Leie River. The view now is as good as it gets. Also visible are the towers of the medieval Gravensteen castle and, closer to hand, the **Graslei (3)**. This much-photographed waterfront promenade is another cherished view but, like in Bruges, it's a medieval fake – the warehouses and townhouses were largely rebuilt for Ghent's 1913 World Fair.

Cross the bridge, then step down to the **Korenlei (4)**, the riverside walkway on the opposite bank. Ghent sprung up along this and nearby

waterways because the Leie and Scheldt rivers, which meet in the city, provided easy access to the North Sea and trading. In summer these two promenades hum with happy students.

Follow the Korenlei north, passing the flower-festooned dock where canal boats moor, cross the next bridge and turn left for the **Groentenmarkt (5)**, the city's former market square (organic produce is still sold here Friday morning). This intimate square houses the **Groot Vleeshuis** (6; Groentenmarkt 7; ⏱ 10am-6pm Tue-Sun), a Middle Ages meat market that is now a promotion and tasting hall for regional products. Cheese, mustards and beers are all offered – pull up a chair beneath a leg of ham that's being hung and dried here as in earlier times.

Continue north and cross the river once more to arrive at the Kraanlei. This is the start of **Patershol (7)**, the city's only remaining fully preserved medieval quarter. The gaggle of twisting cobbled lanes is very old-world – leather tradesmen once lived here, as did the religious order of the Carmelites (the *Paters*, ie Fathers, gave the quarter its name). After years of neglect, the area was renovated in the 1980s and is now home to many restaurants and B&Bs.

WALK FACTS

Start Korenmarkt
Finish Belfort
Distance 3km
Duration About two hours

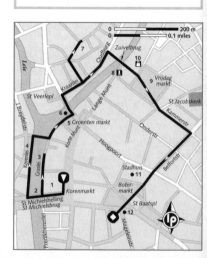

Get lost in the Patershol's labyrinth of alleys before crossing Zuivelbrug back to the east bank, en route passing **Dulle Griet (8)**, a 5m-long red cannon designed to shoot 250kg balls (but that's never put to the test). The nearby **Vrijdagmarkt (9)**, once the city's forum for public meetings and executions, is lined with *cafés* and shops, including designer boutiques like **Het Oorcussen** (**10**; see p169). The wide square is most animated each Friday when stallholders set up a large food and general goods market.

Head down Kammerstraat, turn right into Belfortstraat, and follow it uphill to the flamboyant Gothic/Renaissance **stadhuis (11)**. Wedding entourages often leave the building – it's a prime spot for marriages. From here it's downhill all the way to the **belfort** (**12**; see p163) – climb or ride to the top for a fabulous view of the city.

Tours

Ghent lends itself to being viewed from the water. The aspects only seen from a **canal cruise**, and the relative serenity of being on a boat, lend the city a whole new persona. Boats depart every 15 minutes between 10am and 6pm.

Canal-cruise companies:

De Bootjes van Gent (☎ 09 223 88 53; Korenlei 4a; adult/child per 40min €4.50/2.50, per 90min €9/4.50; ◷ Mar–mid-Nov)

De Gentenaer Rederij (☎ 0473 48 10 36; Vleeshuisbrug; adult/child per 55min €5/2.50; ◷ daily Apr–mid-Oct, Sat & Sun mid-Oct–Mar)

Gent Watertoerist (☎ 09 269 08 69; Graslei 7; adult/child per 40min €5/2.50, per 90min €9/4.50; ◷ Mar-Nov)

Festivals & Events

De Gentse Feesten (Ghent Festivities; www.gentse feesten.be in Flemish) Annual 10-day festival in mid-July in which the heart of Ghent is transformed into a good-hearted party of music and street-theatre. Started over 30 years ago, it's still characterised by lots of fun, drinking, loud music and packed streets. The city's many squares become venues in themselves, with tents set up for street-theatre performances and puppet buskers. The *feesten* include '10 Days Off…' (www.10daysoff.be), one of the Europe's biggest techno parties, attracting up to 50 of the world's top DJs, as well as the Blue Note jazz festival (www.bluenotefestival.be). Most of the events (except the jazz and techno fests) are free.

Filmfestival Gent (www.filmfestival.be) Well-attended festival in mid-October that has grown from humble beginnings in '74. Strong focus on music in film.

GAY & LESBIAN GHENT

Flanders' biggest gay, lesbian and bisexual organisation is **Holebifederatie** (www.hole bifederatie.be in Flemish; Kammerstraat 22). It has a popular *café*, **Foyer Casa Rosa** (☎ 09 269 28 16; Belfortstraat 39), and an information shop, **Casa Rosa Infowinkel** (www.casarosa .be/infowinkel in Flemish; ◷ 6-10pm Mon, 3-9pm Wed, 4-7pm Sat), where you can pick up a free guidebook (in Flemish) listing organisations, bookshops and *cafés* throughout Flanders and Brussels. Holebifederatie also operates an information/help hotline called **Holebifoon** (☎ 09 238 26 26; ◷ 6-10pm Mon & Thu, 2-10pm Wed).

Sleeping

Ghent offers innovative accommodation. All budgets are catered for, but book at least a month in advance for the Gentse Feesten (see left). The thriving B&B scene is organised by **Bed & Breakfast Ghent** (www.bedandbreakfast-gent.be).

BUDGET

Camping Blaarmeersen (☎ 09 266 81 60; camping.blaar meersen@gent.be; Zuiderlaan 12; camp sites per adult/car/tent €4.50/2.50/4.50) Pleasant ground located a long way west of the city. Take bus 9 (direction Mariakerke) from St Pietersstation to the Europabrug stop, then take bus 38 or 39, which stop out the front.

De Draecke (☎ 09 233 70 50; www.vjh.be; St Widostraat 11; dm/tw €16.60/42; ✗) A great place to stay. This attractive hostel occupies a renovated warehouse in the heart of town – the rooms are clean and modern, no dorm has more than six beds (each dorm has a private bathroom), and the breakfast is a self-serve buffet. From the train station, take tram 1, 10 or 11 to St Veerleplein.

Brooderie (☎ 09 225 06 23; www.brooderie.be; Jan Brey delstraat 8; s/d/t €40/60/80; ✗) Also recommended. It has three simple rooms (shared bathroom facilities) located above a bakery and tearoom. Unpolished wooden floors, earthy furniture, and a fabulous location are the salient features.

Atlas B&B (☎ 09 233 49 91; www.atlasbenb.be; Rabotstraat 40; s/d/t €55/68/88; ▯) Globetrotters are the *raison d'être* of this delightful B&B, and the rooms succinctly reflect this – try Asia, Africa, America or Europe. The latter is the pick of the bunch, with a warm-toned Tuscan feel that's perfect on a cold grey day. Unless you're into small rooms, avoid Africa or America. Tram 1 from the train station stops outside the front door.

MIDRANGE

In's Inn (☎ 0494 36 18 61; insinn@pandora.be; Corduwaniersstraat 11; r €75) There's a self-contained groundfloor studio room in this little B&B, located in the charming Patershol quarter. In (the vibrant host) and her architect husband have managed to squeeze every conceivable appliance (including washing machine and clothes dryer) into the studio's kitchen/laundry – and it still looks good. There are two free bikes, and young children and babies are welcome.

Chambre Plus (☎ 09 225 37 75; www.chambreplus .be; Hoogpoort 31; d from €75, ste €125; 🗶) Gorgeous B&B with a fab location on a pedestrianised street right in the city centre. Choose from Sultan, Congo or Côte Sud – all exotic themed rooms complemented by convivial hosts and an unbelievably gastronomic breakfast.

Verzameld Werk (☎ 09 224 27 12; www.verzameldwerk .be; Onderstraat 23a; r €95, 15% extra for 1-night stay) Spartan doesn't begin to describe this avant-garde B&B located in what is now the shell of an old townhouse right in the centre. 'Art&design and movements inbetween' is the owner's description of the place. Come without expectations (easy enough considering Ingrid's and Frank's website gives nothing away) and you may just enjoy it. Breakfast is taken in your room – just open the fridge to find it.

Monasterium PoortAckere (☎ 09 269 22 10; www .monasterium.be; Oude Houtlei 50-58; hotel s/d/tr €60/90/125, guesthouse s/d without bathroom €45/90, d/tr with bathroom €100/125) A night with the nuns…well, not quite, but it's close. This hotel/guesthouse occupies a former convent near the historic centre. The rooms, all once nuns' quarters, have been given the odd decoration, but all in all it's pretty bare. Rooms in the hotel section are spacious, but those in the 1st-floor *gastenverblijf* (guest-

house) are small and sober with little neogothic windows. It's definitely out of the ordinary.

Hotel Erasmus (☎ 09 224 21 95; www.proximedia.com /web/hotel-erasmus.html; Poel 25; s/d/f €75/95/150, luxury s/d €85/110) Renovated 16th-century house with a dozen rooms, some with stained-glass windows and oak-beamed ceilings. The cheaper rooms are twee rather than antique, but the luxury room is done out as authentic 16th century. The medieval ambience, superb buffet breakfast (€10), friendly staff and central location make it an all-round good option.

Hotel Harmony (☎ 09 324 26 80; www.hotel-harmony .be; Kraanlei 37; s/d from €110/125; 🗶 🖳 🖭 🕭) The Patershol's newest address is Ghent's only 4-star family-run hotel, and a delight to boot. Named after the owner's daughter, it occupies two buildings, including a riverfront mansion dating from 1859, all of which have been lavishly renovated. Book room No 31 to relax in a big bath with a view of the city's historic towers.

Also recommended is **B&B Karavanserai** (☎ 09 233 62 11; Geldmunt 45; s/d/tr €50/65/90). Think 1001 Nights and you're right on track. It has two spacious rooms.

Eating
CAFÉS & BRASSERIES

Brooderie (☎ 09 225 06 23; Jan Breydelstraat 8; light meals €10; ⏰ 8am-6pm Tue-Sun) This rustic tearoom serves wholesome soups as well as sweet and savoury snacks and is a firm local favourite. Beers are available and there is a chessboard for those so inclined.

De Foyer (☎ 09 225 32 75; St Baafsplein 17; mains €9-17; ⏰ 10am-late Wed-Mon) Convivial brasserie on the 1st floor of the Publiekstheater, near the tourist office. Overlooking St Baafskathedraal, dine on an array of Flemish meals and snacks including wicked pancakes. The three-course lunch menu (€11, Monday to Friday only) is great value.

THE AUTHOR'S CHOICE

Engelen aan de Waterkant (☎ 09 223 08 83; www.engelenaandewaterkant.be; Ter Platen 30; s/d/tr €110/120/150; 🗶 🖳) The name translates as 'Angels on the Waterside', and, indeed, you'd be hard-pressed to find a more angelic or romantic B&B in Belgium. Interior designer Ann Willems started this B&B after falling in love with a statue of a little wooden angel that she found in an antique shop. From there the angels took flight, resulting in two luxuriously spacious rooms that are beautifully thought out and magically understated.

The B&B is about 1.5km from both the city centre (tram 40 from the Korenmarkt stops about 500m away at Ter Platenbrug) and the train station (take one of buses 70 to 79 to the stop Ter Platenbrug). Price-wise it's hardly top-end material; quality-wise it's superb.

THE AUTHOR'S CHOICE

't Velootje (☎ 09 223 28 34; Kalversteeg 2; ☽ from 9pm but variable) Unique doesn't begin to describe this extraordinary Patershol pub. It started life as a bike-rental shop and, somewhere in its convoluted past, it morphed into a boozer. Don't even think of visiting if you're even slightly claustrophobic: the interior is crammed from floor to ceiling with all manner of junk and riches including, in reference to past-life experiences, antique bikes (one of which is apparently of great historic value).

To find the pub, walk north along Oudburg until you see a pile of junk leaning against the wall in one of the pedestrianised lanes on your left. There's no sign out the front, just a Westmalle hoarding attached to the wall.

ESTAURANTS

ethuis Avalon (☎ 09 224 37 24; Geldmunt 32; dagschotel .50, 3-course menu €11.50; ☽ lunch Mon-Sat) Spacious, ell-priced vegetarian restaurant with modest écor located close to the Gravensteen. Inside, 's a warren of little rooms, or you can dine utside on a small terrace.

Panda (☎ 09 225 07 86; Oudburg 38; mains €9-11, 3-urse menu €16; ☽ lunch & dinner Mon-Sat; ✗) For a ore formal vegetarian setting than that of ethuis Avalon, there's the excellent Panda, idden behind an organic food shop. Step own to canalside for a cosy and peaceful cation, and enjoy a good selection of well-resented, tasty dishes.

Marco Polo Trattoria (☎ 09 225 04 20; Serpentstraat |; mains €13-18; ☽ lunch Tue-Fri, dinner Tue-Sun) Part f the Italian 'slow food' drive, combining rganic produce and candlelit surroundings. oth the atmosphere and the well-priced eals are highly recommended.

La Malcontenta (☎ 09 224 18 01; Haringsteeg 7; mains 4-20; ☽ dinner Wed-Sat) One of many restaurants the quaint Patershol quarter. This one spe-alises in high-quality cuisine from Spain and e Canary Islands.

Tête-à-Tête (☎ 09 233 95 00; Jan Breydelstraat 32; mains 7-24; ☽ lunch Thu-Sun, dinner Tue-Sun) Stars twinkle nd candles shine in this refined little restau-unt that manages to marry lace curtains and odern décor in a winning way. Book a table in e enclosed terrace for canal views, and enjoy pical Belgian cuisine made with aplomb.

Belga Queen (☎ 09 280 01 00; Graslei 10; mains €16-30; ☽ lunch & dinner) A couple of years old but still earing the crown around town. This big rasserie/restaurant occupies a 13th-century arehouse with a prized canalside position. eafood lovers, vegetarians and carnivores are ll copiously catered for.

Faim de Toi (☎ 09 223 63 93; Belfortstraat 10; mains €22-; ☽ lunch Tue-Fri, dinner daily) New and immensely opular designer restaurant/lounge bar serv-

ing contemporary versions of classic cuisine spiced for world tastes. As you'd expect from this burgeoning breed of restaurants, the tone is cool (and the seats are hard plastic).

QUICK EATS

Souplounge (☎ 09 223 62 03; Zuivelbrugstraat 6; small/large soup €3/4.50; ☽ 10am-7pm) One of the new breed of modern soup kitchens and great for a light, fast meal.

Tasty (☎ 09 225 74 07; Hoogpoort 11; light meals €3-7; ☽ 11.30am-9pm Mon-Sat) Good variety of light meals and delicious fresh juices are available at this little funky eat-in/takeaway joint.

SELF-CATERING

Contact GB (Hoogpoort 42; ☽ 9am-6pm Mon-Sat) Supermarket.

Market (Vrijdagmarkt; ☽ 7.30am-1pm Fri) Food market.

Market (St Michielsplein; ☽ 7.30am-1pm Sun) Food market.

Organic market (Groentenmarkt; ☽ 9am-1pm Fri)

Drinking

The canalside Graslei is adorned with terrace *cafés* throughout summer. The Vrijdagmarkt is just one of the nightlife hubs. Another is St Pietersnieuwstraat, good for dingy student hang-outs that stay open into the wee hours.

THE AUTHOR'S CHOICE

Pakhuis (☎ 09 223 55 55; Schuurkenstraat 4; mains €15-25; ☽ noon-midnight Mon-Sat) This huge brasserie/restaurant occupies a beaut-ifully restored textile warehouse on a dog-eared backstreet and, for years now, has drawn young and old alike. Pop in for a post-movie drink and end up supping on warm oysters at midnight – it's that sort of place. The cuisine is eclectic and the kitchen is open until 11.45pm.

Café Trefpunt (☎ 09 233 58 48; Bij St Jacobs 18; ⏰ from 7pm) Run by the organisers of the Gentse Feesten (see p165), most of the week this is a laid-back pub, but on Mondays there are DJs, jam sessions or live concerts.

't Dreupelkot (☎ 09 224 21 20; Groentenmarkt 12; ⏰ 11am-1am Tue-Sun) An austere bar that majors in *jenever* and packs in the punters. Shares the same enticing waterfront location as Het Waterhuis aan de Bierkant (see below).

't Galgenhuisje (☎ 09 233 42 51; Groentenmarkt 5; ⏰ from 3pm Tue-Sun) The city's smallest pub. It dates back to the 17th century, and its name means 'the gallows' (that's what went down on this square in times past). It's formidable how many people squeeze in here on Friday and Saturday nights.

Herberg De Dulle Griet (☎ 09 224 24 55; Vrijdagmarkt 50; ⏰ noon-1am) One of Ghent's best-known beer pubs. Local brews include Guillotine (9.3%), Delirium Tremens (9.5% – watch out for pink elephants if you down too many of these) and the city's strongest beer, Piraat (10.5%). The tables are old *kriek* (cherry lambic beer) barrels and the beer list makes for solid reading.

Limonada (☎ 09 233 78 85; Heilige Geeststraat 7; ⏰ 10pm Mon-Sat) Go retro at this stylish '70s lounge bar. Luminous furniture – designed on-site – is one of the attractions.

Pink Flamingo's (☎ 09 233 47 18; Onderstraat 55; ⏰ noon-midnight Sun-Thu, 2pm-3am Fri & Sat) Barbie meets Princess Di at this knowingly kitsch *café*. The décor changes every three months, and you can rest assure it'll be bad taste. Even if its aesthetics aren't your thing, the funky background tunes will win you over.

Het Waterhuis aan de Bierkant (☎ 09 225 06 80; Groentenmarkt 9; ⏰ 11am-late) Another port o' call for beer lovers. Offers a pleasant canalside terrace and a popular bar draped with dried hops. It's definitely on the tourist circuit.

Entertainment

Pick up free entertainment guides from the tourist office or in pubs. Many concerts and theatre performances can be booked through **FNAC** (☎ 09 223 40 80; Veldstraat 88).

CINEMAS
Sphinx (☎ 09 225 60 86; St Michielshelling 3) Cinema close to the Korenmarkt that majors in art-house films.

Studio Skoop (☎ 09 225 08 45; St Annaplein 63) This is a five-screen cinema with a cosy old atmosphere.

LIVE MUSIC & NIGHTCLUBS
Culture Club (☎ 09 267 64 41; www.cultureclub.be; Afrikalaa 174; ⏰ from 7pm Wed-Sun) According to one Britis magazine, this is the 'world's hippest club'. It roughly 2km to the northeast of the centre.

Hotsy Totsy (☎ 09 233 47 18; Onderstraat 55; ⏰ noon midnight Mon-Fri, 8pm-3am Sat & Sun) The unassumin façade of this bar belies its local standing. It one of the city's most popular small venue for everything from jazz to poets.

Café Den Turk (☎ 09 233 01 97; Botermarkt 3; ⏰ 4pm 2am Wed-Mon) Dates from 1228 and naturall prides itself on being Ghent's oldest pub. It tiny, and inside it's nothing special, but occa sionally there's a night of live jazz or blues.

Flanders Expo (☎ 09 241 92 11; Maaltekouter 1) Al though Brussels is the premier destinatio for international rock bands, Ghent does ge a fair share. Performances are usually stage at the Expo, a couple of kilometres southwe of the centre.

Oude Beestenmarkt is where some c Ghent's best DJs got their start. The string c little venues here includes **Video** (Oude Beestenmar 7; ⏰ Thu-Sat), a tiny boutique club that attract a like-to-be-seen clientele, and **Chocolat** (Oud Beestenmarkt 4; ⏰ 7.30pm-5am Thu-Sat). Both are bi on everything from techno to drum'n'bass.

For dancing in town, head to **Charlatan** (Vla markt 6). This is Ghent's biggest music bar, wit live gigs most Thursdays and Sundays.

PERFORMING ARTS
Vooruit (☎ 09 267 28 28; www.vooruit.be in Flemish; St Pie tersnieuwstraat 23) Excellent arts centre, and th city's main venue for dance and performance by visiting theatre companies. This impressiv building, on the edge of the student quarter an close to the revamped Zuid district, was built i 1912 as a cultural centre for the Socialist Part and is worth a look in itself. From the Kore nmarkt it's about 1km, or take tram 41 to th stop 'Zuid' at Graaf van Vlaanderenplein.

De Bijloke (☎ 09 269 92 92; www.debijloke.be in Flem ish; Jozef Kluyskensstraat 2) Classical music buffs wi find a good selection of concerts held in thi hall, which is within the Bijloke complex.

De Vlaamse Opera (☎ 070 22 02 02; www.vlaams opera.be; Schouwburgstraat 3) Ghent's main venu for opera performances. It was built in 184 and boasts horseshoe-shaped tiered balconie and elegant salons.

NT Gent Schouwburg (☎ 09 225 01 01; St Baafsple 17) The Nederlands Toneel Gent is the city premier theatre company, and performance (exclusively Flemish-language) can be seen here at the company's home.

Shopping

Local shoppers head for Veldstraat, which leads off immediately south of Korenmarkt. It's pedestrianised (except for trams), and is where you'll find department stores like FNAC, Inno and C&A. Mageleinstraat (east of Veldstraat) and its offshoots are fashion hunting-grounds.

Sunday morning is market time, with the following markets operating from 7am to 1pm: *kunstmarkt* (art market) at Korte Munt; *bloemenmarkt* (flower market) on Kouter; *vogelmarkt* (bird market) at the Vrijdagmarkt; and *prondelmarkt* (flea market; also operates Friday and Saturday mornings) on Steendam.

Other recommendations:

Belgian Treasures (☎ 09 223 16 43; St Baafsplein 6) Sells all manner of Flemish tapestries, many made nearby at St Niklaas.

Het Oorcussen (☎ 09 233 07 65; Vrijdagmarkt 7) Unimposing shop that's home to top Flemish fashion designers including Ann Demeulemeester and Dries Van Noten.

Home Linen (☎ 09 223 60 93; Korenlei 3) Large collection of handmade Belgian linen.

Stripwinkel Adhemar (☎ 09 224 32 39; Kammerstraat 25) Comic-strip shop.

Tierenteijn-Verlent (☎ 09 225 83 36; Groentenmarkt 3) Mustard makers who've been around since 1790.

Getting There & Around

The **Eurolines office** (☎ 09 220 90 24; Koningin Elisabethlaan 73) is 100m from St Pietersstation. Buses leave from this office. For details on services see boxed text, p317.

Ghent has two train stations. The main one, **St Pietersstation** (☎ 02 528 28 28), is a distinct, fortresslike affair about 2km south of the city centre. Some trains also stop at Gent-Dampoort to the east of the city. From St Pietersstation there are trains every half-hour to Antwerp (€7.80, 45 minutes), Bruges (€5.40, 20 minutes), Brussels (€7.40, 45 minutes), Kortrijk (€5.70, 20 min-

utes) and Ostend (€7.80, 50 minutes), as well as hourly connections to Oudenaarde (€3.70, 35 minutes) and Ypres (€9.50, one hour).

The city's public transport network is operated by **De Lijn** (☎ 070 22 02 00). Its information kiosks (train station ⟨⟩ 7am-7pm Mon-Fri; Korenmarkt ⟨⟩ 7am-7pm Mon-Fri, 10.30am-5.30pm Sat) sell bus and tram tickets and have free transport maps. Trams to the town centre (1, 10, 11, 12 and 13) depart from the tram station in the tunnel to the left as you exit the train station. Free night buses operate from 11.30pm to 2.30am on Friday and Saturday nights.

Bikes can be rented either from the luggage room at the **train station** (☎ 09 241 22 44; per day €9.50, plus €12.50 deposit) – remember to bring your passport for identity – or from **Biker** (☎ 09 224 29 03; Steendam 16; half-/full day €6.50/9; ⟨⟩ 9am-12.30pm & 1.30-6pm Tue-Fri, to 5pm Sat), located in the town centre.

ST MARTENS-LATEM

pop 8300

From 1904, St Martens-Latem, 10km southwest of Ghent, was home to symbolists and later to expressionist artists whose works are now displayed in a trio of museums. The **Museum Dhondt-Dhaenens** (☎ 09 282 51 23; www.museumdd.be; Museumlaan 14; adult/child/concession €3/free/2; ⟨⟩ 11am-5pm Tue-Sun) is the principal attraction with a rich collection of paintings by Gustave De Smet and Constant Permeke, leaders of that time, as well as works by Ensor and many others. As museums go, it's fairly small and can be covered easily in an hour or so. The other museums, **Museum Leon De Smet** (☎ 09 282 30 90; Museumlaan 18; admission free; ⟨⟩ 2.30-6pm Sun Jul & Aug, 2.30-6pm Sat & Sun Easter-Jun, Sep & Oct, 2.30-5pm Sat & Sun Nov-Easter, closed Jan) and the nearby **Museum Gustave De Smet** (☎ 09 282 77 42; Gustaaf De Smetlaan 1; adult/concession €2.50/free; ⟨⟩ 2-6pm Wed-Sun May-Sep, 2-5pm Wed-Sun Oct-Apr, closed Jan), are even smaller, each devoted to works by these expressionist brothers.

Buses 34, 35 or 36 from Ghent stop about 400m from the Museum Dhondt-Dhaenens.

Eastern Flanders

Eastern Flanders takes in the Flemish-speaking provinces of Antwerpen, Vlaams-Brabant and, away to the east, Limburg. Its immediate pull is Antwerp, the region's largest centre and a dynamic and immediately likable city. Worldly and seedy, historic and hip, Antwerp is currently basking in a third Golden Age that has made it one of Europe's most fashionable getaways.

Within easy striking distance of Antwerp are the towns of Mechelen and Lier. Both are decidedly provincial, but they've got enough attractions to warrant an overnight halt, and Mechelen bathes in history.

Move south into the province of Vlaams-Brabant and there's Leuven, one of Flanders' leading university towns. Scholars have met here since the 15th century, and these days it's still alive with students, bars and cafés. Architecturally, it's home to one of Belgium's finest town halls. Nearby, forgotten little Diest has arguably the country's best *begijnhof*.

East of Diest is the agricultural province of Limburg. Its workaday capital is Hasselt, a pleasant if unexceptional town, whose main claim to fame is *jenever* (gin). A short drive from Hasselt is the Bokrijk Openluchtmuseum, an open-air museum that re-creates old Flemish lifestyles and is a hit with families.

South of Hasselt, the flat landscape changes to the undulating hills of the fertile Haspengouw region based around the towns of Zoutleeuw, Sint Truiden and Tongeren. Of this trio, Tongeren is the obvious attraction. It's Belgium's oldest settlement, dating to Roman times, and sellers and buyers from neighbouring countries come here weekly to unearth treasures at its bustling antique market.

HIGHLIGHTS

- **Master Class** Rubens (p181) meets avant-garde fashionistas (p197) in Antwerp
- **Sunday Shopper** Antiques in Tongeren (p214)
- **Gothic Excess** Leuven's ornate stadhuis (p205)
- **In a Shot** Hasselt's Gin Museum (p211)
- **Architectural Gem** Diest's charming *begijnhof* (p209)
- **Pilgrim Pull** Scherpenheuvel's basilica (p210)
- **Carillon Chimes** Concerts in Mechelen (p201)
- **Yesteryear Revisited** Bokrijk Open-Air Museum (p212)

- PROVINCES: ANTWERPEN (CAPITAL ANTWERP), LIMBURG (CAPITAL HASSELT), VLAAMS-BRABANT (CAPITAL LEUVEN)
- LANGUAGE: FLEMISH

ANTWERP

pop 455,000

Even the *New York Times* agrees – Antwerp (Antwerpen in Flemish, Anvers in French) is Europe's place to be. Appreciated by mode moguls, club queens, art lovers and diamond dealers, Belgium's capital of cool and the country's second-biggest city once again revels in fame and fortune.

Antwerp has a rollcall of drawing cards. Start with its manageable size and timeless quality. The old city centre, built around the country's most impressive cathedral, is as beautiful and intimate as it was centuries ago. Tucked away in cobbled lanes and backstreets are thousands of restaurants and bars, antique shops, art galleries, exclusive chocolate outlets, designer boutiques and diamond shops where Antwerpenaars enjoy spending money.

The whole city is something of an architectural museum, from the medieval riverside fortress to modern waterfront creations and the famous Cogels-Osylei, where architects ran riot. Most distinctive is its Gothic and Flemish baroque architecture; it was the home of Pieter Paul Rubens, northern Europe's greatest baroque artist. A visit to his home and studio in the city centre gives fabulous insight into the painter's personal life, after which you can track down some of his most acclaimed works in churches and museums dotted around the city.

Antwerp's role as a celebrated fashion hub means it's a magnet for shoppers. For a city of its size, it boasts an astonishing number of world-acclaimed fashion designers and many have set up boutiques here. Designer-led stores buzz with shoppers looking for the latest in hip clothing and accessories.

On the backbone of the fashion and growing gay scenes, Antwerp's club culture has expanded. The city runs on party time. Club extravaganzas burst out in summer and the nightly scene in the regenerated docklands to the north and south of town beat to the coolest vibes.

It doesn't end there. The world's largest diamond-cutting industry operates behind discreet façades in the Jewish neighbourhood. In the sailors' quarter just north of the city centre, bored women sit framed in red lights while itinerant Philippino, Sri Lankan and East European seaman wander the seedy streets. Turkish, African and Chinese communities live northwest of Franklin Roosevelt-plaats, ultratrendy style victims have taken over the fashion district, and businessmen and upper-class Flemish hang out around Koning Albertpark.

Cosmopolitan, confident and full of contrasts…Antwerp's an essential stop on your Belgium itinerary.

History

Sailors from a north Germanic Frisian tribe are believed to have settled in Antwerp as far back as the 2nd and 3rd centuries AD. It later attracted the Franks, who were Roman mercenaries before gaining power following the Romans' fall. During Charlemagne's time (768–814) a fort was built, which was visited by such noted Christian missionaries as St Amand and St Bavo, but destroyed by the Vikings in 836.

With a prime spot on the Scheldt River (Schelde in Flemish), Antwerp rapidly came to the fore as Western Europe's greatest economic centre. By the end of the reign of Charles V in 1555, the city was a trading, cultural and intellectual headquarters with a population of 100,000 and bustling docks and new mansions.

But the times of prosperity were ruthlessly cut short. When Protestants smashed up the city's cathedral in 1566 as part of the Iconoclastic Fury, the fanatically Catholic Spanish ruler Philip II sent troops to take control. Ten years later the unpaid garrison mutinied, ransacking the city and massacring 8000 people in three nights in what has become known as the 'Spanish fury'. Although the Spanish were driven out after the massacre, they besieged the city again in 1585. Antwerp held out for a year, but was finally forced to surrender and was incorporated into the Spanish Netherlands. As part of the peace deal, Philip II demanded that Antwerp become a Catholic city. Thousands of Protestants, including many skilled workers, headed north to the relative safety of the United Provinces (ie today's Netherlands). By 1589 Antwerp's population was more than halved to 42,000.

A second flush of prosperity came in 1609 with the Twelve Years' Truce, signed by the rulers of the United Provinces and the Spanish Netherlands. No longer cut off from the rest of the world, trade and the arts flourished with new industries such as diamonds and master

EASTERN FLANDERS

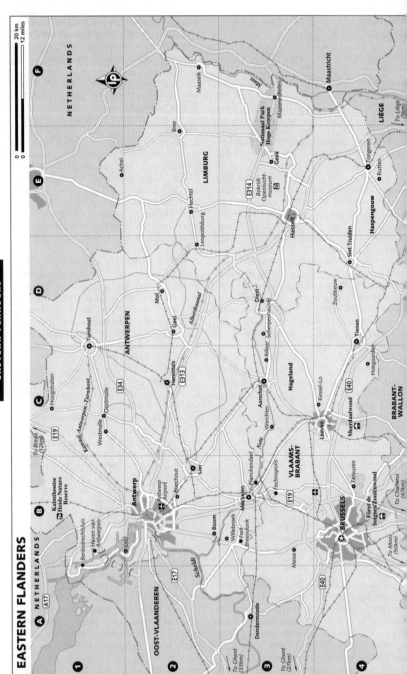

painters, including Rubens who had gained an international reputation. The city's printing houses also became known throughout Europe.

But the final blow came in 1648 when, under the Treaty of Westphalia which concluded the Thirty Years' War, the Scheldt was closed to all non-Dutch ships. Antwerp's vital link to the sea was lost and the city ruined. Amsterdam rose as the region's trade capital, and it wasn't until Napoleon arrived in 1797 and the French rebuilt the docks that Antwerp got back on its feet.

By the second half of the 19th century Antwerp had become the world's third-largest port after London and New York, due largely to new rail links connecting other parts of Europe. The city hosted the Olympic Games in 1920 and, in 1928, construction began on Europe's first skyscraper, the 27-storey Torengebouw.

Immigration in the 1960s saw many Moroccans settle in Antwerp, but racial tensions have risen sharply in recent years. These days the city is a tight package of cultural diversity. For more on the city's multicultural make-up, see p32.

Orientation

Antwerp flanks the Scheldt River and is bordered by the Ring, a motorway that skirts three-quarters of the city. The old city centre, based around the Grote Markt on the right bank of the river, is 1km from the impressive Centraal Station. The two are linked by the pedestrianised Meir (pronounced 'mare'), a bustling shopping thoroughfare.

Many of the city's major sights are concentrated between Centraal Station and the old city centre, an area easily covered on foot, although the attractions outside the old city centre should not be overlooked.

St Andries, a relatively down-at-heel quarter close to the old city centre, is the fashionista hub. Het Zuid (The South), commonly abbreviated as 't Zuid, is one of the nightlife zones. This area, first developed as a dockland in the latter half of the 19th century, now sports museums, art galleries, trendy restaurants and clubs. Focal points are the Koninklijk Museum voor Schone Kunsten (Royal Museum of Fine Arts) and, way to the south, the city's brand-new Justitiepaleis (Justice Palace).

North of the Grote Markt, between the city and the massive modern-day port, is the sailors' quarter, 't Schipperskwartier, and, a little further north, the regenerated 19th-century docklands known as 't Eilandje (Little Island). A small red-light district is based around St Paulusplaats. Much of the sailors' quarter has a seedy, dog-eared feel, although gentrification is becoming increasingly evident.

Immediately south of Centraal Station is the Jewish neighbourhood, with its diamond industry based around Hoveniersstraat.

see p32.

EASTERN FLANDERS

ANTWERP IN...

One Day
Start with the **Grote Markt** – the city's opulent central square – and then indulge in masterpieces by Rubens at **Onze Lieve Vrouwekathedraal**. Soak up the old city centre's ambience in an idle wander that finishes at **Zuiderterras**, a fab riverside spot for lunch or a drink. In the afternoon, weave your way through **St Andries'** fashion quarter, popping into **MoMu**, before continuing through the intimate backstreets to **Rubenshuis**, where the master lived and worked. For a late-afternoon drink there's **Oud Arsenaal**. Dine at one of the many restaurants in the old city centre before embarking on a seemingly never-ending pub crawl.

Two Days
Day two is devoted to **'t Zuid**. Start with the **Koninklijk Museum voor Schone Kunsten** (Royal Museum of Fine Arts), then lunch at one of the many nearby eateries – **Patine** is highly recommended. In the afternoon there's either the **Museum Voor Hedendaagse Kunst Van Antwerpen** (Museum for Contemporary Arts of Antwerp) or the excellent **FotoMuseum**, followed by a browse past some **Art Nouveau buildings** and a look at avant-garde fashions at **Ann Demeulemeester's** boutique. Further afield is the new **Justitiepaleis** (Justice Palace). While in 't Zuid, suss out a restaurant and return in the evening for dinner, followed by a movie at the FotoMuseum and some nightclubs and bars.

EASTERN FLANDERS

ANTWERP

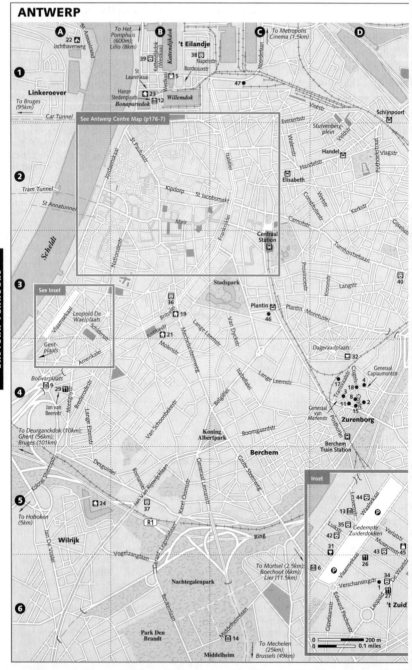

To Het
Pomphuis
(600m);
Lillo (8km)

'␣t Eilandje

38 Napelsstr

Bordeauxstr

5

39 Kattendijkdok
(Westkaai)

St
Laurerkaai

St Annastrand

22 Jachthavenweg

To Metropolis
Cinema (1.5km)

Noorderlaan

47

Schijnpoort

Linkeroever

To Bruges
(95km)

Hanze
Stedenplaats

Bonapartedok

23

12

Willemdok

Viséstr

Everaertsstr

Stuivenberg-
plein

Veldstr

Handel

Pothoekstraat

Vlagstr

Car Tunnel

See Antwerp Centre Map (p176-7)

St Paulsstr

Jordaenskaai

Kipdorp

St Jacobsmarkt

Meir

Italiëlei

Handelstr

Elisabeth

Westr

Constantstr

Carnotstr

Kerkstr

Gijselstr

Tram Tunnel

St Annatunnel

Nationalestr

Frankrijklei

Centraal
Station

Provinciestr

Turnhoutsebaan

Kroonstr

Langstr

40

Scheldt

See Inset

Leopold De
Waelplaats

Stadspark

36

Brits...

19

Plantin

46

Plantin-Moretuslei

Dageraadplaats

32

Generaal
Capiaumontstr

Vlaamsekaai

Schildersstr

Gent-
plaats

Amerikalei

21

Molenstr

Lange Leemstr

Van Dijckl...

Lange Leemstr

Cogels...

Transvaalstr

17

18

4

8

11

15

2

Bolivarplaats

9

29

Jan van
Beerstr

Bredarodestr

Montigny...

Lange Elzenstr

Van Schoonbekestr

Begijnen...

Isabellalei

Generaal
van
Merlenstr

Zurenborg

To Deurganckdok (10km);
Ghent (56km);
Bruges (101km)

Koning
Albertpark

Boomgaardstr

Berchem

Berchem
Train Station

Desguinlei

Kolonel Silvertoplaan

Bossenstein

Jan Van Rijswijcklaan

Karel Oomsstr

Generaal Lemanstr

Grote Steenweg

Inset

44

Waterlokaal

13

35

Gedempte
Zuiderdokken

Verlatstr

42

Luiksstr

Museumstr

45

To Hoboken
(5km)

24

37

R1

Ring

31

43

26

Wilrijk

Vogelzangdaan

6

Vlaamsekaai

34

1

27

Verschansingstr

'␣t Zuid

Edward Pecherstr

Cogelsstr

Leopold...

Nachtegalenpark

To Mortsel (2.5km);
Boechout (6km);
Lier (11.5km)

Park Den
Brandt

14

Middelheim

Middelheimlaan

Berkenlaan

To Mecheler
(25km);
Brussels (49km)

0   200 m
0   0.1 miles

INFORMATION		
Wassalon	1	D6
SIGHTS & ACTIVITIES		
De Morgenster	2	D4
De Vier Seizoenen	3	D4
Euterpia	4	D4
Flandria (Quay 14)	5	B1
FotoMuseum	6	D6
Help U Zelve	7	E5
Huize Zonnebloem	8	D4
Justitiepaleis	9	A4
Koninklijk Museum voor		
Schone Kunsten	10	E6
Les Mouettes	11	D4
Museum aan de Stroom	12	B1
Museum voor Hedendaagse		
Kunst van Antwerpen	13	D5
Openluchtmuseum voor		
Beeldhouwkunst		
Middelheim	14	C6
Quinten Matsys	15	D4
't Bootje	16	E6
Twaalf Duivels	17	D4
Witte Paleizen	18	D4
SLEEPING 🏠 🏨		
Aan de Leien B&B	19	B3
B&B Charles Rogier XI	20	E5
Bed, Bad & Brood	21	B3
Camping De Molen	22	A1
Floatel Diamond Princess	23	B1
Hostel Op Sinjoorke	24	A5
Patine	(see 27)	
Slapenenzo	25	E5
EATING 🍴		
L'Entrepot du Congo	26	D6
Patine	27	D4
Soeki	28	E5
Walrus	29	A4
DRINKING 🍸 🍺		
Atthis	30	E5
Bar Tabac	31	D5
Den Draak	32	D4
Mogador	33	E5
ENTERTAINMENT 🎭		
Café Hopper	34	D6
Café Local	35	D5
Crossroads Café	36	B3
deSingel	37	B5
FotoMuseum	(see 6)	
Kaaiman	38	B1
Koninklijk Ballet van		
Vlaanderen	39	B1
Roma	40	D3
Sportpaleis	41	E1
Stereo Sushi	42	D5
Studio Tokio	43	D5
Zuiderpershuis	44	D5
SHOPPING 🛍		
Ann Demeulemeester	45	D5
TRANSPORT		
Avis	46	C3
Budget	47	C1

Further southeast is Zurenborg, today considered one of the city's finest neighbourhoods. The area is famed for its rich *belle-époque* quarter, based around a street called Cogels-Osylei.

From the Ring, Antwerp fans out into suburbs, such as Berchem, Deurne, Hoboken and Wilrijk. It also extends west to Linkeroever (Left Bank), easily accessible via the pedestrianised St Annatunnel under the Scheldt.

MAPS

Many maps of Antwerp are very poor quality and prove quite useless for navigating the maze of streets in the old city centre. The detailed maps in this book should stand you in good stead. For exploring further afield, Geocart's *Super Plan No 69* (scales 1:17,500 and 1:10,000) of Antwerp and its environs also lists streets and useful addresses.

Information
BOOKSHOPS
Copyright (Map pp176-7; ☎ 03 232 94 16; Nationalestraat 28a; ⊗ 11am-6.30pm Tue-Sat, 11am-5.30pm Sun) Specialises in fashion, art and architecture; located next to MoMu.

De Slegte (Map pp176-7; ☎ 03 231 66 27; Wapper 5) Secondhand books, including English-language novels.

FNAC (Map pp176-7; ☎ 03 231 20 56; Groenplaats; ⊗ 10am-6.30pm Mon-Sat, 10am-7pm Fri) On 1st floor of the Grand Bazar shopping centre. All-round bookshop with a strong travel section.

International Magazine Store (Map pp176-7; ☎ 03 233 16 68; Melkmarkt 17; ⊗ 7.30am-7pm Mon-Fri, 8.30am-7pm Sat, 11am-6.30pm Sun) The place for foreign and local newspapers and top-selling magazines.

Mekanik Strip (Map pp176-7; ☎ 03 234 23 47; St Jacobsmarkt 73; ⊗ 10am-6pm Mon-Sat) Excellent comic-strip shop with a little art gallery upstairs.

Stripwinkel Beo (Map pp176-7; ☎ 03 233 25 36; Oude Vaartplaats 16; ⊗ 10am-6.30pm Tue-Sat, 10am-2pm Sun) City's largest comic-strip shop.

EMERGENCY
Ambulance/Fire (☎ 100)
Police (☎ 101)

INTERNET ACCESS
2Zones (Map pp176-7; ☎ 03 232 24 00; Wolstraat 15; per hr €4.50; ⊗ 11am-midnight) Cool internet bar with a dozen terminals. Under 26 year olds get a 50% discount.

LAUNDRY
Netezon (Map pp176-7; Nationalestraat 18) Near MoMu.
Wassalon (Map pp174-5; Verschansingstraat 13) In 't Zuid.

ANTWERP CENTRE

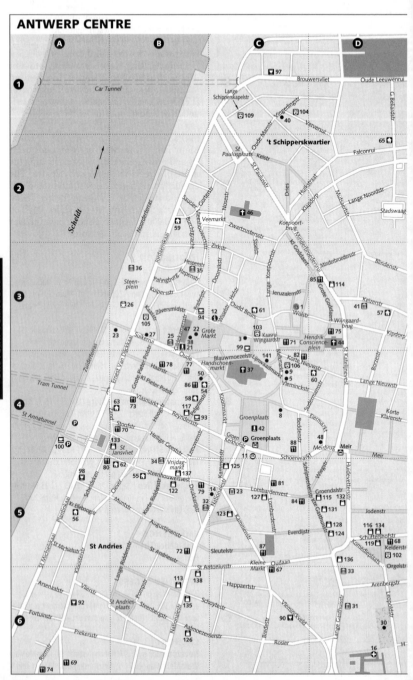

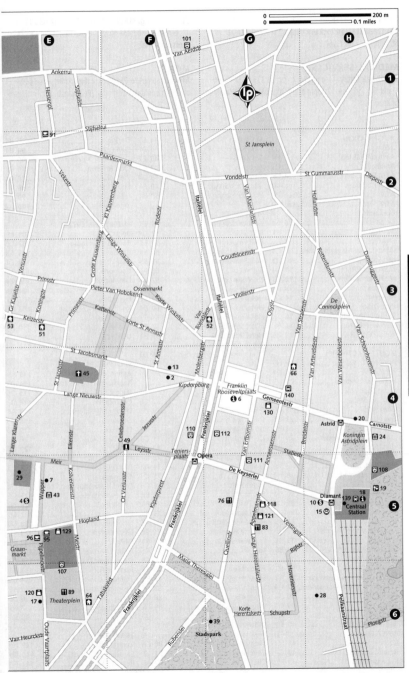

LEFT LUGGAGE
Centraal Station lockers (Map pp176-7; Centraal Station; per 24hr €2.60-3.60)

MEDICAL SERVICES
Apotheek Lotry (Map pp176-7; ☎ 03 233 01 86; Grote Markt 56; ⏰ 9am-12.30pm & 2-7.30pm Mon-Fri) Handy pharmacy.

St Elisabethgasthuis (Map pp176-7; ☎ 03 234 41 11, emergency 03 234 40 50; Leopoldstraat 26; ⏰ 24hr) Central hospital.

MONEY
ATMs (Map pp176-7) KBC Bank (**Eiermarkt**); main post office (**Groenplaats**); post office (**Pelikaanstraat**); Fortis Bank (**Wapper**)

INFORMATION
2Zones.................................1 C3
Airstop/Taxistop.................2 F4
Apotheek Lotry...................3 C3
ATM Fortis Bank.................4 E5
ATM KBC Bank................(see 48)
ATM...............................(see 11)
ATM...............................(see 15)
Connections........................5 C4
De Lijn................................6 G4
De Slegte...........................7 E5
FNAC..................................8 C4
International Magazine Store.....9 C4
Leo Stevens......................10 H5
Main Post Office...............11 C4
Main Tourist Office...........12 C3
Mekanik Strip....................13 F4
Netezon............................14 C5
Post Office.......................15 H5
St Elisabethgasthuis..........16 D6
Stripwinkel Beo.................17 E6
Tourist Office....................18 H5

SIGHTS & ACTIVITIES
Antwerp Zoo.....................19 H5
Aquatopia.........................20 H4
Bag Bearer Statue..............21 B3
Brabo Fountain..................22 B3
Centraal Station..............(see 139)
Copyright........................(see 32)
Dagbladmuseum................23 C5
Diamantmuseum................24 H4
Etnographisch Museum.......25 B3
Flandria............................26 B3
Het Ruihuis.......................27 B3
Het Steen.......................(see 36)
Hoge Raad voor Diamant....28 H6
Koninklijk Paleis.................29 E5
Kruidtuin..........................30 D6
Maagdenhuis.....................31 D6
ModeNatie.....................(see 32)
MoMu................................32 E5
Museum Mayer Van den
  Bergh............................33 D6
Museum Plantin-Moretus......34 B5
Museum Vleeshuis/Kank
  van de Stad....................35 B3
Nationaal Scheepvaartmuseum.36 B3
Onze Lieve Vrouwekathedraal.37 C4
Peerdentram......................38 B3
Playground........................39 G6
Prospekta........................(see 12)
Red-Light District................40 C1
Rent A Bike....................(see 141)
Rockoxhuis........................41 D3
Rubens Statue....................42 C4
Rubenshuis........................43 E5

St Carolus-Borromeuskerk........44 D3
St Jacobskerk.....................45 E4
St Pauluskerk.....................46 C2
Stadhuis............................47 B3
Torengebouw......................48 D4
Van Dyck Statue..................49 F4
Vlaeykensgang....................50 B4

SLEEPING 🏠
Aandekeizer B&B.................51 E3
B&B 2000..........................52 G3
B&B Emperor's 48................53 E3
B&B Le Patio......................54 B4
B&B Siddartha.....................55 B5
Big Sleep...........................56 A5
De Witte Lelie.....................57 D3
Den Heksenketel..................58 B4
Hotel Antigone....................59 B2
Hotel Julien........................60 D4
Hotel Rubens......................61 C3
Hotel Scheldezicht................62 B5
Hotel 't Sandt.....................63 B4
Ibis Antwerpen Centrum.......64 E6
International Zeemanshuis......65 D2
Vlaamse
  Jeugdherbergcentrale.........66 G4

EATING 🍴
Berlin................................67 C6
Bourla & Mares....................68 D5
Dansing Chocola..................69 A6
De Kleine Zavel...................70 B4
De Peerdestal......................71 C3
Delhaize............................72 B5
Eethuisje De Stoemppot........73 B4
El Pintxo's..........................74 A6
Façade..............................75 D3
Faites simple......................76 C5
Frituur No 1........................77 B4
Gin Fish.............................78 B4
Het Dagelijks Brood.............79 B5
Het Nieuwe Palinghuis..........80 A5
Hungry Henrietta.................81 C5
La Cuisine..........................82 C4
Lamalo..............................83 G5
Lombardia..........................84 C5
Pottenbrug........................85 D3
Sir Anthony Van Dyck..........86 B4
Soep & Soup.......................87 C5
Super GB...........................88 C4
Vogelmarkt........................89 E6

DRINKING 🍷 🍺
Boekhandel 't Verschil.........(see 114)
Bierhuis Kulminator.............90 C6
Café Hessenhuis..................91 E2
Chez Fred..........................92 A6

De Vagant..........................93 B4
Den Engel..........................94 B3
Grand Café Horta................95 E5
Oud Arsenaal......................96 E5
Pier 19..............................97 C1
Popi Café...........................98 A5
't Elfde Gebod....................99 C3
Zuiderterras.......................100 A4

ENTERTAINMENT 🎭
Boots...............................101 F1
Bourlaschouwburg..............102 D5
Buster..............................103 C3
Café d'Anvers....................104 C1
Cartoons...........................105 B3
De Muze...........................106 C4
FNAC Ticket Service...........(see 8)
Het Paleis.........................107 E6
Koningin Elisabethzaal..........108 H5
Red & Blue........................109 C1
Space...............................110 F4
UGC.................................111 G5
Vlaamse Opera...................112 G4

SHOPPING 🛍
Annemie Verbeke................113 B6
Boekhandel 't Verschil..........114 D3
Burie...............................115 D5
Coccodrillo........................116 D5
De Vagant Slijterij...............117 B4
Del Rey............................118 G5
Delvaux............................119 D5
Den Dorstvlegel.................120 E6
Diamondland......................121 G5
Episode............................122 B5
Fish & Chips......................123 C5
Goossens..........................124 D5
Grand Bazar Shopping Centre..(see 88)
Het Modepaleis...................125 C5
Labels Inc..........................126 B6
Louis...............................127 C5
Nico Taeymans...................128 D5
Olivier Strelli.....................129 E5
Pardaf..............................130 G4
Philip's Biscuits..................131 D5
Pierre Marcolini..................132 D5
Rommelmarkt.....................133 B4
Temmerman.......................134 C5
Veronique Branquinho..........135 B6
Verso...............................136 D5
Vrijdagmarkt......................137 B5
Walter..............................138 B6

TRANSPORT
Centraal Station.................139 H5
Eurolines..........................140 G4
Rent A Bike.......................141 C4

Leo Stevens (Map pp176-7; ☎ 03 232 18 43; De Keyserlei 64; ☯ 9.30am-4.30pm Mon-Fri) Excellent exchange rates, but handles cash only. Opposite Centraal Station.

POST
Main post office (Map pp176-7; Groenplaats 43) Handy to the Grote Markt.
Post office (Map pp176-7; Pelikaanstraat 16) Opposite Centraal Station.

TOURIST INFORMATION
Main tourist office (Map pp176-7; ☎ 03 232 01 03; www.visitantwerpen.be; Grote Markt 13; ☯ 9am-6pm Mon-Sat, 9am-5pm Sun)
Tourist office (Map pp176-7; Centraal Station; ☯ 9am-6pm Mon-Sat, 9am-5pm Sun)

TRAVEL AGENCIES
Airstop/Taxistop (Map pp176-7; ☎ 070 23 31 88; St Jacobsmarkt 84)
Connections (Map pp176-7; ☎ 070 23 33 13; Melkmarkt 23)

Sights
OLD CITY CENTRE
As in every great Flemish city, life in Antwerp radiates out from the **Grote Markt** (Map pp176-7), a vast, pedestrianised, triangular market square presided over by the impressive Renaissance-style **stadhuis** (town hall; Map pp176-7). Designed by Cornelius Floris De Vriendt and completed in 1565, the stadhuis' palatial façade is a blend of Flemish and Italian styles, an innovative departure from the standard Gothic architecture prevalent at the time of construction. The commanding gable is topped by a fine gilded eagle and flanked by statues representing wisdom and justice.

The Grote Markt is lined on two sides by Renaissance-style **guildhalls**, most of which were reconstructed in the 19th century. The tallest and most impressive is No 7, topped by a gilded statue of St George astride a rearing horse as he spears a dragon.

The voluptuous, baroque **Brabo Fountain** (Map pp176-7) rises from a rough pile of rocks in the centre of the Grote Markt. Crafted in 1887 by Jef Lambeaux (who lived at Grote Markt 44), it depicts the legend of Antwerp's name (see boxed text, p180).

Next to the stadhuis entrance, the **Etnografisch Museum** (Ethnographic Museum; Map pp176-7; ☎ 03 220 86 00; www.museum.antwerpen.be/etnografisch_museum; Suikerrui 19; adult/concession €4/3; ☯ 10am-5pm Tue-Sun) contains a highly respected col-

lection of traditional artefacts from around the world.

Next door again is the city's newest attraction, **Het Ruihuis** (Map pp176-7; ☎ 03 232 01 03; Suikerrui 21; ☯ 9.30am-5.30pm Thu-Tue), an adventure through the city's underground sewer system. Expect things to be a bit pongy at the start, but then highly sanitised. Choose a three-hour guided tour (€14.50), or pop in for a visit *zonder gids* (without guide; €2.50).

The splendid **Onze Lieve Vrouwekathedraal** (Cathedral of Our Lady; Map pp176-7; ☎ 03 213 99 51; Handschoenmarkt; adult/concession €2/1.50; ☯ 10am-5pm Mon-Fri, 10am-3pm Sat, 10am-4pm Sun) is the largest and finest Gothic cathedral in Belgium. It was 169 years in the making (1352–521) and the work of several architects (Appelmans, Domien and Keldermans). Its graceful 123m-high spire was a mighty landmark in early times and is still visible from kilometres around today. The combined effects of a fire in the Middle Ages, the Iconoclastic Fury and plundering during the French occupation mean that little of what you see today inside the cathedral is original Gothic. Instead, baroque decorations – notably four early canvases by Rubens – adorn its light but imposing interior. From the centre of the seven-aisled nave, look straight down to the high altar and Rubens' *Assumption* (1625). Although impossible to view up close, this painting's radiance is profound. To the left of the central crossing is *The Raising of the Cross* (1610), while the much smaller *Resurrection* (1612) hangs in a small chapel to the right of the high altar. The most celebrated of Rubens' four paintings is *The Descent from the Cross* (1612) immediately to the right of the central crossing. In this sensitive triptych, the deathly grey Christ is lowered by mourners while the Virgin reaches to touch her son.

Fashion followers must start with Antwerp's mode museum, **MoMu** (Map pp176-7; ☎ 03 470 27 70; www.momu.be; Nationalestraat 28; adult/concession €7/5; ☯ 10am-6pm Tue-Sun). It's located in the much-celebrated **ModeNatie** (www.modenatie.com) complex, home also to both the Flanders Fashion Institute and the fashion department of the Royal Academy of Fine Arts. Sticking firmly to avant-garde, MoMu changes its exhibits every six months. For more on Antwerp fashion, see boxed text (p197).

The World Heritage–listed **Museum Plantin-Moretus** (Map pp176-7; ☎ 03 221 14 50; www.museum.antwerpen.be/plantin_moretus; Vrijdagmarkt 22; adult/concession €5/3; ☯ 10am-5pm Tue-Sun) is home to the

EASTERN FLANDERS

THE LEGEND LIVES ON

Two stories tell the origins of Antwerp's name.

The not so popular, but more likely, explanation lies with archaeological remains found near the riverside castle, Steen. The findings proved that a Gallo-Roman settlement existed on a mound *(aanwerp)* that partly vanished when the quays were straightened in the 1880s.

The legend, of course, is much more colourful. It tells of Druon Antigoon, a giant, who lived at the bend of the Scheldt and forced passing shipmasters to pay a toll. Those who refused lost a hand. Along came Silvius Brabo, a Roman warrior, who killed the giant, chopped off his hand and chucked it in the river. *Hand werpen* (hand throwing) subsequently evolved into Antwerpen.

Today the city uses *Antwerpse handjes* (Antwerp hands) to symbolise friendship. All manner of gift items are made in the shape of little hands, from butter biscuits to chocolates.

world's first industrial printing works. This fascinating museum deals with a prosperous 16th- and 17th-century printing family headed by Christoffel Plantin. Plantin moved from France to Antwerp where he set up as a bookbinder in 1548. Eight years later he started a printing business that eventually became the Low Countries' largest printing and publishing concern and a magnet for intellectuals, scientists and humanists. On Plantin's death, the business passed to his son-in-law, Jan Moretus, and later to Jan's son, Balthasar, a friend of Rubens. Some of the family portraits exhibited inside this museum are the master's works.

Built around a central courtyard, the museum is worth visiting for the mansion alone, but also for insight into old typesetting, proof-reading and printing processes. Room after room is filled with ancient presses, copper plates, old globes, Flemish tapestries and, of course, splendid manuscripts, including a rare copy of the Gutenberg Bible. In the age of email, it's hard not to admire the painstaking effort and dedication that was once needed to produce a 'simple' book.

Those really into printing should consider visiting the nearby **Dagbladmuseum** (Newspaper Museum; Map pp176-7; ☎ 03 887 01 78; www.dagbladmuseum .be in Flemish; Lombardenvest 6; admission €5). It was here that the world's first newspaper, *Nieuwe Tydinghen*, was invented by Abraham Verhoeven in 1606. The museum doesn't have standard opening hours, so call ahead.

By the waterfront is the engaging **Nationaal Scheepvaartmuseum** (National Maritime Museum; Map pp176-7; ☎ 03 201 93 40; www.museum.antwerpen .be/scheepvaartmuseum; Steenplein 1; adult/concession €4/3; ☺ 10am-5pm Tue-Sun). Model ships, maritime maps and instruments are exhibited in the gatehouse and front section (which is all that remains) of the 13th-century castle, Steen. Highlights

include an intriguing nautical totem shaped like a snake's head and boats from around the world, including an 18th-century coracle or skin boat. Beneath the next-door raised promenade is the museum's open-air collection of river barges, canal boats and *De Schelde P905*, a 1950's Belgian navy patrol ship.

Due east of the Steen is the striking Vleeshuis, or **Museum Vleeshuis/Klank van de Stad** (Butchers' Hall; Map pp176-7; ☎ 03 233 64 04; www.museum vleeshuis.be; Vleeshouwersstraat 38-40; adult/concession €5/3; ☺ 10am-5pm Tue-Sun). This building, with its red-and-white layered stonework reminiscent of rashers of bacon, was the 14th-century headquarters of the butchers' guild. It's now a new music museum, known as Klank van de Stad, home to instruments specifically related to Antwerp. Time a visit with a concert given on one of the old instruments – the tourist office has the schedule.

The **Rockoxhuis** (Rockox House; Map pp176-7; ☎ 03 201 92 50; Keizerstraat 10-12; adult/concession €4/3; ☺ 10am-5pm Tue-Sun) is a 17th-century mansion that once belonged to Nicolaas Rockox, a former city mayor and friend and patron of Rubens. It's built around a central courtyard, is furnished in classical Flemish style, and holds a small but esteemed collection of paintings, including works by Rubens, Jordaens, Van Dyck and Pieter Breughel the Younger. Seek out the latter's *Proverbs (De Spreekwoorden)*. This engaging work is no run-of-the-mill village scene – it depicts 108 Flemish proverbs. Find the man bashing his head against a brick wall (ie symbolising stupidity) or the guy peeing on the moon (ie trying to do the impossible). The museum sells a card (€1.25) explaining each proverb, but unfortunately it's not in English.

The stunning Flemish baroque **St Carolus-Borromeuskerk** (Map pp176-7; Hendrik Conscienceplein 6; admission free; ☺ 10am-12.30pm & 2-5pm Mon-Sat) was built n 1621 by the Jesuits on one of the city's most beautiful public squares. Much of the church, including the façade and tower, was designed by Rubens. Unfortunately, most of the marble interior and 39 ceiling paintings by Rubens and his colleagues were destroyed by fire in 1718. Baroque art at its prime can still be seen in the small Onze Lieve Vrouwekapel (Chapel of Our Lady), inside to the right of the entrance, which was spared by the flames.

MEIR AREA

Just off the Meir, on a nondescript square known as Wapper, is the prestigious **Rubenshuis** (Rubens' House; Map pp176-7; ☎ 03 201 15 55; http://museum .antwerpen.be/rubenshuis; Wapper 9-11; adult/concession €5/2.50; ☻ 10am-5pm Tue-Sun). The home and studio of the city's most celebrated painter, Pieter Paul Rubens (below), it was little more than a ruin when acquired by the city in 1937. Superbly restored along original lines, it's now Antwerp's chief attraction, despite the fact that only a handful of Rubens' lesser works are exhibited

here. Rubens built this beautiful Flemish baroque mansion in 1611 when he was 34 years old; he died here 29 years later. The building is divided in two: on the left are the living quarters and an elaborate art gallery where Rubens displayed sculptures and paintings by artists he admired; to the right you'll see the master's studio where he taught and worked. Near the entrance is a baroque portico, and beyond this lies a formal garden. Much of the furniture inside the house dates from Rubens' era but was not part of the original décor.

The tomb of Rubens and his family is the reason most visitors come to **St Jacobskerk** (St James' Church; Map pp176-7; Lange Nieuwstraat 73; adult/concession €3/2; ☻ 2-5pm Mon-Sat Easter-Oct, 9am-noon Nov-Easter). The tomb, in a small chapel behind the high altar, is adorned with a painting, *Our Lady Surrounded by Saints*, which Rubens executed specifically for his tomb and which is a family portrait, with the master as St George and his wives and father the other figures. The church was *the* place of worship for the

---

PIETER PAUL RUBENS

Pieter Paul Rubens (1577–1640) was Belgium's most influential early 17th-century artist. His paintings fused Flemish and Italian influences and his enormous canvases, with their glowing colours and animated forms, are baroque masterpieces. Rubens is best remembered for his sensuous women inspired by Greek mythology, but he's also noted for religious works. In the latter he combines a technical mastery of musculature with a deep sense of the spiritual, and these paintings may appeal to those who aren't fans of his ample nudes.

Rubens was born in Siegen (in Germany) in 1577 after his parents fled Antwerp due to religious turmoil. When his father died a decade later, the family returned to Antwerp, where Rubens started painting – by the age of 21 he was a master in the Antwerp Guild of St Lukas. In 1600 he journeyed to Italy and was soon appointed court painter to the Duke of Mantua. For the next eight years he travelled extensively in Italy and Spain, all the while painting for the wealthy and soaking up the rich Renaissance art and architecture.

When his mother died in 1608, Rubens returned to Antwerp. He worked on religious canvases, such as *The Descent from the Cross*, a huge painting filled with saints, muscular soldiers and distraught women that earned him immediate success. Today it's displayed in Onze Lieve Vrouwekathedraal, the city's cathedral. With commissions pouring in, he established a studio in his house in the city centre from where he proceeded to paint portraits of Europe's royalty and a series of grand religious canvases. Joined by contemporaries such as Antoon (Anthony in English) Van Dyck and Jacob Jordaens, the studio's output was staggering.

In the 1620s Rubens broadened his painting repertoire and also took on diplomatic missions, including a visit to England where he was commissioned to paint part of the ceiling of the Banqueting House in London's Whitehall Palace and was knighted by Charles I.

During his last decade he married Hélèna Fourment, his second wife, whom he used as a model for some of his later, largely allegorical paintings.

Rubens' works are dotted around Antwerp, including Onze Lieve Vrouwekathedraal (p179), Koninklijk Museum voor Schone Kunsten (p182), Rockoxhuis (opposite) and St Jacobskerk (above), and are also superbly exhibited in Brussels' Musées Royaux des Beaux Arts (p83). To discover the city in his footsteps, pick up one of the three walking-tour booklets (€4) sold at the tourist office.

aristocracy and is a showcase of their wealth. Started in 1491, it took nearly 150 years to build and the result is a Gothic façade cloaking mainly baroque embellishments inside.

Museum Mayer Van den Bergh (Map pp176-7; ☎ 03 232 42 37; www.museum.antwerpen.be/mayervandenbergh; Lange Gasthuisstraat 19; adult/concession €4/3; ☽ 10am-5pm Tue-Sun) occupies a simulated 16th-century townhouse, built in 1904 by the mother of Fritz Mayer Van den Bergh, a prosperous art connoisseur who had died a few years earlier aged 41. His highly prized collection of sculptures and paintings, including works by Quinten Matsijs and Cornelius De Vos, form the core of the museum. The collection's most famous piece is Pieter Breugel the Elder's *Dulle Griet* (Mad Meg), an allegorical painting in which a demented woman roams a grotesque war-torn landscape marked by demons and monsters. This is one of Breugel's most Bosch-like paintings and interpretations of its meaning vary – some say it's an allegory of misogyny, others of human madness.

Just down the road from Museum Mayer Van den Bergh is the **Maagdenhuis** (Maidens' House; Map pp176-7; ☎ 03 223 53 20; Lange Gasthuisstraat 33; adult €3; ☽ 10am-5pm Wed-Mon, 1-5pm Sat & Sun). In the 16th and 17th centuries this building was an orphanage and refuge for girls of poor families. Today it's home to a small art collection. As you enter, note the sandstone carvings of young girls above the archway. Of the museum's exhibits, the most nostalgic items are the playing cards, or identification tokens. These cards were cut in half when girls were brought into the refuge – one piece was retained by the parent and the other kept with the child.

Secret garden fans shouldn't miss the city's tiny **Kruidtuin** (botanical garden; Map pp176-7; Leopoldstraat). Originally the herb garden of St Elisabethgasthuis, a hospital that dates back to medieval times, this informal garden has 2000 plant species and, despite its diminutive size, is a great getaway from crowds and vehicles.

CENTRAAL STATION QUARTER

One of the city's premier landmarks is the extraordinary **Centraal Station** (Map pp176–7), designed by Louis Delacenserie at the start of the 20th century in a harmonious blend of styles. Steps lead from the main hall with its enormous dome up to the glass-covered train platforms. The station and adjoining Koningin Astridplein have been undergoing massive works for years to accommodate the Eurostar and Thalys fast

trains, thus directly linking the city to London and the rest of Europe. All is due to be finished by the time you read this. The station is also diamond central (see opposite).

Antwerp Zoo (Map pp176-7; ☎ 03 202 45 40; www.zoo antwerpen.be in Flemish & French; Koningin Astridplein 26; adult/concession €16/11; ☽ 10am-7pm Jul-Aug, 10am-6pm May-Jun & Sep, 10am-5.30pm Mar-Apr & Oct, 10am-4.45pm Jan-Feb & Nov-Dec) ranks among the world's oldest. It opened in 1843 during Belgium's colonial heyday – its age is immediately evident by the striking lion and tiger mosaic panels that greet visitors. The 10-hectare park is home to an extremely diverse range of animals; some (such as the penguins) live in state-of-the-art enclosures but others are still in shoddy cages. The zoo is constantly upgrading accommodation and it also has a good reputation for its breeding programme.

Immediately southwest of Centraal Station is the **diamond district** (see opposite). The first things most people see of this quarter are the gold and diamond shops newly located inside Centraal Station. Here you'll find people from all over the world, including plenty of newly engaged Brits (prices here average 30% lower than in UK High Sts) browsing the bright lights and gleaming displays. But outside, it's a vastly different world. Orthodox Jewish men clad in distinctive black coats and hats shuffle around the lacklustre quarter, traders with briefcases handcuffed to their wrists hurry into diamond exchanges and armed guards keep watch over the little huddle of streets where multimillion-euro deals are going down.

The city's role as a world diamond centre can be explored at the **Diamantmuseum** (Diamond Museum; Map pp176-7; ☎ 03 202 48 90; www.diamant .provant.be; Koningin Astridplein 19-23; adult/concession €5/3; ☽ 1-6pm Mon, 10am-6pm Tue-Sun May-Oct, 1-5pm Mon, 10am-5pm Tue-Sun Nov-Apr). With an English-language audio guide in hand, start on the 3rd floor and let one of seven virtual guides assist in your quest for the perfect stone. The whole thing is very Antwerp – from the sultry fashions worn by the guides to the proud exhibits showing diamond-studded jeans.

'T ZUID

Koninklijk Museum voor Schone Kunsten The **Koninklijk Museum voor Schone Kunsten** (Royal Museum of Fine Arts; Map pp174-5; ☎ 03 238 78 09; www.antwerpen.be/cultuur/kmska; Leopold De Waelplaats; adult/concession/child €6/4/free, last Wed of the month free; ☽ 10am-5pm Tue-Sat, 10am-6pm Sun) is a monumen-

DIAMONDS

Diamonds have been changing hands in Antwerp for more than 500 years. As the world's uncut diamond capital, 80% of the world's rough diamonds are traded in the city's diamond quarter, an unassuming cluster of streets near the Centraal Station, and the industry employs some 30,000 people. But insiders are wondering whether things are on the rocks? Where once 25,000 skilled cutters and polishers were employed, now only 2000 struggle on. For hundreds of years the domain of Orthodox Jews, Indians now account for 60% of the district's trade and much of the manufacturing work has shifted to low-cost Asian countries. Dubai, the Middle Eastern business capital, is actively trying to snare Antwerp's trade. And the once laissez-faire attitude of the Belgian government, a boon to traders, has been replaced by strict EU regulation and tight customs procedures. These changes have come about partly to end the crisis of 'blood diamonds', stones which have been smuggled across borders in conflict zones in Africa, and which are used to fuel the arms trade and finance civil wars. Time will tell whether such measures will end this trade.

To get a glimpse of the amount of diamonds (and gold) being traded, just wander along Pelikaanstraat, Vestingstraat or Hoveniersstraat at any time during the day (on Saturday many shops are closed for Sabbath, the Jewish holy day). Don't expect fanfare or glitz – most of the trade goes on behind discreet, even shabby, façades and in the four *beurzen voor diamanthandel* (diamond exchanges) dotted along two pedestrianised streets – Hoveniersstraat and Rijfstraat. These high-security streets are also home to important financing banks and the industry's governing body, the **Hoge Raad voor Diamant** (Diamond High Council; Hoveniersstraat 22).

tal neoclassical edifice built at the end of the 19th century. Its stately rooms house an impressive collection of paintings dating from the 14th century to contemporary times and include works by Flemish masters.

The size of the museum's collection means that paintings are sometimes rotated. To find the highlights you'll need to pick up a museum plan and audio headset (both free) from reception.

The Flemish Primitives are represented by Jan Van Eyck, Hans Memling, Rogier Van der Weyden and Gerard David. Highlights include Van Eyck's unusual, almost monotone *Saint Barbara* (1437), Memling's rich *Christ among Angels Singing and Playing Instruments* and Van der Weyden's portrait of *Filips Van Croy*.

Sixteenth-century works to seek out include Quinten Matsijs' profound triptych *The Lamentation of Christ* (also called the *Triptych of the Joiners' Guild*). Matsijs, spelt Matsys in English, founded the Antwerp school of painting and his works reflect a deep understanding of landscape perspective. There are no originals by Pieter Breugel the Elder; however, paintings by his followers detail the enchanting peasant scenes for which Breugel was famous.

The museum's best section is undoubtedly the 17th-century Flemish baroque masters display. There are several enormous canvases by Rubens, including his famous *Adoration of the Magi* (1624), a hugely expressive and ani-

mated work, as well as a selection of smaller, preparatory paintings and oil sketches. The other local players of that time, Jacob Jordaens and Antoon Van Dyck, are also well represented. Watch out for Jordaens' *As the Old Sing, the Young Play Pipes* (1638), in which senior citizens are shown setting a good example to the young. Van Dyck was best known for his portraiture, a fine example of which is *Portrait of Maarten Pepijn* (1632).

Moving on to modern art, the museum has a diverse collection of paintings by James Ensor that traces his conservative beginnings – such as the *Woman Eating Oysters* (1882) – to his disturbing later works, exemplified here by *Masks Fighting over a Hanged Man* (1891).

Other Belgian artists of note whose works are exhibited include Constant Permeke and Rik Wouters, as well as surrealists René Magritte and Paul Delvaux.

Tram 8 from Groenplaats or bus 23 (direction Zuid) from Franklin Rooseveltplaats both stop out the front.

Other Sights

The **Museum voor Hedendaagse Kunst Van Antwerpen** (MuHKA; Museum for Contemporary Arts of Antwerp; Map pp174-5; ☎ 03 238 59 60; www.muhka.be in Flemish; Leuvenstraat 23; adult/concession €4/3; ☺ 10am-5pm Tue-Sun) is housed behind an Art Deco façade in a building that started life as a grain silo. It contains a permanent collection of Belgian and international art dating from the 1970s onwards, although only a fraction is displayed at any one time. Temporary exhibitions are often staged. Bus 23 (direction Zuid) from Franklin Rooseveltplaats stops nearby.

Five blocks south of MuHKA and with an excellent reputation is the newly renovated and expanded **FotoMuseum** (Map pp174-5; ☎ 03 242 93 00; www.fotomusuem.be; Waalsekaai 47; adult/concession €6/4; ⌚ 10am-5pm Tue-Sun). Once again housed in a renovated warehouse, this museum has a huge collection of B&W photographs, old portraits and ancient cameras. One of the highlights is the Keizerspanorama, a huge, motorised, slide-viewing contraption built in 1905 for Antwerp Zoo. In the evening you can take in a golden-oldie film in one of two auditoria. To get to the museum, take bus 23 (direction Zuid) from Franklin Rooseveltplaats.

Although Zurenborg (right) has the city's most dense concentration of Art Nouveau architecture, two other fine examples can be seen in 't Zuid and both are just short walks from the Koninklijk Museum voor Schone Kunsten. **Help U Zelve** (Map pp174-5; Volkstraat 40) is arguably the city's most beautiful and harmonious Art Nouveau façade. Built in 1901 by architects Van Asperen and Van Averbeke, it features mosaics and strongly geometric wrought-iron work. It's now used as a Rudolph Steiner school. **'t Bootje** (Map pp174-5; cnr Schildersstraat & Plaats-nijdersstraat) has a little ship-shaped balcony that is part of a 1901 townhouse called De Vijf Continenten (The Five Continents).

The city's new **Justitiepaleis** (law court; Map pp174-5; Bolivarplaats), reminiscent of Sydney's Opera House, will blow away any preconceptions that architecture in Antwerp is all old hat. The work of renowned British architect Richard Rogers, the man behind London's Lloyd's building and Paris' Pompidou Centre, its gleaming sails can easily be seen rising at the end of Amerikalei, down the southern end of 't Zuid. This area has largely been left begging in recent decades, but this flashy new addition has already sparked a real-estate boom. During its construction in 2005, controversy reigned over its cost – quoted at €75 million but eventually coming in at around €250 million. Take tram 12 (direction Bolivarplaats) from Gemeentestraat, next to Koningin Astridplein, to its terminus to get there.

'T SCHIPPERSKWARTIER

Marking the start of the sailors' quarter, or 't Schipperskwartier, is **St Pauluskerk** (St Paul's Church, Map pp176-7; Veemarkt; admission free; ⌚ 2-5pm May-Sep). The proud, white Gothic church was built for the Dominicans and dates from 1517. It suffered over the years due to fires, the latest in 1968 when locals rallied to save the art treasures inside. The baroque interior is resplendent with a stunning procession of wooden confessionals and carvings, altars, a (partly) ancient organ and marble embellishments, as well as paintings by the 17th-century masters and lesser artists.

Antwerp's **red-light district** (Map pp176–7) is Belgium's largest, but it's small fry compared with neighbouring Amsterdam. It is based between St Paulusplaats and Verversrui and includes the appropriately named Oude Manstraat (Old Man St). Much of the quarter has a dog-eared feel, and the fanfare and crass consumerism that makes its counterpart in the Netherlands so famous is noticeably absent here.

'T EILANDJE

Due to open in 2008, the purpose-built multi-storey **Museum aan de Stroom** (MAS; Map pp174-5; ☎ 03 206 09 40; www.museumaandestroom.be; Hanze Stedenplaats) is located between two docks – Bonapartedok and Willemdok – in the flourishing 't Eilandje district. Architecturally it's expected to be a big draw, designed like a modern spiral tower with a panorama platform offering city views. It will bring together exhibits of the city's history from its earliest beginnings to recent times, which means some existing museums – like the Scheepvaartmuseum – will lose all or some of their content.

Another museum in the pipeline for this district is the **Red Star Line Museum**. It will tell the story of the three-million Europeans who immigrated via Antwerp to the US and Canada. Ask the tourist office (p179) for up-to-date details on both museums.

ZURENBORG

This area, about 2km southeast of Centraal Station, is famed for the eclectic architecture found in a handful of streets. The showcase is **Cogels-Osylei** (Map pp174–5), a bazaar of all possible house styles. Here the city's affluent citizens went wild a century ago, creating competing and highly contrasting façades ranging in style from Art Nouveau and Flemish baroque to

EASTERN FLANDERS

neoclassical and neo-Renaissance. Roofs and towers spiked with onion tops or witches' hats, wrought-iron balconies, bay windows, slate tiles, stained glass and mosaics…you name it, this street's got it. Most of the buildings were constructed between 1894 and 1914 and involved many architects. In the 1960s the houses faced demolition but were saved thanks to protests by artists and hippies.

The area's focal point is the small round-about on Cogels-Osylei, which is flanked by the **Witte Paleizen** (White Palaces; Map pp174-5), grand façades resembling chateaux in France's Loire Valley. Three exquisite Art Nouveau examples along Cogels-Osylei are the **Huize Zonnebloem** (Sunflower House; Map pp174-5; 50 Cogels-Osylei), built by Jules Hofman in 1900, **De Morgenster** (The Morning Star; Map pp174-5; 55 Cogels-Osylei) and **Quinten Matsys** (Map pp174-5; 80 Cogels-Osylei), both built in 1904.

More nearby Art Nouveau swirls and mosaic façades include **Les Mouettes** (Waterloostraat 39), built in 1905. Mosaics are at their best at **De Vier Seizoenen** (The Four Seasons; Map pp174-5; cnr Waterloostraat & Generaal Van Merlenstraat), designed in 1899 by the architect Bascourt. The **Euterpia** (Map pp174-5; Generaal Capiaumontstraat 2), from 1906, follows Greek neoclassical lines – the door handle even resembles an Olympic torch. The **Twaalf Duivels** (Map pp174-5; Transvaalstraat 59 & 61), built in 1896 by Jules Hofman, has a timber façade that gives way to 12 wooden devils that leer at passers-by.

Zurenborg is easily reached by tram 11 (direction Eksterlaar), which runs right along Cogels-Osylei.

GREATER ANTWERP

Some 4km south of the city centre is a large, landscaped park known as the **Openluchtmuseum voor Beeldhouwkunst Middelheim** (Middelheim Open-Air Sculpture Museum; Map pp174-5; ☎ 03 828 13 50; Middelheimlaan 61; admission free; ☯ 10am-9pm Jun & Jul, 10am-8pm May & Aug, 10am-7pm Apr & Sep, 10am-5pm Oct-Mar, closed Mon). It contains more than 300 works by sculptors, including notable nationals (Rik Wouters) and influential internationals (Auguste Rodin and Henry Moore). To get there take bus 17 (direction Wilrijk Universitair Ziekenhuis) from in front of Centraal Station, get off at Beukenlaan and walk 500m east.

Walking Tour

This walk takes in the Grote Markt to the so-called Quartier Latin, a huddle of pedestrianised shopping streets close to the Meir. If you don't linger too long or get sidetracked, it'll take one

to 1½ hours (allow at least another 20 minutes if you cross under the river to the Linkeroever).

The **Grote Markt** (1; p179) is the obvious starting point. From here, head down Suikerrui towards the river, noting Constantin Meunier's proud 19th-century bronze **statue** (2) entitled *Bag Bearer*, paying tribute to the city's dock workers.

At the waterfront is **Steenplein (3)**, a tree-lined square home to the city's oldest building, **Het Steen (4)**. This castle, dating from 1200, has been much restored; it is also a vestige of the 9th-century fortifications that once stood here. The Steen is now home to the **Nationaal Scheepvaartmuseum** (4; p180), marked by a statue of the mischievous Lange Wapper, a tall folkloric figure who is little more than a Peeping Tom.

On both sides of Steenplein are raised promenades known as *wandelterrassen*, built three-quarters of a century ago alongside the city's main dock so that townsfolk could view the exotic cargoes coming in from the Congo. The promenades are still immensely popular on weekends, and from **Zuiderterras (5)**, the south promenade, there is a great skyline view plus an essential **café pitstop** (6; p193).

Wander the full length of the Zuiderterras then descend to St Jansvliet, a small tree-lined square best known as the entrance to the **St Annatunnel (7)**. This 572m-long pedestrian tunnel, built in the 1930s, links the city centre with the Linkeroever, or Left Bank, from where there's an excellent waterfront panorama.

Back at St Jansvliet, take Steenhouwersvest all the way to Nationalestraat, the heart of the **St Andries (8)** mode quarter. From this five-ways, any street will deposit you at fashion outlets (p196). Continue north along Kammenstraat, turn left into Reyndersstraat and then right into **Pelgrimsstraat (9)**, where an overpowering view of the cathedral spire awaits.

Just around the corner is the entrance to **Vlaeykensgang (10)**, one of the few 16th-century alleys that have survived in Antwerp. Originally these tiny streets were the domain of the city's most impoverished citizens (in this case cobblers); today Vlaeykensgang is synonymous with one of the most expensive restaurants in town **Sir Anthony Van Dyck** (11; p191).

The picturesque **Handschoenmarkt (12)** is a tiny square that takes its name from the glove market that once thrived here. It's lined with gabled houses and terrace *cafés* (pub/bar), all dwarfed by the majestic **Onze Lieve Vrouwekathedraal (13**; p179). In a corner stands a well

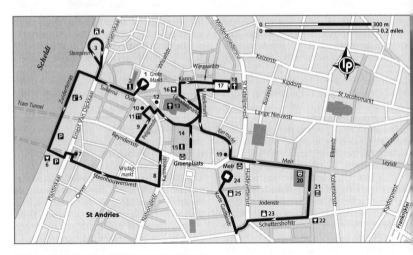

EASTERN FLANDERS

WALK FACTS

Start Grote Markt
Finish Quartier Latin
Distance 2km
Duration About 1½ hours

with wrought-iron work attributed to a 16th-century painter Quinten Matsijs. So the story goes, Matsijs (from a blacksmith family) became an artist simply to marry the daughter of a painter as, in those days, marriage between families of different guilds didn't occur.

Pass along the cobbled street on the southern side of the cathedral (named 't Waaigat by locals) to view **Groenplaats (14)**. This square was the town's graveyard until the 18th century. A much-photographed **statue of Rubens (15)**, built in 1840, commands centre stage; popular terrace *cafés* flank the northern side.

Continue around the base of the cathedral and follow Lijnwaadmarkt to **'t Elfde Gebod (16**; p193), an ivy-clad *café* that's worth a peek for its astounding interior. Turn right along Kaasrui, cross the tram tracks and follow cobbled Wijngaardstraat to the secluded square **Hendrik Conscienceplein (17)**. Arguably the most handsome square in the city, it is named after the revered 19th-century Flemish writer Hendrik Conscience, whose statue graces the square. More commanding is the stunning façade of **St Carolus-Borromeuskerk (18**; p180).

Join Melkmarkt and follow it along to Eiermarkt, which curves around at the base of the

Torengebouw (19). This stocky Art Deco building, completed in 1932, was Europe's first skyscraper. However, it's better known by its nickname 'Boerentoren' (Farmers' Tower), a snide reference to its blunt appearance.

The Torengebouw marks the western end of the pedestrianised Meir, the city's stately main artery and shopper's hive. Gilded, allegorical statues top many of the classical and rococo-style buildings that line this thoroughfare. Look out for the **Koninklijk Paleis (20)**, a palatial building used at various times by Napoleon and the Belgian royal family.

Just off the Meir is the prestigious **Rubenshuis (21**; p181) and nearby the **Grand Café Horta (22**; p193). Wander west now along Schuttershofstraat, one of the city's most vaunted shopping streets, and with plenty of euros to spare stop at Belgium's best shoe shop, **Coccodrillo (23**; p196). Round the corner into Korte Gasthuisstraat and the start of the pedestrianised **Quartier Latin (24)**, a huddle of small streets where shopping is on everyone's list. Don't miss the window display at discreet **Burie (25**; p196), a top-class chocolate boutique.

Antwerp for Children

Kids love **Antwerp Zoo** (p182), and many enjoy **Flandria boat trips** (opposite), walking through **St Annatunnel** (p185) underneath the Scheld or riding the **Peerdentram** (opposite).

Aquatopia (Map pp176-7; ☎ 03 205 07 40; www.aquatopia.be; adult/child €12/8; ☺ 10am-6pm), inside the Astrid Park Plaza Hotel near Centraal Station is a watery hit. Newly revamped, it's now one of the most interactive and realistic marine theme parks in Europe. Let multilingual Fibu the octopus guide the kids.

The **playground** (Map pp176–7) at the northern corner of Stadspark is good for littlies.

Remember, too, that **Technopolis** (p204) and **Planckendael animal park** (p205) are within easy striking distance just outside Mechelen.

Tours

Diamond Bus (☎ 0478 48 28 20; adult/concession/child €11/10/6; ☼ 10.30am-5pm Jul-Aug, 10.30am-5pm Sat & Sun Sep-May) Hop-on hop-off double-decker bus that runs continuously around the city.

Flandria (Map pp176-7; ☎ 03 231 31 00; www.flandria boat.com; Steenplein; adult/concession €7.50/6; ☼ Easter-Oct) One for boaties. The 50-minute Scheldt excursion departs from Steenplein and affords great views of the city skyline. The 2½-hour harbour cruise (adult/concession €12/6) departs from *kaai* (quay) No 14 (Map pp174–5) in 't Eilandje, 1km north of the Grote Markt, daily at 2.30pm from May to September and 2.30pm Friday to Sunday in October.

Peerdentram (Grote Markt; tour €5; ☼ from noon Apr-Oct) Old-fashioned coach drawn by two stocky Brabant horses. Does a 40-minute tour of the old city centre, departing hourly from the Grote Markt.

Rent A Bike (Map pp176-7; ☎ 03 290 49 62; www .antwerpbikes.be; Lijnwaadmarkt 6; tour €16.50; ☼ 9am-6pm) This bike-rental company also runs good two-hour guided tours around town.

Festivals & Events

For details on summer music parties, see boxed text (p194).

Beerpassie Weekend (www.beerpassion.com) Late June sees Antwerp extol the virtues of Belgian beer. In 2006, 35 brewers set up, and visitors could taste 156 beers – €2 for a 20mL *proefglas* (tasting glass).

Sfinks Festival (www.sfinks.be) This four-day world-music celebration is held in Boechout, near Antwerp, at the end of July.

Jazz Middelheim (www.jazzmiddelheim.be) Biennial (in odd years), week-long jazz festival in the second week of August, held in Park Den Brandt (Map pp174–5) in Antwerp. One of the city's biggest shindigs.

Sleeping

Antwerp's scene is on the up. Designer B&Bs have taken off in recent times as locals convert homes into cutting-edge accommodation to keep abreast with the city's image. Check out what's on offer at **Gilde der Antwerpse Gastenkamers** (www.gastenkamersantwerpen.be). A new, ecofriendly HI hostel will open in 2009 in the city's heart. And hotels offering hefty weekend reductions

mean great last-minute deals for visitors (book via the internet or tourist office).

BUDGET

Camping De Molen (Map pp174-5; ☎ 03 219 81 79; Thonetlaan; camp sites per adult/car/tent €2/1/2.50; ☼ Apr-Sep) One of two camping grounds in the city. This one is pleasantly sited on the Linkeroever (Left Bank) of the Scheldt River; take bus 81 or 82 (direction Linkeroever).

Hostel Op Sinjoorke (Map pp174-5; ☎ 03 238 02 73; www.vjh.be; Eric Sasselaan 2; dm/s/d €14.50/29/42; ☼ closed Dec; ✗) Run-of-the-mill HI-affiliated hostel nearly 3km south of the city centre. To get there take tram 2 (direction Hoboken). A new hostel, with an inner garden, rooftop terrace and much better location, is due to open on Bogaardeplein in early 2009.

Den Heksenketel (Map pp176-7; ☎ 03 226 71 64; www .heksenketel.org in Flemish; Pelgrimstraat 22; dm €19) The only cheap accommodation in the city's heart and located on a street with an unbeatable cathedral view. Three simple but fresh dorms are situated above a small folk-music club (concerts Monday, jam sessions Thursday). Take *premetro* (a tram that runs underground for part of its journey) tram 2 or 15 to Groenplaats.

MIDRANGE

Internationaal Zeemanshuis (Map pp176-7; ☎ 03 227 54 33; www.zeemanshuis.be; Falconrui 21; s/d from €39/61; ▯) Large hotel originally built for visiting seamen. This efficiently run complex with polished rooms welcomes women and land-lubbers these days, too.

B&B Emperor's 48 (Map pp176-7; ☎ 03 288 73 37; www .emperors48.com; Keizerstraat 48; s/d €45/65, apt €130; ▯ ✗) Well-located B&B halfway between Centraal Station and the Grote Markt sporting two rooms plus a self-contained apartment. If you're here with a handful of friends, book the whole place. The furnishings are sober but stylish, and the owner's a respected photographer.

Hotel Scheldezicht (Map pp176-7; ☎ 03 231 66 02; www.hotelscheldezicht.be; St Jansvliet 2; s/d/tr from €45/65/85; ▯) Old-style hotel, well sited on a tree-lined square close to the river in the old city centre. The spacious rooms have private shower cubicles, but the toilets are shared. Breakfast is taken in a quaint room loaded with old paintings and B&W photos. Rooms with a view of the square are €5 dearer.

Big Sleep (Map pp176-7; ☎ 0474 84 95 65; www .intro04.be/thebigsleep; Kromme Elleboogstraat 4; s/d/t/q €45/65/85/100) Appropriately named B&B that

---

GAY & LESBIAN ANTWERP

Antwerp's gay and lesbian scene is small, discreet and vibrant. Unlike Brussels, there's no focal point – bars, *cafés* (pub/bar) and clubs are dotted around town, and the city hosts one of the biggest gay nightclubs in this corner of Europe.

Den Draak (Map pp174-5; ☎ 03 288 00 84; www.hetrozehuis.be in Flemish; Draakplaats 1; ☻ 3pm-midnight Tue-Fri, noon-midnight Sat & Sun) *Café* and community centre, also known as Het Roze Huis (the Pink House), for Antwerp's gay and lesbian community. It's located in the Zurenborg (take tram 11 direction Eksterlaar).

Atthis (Map pp174-5; ☎ 03 216 37 37; www.atthis.be in Flemish; Geuzenstraat 27; ☻ from 8.30pm Fri & Sat) Meeting place and bar for Belgium's longest-running lesbian group. Celebrates 30 years in 2008.

Café Hessenhuis (Map pp176-7; ☎ 03 231 13 56; Falconrui 53; ☻ 10am-late) Popular *café* in the old Hessenhuis building, an historic 16th-century warehouse that was rediscovered by a group of artists in the 1950s and given a total makeover. The *café's* cool, modern interior attracts a trendy mixed clientele during the day, but evenings tend to be exclusively for gay men.

Popi Café (Map pp176-7; ☎ 03 238 15 30; Plantinkaai 12; ☻ from noon) Big stylish *café*-brasserie near the river and popular with a gay/mixed bunch. Serves light meals (€9 to €14).

Chez Fred (Map pp176-7; ☎ 03 257 1471; Kloosterstraat 83; mains €15) Little resto-bar with an outside terrace good for watching the *brocante* (bric-a-brac) shoppers.

Red & Blue (Map pp176-7; ☎ 03 213 05 55; www.redandblue.be; Lange Schipperskapelstraat 11; ☻ 11pm-7am Sat) Bills itself as 'the biggest gay disco in Benelux' (that is, Belgium, the Netherlands and Luxembourg). True or not, it's the city's hottest gay (only) nightclub and certainly draws punters from kilometres around. On Friday night it draws a mixed crowd to the sounds of house, techno, rap and soul.

Boots (Map pp176-7; ☎ 03 231 34 83; Van Aerdtstraat 22; ☻ 10.30pm-late Fri & Sat) Has the distinction of being the country's most disreputable nightclub, with rooms devoted to fulfilling almost every imaginable sexual fantasy.

Boekhandel 't Verschil (Map pp176-7; ☎ 03 226 08 04; Minderbroedersrui 33; ☻ noon-6pm Wed-Sun) Gay and lesbian bookshop plus a *café*.

B&B 2000 (Map pp176-7; ☎ 03 234 12 10; http://guestrooms.happygays.be; Van Boendalestraat 8; s/d €30/42; ▯) A rainbow flag flying from the top floor announces B&B 2000 to those in search of this pokey backstreet. The friendly owners, Luc and Steven, and their big dog Jack have four rooms with shared bathroom in this whitewashed townhouse. The rooms are small and ordinary, reflecting the price.

---

occupies part of a mustard-toned family home close to the river in the *brocante* (bric-a-brac) quarter. A grey-grill door opens to a huge ground-floor bedroom that stretches from a whitewashed breakfast salon and lounge area to a wood-decked courtyard. Another smaller room for guests is located upstairs.

Aan de Leien B&B (Map pp174-5; ☎ 03 288 66 95; tony.vandepitte@telenet.be; Britselei 49 bte 6; s/d €55/62, penthouse €100; ☒) This is one of the most sought-after addresses in Antwerp – take the lift to the 6th floor of an ugly apartment block and you'll soon see why. This B&B offers two small rooms and a penthouse suite – it's the latter you're after. Oodles of private space ends with a panoramic terrace specially designed for sipping sundowners. Located just over 1km from Centraal Station – take tram 8 from Berchem train station or bus 23 from Centraal Station.

Floatel Diamond Princess (Map pp174-5; ☎ 03 227 08 15; www.diamondprincess.be; Bonapartedok; s/d/ste €57/77/139; ☒) Former 1952 Norwegian passenger ship that's been transformed into a hotel complete with piano bar and disco. It's moored in a dock in 't Eilandje, right next to the new MAS museum. Though hard to believe, there are 52 cabins on board: all pretty small but pleasantly decorated. The most unusual is the suite – it tries hard to be romantic but the bed would defeat even Simenon.

Ibis Antwerpen Centrum (Map pp176-7; ☎ 03 231 88 30; www.ibishotel.com; Meistraat 39; s/d from €79/82; ☒ ▯ ☖) Modern chain hotel (Accor group) that offers standard facilities and a central location. Handy to Rubenshuis and the fashion quarter, though the immediate area is nondescript and the view of Het Paleis theatre ghastly. It's particularly interesting for late risers or those into dancing until dawn – the buffet reakfast (€10) goes from 6.30am to 10am ter which coffee and croissants are offered ntil noon.

B&B Le Patio (Map pp176-7; ☎ 03 232 76 61; www.lepa .be; Pelgrimstraat 8; r €90; 🖳) Step up to the door of e Patio and swoon at the unbeatable cathedral ew. Located smack in the very heart of the city n a pedestrianised street brimming with res- .urants and *cafés*, this friendly place has three ●odern rooms – blue, red or yellow – all built ●ound a small inner courtyard. And, unusual ●r Belgium, the only stairs you'll climb are ●ose to the old beamed breakfast room with its ●g communal table, located on the 1st floor.

Patine (Map pp174-5; ☎ 03 257 09 19; www.wijnbistro tine.be; Leopold de Waelstraat 1; r €100) Fabulous B&B ddress, located at the epicentre of 't Zuid, ●ove one of the quarter's best-known eateries ●ee p192). Just one spacious 1st-floor room ●available, offering simple, white décor with corner living area overlooking the heart of p. A great address for families (double bed us sofa bed plus kitchenette) or those into ●room with a view.

B&B Siddartha (Map pp176-7; ☎ 03 232 97 44; www azarbizar.be in Flemish; Steenhouwersvest 18; d/tr/f €122/ 2/212) There's nothing understated about Sid- ●rtha. Awaken senses as you climb two flights ● a world of colour and vitality – romantic ●chsia for the main room, apple green for ●e adjoining twin. The immediately likeable ●vner, Els Ongenae, has similar flair. She runs ● Asian gift shop on the ground floor, and has ●corated her B&B with wares from the shop. ●s conveniently located in the fashion quarter ●d, for those with a car, Els provides a free ●rking card for the nearby car park.

Slapenenzo (Map pp174-5; ☎ 03 216 27 85; www.slap ●enzo.be; Karel Rogierstraat 20; r from €130; ✂ 🖳) New ●signer hotel that's simply got the sexiest ●el. It occupies two adjoining century-old

townhouses on a quiet street near 't Zuid's Koninklijk Museum voor Schone Kunsten. Step inside to a world of virginal white, backed by walls decorated with suggestive art and faux-fur throws over the beds. By the time you read this 15 rooms should be up and running, all with monochrome colours – black, white or mocha – some with marble baths and open fires, plus a cellar spa and sauna. And it has all been done by one friendly couple with a flair for cutting-edge cool. Tram 8 from Groenplaats stops nearby.

Also recommended:

Hotel Antigone (Map pp176-7; ☎ 03 231 66 77; www .antigonehotel.be; Jordaenskaai 11-12; s/d/tr €85/95/115; ✂) Waterfront hotel, close to 't Schipperskwartier, that's popular with a clubbing crowd. The sugary-sweet baroque reception contrasts with '70s rooms – pink fans and green bedspreads.

Aandekeizer B&B (Map pp176-7; ☎ 03 225 22 96; www.aandekeizer.be; Keizerstraat 62; s/d €92/100; ✂) Old-world charm and fabulous hosts are the watchword at this central B&B located on a quiet backstreet.

TOP END

Hotel 't Sandt (Map pp176-7; ☎ 03 232 93 90; www.hotel -sandt.be; Zand 17; s/d from €135/150; 🖳) Classy clas- sified hotel down by the Scheldt that was once a customs house and later a soap factory. The rooms are a tasteful marriage of modern and old, and some on the top floor have charm- ing beamed ceilings. There are also some duplexes.

Hotel Rubens (Map pp176-7; ☎ 03 222 48 48; www .hotelrubensantwerp.be; Oude Beurs 29; s/d Mon-Fri €160/188, r front/back Sat & Sun €150/170; ✂ ✂) Old-fashioned hotel with 36 rooms, just a stone's throw from the Grote Markt. The mellow-toned rooms have floral prints and classical furniture.

B&B Charles Rogier XI (Map pp174-5; ☎ 0475 29 99 89; www.charlesrogierxi.be; Karel Rogierstraat 11; d €180; ✂ ✂)

THE AUTHOR'S CHOICE

Hotel Julien (Map pp176-7; ☎ 03 229 06 00; www.hotel-julien.com; Korte Nieuwstraat 24; r from €165; ☒ ☒ ☐) New and very discreet design hotel, and a dream come true for former interior designer Mouch Van Hul. Mouch has renovated two historic houses on a ragged unloved little street right in the city's heart. The 11 contemporary rooms exude her love of understated elegance and subtle style. The approach is intimate and informal, and highly romantic. Choose an outback 'Patio' room, situated around a green courtyard, for real seclusion. Closest metro is Meir, or take tram 10 (direction Melkmarkt) from Gemeentestraat next to Koningin Astridplein.

Urked by modern minimalism? Then step into a world away from current reality…a place where beds were high, phones didn't exist and an afternoon snooze on a daybed was mandatory. This 't Zuid townhouse has three rooms – English (1st floor), Scottish (2nd floor) and French (3rd floor) – all loaded with antiques, heavy fabrics and floral designs. Sunken baths, handmade linen, red wine, a Belgian chocolate before bed and a fine breakfast are other enticements. Oh, and if you're not into stuffed foxes and pheasants, ask for the French room (it's also the only room that's air-conditioned). Tram 8 from Groenplaats stops nearby.

De Witte Lelie (The White Lily; Map pp176-7; ☎ 03 226 19 66; www.dewittelelie.be; Keizerstraat 16-18; s/d €195/265, ste from €275; ☒ ☒ ☐) Push the gold button and wait to be ushered into this gorgeous hotel. Occupying three renovated 16th-century mansions built around a central courtyard on a quiet backstreet not far from the Grote Markt, it has just 10 luxurious rooms, individually furnished with an outstanding mix of modern and antique. The blend of white décor, polished wooden floors and exposed oak beams creates an atmosphere of peace and calm. Breakfast is taken in the big open kitchen on the ground floor. There's no bar, but that's hardly a problem in Antwerp. Babies (cot €10) and children (prices vary depending on age) are welcome; reservations wise.

Eating

Foodies love Antwerp. Dining out is a favourite local pastime, resulting in a staggering number of restaurants. The old city centre is well endowed with eateries in all price categories. Suikerrui is the street for mussels, Grote Pieter Potstraat has funky *cafés* and bistros, Pelgrimstraat is popular with tourists and the cobbled streets around Hendrik Conscienceplein are dotted with intimate restaurants. In between all of these are quiet side streets and cobbled lanes where restaurants of all description thrive. Outside the old city centre there's also plenty on offer: 't Zuid has an ever-increasing line-up of trend-setting establishments, 't Eilandje calls with monumental restaurants and St Andries allures with food alongside fashion. Visit **Out in Antwerp** (www.outinantwerp.be in Flemish) for the latest on dining.

QUICK EATS

Soep & Soup (Map pp176-7; ☎ 03 707 28 05; Kammenstraat 89; small/large bowl €4.25/5.50; ☒ 11am-6.30pm Mon-Sat) At this buzzing soup bar in trendy St Andries, five pots of soup, all made with fresh ingredients, simmer away. Vegos can ask to hold the meatballs.

Het Dagelijks Brood (Map pp176-7; ☎ 03 226 76 14; Steenhouwersvest 48; light meals €5-9; ☒ 7am-7pm Mon-Fri, 7.30am-6.30pm Sat & Sun) This bakery/tearoom located in the heart of St Andries, is part of a successful chain (see p103). The house speciality is *boterhammen* (slices of bread with exotic toppings), but there's also a good range of soups and salads.

Also recommended:

Frituur No 1 (Map pp176-7; Hoogstraat 1) Makes the city's finest *frites* (fries). Close to the Grote Markt.

La Cuisine (Map pp176-7; ☎ 03 226 42 71; St Pieter & Paulusstraat 7; mains €6-7.50, 3-course menu €7.50; ☒ noon-2.30pm & 4-7pm Mon-Sat) The cheapest eatery in town is run by youth learning the trade.

RESTAURANTS
Old City Centre

Façade (Map pp176-7; ☎ 03 233 59 31; Hendrik Conscienceplein 18; mains €9-18; ☒ 11am-10.30pm) Unpretentious little restaurant that occupies two quaint houses on one of the most delightful public squares in Antwerp. Comprises two rooms plus a tiny mezzanine and an outdoor terrace. The French-Belgian cuisine is well priced and beautifully presented – the *scampis in look* (garlic prawns) are divine. Love the modern touches around the bar, and the gorgeous lamps suspended from the old timber ceiling.

Berlin (Map pp176-7; ☎ 03 227 11 01; Kleine Markt 3; dagschotel €9, mains €12-17; ☒ 7.30am-1am Mon-Wed, 10am-3am Fri-Sun) Spacious brasserie underneath

---

THE AUTHOR'S CHOICE

Lombardia (Map pp176-7; ☎ 03 233 68 19; Lombardenvest 78; light meals €4-8; ⏰ 8am-6pm Mon-Sat) A legendary health-food shop and *café* located at the heart of the pedestrianised Quartier Latin shopping district. It's run by a hip crew, the décor's way out and the food's all *bio* (organic). Sells a bit of everything, has English-language newspapers, snappy service and a few tables for diners (plus a huge summer terrace under a shady tree). *Bio* milkshakes – either beastie or vegan – go for €6, fresh juices are €4.50, and there's a range of salads, vegetable pies and sandwiches. The sign above the counter asks that customers 'Do not spit' – now that's health conscious.

---

he police tower in St Andries, with bold design features and black and tan décor. Attracts an eclectic crowd from jeans-minded teens to the old lady who lives round the corner. Simple honest bistro fare is served, including homemade shrimp croquettes. Great place to drop in for a drink, snack or meal.

Bourla & Mares (Map pp176-7; ☎ 03 232 16 32; Kelderstraat 3; mains €16-25; ⏰ 11am-1am Mon-Sat) Excellent bistro-restaurant on a pedestrianised backstreet in the shadow of the Bourlaschouwburg. Ultramodern with a touch of antique and Art Nouveau. The cuisine is predominantly Italian with a seafood slant. Pop in any time – the kitchen is open from noon to midnight.

Hungry Henrietta (Map pp176-7; ☎ 03 232 29 28; Lombardenvest 19; mains €17-21, ⏰ lunch & dinner Mon-Fri) Three different locations in 35 years but none nothing to deter the fans. The strong dark décor – all black – contrasts with the light Flemish cuisine. The *dagschotel* (dish of the day; €13) is well priced.

Pottenbrug (Map pp176-7; ☎ 03 231 51 47; Minderbroedersrui 38; mains €17-27; ⏰ lunch Mon-Fri, dinner Mon-Sat) Old bistro that has changed little over the years and still gets rave reviews. Tables close together, antique posters and a terrace in summer.

THE AUTHOR'S CHOICE

Walrus (Map pp174-5; ☎ 03 238 39 93; Jan van Beersstraat 2; mains €11-16; ⏰ from noon) Modern atmospheric *eetcafé* (eating café) at the southern end of 't Zuid, in an area ripe to take off. Its out-of-the-way location means few tourists come here – this is local central. Sit on the terrace to see the sails of the controversial new Justitiepaleis, or dine inside on dishes any Belgian Mum would be proud to serve. Very kid friendly, too. To get here take tram 12 (direction Bolivarplaats) from Gemeentestraat near Koningin Astridplein.

De Kleine Zavel (Map pp176-7; ☎ 03 231 96 91; Stoofstraat 2; mains €20-27; ⏰ lunch Sun-Fri, dinner daily) *Gezellig* (cosy, convivial atmosphere) bistro-style décor and an informal atmosphere belie this restaurant's standing as one of the most sought-after and reliable eateries in the whole country. Fusion cooking with an accent on fish and Mediterranean flavours are the go. For wine lovers there's an extensive world list, and those into beer will find old wooden crates incorporated into the rustic décor. Parking is handy on the nearby quays.

Sir Anthony Van Dyck (Map pp176-7; ☎ 03 231 61 70; Oude Koornmarkt 16; mains €24-32, 4-course menu €44; ⏰ lunch & dinner Mon-Sat) Named after a local baroque artist, this is one of the city's finest restaurants, with innovative Flemish cuisine and a secretive location in the Vlaeykensgang, a tiny, cobbled 16th-century alley. Inside the décor is modern but calm. Booking is necessary.

Het Nieuwe Palinghuis (Map pp176-7; ☎ 03 231 74 45; St Jansvliet 14; mains €25-32; ⏰ lunch Wed-Sun; ✖) Seafood restaurant well known for its attentive service and seasonal food. Mussels go for around €25.

Also recommended:

Eethuisje De Stoemppot (Map pp176-7; ☎ 03 231 36 86; Vlasmarkt 12; mains €7.50-15; ⏰ dinner Thu-Mon) Granny would feel right at home in this place. Big portions of *stoemp* (mashed potatoes) are slapped onto plates and paired with a *boerenworst* (sausage) or a *spiegelei* (fried egg).

De Peerdestal (Map pp176-7; ☎ 03 231 95 03; Wijngaardstraat 8; mains €15-22; ⏰ lunch & dinner) One of many restaurants in this atmospheric cobblestone quarter. This one caters to tourists keen to sample the house speciality – horse (*paard* in Flemish). A *filet van paard* costs €21, while a regular horse steak is a bit cheaper.

't Zuid

L'Entrepot du Congo (Map pp174-5; ☎ 0475 52 82 15; Vlaamsekaai 42; snacks €3-5, mains €8-12; ⏰ 7.30am-2am Sun-Thu, 7.30am-4am Fri & Sat) The first bistro to open in 't Zuid and it still pulls the locals. Occupies a renovated stone warehouse and is

(sidebar) **EASTERN FLANDERS**

THE AUTHOR'S CHOICE

Gin Fish (Map pp176-7; ☎ 03 231 32 07; Haarstraat 9; 4-course menu excl/incl wine €60/75; ☯ dinner Tue-Sat; ☒) Didier Garnich knew it was risky closing his seafood restaurant De Matelote and relinquishing its Michelin star. But he longed for the pre-Michelin days, when an open kitchen allowed him to laugh with the people whose meals he was preparing, and there was no mandate to slavishly follow classic formulas. So he took the gamble and opened Gin Fish. Same address, same attention to quality, same devotion to fish… only this time he's doing it his way. There's no exhaustive seafood menu, as out-of-season fish is not an option. Instead, only the freshest catch is cooked, and only one menu-of-the-day is offered: two entrées, a main and dessert. Each evening has three sittings – 6pm, 8.30pm and 10pm. And for pre- or post-dinner drinks, hit the cosy lounge next door. Bookings are essential.

noticeably less pretentious than other eateries in this area. Drinks are reasonably priced and the bistro-style food – sandwiches, pasta dishes, steaks and salads – is a cut above the average. The kitchen closes at 10.30pm.

Patine (Map pp174-5; ☎ 03 257 09 19; Leopold de Waelstraat 1; mains €7-11; ☯ 8am-1am Mon-Fri, 9am-2am Sat & Sun) Give minimalism the flick in this bohemian little wine bar-restaurant-tearoom that also doubles as a B&B (see p189). The décor is warm and soothing, the clientele's a mix of everyone (including poodles), and the cuisine is light and healthy – salad, quiche and pasta dishes.

El Pintxo's (Map pp176-7; ☎ 03 237 06 00; Riemstraat 49; lunch/dinner menu €10/20; ☯ lunch & dinner Mon-Sat) Antwerp's first *pintxo* (the Basque version of tapas) bar has a cool, sober interior lorded over by a big red bull. The *pintxos variados* dinner menu (€20) includes five cold and four warm servings – great for satisfying those who want to test the lot.

Dansing Chocola (Map pp176-7; ☎ 03 237 19 05; Kloosterstraat 159; mains €11-15; ☯ 10am-1.30am) Another *eetcafé* (*café* serving food) but this time things are decidedly old fashioned. Excellent spot for a simple Belgian bite before or after trawling the nearby *brocante* shops on Kloosterstraat and Oever. The kitchen closes at 10pm.

Soeki (Map pp174-5; ☎ 03 238 75 05; Volkstraat 21; assortment of tapas plus glass of champagne €15-25; ☯ dinner Wed-Sun) Tiny tapas and champagne bar that seduces passers-by with smooth velvet décor, multinational tapas and champagne by the glass.

Centraal Station Quarter

Faites Simple (Map pp176-7; ☎ 03 232 64 67; Quellinstraat 30; mains €10-15; ☯ lunch Tue-Fri, dinner Tue-Sat) Organic vegetables, hormone-free meat and artisanal products are the mainstay of this stylish (mainly) vegetarian restaurant. Th interior is an arty blend of glass, light an Art Nouveau. In summer the garden terrac at the back makes a welcome respite in th busy part of town.

Lamalo (Map pp176-7; ☎ 03 213 22 00; Appelmansstra 21; mains €20-30; ☯ lunch & dinner Mon-Thu & Sun; ☒ For many years this kosher Mediterranea restaurant was one of the area's best-kept se crets. Relocation and an image (and pric hike means it's now well known outside th quarter. The cuisine is from Israel, Leban and Morocco. The plate of 10 assorted me (€20 for two people) is excellent. Décor-wi it's warm but suffers no nonsense.

't Eilandje

Het Pomphuis (☎ 03 770 86 25; Siberiastraat; mains € 25; ☯ 10am-midnight Mon-Sat, noon-11pm Sun) Mon mental restaurant-brasserie-bar that occupi an old pump house located on a spit way the north of the old city centre in the surre world of Antwerp's mammoth harbour. Insi it's one big glassy space, overseen by eclect architectural features, including Art Nouvea elements. Enter and come face-to-face with 7m deep pit where the pumps once turne The restaurant does Belgian and world cu sine, and the service is friendly and attentiv If you're without a car, a taxi's a must.

SELF-CATERING

Delhaize (Map pp176-7; Nationalestraat 52) Supermarke in St Andries.

Super GB (Map pp176-7; Groenplaats; ☯ 8.30am-8pm Supermarket in the basement of the Grand Bazar shoppi centre.

Vogelmarkt (Map pp176-7; Theaterplein; ☯ 6am-3p Sat & Sun) Antwerp's principal food market takes over th huge square behind Het Paleis theatre every weekend. Saturday is the big day.

Drinking

The only thing better in Antwerp than eating is drinking. Small convivial pubs, converted warehouses and grand *cafés* abound. Excellent terrace *cafés* for soaking up the city's atmosphere are scattered around Handschoenmarkt, Groenplaats, Hendrik Conscienceplein and Wapper.

Zuiderterras (Map pp176-7; ☎ 03 234 12 75; Ernest van Dijckkaai 37; ☑ 9am-midnight) Modern landmark *café*-restaurant located at the southern end of the riverside promenade. Designed by the city's eminent contemporary architect, bOb (sic) Van Reeth, it mixes black, white and metal, and the enormous plate-glass windows provide superb river views. In summer a terrace fans out onto the walkway and it makes a superb place to while away an hour or two watching Antwerpenaars wandering the quayside.

Den Engel (Map pp176-7; ☎ 03 233 12 52; Grote Markt 3; ☑ 9am-late) Located in a guildhall and one of the city's oldest watering holes. A reasonable number of tourists dilute the locals – join them in downing a *bolleke* (little bowl) of De Koninck (The King), the city's favourite ale.

Grand Café Horta (Map pp176-7; ☎ 03 232 28 15; Hopland 2; ☑ 9am-9pm Tue-Sun) Much vaunted *café*-restaurant that incorporates iron girders salvaged from Victor Horta's ill-fated Maison du Peuple (see boxed text, p88). It's a good place to sip an Élixir d'Anvers, a saccharin-sweet, bright-yellow liqueur made in Antwerp since 1863 and reputed to aid digestion – Louis Pasteur even awarded it a diploma in 1887.

De Vagant (Map pp176-7; ☎ 03 233 15 38; Reyndersstraat 21; ☑ noon-late) Those into *jenever* (Belgian gin)

should make a beeline here. More than 200 *jenever* are served in this humble *café*. The house cocktail – a potent mix of white and lemon *jenever* plus a few other liqueurs and fruit juice (€4.50) – is worth trying.

't Elfde Gebod (The 11th Commandment; Map pp176-7; ☎ 03 232 36 11; Torfbrug 10; ☑ noon-late) A real tourist trap (ie…expensive beers), but worth a look for its angel-adorned interior.

Bierhuis Kulminator (Map pp176-7; ☎ 03 232 45 38; Vleminckveld 32; ☑ from 8pm Mon, from 11am Tue-Fri, from 5pm Sat) The place to sink a host of Belgian beers. It has been around for years and boasts 700 types of beer, many of them stacked up behind the counter. Don't bother deciphering the beer list – just point.

Bar Tabac (Map pp174-5; www.bartabac.be; Waalsekaai 43; ☑ 8pm-7am Wed-Sun) Tiny bar that looks like it was plucked from a village in rural France and plonked in 't Zuid. The odd thing is it has been going for years and is always packed. The décor's no more than a faded Michelin map and two old cigarette vending machines, plus a hotchpotch of old metal tables and chairs. In summer there's a terrace section for relaxing on crusty cinema seats; in winter everyone's jammed inside. 'Drunk Wednesdays' see beers going for €1 and a DJ spinning tracks.

Mogador (Map pp174-5; ☎ 03 238 71 60; Graaf van Egmontstraat 57; ☑ 6pm-3am Wed-Sun) It's back to black in this champagne bar in 't Zuid – a real gossip den for the bold and beautiful.

Entertainment

Antwerp's entertainment scene lacks nothing. Several free entertainment guides list what's happening, but the most concise for non-Flemish speakers is *Week Up*. It's available from the tourist office and many *cafés*.

Tickets for concert, opera, theatre and dance performances can be bought from two locations:

FNAC (Map pp176-7; ☎ ticket office 0900 006 00; Groenplaats; ☑ 10am-6.15pm) Inside the Grand Bazar shopping centre.
Prospekta (Map pp176-7; ☎ 03 203 95 86; Grote Markt 13; ☑ 10am-6pm Tue-Fri, noon-5pm Sat) Shares a guildhall with the tourist office.

CINEMAS

Cartoons (Map pp176-7; ☎ 03 232 96 32; Kaasstraat 4-6) The place to get away from general release Hollywood pulp. Art-house movies and quality foreign films are screened in its three auditoriums. Tickets are discounted on Monday.

Roma (Map pp174-5; ☎ 03 235 04 90; Turnhoutsebaan 286) Antwerp's last old cinema and concert hall. It dates from 1928, and in the '70s was a popular venue for international artists – AC/DC, Lou Reed and James Brown all played here. Recently returned to life thanks to determined community effort, it now screens a varied line-up of off-beat films, Hollywood hits and kids' matinees. It's located east of Centraal Station in Borgerhout, a suburb that's chiefly home to Moroccan immigrants, and is rarely visited by tourists. Tram 10 or 24 stops out the front.

Also recommended:

FotoMuseum (Map pp174-5; ☎ 03 242 93 00; www .fotomusuem.be; Waalsekaai 47) Golden oldies screened nightly.

Metropolis (☎ 0900 005 55; Groenendaallaan 394) Twenty four–screen monstrosity way to the north of the city. Take bus 720 from Franklin Rooseveltplaats.

UGC (Map pp174-5; ☎ 0900 104 40; Van Ertbornstraat 17) Seventeen-screen cinema complex near Centraal Station.

LIVE MUSIC

Café Hopper (Map pp174-5; ☎ 03 248 49 33; Leopold De Waelstraat 2) One of the city's most popular jazz venues, located in 't Zuid. There's usually live sessions on Sunday, Monday and Wednesday. It's small, so come early if you want to get your foot in the door. Admission costs around €8 for established acts.

Buster (Map pp176-7; www.busterpodium.be; Kaasrui 1; ☺ 8pm-late) Little place, just off the Grote Markt, that stages live concerts on Tuesda (mainly jazz and rock'n'roll; admission €7 t €10) as well as jam sessions (Thursday from 8pm; free admission) when anyone can tak to the podium.

Crossroads Café (Map pp174-5; www.crossroadsca .be; Mechelsesteenweg 8; admission €2.50-10) The city' chief exponent of the blues, this unpretentiou *café* features regular live concerts (from 5pm t 8pm most Sundays) by local or visiting bands There's also a free concert at 8pm most Mon days. It's about 1km from the Grote Markt tram 7 (direction Mortsel) stops at the front

De Muze (Map pp176-7; ☎ 03 226 01 26; Melkmarkt 1; ☺ noon-4am) In the early '70s this was the meet ing place for the city's free-thinking youth The radical edge is gone, but it's still an im mensely popular *café* spanning three floor with an Escher-like interior and a bastion o live jazz (from 10pm Monday to Saturday).

NIGHTCLUBS

Antwerp's club scene begins with smooth lounges featuring in-house DJs and ends wit high-octane house parties. The scene meld permanent with one-off in a mix that hold both mainstream and alternative. Trance an experimental electronica are big – check ou **Noctis** (www.noctis.com) to track down clubs, one off parties or festivals. Alternatively, pick u fliers at **Fish & Chips** (Map pp176-7; ☎ 03 227 08 2 Kammenstraat 36-38) and see boxed text (below)

Café d'Anvers (Map pp176-7; www.café-d-anvers.con Verversrui 15; ☺ 11pm-7.30am Fri & Sat) Well over

---

PARTY ON

Antwerp rocks. The city lives on party time, with nightclubs (above) that have produced some of the country's most revered DJs, and a host of parties that see summer out with a bang.

One of the best known is **Antwerp is Burning** (www.antwerpisburning.be). It takes over a huge field on the Linkeroever, converting the left bank of the river into a one-night party bash in early September. Half a dozen clubs band together, and more than 30 artists beat out hard dance, trance, techno, house and drum'n'bass until well into the next day.

A week later there's **Laundry Day** (www.laundryday.be). Smack in the heart of Antwerp's St Andries fashion district, this party with an unlikely name sees seven stages set up on and around Vrijdagmarkt and Oudaan, with 50 DJs pulsing throughout the day and into the night.

Illusion (www.illusion.be), a trance odyssey, takes over Antwerp's Sportpaleis (Map pp174–5) for one full night in late September. This party is legendary.

Throughout the year check out **Partyguide** (www.partyguide.be); it's in Flemish but it's easy enough to get the gist of the party agenda.

A good way to taste the scene before even hitting Antwerp is to catch *Anyway the Wind Blows*. This 2003 film was the directorial debut of dEUS front man, Tom Barman. It follows 32 hours in the lives of eight interconnected characters, set against the backdrop of Barman's hometown, Antwerp. The eight all end up at a party one summer night. The music's great.

decade old and still going strong, this legendary club does funk and house, disco and soul in a refurbished church in the city's red-light district. Many of Belgium's top DJs started here, and more are breeding. Every Friday night in July and August the club puts on Free Vibes, free dance nights featuring new, resident and visiting DJs.

Café Local (Map pp174-5; www.cafélocal.be; Waalsekaai 25; ☾ from 10pm Tue-Sat) A long-time favourite, in 't Zuid, Café Local was once known for its techno parties but these days it prefers the sounds of salsa and global grooves.

Kaaiman (Map pp174-5; www.kaaiman.be; Napelsstraat 57; ☾ 10pm-late Fri & Sat) Alternative types flock to this small club occupying a converted red-brick garage in 't Eilandje. Music is eclectic with a lean to house and drum'n'bass.

Pier 19 (Map pp176-7; ☎ 03 288 78 61; Brouwersvliet 19; ☾ midnight-5am Thu-Sat) Small cellar club on the edge of 't Eilandje that's done out in pristine white with a glass bar and laid-back lounge music. Attracts a 25 to 40ish crowd.

Space (Map pp176-7; Frankrijklei 53; ☾ 6am-2pm Mon, Tue & Sat, 8am-6am Sun) Down near Centraal Station, this is the after-club club. Dancing starts when the streetlights go out.

In 't Zuid, check out Luikstraat for the line-up of lounges/clubs/restaurants that are forever reincarnating here – at last count **Stereo Sushi** (Map pp174-5; Luikstraat 6) was leading the pack.

For details on Red & Blue, see boxed text (p188) and for La Rocca, see p201.

SPORT

Antwerp traditionally had two top competing football clubs, Antwerp and Beerschot. Both are now so degraded that Beerschot amalgamated with a suburban soccer club to become Germinal Beerschot and Antwerp kicks along on its own. You'd have to be mad keen to bother with a game here.

THEATRE, DANCE & OPERA

deSingel (Map pp174-5; ☎ 03 248 28 28; www.desingel be; Desguinlei 25) This is the city's chief venue for classical music, international theatre and modern dance. It has two concert halls, and a highly innovative programme is offered throughout the year.

Bourlaschouwburg (Map pp176-7; ☎ 03 224 88 44; Komedieplaats 18) Beautiful old theatre with a rounded façade topped by statues of nine muses, composers and writers. Built in the 1830s for the city's French-speaking elite by architect Pierre

Bourla, it eventually fell into disuse and was on the brink of demolition only a decade or so ago. It's now home to Het Toneelhuis theatre company. This company also commonly plays at a second venue, Studio Tokio (Map pp174–5) on Museumstraat in 't Zuid.

Koninklijk Ballet van Vlaanderen (Map pp174-5; ☎ 03 234 34 38; www.koninklijkballetvanvlaanderen.be; Westkaai 16) The Royal Flanders Ballet, founded in 1960, is the nation's only classical dance company. It moved to 't Eilandje in the late 1990s, and its impressive home – a purpose-built palatial grey building – harmonises perfectly with the area's maritime architecture. The ballet performs both here and at the Vlaamse Opera.

Vlaamse Opera (Flemish Opera House; Map pp176-7; ☎ 03 233 66 85; Frankrijklei 3) A stunning building and a fitting place to hear a performance by the highly regarded Koninklijke Vlaamse Opera (Royal Flemish Opera). Built in 1907, the building's majestic façade is unfortunately diminished by the mirrored monstrosity built next to it in the 1960s. Still, the marbled interior is sumptuous and the quality of the performances superb. Tickets generally cost €10 to €60.

Zuiderpershuis (Map pp174-5; ☎ 03 248 01 00; www .zuiderpershuis.be; Waalsekaai 14) This cultural centre in 't Zuid specialises in music, dance, theatre and workshops from non-Western cultures. An impressive calendar of events includes at least three artists or groups performing weekly. Tickets generally cost €10 to €20. There's also a popular *café* attached to the venue.

Koningin Elisabethzaal (Queen Elisabeth Concert Hall; Map pp176-7; ☎ 0900 260 00; Koningin Astridplein 23-24) Classical music concert hall located next to Centraal Station. Flanders' philharmonic orchestra, De Filharmonie (www.defilharmonie .be), plays here.

Het Paleis (Map pp176-7; ☎ 03 248 28 28; Theaterplein 1) This venue is an ugly cement eyesore built in 1980 and commonly called the Bunker.

Shopping

Antwerp has something for every shopper – gourmet chocolates, world-class diamonds, quality antiques, high-profile designers and streets lined with *brocante* shops. The pedestrianised Meir is first cab off the rank for most people – after Centraal Station's diamond shops. For more intimate shopping, head to the small cluster of streets on either side of Huidevettersstraat. This so-called Quartier Latin is home to some of the city's most exclusive shops; Schuttershofstraat and Korte Gasthuisstraat are the best places to start.

ANTIQUES

Antwerp deservedly has a fine reputation for antique shops. Steenhouwersvest, Schuttershofstraat, Komedieplaats and Leopoldstraat are the streets to go hunting. Also visit the Vrijdagmarkt (see p198).

BEER & JENEVER

Den Dorstvlegel (Map pp176-7; ☎ 0485 50 48 80; Oude Vaartplaats 12; ⏰ 10.30am-5.30pm Mon, Wed & Fri, 10.30am-4pm Sat & Sun) Excellent beer shop.

De Vagant Slijterij (Map pp176-7; ☎ 03 233 15 38; Reyndersstraat; ⏰ 11am-6pm Mon & Wed-Sat) A shop selling strong alcohol is called a *slijterij* in Flemish. This shop sells more than 200 types of *jenever*, and is across the street from a pub that's similarly obsessed.

BROCANTE

Brocante (bric-a-brac) traders have taken over Kloosterstraat and Oever (south of St Jansvliet; Map pp176–7). For more options, see Markets (p198).

CHOCOLATES & SWEETS

Burie (Map pp176-7; ☎ 03 232 68 88; Korte Gasthuisstraat 3) Famous artisan *chocolaterie*. For years this little shop has been known for the intricate marzipan and chocolate sculptures displayed in the window. Those after diamond-shaped chocolates or *Antwerpse handjes* (see boxed text, p180) will find them here.

Del Rey (Map pp176-7; ☎ 03 233 29 37; Appelmansstraat 5-9) A top-rate chocolate shop, located on the edge of the diamond district near Centraal Station. A mouth-watering assortment of pralines (filled chocolates), exquisite pastries and biscuits beckon from sumptuous displays. Sampling is done at the neighbouring degustation salon, where an espresso, plus one praline and a biscuit, costs €4.15.

Pierre Marcolini (Map pp176-7; ☎ 03 226 50 01; Huidevettersstraat 38-40) Join the queues at this Belgian high flier (for more information, see p113).

Goossens (Map pp176-7; ☎ 03 226 07 91; Korte Gasthuisstraat 31) One of the city's best bakeries. It's teensy, so you'll probably have to join the queue on the street. Try its rye-and-raisin bread (€2.25) or a *suikerbrood* (sugar bread).

Philip's Biscuits (Map pp176-7; ☎ 03 231 26 60; Korte Gasthuisstraat 11) Exclusive biscuit shop specialis-

ing in *speculaas* (cinnamon-flavoured biscuits) and *peperkoek* (honey cake).

Temmerman (Map pp176-7; ☎ 03 227 03 90; Schutershofstraat 13; ⏰ Tue-Sat) Sweet shop with a tiny café.

FASHION & ACCESSORIES

The heart of Antwerp's fashion quarter is St Andries. Head to Nationalestraat, Lombardenvest, Huidevettersstraat and Schuttershofstraat for designer gear; Kammenstraat has streetwear stuff. The tourist office publishes a booklet *Antwerp Fashion Walk* (€3) containing five self-guided tours of the area and a rundown on many of the designers. Also see boxed text, opposite.

The following shops open from around 11am to 6pm, and all are closed Sunday.

Ann Demeulemeester (Map pp174-5; ☎ 03 216 00 33; Verlatstraat 38) Demeulemeester's shop in 't Zuid stocks her complete line of men's and women's clothing. Despite occasional bursts of colour, her collections are usually monochrome based.

Annemie Verbeke (Map pp176-7; ☎ 03 226 35 60; Nationalestraat 76) Highly successful Ypres-born designer who sells internationally. She opened this shop in 2005.

Coccodrillo (Map pp176-7; ☎ 03 233 20 93; Schuttershofstraat 9a) No-frills shoe boutique that's an institution in Antwerp. Stocks big-name internationals as well as all the local designers, including Branquinho and Van Noten. A word of warning: Saturday afternoon's crowds make browsing hard.

Episode (Map pp176-7; ☎ 03 234 34 14; Steenhouwersvest 34a) Vintage clothes with bottom-line prices deck out this cavernous shop.

Fish & Chips (Map pp176-7; ☎ 03 227 08 24; Kammenstraat 36-38) The place to collide with youth culture. This department-sized store woos the young with retro labels and urban scrawl. Go for a fresh fruit and veg juice at the upstairs bar, or groove to the sounds of the in-store DJs.

Labels Inc (Map pp176-7; ☎ 03 232 60 56; Aalmoezenierstraat 4) End-of-line designer wear – including pieces by Belgium's big names – are sold in this famous little backstreet boutique at prices that won't send you bankrupt.

Louis (Map pp176-7; ☎ 03 232 98 72; Lombardenstraat 4) Great introduction to various Belgian players, with collections by Ann Demeulemeester, Martin Margiela, Jurgi Persoons, Véronique Branquinho and Raf Simons.

AT THE CUTTING EDGE

Mention Belgium in the right circles and the immediate word association will be 'fashion'. Designers from Antwerp have been avant-garde leaders since 1987 when a handful of graduates from the city's Royal Academy of Fine Arts loaded a truck with designs and sped over to a showing in London. Their ideas were collectively daring, provocative and extreme, but markedly different from each other. They were soon labelled the 'Antwerp Six' – Ann Demeulemeester, Dries Van Noten, Walter Van Beirendonck, Dirk Van Saene, Dirk Bikkembergs and Marina Yee – and, thanks largely to them, Belgian fashion has never looked back.

With designers from Brussels now picking up the slack (see boxed text, p114), Belgium's fashion industry is worth millions. But despite big turnovers, many of the nation's designers have remained independent of large fashion houses, preferring to call the shots themselves. Belgian designers also have a strong sense of place – instead of reaping rewards by moving to Paris or Milan, five of the Antwerp Six set up in their home town and three still live there.

Belgium is often regarded as one of fashion's intellectual breeding grounds. What happens here is done relatively quietly, without red carpet or fanfare – like so much in this modest little country – but the ideas of the country's designers are keenly watched by fashion houses the world over.

The best known of the Antwerp Six is the bald and bearded Walter Van Beirendonck – he has designed outfits for rock supergroup U2 and is definitely wild and futuristic. His fashions are a favourite among the clubbing crowd, merging clubwear with post-modern ideas about everything from bio-technology to aliens. But he also recently surprised the fashion world with a childrenswear collection for high-street chain JBC that has branches across Belgium and Luxembourg. Van Beirendonck's latest collections are on show at his shop, Walter (p198). Here, too, you'll find soft women's wear designed by Dirk Van Saene and other selected friends.

Ann Demeulemeester's designs are timeless, often crafted in black. Her shop (opposite) in 't Zuid in Antwerp is the best place to explore her creations. Dries Van Noten is the group's commercial leader. His colourful bohemian clothes are sold in more than 500 shops around the world, but buyers love his Antwerp flagship, Het Modepaleis (below). Dirk Bikkembergs left Antwerp for Germany and his designs can now only be found at Verso (below) in Antwerp or L'Héroïne (p138) in Bruges. In 2006 Bikkemberg launched the Bix – the first professional football boot to be designed by a fashion house. Made from kangaroo leather, a pair sells for a cool €320. Marina Yee is the least known of the Six and, until recently, her creations were hard to find. But since opening a store in Brussels' designer heartland (p114) she's now much more accessible. The group's unofficial seventh member is Martin Margiela, who graduated from the Royal Academy in 1980 and set up in Paris soon after. Margiela's clothes are conceptual with subtle details. He uses the body as an exhibition space, turning old clothes inside out to make something unique and producing works that are part fashion, part art. He, too, has a shop in Brussels (p114).

The talent hasn't ended there. The Royal Academy continues to spawn designers who have made names for themselves – Raf Simons, Véronique Branquinho, Bernhard Willhelm and Jurgi Peersons are a few. To see some of these names head to the shop that first waved Belgian fashion to the world, Louis (opposite).

If fashion's your passion, time a visit for early September when a 10-day event known as Vitrine takes over the city; for details see **Modenatie** (www.modenatie.com). And there's no shortage of shops handling designer gear.

Het Modepaleis (Map pp176-7; ☎ 03 470 25 10; Nationalestraat 16) Headquarters and shop of Dries Van Noten, located in a distinct, 19th-century, domed building in the heart of St Andries.

Véronique Branquinho (Map pp176-7; ☎ 03 233 66 16; Nationalestraat 73) One of the newer set of Antwerp designers, but already a part of the international scene. She's known for her clas-sic tailoring skills, and opened this, her flagship store, a few years back.

Verso (Map pp176-7; ☎ 03 226 92 92; Lange Gasthuisstraat 11) Fantastic location – an old bank building with a gorgeous stained-glass cupola – for this large boutique, which specialises in Italian designers, although there are also a few French names and one Belgian (Dirk Bikkembergs). Women's and men's collections, cosmetics and accessories, plus a hip *café*.

Walter (Map pp176-7; ☎ 03 213 26 44; St Antoniusstraat 12) This former garage on a quiet backstreet looks more like an exhibition space than somewhere to buy clothes. Van Beirendonck's styles sit mighty comfortable here.

Also recommended:

Delvaux (Map pp176-7; ☎ 03 232 02 47; Komedieplaats 17) Belgian leather handbags plus accessories.

Nico Taeymans (Map pp176-7; ☎ 03 231 82 18; Korte Gasthuisstraat 23) Noted Antwerp jewellery designer.

Olivier Strelli (Map pp176-7; ☎ 03 231 81 41; Hopland 6) Fashions by Belgium's most accessible designer.

Pardaf (Map pp176-7; ☎ 03 232 60 40; Gemeentestraat 8) Huge townhouse full of secondhand clothes for women and men.

DIAMONDS
Diamond and gold traders line up inside the newly expanded Centraal Station, as well as in showrooms along nearby Pelikaanstraat, Hoveniersstraat, Vestingstraat and Appelmansstraat.

Diamondland (Map pp176-7; ☎ 03 229 29 90; Appelmansstraat 33a; ⊗ 9.30am-5.30pm Mon-Sat, also 10am-5pm Sun Apr-Oct) Watch workers cutting diamonds and ogle the huge range of stones for sale. For more information on the history of diamond trading in Antwerp, see boxed text (p183).

MARKETS
Vrijdagmarkt (Map pp176-7; Vrijdagmarkt; ⊗ 6-11am Fri) The city's oldest antique flea market has been operating on this square every Friday morning since the 16th century. Everything is sold by auction, with sales going down in fast guttural Flemish. Feel free to throw in an English bid if you see an irresistible antique – the dealers will readily accept it.

Rommelmarkt (Map pp176-7; St Jansvliet; ⊗ 7am-3pm Sun) Weekly *brocante* market on a small square close to the river.

For details on the city's main food market, Vogelmarkt, see p192.

Getting There & Away
AIR
Four kilometres southeast of the city centre in the suburb of Deurne, **Antwerp airport** (☎ 03 285 65 00; www.antwerpairport.be) services a very limited number of flights to London City, as well as to Liverpool and Manchester via London City.

BUS
The arrival and departure point for **Eurolines** (Map pp176-7; ☎ 03 233 86 62; www.eurolines.be; Van Straelenstraat 8) buses is from this office near Franklin Rooseveltplaats. For information on services, see p317.

CAR & MOTORCYCLE
Car-rental companies in Antwerp include **Budget** (Map pp174-5; ☎ 0800 155 55; Noorderlaan 32), which also has an office at **Antwerp airport** (☎ 03 213 79 60), and **Avis** (Map pp174-5; ☎ 03 218 94 96; Plantin-Moretuslei 62).

TRAIN
Antwerp's main train station, **Centraal Station** (Map pp176-7; ☎ 03 204 20 40), is about 1.5km from the old city centre; another station, Berchem, is 2km southeast of Centraal Station. For details on Centraal Station, see p182.

National connections from Antwerp include IC trains every half-hour to Brussels (€6.10, 35 minutes), Ghent (€7.80, 45 minutes) and Mechelen (€3.20, 15 minutes), and hourly trains to Bruges (€12.40, 70 minutes), Hasselt (€9.50, 65 minutes), Leuven (€6, 45 minutes) and Lier (€2.30, 15 minutes).

Getting Around
TO/FROM THE AIRPORT
Bus 16 connects Antwerp airport with Quellinstraat (20 minutes), two blocks west of Centraal Station. Taxis cost about €10 one way.

BICYCLE
Antwerp is cycle friendly. Motorists are used to throngs of cyclists and, although there aren't heaps of cycle paths, the city can be safely navigated by bike. Be aware of trams and their slippery tracks, and ensure you double lock your bike as theft is common.

In summer bikes can be hired from **Rent A Bike** (Map pp176-7; ☎ 03 290 49 62; www.antwerpbikes.be in Flemish & French; Lijnwaadmarkt 6; ⊗ 9am-6pm), a new outfit barnacled to the side of the cathedral, from €6/8.50 per half-/full day. Note, full-day rental here means 24 hours.

CAR & MOTORCYCLE
A great place to park is on the covered riverside quay (in the Zuiderterras hangar) near the city centre. The northern section is for paid parking but the southern end (and all the open-air parking next to it) is free. The entrance is opposite Fortuinstraat. There's also free parking

in 't Zuid on the Gedempte Zuiderdokken, the square between Vlaamsekaai and Waalsekaai. From here, it's a 15- to 20-minute walk to the Grote Markt. Alternatively buses 6 and 34 go to Steenplein near the Grote Markt, and bus 23 runs to Franklin Rooseveltplaats.

The easiest central parking garage to access is the 24-hour underground car park at Groenplaats.

PUBLIC TRANSPORT

A good network of buses, trams and a *premetro* (a tram that runs underground for part of its journey) is run by **De Lijn** (☎ 070 220 200; www.delijn.be in Flemish). Free public transport maps covering the city centre are available from De Lijn ticket and information kiosks – the most useful are located at the *premetro* stations Diamant (below Centraal Station), Groenplaats and on Franklin Rooseveltplaats (all on Map pp176–7). These kiosks are generally open 8am to 4pm weekdays (also 9am to noon Saturday and Sunday).

Both *stad* (city) and *streek* (regional) buses leave from one of the city's main bus hubs, Franklin Rooseveltplaats and Koningin Astridplein. Make sure you know in which direction you're heading. As many bus (and tram) routes start at one side of the city and finish on the other, it's possible to be on the right-numbered bus (or tram) but travelling in the wrong direction.

The tram network is well established with routes as far out as Hoboken, Deurne and Mortsel.

The tiny, two-line *premetro* simply consists of above-ground trams that dive underground. Handy *premetro* trams include 2, 3, 5 and 15, which run underground along the main drag – Diamant (under Centraal Station) to Groenplaats – before continuing under the Scheldt River to surface on the Linkeroever.

The same tickets can be used for buses, trams and *premetro*. A single ticket (valid for one hour) bought at De Lijn's information office costs €1.20 (or €1.50 on the bus), a *dagpas* (day ticket) is €5 (€6 on the bus) and a 10-journey *lijnkaart* (network card) is €8 (€10 on the bus). Public transport generally runs from about 6am to midnight. There's also a *nachtlijn* (night bus) service on weekends.

TAXI

Taxis wait at Groenplaats, outside Centraal Station and on Koningin Astridplein. Otherwise call **Antwerp Taxi** (☎ 03 238 38 38). An extra €2.50 is added to fares between 10pm and 6am.

AROUND ANTWERP

Pick up any tourist map of Antwerp and a few small blue patches in the northwest corner will indicate **Antwerp port**. Believe us – these areas are just the tip of the iceberg. Likewise, stand on the riverside Zuiderterras promenade in Antwerp and the cranes you can see in the distance are just the beginning of the world's fourth-largest port.

It wasn't all that long ago when the city's port did cover a relatively small area. But massive transformation of the surrounding farmlands and polders in the 20th century, including the annihilation of whole villages, has seen the port grow from a prosperous medieval harbour based around waterways (now filled in) in the heart of the old city centre to a giant that stretches to the Dutch border.

Napoleon initiated this expansion with the creation of two huge docks – Bonapartedok and Willemdok. These docks are now the focus of 't Eilandje district – it's between them that the new MAS museum is being built. Towards the end of the 19th century, the nearby Kattendijkdok was constructed and from there the port has soared. In 2005 King Albert II opened the port's latest expansion, Deurganckdok, doubling the port's holding capacity to 12 million containers.

Tours through the port are surreal – a maze of cranes and loading yards, docks and warehouses, railway lines and industrial estates, the latter belonging to petroleum refineries, car-assembly plants and petrochemical industries. More picturesque is the polder village of **Lillo**, one of the lucky survivors and home to a little museum devoted to life before the great transformation.

Without your own car, the best way to explore this area is on a Flandria boat trip (see p187).

LIER

pop 32,800

The small town of Lier, or Pallieterstad as it's also known, sits 17km southeast of Antwerp near the confluence of two rivers – the Grote and Kleine Nete. Its nickname comes from *Pallieter,* a jovial character invented by local writer Felix Timmermans. The people of Lier also have a less-charming nickname – see boxed text (p215).

Lier is a tranquil and typically Flemish provincial town. It was founded in the 8th century as a place of worship for St Gummarus, a nobleman from King Pepin's court in France who settled and eventually died here in 775. The town has a smattering of interesting – and unique – sights, making it a popular day trip from Antwerp, or a charming little place to hole up for a night.

The **tourist office** (☎ 03 800 05 05; www.lier.be; Grote Markt 57; ⏰ 9am-12.30pm & 1.30-5pm, Mon-Fri only Nov-Mar) is in the heart of town, in the basement of the town hall.

Sights

Central Lier is dominated by the **Grote Markt**, at the heart of which sits its refined **stadhuis** and adjoining turreted, 14th-century **belfort** (belfry), whose carillon chimes melodiously every quarter of an hour.

Close by is the town's most famous sight – the **Zimmertoren** (☎ 03 800 03 95; Zimmerplein; adult/child €2/1; ⏰ 9am-noon & 1-6pm Apr-Sep, 9am-noon & 1.30-5.30pm Oct-Mar). This former 14th-century tower, once part of the town's ramparts, was converted into the *Centenary Clock* in 1930 by a prosperous local Lodewijk Zimmer. The marvellous timepiece contains a central dial surrounded by 12 smaller dials each conveying bits of information, such as the ages of the moon and the signs of the zodiac. Hang around for the hour if you want to see the side figures donging the bells. In the pavilion next door is Zimmer's studio and another of his works – the astronomical *Wonder Clock* that featured at World Fairs in Brussels in 1935 and New York in 1939.

Go along Schapekoppenstraat (Sheep Heads St) to the monumental portal announcing the entrance to the **begijnhof**, a charming cluster of cottages founded in the 13th century. Most of the houses, as well as **St Margarethakerk** at the heart of the community, date from the 17th century.

From Zimmertoren, cross the river at Zimmerplein to reach the **Timmermans-Opsomerhuis** (☎ 03 800 05 55; Netelaan 6; admission €1; ⏰ 10am-noon & 1-5pm Tue-Sun). This museum is devoted to local 19th- and 20th-century writers and artists, particularly writer Felix Timmermans (1886–1947), artist Isidoor Opsomer (1878–1967) and sculptor Lodewijk Van Boeckel (1857–1944).

The creamy-toned **St Gummaruskerk** (Kardinaal Mercierplein; admission €1.25; ⏰ 10am-noon & 2-5pm Mon-Sat) was gradually built from the late 14th to early 16th century. The elegant tower is a mix of Gothic and baroque, topped by a rococo cupola (the tower was rebuilt in the 18th century after being struck by lightning). The church's most important treasures are its 16th-century stained-glass windows, which are among Belgium's oldest.

To explore Lier's central waterways, hop on board a former eel-fishing **boat**. Forty-minute trips (€2.50/1.50 per adult/child) depart from the quay at the *begijnhof's* back entrance at 2.30pm and 3.30pm on Saturday, and 2pm to 6pm on Sunday from May to October.

Sleeping & Eating

Hof van Aragon (☎ 03 491 08 00; www.hofvanaragon.be in Flemish; Mosdijk 1-6; s/d from €60/70; ✖) Those into old-world style will find this well-established hotel-restaurant the pick of Lier's accommodation scene. It's flanked by the peaceful river and has spacious rooms.

Hotel Florent (☎ 03 491 03 10; www.hotelflorent.be in Flemish; Florent Van Cauwenberghstraat 45; s/d €70/90) Relatively new, but very discreet, corner hotel that offers modern rooms with rich colour schemes and spacious bathrooms.

Zuster Agnes (☎ 03 288 94 73; Schapenkoppenstraat 16; mains €14-18; ⏰ from 10am) At the rear of the *begijnhof*, Sister Agnes is a modern wok brasserie and well-hidden local favourite offering intimate interior dining or outdoor tables overlooking the town's mascot – those sheep.

De Oude Komeet (☎ 03 488 21 56; Florent Van Cauwenberghstraat 18; mains €14-20; ⏰ lunch & dinner Tue-Sun) Likable *eetkafee* with organic produce and a good range of wholesome vegetarian meals. There's also a garden terrace.

Cuistot (☎ 03 488 46 56; Antwerpsestraat 146; mains €20-29; ⏰ Thu-Mon) Located in a big townhouse at the end of one of the main shopping streets, this modern restaurant does a very limited range of dishes marrying world flavours. The chef learnt his stuff at Villa Lorraine, one of Brussels' top restaurants, and he's impressed the locals.

De Werf (☎ 03 480 71 90; Werf 17; mains €20-30, three-course menu €33; ⏰ lunch Tue-Fri, dinner Tue-Sat) A great restaurant serving excellent French/Flemish cuisine. Very cosy – just 10 tables – with attentive service.

For a sweet treat try a *Liers vlaaike* sold in any bakery. These fat little tarts are a mix of syrup, cinnamon and flour, and have been made in Lier since the 13th century.

For self-caterers, there's an **AD Delhaize** (Eikelstraat 26) supermarket with entrances on Grote Markt and Eikelstraat.

Entertainment

Lier's biggest music event is the **Jazzkroegentocht** (www.lier.be), a night of unremitting live jazz held in *cafés* around town in early November.

Lively student bars and cheap pitta/*shwarma* (doner kebab) places coexist on Eikelstraat and Zimmerplein.

Café St Gummarus (☎ 03 489 05 15; Timmermansplein 2; ❤ 2pm-2am Tue-Sun) Small bar on a square next to the river. It attracts an arty crowd and is a good place to try the local Lierse Caves, a gueuze-style lambic beer.

La Rocca (www.larocca.be; Antwerpsesteenweg 384; ❤ from 11.30pm Fri-Sun) Legendary nightclub celebrating its second decade in 2008. Its close proximity to Antwerp (just 17km away) means it's regularly frequented by Antwerpenaars.

Mister 100 (☎ 03 489 11 16; Grote Markt 28; ❤ 11am-9pm Tue-Sun) Huge billiard salon set up by Raymond Ceulemans, Belgium's world billiard champion. It's now run by his son, Kurt, and attracts billiard buffs from afar. All kinds of games are available, including billiards (€4/5 per hour per small/large table) and pool/snooker (€6/7 per hour).

Getting There & Away

Lier is well connected on the regional train circuit. The **train station** (☎ 03 229 55 03) and adjoining **bus station** (☎ 070 22 02 00) are 1km northeast of the Grote Markt. Trains run every half-hour to Antwerp (€2.30, 15 minutes), Diest (€5.70, 30 minutes), via Aarschot to Leuven (€5.70, 45 minutes) and to Mechelen (€2.60, 20 minutes). Bus 55 goes to Mechelen.

MECHELEN

pop 77,000

Mechelen (Malines in French, Mechlin in English) sits equidistant between Antwerp and Brussels – or just 20km from either – and is completely overshadowed by both. Like Ghent, it has long been bypassed by tourists doing the hop between the bigger, better-known Flemish cities. But recent revamping means it's now ringing its own bell and, considering the town is home to the country's heaviest carillon, the call is being heard far and wide. Newly pedestrianised areas and a new generation of B&Bs, hotels and fashionable shops are drawing visitors and locals alike. But even with this influx, the town is never uncomfortably crowded on weekends. For an authentic taste of Flanders minus any tourist hype, Mechelen's a must.

History

The town's history is surprisingly rich. Converted to Christianity by 8th-century evangelist St Rombout, Mechelen went on to become the country's religious capital and is home of the primate (archbishop) of the Catholic church.

In 1473 Charles the Bold chose Mechelen as his administrative base and the town became the thriving capital of the Burgundian Low Countries. Although Charles was killed in battle in France four years later, his widow, Margaret of York, decided to make Mechelen her permanent residence. In 1506 her step-granddaughter Margaret of Austria, the daughter of Maximilian I, was appointed governor and her glamorous court became one of the most famous of its day. Science, literature and the arts thrived, and many elaborate buildings, including a palace (now used as a courthouse), were constructed. A statue in her memory now stands at the edge of the Grote Markt. When Margaret died in 1530, the capital was moved to Brussels and Mechelen never regained the spotlight.

Information

ATM (Grote Markt 27) Attached to the KBC Bank.
In&Uit Mechelen (☎ 070 22 28 00; www.inenuit mechelen.be; Hallestraat 2; ❤ 9.30am-5.30pm Mon-Fri, 10am-4.30pm Sat & Sun Apr-Sep, 9.30am-4.30pm Mon-Fri, 10.30am-3.30pm Sat & Sun Oct-Mar) Tourist office newly located just off the corner of the pedestrianised Grote Markt.

Sights

It's impossible to miss **St Romboutskathedraal** (Grote Markt; admission free). This robust cathedral features a gigantic, 97m-high tower that was completed in the middle of the 16th century and in fine weather can be seen from Brussels. It's due to this tower that the residents of Mechelen are nicknamed Maneblussers (see boxed text, p215). It's possible to climb the tower (514 steps; €5) at certain times; the tourist office has details.

The cathedral is topped by the country's heaviest **carillon** – appropriately enough considering Mechelen boasts the world's most prestigious school of campanology (bell-ringing), and students come from far and wide to learn the art. The carillon master is Jo Haazen, and he plays the 49 bells (that date from the 15th to 18th centuries) for an hour-long concert at 8.30pm on Monday from June to mid-September.

For its size, Mechelen is overly endowed with churches – testimony to the town's rich religious history. Some, including the white sandstone **St Janskerk** (Klapgat), can only be visited by prior arrangement (ask at the tourist office).

Splayed in front of the stadhuis is a **statue of Op-Sinjoorke**, the town's mascot, being hurled into the air from a blanket. The real mascot, a wooden dummy carved in 1647, is kept in **Museum Hof van Busleyden** (☎ 015 29 40 30; Frederik De Merodestraat 65; adult/child €2/free; ☷ 10am-5pm Tue-Sun), the town's municipal museum. It occupies a high-Gothic-style mansion built during Margaret of Austria's rule and is full of historical bits and pieces, including bells, paintings and furniture.

Tapestry lovers must tour **De Wit Royal Manufacturers** (☎ 0475 52 29 05; www.dewit.be; Schoutestraat 7; adult/child €6/2). This well-established work-shop is one of the few places in Belgium where you can see contemporary tapestries being woven and antique ones from all over the world being repaired. There's a 1½-hour tour at 10.30am on Saturday.

The **Joods Museum van Deportatie en Verzet** (Jewish Museum of Deportation & Resistance; ☎ 015 29 06 60; www .cicb.be; Goswin de Stassartstraat 153; admission free; ☷ 10am-5pm Sat-Thu, 10am-1pm Fri) is housed in a former Nazi deportation centre. It movingly tells the Belgian chapter of Jewish persecution in WWII (see boxed text, opposite) and chronicles the resist-ance movement that sprang up. The museum is best toured with a guide – phone an hour or two ahead to arrange an English-speaking tour.

Trainspotters must time a visit to **De Mijlpaal** (☎ 015 41 65 68; Leuvensesteenweg 30; admission €2.50;

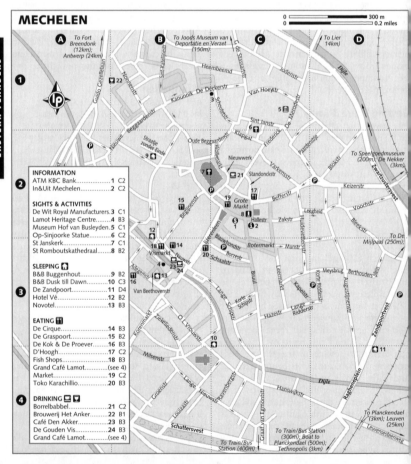

MECHELEN

INFORMATION
ATM KBC Bank..................1 C2
In&Uit Mechelen.............2 C2

SIGHTS & ACTIVITIES
De Wit Royal Manufacturers.3 C1
Lamot Heritage Centre........4 B3
Museum Hof van Busleyden.5 C1
Op-Sinjoorke Statue..........6 C2
St Janskerk.....................7 C1
St Romboutskathedraal......8 B2

SLEEPING
B&B Buggenhout................9 B2
B&B Dusk till Dawn..........10 C3
De Zandpoort.................11 D4
Hotel Vé........................12 B2
Novotel........................13 B3

EATING
De Cirque......................14 B3
De Graspoort...................15 B2
De Kok & De Proever......16 B3
D'Hoogh........................17 C2
Fish Shops.....................18 B3
Grand Café Lamot...........(see 4)
Market.........................19 C2
Toko Karachillio.............20 B3

DRINKING
Borrelbabbel...................21 C2
Brouwerij Het Anker........22 B1
Café Den Akker................23 B3
De Gouden Vis................24 B3
Grand Café Lamot............(see 4)

0   300 m
0   0.2 miles

To Fort Breendonk (12km); Antwerp (24km)

To Joods Museum van Deportatie en Verzet (150m)

To Lier 14km

To Speelgoedmuseum (200m); De Nekker (3km)

To De Mijlpaal (250m)

To Planckendael (3km); Leuven (25km)

To Train/Bus Station (300m); Boat to Planckendael (500m); Technopolis (3km)

To Train/Bus Station (400m)

⊙ 2-6pm Sat May-Sep), an essential railway museum on the outskirts of town. It tracks back in time to when Continental Europe's first train journeyed from Brussels to Mechelen.

The **Speelgoedmuseum** (Toy Museum; ☎ 015 55 70 75; Nekkerstraat 21; adult/child €5.50/3.80; ⊙ 10am-5pm Tue-Sun) is chock-full of games and toys, including a 17m-long train table complete with working engines and a model replica of the battle of Waterloo. In parts it's dark and old fashioned but the collection is impressive.

Check with the tourist office to find out what's on at the new **Lamot Heritage Centre** (☎ 015 29 49 10; www.lamot-erfgoedcentrum.be in Flemish; Van Beethovenstraat 8; admission free). This place is a first in Flanders, looking not only at history but where Flemish society is bound. Visitors are welcome.

Festivals & Events

Mechelen's biggest annual shindig is the **Hanswijkprocessie** (Procession of Our Lady) in which thousands dress up in medieval-style garb and parade through the town at 3pm on the last Sunday in May.

Sleeping

De Zandpoort (☎ 015 27 85 39; www.mechelen-hostel .com; Zandpoortvest 70; dm/s/d €16.6/29/45; ✕ 🖳) Modern, spic-and-span youth hostel next to the railway lines.

B&B Buggenhout (☎ 015 20 97 21; fran.ronny@skynet .be; Straatje zonder Einde 3; small studio s/d €40/50, large studio €50/60) Family home with a separate holiday cottage tucked away at the back of the garden. It contains two cosy, impeccable studios, both with cooking facilities.

B&B Dusk till Dawn (☎ 015 41 28 16; www.dusktill dawn.be; Onze Lieve Vrouwestraat 81; Dusk €100, Dawn €130; 🖳) Turn the age-old grey handle to ring the bell at this delightful B&B, which occupies a big grey building directly opposite the Onze Lieve Vrouwekerk (Church of Our Lady). Inside awaits a muted world of subtle colours and discerning décor. It's impossible not to sleep well in an environment like this. Children and babies welcome. Bus 4 from the train station stops out the front.

Hotel Vé (☎ 0479 49 66 82; www.hotelve.com; Vismarkt 14; s/d €128/154; ✖ 🖳) Located in a former fish-smoking factory (there's not a whiff to remind overnighters of its former occupation), this is Mechelen's most spunky new address, opened to rave reviews in 2006. Its 36 rooms – all done in sombre brown, grey or beige – range from cosy (the cheapest) to luxe. Its discreet location on the Vismarkt in the heart of the town's riverside nightlife area is another big plus.

Novotel (☎ 015 40 49 50; www.novotel.com; Van Beethovenstraat 1; r €159; ✖ ✖ 🖳 ⚿) Brand-new hotel in a modern nondescript grey-brick building smack bang in the town's newly revitalised riverside quarter.

Eating

Mechelen is right in the heart of Belgium's asparagus-growing belt and the 22cm-long 'fat white' from here are considered by gourmets to be the best – smooth, juicy and soft. The season runs from about mid-April to late June and during this time restaurants put *asperges* high on their menus. Another home-grown speciality is *witloof* (chicory), often presented as a soup or gratin.

HOLOCAUST IN BELGIUM

About 57,000 Jews were living in Belgium (mainly in Brussels and Antwerp) on 27 May 1942, the date when Jews were forced to start wearing a yellow Star of David as identification. Many had sought refuge here after the outbreak of WWII and Nazi persecution in their home countries of Germany, Austria and Poland.

In the summer of '42 the Nazis called for volunteers for labour camps in the east; many Jews boarded trains in the hope of safety, only to be transported to death camps, such as Auschwitz. These camps were designed specifically to rid Europe of people considered undesirable according to racist Nazi doctrine.

Over the next two years, 25,000 Jews were sent from the Nazi deportation centre in Mechelen; 15,000 of them were gassed upon arrival at the camps and only 1400 returned. None of the Jewish children deported survived, although several thousand children hidden by the Resistance in Belgium made it through the war.

Belgium's small Roma (gypsy) population suffered similarly, with about 500 of the country's 600 Roma deported to their deaths.

Toko Karachillio (☎ 015 34 60 12; IJzerenleen 35; focaccia €7-9, pasta €12-16; ☺ Mon-Sat) Since opening a few years back, Toko has remained one of the toasts of the town. Light and trendy, with a prime terrace location, it attracts a chatty mix for its quick, playful and contemporary cooking. There's also a lounge bar on the 1st floor.

De Graspoort (☎ 015 21 97 10; Begijnenstraat 28; mains €10-18; ☺ from 11.30am Mon-Sat, from 3pm Sun) This rustic place fills up quickly. It's tucked away at the end of an alley, but is well known by locals for its seafood and vegetarian meals.

De Kok & De Proever (☎ 015 34 60 02; Adegemstraat 43; mains €15-23, menus from €27; ☺ lunch Mon-Fri, dinner Mon-Sat) Its romantic interior, with creamy-toned décor, candles and lanterns, hides behind a 17th-century façade. The cuisine fuses French/Belgian classics, including recipes with local beer-based sauces. It's owned by the same chef as Toko Karachillio, but on a more serious note.

Grand Café Lamot (☎ 015 20 95 30; Van Beethovenstraat 8; mains €15-18; ☺ from 9am) Newest kid on the riverfront, and a big yahoo at that. This brasserie, attached to the recently renovated Lamot Heritage Centre, was part of a former brewery and the big brass brewing cauldron is still there for all to see. Wok, veggie and Belgian fare make up the sizable menu.

D'Hoogh (☎ 015 21 75 53; Grote Markt 19; mains €29-46, four-course menu €48; ☺ lunch & dinner Mon-Fri) Requires formal attire (yep, ties for the guys) if you want to blend in with the well-heeled locals at this Michelin-starred restaurant. Seasonal produce and hormone-free meats are the mainstay of the Flemish cuisine.

Also recommended:

De Cirque (☎ 015 20 77 80; Vismarkt 8; mains €14-18; ☺ Mon-Sat) Bistro, almost devoid of décor, serving well-priced pasta dishes, snacks and homemade *frites*. The terrace overlooks the new Lamot Heritage Centre.

Fish shops (Vismarkt) For self-caterers.

Market (Grote Markt; ☺ Sat) Fresh produce; held during the morning.

Drinking

The revitalised riverside quarter based around Vismarkt and Van Beethovenstraat is the city's chief nightlife zone. **De Gouden Vis** (☎ 015 20 72 06; Nauwstraat 7) is a happening *café* that draws an eclectic late-night crowd. Note the pure Art Nouveau window. Almost next door is the equally pleasant **Café Den Akker** (☎ 015 33 10 78; Vismarkt 11). Cross the river to reach **Grand Café Lamot** (☎ 015 20 95 30; Van Beethovenstraat 8; ☺ from 9am).

Borrelbabbel (☎ 015 27 36 89; Nieuwwerk 2; ☺ from 5pm Thu-Mon) It's generally standing room only at Mechelen's smallest pub, shoehorned into a corner of a lovely square behind the cathedral. It's the place in town for a shot of *jenever* and also good for any local beer.

Brouwerij Het Anker (☎ 015 20 38 80; Guido Gezellelaan 49) Mechelen's local brewery is located in the heart of town and has a rambling brasserie serving the brewery's four beers. Blusser (5.4%) is a standard lager, Mechelschen Bruynen (6%) is the brewery's oldest with a recipe dating to 1421, Triple Toison d'Or (7%) is a blond beer spiced with herbs, and Gouden Carolus (7.5%) is dark with a rich flavour of caramelised malt and hops. The family-owned establishment brews once a week but visits are open only to groups of 25 or more.

Getting There & Around

Mechelen's **train station** (☎ 02 528 28 28) and adjoining **bus station** (☎ 070 22 02 20) are 1.25km south of the Grote Markt – just head straight up Hendrik Consciencestraat or jump on bus 1, 2, 3, 4, 5 or 7. There are IC trains every half-hour to Antwerp (€3.20, 15 minutes) and Brussels (€3.70, 15 minutes).

Bikes can only be rented from **De Nekker** (☎ 015 55 70 05; Nekkerspoel-Borcht 19; ☺ 8am-10pm Mon-Fri, 9am-9.30pm Sat & Sun), a provincial sports/recreation centre 3km from town. Bike rental costs €8 per day.

AROUND MECHELEN
Technopolis

The **Technopolis** (☎ 015 34 20 01; www.technopolis .be; Technologielaan; adult/concession/child €9/8/6.50; ☺ 9.30am-5pm) sets out to amaze through educational but fun interactive experiences. It opened in 2000 and has been a runaway hit among school kids and families ever since. It's designed for ages six to 96 (although toddlers love it, too) and includes several hundred permanent exhibits – from wind and water play to invisible or hair-raising feats. Try to time your visit when it's not overrun with screaming kids (it's worth ringing to find out how many schools are booked in that day), and allow two to three hours.

The centre is about 3km from Mechelen train station – take bus 282 or 283 (every 30 minutes, less frequent on weekends). If you're coming by train, it's worth inquiring about a B-Dagtrip (see boxed text, p324). By car, it's halfway between Brussels and Antwerp, just off the E19 motorway (take the Mechelen-Zuid exit – it's well signposted).

Planckendael

This much-loved 40-hectare **animal park** (☎ 015 41 49 21; www.planckendael.be; Leuvensesteenweg 582; adult/child €16/11; ☒ 10am-7pm Jul-Aug, 10am-6pm May-Jun & Sep, 10am-5.30pm Mar-Apr & Oct, 10am-4.45pm Jan-Feb & Nov-Dec) is located about 3km southeast of Mechelen. Exhibits include bonobo (dwarf chimpanzee from central Africa) and koalas, among a host of other critters. Many of the enclosures are innovative but others, particularly the bird cages, are depressingly small. The park has a respected breeding programme and koala births always make national news.

Planckendael can be reached by **boat** (☎ 015 43 22 65), along the Leuven-Dijle Kanaal, which depart every 30 minutes from Hanswijkvaart 13 (at the Como Bridge behind Mechelen train station). Boats (€5/4.50 per adult/child, 25 minutes one way) leave daily from July to August, and on Saturday and Sunday from April to June and September. Alternatively, take bus 284 or 285 (€0.60, every 30 minutes) from Mechelen bus station.

Fort Breendonk

About 12km west of Mechelen is **Breendonk Fort** (☎ 03 886 75 25; www.breendonk.be; Brandstraat 57, Willebroek; adult/child €6/5; ☒ 9.30am-5.30pm, last visit 4.30pm), built in 1906 as an outlying defence post for Antwerp. In WWII it was converted into a Nazi concentration and deportation camp. Political prisoners were held here and, of the 3456 prisoners who passed through, less than half survived. The torture room, cells and dark dank corridors have all been preserved, and a section of the fort has been turned into a museum. Even in summer, this place chills to the bone.

The fort is just off the A12 highway linking Antwerp–Brussels and is well signposted. Without your own vehicle, access is more difficult – from Mechelen take the train to Willebroek (€2.30, 10 minutes), from where it's a 20-minute walk.

LEUVEN

pop 89,800

Picturesque, intimate and lively… Leuven is yet another fabulous Flemish city, and again it's just a hop, skip or jump from Brussels (25km). Leuven (Louvain in French) is the chief town of the province of Vlaams-Brabant. It's an ancient capital – the home of the Dukes of Brabant

since 1200 – and in medieval times an important cloth trading centre. Today it boasts one of Belgium's most ornate town halls and is Flanders' oldest university town (see boxed text, p208). Some 25,000 students – more than a quarter of the town's population – zoom around by pushbike here, giving the city an upbeat, creative air. Leuven is also Belgium's beer capital, home to the internationally known red-label Stella Artois.

Orientation & Information

Central Leuven is easily covered on foot. Its heart is the Grote Markt and immediately behind it the Oude Markt, which transforms into one enormous open-air terrace for socialising and drinking in fine weather.

Barak Telecom (Tiensestraat 24; per hr €1.50; ☒ 9am-midnight Mon-Sat, 10am-midnight Sun) Internet access.

Café Apero (☎ 016 22 37 76; Oude Markt 52; ☒ 11am-11pm) Has one terminal, with free access, otherwise a normal pub.

In&Uit Leuven (☎ 016 20 30 20; www.inenuitleuven.be; Naamsestraat 1; ☒ 9am-5pm Mon-Sat, 10am-5pm Sun Apr-Oct) Tourist office newly relocated around the side of the stadhuis.

Post office (☎ 016 22 30 51; Jan Stasstraat)

Sights

Leuven suffered heavy damage in both world wars and the city centre has relatively few remains of early times. That said, it's still as pretty as a picture, and the buildings that survived are well worth seeing.

Leuven's main sight is the 15th-century **stadhuis** (town hall; Grote Markt; ☒ tours at 11am & 3pm Mon-Fri, 3pm Sat & Sun Apr-Sep, 3pm daily Oct-Mar). This flamboyant late-Gothic structure resembles an overblown wedding cake full of terraced turrets, delicate statues, fancy stonework and colourful flags. The 236 statues represent prominent locals throughout the ages – scholars, artists and nobility – but were added as an afterthought in the mid-19th century. Incredibly, the stadhuis survived relatively unscathed during the wars (although a bomb, which failed to explode, scoured part of the façade). There's not all that much to see inside; most notable are the few sculptures by Constantin Meunier (see p87). More of Meunier's work is located in Minderbroedersvest, where he had a workshop, and there's another statue, Pater Damiaan, in Brusselsestraat.

The other main edifice is **St Pieterskerk** (St Peter's Church; Grote Markt; free admission; ☒ 10am-5pm Mon-Sat,

2-5pm Sun, closed Mon mid-Oct–mid-Mar), another late-Gothic structure. Construction started in 1425, the same year that the university was founded, but the church never reached full throttle as unstable subsoil forced the builders to abandon a 170m-high tower. Inside, highlights include an elaborately carved stone rood screen and an equally impressive wooden baroque pulpit. However, it's the church's **treasury** (adult/student €5/2.50 incl entry to the Museum Van der Kelen-Mertens) that most people come to see. It boasts two triptychs by Flemish Primitive artist Dirk Bouts (c 1415–75), who spent much of his life in Leuven. The *Martyrdom of St Erasmus* records the gory death of the patron saint of mariners, while *Het Laatste Avondmaal* (The Last Supper) shows the purple-clad Christ surrounded by his disciples in a typical Flemish dining hall. Bouts painted this between 1464–67 and it is considered to be one of the period's masterpieces, mixing the Biblical theme with contemporary Gothic architecture. Strictly controlled paintings with rich, broad landscapes and static, unmoving figures were his passion. The panels have a lively history: they were sold off several times and ended up in Germany; they

were returned to Leuven after WWI as part of the war reparations package; and they were carted off again during WWII and saw the war out in a salt mine.

Behind the town hall is the 14th-century **Lakenhal** (Naamsestraat) where cloth was traded centuries ago. It's now used as the official headquarters of the university.

The **Museum Van der Kelen-Mertens** (☎ 016 22 69 06; Savoyestraat 6) holds, among other things, a vast collection of religious art from the 15th to 18th centuries. The museum is closed until 2009 due to major expansion and renovation. Until then a representative sample of its collection will tour temporary sites around town – ask the tourist office for the current location.

The cobblestoned **Groot Begijnhof**, a Unesco World Heritage site, is secured behind large walls near the Dijle River to the south of the city centre. It was founded by the Beguines in 1232, though most of the houses date from the 17th century when around 300 Beguines still lived here. The restored, somewhat sober houses are now a university residential quarter. Visit the church, **St Jan de Doperkerk** (1.30-

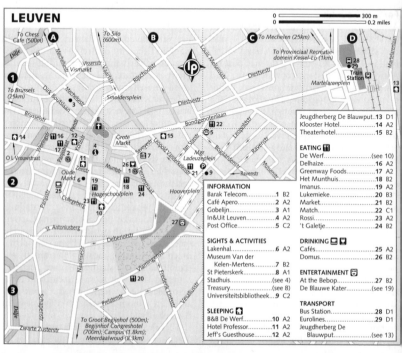

LEUVEN

Jeugdherberg De Blauwput..**13**	D1
Klooster Hotel..............................**14**	A2
Theaterhotel...............................**15**	B2

EATING 🍴
De Werf..........................(see 10)	
Delhaize......................................**16**	A2
Greenway Foods.........................**17**	A2
Het Munthuis..............................**18**	B2
Imanus...**19**	A2
Lukemieke...................................**20**	B3
Market..**21**	B2
Match..**22**	C1
Rossi...**23**	A2
't Galetje......................................**24**	A2

INFORMATION
Barak Telecom.............................**1**	B2
Café Apero...................................**2**	A2
Gobelijn......................................**3**	A1
In&Uit Leuven.............................**4**	A2
Post Office...................................**5**	C2

SIGHTS & ACTIVITIES
Lakenhal......................................**6**	A2
Museum Van der	
Kelen-Mertens.........................**7**	B2
St Pieterskerk.............................**8**	A1
Stadhuis..............................(see 4)	
Treasury.............................(see 8)	
Universiteitsbibliotheek...**9**	C2

DRINKING 🍷 🍸
Cafés..**25**	A2
Domus..**26**	B2

ENTERTAINMENT 🎭
At the Bebop...............................**27**	B2
De Blauwe Kater.................(see 19)	

SLEEPING 🏠
B&B De Werf................................**10**	A2
Hotel Professor...........................**11**	A2
Jeff's Guesthouse.......................**12**	A2

TRANSPORT
Bus Station..................................**28**	D1
Eurolines.....................................**29**	D1
Jeugdherberg De	
Blauwput............................(see 13)	

4.30pm Tue-Sun Apr-Sep), whose Gothic façade hides an elaborate baroque interior.

The imposing **Universiteitsbibliotheek** (University Reference Library; ☎ 016 32 46 60; Monseigneur Ladeuzeplein 21) was rebuilt in Flemish Renaissance style after a fire raged through it during WWI. Rebuilt from the charity of 400 American universities, it again burnt down in WWII and was rebuilt yet again. The tower rising in the rear breaks the façade's symmetry and houses a carillon.

Festivals & Events

Werchter (www.rockwerchter.be) Together with Glastonbury (England) and Roskilde (Denmark), this is one of Europe's biggest 'field' rock festivals. Takes over paddocks in Werchter north of Leuven for four days over the first weekend of July.

BeLEUVENissen (www.beleuvenissen.be) Free concerts – jazz, folk and tropical music – are staged on the first four Fridays in July at diverse locations around Leuven.

Klapstukfestival (www.stuk.be) Month-long international contemporary dance festival from mid-October.

Sleeping

Jeugdherberg De Blauwput (☎ 016 63 90 62; www.vjh .be; Martelarenlaan 11a; dm/s/d €19.60/24/48; ✕ ▯ ᕆ) Modern HI-hostel with spunky décor and good vibes, a one-minute walk behind the train station. No room has more than six beds, and there are showers and toilets inside each room. There's a good bar, courtyard, internet access (per hr €2) and a conscious effort to be green (composting and recycling).

B&B De Werf (☎ 016 23 73 14; www.dewerf-leuven .be; Hogeschoolplein 5; s/d €30/45; ▯) Three rooms located above a rustic café (right) overlooking a charming tree-lined square and with a handy central location. It's more like a cheap hotel than a B&B. Breakfast (€5) is taken downstairs in the café.

Hotel Professor (☎ 016 20 14 14; fax 016 29 14 16; Naamsestraat 20; s/d €65/80) Above a corner cocktail bar in the city centre, this nondescript hotel has just eight simple rooms (No 5 is the biggest). Take heart on arrival – the rooms are nicer than the mundane ground-floor bar would suggest.

Theaterhotel (☎ 016 22 28 19; www.theaterhotel.be; Bondgenotenlaan 20; s/d Mon-Thu €129/149, Fri-Sun €89/109; ✕) Just skipping distance from the Grote Markt, this discreet hotel offers huge bathrooms, small beds and soothing décor, and it's child friendly (free cots and highchairs).

Klooster Hotel (☎ 016 21 31 41; www.kloosterhotel .com; Onze Lieve Vrouwstraat 22; r Mon-Thu from €205, Fri-Sun from €155; ✕ ▯ ᕆ) Hidden on a small cobbled street in the old city centre, this relatively new hotel is Leuven's most atmospheric address. It occupies an historic building that did time as a cloister; the last nun left in 1999. It opened as a four-star hotel in 2003, and maintains serenity and ties to its earlier life with understated furnishings and subtle details. Book room No 7 to live like Mother Superior.

Eating

Take to pedestrianised Parijsstraat or Muntstraat, or the area around the stadhuis, for wall-to-wall eateries – everything from gastronomic to student fare rubs shoulders and nonchalantly complements each other. Further afield you'll find local favourites.

De Werf (☎ 016 23 73 14; Hogeschoolplein 5; snacks €4, mains €9-13) All-time student favourite, with a big terrace occupying a quiet tree-lined square on one of the town's backstreets. Pull off a serviette from a kitchen roll, drink out of pink plastic tumblers and try to get your lips around one of the house specialities, wraps. The service is not fast, but no-one minds – chill out looking at the wacky décor.

Lukemieke (☎ 016 22 97 05; Vlamingenstraat 55; mains €9; ☺ noon-2pm & 6-8.30pm Mon-Fri) Casual, friendly vegetarian eatery that has been around for donkey's years and still draws locals to its out-of-the-way location. A *dagschotel* goes

---

THE AUTHOR'S CHOICE

Jeff's Guesthouse (☎ 016 23 87 80; www.jeffsguesthouse.be; Kortestraat 2; d without bathroom €80, d with bathroom & view €90, ste €95; ✕) 'Simple but beautiful' – that's the motto at this guesthouse, hidden above an *oliveria* (shop selling olive-oil based products) just metres from the Grote Markt. It's shoes off to enter the six rooms, each named after a woman and where linen sheets sprayed with lavender awaken the senses. Spacious and free of clutter, the pervading theme is Mediterranean – sand-coloured walls with Venetian stucco and a Moroccan lounge with lanterns and rugs. Breakfast (€8, brunch €25) is taken on big tables in a room lit by stained glass at the rear of the shop. All in all it's a gem.

EASTERN FLANDERS *(vertical, left margin)*

THE KUL

Within a century of being founded in 1425, the Katholieke Universiteit van Leuven (KUL) had become one of Europe's most highly regarded universities. It attracted famous academics and freethinkers, such as the cartographer Mercator, Renaissance scholar Desiderius Erasmus and the father of anatomy, Andreas Vesalius.

Its history, however, has been far from smooth, with disputes arising over both religion and language. In response to suppression by French and Dutch rulers during the 18th and 19th centuries, the university became a bastion of Flemish Catholicism and these days is still at the heart of Flemish thinking.

Language issues came to a head in the late 1960s when Flemish students protested over the absence of lectures in their mother tongue, eventually forcing their French-speaking counterparts to set up a new Francophone university at the town of Louvain-la-Neuve, southeast of Brussels. In one of those typically Belgian scenarios, the university then split its reference library in two – the KUL kept everything from A to L, and Louvain-la-Neuve took M to Z!

---

for €9, the child's *peuterschotel* costs €5. The garden terrace, with its trellised grapevines, is great in summer.

Greenway Foods (☎ 016 30 97 35; Parijsstraat 12; mains €7) Bright green décor immediately tells you this place is vegetarian – *bio* (organic) burgers, soups, pasta dishes and noodles are the mainstays. It's smack on one of the city's main restaurant strips, and is also great for kids and babies.

Rossi (☎ 016 62 48 48; Standonckstraat 2; antipasti €7.50-12.50, secondi €16; ✆ dinner Tue-Sat) Ten tables, no décor, sacks of onions waiting to be put away and garlic wafting from the kitchen. This little Italian eatery is hugely popular, great value and as authentic as they come. The gent who runs it is a gem.

Het Munthuis (☎ 016 29 29 41; Muntstraat 20; mains €17-20; ✆ lunch & dinner, closed Wed & lunch Sat) One of the classiest acts on this intimate restaurant-lined street. Italian/Belgian cuisine is the go.

Chess Cafe (☎ 016 22 28 88; Fonteinstraat 1a; mains €18; ✆ closed lunch Sat) The table reserved for chess players at the back of this buzzing wok eatery provided the restaurant's name. It's located in an old grain silo in a semi-industrial and somewhat unloved part of town, about 1km from the Grote Markt. Wok *à volonté* for €18 – pick your ingredients from the self-service buffet bar and watch the team sizzle and spice your meal with beer-laced sauces.

Also recommended:

Imanus (☎ 016 29 10 82; Naamsestraat 17; sandwich €2.50-4.50; ✆ Mon-Sat) Best sandwich bar in town.

't Galetje (☎ 016 29 22 24; Tiensestraat 44) The place to join summer ice-cream queues.

Match (Bondgenotenlaan 50) Supermarket.

Delhaize (Wieringstraat 31) Supermarket.

Market (Monseigneur Ladeuzeplein; ✆ Fri) Sells fresh produce; held during the morning.

Drinking & Entertainment

You'd be forgiven for mistaking central Leuven for the world's biggest bar. The Oude Markt literally hums with terrace *cafés* where students hang out until the wee small hours. And we're not talking lager louts here – these are young people having a good but respectful time, and it's certainly not a threatening environment. Belgian students, it seems, have already learnt the national art of socialising with a long beer or two.

Domus (☎ 016 20 14 49; Tiensestraat 8; ✆ Tue-Sun) Old-fashioned ale house attached to a rambling brewery where several tasty beers are brewed – try the Nostra Domus (amber beer with 5.8% alcohol and a light, smoky taste) or ConDomus (5% alcohol and bitter flavour).

At the Bebop (☎ 016 20 86 04; www.atthebebop.be; Tiensestraat 82) Popular atmospheric jazz *café* with occasional live gigs.

De Blauwe Kater (☎ 016 20 80 90; Hallengang 1) Well-hidden little pub, in an alley off Naamsestraat. Has jazz and blues performances on most Monday nights.

Silo (www.silo.be; Vaartkom 39; ✆ Fri & Sat) High-tech club that rates highly among Belgian clubbers, down by a canal in a former industrial building.

Shopping

Gobelijn (☎ 016 23 55 86; Mechelsestraat 35) Cartoon shop tucked away on a backstreet. It sports a solid line-up of Belgian and international cartoons.

Getting There & Around

Leuven's modern **train station** (☎ 016 21 21 21) is 800m east of the Grote Markt. There are frequent connections to Brussels (€4.30, 30 minutes), Mechelen (€3.70, 15 minutes), Antwerp (€6, 45 minutes), Diest (€4.30, 30 minutes), Lier (€5.70, 45 minutes) and Liège (€9, 50 minutes). There's also now a direct line to Brussels airport (€3, 15 minutes).

Eurolines (www.eurolines.be) buses and **De Lijn** (☎ 016 31 37 37) local buses depart from the big new red bus station to the right as you exit the train station; there's also an information office here. Buses 1 and 2 shuttle to the Grote Markt. A *dagkaart* (day card) can be bought from the info kiosk (€5/1.5 per adult/child) or on the bus (€6/2).

Bikes can be rented from **Jeugdherberg De Blauwput** (☎ 016 63 90 62; www.vjh.be; Martelarenlaan 11a; ☽ 8am-10pm) for €10 per day (deposit €150).

AROUND LEUVEN
Meerdaalwoud

Brussels has the Fôret de Soignes at its doorstep, Leuven has the **Meerdaalwoud**. This deciduous and conifer forest covers about 50 sq km to the south of Leuven and offers pleasant walking and cycling paths. Take the TEC bus 18 (direction Jodoigne).

Provinciaal Recreatiedomein Kessel-Lo

This 100-hectare **recreational park** (☎ 016 25 13 92; Holsbeeksesteenweg 55; ☽ 9am-7pm) is east of Leuven and is one of the biggest playgrounds for kids in Belgium. The playground is free, but admission is charged for other attractions, such as the rowboats, the heated swimming pool and the mini-cars. From Leuven, take bus 2 or the train to Kessel-Lo, from where it's a 15-minute walk.

DIEST
pop 22,500

The ancient town of Diest has been saved from mediocrity thanks to its *begijnhof,* one of the best-preserved examples in Belgium, together with its association with the House of Orange-Nassau. Princes from this ruling Dutch family were the lords of Diest from 1499 to 1794 – Philip, the eldest son of William the Silent, is buried in the church here.

Diest sits just south of the Demer River in a rural corner of Vlaams-Brabant. As small towns go, it's decidedly pleasant and the people particularly good humoured – they'd have to be with the nickname they bear (see boxed text, p215).

Information

Main tourist office (☎ 013 35 32 74; www.tourisme diest.be; Grote Markt 1; ☽ 10am-noon & 1-5pm Mar-Sep, closed Sun Oct-Feb) In the basement of the stadhuis.
Tourist office (Kerkstraat 21; ☽ 2-5pm Jul-Aug, 2-5.30pm Sat & Sun Apr-Jun & Sep–mid-Nov, Sun only mid-Nov-Mar) At the *begijnhof.*

Sights & Activities

Smack on the Grote Markt is the 18th-century **stadhuis**, home to the main tourist office and, in the adjoining vaulted cellars, the **Stedelijk Museum** (☎ 013 35 32 70; Grote Markt 1; admission €1.50, combination ticket for Stedelijk Museum plus Religious Art Museum €2; ☽ 10am-noon & 1-5pm Mar-Sep, closed Sun Oct-Feb). Small but rich, this museum houses artefacts from the days of Orange-Nassau as well as a wealth of religious relics. Note the 15th-century painting *Het Laatse Ordeel,* believed to be a work of Gerard Brunen, the town's best-known artist. Also worth seeking out are the two *Besloten Hofkens* (literally, private gardens). Created by the Beguines, these are large, glass-covered wooden frames containing religious bits and pieces and hung on the wall as decoration. Only a few still exist in Belgium.

Dominating the Grote Markt is **St Sulpitiuskerk**, a huge church, built from a distinct rusty-brown iron-sandstone cut from the Hageland hills. Constructed between 1321 and 1533, it replaced an older Romanesque church. It houses the tomb of Prince Philip, exotically carved *koorgestoelte* (choir stalls) and the **Museum voor Religieuze Kunst** (Religious Art Museum; admission €1.25; ☽ 2-5pm Tue-Sun Jul-Aug, Sun only mid-May–mid-Sep), whose pride is a monstrance embedded with 220 diamonds.

The **St Katharinabegijnhof** is at the far end of Begijnenstraat, a 10-minute walk from the Grote Markt. A splendid baroque portal marks the *begijnhof*'s main entrance. Founded in 1252, some of the well-preserved buildings date to this time. About 300 Beguines lived here in the Middle Ages, though now it's home to ordinary folk and a few artists. Its aura is charmingly authentic and most of the houses still display religious statues in the alcove above the door – a means of identification at a time when street numbering didn't exist. For more, see boxed text, p129.

If you're travelling with kids, head to **Provinciedomein Halve Maan** (☎ 013 31 15 28; Leopoldvest

48; admission May–mid-Sep €3, Oct-Apr free; 9am-9pm Apr-Sep, 9am-4pm Oct-Mar). This recreational park covers a large area immediately east of the town's main ring road, and includes a big pool, a white-sand beach, waterways topped with swan-shaped boats and a playground. It's a bit of an institution in Diest, having been around since the days of B&W photos.

Sleeping & Eating

B&B Tonet (013 31 14 39; marthe.tonet@pandora.be; Schaffensesteenweg 55; s/d/tr €35/50/75) Three bright, zany rooms, all completely different, with shared bathroom facilities. Run by an extremely welcoming woman, and great value to boot.

Hotel De Fransche Croon (013 31 45 40; www.defranschecroon.be; Leuvensestraat 26; s/d/tr €75/95/115;) Two blocks from the Grote Markt, this friendly and efficient hotel-restaurant is a stylish rabbit warren of rooms. They come in a variety of colour schemes, from neutral tones to busy florals. The buffet breakfast is excellent. Attached to the hotel is the popular and folksy Herman's Eetcafé, serving well-priced local fare and Diest's main beer, Gildenbier.

The Lodge (013 35 09 35; www.lodge-hotels.be; Refugiestraat 23; s/d €85/120, ste from €110/155;) Best address in town. This charming hotel occupies a small, restored castle. There are 20 rooms, all with different colour schemes and décor, including beautiful old furnishings. Some of the beds are a bit narrow, but that's the only gripe. Well located on a quiet backstreet in the heart of town. Bikes can be rented for €7 per day. Kids and babies are welcome.

La Bas (013 32 30 32; Koning Albertstraat 11; mains €10; until 6pm Tue-Sun) Ultramodern café with a strong emphasis on light healthy cuisine –

juices, soups and yummy fresh-baked breads Located about 100m from the church on the road to the *begijnhof* – you can't miss the striking red-and-black décor.

Gasthof 1618 (013 33 32 40; Kerkstraat 8; snack €3-6, mains €11-13) This is the only eatery in the *begijnhof* and is often full to bursting with coach loads of elderly tourists. The Middle Ages ambience is its draw, although it also bakes a seasonal, tasty *Diestse cruydtcoech* (€3.75), a pancake made from a herb known locally as *boerenwormkruid* (tansy). Particularly enticing on a cold winter's day.

Market (Kaai; Wed) Located behind the town hall, this food market is held during the morning.

Getting There & Away

Diest is on the railway line between Liege (€5.30, 30 minutes) and Hasselt (€3.10, 15 minutes). The train station is about 1.25km north of the Grote Markt. To get there, turn left out of the station building, veer right (crossing the Demer) then continue down Statiestraat, which leads to Demerstraat and eventually the Grote Markt.

HASSELT
pop 69,100

The capital of Limburg province, Hasselt is well and truly off the foreign tourist track This modern town acts as the workaday centre for the agricultural lands surrounding it – the soils here are well suited to fruit growing and apple and cherry orchards burst into a mass of delicate white-and-pink blossoms in spring. It's also the unofficial *jenever* capita of Belgium, and the town celebrates the white spirit with a two-day festival every October.

On a daily level, Hasselt's user-friendly own centre, bristling with shops and restaurants, is firmly entwined in the day-trip circuit for shopaholic, food-mad Flemish. And if you're travelling with kids, it's well worth detouring here to explore the open-air museum of Bokrijk (see p212).

Orientation & Information

Hasselt sits just south of the Albertkanaal and is encircled by a one-way ring road. As always the bull's-eye is the Grote Markt, but don't expect architectural grandeur – this place pulses with people and terrace *cafés*, but that's all.

Huis van het Kind (House of the Child; ☎ 011 21 14 7; Maastrichterstraat 65; ☟ 1-6pm Wed, 10am-6pm Sat, 10am-6pm in school holidays) Day-care centre for children from 2½ to 12 years. The only such centre in Belgium that can be easily accessed by visitors travelling with kids.

In&Uit Hasselt (☎ 011 23 95 40; www.hasselt.be; Lombaardstraat 3; ☟ 10am-6pm Mon-Sat, 10am-2pm Sun, closed Sun Nov-Mar) Newly revamped tourist office next to the stadhuis.

Sights

A must see is the **Nationaal Jenevermuseum** (National Gin Museum; ☎ 011 23 98 60; www.jenevermuseum.be; Witte Nonnenstraat 19; adult/concession €3/1; ☟ 10am-5pm Jul & Aug, closed Mon rest of the year, 10am-5pm Tue-Fri, 1-5pm Sat & Sun Nov-Mar). Hasselt has been at the centre of the *jenever* industry since the 17th century and this beautifully restored 19th-century distillery houses a comprehensive and well-presented museum on the history of *jenever* and its distilling process, as well as produces 1000 bottles of *jenever* annually. At the end of your visit, pop in to the museum's café for a free shot of the '*jenever* of the week'. It's also a good place to buy, with one of the country's best *jenever* selections, all at normal retail prices.

The importance of *jenever* to Hasselt is symbolised by the **Borrelmanneke** (St Jozefsstraat) fountain. Here, a little guy lying on a cow pours liquid from a leaking barrel to a gang of delighted pigs. During the *jenever* festival in October, the fountain spurts *jenever* rather than water, and the little man is presented with an article of clothing (Manneken Pis revisited, see p80) from the visiting *jenever* brotherhood.

Het Stadsmus (☎ 011 23 98 90; Guido Gezellestraat 2; admission free; ☟ 10am-5pm Tue-Sun, from 1pm Sat & Sun Nov-Mar) exhibits decorative arts and religious relics, all linked with the history of the town.

The **Stedelijk Beiaardmuseum** (☎ 011 24 10 70; Fruit-markt; adult/concession €1.50/1; ☟ 10am-5pm Sun Jul-Aug) is a carillon museum in the tower of St Quintinuskathedraal, the town's main cathedral.

Fashion followers shouldn't miss the **Mode-museum** (☎ 011 23 96 21; Gasthuisstraat 11; adult/concession €3/1; ☟ 10am-5pm Tue-Sun Apr-Oct, 10am-5pm Tue-Fri, 1-5pm Sat & Sun Nov-Mar). This museum occupies part of a former abbey and has been tastefully renovated to allow (partial) illumination by natural light. The permanent display features fashion from the 18th century onwards, but more riveting are the many temporary exhibitions.

Like Brussels, Hasselt has been spruced up with huge **murals** of popular comic-strip characters, such as Suske & Wiske, Nero, Lucky Luke and Jommeke. You'll find them dotted around town.

About 1.5km east of the town centre is the **Japanse Tuin** (☎ 011 23 52 00; Gouverneur Verwilghensingel; adult/concession €3/2; ☟ 10am-5pm Tue-Fri, 2-6pm Sat & Sun Apr-Oct). Hasselt and its sister city, Itami, got together to establish this picturesque Japanese garden, the largest in Europe. From the train station, take free bus H3 (direction Trichterheide).

Kids already familiar with Plopsaland (see p148) will be thrilled to know Hasselt has a new indoor version, appropriately titled **Plopsa Indoor** (☎ 011 29 30 40; www.plopsa.be; Gouverneur Verwilghensingel 70; admission over/under 1m €14/5; ☟ 10am-6pm Wed-Sun, daily in school holidays). It's opposite the Japanse Tuin, 1.5km east of the town centre on the outer ring road – from the train station, take free bus H3 (direction Trichterheide).

Festivals & Events

Hasselt gets into two days of serious *jenever* drinking on the third weekend in October for the **Hasseltse Jeneverfeesten**. Events include a waiters' race and distillery tours and, for a few short hours, free *jenever* pours forth from the town's Borrelmanneke statue (see left).

Sleeping

The dearth of overnight visitors is reflected in Hasselt's lacklustre hotel scene.

B&B Emily's Place (☎ 011 82 12 50; www.emilysplace .be; Kneuterweg 5, Zonhoven; s/d €40/56; ☒) With your own transport, this is one of the most characterful accommodation options in the area. Just one spacious room is on offer in this delightful family home, 8km from Hasselt and close to the Bokrijk Openluchtmuseum. Depending on the weather, breakfast is taken either at the family's dining table or on the terrace and, in true Limburg style, it's a feast.

Guesthouse Kattegatt (☎ 011 21 44 21; www.katte gatt.be; Congostraat 9; s/d €41/77; 🖳) Well located just outside the inner ring road – a five-minute walk from the town centre – this little B&B/brasserie has four pleasant, modern and spacious rooms, all individually styled and each with a kitchenette with microwave.

Hassotel (☎ 011 23 06 55; www.hassotel.be; St Jozefsstraat 10; s/d from €70/93; 🖳 ♿) Modern but unremarkable, this hotel is centrally located and has a nondescript restaurant. Inquire about weekend discounts. Children and babies are welcome.

Hotel Portmans (☎ 011 26 32 80; www.walputsteeg .com; Minderbroederstraat 12; s/d/tr from €80/85/90; 🐾 🖳) Friendly and efficient establishment in the heart of town, with just 14 rooms built around an atrium.

Radisson SAS (☎ 011 77 00 00; www.hasselt.radissonsas .com; Torenplein 8; s/d Mon-Thu from €130/145, Fri-Sun r from €89; 🗙 🐾 🖳 ♿) This new top-ender occupies the only twin towers on Hasselt's skyline and is impossible to miss.

Eating

Hasselt has a reputation for townsfolk who enjoy the art of good eating…and that's in a nation of good eaters. Wander along Ridderstraat to see an enormous mural entitled *Hasselt Stad voor Lekkerbekken,* which graphically highlights the locals' love of dining. Zuivelmarkt and Fruitmarkt, two streets lined with restaurants and hip brasseries, are good places to start hunting, but there are plenty of backstreet options as well.

't Pandje (☎ 011 22 38 37; Paardsdemerstraat 3; 🕑 10am-6.30pm Tue-Sat) Decorator's shop and tearoom, and *the* place to try a Hasselt *speculaas.* These cinnamon-flavoured biscuits are devoured nationally; however, they supposedly originated in Hasselt where the fat, chewy versions are still baked and sold.

Blue Olive (☎ 011 72 72 70; Zuivelmarkt 22; bistro mains €14-21) Big, hip bistro-bar with lampshades that have to be seen to be believed. Serves a good selection of pasta dishes, salads and typical bistro cuisine, and has an impressive wine list.

De Goei Goesting (☎ 011 32 52 82; Zuivelmarkt 18; mains €17-26; 🕑 lunch & dinner) Generally regarded as Hasselt's best restaurant and newly relocated to the dining heart of town. Belgian cuisine spiced with Mediterranean influences is prepared in an open kitchen and makes for delectable dining.

Also recommended:

Panos (☎ 011 22 22 59; Maastrichterstraat 22) Good for a quick croissant or takeaway sandwich.

Market (Kolonel Dusartplein; 🕑 Tue & Fri) Food market; held during the morning.

Getting There & Around

Hasselt is on two main railway lines and has convenient links in all directions. The **train station** (☎ 011 29 60 00) is about 1km west of the town centre. Local connections include to Tongeren (€3.70, 20 minutes), Leuven (€6.70, 50 minutes) and Diest (€3.10, 15 minutes), or there are IC trains further afield to Brussels (€10.70, 1¼ hours), Antwerp (€9.50, 65 minutes) and Liège (€6.70, 55 minutes).

Like Mons in Wallonia, Hasselt has free city buses. Many buses circle the town on the one-way ring of boulevards that encompass the old centre; these buses are marked Boulevardpendel (or 'BP'). Other buses, marked Centrumpendel (or 'CP'), cross through the old centre, running between the bus/train station and the Grote Markt every 10 minutes.

Local information can be obtained from **De Lijn** (☎ 070 220 220), which has a kiosk to the left as you exit the train station.

Free bikes are available from what's called the **Stadswachten** (City Watch; 🕑 10am-5pm Mon-Sat) behind the old stadhuis.

AROUND HASSELT
Bokrijk Openluchtmuseum

One of Europe's largest open-air museums, the **Bokrijk Openluchtmuseum** (☎ 011 26 53 00; www .bokrijk.be; adult/concession/child €10/8.50/5 Jul, Aug & Sun, €5/4.50/2.50 Mon-Sat Apr-Jun & Sep; 🕑 10am-6pm Apr-Sep) is a nostalgic and enjoyable look at Flanders' past. It's spaced over 60 hectares and contains over 100 old buildings from several areas – the Kempen (east of Antwerp), Haspengouw (in Limburg), and the provinces of Oost-Vlaanderen and West-Vlaanderen – as well as old townhouses from Antwerp. The buildings – village churches, an ancient *herberg* (pub), farmhouses and windmills – are all originals, dismantled and reassembled here since 1958 when the museum was established. Local people dressed in traditional garb are employed to tend veggie gardens and bake bread, evoking yesteryear's village life.

The museum, situated 7km northeast of Hasselt, is surrounded by forest that forms part of a larger public domain. Within the forest is a splendid **arboretum**, where pink and white magnolias burst into colour in early spring. Next to the museum's main entrance is Belgium's biggest open-air kids' **playground** (*speeltuin* in Flemish). Both the arboretum and the playground are free to enter.

A small green **train** (adult/child €2.50/1.50; ☺ daily Jul & Aug, Sun only rest of year) shuttles through the museum and past the arboretum and playground. Another way to move around is by **horse-drawn cart** (per 20min adult/child €3/2).

Bokrijk has two entrances: the main gate is to the north and is marked by the Kasteel Bokrijk, a 19th-century mansion; the southern entrance is the first you come to when arriving either by car or public transport from Hasselt. If you've got your own transport, it's best to head to the main entrance (follow the signs 'Kasteel & Museum'), where you can get an overview of the museum via a seven-minute aerial film (screened in English). Also use this entrance if you're travelling with kids as the playground is next door.

Using public transport, the easiest way to get there is by bus 1 from Hasselt train station. They depart hourly (Monday to Saturday) and take 20 minutes. On Sunday take the Genk-bound train (10 minutes, hourly), which stops 500m from the southern entrance. By car, take the N75 (direction Genk) and then the N726 (follow the signs 'Park Midden-Limburg').

TONGEREN

pop 29,500

The town of Tongeren laps at Belgium's linguistic divide. It sits roughly equidistant between Flemish-speaking Hasselt and the Walloon city of Liège, and is the last major settlement before the frontier with the Netherlands. Together with Tournai in Hainaut it has the honour of being Belgium's oldest town but, unlike Tournai, Tongeren has lots to show for it. Its Gallo-Roman museum is the finest in Belgium.

When this area was invaded by Roman troops in 54 BC, the original locals (known as the Eburones) successfully ambushed the

Romans under the leadership of Ambiorix, a local chieftain commemorated by a statue in the town centre. The following year Caesar's troops fought back and conquered the area, which then became known as Aduatuca Tungrorum. Within a hundred years it was a thriving settlement on the road to Germany and was protected by enormous stone ramparts, some of which remain. This was the first of three walls to surround the town. Despite these walls, subsequent centuries saw invasions by the Franks, Normans and, in the 17th century, the French armies of Louis XIV who set much of the town ablaze.

Tongeren's rich history is one of its present-day drawing cards; the other is the weekly antique market that attracts buyers from far and wide.

Information

The **tourist office** (☎ 012 39 02 55; www.tongeren.be in Flemish; Stadhuisplein 9; ☺ 8.30am-5pm Jul-Aug, 8.30am-noon & 1-5pm Mon-Fri, 10am-4pm Sat & Sun Sep-Easter, 8.30am-noon & 1-5pm Mon-Fri, 9.30am-5pm Sat & Sun Easter-Sep) is in the town centre.

Sights & Activities

Overshadowing the Grote Markt is the elegant **Onze Lieve Vrouwebasiliek** (Basilica of Our Lady; ☺ 10am-noon & 1.30-5pm). A church has stood on this site for at least 1200 years, possibly longer. Historians believe a place of worship existed here as early as the 4th century and that it was the first church north of the Alps to be dedicated to the Virgin. Due to its rich history, the basilica is now the subject of a decade-long excavation project, expected to finish in 2009. Tourists have been well accommodated during this lengthy process and only a part of the basilica is ever off limits at any one time. As for the basilica itself, little of its 11th-century origins are visible; most of what you see today is from the 14th to 16th centuries. The church's most prized possession is Our Lady of Tongeren, a delicate walnut statue of the Virgin and Child from 1479 that is kept in a glass case and is paraded through the streets during the Kroningsfeesten (see p215). Other treasures to keep an eye out for are the 16th-century Antwerp-made retable (screen) depicting scenes from the Virgin's life and, in the **Schatkamer** (Treasury; adult/concession/child €2.50/2/0.50; ☺ closed 8am-noon Mon), a pious 11th-century Head of Christ.

Immediately outside the basilica is a small open-air **archaeological site** containing the foundations of medieval buildings and a section of the 4th-century second Roman wall that once encircled the town. Walk through the site to see how towns have been layered like lasagne throughout history.

Smack in the heart of town, the **Gallo-Roman Museum** (☎ 012 67 03 32; www.galloromeinsmuseum.be; Kielenstraat 15; adult/concession/child/family €5/4/2/10; ☻ noon-5pm Mon, 9am-5pm Tue-Fri, 10am-6pm Sat & Sun) displays findings from the town's Gallo-Roman and Merovingian periods. Closed for renovation and expansion until early 2008, if the previous exhibits are anything to go by, it's bound to be impressive.

Tongeren's **antique and brocante market** is billed as the Benelux's biggest. It has been going for nearly 30 years and today attracts hundreds of traders who take over Veemarkt (and most of Maastrichterstraat and Leopoldwal) every Sunday morning from about 5am – be here early if you're seriously hunting antiques. Much of the antique trade goes on in the sprinkling of permanent shops dotted around this area – the tourist office's free booklet *A Round of Antiques* details many of these outlets (mostly open Wednesday to Sunday).

Tongeren's **begijnhof** is no longer an enclosed affair and is largely overshadowed in this part of Flanders by the superbly preserved *begijnhof* at Diest. Still, it's a pretty part of town and well worth a wander. There's also a rustic little tavern here that makes a great pitstop (Herberg De Pelgrim, p216).

Tongeren's new **Het Land van Ooit** (Once Upon A Time Land; www.landvanooit.be), just to the northwest of town, will be open by the time you read this. It's a clone of the highly successful Land Van Ooit in the Netherlands but, in keeping with local history, this one takes visitors back into Roman times. Kids will love it – expect lots of fancy dress, make-believe and role playing. The tourist office will have full opening hours and details.

Those travelling with young kids will delight at the **Stadspark de Motten** (Kastanjewal) at the southern end of town, a five-minute walk from the Grote Markt. This huge, extremely well-equipped playground is free; there are also go-carts, minigolf and boats. Parents can

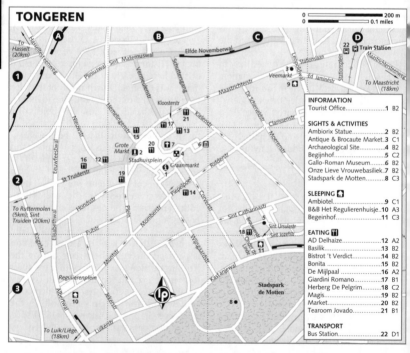

TONGEREN

0 —————— 200 m
0 —————— 0.1 miles

INFORMATION
Tourist Office.....................1 B2

SIGHTS & ACTIVITIES
Ambiorix Statue.................2 B2
Antique & Brocante Market.3 C1
Archaeological Site.............4 B2
Begijnhof..........................5 C2
Gallo-Roman Museum........6 B2
Onze Lieve Vrouwebasiliek.7 B2
Stadspark de Motten..........8 C3

SLEEPING
Ambiotel...........................9 C1
B&B Het Regulierhuisje...10 A3
Begeinhof........................11 C3

EATING
AD Delhaize.....................12 A2
Basilik.............................13 B2
Bistrot 't Verdict..............14 B2
Bonita............................15 B2
De Mijlpaal......................16 A2
Giardini Romano..............17 B1
Herberg De Pelgrim.........18 C2
Magis.............................19 B2
Market............................20 B2
Tearoom Jovado..............21 B1

TRANSPORT
Bus Station.....................22 D1

have time out at the terrace *café* next to the climbing frames.

Festivals & Events

The **Kroningsfeesten** (Coronation Celebration; www.kronings feesten.be) celebrates the town's historic religious status – Tongeren is believed to be the first place of worship of the Virgin Mary north of the Alps – and takes place just once every seven years (next on 5 to 12 July 2009). During the last event, 600,000 people lined the streets to watch the venerated 15th-century statue of the Virgin and scores of participants clad in medieval-style garb parade through town. Due to the event's popularity, the procession is performed on four days.

Sleeping

Begeinhof (☎ 012 39 13 70; www.vjh.be; St Ursulastraat 1; dm per person €16.60; 🖳) A modern youth hostel in an antique frame. It's pleasantly sited in the heart of the *begijnhof*, about 900m from the train station, and has good rooms (maximum six beds). The hostel's colourful café is fine for a snack.

B&B Het Regulierenhuisje (☎ 012 23 76 62; Regulierenplein 30; s/tw €35/60; 🗶) Two clean simple rooms, each with bathroom, are located on the 1st and 2nd floors of the house next door to the owners. Babies and children are welcome. It's about a three-minute walk from the Grote Markt and, for families, is wonderfully handy to Stadspark De Motten. There's a shed for securing bikes at night.

Ambiotel (☎ 012 26 29 50; www.ambiotel.be; Veemarkt 2; s/d/tr Sun-Fri €75/100/125, Sat €85/110/135; 🗶 🖳 🖳) An unremarkable address, located dead centre in the antique area and charging accordingly.

Ruttermolen (☎ 012 24 16 24; www.ruttermolen .be; Ruttermolenstraat 20; studio per night €90, per weekend 2/4/6 persons €170/185/220, per week €295/310/370; 🖳) With a car, this B&B is a fabulous address, especially for travelling families. It's part of an old mill located alongside the River Jeker and the welcoming family who run it have converted the old stables into three modern self-contained studios. There's a large aboveground pool for summer, and plans are afoot for an all-weather indoor pool in what was once a bakery. It's 5km from Tongeren – follow the signs to Borgworm for 4km, then turn left (direction Rutten), from where it's 1km along this road, on the right.

ALL IN JEST

Belgians are good at laughing at themselves, and the Flemish language is full of derisive expressions that hark back to the days of Breugel or beyond. Where else in the world, for example, would you find 'cobblestones' referred to as *kinderkopkes* – literally 'the heads of little children'?

Maneblussers is the popular name for the citizens of Mechelen. It comes from a local legend in which a 17th-century reveller had one-too-many at the pub and then thought the tower of St Romboutskathedraal, the city's cathedral, was on fire. He raised the alarm and townsfolk rallied to put out the blaze. It soon became apparent that the 'fire' was simply the light of the moon casting an unusual reddish glow around the tower. Hence their nickname Maneblussers, or 'Extinguishers of the Moon'.

The people of Ghent are known as the Stropdragers because Emperor Charles V humiliated the rebellious townsfolk by forcing them to wear a *strop* (noose) around their neck.

Antwerp folk are sometimes referred to as Sinjoren, which comes from the Spanish *señor* ('Sir'), and originated during the 16th century when Spain ruled the region. So the story goes, the people of Antwerp were gentrified enough to receive this accolade.

But not all the nicknames are so endearing or complimentary. The people of Lier are known as the Schapekoppen, or 'Sheepheads', due to their reputation for being stupid, and there's even a street in Lier named Schapekoppenstraat. Similarly, those from Poperinge in West Flanders are nicknamed Keikoppen, or 'Pigheads'.

From here the names go downhill fast. The citizens of Diest are the Mosterdschijters ('Mustard Shitters'), while Tongeren inhabitants have what must be the nation's worst appellation – the Schoepschijters, or 'Shovel Shitters'.

Hardly surprisingly, the origins of these last two seem lost in time – at least none of the locals we asked knew how the names came about but, true to character, they had a good chuckle when the subject was raised.

EASTERN FLANDERS

Eating

Tearoom Jovado (☎ 012 23 43 40; Maastrichterstraat 35; ☺ 9am-6pm Wed-Mon) Old-fashioned café known for its freshly ground coffee and calorific cakes. Stock up on pralines from Neuhaus next door before settling in.

Giardini Romano (☎ 012 23 04 85; Maastrichterstraat 17; pizza €7.50-9, mains €10-21; ☷) Long-established Italian restaurant with a pretty gaudy interior but superb fresh homemade pasta. Kids are most welcome.

Herberg De Pelgrim (☎ 012 23 83 22; Brouwerstraat 9; mains €9-17; ☺ Wed-Sun) Snuggled into the *begijnhof* quarter, this is a great spot for a light meal or snack. The building dates from 1632 and is disgustingly quaint. It's well priced, and offers salads (€7 to €9), pasta dishes (€7 to €12) and Flemish staples.

Basilik (☎ 012 21 33 24; Kloosterstraat 2; mains €11-21) Big buzzing split-level brasserie hidden away in a tiny lane next to the basilica. Locals love the mocha tones and wood feel. Great for a snack or meal at any time.

Bistrot 't Verdict (☎ 012 26 42 24; Piepelpoel 3; mains €15-20; ☺ lunch Thu-Sun, dinner Wed-Mon) Backstreet bistro with subtle décor and a limited range of excellent Belgian dishes. It's popular with the locals and comes highly recommended.

Magis (☎ 012 74 34 64; Grote Markt 31; mains €25; ☺ lunch & dinner Thu-Mon) Small corner restaurant just down from the Ambiorix statue that does excellent Belgian/French cuisine. The décor's subtle, the staff friendly and the location superb. There's also a tiny terrace in fine weather.

De Mijlpaal (☎ 012 26 42 77; St Truiderstraat 25; 3-course lunch menu €38, dinner menus €38-51; ☺ Fri-Wed) One of the first restaurants to bring 'modern' to Tongeren. Features strong colours, inventive Belgian cuisine (vegetarians aren't forgotten) and a chef, Jan Menten, who knows his stuff (he worked for two years in Brussels' Comme Chez Soi, Belgium's most famous restaurant).

Also recommended:

AD Delhaize (Sint Truiderstraat 7; ☺ 9am-7pm Mon-Sat) Supermarket.

Bonita (☎ 012 23 31 22; Hemelingenstraat 9-11; snacks €2.50-4; ☺ Tue-Sun) The place for a *baguette* sandwich, panini, pancake or ice-cream; dine in or take away.

Market (Grote Markt; ☺ Thu) Held during the morning.

Getting There & Around

Hourly trains depart from Tongeren's **train station** (☎ 02 528 28 28) for Hasselt (€3.70, 20 minutes), Liège (€3.80, 30 minutes) and Sint Truiden (via Hasselt; €5.70, 45 minutes). **De Lijn** (☎ 070 220 220) buses depart from the bus station, located next to the train station – bus 23A goes direct to Sint Truiden (€2.50, 35 minutes).

Free **bikes** (☺ 8.30am-4.30pm Apr-Sep) are available from the tourist office (deposit €10). Bikes can be reserved in advance. A few have baby seats, but there are no children's bikes.

ZOUTLEEUW

pop 7900

The sleepy Brabant village of Zoutleeuw, 7km west of Sint Truiden, sits on the edge of the Hageland wine-producing region. Once a prosperous medieval cloth-making centre, it fell into decline along with that industry in the 15th century. It's now best known for the rich art collection housed in the turreted **St Leonarduskerk** (admission €1.50; ☺ 2-5pm Tue-Sun Easter-Sep), a huge Gothic structure that seems overblown in its present-day context at the heart of such a small village. St Leonarduskerk was the only significant church in the country to escape untouched during the religious wars and invasions that swept this part of Europe between the 16th and 18th centuries, and its interior is adorned with many medieval art treasures.

Opposite the church is the **tourist office** (☎ 011 78 12 88; www.zoutleeuw.be in Flemish; ☺ 10am-noon & 1-4pm Tue-Fri, 1-5pm Sat & Sun Apr-Sep, 10am-noon & 2-4pm Tue-Fri Oct-Mar), a good place to buy some of the local Hageland wine.

The best bet for overnighters is **Hof ter Wallen** (☎ 011 78 03 43; Stationstraat 44; r per person €34). This B&B occupies part of a restored farmhouse with a beautiful rose garden and is situated alongside the 16th-century fortification walls.

For a bite or a slurp head to the local favourite, **De Cleyne Taefel** (☎ 011 78 43 43; Prins Leopold-plaats 4; snacks €4-10; ☺ 8am-6.30pm Tue-Fri, 8am-9.30pm Sat & Sun). This cheery little place churns out waffles, sandwiches and pancakes. More substantial fare can be had at **Pannenhuis** (☎ 011 78 50 02; Grote Markt 25; mains €12-20; ☺ closed Tue evening Jun-Aug), a whitewashed restaurant serving typical Flemish food.

To get to Zoutleeuw, take bus 25 from Sint Truiden (direction Tienen; 20 minutes, every two hours). For details on getting to Sint Truiden, see left.

Hainaut & Brabant-Wallon

With the exception of Waterloo, Wallonia's western provinces of Hainaut and Brabant-Wallon are largely overlooked by foreign visitors. After the hubbub of the country's more touristy spots, this little corner of French-speaking Belgium is refreshingly ordinary.

Two cities in Hainaut make excellent exploration bases – choose between Mons, the province's capital, or Tournai, one of Belgium's oldest settlements. With good timing, your own wheels and a passion for beer, don't miss Brasserie à Vapeur, a steam-driven brewery close to Tournai. Nearby, too, are the giants of Ath. Halfway between Mons and Charleroi is Binche, where the Gilles (local men) take centre stage during carnival. Move north into Brabant-Wallon and there's Nivelles with its impressive Romanesque church. Close by are the haunting ruins at Villers-la-Ville and, to the north, the great battlefield of Waterloo.

Back in Hainaut, Charleroi is a city on the edge – its heavy industry long gone and its future uncertain. This area's unappealing landscape gradually gets better the more you descend into the Botte de Hainaut (Boot of Hainaut), a chunk of land that extends into France. The Boot is an extension of the forested Ardennes and contains a slab of Namur province, included in this chapter for convenience. The little towns of Couvin and Chimay are the focal points, both accessible by public transport. Keep in mind that accommodation is thin on the ground in this southern quarter and advance planning might be wise in summer.

HIGHLIGHTS

- **Carnival Capers** The Gilles of Binche (p223)
- **History Buffs** The battlefield of Waterloo (p225)
- **Dance Demons** The avant-garde Charleroi/ Danses (p226)
- **Evocative Ruins** The Cistercian abbey (p225) at Villers-la-Ville
- **Dragon Slayers** Mons' La Doudou (p222)
- **Art & Art Nouveau** The Musée des Beaux-Arts (p219) in Tournai
- **Steam Blower** Brasserie à Vapeur (p51), Pipaix
- **Big Weekend** The giants of Ath (p222)

★ Waterloo

★ Tournai ★ Ath
★ Pipaix
★ Villers-la-Ville

Mons ★
★ Charleroi
Binche ★

- PROVINCES: HAINAUT (CAPITAL MONS), BRABANT-WALLON (CAPITAL NIVELLES)
- LANGUAGE: FRENCH

TOURNAI
pop 67,300

As provincial towns in Wallonia go, Tournai (Doornik in Flemish) is decidedly pleasant. Situated on the Scheldt River (known as L'Escaut in French), just 10km from the French border and 80km from Brussels, its air is distinctly French and it offers a gaggle of great museums plus one of the country's finest cathedrals.

Together with Tongeren in Flanders, Tournai rates as Belgium's oldest city. It started life as a Roman trading settlement known as Tornacum but, unlike Tongeren, it has little to hark back to these times. The rest of its history is as chequered as Belgium's – the counts of Flanders as well as the French, English, Spanish and Austrians have all had a hand in ruling it over the centuries. In the 5th century it was the relatively short-lived capital of the Merovingians, a Frankish dynasty that reigned in France. Their most celebrated king, Clovis, was born here in 465. In the early 14th century, in Henry VIII's time, it had a brief spell as an English city, but five years later was sold back to France. The city, in 1521, was then swallowed by the Hapsburg empire, after which it became an important tapestry-making centre.

Information

Internaute (☎ 069 84 67 43; info@internaute.be; Rue du Château 63; per hr €3; ⊗ 11am-midnight) Funky internet bar.

Office du Tourisme (☎ 069 22 20 45; www.tournai .be; Vieux Marché aux Poteries 14; ⊗ 8.30am-6pm Mon-

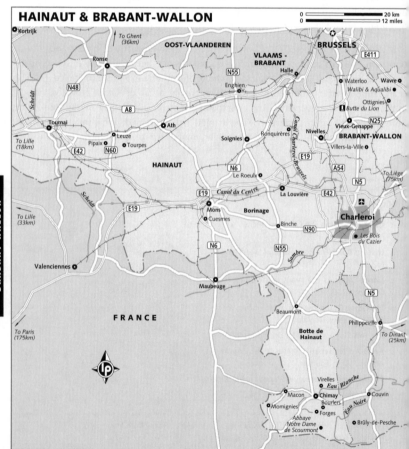

HAINAUT & BRABANT-WALLON

0 — 20 km
0 — 12 miles

To Ghent (36km)
Kortrijk
OOST-VLAANDEREN
Ronse
N48
Scheldt
A8
Tournai
To Lille (18km)
Leuze
Pipaix
E42
N60
Tourpes
Ath
HAINAUT
Scheldt
To Lille (33km)
E19
Valenciennes

VLAAMS - BRABANT
Enghien
N55
Halle
BRUSSELS
E411
Waterloo
Wavre
Walibi & Aqualibi
Ottignies
Butte du Lion
N25
Vieux-Genappe
BRABANT-WALLON
Villers-la-Ville

Soignies
Ronquières
Nivelles
N6
Le Roeulx
E19
A54
To Liège (75km)
N5

Canal du Centre
La Louvière
E42

Mons
Cuesmes
Borinage
Charleroi
Binche
N90
Les Bois du Cazier

N6
N55
Sambre

Maubeuge
N5

Beaumont
Philippeville
To Dinant (25km)

FRANCE

To Paris (175km)

Botte de Hainaut

Virelles
Eau Blanche
Macon
Chimay
Couvin
Momignies
Bourlers
Forges
Eau Noire
Abbaye Notre Dame de Scourmont
Brûly-de-Pesche

ri, 9.30am–noon & 2–5pm Sat, 10am–noon & 2.30–6pm
un) Catch the 20-minute movie (in English; €2) tracing
ournai's history.

Post Office (Rue des Chapeliers)

Sights

The five towers of the striking but sober
Cathédrale Notre Dame (Our Lady's Cathedral; Grand Place;
admission free; 9.30am–noon & 2–5pm Apr–Oct, 10am–noon
& 2–4pm Nov–Mar) have long been the trademark
of Tournai's skyline. Completed in the 12th
century, it's an enormous Romanesque affair
but its fine proportions are difficult to ap-
preciate as it's encrusted by buildings on all
but one side. Pummelled by a freak tornado
in 1999, parts of the World Heritage–listed
cathedral are still off-limits to tourists due to
major works to realign the towers.

Worth seeking on the outside is the **Porte
Mantile**, a two-tiered Romanesque archway
adorned with carvings. Better still is the west
façade, festooned with carvings from the 14th
to 17th centuries and, due to the relative protection, not nearly so weathered. Inside, the
Trésor (treasury; admission €2; 10am–noon & 2–5.45pm
Mon–Fri, 2–4.45pm Sat & Sun Apr–Oct, 10am–noon & 2–4pm

Mon–Fri, 2–4pm Sat & Sun Nov–Mar) is loaded with religious bits and pieces.

Tournai's 72m-high World Heritage–listed
Beffroi (belfry; Grand Place; admission €2; 10am–1pm &
2–6pm Tue–Sun Mar–Oct, 10am–noon & 2–5pm Tue–Sat, 2–5pm
Sun Nov–Feb) is Belgium's oldest, dating from
1188. It was built to house a bell given to the
city as a symbol of freedom by the king of
France during one of Tournai's bouts of independence. Some 257 steps lead up to it.

The **Musée des Beaux-Arts** (069 22 20 43; Enclos
St Martin; admission €3; 9.30am–12.30pm & 2–5.30pm
Wed-Mon Apr–Oct, 10am–noon & 2–5pm Mon, Wed-Sat, 2–
5pm Sun Nov–Mar) is housed in an airy building
designed by Art Nouveau architect Victor
Horta. The impressive collection includes
paintings and sculptures by local, national
and international artists. Of the local works,
look out for those by Louis Gallait (1810–87),
whose enormous canvas *La Peste de Tournai*
is a harrowing account of the plague of 1092;
considerably more enchanting is *En ballon*
by Roméo Dumoulin (1883–1944). Tournai's
best-known artist, Rogier Van der Weyden
(also known as Roger de la Pasture) is also
well represented. Other artists of note include

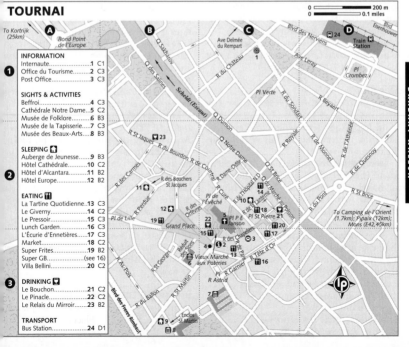

TOURNAI

INFORMATION
Internaute.........................1 C1
Office du Tourisme...........2 C3
Post Office.......................3 C3

SIGHTS & ACTIVITIES
Beffroi..............................4 C3
Cathédrale Notre Dame....5 C2
Musée de Folklore.............6 B3
Musée de la Tapisserie......7 C3
Musée des Beaux-Arts......8 B3

SLEEPING
Auberge de Jeunesse.........9 B3
Hôtel Cathédrale..............10 C2
Hôtel d'Alcantara.............11 B2
Hôtel Europe...................12 B2

EATING
La Tartine Quotidienne....13 C2
Le Giverny.......................14 C2
Le Pressoir.......................15 C3
Lunch Garden..................16 C3
L'Écurie d'Ennetières........17 C3
Market.............................18 C3
Super Frites.....................19 B2
Super GB...................(see 16)
Villa Bellini......................20 C2

DRINKING
Le Bouchon......................21 C1
Le Pinacle........................22 C2
Le Relais du Miroir..........23 B2

TRANSPORT
Bus Station......................24 D1

Pieter Breughel the Younger, Jacob Jordaens and French impressionist Edouard Manet, who painted the serene *Argenteuil*.

The **Musée de Folklore** (☎ 069 22 40 69; Réduit des Sions; admission €2.50; 9.30am-12.30pm & 2-5.30pm Wed-Mon Apr-Oct, 10am-noon & 2-5pm Mon, Wed-Sat, 2-5pm Sun Nov-Mar) is a rabbit warren of fascinating relics from Tournai's past, including religious *brocante* (bric-a-brac) and old posters. The museum also keeps a *jeu de fer* table (see below) for posterity.

Tapestry lovers should not miss the **Musée de la Tapisserie** (☎ 069 84 20 73; Place Reine Astrid; admission €2.50; 9.30am-12.30pm & 2-5.30pm Wed-Mon Apr-Oct, 10am-noon & 2-5pm Mon, Wed-Sat, 2-5pm Sun Nov-Mar). In the 15th and 16th centuries Tournai was one of Belgium's most important tapestry-making cities, and this museum contains a handful of enormous works from that time as well as contemporary pieces. On the top floor, pop into the restoration room to see revamping techniques.

Festivals & Events

Triënnale de la Tapisserie (☎ 069 21 64 34) International tapestry festival, held every three years. The next is June to September 2008.

Jeu de Fer World Championships Annual folkloric gathering held on the second weekend in September. Hundreds of participants gather on the Grand Place to contest this so-called 'game of iron', which melds billiards with curling and boules (an outdoor game using big metal balls that's popular in the south of France).

Sleeping

Camping de l'Orient (☎ 069 22 26 35; Vieux Chemin de Mons; camp sites per adult/child/tent €3/2.50/2.50) Part of the huge Aqua Terra swimming complex, 2km from the train station. Bus W stops out the front.

Auberge de Jeunesse (☎ 069 21 61 36; www.laj.be; Rue St Martin 64; dm/s/d €16.60/29/42) Modern and pleasant hostel around the corner from the Musée des Beaux-Arts. It's a 20-minute walk from the train station – take bus 4 (direction Baisieux).

Hôtel d'Alcantara (☎ 069 21 26 48; www.hotelalcantara .be; Rue des Bouchers St Jacques 2; s/d from €75/85) Not the most expensive hotel in the city but certainly the most charming. This discreet four-star abode has attentive service and 15 well-priced, modern rooms set behind a pleasant courtyard. Families are welcome.

Also recommended:

Hôtel Europe (☎ 069 22 40 67; www.europehotel.be; Grand Place 26; s/d €50/65) Few cities in Belgium have

hotels right on their main square – it's worth suffering this hotel's drab décor for its sublime spot.

Hôtel Cathédrale (☎ 069 21 50 77; www.hotelcathe drale.be; Place St Pierre 2; s/d from €105/116;) Comfortable hotel close to the river.

Eating

La Tartine Quotidienne (☎ 069 23 35 88; Rue de Paris 7; light meals €8; lunch Mon-Sat, dinner Fri) Rustic café doing salads, quiches and sandwiches and where no two chairs are alike. The ivy-clad courtyard out the back is perfect in summer.

L'Écurie d'Ennetières (☎ 069 21 56 89; Ruelle d'Ennetières; mains €12-15, 3-course menu €24; lunch Tue-Sun, dinner Wed-Sun) Occupies a renovated old building in the river quarter of the city and does affordable French cuisine.

Le Giverny (☎ 069 22 44 64; Quai du Marché au Poisson 6; mains €13-20, menus from €40; closed Mon, lunch Sat & dinner Sun) Down by the river, this refined restaurant occupies an old bakery and has two sections, one with authentic tiling. A lovely eating space and great classic French food.

Le Pressoir (☎ 069 22 35 13; Vieux Marché aux Poteries 2; mains €15-23, menu from €45; lunch daily, dinner Fri) Arguably the city's best restaurant, tucked away next to the cathedral and serving innovative French cuisine.

Also recommended:

Lunch Garden (☎ 069 54 57 46; Rue Tête d'Or 669; plat du jour €5; 9am-9pm Mon-Sat, 11.30am-9pm Sun) Self-service cafeteria.

Villa Bellini (☎ 069 23 65 20; Place St Pierre 15; pizza €7-10, pasta €8-12) Pleasant interior and good Italian fare.

Super GB (Rue Tête d'Or 669; 8am-8pm) Supermarket.

Market (Place St Pierre; Sat) Food market held during the morning.

Drinking & Entertainment

Tournai's nightlife hubs are Quai du Marché au Poisson, the nearby Place St Pierre and, of course, the Grand Place.

Le Pinacle (☎ 0475 83 49 65; Vieux Marché aux Poteries ; ☺ 11am-11pm Tue-Sun) Overlooking the cathedral, this tavern is great for a cool beer on a shady terrace during a hot afternoon.

Le Bouchon (☎ 069 21 54 36; Quai du Marché au Poisson 23; ☺ 3pm-1am Tue-Sun) Tiny pub with a nautical theme and patrons who cling like barnacles to the side of the bar. Note the disgusting things preserved in bottles above the counter.

Le Relais du Mirroir (☎ 069 21 10 79; Rue St Jacques 5; ☺ 2pm-1am Tue-Sun) Atmospheric pub with an enormous fireplace and a billiard table out the back.

Getting There & Away

Tournai's **train station** (☎ 02 528 28 28) is 900m from the heart of the city, the Grand Place. There are regular trains to Mons (€6, 30 minutes), Brussels (€10.70, one hour), Kortrijk (€4.30, 40 minutes) and Ypres via Kortrijk (€7.80, one hour).

AROUND TOURNAI

For details on **Brasserie à Vapeur** and **Brasserie Dubuisson**, two local breweries in nearby Pipaix, see p51.

MONS

pop 91,200

Calling all dragon slayers. Once a year Mons (Bergen in Flemish) shakes off its workaday role as the capital of Hainaut to take on one of Belgium's most riotous battles, the Lumeçon (see boxed text, p222). For the rest of the year this outwardly humdrum town is simply a likeable place, built on a hill, and dotted with interesting sights and more than its fair share of great eateries.

Historically, Mons is associated with war – it was here that the battles that marked the beginning and end of WWI for the British were fought. During WWII the American liberation campaign had its first victory here. Since 1967 Mons has been home to the Supreme Headquarters of the Allied Powers in Europe (Shape), which employs some 3000 Americans and NATO officials and is based 5km north of town.

To the Brits, Mons is often best remembered for the Angels of Mons, a legend that arose in 1914 based around a host of heavenly archers. Ex-Genesis guitarist, Steve Hackett, evoked the fable in more recent times with his song 'Clocks – The Angels of Mons'.

Information

Maison du Tourisme (☎ 065 33 55 80; www.pays demons.be, in French; Grand Place 22; ☺ 9am-7pm Apr-Oct, 9am-6.30pm Mon-Sat, 9.30am-6.30pm Sun Nov-Mar) Don't miss the 15-minute video (in English) introducing the town.

Sights & Activities

Ensure good luck by making straight to the 15th-century **Hôtel de Ville** (Town Hall) on the **Grand Place** where you'll find a small iron **monkey** that beckons to be stroked.

From the Grand Place, head up Rue des Clercs to Mons' World Heritage–listed baroque **beffroi** (belfry), a black-domed gilded affair standing amid gardens from where there's a good rooftop view.

A few streets further west is the **Collégiale St Waudru**, a 15th-century church of huge proportions and home to the Car d'Or, a gilded chariot from 1781 that's festooned with cherubs. It used to carry the remains of St Waudru during La Doudou (see boxed text, p222).

Decorative arts is the theme of the **Musée François Duesberg** (☎ 065 36 31 64; Square Franklin Roosevelt 12; admission €4; ☺ 2-7pm Tue, Thu, Sat & Sun), located opposite St Waudru church. The late-18th-century clock collection gets a big tick.

Two of the town's principal museums, the **Musée des Beaux-Arts** (☎ 065 40 53 06; Rue Neuve 8) and the **Musée du Folklore** (☎ 065 31 43 57; Rue Neuve), are expected to reopen by the time you read this, following restoration.

Sleeping & Eating

Mons is stuffed with restaurants, but is light on accommodation. While away the evening on the Grand Place or Marché aux Herbes, both lined with informal cafés.

Auberge de Jeunesse du Beffroi (☎ 065 87 55 70; www.laj.be; Rampe du Château 2; dm/s/d/f €17/30/44/74; ☒ ☐) Modern hostel located at the base of the belfry. Its attractive tiered design makes good use of the sloping terrain, and the inner courtyard has a bend-over-backwards belfry view. It's family friendly, and the good facilities include a kitchen, restaurant and bar, and free parking.

Hôtel Ibis (☎ 065 84 74 40; www.ibismons.be; Blvd Charles Quint 27; s/d/t €68/68/80) Chain hotel with a handy location opposite the train station.

Hôtel Infotel (☎ 065 40 18 30; www.hotelinfotel.be; Rue d'Havré 32; s/d from €75/85) Respectable midrange hotel with modern décor, though you may need to don sunglasses before entering your room. Just footsteps from the Grand Place.

LA DOUDOU

Known locally as La Doudou, **La Ducasse** (www.ducassedemons.be) is Mons' biggest annual shindig. Even King Albert and Queen Paola turned up in 2006, and the event has made it onto Unesco's World Heritage list. Held on Trinity Sunday (3 June 2007, 18 May 2008 and 7 June 2009), it begins with the morning's **Procession du Car d'Or**, which sees the remains of St Waudru, a 7th-century female miracle worker and the city's patron saint, paraded through town in time-honoured tradition. But the jamboree's highlight comes at lunchtime on the Grand Place with the **Lumeçon**, a legendary battle between good and evil in the form of St George astride his black horse against a 9.4m-long wicker-work dragon. Lesser characters include St George's sidekicks, the Chinchins, and, on the dragon's side, some *diable* (devils). Join the crowd as it surges forward to grab sheaves of brushwood from the 200kg-dragon's tail – life-threatening stuff, really – or watch from the sardined sidelines.

L'Excelsior (☎ 065 36 47 15; Grand Place 29; mains €15-20; ⏰ from 9.30am) Long, wood-panelled bistro that faithfully reproduces Belgian classics. Good also for some lesser-known regional beers.

Sel & Sucre (☎ 065 59 05 07; Rue de Nimy 6; 3-course lunch/dinner menu €17/35; ⏰ lunch & dinner Tue-Sat, lunch Sun) Modern little resto just off the Grand Place, where the young chef is noted for his spontaneous cooking.

La Cinquième Saison (☎ 065 72 82 62; Rue de la Coupe 23; mains €20-30, menus from €30; ⏰ lunch & dinner Tue-Sat) Relatively new addition to Mons' range of fabulous eateries. This classy little place does French/Belgian cuisine in style, served in just one small room (or on an even tinier courtyard). Dig around down the end of a cobbled alley to find it.

Devos (☎ 065 35 13 35; Rue de la Coupe 7; mains €28-32, menu gastronomique €75; ⏰ closed Wed & dinner Sun) Refined establishment serving seasonal French/Belgian haute cuisine.

Also recommended:

Camping du Waux-Hall (☎ 065 33 79 23; Ave St Pierre 17; camp sites per adult/child/tent €3.40/2.20/2; ⏰ year-round) Camping ground just outside the town centre on the road to Binche.

Sandwicherie Henri (☎ 065 36 18 68; Grand Place 1; baguettes €2-2.70; ⏰ 9am-10pm) Pumps out enormous filled baguette sandwiches.

Market (Marché aux Herbes; ⏰ 6am-2pm Fri & Sun) Fresh produce.

GB Express (Rue d'Havré 16) Supermarket.

Getting There & Around

Mons' **train station** (☎ 02 528 28 28) and neighbouring **TEC bus station** (☎ 065 38 88 15) are at Place Léopold, 700m from the Grand Place. Regular connections include to Brussels (€7.80, 45 minutes), Charleroi (€5.40, 30 minutes) and Tournai (€6, 25 minutes).

Free public **minibuses** (⏰ 7am-9pm Mon-Sat) shuttle every 15 minutes between the train/bus station and the Grand Place.

AROUND MONS

The area between Mons and Charleroi is known as the Borinage. This unappealing sprawl of factories, chimneys belching black smoke and old slag heaps was Belgium's industrial powerhouse up until the decline of the steel and coal industries in the 1970s. Among these former coalfields is the **Maison Vincent van Gogh** (☎ 065 35 56 11; Rue du Pavillon 3; admission €2.50; ⏰ 10am-6pm Tue-Sun), in the village of **Cuesmes**, a few kilometres southwest of central Mons. Van Gogh lived in this house in 1879 and was inspired to start seriously drawing after watching the local miner's toil. The house accommodates reproductions of his work. From Mons' bus station take TEC bus 20 (€1.30, 10 minutes, hourly).

Sixteen kilometres east of Mons is **Binche**, a grim little town that bursts into life once a year for one of the world's most unusual carnivals (see boxed text, opposite). If you're around at this time, it's a must. Otherwise, get a feel for what it's about at the **Musée International du Carneval et du Masque** (☎ 06 433 57 41; Rue Saint Moustier 10; adult/child €6/3.50; ⏰ 9.30am-12.30pm & 1.30-6pm Sun-Thu, 2-6pm Fri & Sat). From Mons, TEC bus 22 goes to Binche (€3.25, 40 minutes, every 30 to 40 minutes).

Ath, 21km northwest of Mons, is famed throughout Belgium for its **Procession of the Giants**, held on the last weekend in August. Enormous World Heritage–listed models with biblical and folkloric connections wind through town to the Grand Place, where two of the giants wed. The **Maison des Géants** (☎ 068 26 51 70; www.maisondesgeants.be; Rue de Pintamont 18; admission €2.50; ⏰ 10am-noon & 1-6pm Tue-Fri, 2-6pm Sat & Sun Apr-Sep, 10am-noon & 1-5pm Tue-Fri Oct-Mar) intro-

CARNIVAL CAPERS

Carnival is a fabulous way to experience Belgium's love of folklore and pageantry. Steeped in religious traditions, festivities trace back to the Middle Ages and include goings-on that defy modern imagination.

Locals batten down the hatches and visitors come prepared for a bruising at **Binche** (www .carnavaldebinche.be, in French; ⊙ 3-5 Feb 2008, 22-24 Feb 2009), Belgium's most bizarre carnival celebration and recently World Heritage listed. On Shrove Tuesday local men, known as Gilles, stomp around to the ominous beat of drums while wearing strange green-eyed masks and shaking sticks to ward off evil spirits. After lunch the Gilles slow dance through town, decked out in all their finery, including enormous ostrich-feather headdresses, and accompanied by local lads laden with baskets of oranges. From here things get messy as the crowd is pelted with oranges to bless the forthcoming summer. No matter how tempting, don't hurl one back – it's a gift! Despite what you may think, carnival in Binche is actually a serious celebration, taking months of preparation and involving strict rules of conduct. The rituals surrounding it date back hundreds of years and the Gilles' costumes, some of them 150 years old, are thought to be modern-day interpretations of the elaborate, Inca-inspired dress worn by courtiers at a feast to honour Emperor Charles V in 1549.

Carnival at **Malmédy** (www.malmedy.be; ⊙ 3-5 Feb 2008, 22-24 Feb 2009) is known as Cwarmé and it's held over several days from the Saturday before Shrove Tuesday. The focus is Sunday's parade, which is dominated by the Haguète, masked characters who wander around wielding *hapes-tchâr*, great extendible wooden pincers that fly out and grab bystanders around the throat. So the story goes, these exceedingly useful implements were originally designed to feed lepers. The Haguète immobilise bystanders, then force them to their knees and make them demand forgiveness. For what? Who knows, but if you were caught around the throat by a pincer-wielding figure wearing a pirate hat stuffed with ostrich feathers and draped in a blood-red cape, you'd probably make amends without asking too many questions. (For information on the town of Malmédy, see p258.)

To top it off, there's the three-day Laetare at **Stavelot** (www.laetare-stavelot.be; ⊙ 1-3 March 2008, 20-22 March 2009), based around the fourth Sunday in Lent. Legend has it that this festival dates back to the 16th century when the principality's Prince Abbot forbade local monks from taking part in festivities. The local people reacted by wearing white costumes recalling the Benedictine's habit. Whatever its origins, local students revived tradition soon after WWII, and today the festival's big event is a colourful street parade full of floats and oompapa bands. Bringing up the rear are the highlights, the Blancs Moussis, a brotherhood of local men clad in white cloaks and capes and each sporting a mask with an extravagantly long red nose. These characters emit sinister half-grunt, half-laugh noises while stuffing confetti down women's clothes, dangling smelly dried herrings in people's hair and beating up bystanders with dried pigs' bladders! (For information on the town of Stavelot, see p257.)

Now, really, whoever said Belgians were boring?

duces their world. Brussels-bound trains from Mons stop in Ath (€3.60, 15 minutes).

NIVELLES

pop 24,100

The ancient town of Nivelles (Nijvel in Flemish) grew up around its abbey, founded in 648, and is still presided over by a magnificent and unusual church. About 35km northeast of Mons, it's Brabant-Wallon's main town and, if nothing else, makes a pleasant and convenient pit stop en route to the ruins at Villers-la-Ville. It's also an easy day trip from Brussels (30km away).

The **Office du Tourisme** (☎ 067 84 08 64; www tourisme-nivelles.be; Rue de Charleroi 25; ⊙ 9am-5pm Mon-

Sat, 1-5pm Sun) is housed under the arcade just off the main square.

The **Collégiale Ste Gertrude** is Nivelles' only sight. This Rhineland Roman–style church was built in the 11th century as the abbey church and is named after the first abbess, daughter of Itte the abbey's founder. Successively altered and repaired (some 19 fires over the centuries as well as WWII bombing) means it's now a hotchpotch of styles, but it's impressive nonetheless.

The church contains fine sculptures by 18th-century artist Laurent Delvaux, including a lavish oak-and-marble pulpit. Look out, too, for the old wooden chariot that is used to carry Ste Gertrude's shrine in the town's age-old annual procession (late September or early October). The crypt, an archaeological site and the treasury can all be visited.

The church's history is so varied that it's well worth taking a 1½-hour **guided tour** (admission €5). Tours can be arranged at the small office inside the church; if you want to be sure of an English-speaking guide, telephone the tourist office in advance. Tours are held at 2pm Monday to Friday, and 2pm and 3.30pm Saturday and Sunday.

Overnighters will find **Hôtel du Commerce** (☎ 067 21 12 41; fax 067 84 17 04; Grand Place 7; s/d €35/65, mains €14-18, menu €27) has basic rooms and a good, well-priced restaurant.

Nivelles is on the Brussels–Charleroi railway line, and there are hourly connections to Brussels (€4.70, 20 minutes) and Charleroi (€3.80, 20 minutes). The train station is a 10-minute walk from the town centre.

WATERLOO
pop 29,000

Waterloo lies 18km south of Brussels in Brabant-Wallon and is easily visited on a day trip from the capital. It's one of Belgium's main tourist attractions, with hundreds of thousands of visitors coming each year to look out over the plains from the Lion of Waterloo – the site of the battle on 18 June 1815 that changed the course of European history (see boxed text, opposite).

Reactions to the various sights are generally divided into two camps – history and war buffs find it exciting, others may wonder why they came. The most important sights are spread over several kilometres, making it tedious, but not impossible, to get around without your own transport (for more details, see opposite). Many of the displays have both feet firmly in the 19th century, though this will change once the site's €20 million facelift, announced in 2006, is completed.

The best place to start a visit is at the **Office du Tourisme** (☎ 02 352 09 10; www.waterloo-tourisme.be; Chaussée de Bruxelles 218; ♡ 9.30am-6.30pm Apr-Sep, 10am-5pm Oct-Mar), in the village of Waterloo. The helpful staff will know the state of play regarding the facelift – what's open and what's not.

Sights & Activities

Opposite the Waterloo tourist office is the **Musée Wellington** (☎ 02 354 78 06; www.museewellington.be; Chaussée de Bruxelles 147; adult/child €5/2; ♡ 9.30am-

6.30pm Apr-Sep, 10am-5pm Oct-Mar). Wellington spent the eve of the battle in this old inn and it was here that his aide-de-camp, Alexander Gordon, died. It contains well laid-out exhibits including battle plans, weapons and personal effects. An audio-guide takes you around.

From here proceed to the battlefield, some 5km south of Waterloo centre, where a clutch of sights compete for the attention of visitors. The first stop is generally the **visitors centre** (☎ 02 385 19 12; www.waterloo1815.be; Route du Lion 254; adult/child/concession €5/3.35/4.20; ♡ 9.30am-6.30pm Apr-Sep, 10am-5pm Oct-Mar). This place is slated to be torn down as part of the site's facelift, with an underground memorial to be built instead.

Rising behind the visitors centre is the **Butte du Lion** (Lion's Mound; admission €2; ♡ 9.30am-6.30pm Apr-Sep, 10am-5pm Oct-Mar), a 40m-high mound marking the site where the allies' William of Orange (who became King William II of the Netherlands) was wounded. Women carting baskets of soil took two years to build the impressive mound, constructed soon after the battle at a time when the Dutch ruled Belgium. It's usually possible to climb the 226 steps to the massive bronze lion at the top.

Next to the visitors centre is the **Panorama de la Bataille** (Battleground Panorama; ☎ 02 384 31 39; Route du Lion 252; adult/child/concession €5/3/4; ♡ 9.30am-6.30pm Apr-Sep, 10am-5pm Oct-Mar), a domed building with an elevated gallery containing a circular painting (110m in circumference) of the battlefield. Painted by Louis Dumoulin, it dates from 1912 and is one of the world's last such panoramas. Brace the cold to see this slice of history.

Opposite the Panorama is the **Musée de Cire** (Wax Figures Museum; ☎ 02 384 67 40; Route du Lion 315; adult/child €2/1.50; ♡ 10am-5pm Apr-Nov, 10am-5pm Sat & Sun Dec-Mar), a dreadful waxworks museum with 500-year-old mannequins that should be melted.

The last sight, the **Dernier Quartier Général de Napoléon** (Napoleon's Last Headquarters; ☎ 02 384 24 24; Chaussée de Bruxelles 66, Vieux-Genappe; adult/child €2/1; ♡ 10am-6.30pm Apr-Oct, 1-5pm Nov-Mar) is 4km south of the visitors centre in Vieux-Genappe. Napoleon spent the night before the battle at this former farmhouse, which now accommodates some relevant memorabilia, such as his camp cot. The Brussels–Charleroi bus 365 passes by every two hours – ask for details at the Waterloo tourist office.

Eating

Le Pain Quotidien (☎ 02 354 59 90; Chaussée de Bruxelles 139; breakfast €7.70; ♡ 7am-6.30pm Mon-Sat, 7am-4.30pm

THE BATTLE OF WATERLOO

On 1 March 1815 the legendary French emperor Napoleon Bonaparte landed in the south of France after escaping from the island of Elba, where he'd been imprisoned following his abdication the previous year. Despite defeat at Trafalgar, being driven out of Russia and the dissolution of his empire, Napoleon quickly reignited his peoples' passions. The major European powers declared war, and chose Brussels as their base. The Duke of Wellington's allied force of British, Belgians, Dutch and Germans began assembling in Brussels in April, backed by a Prussian army commanded by Marshal Blücher.

Napoleon knew he had to attack swiftly and decisively against such an alliance. On 15 June he crossed into Belgium with 130,000 men – a force larger than either opposing army – took Charleroi and continued towards Brussels. His strategy was to prevent his opponents joining forces. On 16 June he struck the Prussians at Ligny. Believing them to be fleeing, he turned his attention to Wellington, whose troops were assembling at Waterloo, a defensive position just south of the capital.

At sunrise on Sunday 18 June the two armies faced off, just 1500m apart. Wellington's force of 68,000 were lined up on a ridge facing south; Napoleon's 72,000 men had an uphill battle.

Due to heavy overnight rain, the start of the battle was delayed to allow the ground to dry out. At 11.30am the French attacked, moving round to the west to a farm at Hougoumont that was vital for the defence of Wellington's right. The assault failed, and by 1pm Napoleon had word that the Prussian army was not routed, but in fact just 6km away and moving in fast. Napoleon detached a force to meet it and at 2pm he sent a massive wave of infantry to attack Wellington's left, a confrontation that also proved indecisive.

At 4pm the French cavalry charged Wellington's centre but were unable to break through the infantry formations. By early evening, with the Prussians arriving to the east, Napoleon ordered his Imperial Guards, the army's best soldiers, to break through Wellington's centre. It was a desperate last-ditch effort – the guards had to slog uphill through mud churned up by the cavalry's previous attempt and were mown down by the opposing infantrymen from their protected high-ground position.

At 8.15pm Wellington stirred his men into a full-scale advance and within minutes the nine-hour battle that cost the lives of 15,000 men was over. Napoleon was forced to abdicate and spent the rest of his life in exile on St Helena. The emperor's defeat spelt the end of France's military prowess in Europe and of its rule in Belgium.

Every year or five (there's no set schedule), the famous battle is replayed on the battlefield at Waterloo – check with the tourist office for the next re-enactment. For armchair travellers, *Waterloo – The Hundred Days* by David Chandler is an illustrated account of this decisive battle.

Sun) Good for an informal bite (see boxed text, p103) before setting off to the main cluster of sites south of Waterloo village. It's diagonally across the road from the tourist office.

Getting There & Around

Catch TEC bus W (Map pp76–7) from Ave Fonsny at Brussels' Gare du Midi; ask the driver for a day card (€6). This ticket will get you to Waterloo, around most of the sights and back to the capital. Bus W runs every half-hour from Brussels and stops outside the Waterloo tourist office/Musée Wellington (40 minutes). After visiting Musée Wellington, catch bus W to the vicinity of the visitors centre. Ask either the bus driver or the Waterloo tourist office for a bus timetable.

VILLERS-LA-VILLE
pop 9400

The ruined **Abbaye de Villers** (☎ 071 88 09 80; Rue de l'Abbaye 55, Villers-la-Ville; adult/child/concession €4.50/2/3.50; 🕙 10am-6pm Wed-Mon Apr-Oct, 10am-5pm Wed-Mon Nov-Mar) has no equal in Belgium. About 15km east of Nivelles (and 25km south of Brussels), it awaits discovery in a forested dell and is unquestionably Brabant-Wallon's most engaging site. The local **Office du Tourisme** (☎ 071 87 98 98; www.villers.be; 🕙 9am-1pm Mon & Tue, 10am-6pm Wed-Sun) occupies a small building next to the ruins.

The abbey was founded in this isolated spot by a small religious community – an abbot and a handful of monks – in 1147. It was St Bernard who ruled that his followers should settle in a beautiful location in a peaceful valley. The community flourished, and by the

13th century, when the bulk of the buildings were constructed, it had attracted several hundred devotees, owned a vast tract of land and had fulfilled its aim of living self-sufficiently under Cistercian rules. It continued to thrive, initiating another burst of building activity in the 18th century. But in 1794 French revolutionaries plundered the monastery; four years later it was sold off and in the 1850s a railway line was built through the site. Today evocative ivy-clad ruins are all that remain.

The church is the most striking feature, but it's also possible to make out the old warming room (the only part of the complex to be heated in winter), brewery and kitchen. The hilltop chapel offers the best view.

For a bite to eat, there's **Le Cigalou** (☎ 071 87 85 54; Ave Arsène Tournet 47; mains €13-16, menus from €20; ❧ lunch Wed-Sun, dinner Wed-Sat), a rustic restaurant about 800m from the ruins.

Getting here without a car is an adventure. Villers-la-Ville is on the Brussels–Ottignies–Charleroi railway line and there are hourly connections from Brussels (€5, one hour) or trains every two hours from Charleroi (€3.60, 30 minutes). From Nivelles (€6.40), get a train to Charleroi and take another train from there – it'll take about 1½ hours all up to get to the ruins (and you'll need to time it properly in order to get the train connection in Charleroi).

The Villers-la-Ville train station is 1.6km from the ruins. Turn left out of the train station and continue until reaching a T-junction. Turn right and then simply follow the main road to the ruins.

CHARLEROI
pop 200,600

Born of coal, iron and glass, the city of Charleroi is a modern-day metropolis at the heart of the Pays Noir (Black Country). It flanks the formerly coal-rich Sambre Valley and was the powerhouse of the steel industry up until the 1970s. Today a blackened industrial landscape with belching chimneys greets visitors arriving by train. Although the area around the main train station, Gare du Sud, has been revamped, you only have to cross the Sambre River en route to the city centre at Place Charles II to find run-down streets and a desolate air.

Charleroi has a couple of worthwhile museums that can easily be seen as a day trip from Mons (36km away) or Brussels (55km). On arrival, pick up a city map from the **Pavillon du Tourisme** (☎ 071 31 82 18; www.charleroi.be; Gare du Sud;

❧ 9.30am-12.30pm & 1-5.30pm Mon-Fri) on the square in front of Gare du Sud.

The **Musée des Beaux-Arts** (☎ 071 86 11 34; Place Charles II; admission free; ❧ 9am-12.30pm & 1.15-5pm Tue-Sat) is on the 2nd floor of the Hôtel de Ville. It's home to an excellent collection of works by artists who were born or have lived for a time in Hainaut. Though this may at first seem rather limiting, the province was the birthplace of Pierre Paulus, René Magritte and Paul Delvaux, and attracted artists such as Constantin Meunier, Félicien Rops and James Ensor. Lesser-known local artists include François Navez (1787–1869) and Jean Portaels (1818–95). Upstairs is an exhibition devoted to Jules Destrée, a key socialist politician who fought to improve local working conditions. In all, it makes for a fascinating collection.

To explore Charleroi's industrial heritage, head south of town to the new museum complex, **Le Bois du Cazier** (☎ 071 88 08 56; www.leboisducazier .be; Rue du Cazier 80, Marcinelle; adult/child €5/4; ❧ 9am-5pm Tue-Fri, 10am-6pm Sat & Sun). This converted mine site at Marcinelle opened in 2006 to mark the 50th anniversary of an underground mining accident that killed 262 miners. The complex incorporates three sections – glass, industry and the Marcinelle tragedy. Charleroi was once a world centre for glass production but, as with steel and coal, market changes forced its decline. The industry section involves plenty of old machines, some of which are brought back to life, as well as landscaped walks up old slag heaps. To get there, take bus 52 (10 minutes) from Gare du Sud.

Charleroi's international reputation stands on its avant-garde dance company, **Charleroi/Danses** (www.charleroi-danses.be). One of the jewels in Belgium's cultural crown, it was directed until 2004 by Belgian choreographer Frédéric Flamand. His departure to the Ballet National de Marseille in France saw the company in limbo for a year or so, but it's now headed by a four-prong artistic team whose collaboration has already proved a success. The company performs at its Charleroi base, **Les Écuries** (☎ 071 20 56 40; Blvd Pierre Mayence 65), as well as in Brussels (see p109) and abroad.

A light-lunch option is **Le Pain Quotidien** (☎ 071 32 27 82; Blvd Tirou 79; soups €3-5; ❧ 7.30am-6pm Mon-Sat, 7.30am-3pm Sun; ✗), relaxed and ideal for a bowl of soup or a sandwich (for more details, see p103).

For more serious dining head to **L'Opéra Bouffe** (☎ 071 33 17 57; Rue de la Régence 10; menus €45-

75; ⏰ closed Sun & Tue dinners), a top-notch restaurant one block north of Place Charles II.

Charleroi's main train station, **Gare du Sud** (☎ 02 528 28 28), is a 15-minute walk from Place Charles II. Half-hourly trains run to Brussels (€7.80, 55 minutes), Mons (€5.40, 30 minutes) and Nivelles (€3.70, 20 minutes). To Villers-la-Ville (€3.60, 30 minutes) there is one train every two hours.

Charleroi airport (www.charleroi-airport.com), sometimes called Brussels-Charleroi, is 6km north of the city and is serviced by budget airlines (eg Ryanair) from Ireland, Britain and European destinations. Construction of a new terminal started in mid-2005, and is expected to take a couple of years. A bus (€10.50 one way) connects the airport with Brussels' **Gare du Midi** (p115) train station. Bus A or 68 runs from Charleroi airport to the city's Gare du Sud train station.

BOTTE DE HAINAUT

The oft-overlooked Botte de Hainaut (Boot of Hainaut) extends south from Charleroi and kicks on firmly into France. Geologically it's an extension of the Ardennes, though the landscape is more gentle and the hills an undulating mix of farms and, to a lesser extent, forests. The Boot is shared by Hainaut and Namur provinces, but travelling through here you'll soon see it has little in common with the rest of industrialised Hainaut. Throughout the years it has remained a forgotten sliver of Belgium and today attracts Flemish families in search of a quiet roost for the summer holidays.

The main points of interest for tourists are Couvin and Chimay. The former is easily accessed by public transport, as it marks the end of the railway line from Charleroi. Chimay is accessible by bus from Couvin.

Couvin

pop 13,400

Couvin is a tiny town that lives more and more from its tourist pull. It's actually part of Namur province and is the Boot's southern base for exploration, just 11km from the border with France. It was close to Couvin that Hitler set up a command station in WWII. The town straddles the Eau Noire, a fast-flowing river that separates the picturesque Old Town from the modern hub at Place Général Piron.

The **Maison du Tourisme** (☎ 060 34 01 40; www.couvin.be; Rue de la Falaise 3; ⏰ 9am-5pm Mon-Sat, 10am-4pm Sun) is at the base of the old town.

SIGHTS

There's little to do in Couvin itself, except wander the streets of the Old Town or duck into the **Cavernes de l'Abîme** (☎ 060 31 19 54; Rue de la Falaise; adult/child €4.80/2.80; ⏰ 10am-noon & 1.30-6pm Jul–mid-Sep, Sat & Sun only Apr–Jun & mid-Sep–Oct), a series of caves accommodating a prehistoric display and a sound-and-light show.

The area's main sight is the **Grottes de Neptune** (☎ 060 31 19 54; Route de l'Adugeoir 24; adult/child €7.50/4.50; ⏰ 10am-noon & 1.30-6pm Apr-Sep, Sat & Sun only Oct-Mar), 3km north of town in the hamlet of Pétigny. Here guided visits (45 minutes) follow the underground course of the Eau Noire, and include a 20-minute boat ride. The caves are extremely popular in summer and people queue for hours. They're located 500m off the main road; there's no public transport from Couvin.

Those with a car may want to go back in time to WWII when Hitler established his **Grand Quartier Général Allemand** (German Headquarters; ☎ 060 37 80 38; Place St Méen, Brûly-de-Pesche; adult/child €4/3.50; ⏰ 10.30am-5pm Tue-Sun Easter-Sep) at Brûly-de-Pesche, 8km south of Couvin. Hidden deep in the forest close to the French border, the Nazi leader only commanded from here for a few months in 1940, but in so doing he put the site on the map. Two pavilions and an underground bunker take visitors on an eerie journey.

SLEEPING & EATING

Maison St Roch (☎ 060 34 67 96; maisonsaintroch@hotmail.com; Rue de la Gare 34; d €52; ⏰ closed end Sep–mid-Oct) B&B located in a lovely townhouse on the main road opposite the train station. The four rooms are a tad old-fashioned – pink curtains and floral designs – but they're big and comfy, and the atmosphere is friendly. It's a good overnight bolt for families, as there's a separate kids' bedroom with a bunk bed. The maison's small restaurant (three-course menu €40; closed Monday and Saturday) does regional French/Belgian cuisine.

Au Milieu de Nulle Part (☎ 060 34 52 84; Rue de la Gare 10; s/d €58/70; mains €14-22; ⏰ bistro lunch & dinner Wed-Sun) This B&B and bistro offers sober rooms at the back of its cosy, twin-salon bistro. Rooms have a view of the garden and river, while in the bistro the décor's mix'n'match with a heavy accent on roosters and dried flowers. It's located halfway between the town centre and the train station.

Brasserie Jeanne (☎ 060 34 59 41; Place Général Piron 2; mains €14-20, 3-course menu €25; ⏰ lunch & dinner Fri-Sun; 🖥) Subtle décor, a large terrace and a good selection of Belgian meals, including dishes made with beer-based sauces, are the salient features of this split-level brasserie.

GETTING THERE & AWAY
Couvin's train and bus station sits at the end of the railway line from Charleroi (€6.70, 65 minutes). The station is a five-minute walk from Place Général Piron – head straight along Rue de la Gare.

Chimay
pop 9700

The picturesque town of Chimay, 14km west of Couvin, is most often associated with the Trappist beer brewed here by local monks. The town slopes gently down a hillside to meet the valley of the Eau Blanche River; its hub is the Grand Place, close to which sit a few interesting sights.

The **Maison du Tourisme** (☎ 060 21 18 46; www.ville -de-chimay.be, in French; Rue de Noailles 4; ☺ 9am-6pm Mon-Fri, 10am-6pm Sat & Sun Jul-Aug, 9am-5pm Mon-Fri, 10am-6pm Sat & Sun Apr-Jun & Sep, 9am-noon & 1-4.30pm Mon-Sat Oct-Mar) is in the heart of town, located in a picturesque old stone tower.

SIGHTS
The grey-stone **Château de Chimay** (☎ 060 21 44 44; Rue du Château 18; admission €7) overlooks the river valley on the western side of town and was home to the De Croy family, the town's medieval rulers. It was built in the 15th century, but was gutted by fire in 1935. Faithfully rebuilt, today it hosts occasional classical-music events. One-hour guided tours are held at 10am, 11am, 3pm and 4pm from Easter to October.

The only other sight within the town is the **Collégiale des Saints Pierre et Paul**, a 16th-century church where many of the De Croy family are buried.

The **Abbaye Notre Dame de Scourmont** (☎ 060 21 05 11; Rue du Rond Point 294, Forges) is home to Chimay's Trappist monks. The abbey is 9km south of town and sits on a gentle hill overlooking farmlands and woods. It's not open to visitors but you're free to wander around the peaceful gardens and cemetery and into the abbey church. Beer has been made at the abbey since 1862, but it's now bottled in a modern plant in an industrial estate 5km east of Chimay.

Kids will enjoy **La Grange aux Papillons** (☎ 060 21 99 89; Rue de l'Estrée 4, Virelles; adult/child €4/2.50; ☺ 10am-5.30pm May-Sep, closed Mon May, Jun & Sep), a

tropical butterfly garden located a few kilometres outside town.

SLEEPING & EATING
Though there's only one option in town, there are several good accommodation possibilities in the countryside, but you'll need a car.

Le Petit Chapitre (☎ 060 21 10 42; Place du Chapitre 5; d/ste €70/95) An over-the-top B&B that offers Chimay's only accommodation. It's a small red-stone turreted building on the square behind the church and has four rooms and one suite, all decked out in antiques and flamboyant furnishings – read gold filigree and lacquered furniture. Each room is different – the blue room with its stained glass is a favourite.

Auberge de Poteaupré (☎ 060 21 14 33; www.chimay .com; Route de Poteaupré 5, Bourlers; s/d €76/82) A big place very close to the French border, 9km south of Chimay. It's real attraction, rather than accommodation, is its status as official watering hole for Chimay beers. It also contains a shop (open Tuesday to Saturday) selling the three brews plus other local products like cheese and honey.

Hostellerie du Gahy (☎ 060 51 10 93; fax 060 51 30 05; Rue du Gahy 2, Momignies; s/d €77/90; ☺ Mon-Fri) A delightful place – a converted 300-year-old dairy farm – with six lovely rooms and superb intimate dining, all handled by the wonderfully vibrant owner and chef, Réjane Bouillon. It's 12km southeast of Chimay, in the village of Momignies.

Gîte Rohies (☎ 060 51 23 46; bernardjacquelot@hotmail .com; Place Falleur 9, Macon; apt Mon-Fri €215, Sat & Sun €100) Offers two modern, fully furnished, self-contained apartments in a renovated building. It's in the farming hamlet of Macon, 8km east of Chimay.

Also recommended:

Camping de Chimay (☎ 060 21 18 43; Allée des Princes 1; ☺ Apr-Oct) Close to the town centre, on a plateau next to the river.

Aux Armes de Chimay (☎ 060 21 10 21; Grand Place 35; mains €12-20) Decent local cuisine is served up in this Grand Place setting.

Market (Grand Place; ☺ Sat) Fresh produce; held during the morning.

GETTING THERE & AWAY
Chimay's bus station is a five-minute walk from the Grand Place. From here, bus 60/1 runs to Couvin (€1.50, 40 minutes, 10 times daily), from where there are trains back to Charleroi or Brussels.

The Ardennes

Scenically, the Ardennes is Belgium at its best. This southeastern corner is home to deep valleys, forested hills, meandering rivers and, in its quieter recesses, tranquil stone villages and ancient castles. For those into nature, this is as wild as Belgium gets. The region comprises three Walloon provinces – Namur to the west, Luxembourg to the south and Liège in the east.

By and large, the first port of call is Namur, the capital of Wallonia and a positively pleasant riverside town. From here, the Meuse River (Maas in Flemish) winds along to the tourist town of Dinant. The Ardennes' most inspiring stretch reaches to the villages of Rochefort and Han-sur-Lesse, both known for ancient caves that drip with enormous natural sculptures. Near the French border is Bouillon, an old town dominated by its fine castle, and a superb base for hiking and kayaking. Another outdoor playground and picturesque riverside retreat is La Roche-en-Ardenne. It's also close to the marvellous caves at Hotton.

In the north is industrial Liège, the Ardennes' largest city. Staunchly parochial, it has long been at the heart of life in this area. Within easy striking distance of Liège is the revamped resort of Spa and, nearby, the twin towns of Stavelot and Malmédy, which both burst with revelry around carnival time. A short hop east of Liège is Verviers, a former industrial town that has keenly kept abreast of modern times. Nearby is Eupen, the capital of Belgium's German-speaking Ostkantons (Eastern Cantons). Here too lies the windswept plateau of the Hautes Fagnes.

In a nutshell, the Ardennes is a place to relax – even if you're travelling with kids.

HIGHLIGHTS

- ▪ **Art Treasures** Mosan art at the Trésor du Prieuré d'Oignies (p232) in Namur
- ▪ **Carnival Celebrations** Stavelot's Laetare festivities (p257)
- ▪ **Bubble Forth** Spa (p254), Europe's first health retreat
- ▪ **High Spot** The Hautes Fagnes' fascinating landscape (p259)
- ▪ **Forest Hikes** La Roche-en-Ardenne (p246)
- ▪ **Scenic Cycling** Rochefort's RAVeL bike path (p238)
- ▪ **Natural Gem** Ancient formations in the grottoes at Hotton (p248)
- ▪ **Trappist Brew** The Abbaye Notre Dame d'Orval (p243)
- ▪ **Time-Warp Experience** The castle at Bouillon (p241)

★ Namur   Spa ★   ★ Hautes Fagnes
★ Stavelot
★ Hotton   ★ La Roche-en-Ardenne
★ Rochefort
★ Bouillon
★ Orval

- ▪ PROVINCES: LIÈGE (CAPITAL LIÈGE), LUXEMBOURG (CAPITAL ARLON), NAMUR (CAPITAL NAMUR)
- ▪ LANGUAGES: FRENCH, GERMAN

THE ARDENNES

THE ARDENNES

0 — 20 km
0 — 12 miles

GERMANY

ANTWERPEN

NETHERLANDS

LIMBURG

Hasselt

St Truiden

Tongeren

E13

Maastricht

Lanaye

Aachen

E40

Liège

Jupille

E40

Eupen

Barrage
de la Vesdre

Verviers

Lac de
Gilleppe

Hautes Fagnes-
Eifel Nature Park

Meuse

Hony

Vesdre

N68

Signal de
Botrange

Monschau

Marche-les-
Dames

N63

E25

LIÈGE

Hautes
Fagnes

Hautes Fagnes
Nature Reserve

Herzogenhügel

Namur

Sombre

Spa

E42

Botrange
Nature Centre

Wépion

N97

Francorchamps

N95

Profondeville

Coo

Malmédy

Rocherath

Rivière

Trois Ponts

Stavelot

Bütgenbach

Les Jardins
d'Annevoie

E411

NAMUR

N4

Radhadesh

Durbuy

Petit Somme

Barvaux

Amblève

Dinant

Parc et Réserve
Naturelle
de Furfooz

N63

Melreux

St Vith

Anseremme

Freyr

Domaine de
Chevetogne

Hotton

Gendron

Houyet

Marche-en-
Famenne

N89

N68

Wanlin

Rochefort

Jemelle

Marloie

Villers-sur-Lesse

Maboge

Givet

Han-sur-Lesse

La Roche-
en-Ardenne

Nadrin

Champlon

GERMANY

LUXEMBOURG

Clervaux

Redu

Euro Space
Center

St Hubert

N4

Bastogne

Transinne

Libramont

N95

N89

Rochehaut

Frahan-
sur-Semois

Poupehan

Martelange

Corbion

Bouillon

Semois

E25

N4

LUXEMBOURG

Florenville

Arlon

Abbaye Notre Dame d'Orval

LUXEMBOURG
CITY

FRANCE

Virton

THE ARDENNES

NAMUR

pop 106,200

Namur (Namen in Flemish) is a great jumping-off point for exploring this part of the Ardennes. Some 60km southeast of Brussels, it's a picturesque town, built at the confluence of the Meuse and Sambre Rivers and presided over by a citadel that, in times gone by, ranked as one of Europe's mightiest. Good transport connections to more-remote parts of the Ardennes puts it on the map for travellers without their own vehicle. And for those simply into wining, dining and visiting, it has a lively restaurant and *café* (pub/bar) scene, and a clutch of interesting museums.

History

Namur has been shaped by its strategic military position on the rivers. The Celts first established a fortification here, and later the Romans set up camp. In the Middle Ages, the counts of Namur built a well-protected castle on the craggy rocks overlooking the rivers. Under Spanish rule in the 1640s, the castle was strengthened and thus brought to the attention of the French, who captured the town in 1692; Louis XIV's renowned military engineer Vauban set about redesigning and rebuilding it as the perfect fortification. During the next hundred or so years, the fort was razed and rebuilt, this time by Dutch military prowess.

In WWI, the so-called impregnable fort was taken within three days of the German invasion. With a history like this, there was no way WWII could pass Namur by; the town was bombed and extensively damaged. Its military connections continued right up until 1977, when Belgian army paratroopers packed up and moved out of the citadel.

Although Namur is far from being Wallonia's largest city, it proudly holds the seat of the Conseil de la Région Wallonne, the region's parliament, housed in a former hospice beside the Meuse River.

Orientation

The citadel sits above the meeting of the rivers, a point known as Port du Grognon and marked by a statue of King Albert I on horseback. It was not far from here, in Marche-les-Dames, that the king came to his end while climbing the cliffs along the Meuse.

The town centre stretches north from here along the main shopping streets – Rue de l'Ange and its continuation Rue de Fer –

before abruptly ending at the train station. Pl d'Armes, a largely unattractive square, is the town's nominal heart, and immediately west of here is Namur's good-looking ancient quarter, home these days to some hip pubs and casual eateries.

Information

Ambulance/Fire (☎ 100)
ATM (Post office, Pl d'Armes)
Laverie (Rue Borgnet 18) Self-service.
Main post office (Blvd E Merlot)
Net@Food (☎ 081 22 62 49; Rue Godefroid 1; per hr €2; 9am-11.30pm Mon-Sat, noon-11.30pm Sun) Internet.
Office du Tourisme (☎ 081 24 64 49; www.pays-de -namur.be; Sq Léopold; 9.30am-6pm) Near the train station. Pick up a copy of the free *Storming the Citadel of Namur* brochure – it has an excellent map showing five self-guided walking tours ranging from one to three hours.
Police (☎ 101)
Post office (Pl d'Armes)
Tourist office kiosk (☎ 081 24 64 48; Pl du Grognon; 9.30am-6pm Apr-Sep) At the citadel's base.

Sights & Activities

What remains of Namur's once-mighty **Citadelle De Namur** is slung high above the town on a rocky outcrop. Due to centuries of military expansion (see left), it covers a huge area, though only towers, tunnels and much of the outer walls exist today. Visitors are free to wander around, and access is possible by car, bike, foot or minibus (one way €1.50). The latter depart regularly from the tourist office and stop at Terra Nova. To reach the citadel on foot, head up from the path on Pl St Hilaire; by car or bike follow the Rte Merveilleuse. The best place to start is the new information point, **Terra Nova** (☎ 081 65 45 00; www.citadelle.namur .be; Route Merveilleuse; 11am-6pm). Oddly, it's not signposted as such – instead, look out for the sign 'Domaine fortifié'. Attractions here include a **petit train** (Apr-Nov) that shuttles around parts of the citadel and is well worth taking if you're without wheels, and the **souterrains**, underground galleries used over the centuries for all manner of wartime purposes. A combination ticket (adult/child €6/3) for the petit train and the souterrains also includes entry to the nearby paratrooper's museum. Terra Nova is also home to a *café*/brasserie. About 200m down the road from Terra Nova is a section of the citadel known as **Château des Comtes**. There's not much here besides another *café*/restaurant and, nearby, Belgium's only perfume-maker, **Parfumerie Guy Laforge** (☎ 081 22 12 19; www.delforge.com; Route Merveilleuse; admission free, guided tour 3.30pm Sat €3; ☉ 9.15am-5.30pm Mon-Sat, 2.15-5.30pm Sun). Tours take in the cold Charles V galleries where the perfumes are stored.

Don't miss the **Trésor du Prieuré d'Oignies** (Treasury of the Priory of Oignies; ☎ 081 23 03 42; Rue Julie Billiart 17; admission €2; ☉ 10am-noon & 2-5pm, closed Sun & Mon). This one-room treasury is housed in a modern convent and is guarded by the Sisters of Our Lady. Ring the bell to be taken on a guided tour of the exquisite hoard of Gothic religious treasure (chalices, crosses and reliquaries), much of which was created by Brother Hugo d'Oignies (see boxed text, opposite). Like other famous artworks in Belgium, this collection has a colourful his-

tory. During the French Revolution, when art treasures were being carted off to Paris, the monks in charge of the priory where Brother Hugo had lived took the artworks to a local farmer who walled them up in his house. When the last monk died in 1818, the treasure was given to the Sisters of Our Lady in Namur. During WWI, the Germans destroyed the sisters' convent but the treasure remained intact, wisely buried at the outbreak of war. These days it's kept behind barred doors, though many pieces travel the world as part of international exhibitions.

Housed in an 18th-century mansion just a few minutes' walk from the Trésor du Prieuré d'Oignies, the small **Musée des Arts Anciens du Namurois** (Museum of Ancient Art; ☎ 081 22 00 65; Rue de

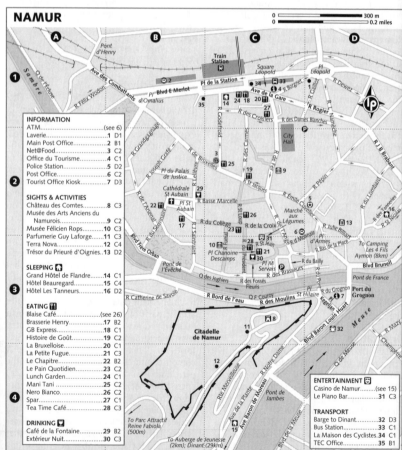

NAMUR

0 .... 300 m
0 .... 0.2 miles

INFORMATION	
ATM	(see 6)
Laverie	1 D1
Main Post Office	2 B1
Net@Food	3 C2
Office du Tourisme	4 C1
Police Station	5 D2
Post Office	6 C2
Tourist Office Kiosk	7 D3

SIGHTS & ACTIVITIES	
Château des Comtes	8 C3
Musée des Arts Anciens du Namurois	9 C2
Musée Félicien Rops	10 C3
Parfumerie Guy Laforge	11 C3
Terra Nova	12 C4
Trésor du Prieuré d'Oignies	13 D2

SLEEPING	
Grand Hôtel de Flandre	14 C1
Hôtel Beauregard	15 C4
Hôtel Les Tanneurs	16 D2

EATING	
Blaise Café	(see 26)
Brasserie Henry	17 B2
GB Express	18 C1
Histoire de Goût	19 C2
La Bruxelloise	20 C1
La Petite Fugue	21 C3
Le Chapitre	22 B2
Le Pain Quotidien	23 C2
Lunch Garden	24 C1
Mani Tani	25 C2
Nero Bianco	26 C2
Spar	27 C1
Tea Time Café	28 C1

DRINKING	
Café de la Fontaine	29 B2
Extérieur Nuit	30 C3

ENTERTAINMENT	
Casino de Namur	(see 15)
Le Piano Bar	31 C3

TRANSPORT	
Barge to Dinant	32 D3
Bus Station	33 C1
La Maison des Cyclistes	34 C1
TEC Office	35 B1

To Parc Attractif Reine Fabiola (500m)

To Auberge de Jeunesse (2km); Dinant (29km)

MOSAN ART

In the early Middle Ages, the Meuse River valley in Belgium (basically from Dinant to Liège) was well known for its highly skilled artisans, particularly those who worked in metals – copper, bronze, brass and gold. Their works are now called Mosan art, and several fine museums throughout this region devote themselves to this art form.

Brother Hugo d'Oignies was one of the region's most masterful medieval metal smiths. With his three brothers, Hugo founded a priory at Oignies (on the nearby Sambre River) in the 12th century and spent his life making religious works of art, many of which are now exhibited in Namur's Trésor du Prieuré d'Oignies (opposite). His works mirror the transition from Romanesque to Gothic, and he's best known for pieces like jewel-studded crosses and elaborate reliquaries with beaded gold rims; the latter were used to hold religious relics brought back from the Holy Land by Jacques de Vitry, a Frenchman whom Hugo had met. Hugo perfected the use of filigree, giving the decorative features – be it animals, people or leaves – depth when raised from the background. He also worked with a technique called *niello,* which allowed delicate lines to be created on a gold background.

Two other museums well worth exploring are the Musée de la Vie Wallonne (p251), which recreates the lifestyles of early Mosan artisans, and the Musée d'Art Réligieux et d'Art Mosan (p251), chock-full of Mosan art from the 11th century onwards. They're located almost side by side in Liège.

Fer 24; adult/child €3/free; ☉ 10am-6pm Tue-Sun) holds a simple but pleasant collection of old artworks from the region, including paintings, religious pieces and Mosan metalwork (see boxed text, above).

The **Musée Félicien Rops** (☎ 081 22 01 10; www .ciger.be/rops; Rue Fumal 12; adult/child €3/1.50; ☉ 10am-6pm Tue-Sun, daily Jul & Aug) is devoted to 19th-century Namur-born artist Félicien Rops (1833–98), who fondly illustrated erotic lifestyles and macabre scenes. Born a few streets away at Rue du Président 33 (the house is marked with a plaque), Rops worked mainly in Paris and Brussels. He was never embraced by the art worlds in either city and became highly critical of them.

Children's amusement park **Parc Attractif Reine Fabiola** (☎ 081 73 84 13; Rond Point Thonar; adult/ child under 1m €3/free; ☉ 11am-6pm mid-Apr–mid-Oct) is located on top of the hill near the citadel.

The **bike ride** to Dinant (28km) is popular with casual cyclists (for bike-rental details, see p235). Flat riverfront bike paths trace some of this scenic route, though there are also stretches where cyclists must join the busy main road. You can also combine cycling with a train trip – ride to Dinant, then return to Namur by train.

Festivals & Events

Namur's most famous annual shindig is the **Combat de l'Échasse d'Or** (Fight for the Golden Stilt), held on the third Sunday in September. Two teams of stilt-walkers – the Mélans (with

yellow and black stilts) and the Avresses (red and white) – joust in medieval garb on Pl St Aubain.

Sleeping

Namur's proximity to Brussels has long made it a daytrip destination. The town's overall dearth of decent accommodation is luckily counterbalanced by a couple of inspiring places to stay.

Camping Les 4 Fils Aymon (☎ 081 58 02 94; Chaussée de Liège; camp sites per adult/tent €3.50/3; ☉ closed Oct-Mar) Pleasant ground located about 8km east of Namur – bus 12 departs hourly from the bus station.

Auberge de Jeunesse (☎ 081 22 36 88; www.laj .be; Rue Félicien Rops 8; dm/s/d €16.60/29/42; ✄ ▦) Attractive riverfront hostel located about 3km southwest of the train station. The main building occupies a distinct red-brick mansion that was formerly a studio of Félicien Rops (see Musée Félicien Rops, left). There's also a series of modern, interconnecting bungalows out the back. It has a quiet location and a view over the Meuse; there's also a kitchen, bar and small terrace. Babies (cot provided) and children are welcome. It's a good place to stay with kids as there's a playground just 100m away. Buses 3 and 4, which both depart hourly from Pl de la Station, stop nearby.

Hôtel Les Tanneurs (☎ 081 24 00 24; www.tanneurs .com; Rue des Tanneries 13; s €45-200, d €60-215, breakfast €10; ✄ ▦) Unique hotel situated on a shabby

THE ARDENNES

street in the heart of town. It unites modern comfort with 17th-century charm. The 30 rooms are part of a renovated tannery and each is totally different – some have water beds, private Jacuzzis or rambling rooftop views. The cheaper rooms are very small and less atmospheric, but are still good value. Children and babies are welcome. Book well ahead.

Hôtel Beauregard (☎ 081 23 00 28; hotel.beauregard@ skynet.be; Ave Baron de Moreau 1; r €70; breakfast €8.50) Big, tired hotel draped along the base of the citadel. Tries to be flash but ultimately it's mutton dressed as lamb. The rooms are good value – comfortable and light with views over the river – and, if insomnia sets in, you can pop into the attached casino. Ask about weekend discounts.

Grand Hôtel de Flandre (☎ 081 23 18 68; www.hotel flandre.be; Pl de la Station 14; s/d/tr €72/80/96; ✕ ▯) This place is anything but grand, but it is centrally located and comfortable enough, with 33 large, modern rooms boasting double-glazed windows to keep train and traffic noise at bay.

Eating

Namur has an excellent range of options to suit all budgets.

CAFÉS & BRASSERIES

Tea Time Café (☎ 0496 52 44 22; Rue St Jean 35; ⏱ 8.30am-5.30pm Tue-Sat) Stylish sandwich shop/tearoom that serves mean crepes (€3.50), waffles and salads (€6.50 to €8.50), and has a pleasant outdoor terrace. Also good for takeaway baguette sandwiches.

Le Pain Quotidien (☎ 081 22 16 66; Rue du Collège 5; snacks €4-10; ⏱ 7.30am-5.30pm) Atmospheric option for a light bite to eat at any time of the day (for more, see p103).

Brasserie Henry (☎ 081 22 02 04; Pl St Aubain 3; mains €10-27; ⏱ noon-midnight Mon-Thu, to 1am Fri & Sat) Sociable brasserie that's become an institution among Namur's late eaters. Expect well-priced Belgian cuisine (vegetarian offerings, too), efficient service and spacious surroundings. It's child friendly and highly recommended.

RESTAURANTS

Histoire de Goût (☎ 081 26 03 30; Rue St Jacques 38; mains €13-25; ⏱ lunch Mon-Sat, dinner Fri & Sat) Cute little French restaurant/tearoom where the house speciality is homemade foie gras. Make sure

THE AUTHOR'S CHOICE

Le Chapitre (☎ 081 22 69 60; Rue du Seminaire 4; mains €10; ⏱ lunch Mon-Sat, dinner Thu-Sat) Convivial and very cosy restaurant huddled in a corner beneath the tower of Cathédrale St Aubain. Specialises in regional cuisine, Breton crepes, and Belgian beers, all at very affordable prices. A blackboard lists the available brews (usually around 30), and the décor's charmingly rustic.

you order the coconut-tinged *crème brûlée* for dessert.

La Bruxelloise (☎ 081 22 09 02; Ave de la Gare 2; mains €16-25; ⏱ lunch & dinner; ✕) Don't come for the '70s décor – it's the plump and succulent mussels, claimed by some to be Wallonia's best, that attract diners from far and wide. Belgian specialities are the staple – *filet américain* (a blob of minced beef served raw) is also on the menu.

La Petite Fugue (☎ 081 23 13 20; Pl Chanoine Descamps; mains €17-28; ⏱ lunch & dinner, closed lunch Sat) Oozes understated chic. Just two small rooms (and a terrace in summer), personal service and modern interpretations of classic French cuisine have made it a winner among locals.

Blaise Café/Nero Bianco (☎ 081 26 25 25; Rue St Loup 4; café mains €10-16; ⏱ noon-2.30pm Tue-Sat; restaurant mains €35; ⏱ lunch & dinner Tue-Sat) This duo doing modern Italian cuisine occupies an elite corner of Namur. Delvaux and Pierre Marcolini are also present, making it *the* spot to dine and shop. The ground-floor Blaise Café has a semiprivate courtyard, or you can take to the soft seats inside, watched by military mannequins. Upstairs, Nero Bianco's modern décor is accentuated by lamps that hang over the tables like great praying mantises.

QUICK EATS

Mani Tani (☎ 081 22 74 37; Rue Godefroid; sandwiches €2.15-2.85; ⏱ 7am-6pm Mon-Sat, closed mid-Jul—mid-Aug) This takeaway joint in the student quarter does the best baguette sandwich (known here as a *dagobert*) in town.

Lunch Garden (☎ 081 41 49 35; Passage de la Gare; plat du jour €5; ⏱ 9am-6pm Mon-Sat, 11am-4pm Sun) Self-service cafeteria that's good if euros are short or the kids are starving.

SELF-CATERING

GB Express (Pl de la Station 2) Supermarket.

Spar (Rue des Croisiers 8) Supermarket.

Drinking & Entertainment

The cobbled streets around Pl Chanoine Descamps and the nearby tree-lined Pl du Marché aux Légumes make up the town's liveliest quarter.

Le Piano Bar (☎ 081 23 06 33; Pl du Marché aux Légumes 10) Grungy jazz bar that's been going strong for more than two decades and continues to feature live jazz (free) on Thursday, Friday and Saturday nights from 10pm.

Extérieur Nuit (☎ 081 23 09 09; Pl Chanoine Descamps 6; ⊗ 2pm-2am Tue-Sun) Spacious modern brasserie/bar that serves as a popular apéritif pit stop for locals en route to nearby restaurants, and also as a late-night haunt.

Café de la Fontaine (Rue Lelièvre 2; ⊗ 11am-1am, to 3am Fri & Sat) A raw student pub that's considerably more appealing than most of the other dives in this part of town. Has a popular terrace overlooking the great hulk of Cathédrale St Auban.

Casino de Namur (☎ 081 22 30 21; Ave Baron de Moreau 1; ⊗ from 2pm) Riverside casino attached to Hôtel Beauregard.

Getting There & Away

BOAT

Taking the Meuse River from Namur south to Dinant provides one of the most scenic boat rides in Belgium, passing sheer rock faces, forested hillsides and villages such as Wépion, famed for its roadside strawberry stalls in May, and Profondeville, with its distinct turreted river-front mansions. A converted **barge** (Blvd Baron Louis Huart; ⊗ Sat & Sun mid-Jul–mid-Aug) plies the river, departing from the pier in Namur. Choose from a return trip to Wépion (adult/child €9/7.50, 1¾ hours) or Dinant (adult/child €19/16, 3½ hours).

BUS

Local and regional buses are operated by **TEC** (☎ 081 25 35 55; Pl de la Station; ⊗ 7am-7pm). Regional buses leave from either the bus station near the C&A department store or from Pl de la Station. For information on TEC tickets, see p320. Details of bus services to towns and villages in this region are given in the various Getting There & Away sections.

TRAIN

Namur's modern **train station** (☎ 02 528 28 28; Pl de la Station) is a major rail hub in this part of Belgium. Regional connections include the following (the prices listed are full one-way fares):

Destination	Fare (€)	Duration (min)	Frequency
Brussels	7.40	60	2 per hr
Charleroi	4.70	30	2 per hr
Jemelle	7.40	40	1 per hr
Libramont	10.70	60	1 per hr
Liège	7.40	60	2 per hr
Luxembourg City	22.60	120	1 per hr
Marloie	6.70	35	1 per hr
Mons	9.50	60	1 per hr
Villers-la-Ville	5.70	45	1 per 2hr

Getting Around

City buses depart from either Pl de la Station or Ave de la Gare.

Bikes can be hired from **La Maison des Cyclistes** (☎ 081 81 38 48; www.velonamur.be in French; Pl de la Station 2b; per half-/full day/weekend €7/9/14; ⊗ 8.30am-1pm Mon, 1-6pm Wed & Fri), a small kiosk opposite the train station.

AROUND NAMUR

Halfway between Namur and Dinant is **Les Jardins d'Annevoie** (☎ 082 61 15 55; www.jardins.dannevoie. be; Rue des Jardins 37, Annevoie; adult/child/senior €7.50/5/6; ⊗ 9.30-6.30 Jul & Aug, 9.30am-5.30pm Apr-Jun, Sep & Oct). This classical garden was laid out in 1758 around the manor house of Charles-Alexis de Montpellier, and both the house and gardens are still owned by this family. Montpellier blended French, Italian and English styles and incorporated water as the garden's key element – fountains and tree-lined waterways are used extensively.

To get here from Namur's bus station, take bus 21 (€1.60, 30 minutes) to the stop in front of the gardens. This bus continues on to Dinant. During school terms, visitors really need their own transport as there's only one bus per day, and the return bus departs an hour later (leaving little time to visit the gardens). During school holidays (p308) services increase to three per day, with better return connections.

With your own transport, an interesting place to stay or stop in for a bite to eat is **Brasserie/Hôtel les 7 Meuses** (☎ 081 25 75 75; www.7meuses.be; Rue du Sart à Souilles, Rivière; s/d €50/80; ⊗ closed Dec & Jan). A typical of accommodation around here, it's modern, minimal and painted a startling orange. It sits high on the hillside above the Meuse River and has a spacious brasserie and huge terrace that juts out over the forest. The six rooms are done in white and are severely minimal. Avoid rooms one and six because they're at either end of the

SAX APPEAL

Antoine-Joseph Sax (1814–1894), popularly known as Adolphe Sax, invented the musical instrument that has taken centre stage in jazz and other 20th-century musical genres.

Born in Dinant, he inherited a fascination with music from his father, who made wood and brass instruments as well as pianos and harps. He studied at Brussels' Conservatoire Royal de Musique and in 1841 submitted nine musical inventions to the Brussels Industrial Exhibition. However, the organisers considered him too young to be awarded top prize.

In 1842 Sax went to Paris, where he launched one of his inventions, the saxophone – a single-reed instrument made of metal, which he constructed while attempting to improve the sound of his bass clarinet. Though the French were initially less than thrilled by the new instrument, the French army eventually ordered saxophones for its bands. Sax patented the saxophone in 1846 and, a decade later, the Paris Conservatoire inaugurated saxophone classes with Sax as the instructor.

Despite his inventions, Sax never reaped great financial rewards. He died penniless after a decade of legal disputes with rivals who sought to have his patents revoked. Some of Sax's unusual creations, including the saxhorn, are on display at Brussels' Musée des Instruments de Musique (p83).

---

building and don't have views. To get here, take the Namur–Dinant road to the hamlet of Rivière (14km from Namur), where there's a signposted turn-off to the right. From here it's a steep climb.

DINANT

pop 12,700

Pressed between rock and river, Dinant is one of the Ardennes' tourist hot spots. About 28km south of Namur, its bulbous church competes for attention with the cliff-front citadel, while below, a hive of boat operators vie for the Meuse River day-trippers or the Lesse Valley kayakers. In summer the main thoroughfares through town are choked with traffic and the place feels hot and claustrophobic. That, combined with few accommodation options, makes it good for a pit stop, but there are better places deeper in the Ardennes to really kick back.

Historically, Dinant was a major centre for *dinanderie* (copper work), a trade that flourished between the 12th and 15th centuries but shrivelled as mining and textile industries took over.

The **tourist office** (☎ 082 22 28 70; www.dinant.be; Ave Cadoux 8; ⏰ 8.30am-7pm Mon-Fri, 9.30am-7pm Sat, 10am-6pm Sun) is in a whitewashed riverfront building on the opposite side of the river from the cathedral.

Sights & Activities

You don't need to visit Dinant to see its Gothic **Église Notre Dame** (Pl Reine Astrid; admission free; ⏰ 10am-6pm). The onion-topped church must have made the cover of every brochure ever published on the town, but there's actually little to see inside.

The lofty **citadel** (☎ 082 22 36 70; www.citadelle dedinant.be; Le Prieuré 25; adult/child €6.50/4; ⏰ 10am-6pm Apr-Oct, 10am-4pm Sat-Thu Nov-Mar) can be accessed either by 408 steps that were cut centuries ago and lead up from next to the church, or by the neighbouring *téléférique*, a cable car that's been operating for over 50 years. The citadel affords worthy views over the town and the Meuse, though there's little of interest within its sturdy walls aside from a staid museum. Built around 1818 by the Dutch, the citadel was taken by the Germans in WWI; subsequently, nearly 700 townsfolk were killed and much of the town was razed.

Dinant was the birthplace of two well-known Belgians – painter Antoine Wiertz, who lived most of his life in Brussels (where a museum is devoted to his unusual works – see p86) – and Adolphe Sax (above). If you're into jazz memorabilia, wander along Ave Adolphe Sax to No 35, where a **stone plaque** and a little **stained-glass window** commemorate the instrument's inventor. A bit further along the same street is a big sax **statue**.

Belgium's older set loves Dinant for its sedate **boat cruises** down the Meuse. Several companies offer excursions, all departing from Quai de Meuse, on the southern side of the bridge over the river. Voyages include a 45-minute return trip to the town of **Anseremme** (adult/child €5/4; ⏰ every 30min 10am-6.30pm April-Oct) or a 1¾-hour return voyage a bit further upriver to **Freyr** (adult/child €9/7.50; ⏰ 2.30pm May–mid-Sep).

Kids and young families come to Dinant to get wet. The Lesse River is the **kayaking** focus, and several companies have trips departing in the morning from Anseremme. A bus takes you upstream to one of two destinations from where you paddle back to Anseremme. From Houyet it's 22km and takes about five hours; from Gendron it's 12km and can be done in about three hours. You'll be looking at about €17 for single kayaks or €20 for a two-seater for either trip. Be warned, this is one of Belgium's most popular kayaking runs, and on weekends in summer the river is littered with craft and people. For more details contact **Ansiaux** (☎ 082 21 35 35; Rue du Vélodrome 15, Anseremme).

Cycling around this area offers contrasting terrains – either you're cruising along dead-flat riverside bike paths or climbing strenuous hills on small narrow roads shared with cars. Mountain bikes can be hired from **Ansiaux** (☎ 082 21 35 35; Rue du Vélodrome 15, Anseremme; per half-/full day €14/20); normal bikes are available from Dinant train station (€9.50 per day). If you're really into pushing uphill and then coasting down, ride to Brasserie/Hôtel Les 7 Meuses (p235).

Sleeping & Eating

Au Fil de l'Eau (☎ 082 22 76 06; Ave Colonel Cadoux 88; s/d €40/48, child extra €10) Little B&B well located out of the tourist hype and with a privileged view back to town. The squat, whitewashed riverfront building, about 400m from the town's main bridge, has just one homey room full of kitsch. The breakfast compensates. Exiting the train station, turn left, head straight down to the river, and follow the road to the left.

Hôtel Ibis (☎ 082 21 15 00; www.ibishotel.com; Rempart d'Albeu 16; r Sun-Thu €70, Fri & Sat €75, with river view extra €5, breakfast €9; ✖ ⬚ ▢) The only hotel in town, this trim and modern three-storey riverside hotel is shaped like a boat. It's next to the casino, and is 1.2km from the train station – to get here, cross the bridge into town, turn right, and follow the river.

For nearby countryside retreats, see La Ferme des Belles Gourmandes (p238) and Brasserie/Hôtel les 7 Meuses (p235).

Pâtisserie Jacobs (☎ 082 22 21 39; Rue Grande 147; 8am-8pm) For coffee and a *couque* (biscuit), go directly to this pâtisserie/café. Dinant is known throughout Belgium for its *couque de Dinant*, biscuits made in huge wooden moulds of assorted shapes – from kids peeing on chamber pots, to elephants. Unlike Belgium's better-known *speculaas* (cinnamon-flavoured biscuits), Dinant biscuits don't contain sugar – they're honey-based. This

bakery, established in 1860, is worth a look just for the window display.

La Broche (☎ 082 22 82 81; Rue Grande 24; mains €16-22; lunch Thu-Mon, dinner daily) Down the far end of the main drag, this French restaurant is a firm favourite with locals. The décor's an unfussy modern blend of blacks and creams and the prices won't strip your wallet.

Le Jardin de Fiorine (☎ 082 22 74 74; Rue Georges Cousot 3; mains €23-30, multicourse menus from €30; lunch & dinner, closed Wed & dinner Sun) One of the area's best-known gastronomic restaurants, located on the edge of town near Hôtel Ibis. It occupies a century-old riverside mansion, and does classic Belgian cuisine with a modern dash.

Getting There & Away

Dinant's train and bus station is about 300m from the centre of town – turn right when you leave the station and follow the road around to the river. There are hourly trains from Namur to Dinant (€3.90, 30 minutes). Bus 433 (50 minutes, every two hours) also connects the two towns and departs from next to the train station. For bike rental, see left.

AROUND DINANT

Exploring the Lesse River by kayak is one of the most popular excursions from Dinant – see opposite.

However, if you really want to get off the beaten track, head to **Parc et Réserve Naturelle de Furfooz** (☎ 082 22 34 77; www.parcdefurfooz.be in Flemish & French; Rue du Camp Romain, Furfooz; adult/child €2.50/1; 9.30am-6pm Jun-Aug, 10am-5pm Apr, May, Sep & Oct, 10am-4pm Sat & Sun Mar), about 8km upstream from Dinant on a knoll that juts out into the Lesse River. Sprinkled around the forested limestone hillside is a handful of old Roman sites, including a reconstructed bath and the remains of a medieval fortress, as well as caves, *trous* (deep water holes) and cliffs. A 4km marked walking trail winds around most of the sites.

To get here, take the Houyet-bound train from Dinant and get off at the Gendron stop (10 minutes, every two hours) from where it's a 1km walk along the GR126 trail to the park's southern entrance. With a car, go south from Dinant to Anseremme, take the Celles/Houyet turn-off and follow it until just before Celles, where you'll see the signpost for Furfooz. Follow the Furfooz signs for another few kilometres until the road abruptly ends at the park's other entrance.

La Ferme des Belles Gourmandes (☎ 082 22 55 25; www.lafermedesbellesgourmandes.com in French; Rue du Camp Romain 20, Furfooz; s/d €50/55) is a lovely well-priced country retreat about 8km from Dinant. A converted dairy farm, this grey-stone hotel/ restaurant radiates rural tranquillity, and the owners speak English. The rooms are simply furnished and homey.

ROCHEFORT

pop 11,900

As a base in this part of the Ardennes, Roche-fort's hard to beat. Together with its neighbour Han-sur-Lesse, Rochefort is famed for the millennia-old underground limestone grot-toes that attract visitors from all over Belgium. The caves at Han are the more spectacular of the two but that village is a tourist trap. Ide-ally, base yourself in Rochefort and, if you're without a car, bus it to the Han caves.

Rochefort is also well known for the Trap-pist beer brewed by local monks, and there's no shortage of watering holes at which you can sample these brews.

The town is slung along a low hill with the Lomme River passing almost unnoticed in a val-ley below the long main street, Rue de Behogne. The **tourist office** (☎ 084 34 51 72; www.valdelesse.be; Rue de Behogne 5; ⌚ 8am-6pm Mon-Fri, 9.30am-5pm Sat & Sun Jul & Aug, 8am-5pm Mon-Fri, 10am-5pm Sat & Sun Sep-Jun) is in the centre of town and can provide access to the internet (€2 per hour). The **Fortis Banque** (☎ 084 37 03 70; Rue de Behogne 9; ⌚ 8am-5pm Mon-Fri, 9.30am-5pm Sat), next to the tourist office, has an ATM.

Sights & Activities

The premier sight is the **Grotte de Lorette** (☎ 084 21 20 80; Drève de Lorette; adult/child €7.25/4.70; ⌚ 10.30am-4.30pm Mar-Oct), about 600m south of Pl Albert Ier, the town's nominal heart. It was discovered in 1865 and basically comprises one enormous cave, the Salle du Sabbat. The cave's custodians use tricks of the trade to give a sense of its enormous proportions – a sound-and-light show and miniature hot-air balloon are part of the fun. Tours take just over an hour, and run roughly every 60 to 90 minutes, depending on the season. If you plan to visit the Grottes de Han as well, invest in a combination ticket (adult/child €16.50/10.80).

Rochefort takes its name from the Latin *Rocha fortis*. It refers to a rocky outcrop to the south of town that has been partly obscured by buildings in recent times but has been forti-fied since the 12th century, possibly earlier.

On top of it stands the ruins of the **Château Comtal** (☎ 084 21 44 09; Rue Jacquet; adult/child €1.80/1.50; ⌚ 10am-6pm Apr-Oct), a castle built by an 18th-century local count and incorporating some of the earlier fortifications.

Rochefort's Trappist beer is brewed at the **Abbaye de St Rémy**, a Cistercian monastery a couple of kilometres due north of town. The complex is not open to the public, but visitors can enter a small church inside the grounds, and the signposted walk from town to the abbey is decidedly pleasant. For more on Rochefort beer, see p48.

The area is a great base for **walking** and **cy-cling**. The tourist office sells a regional IGN map entitled *Rochefort et ses Villages* (scale: 1:25,000; €7.50), which covers numerous walking trails – all signposted with coloured markers – as well as mountain- and city-bike routes. Seven of the walks originate on the square just outside the tourist office. The 9km walk, **Belvédère de Han-sur-Lesse**, is marked by a green diamond and takes you south to a plateau from where there are magnificent views. For something shorter and less strenuous, the 5km trail, en-titled **Abbaye** (marked with a red rectangle), is a countryside hike to Abbaye de St Rémy and back. The 5km **Rond du Roi** (red diamond) in-volves walking up to the chateau and then mak-ing a steep climb to the wooded plateau above, from where there's a valley panorama.

Cyclists also have plenty of choice, but one highly recommended trail is **RAVel** (www.ravel.wal lonie.be), an 18km-long stretch of disused rail-way line linking Rochefort and Houyet. It's one of Wallonia's four RAVel paths (see boxed text, p301). For those with kids, this path is a boon – there's no traffic danger, it's flat and cemented, and it's wide enough for two bikes to cycle comfortably alongside each other. Count on the round trip taking two to three hours, longer with children or if you stop off for a drink en route (try Le Clé des Champs at Wanlin). The path starts at Rochefort's former railway station, a whitewashed build-ing at the end of Ave de Forest, which has been converted into the local library. **Cycle Sport** (☎ 084 21 32 55; Rue de Behogne 59; rental per morning/ afternoon/full day €10/15/20; ⌚ 9.30am-noon & 1.30-6.30pm Tue-Sat, 9.30am-noon Sun), about 400m downhill from the tourist office, hires out adult bikes, kids' bikes and toddler seats. The tourist office sells a map entitled RAVel (€1).

Parc des Roches (☎ 084 22 12 32; Rue de la Passerelle) has two open-air swimming pools, minigolf and a free playground. It's easily accessed via the path leading down from the square in front of the tourist office.

Sleeping & Eating

Hôtel Le Vieux Logis (☎ 084 21 10 24; www.levieuxlogis.be; Rue Jacquet 71; s/d/tr/f €59/72/92/112) A two-star hotel located near the ruined chateau, roughly 1km from the tourist office. This rustic old place has been around for over three centuries, as is evidenced by the creaky staircase. The 10 rooms – all decorated with old-style furnishings – are modest but comfortable. Some have private bathroom facilities; some have low doorways that command a bow upon entering; some are a bit over the top (pink bathrooms went out in the '70s). A baby cot is available.

La Fayette (☎ 084 21 42 73; www.hotellafayette.be in French; Rue Jacquet 87; s/d/tr/f with bathroom €45/50/65/75, without bathroom €40/45/60/70, breakfast €5, mains €12-25) Yet to emerge from the '70s, this little whitewashed hotel overlooking the chateau has corridors plastered with pink or yellow wallpaper, floors covered in orange lino, and retro rooms. The reception area and adjoining restaurant are posher, but only just.

Hôtel La Malle Poste (☎ 084 21 09 86; www.malleposte.be; Rue de Behogne 46) This survivor from days long past was the town's original stagecoach house. Choose from three different sections: the cute and cosy Maison du Cocher (single/double €60/85), with small beds, whitewashed walls and floral décor; the brand-new Les Thermes (single/double from €75/100) with fabulously large rooms, all with Jacuzzis and stylish understated furnishings; or a room in the original mansion La Malle Poste (single/double €120/150). The hotel's restaurant, La Calèche (mains €16 to €25, open lunch Friday to Wednesday, and for dinner Friday to Tuesday), serves French cuisine.

Couleur Basilic (☎ 084 46 85 36; Sq Crépin 4; mains €18; ☽ lunch & dinner Thu-Mon) Simple but vibrant little restaurant on a quiet tree-lined square one block behind the main street (direction Han-sur-Lesse). It's the best place to get away from weekend crowds, and the French cuisine, spiced with international flavours, is superb. In fine weather the owners set up tables near the bandstand on the square.

Other recommendations:

Camping Communal (☎ 084 21 19 00; Rue du Hableau; camp sites per adult/car/tent €2/3/3; ☽ Easter-Oct) Next to the Lomme River immediately below the main part of town.

Le Vieux Moulin (☎ 084 21 46 04; www.giterochefort .be; Rue du Hableau 25; demi pension under 25yr/over 26yr €18.50/21.25; ☽ year-round) Pleasant *gîte d'étape* (dorm-style) hostel.

Bella Italia (☎ 084 22 15 20; Rue de Behogne 50; pizza & pasta €6.50-12.50) Piping-hot, wood-oven-baked pizzas are the house speciality.

La Gourmandise (☎ 084 21 09 86; Rue de Behogne 24; mains €9-21) Stop in for a Rochefort beer or stay for dinner – local cuisine, such as chicken in Trappist sauce, is served.

Eurospar (Pl du Baty) Supermarket at the northern end of town.

Getting There & Away

Rochefort is linked to the train station of Jemelle. To get here from Namur, take the Luxembourg-bound train to Jemelle (€7.40, 40 minutes, hourly) and from there the hourly bus 29 to Rochefort (€1.20, seven minutes), which continues to Han (€1.50, seven minutes).

AROUND ROCHEFORT
Han-sur-Lesse

This village lives largely off tourism generated by a marvellous underground gallery of limestone caves. Start a visit at the **Domaine des Grottes de Han** (☎ 084 37 72 13; Rue Lamotte 2; ☽ 10am-noon & 1.30-4.30pm Apr-Oct, 11.30am-4pm Nov, Dec, Feb & Mar). This is the information and ticket office for the main attractions – the *grottes* (caves), a nearby animal park and the new Speleogame. Investigate the various combination tickets.

The **Grottes de Han** (☎ 084 37 72 13; www.grotte-de -han.be; Rue Lamotte 2; adult/child €12/7 incl Speleogame; ☽ 10am-noon & 1.30-5.30pm Apr-Oct, 11.30am-4pm Nov, Dec & Mar) are situated a little out of town – a toy train takes you to the entrance from where you walk underground for 2km to the Lesse River. Here, a barge quickly brings you to the exit. The whole excursion takes about 90 minutes. The caves were discovered in the 19th century and tourists have been coming here ever since. Early visitors used fire lamps to explore the many galleries and, as a result, some of the roofs and walls are discoloured. Stalactites and stalagmites are abundant – the oldest stretches for 7m. The Salle du Dôme is the biggest gallery – rising for 20m and impressively dark and dank. As you'd expect, the caves are cold throughout the year – come prepared.

The **Réserve Animalier** (adult/child €8.75/5.25) covers 250 hectares (a sizable park by Belgian standards) and is stacked with deer, wild boar, wild ox, bison, ibex, chamois and donkeys. Green safari trucks loaded with grandparents,

parents and schoolkids drive around for 1¼ hours in search of the critters.

The **Speleogame** (☎ 084 37 82 31; Rue des Grottes 46; adult/child €8.75/5.25; ⊙ noon-6pm) is generally visited on the walk back to town after visiting the caves, and admission is included in the ticket for the caves. It's basically a big-screen computer game.

Han's only other sight is the **Musée du Monde Souterrain** (☎ 084 37 70 07; Pl Théo Lannoy 3; adult/child €3.50/2.50; ⊙ 10am-5pm Apr-Nov), on the square behind the church. The caves' geological formation is explained here, and a few Neolithic relics found locally are displayed.

Han is linked to Rochefort (6km away) and the train stations of Jemelle and Houyet by bus. To get to Han from Namur, take the Luxembourg-bound train to Jemelle (€7.40, 40 minutes, hourly) and then the bus 29 (via Rochefort) to Han (€1.50, 14 minutes, hourly).

Domaine de Chevetogne

Families with a car may want to explore this 550-hectare public **park** (☎ 083 68 88 21; www .province.namur.be/sections/culture/loisirs/; Chevetogne; adult/child under 6yr €5/free Easter-Oct, free for everyone rest of year) located 8km northwest of Rochefort at Chevetogne. It boasts free open-air activities – swimming pools and 10 playgrounds – plus boating, woodland walks, a unicorn garden, restaurants and cafés.

REDU
pop 700

Years ago, if you asked most Belgians to pinpoint the village of Redu, they would have floundered. But in 1984 this little village in Luxembourg province was saved from eternal insignificance by Noel Anselot, an antiquarian bookseller who set up Redu as continental Europe's first book village. It followed in the footsteps of Hay-on-Wye, a dying Welsh town that metamorphosed into a thriving centre for secondhand books in the '60s.

These days this village, on a gently sloping hillside about 18km south of Han-sur-Lesse, attracts 200,000 book-lovers a year. The two biggest events are Easter's **Fête du Livre** and, even more popular, August's one-night festival **La Nuit du Livre**, when bookshops and eateries stay open until dawn and fireworks illuminate the midnight sky.

There's nothing as such to see – people come here to spend a lazy summer weekend trawling bookshops and, for the more energetic, walking

to the Lesse River and nearby villages. Although some of the bookshops are open weekdays, many aren't. The **Maison du Tourisme** (☎ 061 65 65 16; www.redu.info.be; Pl de l'Esro 63; ⊙ 9am-6pm Apr-Oct, 9.30am-4.30pm Nov-Mar), next to the church, hands out a free town map that gives a rundown (in French) of each bookshop.

The best selection of English books is kept by **De Eglantier & Crazy Castle** (☎ 061 65 66 15; Rue de Transinne 34; ⊙ 11am-6pm Jul & Aug, Sat & Sun Sep-Jun).

La Gourmandine (☎ 061 65 63 90; Rue de St Hubert 16; s/d with bathroom €40/60, without bathroom €30/45; ⊙ daily Jul & Aug, Sat-Mon Sep-Jun), directly behind the church, is the most atmospheric option for eating and sleeping. The rooms are spacious and well kept.

Le Fournil (☎ 061 65 56 32; www.le-fournil.be; Pl de l'Esro 58; s/d without bathroom €25/50, mains €14-17), adjacent to the church, is the next best option, with a large terrace and run-of-the-mill rooms.

To get to Redu from Namur, take the Luxembourg-bound train to Libramont (€9.60, one hour, hourly) then bus 61 (€2.10, 1¼ hours, three daily Monday to Friday), which stops at the church.

AROUND REDU

About 6km east of Redu, right next to the E411 motorway, is the **Euro Space Center** (☎ 061 65 64 65; www.eurospacecenter.be; Rue devant les Hêtres 1, Transinne; adult/child €11/8; ⊙ 10am-5pm Jul & Aug, 10am-4pm Tue-Sun Easter-Jun & Sep–mid-Nov). Dedicated to bringing space travel to the armchair viewer, this centre has a full-sized model of a space shuttle, plus movies and gadgets enjoyed by kids of all ages. Belgian families love this place. From Namur, take the Luxembourg-bound train to Libramont (€9.60, one hour), then bus 61 (€1.80, one hour, three daily Monday to Friday), which stops outside the centre. By car from Namur, head south on the E411 to exit 24 (Transinne).

ST HUBERT
pop 5700

Unless you're into hunting, don't bother with St Hubert. This village, 22km southeast of Rochefort, is named after the patron saint of hunters. According to legend, Hubert, a local 7th-century count, was about to do in a stag when Christ appeared between the creature's antlers imploring him to embrace a religious life. The count gave up his land and worldly goods and took to the forest where he lived as a hermit.

Deer and wild boar still live in the region and the town has remained a favourite hunting haunt – so much so that St Hubert bills itself as the 'European Capital of Hunting & Nature'. On the first weekend in September, red-coated horn blowers announce the start of the **Journées Internationales de la Chasse et de la Nature**, a two-day hunting festival complete with medieval pageantry, a hunting dog show, and an elaborate horn-blowers' concert performed in the town's basilica.

The **Maison du Tourisme** (☎ 061 61 30 10; www.saint-hubert-tourisme.be in French & Flemish; Rue St Gilles 12; ☺ 9am-5.30pm) is 100m from Pl du Marché, the town's main square. It hands out a pamphlet for a two-hour walking tour.

The all-dominant **Basilica St Hubert** (☎ 061 61 23 88; Pl de l'Abbaye; ☺ 9am-6pm, to 5pm Nov-Easter) is the only real sight. A great grey slab of a thing, it's the largest place of worship in this corner of the Ardennes – it's drawn pilgrims since the 9th century, when St Hubert's remains were interned here. It's well worth a look if you're passing through town – the late-Gothic interior is much more beautiful than the austere baroque façade would suggest.

The best place to stay is the new **L'Ancien Hôpital** (☎ 061 41 69 65; www.ancienhopital.be; Rue de la Fontaine 23; d from €80, per extra person €25, ste €130; ☐). Once an old hospital, it now offers six rooms with stylish décor. Expect a gourmet three-course breakfast, a smoking salon, a cosy wine bar, free use of mountain bikes and a garden. Book the Jacuzzi suite, if possible – it occupies the old chapel.

At the foot of the basilica, brasserie/restaurant **Le Basilic** (☎ 061 50 48 58; Pl de l'Abbaye 8; mains €15-21, menu €25; ☺ Tue-Sun) has simple décor and a young chef who creates the town's best food.

Taverne Le Dialogue (☎ 061 32 13 91; Pl du Marché 13; snacks €5-10; ☺ 11am-9pm Tue-Sun; ✗) is a modern café set in the traditional surroundings of an 18th-century cellar.

To get to St Hubert from Namur, take the Luxembourg-bound train to Libramont (€9.60, one hour, hourly) and then local TEC buses 51 or 162b (€1.60, 25 minutes, 10 daily) to St Hubert; they stop at Pl du Marché.

BOUILLON
pop 2200
Bouillon is justifiably one of the Ardennes' premier resort towns. It's an immediately likeable place, occupying a loop in the Semois River, lorded over by one of Europe's most impressive medieval strongholds and surrounded by some of the region's wildest scenery. It's the sort of place where you can just chill out and do nothing…though there's actually plenty to do. Hiking and kayaking to nearby villages, exploring the intriguing castle or enjoying a riverfront terrace are all on the cards.

Information
Maison du Tourisme (☎ 061 46 52 11; www.bouillon-tourisme.be; Quai des Saulx 12; ☺ 10am-6pm, to 5pm winter) Tourist information on the town and the region is available at this office inside the Archéoscope (p242).
Syndicat d'Initiative (☎ 061 46 62 57; www.bouillon-sedan.com; Esplanade Godefroid de Bouillon; ☺ 9.30am-7pm Jul & Aug, 10am-6pm Apr-Jun & Sep, 1-5pm Mon-Fri, 10am-5pm Sat & Sun Dec-Feb, 10am-5pm Mar, Oct & Nov) Tourist office at the castle entrance.

Sights & Activities
A **combination ticket** (adult/child/student €13/8.80/11.30) – valid for the castle, the Musée Ducal and the Archéoscope – is available from either tourist office.

Slouching like a great grey dragon on the rocky ridge above town, the **Château de Bouillon** (☎ 061 46 62 57; Rue du Château; adult/child €5.20/3.50; ☺ 10am-6.30pm Jul & Aug, 10am-6pm Apr-Jun & Sep, 1-5pm Mon-Fri, 10am-5pm Sat & Sun Dec-Feb, 10am-5pm Mar, Oct & Nov) is Belgium's finest feudal castle. It commands views over the huddle of houses below and sits rock solid as the town's focal point. Flanked on both sides by the Semois River, a fortress has existed here since about the 8th century, but this castle harks back to 988 and the days of Godefroid de Bouillon (see boxed text, p242). It was expanded in the 15th century, and 200 years later France's military engineer, Vauban, was charged with bringing it up to scratch.

Although much of what exists today dates from Vauban's time, it's still everything you could wish for in a castle – dark, sordid and musty with poorly lit corridors and rough-hewn stairwells winding up and down and around towers, past battlements and through dungeons. Take a **torchlit tour** (€5.20 plus €2 for a mandatory torch; ☺ 10pm Wed & Fri-Sun Jul & Aug) to really give yourself the heebie-jeebies. Access to the castle by car is via Rue du Château; by foot there are steps leading up from both Rue du Moulin and Blvd Heynen (next to the tennis court near Pont de la Poulie).

In the summer months, the castle is home to a small contingent of birds of prey (eagles, hawks, falcons and African vultures), the pets

THE ARDENNES

GODEFROID DE BOUILLON

At the heart of Brussels' busy Pl Royale stands a statue of Godefroid de Bouillon. This 11th-century crusader is seen as one of Belgium's ancient heroes, though the actions of his army would receive few medals today.

Godefroid – or Godfrey in English – was born in 1060 and was the last of the five dukes of Bouillon who lorded over the town from their mighty castle. In 1096 Godefroid sold the ducal castle to the prince-bishop of Liège and, with that money, led one of three Crusader armies across Europe to the Holy Land, which they hoped to recapture from the Muslims. Along the way Godefroid's army of 60,000 seriously degenerated in both number and ethics – his supposedly Christian army slaughtered thousands of Jews in towns across Germany soon after setting off.

It took three years to reach Jerusalem. Godefroid's soldiers breached the city walls on 15 July 1099 and proceeded to massacre an estimated 40,000 Muslims and Jews. According to a contemporary account, six months after the orgy of slaughter the streets still reeked of rotting bodies.

Godefroid declined the title of 'King of Jerusalem' and settled instead for 'Defender of the Holy Sepulchre'. He died a year later in Jaffa, north of Jerusalem.

---

of a local falconer. He organises half-hour feeding shows, known as **Spectacle de Fauconnerie** (11.30am, 2pm & 3.30pm Easter–Jun, plus 5pm Jul & Aug), at a small amphitheatre inside the castle.

Still up on the ridge, but outside the castle walls, is the **Musée Ducal** (061 46 41 89; www .museeducal.be; Rue du Petit 1; adult/child €4/2.50; 10am-6pm Easter-Sep, 10am-5pm Oct–mid-Nov). This museum is spread over two adjoining buildings and contains displays based on Godefroid's life and the Crusade; period rooms highlighting the local metallurgy industry; a room devoted to local artist Albert Raty (1889–1970) and some mean medieval weapons.

Archéoscope Godefroid de Bouillon (061 46 83 03; Quai des Saulx 14; adult/child €6/4.50; 1-4pm Tue-Fri & 10am-4pm Sat & Sun Dec-Feb, 10am-4pm Mar, Apr & Sep, 10am-5pm May-Aug, 10am-4pm Tue-Sun Oct & Nov) is Bouillon's flashiest attraction, located in a renovated 17th-century convent. The film and associated bits and pieces are designed to bring Godefroid's story to life for 21st-century folk. It's multilingual, and kids usually enjoy the sound and lighting effects.

Kayaking on the Semois is organised by **Semois Kayaks** (0475 24 74 23; Rue de Libehan 6; Easter–Sep). Choose from a three-hour trip (Bouillon to Poupehan, one-/two-seater kayak €17/30, 15km) or a one-hour jaunt (Poupehan to Frahan-sur-Semois, €12/18, 5km). Both trips are relaxed and peaceful, and there are far fewer traffic jams on the Semois than on journeys down the Lesse near Dinant. On the whole, the Semois is a gently flowing but wonderfully winding river that meanders through umpteen S-bends before it joins the Meuse across the border in France.

If you're into combining kayaking and **hiking**, you could kayak to Poupehan and then follow one of the paths that circle around Poupehan before returning to Bouillon on a kayaking bus, or alternatively kayak to Poupehan and then walk back to Bouillon via the village of Corbion. For the latter you'll need to pick up the *Cartes des Promenades du Grand Bouillon* walking map (scale 1:25,000, €7) from the tourist office before setting off. This map also details other walks through the oak and beech forests – Belgium's most extensive – that surround Bouillon.

For **cycling**, see opposite.

On warm summer days, a great spot for **swimming** and cooling off with the kids is the stony beach on the bank of the Semois at Pont de la Poulie. It's on the western side of the castle – to get here from the town centre, head up Rue du Nord and then down Rue de la Poulie, or take the centuries-old walking track that leads down from the castle car park.

Sleeping & Eating

Auberge de Jeunesse (061 46 81 37; www.laj.be; Route du Christ 16; dm/s/d €14.50/29/42; closed Nov–mid-Jan) A hostel perched on the ridge opposite the castle and with views over the whole town. Arriving by bus, turn left out of the bus station, follow Rue des Champs to the T-junction, turn right and you'll wind into Rte du Christ. From the town centre, take the short cut via the stairs that lead up from near Pl St Arnould.

B&B Baugard (061 46 78 91; www.chez.com/mbaugard; Rue des Hautes Voies 23a; s/d €35/50) The pick of the town's *chambres d'hôtes* (B&Bs). This place has a superb castle view, especially from the formal dining room, where breakfast is taken. The owner is very friendly and the shared bathroom facilities are well kept. Close to the bus station.

B&B Belle Vue (☎ 061 32 17 71; www.belle-vue.info; Au dessus de la Ville 4; s/d €45/55). Another good place – it's even higher than B&B Baugard, and has lovely rooms and a terrace with a view.

Hôtel Panorama (☎ 061 46 61 38; www.panoramahotel be; Rue au Dessus de la Ville 23; s/d €60/75, mains €21, 3-course menus €28-42; ✗) High above town with forest on one side and the castle on the other. The room décor is modern and warm, there's a great terrace for a drink in summer, there's also a cosy salon, and the hotel is child-friendly.

Hostellerie La Pommeraie (☎ 061 46 90 17; www.hotel pommeraie.com; Rue de la Poste 2; s/d demi-pension May–mid-Sep from €120/160, s/d mid-Sep-Apr from €90/110, mains €20-30) The town's most exclusive hotel/restaurant. A charming ivy-clad mansion with just 10 rooms, all with different furnishings, all individually named after herbs, and some with four-poster beds. The view of the castle is not bad, and on summer evenings you can dine on French cuisine on an old stone terrace with the flood-lit chateau in the background. Superb.

La Vieille Ardenne (☎ 061 46 62 77; Grand Rue 9; mains €14-24; ✗ lunch & dinner, closed Wed Sep-Jun) One of the few pubs/restaurants in town that's not attached to a hotel. It's a friendly old establishment, one block back from the river, that caters mainly for meat-eaters with hearty appetites – the seasonal menu is noted for *gibier* (game) in October and November. Decked out with heavy, typically Ardennes décor, it has a great atmosphere for sampling a local beer such as Cuvée de Bouillon or Godefroy.

Roy de la Moule (☎ 061 46 62 49; Quai du Rempart 42; mussels €12.50-17; ✗ lunch & dinner) Region's best mussel restaurant, with a choice of 32 different varieties – from the traditional white wine to mussels cooked in Trappist beer. Casual and kid friendly, and absolutely chockers on weekends in summer.

Other recommendations:

Camping Halliru (☎ 061 46 60 09; Rte de Corbion 1; camp sites per adult/child/site €3/1.50/4.50; ✗ closed Oct-Mar) One kilometre south of town along the river.

Route66 Burger (Quai du Rempart 21; snacks €4-9) Frites and burgers are the go at this popular snack bar.

Colruyt (Rue du Collège) Supermarket near the Archéoscope.

Getting There & Away
From Namur, take the Luxembourg-bound train to Libramont (€9.60, one hour, hourly),

then bus 8 (50 minutes, six services per day). Buses stop at both Quai du Rempart near Pont de Liège and at the **TEC bus station** (☎ 081 25 35 55) at the southern end of town above Pont de France.

AROUND BOUILLON
The ultracute village of **Frahan-sur-Semois**, 16km northwest of Bouillon, sits in one of the many loops formed by the Semois as it makes its way downriver. It's surrounded by lush green pastures, hedges and forests, and is dotted with whitewashed, grey-tiled-roofed houses and several hotels, all booked way in advance in summer. There are no shops or other facilities and there's absolutely nothing to do but look at the river, eat way too much, walk it off along lovely forested tracks…and then start the whole process over again. One great walk is up to **Rochehaut**, a village high on the plateau overlooking Frahan, where you can get a drink or go **cycling** – mountain bikes can be hired from **Free Time** (☎ 061 46 86 20; Rue Le Routi 22, Rochehaut).

Aux Roches Fleuries (☎ 061 46 65 14; www.auxroches fleuries.be; Rue des Crêtes 32, Frahan; s/d €80/85, menus €20-56; ✗ closed Jan & Mar) is the nicest hotel/restaurant in Frahan. This family-run establishment has a great view down to the river, and the rooms are stylish with individual balconies. Kids are welcome.

Auberge de la Ferme (☎ 061 46 10 00; www.auberge delaferme.be; Rue de la Cense 12, Rochehaut; s/d from €45/85, menus €30-60; ✗ closed Jan) up in Rochehaut has pleasant rooms, some with four-poster beds, as well as a popular tavern and terrace. It also welcomes children.

Public transport from Bouillon to either Frahan (€1.60, 20 minutes) or Rochehaut (€1.80, 35 minutes) is almost zilch – there's just one bus per day (No 45, direction Bertrix), which leaves Bouillon at around 6.30am.

ORVAL
The **Abbaye Notre Dame d'Orval** (☎ 061 31 10 60; www.orval.be; adult/child €4.50/2.50; ✗ 9.30am-6.30pm Jun-Sep, 9.30am-6pm Mar-May & Oct, 10.30am-5.30pm Nov-Feb) lies enclosed by verdant forests 30km southeast of Bouillon on the N88 (heading to Virton). From legendary beginnings, this monastery has grown into a composed complex of mustard-toned buildings that is home to some two dozen Cistercian monks and successful beer-, bread- and cheese-making industries. In international circles, Orval is

best associated with its Trappist brew (p48), but its story is richer than just beer.

The monastery was founded by Italian monks in 1070 and became Cistercian in 1132. In the 11th century the Countess Mathilda of Tuscany accidentally dropped her wedding ring, a present from her dead husband, into a stream here. In despair, she prayed to the Virgin and her ring was returned in the mouth of a fish. Centuries later, a trout carrying a golden ring has become Orval monastery's distinctive logo. The present buildings date from the mid-1920s, when the monastery was totally rebuilt – it had been ransacked and destroyed during the French Revolution, and subsequently abandoned.

Only the ruins of the original 12th-century abbey and a small museum located in an 18th-century cellar are open to visitors. Clear waters still bubble forth from a well hidden among the ruins, and there's a medicinal herb garden and a 300-year-old oak tree. The whole place has an evocative air of centuries long gone and is well worth a visit (providing you have your own wheels; otherwise, it's hard to reach). The brewery is closed to visitors, but samples of the monastery's produce – including young and old cheese, organic wholemeal bread called Miche d'Orval and the famous amber beer – can be bought at the reception shop.

The monastery has its own **guesthouse** (☎ 061 32 51 10; hotellerie@orval.be; r €30) where those interested in learning about monastic life can stay (for two to seven nights).

Alternatively, there's **La Nouvelle Hostellerie d'Orval** (☎ 061 31 43 65; fax 061 32 00 92; Villers-devant-Orval; s/d €38/50, half-pension €55/85, menus €18-30; ☒ closed Dec-Feb). This hotel/restaurant marks a road junction 400m from the abbey and has five basic but clean rooms.

Getting to Orval by public transport is difficult. Bus 24 (€1.50, 10 minutes, one to two daily) runs to Orval from the nearest town, Florenville, 8km northwest.

ARLON
pop 25,800

Down in the deep south, Arlon (known as Aarlen in Flemish) is just kilometres from the border with the Grand Duchy of Luxembourg and is the largest town in Belgium's Luxembourg province. It's an old place, first settled as a Roman trading post, and bits from this time can be seen at the town's only sight, the **Musée Archéologique** (☎ 063 22 61 92; www.ial.be;

Rue des Martyrs 13; adult/child €6/4; ☒ 10am-noon & 1.30-5.50pm Tue-Sat, plus Sun mid-Apr–mid-Sep).

The **Maison du Tourisme** (☎ 063 21 94 54; www.arlon-tourisme.be; Rue des Faubourgs 2; ☒ 8.30am-5pm Mon-Fri, 9am-4pm Sat) is just off the main square, Pl Léopold.

Arlon's train and bus stations are a 10-minute walk south of Pl Léopold. Arlon is a major stop on the railway line between Brussels (€17.70, 2½ hours, hourly) and Luxembourg (€8.60, 20 minutes, hourly). Bus 3 runs to Martelange, from where bus 2 heads to Bastogne.

BASTOGNE
pop 14,100

It was in Bastogne, close to the Luxembourg border, that thousands of soldiers and civilians died during WWII's Battle of the Bulge (see opposite). Today this little town is full of wartime reminders, and the main square – a car park adorned with a tank – has even been renamed Pl McAuliffe after the famous American general whose reply to the German call to surrender was 'Nuts!'. On this square you'll find the **Maison du Tourisme** (☎ 061 21 27 11; www.paysdebastogne.be; Pl McAuliffe; ☒ 9am-6pm mid-Jun–mid-Sep, 9.30am-12.30pm & 1-5.30pm mid-Sep–mid-Jun).

Sights

Bastogne's main attraction is the huge star-shaped **American Memorial** (Colline du Mardasson), just over 2km northeast of town – follow Rue du Vivier, the town's main shopping thoroughfare, downhill until it joins the road to Wiltz/Clervaux in Luxembourg and then follow signs to 'Mardasson'. The memorial was inaugurated in 1950 and is inscribed with the names of the American states as well as principal moments in the course of the battle. In good weather it's possible to climb to the top for local views. A crypt at the memorial's base contains mosaics by Fernand Léger.

Next to the memorial is the **Bastogne Historical Centre** (☎ 061 21 14 13; Colline du Mardasson; adult/child €8.50/6; ☒ 10am-4.30pm Mar, Apr & Oct-Dec, 9.30am-5pm May, Jun & Sep, 9.30am-6pm Jul & Aug). Here the Battle of the Bulge is recounted with a 30-minute film using actual war footage and period displays – Allied and German uniforms, weaponry and a couple of dioramas depicting the freezing conditions of that winter in '44. If you're into buying war-related kitsch, the souvenir shop is full of it.

BATTLE OF THE BULGE

The Battle of the Bulge, officially known as the Battle of the Ardennes, was one of the most fierce confrontations of WWII. In September 1944, both Belgium and Luxembourg were liberated by American troops after four years of occupation. The Allies' plan to continue pushing the Germans back from bases in the Netherlands and France meant there was little defence of their frontline in the forested section of eastern Belgium and into Luxembourg.

On 15 December, in the depths of winter, Hitler launched a surprise raid – the Von Rundstedt Offensive – through the hills and valleys of northern Luxembourg and into Belgium. It was a desperate attempt to capture the River Meuse and the port city of Antwerp, thereby blocking supplies from reaching the Allies. Hitler's army got within sight of Dinant in Belgium, forming a bulge in the Allied line but failing to break through.

The town of Bastogne was surrounded during the invasion but the American 101st Airborne Division stationed in the town repelled the Germans until Allied reinforcements were able to drive Hitler's forces back through Luxembourg into Germany. The battle was over by the end of January 1945, at the cost of nearly 80,000 Americans, 100,000 Germans and many Belgian and Luxembourg civilians.

Many towns in the Belgian Ardennes and Luxembourg suffered heavily in the course of the battle. Memorials to this tragic Christmas are numerous, and include those in Bastogne as well as Luxembourg City's military cemeteries (see p274) and poignant museums in Diekirch (p289), Ettelbrück (p288) and La Roche-en-Ardenne (p246).

Sleeping & Eating

Hôtel Le Caprice (☎ 061 21 81 40; www.horest.be; Pl McAuliffe 25; s/d/tr €55/70/95) Pick of the crop if you're travelling with kids – under-eights stay for free. Handy location and saccharine-sweet pink rooms.

Hôtel Collin (☎ 061 21 43 58; www.hotel-collin.com; Pl McAuliffe 8; s/d/tr €67/85/105) Bastogne's most expensive hotel, with modern rooms fitted out in warm, rustic tones. Baby cots are available (€15).

Restaurant Léo (☎ 061 21 14 41; Rue du Vivier 4; mains €12-20; ♥ 11.30am-9.30pm Tue-Sun) Just off Pl McAuliffe, at the head of Bastogne's main shopping street, this restaurant occupies a renovated yellow-and-blue train carriage and is the most popular eatery in town. There's an extensive menu, good service and an excellent *assiette ardennaise* (plate of mixed local charcuterie), featuring 11 types of meat, for €13.50.

Other recommendations:

Camping de Renval (☎ 061 21 29 85; Route de Marché 148; camp sites per adult/child/site €5.50/3/16) About 1km from the tourist office.

Spar (Rue du Vivier 85) Supermarket.

Bistro Léo (☎ 061 21 65 10; Rue du Vivier 6; ♥ 11am-9.45pm Tue-Sun) More casual than the next-door Restaurant Léo.

Drinking

Le Latino's (☎ 0495 18 58 10; Rue Lamborelle 4; ♥ 11am-11pm Tue-Sun Sep-Jun, 4pm-4am Tue-Sun Jul & Aug) Latino's is the town's coolest bar, located on nightlife street Rue Lamborelle, 100m from Pl McAuliffe (head downhill along Rue du Viver and take the first left).

Brasserie Lamborelle (☎ 061 21 80 55; Rue Lamborelle 5; ♥ 11am-1am Tue-Sun) Rustic stone corner building with warm mustard tones and an excellent list of 80 beers.

Getting There & Away

Bastogne's train line was decommissioned years ago. The closest link is now the rail junction of Libramont, from where bus 163b departs every two hours for Bastogne (€3.20, 45 minutes).

LA ROCHE-EN-ARDENNE

pop 4200

La Roche is a lovely and vibrant little town, hidden in a deep valley, crowned by a ruined castle and surrounded by verdant hills. It hugs a bend in the Ourthe River, 30-odd kilometres northwest of Bastogne, and it is one of the Ardennes' most popular summer resorts. Good eateries, a few lively bars, a smattering of history and the possibility of getting seriously active make La Roche one of the best bases you'll find for a varied few days. Needless to say, it's a great family destination and, for those who are into ham, join the queue – this is where Belgian holiday-makers come to buy up big.

Orientation & Information

Arrive from the west or south and the perfect orientation opportunity presents itself: La Roche suddenly appears in the valley below and from this vantage point it's easy to follow the Ourthe's meandering course through town. The main street – Rue de l'Église – and its continuation Rue Châmont crosses the river and ends at Pl du Bronze, the nominal heart of town (though it's little more than a car park).

The town's **tourist office** (☎ 084 36 77 36; www.la-roche-tourisme.com; Pl du Marché 15; internet access per hr €5; ◷ 9am-7.30pm Jul & Aug, 9.30am-5pm Sep-Jun) is on the main street and can provide internet access.

Sights & Activities

From the main street, steps head up to the ruins of La Roche's picture-postcard medieval **castle** (adult/child €3/2; ◷ 10am-7pm Jul & Aug, 10am-noon & 1-5pm Apr-Jun, Sep & Oct, 1-4.30pm Mon-Fri, 10am-noon & 1-4.30pm Sat & Sun Nov-Mar). Perched on the crag above town, there's not actually much to see – a small museum with a few archaeological relics is the focal point. The castle dates from the 11th century and was expanded throughout the next few centuries. Inhabited until 1780, it was then abandoned and fell into ruin. It's a pleasant spot to wander, and watch out for the ghost in summer (July and August).

Grès de la Roche (☎ 084 41 18 78; Rue Rompré 28; adult/child €4.50/3.25; ◷ 10am-noon & 1.30-5pm Apr-Oct, closed Mon Apr-Jun, Sep & Oct, 10am-noon & 1.30-5pm Sat & Sun Nov-Mar) is upstream from Pl du Bronze. It combines two rather odd bedfellows – blue earthenware and ham. La Roche prides itself on its smoked ham, and huge pigs' shoulders adorn butcher's shops dotted along the main street. At this museum you'll find out what all the fuss is about.

Musée de la Bataille des Ardennes (☎ 084 41 17 25; Rue Châmont 5; adult/child €6/3; ◷ 10am-6pm Wed-Sun Apr-Dec) tells of La Roche's involvement in the

---

GETTING INTO ACTION

Walk, ride or paddle off those breakfast croissants…La Roche offers plenty of activities.

There are two **kayaking** possibilities: a bus takes you to either the Barrage de Nisramont, a dam to the southeast near the village of Nadrin, from where you paddle back (€20, four to six hours, 25km); or to the village of Maboge from where it's a two-hour descent (€15, 12km). Alternatively, you can do a kayaking-cycling combo by mountain biking it to Maboge and kayaking back from there (€25, eight hours). The kayaking season is generally from April to mid-October but, in the height of summer, low water levels sometimes prevent kayaking.

Mountain bikes can be hired for €15/22 for a half-/full day (or €25/45 for 24/48 hours). and the tourist office sells a map (€3.80) detailing good VTT (vélos tout-terrains, or mountain bike) routes. These are marked by a triangle above two circles. Kids' bikes are also available (same price as for adult bikes), but you'd be wise to book ahead, as numbers are limited. Bike helmets cost €1.25 extra.

The town's two kayaking/biking operators are **Ardennes-Aventures** (☎ 084 41 19 00; Rue du Hadja 1), next to the bridge at the northern end of town, or **Les Kayaks de l'Ourthe** (☎ 084 36 87 12; Rue de l'Église 35), near the tourist office.

Horse riding is organised by the **Domaine des Olivettes** (☎ 084 41 16 52; www.lesolivettes.be; Chemin de Soeret 12). You must be experienced, and reservations are necessary; prices are €35 for 2½ hours and €75 for one day. Weekend package deals with accommodation and meals at the hotel are also possible.

The hills around La Roche are crisscrossed by lovely **hiking** trails. Most are numbered, and identified with either a red circle or a shoe-shaped marker. The multilingual Carte de Promenades (€5), sold at the tourist office, gives very basic information (in English) on a dozen popular regional hikes ranging from 6km to 13km (or roughly two to four hours).

Hike No 5 (13km) is the longest and is generally considered the most interesting. It begins at Rue Bon Dieu de Maka near Pl du Bronze and climbs sharply to a plateau east of town. From here you cross forests and fields before descending steeply to the hamlet of Maboge, which contains little more than a couple of terrace cafés nicely positioned along the bank of the Ourthe. Cross the river and follow the road northeast for a few hundred metres before veering left (north) along a small tributary of the Ourthe. This leads to a farm at Borzée where path Nos 5 and 12 intersect. Take the left-hand path (west) to head back to La Roche, a generally easy and pleasant wooded walk that ends with a sharp descent before joining the road that leads back to town.

Battle of the Bulge (see p245). Like other Ardennes villages, La Roche fared badly during this time – 90% of its buildings were flattened, and many townsfolk were killed. This museum spans three floors and includes the new Salle des Vétérans where uniforms donated by veterans have been assembled.

The **Petit Train Touristique** (☎ 084 41 19 00; adult/child €5/4; ☾ hourly 10am-6pm Apr-Sep) is a lazy way to look round town (50 minutes), and is usually brimming with kids and elderly visitors. It departs from the church on Rue de l'Église, but tickets must be bought from Ardennes-Aventures (see boxed text, opposite). It only runs in good weather.

The **Parc à Gibier** (Wildlife Park; ☎ 084 41 23 14; Plateau Dester; adult/child €4/2; ☾ 10am-7pm Jul & Aug, 10am-5pm Easter-Jun & Sep–mid-Oct, 10am-5pm Sat & Sun mid-Oct–Easter), about 2km east of town on the Dester plateau, is home to deer, wolves and wild boars. You can access the park via hiking trail No 4, which winds up from La Roche, or take the tourist train (see above).

Sleeping & Eating

Camping Le Vieux Moulin (☎ 084 41 13 80; www.strument.com; Petite Strument 62; camp sites per adult/child/tent €2.50/2.50/8; ☾ Easter-Oct) Draped for what seems an eternity along a stream next to the Hôtel Moulin de la Strument (right). Great site.

Domaine des Olivettes (☎ 084 41 16 52; www.lesolivettes.be; Chemin de Soeret 12; dm €12, s €50-60, d €60-80) This hotel/hostel/equestrian centre (see boxed text, opposite) offers the only cheap place to sleep in town. It's perched on a hill and has two styles of accommodation – the hotel, which has pleasant rooms (some with great views); or the separate hostel, with dormitory-style accommodation (four to 10 beds).

B&B La Fontanella (☎ 084 41 17 73; www.lafontanella.be; Rue Châmont 32; r €55) New B&B located on the main street, with four rooms situated above a restaurant that's run by the same owners. It's modern and functional and feels more like a tiny apartment than a typical B&B. Don't expect much contact with the owners – breakfast is a self-service affair, taken inside your room.

La Maison au Bord de l'Eau (☎ 084 41 10 88; www.bearadu.be; Clérue 54; apt per day/weekend/week €60/150/350) A self-contained holiday apartment run by a friendly couple and fabulously sited in a cosy V-shaped stone house. The apartment flanks the Ourthe River, just 250m from Pl du Bronze – watch kayakers paddle past from the kitchen window, or step out the front door onto a

riverside footpath that leads into town. Inside, the setup is modern but homey, and includes a double bedroom plus a sofa bed for two. Inquire about seasonal discounts.

Hôtel Moulin de la Strument (☎ 084 41 15 07; www.strument.com; Petite Strument 62; s/d €65/75, 1st night per person extra €5; ☾ closed Jan) The town's most charming hotel. It's part of an old mill (that's now a tiny museum) and is nestled in a secluded, wooded valley next to a babbling stream about 800m from Pl du Bronze. The eight rooms are fitted with country-style décor and there's a matching breakfast room. The attached restaurant has been around for years and has a good reputation.

Le Clos René (☎ 084 41 26 17; Rue Châmont 30; snacks €6-10; ☾ 11am-11pm Jul & Aug, 11am-11pm Fri-Wed Sep-Jun) When you can't stand the sight of another smoked ham, this tasteful brasserie/creperie is the perfect escape. Sweet and savoury crepes are the mainstay, but there are also sandwiches, salads and omelettes. Very child-friendly, and with an innovative interior.

Other recommendations:

La Brasserie Ardennaise (☎ 084 41 28 70; Rue du Pont 1; mains €8-30; ☾ 9am-midnight, kitchen closes 10.30pm) Big brasserie with a prized covered terrace slung next to the river. The food and service are OK but it's the location that's the attraction.

Spar (Quai du Gravier 1) Supermarket close to the tourist office.

Getting There & Away

Buses are the only form of public transport that reaches La Roche. The most convenient central stops are at Quai de l'Ourthe and Pl du Bronze.

From Namur, take the train to Marloie (€6.70, 35 minutes, hourly), from where bus

15 goes to La Roche (€1.80, 35 minutes, seven per day).

From Liège, get a train to Melreux (€6.40, one hour, every two hours) and then bus 3 to La Roche (€1.80, 30 minutes, seven per day).

There are no buses linking La Roche with Bastogne or Durbuy.

AROUND LA ROCHE

The **Grottes de Hotton** (Apr-Nov ☎ 084 46 60 46, Dec-Mar ☎ 083 68 83 65; www.grottesdehotton.com; adult/child €8/6; ☺ 10am-5pm Apr-Nov, 2pm Sat & Sun Dec-Mar), near the pleasant village of Hotton, is 17km northwest of La Roche. Discovered in 1958, the caves have been open since the early '60s but it has taken recent listing as a classified monument to spark public interest. Tours lasting 70 minutes and led by enthusiastic guides delve deep into the underground network – the river cavern has no equal in Belgium and is simply breathtaking. If the hype at caves like Han and Rochefort are not your style, visit Hotton instead. The caves are cold throughout the year – come prepared.

To get here from La Roche, take bus 13 (€1.60, 20 minutes, every two hours). It stops at the bridge in the centre of Hotton. The nearby tourist office will be able to advise whether a footpath leading up to the caves from Hotton's park has been completed (it was expected to be finished in late 2006 and will provide a shortcut for hikers). If not, head through town (direction Marche-en-Famenne) until you reach the signposted turn-off; it's about a 2km walk, all up.

DURBUY

pop 10,300

The smallest 'city' in the world…that's Durbuy's claim to fame and the villagers will hear no ifs or buts about it. This picturesque village flanks the Ourthe River, some 30-odd kilometres northwest of La Roche-en-Ardenne, and is little more than a huddle of quaint cobblestone streets and beautifully kept half-timbered, grey-stone buildings (plus a horde of tourist attractions). It has been around since at least the 11th century. when a local count built a castle here. By 1331 the village had a castle, a courthouse and police – all the prerequisites to be called a 'city' – and was granted city status. Nearly 800 years later, it's still celebrating.

Belgians and Japanese love Durbuy. It has everything for a fun-filled day out or a leisurely weekend – delightful hotels and good restaurants and bars. And extras – a topiary garden, a pint-sized brewery, stuffed *sanglier* (wild boars),

a jam-making shop, an ice-skating rink (in winter), a castle (not open to visitors) and heaps of summer activities from cycling to kayaking to hiking. All this in such a compact area means the village becomes one big amusement park on crowded weekends in summer. At other times it turns back into a pumpkin and becomes the picturesque little village that it always was.

The **tourist office** (☎ 086 21 24 28; www.durbuy.info .be; Pl aux Foires 25; ☺ 9am-12.30pm & 1-5pm Mon-Fri, 10am-12.30pm & 1-5pm Sat & Sun Sep-Jun, 9am-6pm Jul & Aug) is on the main square. There is no ATM or bank in town.

Sleeping & Eating

Camping Le Vedeur (☎ 086 21 02 09; Rue Fond de Vedeur; adult/tent/car €3/5/3) Durbuy unashamedly cashes in on tourists – there's no bottom-end market unless you're equipped to camp at this riverside camping ground.

B&B Au Milieu de Nulle Part (☎ 0476 41 88 21; www .aumilieudenullepart.com; Rue des Recollectines 5; d/ste €125/180; ☺ closed Tue & Wed) Gorgeously rustic B&B on the quaintest pedestrianised backstreet in the middle of town. Subtle grey-and-brown décor, old lamps, flaking paintwork and not a hint of fuss or bother. The five rooms each have different furnishings.

Hôtel Victoria (☎ 086 21 23 00; www.hotel-victoria .be; Rue des Recollectines 4; d Mon-Thu from €60, Fri-Sun from €80) An ivy-clad building dating back some 330 years and situated on one of the nicest streets in town. Creaking wooden steps worn by time lead up to 10 comfortable old-style rooms. Those on the top floor have the charm that comes with exposed timber beams and an A-frame ceiling. The fire escape spoils the overall look, but it's a modern-day necessity.

Les Clos des Recollets (☎ 086 21 79 69; www.closdes recollets.be; Rue de la Prévôte 9; s/d/tr/f €70/85/112/130, mains €18-26) Hotel/restaurant with 14 rooms scattered around three connecting half-timbered houses. The rooms are pleasant but unexceptional – it's the general atmosphere that's so charming. The restaurant dishes up French cuisine and is very popular in summer when you can dine on an intimate tree-lined square across the street from the hotel.

Three of the most expensive hotels in town have formed a pact and reservations for any of them must be made through **Hôtel Le Sanglier des Ardennes** (☎ 086 21 32 62; www.sanglier-des-ardennes.be; Rue Comte d'Ursel 14; s/d/t Mon-Thu €105/105/140, Fri-Sun €140, breakfast Mon-Thu €12, Fri-Sun €15). Of the trio, Hôtel Aux Vieux Durbuy is arguably the most quiet, cosy and rustic, situated on a pedestrianised backstreet and sporting just 12 rooms done out in mellow caramel or apricot tones. To dine, head to the restaurant at **Le Sanglier des Ardennes** (mains €16-24), which has a view over the river and serves regional cuisine such as *côte de sanglier avec stoemp aux choux* (wild boar served with mashed potato and cabbage). This place also serves a popular Sunday brunch (€30).

Le Moulin (☎ 086 21 29 70; Pl aux Foires 17; mains €14-20; ✆ closed Tue) Light and airy French restaurant just footsteps from the main square and specialising in aromatic Provençal cuisine. It was once an old mill and has a lovely calm ambience.

Le Fou du Roy (☎ 086 21 08 68; Rue Comte d'Ursel 4; 2-/3-course menu €28/34; ✆ Wed-Sun) For something more upmarket, head to Le Fou du Roy – housed in the castle's former concierge quarters, this cosy restaurant with its wicker chairs and outback courtyard is noted for original cuisine.

Drinking

La Ferme au Chêne (☎ 086 21 10 67; Rue Comte d'Ursel 115; ✆ closed Wed & Thu Nov-Mar) A tiny brewery/brasserie producing Marckloff, a blond-brown beer (6.5%) with a strong, slightly bitter flavour. This place is pure homespun – the Mrs works behind the bar while Mr Brewer (not his real name) ushers visitors on a tour of the big stainless steel kettles and invites discussions on the merits of his beer.

Getting There & Away

Reaching Durbuy by public transport is possible but, outside the high season, buses are very limited. From Namur, take the train to Barvaux (€9, 50 minutes, every two hours) then a TEC bus to Durbuy (15 minutes). In July and August there are six buses per day; from April to June and September to November there are just three services on Saturdays and Sundays only. No buses run from December to March. Heading back to Barvaux, the last bus departs around 6pm. If you want to stay later into the evening, it's possible to walk the 3km back to Barvaux along a forest track. For bus times and information, contact the **Namur TEC office** (☎ 081 25 35 55; Pl de la Station; ✆ 7am-7pm).

AROUND DURBUY

About 3km west of Durbuy near the hamlet of Petite Somme sits **Radhadesh** (☎ 086 32 29 26; www.radhadesh.com; Château de Petite Somme, Septon; tours adult/child €4.75/2.40; ✆ 10.30am, 11.30am, 3pm, 4pm &

5.30pm Apr–mid-Nov, 11.30am, 3pm & 4pm mid-Nov–Mar), the headquarters of Belgium's Hare Krishna community. It's located on a forested hill in a restored 13th-century castle and is home to about 60 devotees, with more Hare Krishna families living nearby. One-hour tours of the chateau (phone ahead to arrange an English-language tour) are available, and there's a **vegetarian restaurant** (☎ 086 32 14 21; ✆ lunch & dinner Tue-Sun Apr–mid-Nov, Sat & Sun mid-Nov–Mar) serving well-priced Indian-style fare (such as thali for €11). To get here from Durbuy, head south on the N833 to the turn-off – look for the sign 'Château de Petite Somme'.

LIÈGE
pop 185,500

Liège (Luik in Flemish) is one of those cities people love or loathe. Sprawled along the Meuse River about 90km east of Brussels, it's the Ardennes' largest city and the capital of its own province. Industrial, decaying and gritty, it's the sort of place that takes time to get to know – there are quirky charms and some old intimate quarters, but they're not immediately apparent.

The city's museums hold a rich showcase of medieval religious art, the likes of which you won't see elsewhere in Belgium – for that alone Liège merits an overnight stop. Fans of Inspector Maigret may also want to pay homage here, as Liège is the birthplace of writer Georges Simenon (see boxed text, p253).

History

Liège grew from a humble chapel built on the Meuse in 558. In 705 the Bishop of Tongeren-Maastricht was murdered at the chapel and from then on it became a pilgrimage destination. Was his murder the start of the city becoming a capital of crime? Probably not, but Liège did have Europe's highest crime rate in 2001, according to European Commission figures.

In the 10th century, Liège became the capital of a principality ruled by prince-bishops who had both religious and secular powers. It managed to remain independent for the next 800 years, right through the reign of Burgundians, Spanish and Austrians. When rumblings broke out in Paris in 1789, revolutionary desires were whetted in Liège, and the locals, with the assistance of French soldiers, ousted the last prince-bishop, Antoine de Méan. In 1794 the long-independent principality was swallowed by France.

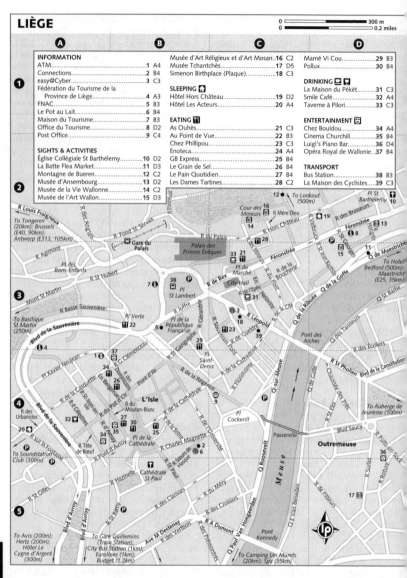

LIÈGE

0 ———— 300 m
0 ———— 0.2 miles

INFORMATION
ATM...1 A4
Connections.......................................2 B4
easy@Cyber..3 C3
Fédération du Tourisme de la
  Province de Liège.............................4 A3
FNAC...5 B3
Le Pot au Lait....................................6 B4
Maison du Tourisme.............................7 B3
Office de Tourisme...............................8 D2
Post Office...9 C4

SIGHTS & ACTIVITIES
Église Collégiale St Barthélemy...........10 D2
La Batte Flea Market...........................11 D3
Montagne de Bueren...........................12 C2
Musée d'Ansembourg..........................13 C2
Musée de la Vie Wallonne....................14 C2
Musée de l'Art Wallon.........................15 D3

Musée d'Art Réligieux et d'Art Mosan..16 C2
Musée Tchantchès..............................17 D5
Simenon Birthplace (Plaque)................18 C3

SLEEPING
Hôtel Hors Château............................19 D2
Hôtel Les Acteurs..............................20 A4

EATING
As Ouhès...21 C3
Au Point de Vue................................22 B3
Chez Phillipou...................................23 C3
Enoteca...24 A4
GB Express..25 B4
Le Grain de Sel..................................26 B4
Le Pain Quotidien...............................27 B4
Les Dames Tartines.............................28 C2

Mamé Vi Cou....................................29 B3
Pollux...30 B4

DRINKING
La Maison du Pékèt............................31 C3
Smile Café..32 A4
Taverne à Pilori.................................33 C3

ENTERTAINMENT
Chez Bouldou....................................34 A4
Cinema Churchill................................35 B4
Luigi's Piano Bar................................36 D4
Opéra Royal de Wallonie......................37 B4

TRANSPORT
Bus Station.......................................38 B3
La Maison des Cyclistes.......................39 C3

Liège entered the industrial age with verve. Coal mining had started here as early as the 12th century, and when the Industrial Revolution swept through in the 19th century, Liège developed its natural assets. Although the steel industry still survives, coal mining has ground to a halt and the city's periphery is dotted with the abandoned remnants of its prosperous past.

The Liègois are known for their liberal, left-wing passions. They were the first to lend their support to Brussels during the 1830 revolution against Dutch rule, and later that century fought heavily for better working conditions. After WWII, they were at the forefront of the campaign that eventually brought down King Léopold III (see p27).

Orientation

The central district is large and initially quite disorientating. The city is strewn along the western bank of the Meuse River, which splits in two, creating the island of Outremeuse. The island is one of the city's original working-class neighbourhoods, and its jumbled streets retain a busy, down-to-earth atmosphere.

The main train station, Gare Guillemins, is 2km south of the huge Pl St Lambert, the city's heart. Pl St Lambert is the main bus hub and is also home to a branch of the tourist office as well as the Palais des Princes Évêques, the former palace of the prince-bishops (now a courthouse). The city's historic quarter is based around a street called Féronstrée, where you'll find another tourist office. The 'newer' hub, with shops and the bulk of the restaurants and lively bars, is centred on Rue Pont d'Avroy and the clutch of little pedestrianised streets leading off it.

Information

ATM (Rue des Dominicains) Attached to Dexia Bank.
Connections (☎ 04 223 03 75; Rue Sœurs de Hasque 7) Travel agency.
easy@Cyber (Rue Léopold 14; per hr €0.50; ☻ 9.30am-8pm Mon-Sat) Cheap, well-patronised internet space.
Fédération du Tourisme de la Province de Liège (☎ 04 237 95 26; www.prov-liege.be/tourisme; Blvd de la Sauvenière 77) Provincial tourist office.
FNAC (☎ 04 232 71 11, ticket sales 04 232 71 12; Rue Joffre 3; ☻ 9.30am-6.30pm Mon-Sat) Department store with a large section of books, including travel guides and maps. FNAC also handles reservations for concerts and theatre.

Le Pot au Lait (☎ 04 222 05 84; Rue Sœurs de Hasque; per hr €2; ☻ from 1pm) At the end of a walkway festooned with psychedelic murals, this loud, smoky student pub has 10 internet terminals in a side room.
Maison du Tourisme (☎ 04 237 92 92; www.liege.be; Pl St Lambert 32; ☻ 9am-6pm Jun-Sep, 9.30am-5.30pm Oct-May) City tourist office.
Office du Tourisme (☎ 04 221 92 21; www.liege.be; Féronstrée 92; ☻ 9am-5pm Mon-Fri) City tourist office.
Post office (Rue de la Régence 26)

Sights & Activities

Liège's museums are regionally based and give good insight into the area's former wealth. The best ones are dotted around the city's historic quarter and are within easy walking distance of one another.

A good starting point, especially for orientation, is **Montagne de Bueren** (Rue Hors Château). This impressive flight of 373 stairs leads up to a former citadel (now a hospital) where a viewpoint, marked by a monument to the two world wars, gives an excellent panorama of the city.

Also worth a wander is **La Batte** (☻ 9am-2pm Sun), a flea market that stretches along 1.5km of river quays.

Close to the base of Montagne de Bueren is the **Musée de la Vie Wallonne** (Museum of Walloon Life; ☎ 04 223 60 94; Cour des Mineurs; adult/child €2.50/1.50; ☻ 10am-5pm Tue-Sat, 10am-4pm Sun). Everything that's Walloon and old-fashioned is extolled here, from 12th-century Mosan metalwork (see boxed text, p233) to old wooden puppets and biscuit moulds (capable of making mega 5kg biscuits). There are reconstructed *ateliers* (workshops) from various trades including candlestick-making, basket-weaving and cooperage, as well as industries specifically associated with this region like glass-blowing and *dinanderie*, a craft that's still practised in Dinant. It's all housed in a restored convent and makes a fascinating amble through the region's past.

Just steps away is the excellent **Musée d'Art Réligieux et d'Art Mosan** (Museum of Religious Art & Art from the Meuse Valley; ☎ 04 221 42 25; Rue Mère Dieu; adult/child €3.80/2.50; ☻ 11am-6pm Tue-Sat, 11am-4pm Sun). Spanning several floors, this museum is chock-full of well-preserved religious relics and paintings from the region. Start on the 3rd floor – home to glowing 16th-century statues of St Hubert, the region's patron saint of hunters – then weave your way down. On the 2nd floor, note the worn but nevertheless delicate wood carving of the *Vierge* (Virgin) that dates right back to 1070.

TCHANTCHÈS

Liège's mascot and oldest 'citizen' is a wooden puppet called Tchantchès, with a big nose and bad behaviour. Supposedly born in the 8th century between two cobblestones in the city's old Outremeuse quarter, he has a penchant for getting riotously drunk on *pékèt* (a light version of gin) and head-butting people but, despite these flaws, is supposedly good-hearted and much loved. According to the Liègois, he typifies their free spirit. Get to know him better at the **Musée Tchantchès** (☎ 04 342 75 75; www.tchantches.be in French; Rue Surlet 56; admission €1; ⏰ 2-4pm Tue & Thu; puppet shows 2.30pm Wed & 10.30am Sun Jun-Sep) in Outremeuse, where you can catch a puppet show and view part of his wardrobe.

Two other museums are located close to the tourist office. Life as it was for some in the 18th century is depicted in the beautiful **Musée d'Ansembourg** (☎ 04 221 94 02; Féronstrée 114; adult/child €3.80/2.50; ⏰ 1-6pm Tue-Sun). If you've just come from either the Musée de la Vie Wallonne or the Musée d'Art Réligieux et d'Art Mosan, you'll find this rich, Regency-styled mansion wonderfully uncluttered. Highlights include four original 17th-century Oudenaarde tapestries, pieces of antique delftware pottery and, upstairs, a six-faced clock. The latter simultaneously shows the time in 50 countries and was invented in 1795 by Hubert Sarton; it still works.

The **Musée de l'Art Wallon** (☎ 04 221 92 31; Féronstrée 86; adult/child €3.80/2.50; ⏰ 1-6pm Tue-Sat, 11am-4.30pm Sun) occupies a modern building that's accessed from Rue St Georges. It accommodates a very enjoyable collection of art by French-speaking Belgians, including 16th-century paintings by Henri Blès (1510–55). There are also works by some of the big guns including Constantin Meunier, Antoine Wiertz, René Magritte and Paul Delvaux.

Romanesque **Église Collégiale St Barthélemy** (Pl St Barthélemy; adult/child €1.25/1; ⏰ 10am-noon Mon-Sat, 2-5pm Sun) has one attraction – a brass baptismal font crafted between 1107 and 1118 and believed to be the work of either Lambert Patras, a coppersmith from Dinant, or Renier, a goldsmith from Huy. This enormous bowl rests on oxen and is adorned with five baptismal scenes (elaborately described in a video screened near the font).

The tourist office has an English-language brochure, the *Simenon Route*, which describes a walking tour around Outremeuse, where writer Georges Simenon (opposite) spent his youth. One of the most tangible references to Simenon is the brass **plaque** marking his nearby birthplace at Rue Léopold 24. Alternatively, a French-language **audio tour** (€6, two

hours) entitled 'Sur les Traces de Simenon' starts at the Maison du Tourisme.

Sleeping

Liège has a smattering of atmospheric hotels, all dotted around the city centre. That said, none are really outstanding, and don't bother looking for a B&B – there's little on offer.

Camping Les Murets (☎ 04 380 19 87; Chemin d'Enonck 57, Hony; camp sites €12.70; ⏰ Apr-Oct) One of the closest grounds to the city, located about 20km to the south. To get here, take a Jemellebound train to Hony (€1.60, 35 minutes), then walk 200m.

Auberge de Jeunesse (☎ 04 344 56 89; www.laj.be; Rue Georges Simenon 2; dm/s/d €16.60/29/42; ✕ 🖵) A modern hostel in Outremeuse. To get here from Gare Guillemins, take bus 4 to Pl St Lambert and change to bus 18, which stops out the front at Pl Léopold.

Hôtel Les Acteurs (☎ 04 223 00 80; www.lesacteurs .be; Rue des Urbanistes 10; s/d €56/77) A comfy modern hotel that tries hard to look artistic. It's well located, and buses 1 and 4 stop about 200m away.

Hôtel Le Cygne d'Argent (☎ 04 223 70 01; www.cygne dargent.be; Rue Beeckman 49; s/d €58/70, breakfast €9) Sits on a quiet backstreet about halfway between Gare Guillemins and the city centre. The 20 rooms are modern, spacious, well presented and have an aura of respectability.

Hôtel Hors Château (☎ 04 250 60 68; www.hors-chateau .be; Rue Hors Château 62; s/d €85/100) Ordinary, small functional rooms are the trademark of this hotel but the excellent central location in the city's historic quarter makes up for the dearth of atmosphere. Take breakfast in the ground-floor bar.

Hotel Bedford (☎ 04 228 81 11; www.hotelbedford.be; Quai St Léonard 36; s/d Mon-Thu €210/235, Fri-Sun €95/115) Liège's best hotel. It's a six-storey affair facing the river and a multilane boulevard – ask for a rear room if traffic noise bothers you. The

LARGER THAN FICTION

Georges Simenon (1903–89), Belgium's most prolific writer, was born in Liège and is best known for his pulp fiction but was also well regarded in some literary circles. His astounding career and exuberant life is most easily summed up in figures:

- Wrote more than 300 novels, including 76 devoted to crime-buster Inspector Maigret, during a 50-year career.
- Sold more than 500 million copies of his works around the world. Published in about 80 languages.
- Worked, on average, six hours a day, during which time he completed 100 pages and smoked six pipes.
- Completed a book in, on average, 11 days (though one novel took just a quarter of that time).
- Left Liège at the age of 19 and lived in far-flung parts of the world, moving house more than 33 times.
- Boasted to have had sex with 10,000 women, though his second wife claims it was only 1200.
- Died in Switzerland in 1989 at the age of 86.

hotel is geared to business people and décor-wise it's bland and functional.

Eating

For serene surroundings, cross the river to Outremeuse, where there's an old cobbled street, Rue Roture, lined with little restaurants. In the city centre, Rue St-Jean-en-Isle and Rue St Paul are also filled with restaurants and brasseries.

Le Grain de Sel (☎ 04 232 03 23; En Bergerue 15; mains 12-16.50, salads €9.50; ☽ lunch Tue-Sat & dinner Mon-Sat) Cheery eatery set up in three connecting rooms. The house speciality is *tartines Corses* (€7.50), sandwiches of sorts with a base of mozzarella cheese and tapenade. A good respite for vegetarians.

Mamé Vi Cou (☎ 04 233 71 81; Rue de la Wache 9; mains €10-20; ☽ closed Wed) Traditional Liègois fare such as *rognon de veau au pékèt* (veal kidneys in a light gin-based sauce) served in cavernous surroundings.

As Ouhès (☎ 04 223 32 25; Pl du Marché 21; mains €14-22, menu €25) Specialises in rich Walloon cuisine with ultragenerous portions, attentive service and reasonable prices. Note the restaurant's apt logo – a gluttonous man sitting on a mound of hams, waffles and sausages.

Au Point de Vue (☎ 04 223 64 82; Pl Verte 10; mussels 16.50-25, mains €13-26) This restaurant occupies a house dating from 1652, and it's busy but informal. A must are the seasonal mussels, shrimps in a cognac sauce and the house peciality, *lapin à la Liègeoise* (rabbit done the local way).

Enoteca (☎ 04 222 24 64; Rue de la Casquette 5; menus €17-31; ☽ closed lunch Sat & closed Sun) The décor's dark and heavy – black marble tables, cushioned brown chairs and wood-panelled walls – but the Italian food is light and luscious, and you can see it being prepared in the white-tiled open kitchen.

Other recommendations:

Les Dames Tartines (☎ 04 232 17 10; Rue des Mineurs 20; snacks €2.75-4.50; ☽ 9am-4pm Mon-Sat) Teensy *sandwicherie* noted for its filled baguette sandwiches.

Le Pain Quotidien (☎ 04 223 60 12; Rue du Mouton-Blanc 19; breakfast €5, lunch €10; ☽ 8am-6pm Mon-Sat, 8am-5pm Sun) Salads, savoury pies and breakfast items. See boxed text, p103, for more on this popular chain bakery/tearoom.

Pollux (Rue du Pont d'Avroy; waffles from €2.10) The best *gaufres Liègeoises* (waffles made the local way).

Chez Phillipou (☎ 04 222 18 22; Rue Souverain Pont 21; mains €15; ☽ Tue-Sun) Simple but very popular Greek eatery.

GB Express (Rue de la Cathédrale) Supermarket.

Drinking

Pick up *La Référence*, a free bi-monthly entertainment booklet (in French) that details everything from rock and jazz to theatre festivals and classical concerts.

Taverne à Pilori (☎ 04 222 18 57; Pl du Marché 7; ☽ 10am-1am) A classic Liègois pub that's pretty much always open. Customers transcend age and class barriers, and regulars mix comfortably with whomever happens upon it.

La Maison du Pékèt (☎ 04 232 04 66; Rue de l'Épée 4; ☽ 11am-2am Tue-Sun) Directly behind the Hôtel de Ville. This bar specialises in *genièvre* (gin – also known as *jenever*) and turns out exotic fruit *genièvre* served in long, tall glasses, or shots of older varieties (€2.60) poured from pottery bottles.

Smile Café (Rue des Célestines 16; ⏰ 5pm-2am Tue-Sun) One of many bars in the city's lively nightlife area. This one has a good ambience and is less intimidating than some of its counterparts.

Entertainment

Cinema Churchill (☎ 04 223 41 07; Rue du Mouton-Blanc 18) Three-screen cinema located behind a grand stained-glass façade and home to quality films. All screenings are in their original language, with French and Flemish subtitles.

Soundstation (☎ 04 232 13 21; Rue Pouplin 6; ⏰ 7.30pm-dawn) A former train station that now sports house parties and live rock most Friday nights.

Chez Bouldou (☎ 0477 78 86 10; Rue Tête de Bœuf 15; ⏰ from 7pm Mon-Sat) Happening cellar venue with acoustic guitar concerts on Monday nights and pop/rock concerts each Thursday from 8pm.

Other recommendations:

Luigi's Piano Bar (Rue Roture 22; ⏰ from 7pm Fri & Sat) Laid-back bar with concerts Friday and Saturday nights.

Opéra Royal de Wallonie (☎ 04 221 47 20; www .orw.be in French; Rue des Dominicains 1)

Basilique St Martin (☎ 04 223 67 74; Mont St Martin) Venue for classical concerts, located west of the city centre.

Getting There & Away

BUS

Eurolines (☎ 04 222 36 18; Rue des Guillemins 94) buses leave from Rue du Plan-Incliné next to the train station.

CAR

Rental outfits:

Avis (☎ 04 252 55 00; Blvd d'Avroy 238b)

Budget (☎ 04 229 96 50; Rue du Plan-Incliné 105)

Hertz (☎ 04 222 42 73; Blvd d'Avroy 60)

TRAIN

Liège is a major international and regional rail junction. The principal train station is **Gare Guillemins** (☎ 02 528 28 28), newly renovated and now accommodating Thalys fast trains.

Sample international and regional connections (the prices listed are full one-way fares):

Destination	Fare (€)	Duration (min)	Frequency
Brussels	12.40	65	2 per hr
Cologne	30.10	90	7 per day
Eupen	5.70	45	1 per hr
Hasselt	6.70	55	1 per hr
Jemelle	9	90	1 per 2 hr
Leuven	9	50	1 per hr
Luxembourg City	32.20	150	7 per day
Maastricht	7.50	30	1 per hr
Namur	7.40	50	2 per hr
Spa	4.30	50	1 per hr
Tongeren	3.80	30	1 per hr
Trois Ponts	7.10	60	1 per 2hr
Verviers	3.40	20	1 per hr

Getting Around

Liège's main train station, Gare Guillemins, is 2km south of Pl St Lambert. To get to the city centre, either take buses 1 or 4 from the bus platforms to the right as you exit Gare Guillemins, or catch another train to the city's most central train station, Gare du Palais, close to Pl St Lambert. The latter option costs nothing (just use the same ticket you purchased for your journey to Liège) and takes an extra seven minutes.

Otherwise, **TEC buses** (☎ 04 361 94 44) are the main form of inner-city transport; the main bus hub is Pl St Lambert.

For a taxi call **Liège Taxi** (☎ 0800 322 00).

La Maison des Cyclistes (☎ 04 222 20 46; www.provelo .org in French; Rue de Gueldre 3; ⏰ 2-6pm Fri-Wed May-Sep) has rental bikes for one hour (€2) or for a half-/ full day (€6/8).

SPA

pop 10,500

Spa, Europe's oldest health resort, is on the up. Just a few years ago, the fortunes of the town that launched a thousand spas were flagging. But thanks to a new generation that's into health and wellbeing (and the opening of the lavish new hilltop Thermes de Spa), the town is seeing a revival – there's just no bursting its bubble.

Spa sits in a valley about 40km southeast of Liège. For centuries it embraced royalty and the wealthy, who came to drink, bathe and cure themselves in the mineral-rich water that bubble forth from 200 springs here. The healing properties of the warm waters were recognised as far back as the 1st century AD. By the 16th century it was an established health resort – Henry VIII, occupying Tournai at the time, praised the waters' curative powers – and by the 18th century the town had become the luxurious retreat for European royalty and intellectuals. A long list of distinguished visitors – from a Russian tsar to Joseph II (former emperor of Austria), and writers Victor Hugo and Alexandre Dumas – came here to rejuvenate themselves. Such was its pull that Spa became known as the 'Café of Europe'. But it didn't last – by the 19th century its popularity had waned and until the recent opening of the new Thermes complex, the town was all but a run-down reminder of what was.

Information

The **Office du Tourisme** (☎ 087 79 53 53; www.spa-info .be in Flemish & French; Pl Royale 41; ☼ 9am-6pm Mon-Fri, 10am-6pm Sat & Sun Apr-Sep, to 5pm Oct-Mar), located in a picturesque pavilion built by Léopold II, sells regional walking maps (€7).

Sights & Activities

The palatial **Thermes de Spa** (☎ 087 77 25 60; www .thermesdespa.com; Colline d'Annette et Lubin; ☼ 10am-9pm) sits on a hillock immediately above central Spa. If you're without a car, it can normally be reached by a state-of-the-art Austrian funicular (one way €1) from near the tourist office. However, the funicular is temperamental, and if it's not working you'll have a 20-minute hike up the next-door footpath.

Peat baths (good for relieving the aches of rheumatism and other disorders), water and beauty treatments, fitness facilities, swimming pools and Jacuzzis are all offered. Go for a three-hour dip in one of the hydrotherapy pools (€17), or submerse yourself for a day (€27). After paying this admission, you can access many of the facilities, including the indoor and outdoor pools, icy plunge pool, saunas, Turkish baths and fitness room. Alternatively, if the shoe fits, join the Institut Maman-Bébé, where new mothers and their babies can mooch around for five days (€695) while mum gets back into shape.

Back down in town, if you'd prefer to simply gulp a mouthful of water, head to the spring, **Pouhon Pierre-le-Grand** (Rue du Pouhon; ☼ 10am-noon & 1.30-5pm Apr-Oct, 1.30-5pm Mon-Fri, 10am-noon & 1.30-5pm Sat & Sun Nov-Mar). It's named after Peter the Great, the Russian tsar who visited in 1717. He found that the iron-rich waters improved his sense of wellbeing; you might find the same after downing a plastic glass (€0.25) of rather vile-tasting water. Better still,

take a bottle (€0.50) back to the hotel and sip at your leisure.

Four other **springs** – Tonnelet, Sauvenière, Géronstère and Barisart – are all a few kilometres out of town. A **petit train** (adult/child €5/4; ☼ 9.30am-6pm Jun-Sep) passes them on its rounds but you can't normally stop to taste the waters.

More water samples can be had at **Spa Monopole** (☎ 087 79 41 11; www.spa.be in Flemish & French; Rue Auguste Laporte 34; ☼ 9am-5pm Mon-Fri), the factory where millions of bottles of Spa water are produced annually. A public gallery overlooks the production floor and at the end you can try either the *plat* (nonsparkling) or *gazeuse* (sparkling) water. It's a 15-minute walk from the tourist office.

The **Musée de la Ville d'Eaux** (☎ 087 77 44 86; Ave Reine Astrid 77; adult/child/concession €3/1/2; ☼ 2-6pm Jul-Sep, 2-6pm Sat & Sun mid-Mar–Jun & Oct-Dec) occupies Villa Marie-Henriette, a former royal abode, and harks back to the good ol' days with posters and memorabilia from the town's past. The only other sight is the **Musée de la Lessive** (☎ 087 77 14 18; Rue de la Géronstère 10; adult/child €2/1; ☼ 2-6pm Jul & Aug, 2-6pm Sat & Sun Apr-Jun, Sep & Oct). Water is the obvious theme of this laundry museum and if you've a yearning to see old tubs and scrubbers, this is the place.

Every Sunday morning there's a **flea market** near the tourist office.

Should you want to hit the world's first **casino** (☎ 087 77 20 52; Rue Royale 4; ☼ from 11am), you'll need to be over 21 years of age and have your passport handy.

About 2km east of town is **Lac de Warfaaz**, a pleasant lake dotted with a few waterfront cafés and restaurants and where **pédalos** (single/double €5/7) can be rented. If you've hired a bike in town, the lake is a good cycling destination as there's a separate bike path most of the way to and around it. **Velodream** (☎ 087 77 11 77; Rue Général Bertrand 6; half-/full day €14/22; ☼ 9am-6pm Tue-Fri, 9am-5pm Sat), behind Pouhon Pierre-le-Grand, rents out mountain bikes.

The **Piscine communale de Spa** (☎ 087 77 21 10; Ave Amédée Hesse 9) comprises an outdoor and indoor swimming pool, plus waterslides, and is set amid the forest en route to Lac de Warfaaz.

Spa's popularity as a resort town is not confined to summer. Besides relaxing in a hot mud bath at the Thermes, the other obvious winter attraction is **skiing**. Several cross-country tracks and a small alpine run are located at the

BOOK AHEAD

The region around Spa, Stavelot and Malmédy is a popular summer resort area. It's normally possible to find accommodation but there are a few annual shindigs that require prior planning and advance hotel bookings.

The pre-Lent carnival celebrations at Stavelot and Malmédy (see boxed text, p223) are immensely popular events, as are some motor-racing meets, which are held at the Circuit de Spa-Francorchamps, halfway between Spa and Stavelot. Of the latter, the three-day Grand Prix de Belgique de Formule 1 in mid-September is the biggest gathering, though other well-attended races include the 24 Heures de Motocross (end July) and the 1000km of Franchorchamps (mid-May).

Pistes de Ski du Thier des Rexhons (☎ 087 77 30 28), 3.5km south of town.

And if you happen to be around at Christmas time, the old hall behind the main spring is transformed into a wonderfully atmospheric *patinage à glace* – **ice-skating rink**.

Festivals & Events

Spa has two main annual events:

Les Francopholies de Spa A few days of exclusively French-language entertainment, from music to theatre and song, in July.

Grand Prix de Belgique de Formule 1 Motor-racing carnival (see boxed text, above) in mid-September.

Sleeping & Eating

B&B La Primavera (☎ 087 77 49 16; www.ives.be; Rue de la Chapelle 2; d €65, studio €85, holiday house weekly €300) Situated on a hillock about 300m from the town centre, this B&B is surrounded by a pleasant garden and is run by a friendly man who imports wines from Spain. The main house, containing one guestroom plus a studio with a kitchenette, is a stone building that's full of character; the rooms are large but not flash. There's also a separate half-timbered holiday house next door that's ideal for families (sleeps four).

B&B L'Étape Fagnarde (☎ 087 77 56 50; www.etape fagnarde.be; Ave Dr Gaspar 14; single/d €65/75, cottage 3/7 nights €450/850) A century-old whitewashed villa on a leafy lane 800m uphill from the tourist office. It's a huge place, with five guestrooms (each named after a spring), a sauna, a big patio and a large rhododendron garden. There's also

a restored self-contained caretaker's cottage for longer stays. The friendly owners take B&B business seriously, and even welcome guests to their dinner table in the evenings.

B&B La Vigie (☎ 087 77 34 97; www.lavigie.be; Ave Professeur Henrijean 129; r from €80) Well-established B&B that's modern and muted, and perfect for a romantic getaway.

Hôtel Cardinal (☎ 087 77 10 64; www.hotel-cardinal .be; Pl Royale 21; s/d/f €105/125/150) With an excellent location opposite the old Thermes in the town centre, this hotel has 29 recently renovated rooms with typical modern décor. The exception is room No 2, a classic. It has a Louis XI style bed and a matching green wardrobe and bedside tables, plus ceiling friezes and a sunken bath – if you're into something different, it's the pick. Ask about discounts during low periods.

Radisson SAS Palace Hotel (☎ 087 27 97 00; www .radissonsas.com; Pl Royale 39; s/d from €125/145) The newest and most luxurious hotel in town located at the base of the Thermes, and with direct funicular access to it. *The* place to stay if your mission is the pools.

Le Jardin des Elfes (☎ 087 77 17 18; Lac de Warfaaz 10am-8pm Tue-Sun) This lake-front café offering standard Belgian snacks – waffles and the *croque monsieur* (grilled ham and cheese sandwich) – is well geared for the summer flocks. In winter there's a heated terrace. The large playground with trampolines keeps youngsters happy.

L'Art de Vivre (☎ 087 77 04 44; Ave Reine Astrid 53; mains €24-35; lunch & dinner Fri-Tue) Refined little family run restaurant about 200m west of the tourist office and housed in a pretty villa. It's out of the main tourist hubbub, and is much loved by locals. Light healthy French cuisine with original twists is the trade and, if the weather's good you can dine on a shady tree-lined square to the trickle of a fountain bubbling nearby.

Other recommendations:

Camping Parc des Sources (☎ 087 77 23 11; Rue de la Sauvenière 141; camp sites per adult/child/tent/car €5/3.30/6/3; closed Dec-Mar)

Glacier Gérard (☎ 087 64 68 64; Rue de l'Hôtel de Ville 8; 10.30am-8.30pm Tue-Sun) Modern ice-cream café.

GB Express (Pl du Monument 9) Supermarket.

Getting There & Away

Spa sits at the end of a train track that branches off from the Liège–Verviers line. The **train station** (☎ 02 528 28 28) and neighbouring bus station are at Pl de la Gare, about 500m from the tourist office – when you exit the station head down

Rue de la Gare, then turn right at the bottom into Ave Reine Astrid. There are trains to Liège (€4.30, 50 minutes, hourly) and Verviers (€2.50, 22 minutes, hourly). Bus 744 runs four times per day to Stavelot (€1.60, 25 minutes).

STAVELOT

pop 6600

Stavelot sits on the slope of a hill above the Amblève River about 24km south of Spa. A summer resort town, it's a delightful place to stay, driven by its proximity to the natural beauty of the nearby Hautes Fagnes. The best time to visit is during the springtime Laetare carnival (see right). Even if you can't be here then, the town is still worth a visit for its interesting history – brought to life in state-of-the-art museums housed in a restored abbey – and for its quaint character, most evident in the 18th-century houses with exposed wooden beams dotted around town.

Orientation & Information

The heart of town is Pl St Remacle, a sloping square at the centre of all the carnival fun. The **Office du Tourisme** (☎ 080 86 27 06; www.stavelot.be; ◷ 10am-5pm Tue-Sun) is inside the abbey, just off Ave Ferdinand Nicolay, the main road through town. For internet access, head to the **library** (access free; ◷ 10am-6pm Mon-Fri) at the abbey.

Sights & Activities

The premier sight is the **Abbaye de Stavelot** (☎ 080 88 08 78; www.abbayedestavelot.be; Ave Ferdinand Nicolay; ◷ 10am-6pm May-Sep, closed Mon Oct-Apr), the unmissable red building in the town centre. Stavelot and its nearby sister town, Malmédy, grew up as a result of this former abbey, which was built in the 7th century. From then on, it was the home to a line of abbot-bishops, founded by St Remacle (also known as the Apostle of the Ardennes), who kept the region independent for over 1000 years and who ruled over the minds and souls of folk in their fiefdom. Their reign came to an end with the French Revolution, and when the region was carved up in 1815, Stavelot was attached to the Netherlands while Malmédy became part of Prussia.

The abbey complex reopened a few years ago after extensive renovation, and houses three **museums** (combination ticket adult/student €6.50/5). The **Musée de la Principauté de Stavelot/Malmédy**, devoted to local history, winds its way around the ground floor, using colour-coded stages to tell Stavelot's story, from the abbey's beginning in 647 to the

abolition of the abbot-bishops' rule in 1794. It's tastefully set out, and it goes out of its way to be clear and engaging. Pick up an English-language audio-guide before setting off.

The second museum, **Musée Guillaume Apollinaire**, occupies a small section on the 1st floor and contains sketches and poetry by French writer Guillaume Apollinaire, who stayed briefly in Stavelot in 1899. Once again, the audio-guide is essential for those who don't speak French. After the serenity of the Musée Apollinaire, descend to the vaulted cellar where the buzz of Formula One racing cars permeates the air in the **Musée du Circuit de Spa-Francorchamps**. Most of the cars here are privately owned and are in working order – the displays change regularly as owners take their vehicles out for a ride or to a rally. Send kids off to the room devoted to PlayStation2, the virtual track.

Some lovely **hiking trails** lead off from the town, and the museum shop sells a map, *Pays de Stavelot – Promenades* (€6), that outlines 14 local walks. Most are marked by green arrows. A good choice is walk No 10 to Coo (7km), which heads west over the hills, passing through the peaceful hamlet of Ster before arriving at Coo (p258).

Festivals & Events

In winter Stavelot falls into a deep slumber and appears almost dead. From this slumber erupts one of Belgium's most colourful celebrations – the **Laetare** carnival, held around the fourth Sunday in Lent. See boxed text, p223, for a full account of the festivities. Without a doubt, this is the best time to be here.

Sleeping & Eating

It's essential to book accommodation in advance if you plan to be here for Laetare.

Hostellerie La Maison (☎ 080 88 08 91; www.hotel lamaison.info in French & Flemish; Pl St Remacle 19; s/d Mon-Thu €65/87, Fri-Sun €69/95, mains €22-25; ◷ closed 2 weeks mid-Sep) This is a Liège-style 19th-century manor house superbly situated at the top end of Stavelot's main square. The whole place radiates a calm, distinguished air – from the classy restaurant to the charming peachy-toned rooms adorned with antiques, colourful ceiling friezes and fireplaces. Note the old oak staircase leading up to the 12 rooms.

Hôtel/Restaurant d'Orange (☎ 080 86 20 05; www .hotel-orange.be; Devant les Capucins 8; s/d/tr/f €70/80/110/120, mains €18-25; ◷ Apr-Nov, weekends & school holidays

THE AUTHOR'S CHOICE

Dufays (☎ 080 54 80 08; www.bbb-dufays.be; Rue Neuve 115; r €105) A new boutique hotel located at the top end of Rue Neuve, just 300m from Pl St Remacle. The exquisitely restored stone building dates back to 1820, and inside there are just six rooms, each individually styled to suit personal taste. Silk cushions await in 1001 Nights, or there's the Deco decadence of *Années 30* (The Thirties). Whichever theme you choose, expect subtle furnishings and graceful high ceilings. Breakfast, too, is a delightful experience, as you'd expect in a place created by so much personal effort. Frank and Ad, the two gents who run it, are delights.

Dec-Mar; 🖥) This place has been owned and run by the same family for five generations, and the current maître d'hôtel is as friendly and jovial as they come. The 17 rooms are decked out with heavy wooden furniture and rose-patterned wallpaper typical of the Ardennes. The restaurant (closed at lunchtime on Wednesday) adapts itself seasonally. It's family-friendly, and cots and highchairs are available.

Auberge St Remacle (☎ 080 86 20 47; www.auberge -stavelot.be; Ave Ferdinand Nicolay 9; s/d €40/50) A standard-issue hotel with just five rooms, done out in pastel tones, ranging from poky to pleasant. No 3 is the largest and has a view over the abbey. The downstairs bar/brasserie can be noisy until the early hours.

Figaro (☎ 080 86 42 86; Pl du Vinave 4; mains €6-9; 🕑 lunch & dinner) This casual Italian restaurant has bright décor, and outdoor tables set up on Pl St Remacle. It's a great spot to eat on a warm summer's evening.

Other recommendations:

Camping de Challes (☎ 080 86 23 31; Rte de Challes 5; camp sites per adult/child/tent/car €5/2.50/1/1.50; 🕑 closed Nov-Mar) Closest ground for campers, located about 2km east of town.

Spar (14 Rue Haute) Supermarket one block uphill from Pl St Remacle.

Getting There & Away

Stavelot is not on a train line. If you're coming from Liège, the closest train station is Trois Ponts (€7.10, one hour, every two hours). From Trois Ponts, bus 294 (€1.20, 10 minutes, hourly) covers the 6km to Stavelot.

From Spa, bus 744 runs four times per day to Stavelot (€1.60, 25 minutes).

COO

Coo (pronounced 'coh') is a tiny hamlet, 7km west of Stavelot, with a handful of buildings clustered around its premier sight – an impressive waterfall built in the 18th century by monks from Stavelot's abbey. The place is popular with summer holidaymakers staying in the nearby towns and has all the aura of a sideshow alley.

Opposite the waterfall is **Plopsa Coo** (☎ 080 68 42 65; www.plopsacoo.be in Flemish & French; person above/ under 1m €15/free), an amusement park including a hillside sled ride (*luge* in French), bumper cars, minigolf and more. Here too is a **télésiège** (chairlift; adult/child €6/4; 🕑 10am-6pm May-Sep, Sat & Sun Oct-Apr) that rumbles up the hillside and provides a pleasant view over a nearby lake and an easy walk (20 minutes) back to Coo. For something more adventurous, there's a plethora of options offered by **Coo Bike Adventure** (☎ 080 68 91 33; Petite Coo 4), located near the bridge over the waterfall – whitewater rafting (€21 for a 23km trip), kayaking (€20) and mountain bike hire (half-/full day €14/20) are all available.

The best bet for dining is **Au Vieux Moulin** (☎ 080 68 40 41; Cascade de Coo 2; mains €12-18; 🕑 closed Tue dinner & Wed), a lovely stone building where typical Walloon cuisine is served. An open fire warms the place on cold days, and some tables have a river view.

Coo is on the Liège–Clervaux train line; the station is about 300m from the waterfall and there are trains from Liège (€6.20, 55 minutes, every two hours) or Trois Ponts (€1.60, three minutes). If you've hiked from Stavelot, you can return by walking (or catching the train) south to Trois Ponts (2km) from where there are hourly buses back to Stavelot.

MALMÉDY

pop 11,600

Malmédy, like Stavelot 12km to the southwest, is a popular summer holiday base for Belgians and is best known for its carnival called Cwarmé (see boxed text, p223). It shares much of its history (right up to the early 19th century) with Stavelot, as both were part of the independent lands overseen for more than a millennium by powerful abbot-bishops who ruled from the abbey at Stavelot. In 1815, after Napoleon's defeat at Waterloo, most of Belgium was incorporated into the Netherlands but Malmédy became part of Prussia and later was incorporated into Germany.

These days, Malmédy is part of the German-speaking Eastern Cantons. However, many of the people living here prefer to speak French. The town's popularity as a holiday destination with folk from Flanders means Malmédy is very much a trilingual town and, perhaps more than anywhere else in the whole country, it has grown to accommodate Belgium's three language groups.

There is very little to actually see in Malmédy – most visitors stay here as it makes a convenient base for exploring the Hautes Fagnes. If you're tossing up between Malmédy and Stavelot, pick the latter – it has more charm and better accommodation.

Information

The **Maison du Tourisme** (☎ 080 33 02 50; www.eastbelgium.com; Pl Albert Ier 29a; ⌚ 9am-6pm Jul & Aug, 10am-6pm Sep-Jun, 10am-6pm Wed-Sun Nov-May) is a big modern building in the heart of town.

Sights & Activities

The town's two main museums are the **Musée du Cwarmé** (☎ 080 33 70 58; Pl de Rome 11; adult/child incl Musée National du Papier €3/2; ⌚ 2-5pm Tue-Sun) and the **Musée National du Papier**, both housed in a former orphanage. Neither is terribly engrossing but they're a good way to spend a rainy hour. The latter is devoted to the town's paper manufacturing industry and the former to the characters who come alive each year at Cwarmé.

Otherwise, the only other so-called 'sight' is the **American Memorial** at a crossroad in the hamlet of Baugnez, about 4km southeast of town on the N62 to St Vith (accessible by bus 395). A tall cross flying the US flag commemorates the 150 servicemen who were captured by a German combat group at this road junction in December 1944 and then gunned down by tank fire; 43 men survived.

For **walking**, the Hautes Fagnes (see p260) is the best area. However, if you decide to stick around town, there are several hiking paths, ranging from 6km to 19km, that start here. Walk M2 (13km, marked with a vertical yellow stripe) and M1 (19km, horizontal yellow stripe) both offer views – the latter climbs Parc de Livremont immediately north of the town centre. Purchase the walking map *Au pied des Fagnes* (€7) from the tourist office before setting off.

Sleeping & Eating

Camping Familial (☎ 080 33 08 62; www.campingfamilial.be in Flemish & German; Rue des Bruyères 19; 2 adults plus tent & car €18.50) Located high on the forest's edge at Arimont, about 3km from Malmédy, this is an excellent spot for hiking. To get here, take bus 745 from Trois Ponts train station to Malmédy (€1.60, 20 minutes, hourly), where the owners will pick you up for free.

Auberge de Jeunesse (☎ 080 33 83 86; www.laj.be; Rte d'Eupen 36, Bévercé; dm/s/d €16.60/29/42) This hostel is 5km north of Malmédy; bus 397 (direction 'Mont', €1.10, three to five services per day) stops out the front.

Hôtel Albert Premier (☎ 080 33 04 52; www.hotel-albertpremier; Pl Albert Ier 40; s/d €60/85, mains €15-25; ⊠) Unquestionably the best hotel/restaurant in town. This modern sliver of a building overlooks the main square and has just six rooms, all spacious and modern, staged between the 2nd and 5th floors. The downside is that there's no elevator. The sleek restaurant dishes up classic French cuisine.

Hôtel St Géréon (☎ 080 33 06 77; fax 080 33 97 46; Pl St Géréon 7; s/d/tr/f €55/65/90/110) Grey-shingled hotel one block behind the tourist office, with 10 tidy modern rooms plus a popular bar.

A vî Mâm'dî (☎ 080 33 96 36; Pl Albert Ier 41; mains €11-18; ⌚ lunch & dinner) This down-to-earth tavern is on the main square. The interior is rustic and the food features typically hearty Ardennes fare such as *jambonneau grillé*, a slab of ham on the bone topped with a mustard-based sauce (€12.50). Kids are most welcome.

Other recommendations:

Taverne St Pierre (☎ 080 33 84 16; Pl Albert Ier 19; menu €15; ⌚ lunch & dinner) Opposite the tourist office, tucked away in a corner of the square, this tavern does well-priced *Ardennaise* cuisine.

Market (Pl Albert Ier; ⌚ 7am-1pm Fri) Fresh produce.

Getting There & Away

Malmédy is not on a train line; regional buses depart from the Gare des Autobus at Rue de la Gare, a few minutes' walk from Pl Albert Ier.

From Verviers, bus 294 (€3.60, 45 minutes, hourly) goes to Malmédy. From Liège, you can get a Clervaux-bound train to Trois Ponts (€7.10, 55 minutes, every two hours) near Stavelot from where bus 745 goes to Malmédy (€1.60, 20 minutes, hourly).

HAUTES FAGNES

The Hautes Fagnes (also known as Hohes Venn in German, or High Fens) is a high plateau that

HAUTES FAGNES NATURE RESERVE

Belgium's Hautes Fagnes area has been twinned with the Nordeifel region in neighbouring Germany to make what's known as the **Hautes Fagnes-Eifel Nature Park** (www.centrenaturebotrange .be in French & Flemish or www.naturpark-eifel.de in French & German) The park covers some 2000 sq km, though only a third of it is in Belgium, and it uses the black grouse as its emblem.

Within this populated park is Belgium's largest nationally protected reserve, the **Hautes Fagnes Nature Reserve**, established in 1957. Its 4000 hectares are a haven for rare fauna and flora such as wild boar, roe deer, tetras lyre bird, hen harrier, black grouse and the *Drosera rotundifolia* (carnivorous sundew plant). The reserve's logo is the *Trientales europaea* (Wintergreen Chickweed), a rare flower with seven petals. Much of the reserve is open to visitors but some areas are accessible only with a registered guide and other areas are closed to the public in order to conduct research and protect delicate ecosystems. During the breeding season of the black grouse (mid-March to mid-June), the whole of the nature reserve is closed to the public.

stretches from south of Malmédy up to Eupen and sweeps over to Germany's Eifel hills. It's a region of swampy heath, woods and wild windswept moors that covers about 300 sq km and signals the end of the Ardennes. Known to be one of the country's coldest and wettest places, it's often shrouded in mist and low cloud, making it the perfect home for the region's ecologically fragile sphagnum bogs. It also makes it one hell of a bleak winter landscape; in summer it's lush, green and picturesque. Belgium's highest point (694m) is here, marked by a tower called the **Signal de Botrange**.

Sights & Activities

Start a visit at the **Botrange Nature Centre** (☎ 080 44 03 00; www.centrenaturebotrange in French & Flemish; Rte de Botrange 31; general admission free, museum adult/child €3/1.20; ☉ 10am-6pm Mon-Fri, 10am-6pm Sat & Sun), located 1km from the sturdy stone Signal de Botrange. It sports an information centre, a café, a huge fireplace and a small museum explaining the Hautes Fagnes' evolution and the impact humans have had on the landscape through sheep grazing, peat extraction and logging.

It's also the best place to investigate hiking, cycling and skiing (cross-country ski hire per half-/full day €6/10) – all possible in certain parts of the park. The centre's staff can tell you which zones are closed to the public and which can be visited freely or in the company of a guide only. A map, *Hautes Fagnes Carte des Promenades* (scale: 1:25,000, €7), also explains (in French, German and Flemish) the various zones and hiking trails. Guided walks are organised from April to November but the base price for a three-/six-hour walk is €45/60 – fine if you're in a group but pricey otherwise.

Those wanting just a short circular walk through this bleak but interesting landscape should head to the **Fagne de la Poleûr** boardwalk at Mt Rigi, 2.5km from the centre. This 4km-long raised boardwalk (accessible to wheelchairs) offers a wonderful introduction to the moorland habitat and allows visitors access to the region while minimising human interference. The path winds past an old peat mine – peat was extracted in this region right up until the 1960s primarily for heating houses. Formed by layers of decaying sphagnum moss, these bogs covered about 1000 hectares of the Hautes Fagnes 5000 years ago; today there are just 125 hectares remaining.

If you want to extend the Fagne de Poleûr walk by 30 minutes or so, follow the path (which is actually part of the GR573 walkway from Liège through Eupen and Spa back to Liège) along the lovely creek to Pont de Bêleu, cross the stream and return to the boardwalk via the track on the opposite bank.

Longer walks include a 16km track to **Herzogenhügel**, a hill to the east, and back. This path crosses the marshes and passes a few old six-sided border stones, used to mark the 1815 frontier between the United Kingdom of the Netherlands and Prussia. It's a mix of mud, turf, wooden boardwalks and tracks through the protected reserve and also takes in part of the GR573.

Other long-distance walks that pass through this beautiful area are the circular GR56 (156km) from Malmédy via Rocherath, Bütgenbach and St Vith; the GRAE (Ardenne-Eifel, 200km), which runs from Monschau (in Germany), via Eupen, Spa and Bastogne to Martelange; and, for those really into a hike, the GR5 from the North Sea to the Mediterranean coast.

Getting There & Away

Botrange Nature Centre is about 13km northeast of Malmédy, 19km south of Eupen and 21km southeast of Verviers. It can be reached by bus 394 from Eupen to St Vith (€3.60, 20 minutes, three daily) or bus 390 from Verviers to Rocherath (€3.60, 30 minutes, five daily).

VERVIERS

pop 52,800

Verviers sits 20-odd kilometres east of Liège, deep in the valley of the Vesdre River. From a modest medieval village it shook hands with the Industrial Revolution to become an international centre for wool processing and textile production in the early 1800s. Although these industries have since declined, the town still has two cloth factories – one processing cashmere and the other producing cloth for billiard tables (Belgium's love of this game makes it a worthwhile endeavour) – and students come from around the globe to attend wool courses at the town's industrial college.

Although Verviers is hardly essential viewing, this French-speaking town is a pleasant enough place for an overnight halt and boasts an excellent museum dedicated to its industrial past.

Information

Espace Full Option (☎ 087 31 19 84; Rue Xhavée 22; per hr €1; ☼ 10am-6pm Tue-Sun) Internet bar, 100m from Pl Verte.

Maison du Tourisme (☎ 087 30 79 26; www .paysdevesdre.be; Rue de la Chapelle 30; ☼ 9.30am-6pm Tue-Sun Apr-Oct, to 5pm Tue-Sun Nov-Mar) Inside the Centre Touristique de la Laine et de la Mode.

Sights

A handful of museums are dotted around town but the most engaging is the **Centre Touristique de la Laine et de la Mode** (☎ 087 35 57 03; www.verviersima.be; Rue de la Chapelle 30; adult/child/concession €6/3/4.50; ☼ 9.30am-6pm Tue-Sun Apr-Oct, to 5pm Tue-Sun Nov-Mar). This 'wool and fashion centre' occupies a 19th-century wool store on a small side street in a formerly run-down part of town. Visitors are taken on a tour using state-of-the-art multilingual headphones that tell the tale of Verviers' rise and fall. Well-preserved equipment – from old wool combs to mechanical spinners – are displayed and there are also examples of equipment invented in Verviers, such as the fouler, a napping machine.

The town's other two museums are the **Musée des Beaux-Arts et de la Céramique** (☎ 087 33 16 95; Rue Renier 17; adult/child/concession €2/free/1.50; ☼ 2-5pm Mon, Wed & Sat, 3-6pm Sun), which houses a small but high-quality collection of paintings from the 14th to 19th centuries and a very good collection of ceramics; and the nearby but less interesting **Musée d'Archéologie et de Folklore** (☎ 087 33 16 95; Rue des Raines 42; adult/child/concession €2/free/1.50; ☼ 2-5pm Tue & Thu, 9am-noon Sat, 10am-1pm Sun).

Sleeping & Eating

Camping Wesertal (☎ 087 55 59 61; Rue de l'Invasion 68, Membach-Baelen; camp sites per adult/child/tent/car €4/2/4.50/2) One of the closest camping grounds to town. It's located about 15km from Verviers in the direction of Lac de Gilleppe.

Chez Paul (☎ 087 23 22 21; www.chezpaul.be; Pl Albert I 5; s/d €95/120, menu €35) Easily the town's most interesting accommodation option. This pricey B&B is located in a hillside mansion above a restaurant of the same name, just out of the town centre but within easy walking distance. The four enormous rooms sport wooden floors and heavy furnishings typical of this region – antique beds and big old bathtubs – and are painted in bright modern colours.

Hôtel des Ardennes (☎ 087 22 39 25; www.hoteldes ardennesverviers.be in French; Pl de la Victoire 15; s/d with bathroom €50/65, without bathroom €35/50) This amiable little hotel is located across the square from the train station. Rooms are done out in creamy, floral tones – a world apart from the reception and 1900s-style brasserie, which feature rich reds, deer antlers and stained-glass windows.

L'Arsène du Pain (Pl Verte 42; ☼ 11am-6pm Mon-Sat) A good range of French-style, lip-smacking baguette sandwiches (€2.20 to €3.50) are available at this takeaway shop on Pl Verte, the town's main square. Also serves pastas and soups.

Brasserie de la Bourse (☎ 087 31 12 71; Rue Xhavée 2; mains €8-15; ☼ closed lunch Sun) A cheap corner *café* flanking Pl Verte, popular with locals for a sausage/chop fry-up. The exterior, with exposed wooden beams, is attractive.

Jean-Philippe Darcis (☎ 087 33 98 15; Rue Crapaurue 121; ☼ 10am-6pm Tue-Sat, 10am-1pm Sun) Modern tearoom and *chocolaterie*/pâtisserie that bills itself as the 'ambassador of Belgian chocolate'. Needless to say, it's firmly entrenched on the ladies' lunch circuit. The fruit tarts and pralines are scrumptious.

La Fourchette (☎ 087 33 52 79; Rue Crapaurue 181; mains €16-22, 3-course lunchtime menu €24) Rustic little French/Belgian restaurant just off Pl Verte. It serves an excellent *waterzooi* (cream-based fish or chicken stew).

Getting There & Away

Verviers' **train station** (☎ 025 28 28 28) is about 500m southwest of Pl Verte, the town's hub. The town is on the main train line between Liège (€3.40, 20 minutes, hourly) and Eupen (€2.90, 20 minutes, hourly). It's also possible to go from here to Spa (€2.50, 22 minutes, hourly), which is on a branch line.

TEC buses also leave from the train station. Bus 390 runs to Rocherath via the Botrange Nature Centre (€3.60, 30 minutes, five daily); and bus 395 heads to Malmédy (€3.60, 45 minutes, hourly).

EUPEN

pop 17,800

Wander into Eupen, and watch Belgium's identity change yet again. German is the language here (though most people understand French as well) and there's an undeniable Germanic feel to the place. Eupen is the capital of Belgium's Eastern Cantons (see boxed text, below), the small parcel of land that flanks Germany and also comprises the towns of Malmédy and St Vith. It's a small town, and pleasant enough, though there's little to do. Visitors mainly come to experience another piece of the Belgian jigsaw.

Information

Call Shop (Paveestrasse 37; per hr €3; ☯ 10.30am-8pm Mon-Sat) For internet access.

Office du Tourisme (☎ 087 55 34 50; www.eupen-info .be in Flemish, French & German; Marktplatz 7; ☯ 9am-5pm Mon-Fri, 9am-3pm Sat & Sun, closed Sun Sep-

---

POEPGELEI

The countryside between Liège and Verviers is known as the Pays de Herve. It's a pretty patchwork of undulating fields, hedges, dairy farms and orchards, and is home to Belgium's much-loved *sirop de Liège*. This sticky black substance is made from apples, pears and dates and is liberally spread on toast every morning in households around the country. Naturally enough, in Flemish kitchens it has a nickname – *poepgelei* or, wait for it, 'arse jelly'.

Jun) In the heart of town on the small main square and not far from the *Rathaus* (town hall). It publishes a free English-language walking-tour brochure that's well worth picking up if you intend wandering.

Sights & Activities

Opposite the tourist office is the office of the *Grenzecho*, Belgium's only German-language newspaper, which occupies a former cloth trader's house. A copy of the newspaper is displayed in a glass cabinet on the building's façade and is a focal point for passers-by.

From the other side of Marktplatz rises the twin-towered **St Nicolas** church, a heavy and distinct 18th-century structure. Inside, things are just as elaborate, with baroque embellishments including a lavish gilded pulpit.

The **Stadtmuseum** (☎ 087 74 00 05; www.eupener -stadtmuseum.org in Flemish, French & German; Gospertstrasse 52; adult/child €1.50/1; ☯ 9.30am-noon & 1-6pm Tue-Fri, 2-5pm Sat, 10am-noon & 2-5pm Sun) holds bits and pieces associated with the town's history. It's a couple of blocks downhill from the tourist office.

EASTERN CANTONS

Belgium's Eastern Cantons (Ostkantons in German, Oostkantons in Flemish or Cantons de l'Est in French) evolved separately from the rest of the country after France's defeat at the Battle of Waterloo. While most of the land now known as Belgium and Luxembourg was incorporated into the United Kingdom of the Netherlands, the towns of Eupen, Malmédy and St Vith were given to Prussia and subsequently became part of Germany.

In 1919, after WWI, the trio were ceded to Belgium under the Treaty of Versailles. But 20 years later, when WWII broke out, Germany claimed them back and the men from these towns were forced to fight alongside soldiers of the Reich throughout this war. In 1945 the Americans liberated the towns and they were handed back to Belgium.

The Hautes Fagnes actually divides the 854-sq-km area into two – the predominantly industrial region close to Eupen and the more-rural area based around St Vith.

Since 1984 the Eastern Cantons has had its own parliament, the *Rat der Deutschsprachigen Gemeinschaft* (Council of the German-speaking Community), as well as its own government.

In an industrial estate on the northern outskirts of town is the **Chokolademuseum** (Chocolate Museum; ☎ 087 59 29 67; www.chocojacques.be in Dutch & French; Industriestrasse 16; admission free; ☺ 9am-5pm Mon-Fri). It's housed within the Jacques chocolate factory, and visitors can learn about the production of chocolate, including cultivation, early machines and present-day methods. Take bus 22 to get here.

Sleeping & Eating

Camping an der Hill (☎ 087 74 46 17; Hütte 46; camp sites per adult/child/tent €3.50/2.50/5; ☺ year-round; ⚲) Closest ground to town, located on the southeastern outskirts of Eupen on the road to Monschau in Germany. Take bus 25 (direction Hütte).

Gîte d'Étape (☎ 087 55 31 26; www.gitesdetape.be; Judenstrasse 79; under/over 26yr €10.90/13.60) A large white hostel on the outskirts of town (10 minutes' walk from the centre), where you can punk down in frugal rooms.

Rathaus Hotel (☎ 087 74 28 12; www.rathaushotel.com; Rathausplatz 13; s/d €60/75) On the main road through town and the most comfortable option, despite its unexciting rooms. The hotel's modern brasserie, La Luna (☎ 087 55 83 85, pizzas €9 to €15, menus €17 to €25), is a popular local meeting place and is good for a drink or meal.

Other recommendations:

Panciera (☎ 087 74 33 42; Marktplatz 3; ☺ 10am-8pm Mon-Sat) Ice-cream parlour two doors from the tourist office, with yummy gelato.

Sandwicherie (☎ 087 56 13 70; Paveestrasse 28; ☺ Mon-Sat) Simple but decent fast-food-style outlet around the corner from the tourist office. Fat sandwiches from €5.

Getting There & Away

The **train station** ('Bahnhof' in German; ☎ 02 528 28 28) is about 10 minutes' walk north of the centre of town – head along Aachenerstrasse until you reach the *rathaus*, then turn left into Klosterstrasse. Eupen is easily reached by hourly train from Liège (€5.70, 45 minutes) or Verviers (€2.90, 20 minutes).

The **bus station** ('Bushof' in German; ☎ 087 74 25 92; Aachenerstrasse) is five minutes' walk from Marktplatz. Bus 394 goes from here to St Vith, calling in on the way at Botrange Nature Centre (€3.60, 20 minutes, three daily) in the Hautes Fagnes.

THE ARDENNES

Luxembourg

LEANNE LOGAN

Luxembourg Snapshot

Luxembourg is fairy-tale stuff…complete with the happy ending. Listen to the story of this land's tumultuous history and be drawn into a tale of counts and dynasties, wars and victories, fortresses and promontories. Only the dragon is missing.

The Grand Duchy stems from the loins of Count Sigefroi of the Ardennes, who raised a castle here in 963 AD. By the Middle Ages, Sigefroi's castle was a highly sought-after fortified city – the Burgundians, Spanish, French, Austrians and Prussians all waged bloody battles to secure it. Besieged, devastated and rebuilt 20 times in 400 years, it became the strongest fortress in Europe after Gibraltar. But it was Luxembourg who had its final say. After the Treaty of London recognised the country's autonomy in 1867, the Grand Duchy declared itself neutral in international affairs and torched its much-contested fort.

For an introduction to the Grand Duchy's nightlife, check out www .luxembourgbynight.com.

German invasion in 1914 squashed Luxembourg's neutrality. It was occupied again in WWII and fared badly throughout those years – local men were conscripted into the Nazi army and in 1944 came the Battle of the Ardennes (see p245).

After the war Luxembourg dumped its neutral status and joined NATO. It became a founding member of the EU, and today plays an active role on its governing bodies. Iron ore discoveries around 1850 started the country's economic success, but when steel slumped a century or so later, Luxembourg wooed foreigners with favourable banking and taxation laws. Today many nations aspire to an economy like this. With per capita GDP among the world's highest, Luxembourg boasts low unemployment and a consistently high standard of living. The country is headed by Grand Duke Henri, who came to the throne in 2000. Prime Minister Jean-Claude Juncker (Christian Social People's Party) has dominated the political scene since 1995.

Luxembourgers are a proud people whose national motto, *Mir wëlle bleiwe wat mir sin* ('We want to remain what we are'), sums up their independent spirit. The population of 469,000 is predominantly rural based – the only centres of any size are the capital, Luxembourg City, followed by Esch-sur-Alzette.

The Duchy's population is 87% Roman Catholic and comprises 30% foreigners – the EU's highest ratio. Luxembourgers are used to their country being held up as a successful multicultural model, though they're also quick to point out that combining a couple of European cultures, in this case Italian and Portuguese, is radically easier than melding different ethnic backgrounds.

FAST FACTS

Population: 469,000

Area: 2586 sq km

Unemployment: 3.5%

Inflation: 1.5%

GDP: US$31 billion

Minimum gross monthly salary: €1467

Most Luxembourgers speak French, German and their national tongue, Lëtzebuergesch, and many are fluent in English. Lëtzebuergesch was only proclaimed the national tongue in 1984, though it's long been an everyday language. The poem *Rénert* (Fox) by Michel Rodange (1827–76) was the first literary work published in Lëtzebuergesch. It takes a teasing look at 19th-century society and has been translated into English. Also worth tracking down is the film *Renart the Fox* by Thierry Schiel, a nomination contender for 2006's foreign-language Academy Awards.

Though too small for its full name to fit on most European maps, pint-sized Luxembourg (2586 sq km, or 82km long and 57km wide) is wonderfully diverse. Lush highlands and valleys in the northern Ardennes merge effortlessly with the Müllerthal's ancient forested landscape to the east. In the southeast snakes the Moselle valley with its steep vineyards and riverside hamlets. In between all this are rolling farmlands dotted with pristine, pastel-toned houses and medieval hilltop castles. Of most concern environmentally are air and water pollution in urban areas.

Luxembourg's cuisine is French and German based. The national dish is *judd mat gaardebounen* – slabs of smoked pork served in a thick cream-based sauce with chunks of potato and broad beans. Other specialities include *ferkelsrippchen* (grilled spareribs), *liewekniddelen mat sauerkraut* (liver meatballs with sauerkraut) and *kachkeis* (a cooked cheese). Beers to sink include Bofferding, Diekirch, Mousel and Simon Pils, after which comes a host of local fruity white and sparkling wines. From 2008 you can enjoy all this in an untainted environment, thanks to recent legislation banning smoking in restaurants and, during dining hours, in *cafés*.

European Capital of Culture in 2007, Luxembourg is sure to shine.

Luxembourg exposes its dining scene at www .resto.lu.

Luxembourg City

Luxembourg City is a storybook beauty. A thousand years old and World Heritage listed, this charming city – often described as Europe's most dramatically sited – radiates a composed air of old and new. Take the glossy art gallery and Philharmonie – stunning new structures that launched the city as European Capital of Culture in 2007. Add to these state-of-the-art museums, chic boutiques and Michelin-starred restaurants. And top it off with a striking location – high on a promontory overlooking deep valleys and sheer-sided gorges. For centuries, these gorges were the key to the city's defence. Nowadays they provide visitors with spectacular vistas over parklands and atmospheric old neighbourhoods like Grund and Clausen.

Start by exploring the neat network of cobbled streets that make up the pedestrianised Old Town – those around the Grand-Ducal palace are particularly appealing. Wander the Chemin de la Corniche, often described as Europe's 'most beautiful balcony' and you'll discover views of a city unrestricted by its tumultuous history or dramatic geography. Cross viaducts and bridges to reach verdant hillsides and neighbouring plateaux. The once boring but now enticing business district of Kirchberg is the outer showpiece. A short distance on, wartime cemeteries recall a bitter time in local and world history.

To fully enjoy the city, allow yourself to simply wander. Snap skylines pierced by turrets and towers, explore quaint riverside quarters, or dine at restaurants with views to make you swoon. Luxembourg City may be pint-sized compared to Paris but it's as romantic as capitals come.

HIGHLIGHTS

- **Art Treasure** The new Musée d'Art Moderne Grand-Duc Jean (p273)
- **Promenade** Europe's 'most beautiful balcony', the Chemin de la Corniche (p275)
- **History Buffs** Dank and dark in the Bock Casemates (p273)
- **War Graves** Patton's last call at the US Military Cemetery (p274)
- **Cycle City** Two wheels (p274) around Luxembourg
- **Wining** *Cafés* and bars (p279) in quaint quarters
- **Dining** Alfresco dining with an unbeatable view at Breedewee (p278)
- **Cinema Delights** Open-air screenings in summer at Cinématèque Municipal (p280)

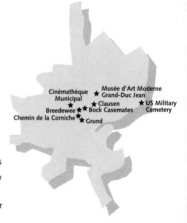

- POPULATION: 85,000

HISTORY

In 963 Sigefroi (or Siegfried, count of the Ardennes) built a castle on a rocky spur, so laying the foundations of the present-day capital. Sigefroi ruled the area as a fiefdom while his successors became vassals of the Holy Roman emperor. In 1354 the region became an independent duchy and its ruler, Wenceslas I, son of John the Blind, vastly extended the duchy's lands, incorporating Metz in the south and Limburg to the north. But the fort's strategic position made it much sought-after and the city's history, from here until 1815, runs largely parallel to Belgium's.

After Napoleon's defeat at Waterloo in 1815, the Congress of Vienna decided Luxembourg should become an independent Grand Duchy. It was ceded to King William I of Orange-Nassau, the ruler of the United Kingdom of the Netherlands, as his personal property; he was installed as the first grand duke. The Grand Duchy remained the property of the Dutch monarchy until 1890 when, due to the lack of a male heir, the crown passed to Duke Adolph of Nassau who headed a branch of the Nassau family and whose descendants rule to this day. For details on Luxembourg's current ducal family, see boxed text (p273).

In 1839, under the Treaty of London, the Grand Duchy was split in two. Belgium received the western portion, while William I kept the eastern side. The present-day borders were set. Recognising Luxembourg's potentially perilous position between France and Germany, Luxembourg was declared neutral in 1867. As a result, much of its historic fortifications were dismantled.

For more on Luxembourg history, see p266.

ORIENTATION

The gorges that hampered invading armies define Luxembourg's modern-day face. The central area neatly divides into four: the Old Town, the train station area, the lower town's river valley quarters and Kirchberg Plateau.

The largely pedestrianised Old Town is where Place d'Armes and Place Guillaume II are based. Although its street plan and aura is somewhat medieval, most of the buildings are 18th or 19th century.

To the south – across Pont Adolphe and Viaduc, two bridges spanning the Pétrusse

Valley – is the train station quarter. This area holds little appeal, and the streets opposite the station are somewhat sleazy. The train station, Gare Centrale, is 1.25km from Place d'Armes.

Below the Old Town's Bock fortifications are the picturesque river-valley quarters of Grund, Clausen and Pfaffenthal. The latter was the birthplace of Robert Schuman, a key instigator of European integration. Easy access to the Grund is provided by an elevator on Plateau du St Esprit (at the time of writing this plateau was one big construction site – skirt the works to reach the elevator).

Across the Alzette Valley is Kirchberg Plateau (see p273).

INFORMATION

Bookshops

Librairie Ernster (Map p272; ☎ 22 50 77 1; Rue du Fossé; ♥ 9am-6.30pm Mon-Fri, 9am-6pm Sat) Best bookshop in the city.

Emergency

Ambulance/Fire (☎ 112)
Emergency Roadside Service (☎ 42 60 00; ♥ 24hr) Club Automobile de Luxembourg's service.
Police (☎ 113)

Internet Access

Cyber Beach (per 15min/hr €1/3; ♥ 10am-8pm Mon-Fri, 1-8pm Sat & Sun) Old Town (Map p270; ☎ 26 47 80 70; 3 Rue du Curé); Train Station quarter (Map p270; ☎ 26 64 95 97; 8 Rue de Bonnevoie) Relaxed internet centre with two handy branches around the city.
Digital World (Map p270; ☎ 26 64 93 49; 45 Ave de la Liberté; per hr €3; ♥ 9am-10pm Mon-Fri, 9am-8pm Sat) At the back of a printing shop.

Laundry

Quick Wash (Map p270; Place de Strasbourg; ♥ 8.30am-6pm Mon-Sat) Provides self-service (per 5kg €10) and service (€12) washes.

Left Luggage

Gare Centrale (Map p270; Place de la Gare; per 48hr €2-4) Luggage lockers available.

Medical Services

Clinique Ste Thérèse (Map p270; ☎ 49 77 61; 36 Rue Ste Zithe) Central hospital providing 24-hour emergency service.
Pharmacie Goedert (Map p272; ☎ 22 23 991; 5 Place d'Armes; ♥ 9am-5.30pm Mon-Sat) Handy pharmacy.

LUXEMBOURG CITY

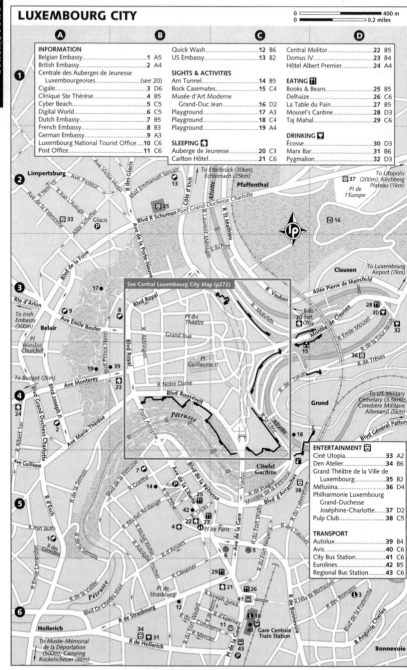

0 ____ 400 m
0 ____ 0.2 miles

INFORMATION
Belgian Embassy.....................1 A5
British Embassy.......................2 A4
Centrale des Auberges de Jeunesse
Luxembourgeoises..........(see 20)
Cigale...................................3 D6
Clinique Ste Thérèse...............4 B5
Cyber Beach..........................5 C5
Digital World.........................6 C5
Dutch Embassy.......................7 B5
French Embassy......................8 B3
German Embassy.....................9 A3
Luxembourg National Tourist Office....10 C6
Post Office...........................11 C6

Quick Wash..........................12 B6
US Embassy...........................13 B2

SIGHTS & ACTIVITIES
Am Tunnel............................14 B5
Bock Casemates.....................15 C4
Musée d'Art Moderne
Grand-Duc Jean...................16 D2
Playground............................17 A3
Playground............................18 C4
Playground............................19 A4

SLEEPING
Auberge de Jeunesse..............20 C3
Carlton Hôtel........................21 C6

Central Molitor......................22 B5
Domus IV..............................23 B4
Hôtel Albert Premier...............24 A4

EATING
Books & Beans.......................25 B5
Delhaize...............................26 C6
La Table du Pain.....................27 B5
Mousel's Cantine....................28 D3
Taj Mahal.............................29 C6

DRINKING
Écosse..................................30 D3
Marx Bar..............................31 B6
Pygmalion.............................32 D3

ENTERTAINMENT
Ciné Utopia...........................33 A2
Den Atelier...........................34 B6
Grand Théâtre de la Ville de
Luxembourg.......................35 B2
Mélusina...............................36 D4
Philharmonie Luxembourg
Grand-Duchesse
Joséphine-Charlotte.............37 D2
Pulp Club..............................38 C5

TRANSPORT
Autolux................................39 B4
Avis.....................................40 C6
City Bus Station......................41 C6
Eurolines..............................42 B5
Regional Bus Station...............43 C6

See Central Luxembourg City Map (p272)

LUXEMBOURG CITY IN...

One Day

The Old Town's pedestrianised core, **Place d'Armes**, is the essential start. From there it's an easy amble to either the **Musée National d'Histoire et d'Art** or the **Musée d'Histoire de la Ville de Luxembourg** – two innovative museums. Attached to the latter is **Café Am Musee**, the city's best (summer) lunch venue. Delve into the dark **Bock Casemates** and then wander along the **Chemin de la Corniche**, an elevated walkway that offers fab views. Take the **elevator** carved into the rock at Plateau du St Esprit down to the **Grund** for an apéritif at **L'Abbaye de Neumünster**. For delicious food and an unbeatable view, dine alfresco at **Breedewee**. If the weather's inclement, choose **Mosconi**. Chill out in the late evening at a pub in **Clausen**.

Two Days

Follow the one-day itinerary. Then, if you're here in summer, add the **Palais Grand-Ducal** to your things to see. The **Cathédrale Notre Dame** is worth a look for its venerated icon. **Brasserie Guillaume** is the spot for an early coffee or lunch. In the afternoon hightail it to the surreal Kirchberg Plateau and explore the new **Musée d'Art Moderne Grand-Duc Jean**. At night eat and drink at one of the many restaurants and *cafés* in the **Old Town**, then take in an outdoor flick at **Cinématèque Municipal**.

Money

Almost every second building in Luxembourg City is a bank – you will have no trouble making a foreign-currency exchange. ATMs are located inside Gare Centrale, outside the main post office and inside Luxembourg airport.

Post

Main Post Office (Map p270; ☎ 47 65 44 51; 25 Rue Aldringen; ☺ 7am-7pm Mon-Fri, 7am-5pm Sat)
Post Office (Map p270; ☎ 40 88 76 10; 38 Place de la Gare; ☺ 6am-7pm Mon-Fri, 6am-noon Sat)

Tourist Information

Interactive Touchscreens Old Town (Map p272; Rue du Curé); Gare Centrale (Map p270; Place de la Gare) Multilingual devices dispensing free tourist information; also located at Luxembourg airport.
Luxembourg City Tourist Office (Map p272; ☎ 22 28 09; www.lcto.lu; Place Guillaume II; ☺ 9am-7pm Mon-Sat, 10am-6pm Sun Apr-Sep, 9am-6pm Mon-Sat, 10am-6pm Sun Oct-Mar) Free city maps, walking-tour pamphlets and event guides.
Luxembourg National Tourist Office (Map p270; ☎ 42 82 82 20; www.visitluxembourg.lu; Place de la Gare; ☺ 8.30am-6.30pm Mon-Sat, 9am-12.30pm & 2-6pm Sun Jun-Sep, 9.15am-12.30pm & 1.45-6pm Oct-May) City and national information, with a handy location inside Gare Centrale.

Travel Agencies

Sotours (Map p272; ☎ 46 15 14 1; 15 Place du Théâtre) Long-established travel agent handling flights and holidays.

SIGHTS
Musée National d'Histoire et d'Art

The **National Museum of History and Art** (Map p272; ☎ 47 93 30 1; www.mnha.lu in French; Marché-aux-Poissons; adult/family €5/10; ☺ 10am-5pm Tue-Sun) is a state-of-the-art affair housed in a startling white building with a glass atrium. Take the glass elevator below ground to the prehistory section before winding up to Gallo-Roman remains. Level 2 is a must, home to the Salles Kutter, two rooms devoted to Luxembourg's Expressionist artist Joseph Kutter (1894–1941). Level 3 does art from the 13th to 20th centuries – look out for a small watercolour of Luxembourg City by William Turner and a drawing of Schengen castle by Victor Hugo.

DISCOUNT CARDS

The **Luxembourg Card** (www.luxembourgcard .lu; adult per 1/2/3 days €9/16/22, family of 2 adults & up to 3 children €18/32/44) gives free admission to country-wide attractions, plus unlimited use of public transport. It's valid from Easter to 31 October, and is available from tourist offices, hotels, train stations and camping grounds.

A good winter alternative is the three-day **Stater Museeskaart** (over 26 yr/under 18 yr/18-26 yr €7/free/5), allowing free admission to museums in Luxembourg City.

CENTRAL LUXEMBOURG CITY

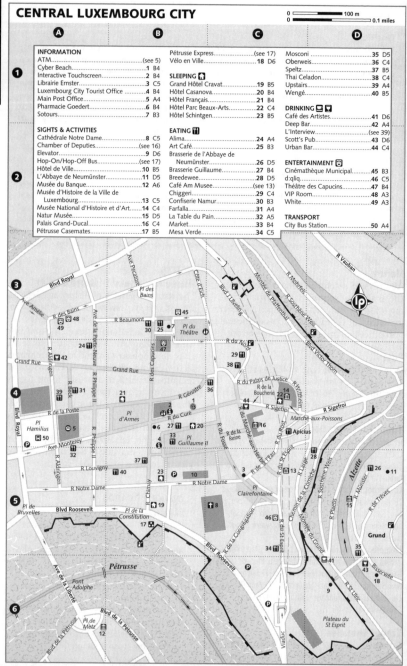

INFORMATION	
ATM	(see 5)
Cyber Beach	**1** B4
Interactive Touchscreen	**2** B4
Librairie Ernster	**3** C5
Luxembourg City Tourist Office	**4** B4
Main Post Office	**5** A4
Pharmacie Goedert	**6** B4
Sotours	**7** B3

SIGHTS & ACTIVITIES	
Cathédrale Notre Dame	**8** C5
Chamber of Deputies	(see 16)
Elevator	**9** D6
Hop-On/Hop-Off Bus	(see 17)
Hôtel de Ville	**10** B5
L'Abbaye de Neumünster	**11** D5
Musée du Banque	**12** A6
Musée d'Histoire de la Ville de Luxembourg	**13** C5
Musée National d'Histoire et d'Art	**14** C4
Natur Musée	**15** D5
Palais Grand-Ducal	**16** C4
Pétrusse Casemates	**17** B5

Pétrusse Express	(see 17)
Vélo en Ville	**18** D6

SLEEPING	
Grand Hôtel Cravat	**19** B5
Hôtel Casanova	**20** B4
Hôtel Français	**21** B4
Hôtel Parc Beaux-Arts	**22** C4
Hôtel Schintgen	**23** B5

EATING	
Alima	**24** A4
Art Café	**25** B3
Brasserie de l'Abbaye de Neumünster	**26** D5
Brasserie Guillaume	**27** B4
Breedewee	**28** D5
Café Am Musee	(see 13)
Chiggeri	**29** C4
Confiserie Namur	**30** B3
Farfalla	**31** A4
La Table du Pain	**32** A5
Market	**33** B4
Mesa Verde	**34** C5

Mosconi	**35** D5
Oberweis	**36** C4
Speltz	**37** B5
Thai Celadon	**38** C4
Upstairs	**39** A4
Wengé	**40** B5

DRINKING	
Café des Artistes	**41** D6
Deep Bar	**42** A4
L'Interview	(see 39)
Scott's Pub	**43** D6
Urban Bar	**44** C4

ENTERTAINMENT	
Cinémathèque Municipal	**45** B3
d:qliq	**46** C5
Théâtre des Capucins	**47** B4
VIP Room	**48** A3
White	**49** A3

TRANSPORT	
City Bus Station	**50** A4

Musée d'Histoire de la Ville de Luxembourg

The **Luxembourg City History Museum** (Map p272; ☎ 47 96 30 61; www.musee-hist.lu in French; 14 Rue du St Esprit; adult/concession/child €5/3.70/free; ☺ 10am-6pm Tue-Sun, 10am-8pm Thu) is another enjoyable multi-level complex, highlighted by a glass elevator that beautifully reveals the Old Town's rocky geology. Lower floors trace the city's history via a series of wooden maquettes, while the upper levels occupy splendid public rooms of a former mansion. Pick up the free English-language guide at reception.

Casemates

The **Bock Casemates** (Map p270; ☎ 22 28 09; Montée de Clausen; adult/child €1.75/1; ☺ 10am-5pm Mar-Oct) is a honeycomb of damp rock galleries and passages carved under the Bock by the Spaniards in 1744. Over the years the casemates have housed everything from bakeries to slaughterhouses and garrisons of soldiers; during WWI and WWII they sheltered 35,000 locals.

The **Pétrusse Casemates** (Map p272; Place de la Constitution; adult/child €1.75/1; ☺ 11am-4pm Easter, Jul & Aug) are much the same, but opening hours are more limited.

Palais Grand-Ducal

This Moorish-style **palace** (Map p272; ☎ 22 28 09; 17 Rue du Marché-aux-Herbes; adult/child €6/3; ☺ mid-Jul–early-Sep) was built during Spanish rule in the 1570s and later expanded. The royals once resided here but today it's used as the Grand Duke's office and for formal receptions (the family lives at the chateau of Colmar-Berg; for more on the ducal family, see boxed text, below). The palace opens for one-hour guided tours (just 40 tickets per tour) in summer; guided tours in English are held at 4.30pm Monday to Friday and 1.30pm on Saturday. Book at the Luxembourg City Tourist Office.

Cathédrale Notre Dame

Peek into the **Cathedral of Our Lady** (Map p272; Blvd Roosevelt; ☺ 10am-noon & 2-5.30pm) to see the nation's most revered idol, the *Lady Comforter of the Afflicted*, a small and elaborately dressed statue of the Virgin and child. The cathedral's black spires add character and balance to the city's distinctive skyline; however, inside it's an ugly hotchpotch of progressive renovations.

Kirchberg Plateau

Pont Grand-Duchesse Charlotte (Map p270), known as the Red Bridge for obvious reasons, connects the Old Town with Kirchberg Plateau. Tall blue-glass buildings announce entry to this ever-evolving business district, home to EU institutions, the Court of Justice, the European Investment bank and others. The newest and most impressive buildings to grace the horizon are the Philharmonie (p280) and the nearby Musée d'Art Moderne Grand-Duc Jean (below). The relative lack of people gives the plateau a surreal feel, like a futuristic cityscape. Pick up Luxembourg City Tourist Office's free booklet *Kirchberg – Art & Architecture in Public Space* before coming here. It includes a colour map and descriptions of some buildings. Bus 18 from Gare Centrale or Place Hamilius does a 45-minute round trip that's good for an overview, but it doesn't stop near either the Philharmonie or Musée d'Art Moderne Grand-Duc Jean.

Musée d'Art Moderne Grand-Duc Jean

Luxembourg's new **Modern Art Museum** (Mudam; Map p270; ☎ 45 37 85 22; www.mudam.lu; 3 Parc Dräi Eechelen; adult/concession €5/3; ☺ 11am-6pm Thu-Mon, 11am-8pm Wed) opened to rave reviews in 2006.

LUXEMBOURG'S ROYALS

In 1919, with the monarchies around them collapsing, the Grand Duchy put its royal family up for referendum. The result was a resounding 'yes', and never again has their existence been questioned. Unlike in England and Belgium, where dissent simmers over how much the royals cost, here their presence is a symbol of stability and prosperity.

Most people in Luxembourg today grew up supporting either Grand Duchess Charlotte, who reigned for 45 years, or her successor, Grand Duke Jean, who abdicated in 2000 at the age of 79 in favour of his eldest son, the current Grand Duke Henri. Henri and Grand Duchess Maria Teresa, a Cuban-born commoner whom Henri met at university in Geneva, married in 1981 and have four sons and a daughter. Their continued acceptance is due in part to their relative 'normality'. Although they inhabit castles, the royal kids go to ordinary schools, and it's possible to bump into a prince at the movies or to see the Grand Duchess out shopping.

Created by Chinese-American architect Ieoh Ming Pei (responsible for the Louvre pyramid in Paris), the magnificent glass-roofed gallery harmoniously blends contemporary and old, with its turreted centrepiece and glass wings sitting back to back with a centuries-old Vauban fortress. The museum's collection includes everything from photography to fashion, design and multimedia. Take bus 125 or 192 from Gare Centrale or Place Hamilius to the stop 'Fort Belaimont'.

Natur Musée

If travelling with kids, make this one of your first stops. Recently given a fabulous facelift, this **Natural History Museum** (Map p272; ☎ 46 22 33 1; www.mnhn.lu in French; 25 Rue Münster; adult/child/family €4.50/3/9; ⊙ 10am-6pm Tue-Sun) in the Grund does dinosaurs, the big bang and other interactive exhibits, all especially designed to keep little hands and curious minds busy. The café has snacks and cheap meals, making it a great lunch spot for families.

L'Abbaye de Neumünster

Still in the Grund and well worth a wander is the newly renovated **Neumünster Abbey** (Map p272; ☎ 26 20 52 1; 28 Rue Münster; ⊙ 11am-6pm). This glass-covered complex houses a temporary exhibition gallery, outdoor performing arts venue, art shop and brasserie (see p278).

Musée du Banque

Where better than Luxembourg to spend an hour browsing through a **Bank Museum** (Map p272; ☎ 40 15 59 03; 1 Place de Metz; admission free; ⊙ 9am-5.30pm Mon-Fri)? It's housed in the headquarters of the Banque et Caisse d'Épargne de l'État, one of Luxembourg's 180 banks, and traces 140 years of tradition and innovation in banking, from piggy banks to ATMs and bank robbers.

Am Tunnel

Appropriate name for an underground **art gallery** (Map p270; ☎ 40 15 24 50; 16 Rue Ste Zithe; admission free; ⊙ 9am-5.30pm Mon-Fri, 2-6pm Sun). Carved 350m through the Bourbon plateau, it's devoted to temporary exhibitions, but also has a permanent display on Edward Steichen (see p287).

Musée-Mémorial de la Déportation

Thousands of Luxembourgers were deported during Germany's WWII occupation of Luxembourg. The train station where their harrowing journey began is now a **Deportation Memorial-Museum** (☎ 48 32 32; Gare de Hollerich, 3a Rue de la Déportation; ⊙ 2-5.30pm Tue-Fri Apr-Oct, 2-5.30pm Thu Nov-Mar). Bus 5 stops out the front.

Military Cemeteries

Only planes taking off from nearby Luxembourg airport disturb the peace at the country's two main war cemeteries.

The easiest to reach and most visited is the **US Military Cemetery** (⊙ 9am-5pm) at Hamm, 4km east of the capital. Here lie more than 5000 US war dead, including famous general George S Patton Jr (see p288). Most of those buried or remembered here were killed during the US' WWII liberation of Luxembourg and the subsequent Battle of the Ardennes (see boxed text, p245). Patton's headstone is easily identified among the rows of white crosses and stars, each marked with flags from the US and Luxembourg. White-stone pylons commemorate the soldiers whose bodies were never found, and enormous wall maps detail the main events from the 1944–45 battles. To get here, take bus 8 from Hôtel Alfa opposite Gare Centrale (15 minutes, hourly Monday to Saturday, every two hours Sunday).

The **Cimetière Militaire Allemand** (German Military Cemetery; ⊙ 9am-5pm) at Sandweiler is 1.5km east of the US Military Cemetery (it's signposted from here). No buses stop nearby, so you'll either need to walk or have your own wheels. Some 11,000 German soldiers lie beneath sombre grey headstones behind an oppressive stone doorway. Established in the 1950s, this cemetery was the first of its kind outside Germany. The caretaker who lives in the nearby house will probably show you around.

ACTIVITIES

The topography's not flat, but those with decent muscles will find Luxembourg City great for biking. The only rental outlet, and it's a good one, is **Vélo en Ville** (Map p272; ☎ 47 96 23 83; 8 Bisserwée; per half-/full day €12.50/20; ⊙ 10am-noon & 1-8pm Apr-Oct). Children's bikes are available (same price as adult bikes), as are toddler seats (per day/week €5/20). Under 26 year olds get a 20% discount (not available on half-day rentals).

An excellent route to start with is the 40km Piste Cyclable du Centre (signposted PC1), which circles the city's outskirts. The Vélo en Ville crew supply a basic B&W map of this route.

WALKING TOUR

This tour winds around much of the Old Town and involves an hour of easy walking (excluding time spent inside museums or attractions).

Start at **Place d'Armes (1)**, an intimate square chock-full with pavement terraces in summer. Head to **Place de la Constitution (2)** for views over the Pétrusse Valley and the imposing spans of Pont Adolphe and Viaduc. The latter dates to 1859 and, unsurprisingly, is known as the Old Bridge. From here it's possible to descend to the **park (3)** that lies in the valley below or to detour into the **Pétrusse Casemates (4**; p273).

Sitting firmly in the background on Place de la Constitution is the city's main church, **Cathédrale Notre Dame (5**; p273). Continue along Blvd Roosevelt to **Plateau du St Esprit (6)**, where superb panoramas up both valleys and over the Grund

have been blocked by a building frenzy. Skirt the construction site to reach the free **lift (7)**, dug in the cliff here, down to the Grund. Stay on the plateau to arrive at the **Chemin de la Corniche (8)** – a pedestrian promenade hailed as 'Europe's most beautiful balcony' – which winds north along the course of the 17th-century ramparts to the **Bock (9)**, the cliff on which Count Sigefroi built his mighty fort. The castle and much of the fortifications were destroyed between 1867 and 1883 following the Treaty of London. There's little left – the main attractions are the view and the nearby entrance to the **Bock Casemates (10**; p273), a 23km network of underground passages spared from destruction because of their delicate position in relation to the town.

From the Bock, it's a short walk to either the **Musée National d'Histoire et d'Art (11**; p271) or the equally impressive **Musée d'Histoire de la Ville de Luxembourg (12**; p273). If you're here in July and August, also visit the **Palais Grand-Ducal (13**; p273). Next to the palace, added as an annexe in 1859, is the **Chamber of Deputies (14)**, where the parliament sits. From here it's a short stroll past formal government edifices to **Place Guillaume II (15)**, lined with 19th-century buildings,

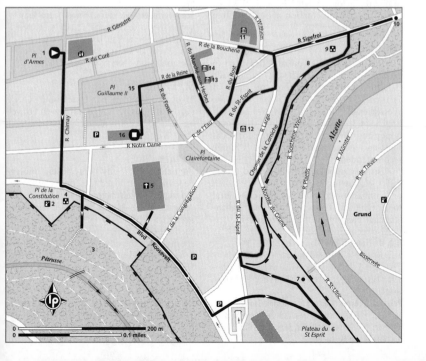

including the neoclassical **Hôtel de Ville** (16; Town Hall), which was largely constructed from the stones of an old monastery.

LUXEMBOURG CITY FOR CHILDREN

To keep toddlers and younger children happy there's the **Natur Musée** (p274), the **Pétrusse Express** (below) or the **Bock Casemates** (p273). Be warned, though, that little legs may soon tire of the steps in the latter. Two **playgrounds** (Map p270) are located in the gardens 500m west of Place d'Armes, and there's another **playground** (Map p270) by the river in the Grund. For kids aged five to 13 years there's **City Safari** (☎ 22 28 09; admission €5), a two-hour discovery tour of the city designed especially for children (unaccompanied or with parents), organised by the Luxembourg City Tourist Office. It's held at 2.30pm Tuesday to Sunday from July to mid-September.

Cycling is a good way to keep kids of all ages on the go – plonk older kids on their own bike or strap younger kids onto yours. For details, see p274.

At the end of July, **Kanner in the City** is a kid's festival held on Place Guillaume II – check the tourist office for the date.

For general information about travelling with children, see p303.

TOURS

The Luxembourg City Tourist Office runs two excellent guided walks. The City Promenade (adult/child €7/3.50; two hours; in English at 1pm daily) covers the Old Town, while the Wenzel walk (adult/child €8/4; two hours; in English at 3pm Saturday) winds through the upper and lower towns, through fortifications and along nature trails, and is highly recommended.

Also very popular are self-guided theme walks – following in the footsteps of Vauban or Schuman for example – or an architectural tour of the Old Town. Pick up free English-language pamphlets from the tourist office.

Also recommended:

Hop-On/Hop-Off Bus (Map p272; ☎ 23 65 11; www.sightseeing.lu; adult/child/family €12/6/30; ☺ 9.40am-5.20pm Mar-May, to 6.20pm Jun-Oct) Double-decker bus that departs every 20 minutes from Place de la Constitution.

Pétrusse Express (Map p272; adult/child/family €8/4/25; ☺ Easter-Oct) Toy train that does a one-hour tour from Place de la Constitution down to the Grund via the Pétrusse and Alzette valleys.

GAY & LESBIAN LUXEMBOURG

Luxembourg's national gay and lesbian organisation is **Rosa Lëtzebuerg** (www.gay.lu in French). It publishes *La Pie qui Chante*, a monthly newsletter in French and German with information on what's happening in Luxembourg City plus a small list of useful addresses.

Cigale (Map p270; 60 Rue des Romains; ☺ 1-5pm Mon & Tue, 4-8pm Wed, 1-7pm Thu) is a gay and lesbian information centre, just east of Gare Centrale.

Luxembourg Pride is a small festival held in mid-June.

FESTIVALS & EVENTS

Octave For details on this annual pilgrimage, see p307.

Luxembourg National Day For details on the Grand Duchy's biggest event, see p307.

Summer in the City (www.summerinthecity.lu) Summer-long series of concerts and street animation. Highlights include: Rock um Knuedler (early July; Place Guillaume II), a one-day rock festival plugging home-grown bands; and Blues 'n' Jazzrallye (mid-July; admission free).

Schueberfouer (www.fouer.lu in French) Annual fortnight-long fun fair with roots stretching to a 14th-century sheep market. Today shepherds still bring their flocks to town on one Sunday, known as the Hammelsmarsch. Takes over Glacis parking station from the last week of August.

SLEEPING

Most accommodation in Luxembourg City is geared towards midrange and top-end travellers. No B&Bs enliven the city centre, though there is one popular hostel.

Budget

For details on the city's only hostel, Auberge de Jeunesse, see boxed text (opposite).

Camping Kockelscheuer (☎ 47 18 15; www.camp-kockelscheuer.lu; 22 Route de Bettembourg; camp site per adult/child/tent €3.75/2/4.50; ☺ Easter-Oct) Pleasantly sited between a forest and a sports centre 4km southwest of the city. To get there, take bus 5 from Gare Centrale (quay No 1) or Place Hamilius (quay No 2).

Midrange

Hôtel Schintgen (Map p272; ☎ 22 28 44; schintgn@pt.lu; 6 Rue Notre Dame; s/d/tr/q €70/85/90/95) Family-run establishment that has the distinction of being the *only* budget hotel in the Old Town.

Choose it for the handy location and friendly staff, not the ordinary rooms.

Hôtel Français (Map p272; ☎ 47 45 34; www.hotel francais.lu; 14 Place d'Armes; s/d Mon-Fri €97/125, Sat & Sun €90/118; 🖥 ♿) Intimate hotel dotted with *objets d'art* and with a prized location on the Old Town's main square. The 24 rooms are a tad small, but they make up for it with calm, modern décor. The hotel is squarely aimed at couples and businesspeople, and the proud staff run a tight ship. Join locals for a cake and coffee in the ground-floor brasserie, one of Place d'Armes most popular spots.

Hôtel Casanova (Map p272; ☎ 22 04 93; www.hotel casanova.lu; 10 Place Guillaume II; s/d €99/130) Fabulously sited on one of the Old Town's two main squares, but otherwise there's little to excite the senses. The rooms are OK, the staff bland. Discounts are available some weekends.

Domus IV (Map p270; ☎ 46 78 78 1; www.domus.lu; 37 Ave Monterey; d with/without kitchen €150/135; ⊠ ⊠ 🖥) Good for longer stays, this hotel offers zany decorations and innovative self-contained rooms – expect beds that fold into the wall, vogue furnishings and modern art. It's on a

busy thoroughfare, two blocks from Place d'Armes. Breakfast is €15.

Central Molitor (Map p270; ☎ 48 99 11; www.hotel molitor.lu; 28 Ave de la Liberté; s/d/tr Mon-Fri €135/160/170, Sat & Sun €95/120/130; ⊠ 🖥) Distinguished little hotel, half-way between the Old Town and the train station quarter, that's been in the business for over a century and now belongs to the Golden Tulip chain. Expect '80s décor, good-sized rooms and a decent restaurant. Families are welcome (there's a baby cot and kids under four years stay for free).

Top End

Hôtel Albert Premier (Map p270; ☎ 44 24 42 1; www.al bert1er.lu; 2a Rue Albert 1er; ste Mon-Thu from €225, continental breakfast €15, ste Fri-Sun incl breakfast from €155; ⊠ 🖥) One for lovers of decoration overkill, this boutique hotel's 14 swanky rooms burst with Gothic excesses. It's located 750m west of Place d'Armes on an unassuming back street. Inquire about summer discounts in July and August.

Grand Hôtel Cravat (Map p272; ☎ 22 19 75; www .hotelcravat.lu; 29 Blvd Roosevelt; s/d Mon-Fri €245/380, Sat & Sun €150/200; ⊠) The six-storey Cravat is a Luxembourg institution favoured by well-off Belgians and Germans enjoying a weekender. Décor-wise it's staid bordering on boring, though the chandeliers, attentive doorman and superb location are redeeming features. Substantial discounts are offered from July to mid-September.

Hôtel Parc Beaux-Arts (Map p272; ☎ 44 23 23 1; www .hpb.lu; 1 Rue Sigefroi; ste Mon-Thu €330, Fri-Sun €190; ⊠ 🖥) Delicious new Old Town address. Press the doorbell to enter the city's most charming hotel, a trio of 18th-century houses converted into 10 gorgeous suites. Elegant creams and caramels are the tones throughout, and the atmosphere exudes understated luxury – expect silk curtains and original artworks, including some by Luxembourg artists.

EATING

The Old Town, Grund and Clausen are the go for dining. In summer these areas turn into open-air terraces as *café* owners roll back the winter canopies, and tables spill onto pavements and tree-lined squares.

Cafés & Brasseries

La Table du Pain Old Town (Map p272; ☎ 24 16 08; 19 Ave Monterey; ☺ 7am-7pm); Train Station Quarter (Map p270; ☎ 29 56 63; 37 Ave de la Liberté; ☺ 7am-7pm; ✗) A small bakery chain that also has convivial, completely nonsmoking cafés. Both branches serve breakfast options, baguette sandwiches (€4.60 to €7.20) and big salads (€12).

Books & Beans (Map p270; ☎ 26 19 64 06; 21 Ave de la Liberté; snacks €5-7; ☺ 7am-6pm Mon-Fri, 10am-5pm Sun) No polished floorboards here. This cosy book café offers a laid-back respite to all that's prim and proper in Luxembourg City. And the locals love it. Go for a hot chocolate and spend an hour or two browsing display books.

Farfalla (Map p272; ☎ 46 51 59; 8 Rue Beck; mains €6-11; ☺ lunch & dinner) Boisterous brasserie that buzzes with happy diners munching on woodfired pizza or steaming bowls of pasta. Absolutely informal (queue at the till when it's time to pay), and a great spot to satisfy spaghetti-starved kids.

Café Am Musee (Map p272; ☎ 26 20 25 95; 14 Rue du St Ésprit; mains €10-12; ☺ 10am-6pm Tue-Sun, 10am-8pm Thu) Well-hidden local favourite, attached to the Musée d'Histoire de la Ville de Luxembourg, but easily overlooked. At its best for a casual lunch (modern international cuisine) on a fine summer day (reservations needed). Big umbrellas and a handful of open-air tables line an old stone wall – kick back and relax with views over the Grund and Alzette Valley. It's also good for young kids – highchairs and coloured pencils are dispensed and, when action's needed, there's a shady garden to explore.

Art Café (Map p272; ☎ 26 27 06 52; 1a Rue Beaumont; plat du jour €10, light meals €11.50; ☺ 8am-7pm Mon-Sat) One in the new wave of lounge bars-*cafés* that's revitalising Luxembourg's eating and entertainment scene. Theatrical velvet décor sets the scene; sandwiches, salads and wok dishes are the mainstays. Head out the back to relax on the enclosed terrace.

Brasserie Guillaume (Map p272; ☎ 26 20 20 20; 12 Place Guillaume II; mains €14-22; ☺ 10am-1am, kitchen closes midnight) The Old Town's best brasserie. Big and brash, it opens out onto Place Guillaume II and is favoured by the city's upper crust on

Saturday mornings when a market takes over the square. It's known for seafood and French cuisine, but caters eclectically – vegetarian and traditional Luxembourg fare also get a look-in. Great spot for a late-night bite, too.

Brasserie de l'Abbaye de Neumünster (Map p272; ☎ 26 20 52 98 1; 28 Rue de Münster; mains €15-22; ☺ 8am-midnight) New brasserie incorporated into the recently renovated Neumünster Abbey complex (p274). Offers French cuisine, a huge open-air terrace and colourful décor. Delightful spot for a drink or well-priced bite while exploring the Grund.

Mousel's Cantine (Map p270; ☎ 47 01 98; 46 Montée de Clausen, Clausen; mains €18-20; ☺ closed Sun & lunch Sat) Rustic *café* attached to the former Mousel brewery. Known for its hearty Luxembourg cuisine and does an excellent plate of assorted specialities for €20. Beer drinkers can sample a *gezwickelte beier*, an unfiltered beer drunk from an old-style crock.

Two tearooms worth a detour are **Oberweis** (Map p272; ☎ 47 07 03; 19 Grand Rue; ☺ 10am-6pm Mon, 7.30am-6pm Tue-Fri, 8am-6pm Sat) and **Confiserie Namur** (Map p272; ☎ 22 34 08; 27 Rue des Capucins; ☺ 2-6pm Mon, 8.30am-6pm Tue-Sat). Indulge in moreish cakes, chocolates and ice cream.

Restaurants

Taj Mahal (Map p270; ☎ 40 59 41; 2 Rue de Strasbourg; mains €13-19; ☺ lunch & dinner Wed-Mon) Authentic Indian restaurant in the train station quarter that looks like nothing but draws a full house. Subtle décor, a large section out the back (good for nonsmokers) and great-value vegetarian/nonvegetarian menus for around €22/25.

Thai Celadon (Map p272; ☎ 47 49 34; 1 Rue du Nord vegetarian mains €13, meat €17-20; ☺ closed Sun & lunch Sat)

THE AUTHOR'S CHOICE

Breedewee (Map p272; ☎ 22 26 96; 9 Rue Large; three-course menu €20, mains €20-32, six-course menu dégustation €55; ☺ lunch & dinner) Wooed by a view? No restaurant in Luxembourg can match it – in fine weather. This modern but elegant little place has a separate terrace perched high on the Corniche in a setting that's quite unique. A dozen tables are serviced by penguin-style waiters who shuttle back and forth to the main building where the French cuisine is prepared. On a warm summer's evening, this is as romantic as they come. Reservations essential.

Excellent Thai food is served in calm minimal surroundings in this Old Town restaurant.

Mesa Verde (Map p272; ☎ 46 41 26; 11 Rue du St-Esprit; vegetarian mains €18, fish €23-25; ⏰ lunch Wed-Fri, dinner Tue-Sat, closed lunch Aug; ✗) Vegetarian and seafood dishes are the mainstay of this exciting restaurant. Exotic colours and imaginative cuisine mean it's often full, and deservedly so.

Upstairs (Map p272; ☎ 26 27 01 12; 21 Rue Aldringen; mains €19-23; ⏰ lunch Tue-Sat, dinner Tue-Fri) Well-hidden, 1st-floor local eatery (entry at the back of the pub, L'Interview) that does great Vietnamese and Japanese dishes in no-fuss surroundings. The lunch-time *plat du jour* (nonvegetarian or vegetarian dishes; €10) is superb value.

Chiggeri (Map p272; ☎ 22 82 36; 15 Rue du Nord; mains €24-32; ⏰ lunch & dinner) Hip street-level *café* topped by a popular 2nd-floor restaurant. The *café* does well-priced bistro fare; the casual but innovative restaurant features an extraordinary wine list (including many by the glass). Summer sees a breezy terrace set up across the road.

Wengé (Map p272; ☎ 26 20 10 58; 15 Rue Louvigny; mains €25-30; ⏰ 8am-6.30pm Mon-Sat plus dinner Wed & Fri) Local lunch favourite. Top-notch, casual restaurant and food shop that serves (and sells) some of the best coffee, cheese, *pâtisseries* and French cuisine in town. All shiny and black inside, or dine at one of the few tables on the pedestrianised street.

Speltz (Map p272; ☎ 47 49 50; 8 Rue Chimay; mains €25-35, 3-/6-course menu €45/75; ⏰ lunch & dinner Tue-Sat) French *haute cuisine* and seafood served with aplomb are the trademarks of this Luxembourg institution. Just three small rooms – all refined and mellow – and a dozen street-side terrace tables mean you'll need to phone ahead.

For restaurant/clubs, see p280.

THE AUTHOR'S CHOICE

Mosconi (Map p272; ☎ 54 69 94; 13 Rue Münster, Grund; mains €24-37, menu degustation €66; ⏰ lunch & dinner Tue-Sat) Come well attired to dine at Luxembourg's first Italian restaurant to be double starred by Michelin. Pasta *gastronomique*, fish and meat dishes are served in old-world surroundings, though it's the home-made ravioli that rates special mention. In fine weather dine on a tiny riverside terrace with the Old Town's cliff-face soaring above. Reservations essential.

Self-Catering

Alima (Map p272; Ave de la Porte-Neuve) Old Town supermarket.

Delhaize (Map p270; Place de la Gare; ⏰ 7am-8pm Mon-Fri, 7am-6pm Sat, 7am-noon Sun) Supermarket near Gare Centrale.

Market (Map p272; Place Guillaume II; ⏰ mornings Wed & Sat) Fresh produce.

DRINKING

The Old Town, Grund, Clausen and Hollerich are the most popular spots for a drink.

L'Interview (Map p272; ☎ 47 36 65; 19 Rue Aldringen; ⏰ 7am-1am) Raw *café* close to Place Hamilius and a great place to simply hang with a drink. In summer the big windows are opened to the street and the atmosphere hums.

Urban Bar (Map p272; ☎ 26 47 85 78; 2 Rue de la Boucherie; ⏰ noon-1am) Unashamedly hip address in the Old Town that draws a cosmopolitan crowd (lots of English spoken).

Deep Bar (Map p272; ☎ 26 20 04 23; 11 Rue Aldringen; ⏰ Wed-Mon) Still in the Old Town, but this time deep and dark. The type of place you end up when all else is closed.

Café des Artistes (Map p272; ☎ 46 13 27; 22 Montée du Grund; ⏰ evenings Tue-Sun) Nostalgic little Grund *café* that's been around since 1968 and has candles to prove it. Brel and Piaf watch from old posters, and the ceiling's about as smoke stained as they come. The *café's* pride and joy is an old piano that bursts into life with folk tunes when the mood's right (usually Wednesday to Saturday).

Scott's Pub (Map p272; ☎ 22 64 75; Bisserwée; ⏰ noon-1am) Typical British pub down in the Grund that's great for a drink while exploring this quaint quarter.

Pygmalion (Map p270; ☎ 42 08 60; 19 Rue de la Tour Jacob; ⏰ 4pm-1am Sun-Thu, 4pm-3am Fri & Sat) Known locally as 'The Pyg', this moody little Irish haunt is one of several good pubs in Clausen, an area favoured by late-night revellers.

Écosse (Map p270; 1 Rue Émile Mousel; ⏰ 4pm-1am) A Scottish pub-brasserie in Clausen, with nonexistent décor and a cherished riverside terrace. Take bus 9 or night bus CN1 from Gare Centrale or Place Hamilius.

Marx Bar (Map p270; 42 Rue de Hollerich; ⏰ from 5pm) Best bet in the alternate nightlife hub of Hollerich.

ENTERTAINMENT

To find out what's on, the weekly English-language magazine *352 Luxembourg News* has extensive entertainment listings plus cinema screenings (including films in English). Also check out **Nightlife** (www.nightlife-mag.lu). Ticket agencies include **Luxembourg Ticket** (☎ 47 08 951; www.luxembourgticket.lu in French) and **E-Ticket** (www.e-ticket.lu).

Cinemas

Cinémathèque Municipal (Map p272; ☎ 29 12 59; 17 Place du Théâtre; adult/concession €4/2.80) Closest thing in Luxembourg to an art-house cinema and cheap to boot. Golden oldies and cult classics line up two or three times daily – the cinema carries 10,000 titles. Also does open-air screenings in July and August at 10pm in the courtyard of nearby Théâtre des Capucins – great atmosphere.

Ciné Utopia (Map p270; ☎ 22 46 11; 16 Ave de la Faïencerie) Ten-minute walk north of the Old Town; five screens and a mix of mainstream and art house.

Utopolis (☎ 42 95 95; 45 Ave J F Kennedy, Kirchberg) Ten-screen multiplex with a solid Hollywood line-up. There are midnight screenings on Saturday and Sneak Previews (newly released surprise film) at 10pm on Thursday. Take bus 18 from Gare Centrale (quay No 3; 23 minutes) or Place Hamilius (quay No 1; 20 minutes).

Live Music

Pubs and *cafés* doing weekly, let alone nightly, live music are a rare breed. Most big names perform at either Kulturfabrik (p296) or the new Rockhal (p296) in Esch-sur-Alzette, Luxembourg's second-largest town, just 25 minutes' away by train.

d:qliq (Map p272; ☎ 26 73 62; www.dqliq.com; 17 Rue du St-Esprit; 5pm-1am Tue-Sat, 5pm-3am Fri) Intimate new bar that's brought life to the Old Town's live music scene. The three floors offer different venues: a cellar bar for experimental acts; free jazz concerts at ground zero; and international bands on the 1st floor (this zone is affectionately known as 'the wardrobe' due to its size – 120 people max). Hip and lesser-known bands from abroad – either jazz, rock, electro or house – are the staples.

Den Atelier (Map p270; ☎ 49 54 66; www.atelier.lu; 56 Rue de Hollerich; generally from 7pm Thu-Sat) The city's main venue for local and visiting groups, located about 500m west of Gare Centrale in Hollerich, an off-the-beaten-track nightlife area. The Luxembourg City Tourist Office sells tickets for some performances and will know what's on.

Nightclubs

White (Map p272; ☎ 26 20 11 40; www.white.lu; 21 Rue des Bains; restaurant-lounge lunch & dinner Mon-Sat, club midnight-6am Wed-Sat) Ever seen one of those insect zappers that uses a blue-fluoro light to lure night-time nasties to a sizzling finale? Well White's the human equivalent, only here the colour is green.

VIP Room (Map p272; ☎ 26 18 78 67; www.viproom.lu; 19 Rue des Bains; restaurant 7pm-midnight Wed-Sat, club from 11pm) A newie in the restaurant-lounge-club genre. This one has sister establishments all round France, and manages to catch visiting international celebs on camera when passing through.

Mélusina (Map p270; ☎ 43 59 22; www.melusina.lu; 145 Rue de la Tour Jacob; Fri & Sat) Restaurant/club in Clausen and one of the city's most popular dance spots. Big on house and even entices guest DJs.

Pulp Club (Map p270; ☎ 49 69 40; www.pulp.lu; 36 Blvd d'Avranches; from 11pm Fri & Sat) Long-standing club across the Pétrusse River from the Old Town.

Theatre, Opera & Dance

Philharmonie Luxembourg Grande-Duchesse Joséphine-Charlotte (Map p270; ☎ 26 32 26 32; www.philharmonie.lu; 1 Place de l'Europe) The Philharmonie is Luxembourg's new concert venue, a stunning oval job that offers jazz, classical and opera, and that has imbued life into boring Kirchberg. The glass building is immediately obvious on the right once across the Red Bridge. Take bus 125 or 192 from Gare Centrale or Place Hamilius to the stop 'Fort Belaimont'.

Grand Théâtre de la Ville de Luxembourg (Map p270; ☎ 47 96 39 00; www.theater-vdl.lu, in French; 1 Blvd R Schuman) Until nudged out of first place by the Philharmonie, this was the nation's premier performing arts complex. It still offers state-of-the-art facilities and an impressive line-up of international dance, opera and theatre.

Also recommended:

Théâtre des Capucins (Map p272; ☎ 47 96 40 54; 9 Place du Théâtre) Small theatre with few offerings in English.

SHOPPING

The pedestrianised streets around Place d'Armes offer chic boutiques (Louis Vuitton, Delvaux and Hermes) on Rue Phillippe II and department stores on Grand Rue.

On the second and fourth Saturday morning of each month, it's *brocante* (bric-a-brac) time on Place d'Armes.

Should you happen to be here on the first Monday in September, watch out for the *braderie*, a big pavement sale.

GETTING THERE & AWAY

For details on Luxembourg airport and airlines flying in and out of the Grand Duchy, see p315.

The main international bus company servicing Luxembourg City is **Eurolines** (Map p270; ☎ 26 29 80; 26 Ave de la Liberté). Destinations include Amsterdam (€22, 8½ hours, one daily), Brussels (€15, 3¾ hours, one or two daily) and Paris (€24, 5½ hours, five weekly). For more details on Eurolines, see p317. Buses to destinations throughout Luxembourg, such as Echternach in the Müllerthal or Remich in the Moselle Valley, leave from Luxembourg City's regional bus station (to the left as you exit the train station).

International train services depart from Luxembourg City's **Gare Centrale** (Map p270; Place de la Gare). Services to neighbouring countries include to Brussels (one way €28.60, three hours, hourly); for other destinations, see p316.

For details on train and bus services to national destinations, see p319, as well as the Getting There & Away sections for each destination.

GETTING AROUND
To/From the Airport

Bus 16 (€1.50, 20 minutes, every 15 minutes) connects Luxembourg airport with Place Hamilius and Gare Centrale. Buses run from 5.40am to 9.40pm.

A taxi to the airport costs €20.

Bicycle

For information on cycling in and around Luxembourg City, see p274.

Car

The cheapest open-air car park is Glacis (Map p270), 800m northwest of Place d'Armes. Convenient underground car parks include Place Hamilius (Map p272; accessed via Rue Aldringen) or the 24-hour parking under Place Guillaume II (Map p272).

Recommended car-rental agencies:
Autolux (Map p270; ☎ 22 11 81; 33 Blvd Prince Henri)
Avis (Map p270; ☎ 48 95 95; Gare Centrale)
Budget (☎ 44 19 38; 300 Route de Longwy)
Hertz (☎ 43 46 45; Luxembourg airport)

Public Transport

A 'light tram' is planned to link the main train station, Gare Centrale, with Kirchberg via Ave de la Liberté and Blvd R Schuman. Until it's built (and that's years off), buses are the most convenient way to cover much of the city.

The main city bus stations are Gare Centrale (Map p270; city buses leave to the right as you exit the train station) and Place Hamilius (Map p272) in the Old Town. Public transport information offices are located inside Gare Centrale and underneath Place Hamilius; for all ticket information, see p320. Most buses run from 5.30am to 10pm, when a limited **night bus service** (☎ 24 89 24 89) takes over (Friday and Saturday nights only). Depending on the route, these buses run every 15 or 30 minutes until about 3.30am.

Around the Grand Duchy

Hop, skip or jump into Luxembourg proper – everywhere is fabulously accessible from the capital.

The Ardennes, the northern region, is spectacular country. Nestled in river valleys throughout this area are beguiling towns and villages such as Vianden, Clervaux and Esch-sur-Sûre, while at almost every second turn a medieval castle, like the magnificent Château de Bourscheid, looms larger than life through the clouds.

Relive fairytales in the Müllerthal, an enchanting pocket of forested land northeast of Luxembourg City. This almost primeval landscape is fab for hikers, and there's no better base than Echternach, an old Christian centre with a strong sense of its past. Cyclists too will find Echternach a superb base for exploration, with flat riverside bike paths linking it with towns and villages along the River Sûre.

The Gutland, a heavily farmed area immediately north of Luxembourg City, is home to Diekirch and its famous war museum. Here it's easy to get a feel of life during Luxembourg's World War II occupation. This bleak period in history came to an end with the Battle of the Ardennes (also known as the Battle of the Bulge) during the deathly cold winter of 1944–45.

For something considerably lighter, tickle your tastebuds with bottles of bubbly or fruity white wines made in the Moselle Valley, one of Europe's smallest wine regions. Remich, with its rock-hewn cellars, is the place to start.

The Grand Duchy's southwest corner is home to the bustling city of Esch-sur-Alzette, one of the country's chief nightlife destinations, and its burgeoning satellite suburb, Belval.

Side margin: AROUND THE GRAND DUCHY

HIGHLIGHTS

- **Medieval Break** Towers in the old Christian town of Echternach (p291)
- **Enchanted Forests** Hikes in the Müllerthal (p290)
- **Castles & More** Vibrant Vianden (opposite)
- **Chill-Out Experience** The ruined Château de Bourscheid (p286)
- **Wining** The Moselle Valley (p293)
- **Artistic Journeys** Clervaux's chanting monks and 'Family of Man' (p287)
- **Wartime Memories** Diekirch's Musée National d'Histoire Militaire (p289)
- **Cycling** The Sûre from Echternach (p291) or Diekirch (p289)

Map labels: Clervaux ★ · Vianden ★ · Château de Bourscheid ★ · Diekirch ★ · Echternach ★ ★ · Müllerthal ★ · Sûre River · The Moselle Valley ★

LUXEMBOURG ARDENNES

Expect highs and lows in the Grand Duchy's northern region – winding valleys with fast-flowing rivers cut deep through green tablelands crowned by castles. Of the three main towns, Clervaux, in the far north, is the most easily accessible by train. Vianden, in the east, is the most visited, while western Wiltz is best timed for its international performing arts festival.

VIANDEN

pop 1600

This is Luxembourg at its most touristy, and understandably so. Round a bend in the road and before you rises the impeccably restored medieval castle of Vianden, framed by forest and shrouded in mist. If this doesn't bring back childhood tales of princes and princesses, baddies and beasts, nothing will.

Vianden's picturesque location – nestled in the valley of the Our River – has made it a summer beehive. On weekends the town buzzes with German, Belgian and Dutch visitors soaking up the village ambience at terrace *cafés* along Grand Rue – the steep, narrow main street. At times the bustle is too much (avoid Sundays in summer when motorcycle troops throttle through town fraying nerves and oscillating eardrums) but mostly it's not so chaotic.

Vianden's **tourist office** (☎ 83 42 57 l; www.tourist -info-vianden.lu; 1a Rue du Vieux Marché; 8am-6pm Mon-Fri, 10am-2pm Sat Apr-Aug, 9am-noon & 1-5pm Mon-Fri Sep-Mar) is down by the river, next to the bridge over the Our. Internet (per hr €2) is available.

Sights & Activities

Looming above all else is the famed **château** (☎ 83 41 08 1; www.castle-vianden.lu; Grand Rue; adult/child €5.50/2; 10am-4pm Nov-Feb, 10am-5pm Mar & Oct, 10am-6pm Apr-Sep). The oldest part dates to the 11th century, although a much older Roman fort is thought to have once occupied the craggy outcrop.

In the 12th century the castle was the residence of the counts of Vianden, who reigned over the town and surrounding lands. They lost control of it in 1264 following an inheritance dispute with the rival House of Luxembourg. In 1417 the castle was absorbed by the Nassau dynasty; however, they abandoned it as a residence, considering it of little worth. Finally,

in 1820, during King William I of Orange-Nassau's reign, the castle was sold to a local merchant, who pulled it down bit by bit and sold almost everything off. What remained fell into ruin until 1977 when ownership was transferred from the Grand Ducal family to the State, which initiated a long-term restoration program. The inside now houses tastefully decorated period rooms, including the massive Counts' Hall and Banqueting Hall.

To reach the castle, either walk up Grand Rue or jump on the **télésiège** (chairlift; ☎ 83 43 23; 39 Rue du Sanatorium; adult/child return €4.50/2.25, one way €2.75/1.50; 10am-6pm Easter-Oct, closed Mon Easter-May & Oct). It climbs a hill behind the château, and takes off from the lower bank of the river at the end of Rue Victor Hugo. From the open-air café at the top, it's possible to follow a forest track down to the castle entrance. Kids love this adventure.

Meander down Grand Rue to find a pathway (off to the left) to a well-restored **belfry** dating to 1603. It's closed to visitors, but the viewing platform affords an excellent town vista.

Further down Grand Rue is **Musée d'Art Rustique et Musée des Poupées et du Jouet** (☎ 83 45 91; 96 Grand Rue; adult/child €2.50/1.50; 11am-5pm Easter-Oct, closed Mon Easter-May & Sep-Oct). This museum is home to a mixed bag of 'rustic arts', furniture, kitchen utensils, dolls, toys and other memorabilia associated with the history of the town.

Back at the river is the **Maison de Victor Hugo** (☎ 26 87 40 88; www.victor-hugo.lu in French; 37 Rue de la Gare; adult/child €4/2.50; 11am-5pm Easter & Jul-Aug, 11am-5pm Sat & Sun May-Jun & Sep-Oct). Vianden was briefly home to author Victor Hugo during his 19-year exile from France and the town makes much ado about the three months he stayed here in 1871. He lived in a small brown waterfront house that reopened as a neat little four-storey museum in 2002. Opposite the house is a bust, created by Rodin, of the famous writer.

A new hop-on hop-off **bus** (☎ 021 70 85 72; www .luxembourg.co.uk/viandenlakesandcastles/; admission €8; Tue-Sun Easter-Sep) offers one-hour regional tours to old copper mines and a low-energy village. The tourist office has the timetable.

For **hiking** information pick up the local walking map (scale: 1:20,000; €3) from the tourist office. It also sells a booklet describing 17 local walks; one of the most popular is to the Bildchen Chapel (about one hour).

Bike rental is available from **Location de Vélos** (☎ 26 87 41 57; Pavillion de la Gare; half-/full day €10/14; Jul-Aug) at the bus station. You'll need good muscles to climb the steep hills around Vianden.

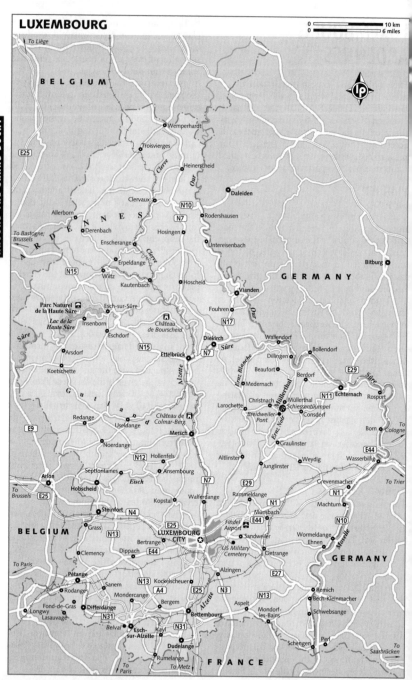

Young kids will enjoy the small riverside **playground** (Rue du Vieux Marché), about 500m past the tourist office. Older kids can test fitness levels at **Parc d'Aventures** (☎ 83 42 57 1; adult/child €10/6; ۞ Apr-Oct, closed Mon-Fri mid-Sep–Oct), located 1.5km from the castle along a forested track.

Sleeping & Eating

Camping de l'Our (☎ 83 45 05; www.camping-our-vianden u in Flemish, French & German; 3 Route de Bettel; camp sites per adult/child/tent €4.50/2/5; ۞ closed Nov-Easter) Pleasant camping ground draped along the riverbank to the south of town.

Auberge de Jeunesse (☎ 83 41 77; www.youthhostels u; 3 Montée du Château; dm/s/d €17.50/29.50/45; ۞ closed ate Dec-early Jan; ✗) In the shadow of the château (and a long 1km uphill walk from the bus station), the nondescript building shelters a modern hostel.

Hôtel La Tourelle (☎ 83 47 07; www.latourelle.lu; 41 Grand Rue; s/d from €40/59; ۞ Apr-Feb) Halfway up the main street. Some rooms have character – an exposed ceiling beam or four-poster bed – but others are ordinary. Ask to see a few.

Hôtel Victor Hugo (☎ 83 41 60; www.hotel-victor-hugo lu; 1 Rue Victor Hugo; s/d €52.50/70; ۞ closed Dec-Easter) Opposite Hugo's house, this corner hotel was where the writer's girlfriend, Juliette Drouet, holed up during her 1871 visit. It's solid and predictable, with clean, functional rooms. The ground-floor bar can get very noisy.

Hôtel Heintz (☎ 83 41 55; www.hotel-heintz.lu; 55 Grand Rue; s/d from €65/80; ۞ Easter-Oct) Back in the Middle Ages, the Heintz was the inn and brewery of Trinitarian monks; today it's a bit like entering a cloister – all white with Gothic arches and a long passage to the re-

THE AUTHOR'S CHOICE

Hôtel Oranienburg (☎ 83 41 53 1; www.oranien burg.lu; 126 Grand Rue, Vianden; s/d/ste from €55/84/130; ۞ Easter–mid-Nov) Arguably the town's most distinguished hotel-restaurant, the Oranienburg enjoys a prime sunny position at the base of the castle. The hotel's known for its gastronomic weekends – room, breakfast and two meals (€160 per person). Expect gilded mirrors and peachy paint jobs in most rooms, and regional cuisine like walnut salad and trout. And don't miss the homemade smoked ham – it's Vianden's best. Families are welcome (kids under two stay for free; from three to 12 years €15).

See p320 for more details.

TRAIN & BUS FARES

The fare system, valid for both bus and train travel, is simple: 1st/2nd class costs €2.25/1.50 for a short trip of about 10km or less (this ticket is valid for one hour) or €7.50/5 for an unlimited day ticket (known as a Billet Réseau).

ception out the back. While the rooms don't quite make the grade, all in all it's a delightful place, and the restaurant (mains €15 to €25) does superb local trout served in a white-wine sauce. Retreat to the tiny garden terrace for a quiet drink.

Economat (1 Rue du Sanatorium) This little supermarket, next to Hôtel Victor Hugo, has picnic supplies.

Getting There & Away

To reach Vianden, take the Luxembourg City–Ettelbrück train (30 minutes, half-hourly) and then a local bus (30 minutes, 10 buses daily).

ESCH-SUR-SÛRE

pop 240

Tiny Esch-sur-Sûre rates as one of Europe's prettiest villages. Built on a rocky loop in the Sûre River off the Wiltz–Ettelbrück road, Esch is surrounded by soft distant hills that drop to steep cliffs as they reach the river. Cushioned in among all this is a true 'crumbly' – a ruined **castle** dating from 927 – around which visitors are free to wander. A new **audio-guide** (€4; in French & German) of the village and surrounding area is available from the Maison du Parc Naturel de la Haute Sûre (p286). A word of warning…summer day-trippers descend on Esch in droves – if possible, time a visit for early spring or out of season.

Camping Im Aal (☎ 83 95 14; fax 89 91 17; camp sites per adult/child/tent €5/1.50/5; ۞ Feb-Dec) is 800m from the village, right on the river, on the road towards Wiltz.

Hôtel-Restaurant de la Sûre (☎ 83 91 10; www.hotel -de-la-sure.lu; 1 Rue du Pont; s/d/tr from €33.50/67/100; ۞ closed mid-Dec–Jan; ✗) is a big place at the top of the village that caters to everyone – there are extra-long beds, nonsmoking rooms, family rooms and baby cots (€13 for the whole stay), vegetarian food and a garage for motorbikes (Dutch bikers love this place.) The bar-restaurant area is nothing special, but the rooms are good. The restaurant (mains

€13 to €22) is noted for its Gourmet vum Séi products (see below).

Hôtel Beau-Site (☎ 83 91 34; www.beau-site.lu; 2 Rue de Kaundorf; s/d without bath €55/75, s/d with bath from €70/96; ☒ Mar-Dec) is a riverside family-run hotel-restaurant. Décor-wise it's all very plain and old-fashioned, but you're here for the castle view, right?

Hôtel Le Postillon (☎ 89 90 33; www.lepostillon.lu; 1 Rue de l'Église; s/d €56/82; ☒ Feb-Dec) has a snug position on the bank of the Sûre underneath the restored tower of the old castle. It's comfortable enough, but the décor is drab.

To get here, take a bus from Ettelbrück (40 minutes, five daily) or from Wiltz (25 minutes, four daily).

AROUND ESCH-SUR-SÛRE

West of Esch, the Sûre River was dammed in the 1960s to form Lac de la Haute Sûre, the country's largest lake (much of the Duchy's drinking water comes from here). Seven local communes have created the **Parc Naturel de la Haute Sûre**, a so-called 'natural park' that promotes environmental awareness, leisure and water activities (no motor boats allowed on the lake), as well as regional produce such as meat, cheese and honey. *Dinkel* (or spelt, as it's known in English), a long-forgotten grain, is also cultivated and used to make everything from organic bread to Simon Dinkel, a full-flavoured beer. Local restaurants supporting this produce will have a 'Gourmet vum Séi' label – try Hôtel-Restaurant de la Sûre (p285) in Esch-sur-Sûre and Hôtel-Restaurant La Diligence (see right) in Arsdorf.

The park's headquarters is the **Maison du Parc Naturel de la Haute Sûre** (☎ 89 93 31 1; www.naturpark-sure.lu in French & German; 15 Route de Lultzhausen;

museum adult/child €2/1.25; ☒ 10am-noon & 2-6pm Mon, Tue & Thu-Fri, 2-6pm Sat & Sun Jul-Aug, 10am-noon & 2-5pm Mon-Fri, 10am-noon Sat Sep-Jun), 500m west of Esch-sur-Sûre and 1km from the dam wall. Occupying an old cloth factory, it contains an information centre, nature museum and boutique, as well as an impressive collection of old looms and other textile-making machines – many of which still work.

The area is impossible to explore without your own wheels. The hamlet of **Arsdorf** makes a good base and has two attractive accommodation options. **Hôtel-Restaurant La Diligence** (☎ 23 64 95 55; www.ladiligence.lu in French; 17 Rue du Lac, Arsdorf; s/d €50/65) sits at the bottom of the village and serves delicious local fare. **Schegdenhaff** (☎ 23 64 90 81; www.schegdenhaff.gites.lu; 1 An der Hiehlt, Arsdorf; apt per week €410, low season €390) is for families planning a longer stay. Two holiday apartments set in a restored farmhouse each accommodate six to eight people, and come complete with a games room, sauna and trampoline in the next-door barn.

WILTZ

pop 4600

Wiltz is not big on the tourist circuit. But come July the town captivates crowds with the **Festival Européen de Théâtre en Plein Air et de Musique** (see boxed text, opposite).

The town has two distinct parts: the Ville Haute (Upper Town), huddled on a rocky crag, and the Ville Basse (Lower Town), sprawled along the river below. The **tourist office** (☎ 95 74 44; www.wiltz.lu in French; ☒ 10am-6pm Jul-Aug, 10am-noon & 2-5pm Mon-Fri, 10am-noon Sat Sep-Jun) is in the Ville Haute's château. As with many of the country's castles, the rather sterile **château** (☎ 95 74 44) has a chequered history: it was originally built as

---

WORTH A TRIP

Roughly halfway between Esch-sur-Sûre and Ettelbrück, a road winds up to the magnificent **Château de Bourscheid** (☎ 99 05 70; www.bourscheid.lu; 1 Schlasswee; adult/child €3.50/2; ☒ 9am-6pm Apr-Sep, 10am-5pm Oct, 10am-5pm Sat & Sun Nov-Mar). This 1000-year-old castle, superbly situated on a rocky bluff overlooking the Sûre River, affords some of the best views in Luxembourg. Although parts of the castle have been restored, it's nowhere near as complete as the castle in Vianden, but is ultimately more attractive due to its outstanding location. A good audio-guide (in English) recounts its place in history. Listen to it as you perch like a princess on one of the cold stone ledges, letting the evocative setting conjure up images of horses, knights and invading armies crossing the distant windswept hills. The castle is accessible only by foot or car.

Families or hikers looking to bunk down nearby can stay at **Camping Um Gritt** (☎ 99 04 49; www.camp.lu in Flemish, French & German; Bourscheid-Moulin; camp sites per adult/child/tent €5/2.50/7.50, hikers' hut €45; ☒ closed mid-Oct–Easter) at the foot of the bluff. (For details on hikers' huts, see p298.)

WILTZ'S EXTRAVAGANZA

The **Festival Européen de Théâtre en Plein Air et de Musique** (www.festivalwiltz.online.lu in French) is the Grand Duchy's biggest musical event. This festival of open-air theatre plus jazz and classical music concerts takes over Wiltz for the whole of July. Performances are held in the evocative setting of the amphitheatre and formal grounds of the town's chateau. If ever there's a time to visit Wiltz, this is it.

---

a count's residence, but in the 19th century became a girl's boarding school and later was converted into a home for elderly.

The château houses two museums, neither of which are much chop. The **Musée de la Bataille des Ardennes** (☎ 95 74 42; adult/child €1.50/0.75; ☺ 1-5pm Jul & Aug) is a less-than-gripping account of the 1944 Battle of the Bulge (see boxed text, p245). The other attraction is the **Musée National d'Art Brassicole et des Arts et Métiers Anciens** (☎ 95 74 44; adult/child €2.50/1.50; ☺ 10am-6pm Jul & Aug), devoted to brewing, arts, handicrafts and machinery from earlier times.

Head down the main road from the château to see Wiltz's only other sight – a stone-sculpted **tower** that commemorates those who died or were sent to concentration camps as a result of a national strike in 1942 to protest the Nazi's introduction of conscription. The people of Wiltz instigated the strike, which lasted three days before being brutally suppressed. The memorial was designed by Luxembourg sculptor Lucien Wercollier.

The **Auberge de Jeunesse** (☎ 95 80 39; www.youth hostels.lu; 6 Rue de la Montagne; dm/s/d €17.50/29.50/45; ☺ closed mid-Nov–Dec, early Feb & late Apr; ☒ ☺) is a 1km climb from the train station, behind the Ville Haute. The distinguished building has character and a pleasant internal courtyard. It's a good hostel for families – there's a playroom plus a nearby playground.

Aux Anciennes Tanneries (☎ 95 75 99; www.aux anciennestanneries.com, in French; 42a Rue Jos Simon; s/d from €73/98; ☺ closed late Aug & late Dec; ☒), in the Ville Basse, is the town's most engaging hotel-restaurant. Modern rooms in a renovated tannery overlook a babbling stream – on summer days you can dine outside on a tranquil terrace. The three-course lunchtime menu (€11.50; Monday to Friday) is great value (regular mains €13 to €20). Kids and babies are welcome.

Wiltz is easily accessible by train from Luxembourg City or anywhere along the northern railway line. The train station is in the Ville Basse. From Luxembourg City, take the train (direction Clervaux) to Kautenbach and catch another train from there (total 1½ hours).

CLERVAUX
pop 1800

Far, far to the north of Luxembourg, hidden deep in the valley of the Clerve River, is a little town that plays second fiddle in most things tourism. Its castle isn't as grand or crumbly as others in the region. No artists of renown have graced its streets. And it doesn't boast a flashy chairlift or hop-on hop-off bus. But Clervaux does have two aces – a permanent photographic exhibition that draws visitors from all over the country and further afield, and some of the best chanting monks this side of the Rhine. If either of these are your thing, make this cosy town first string.

The **tourist office** (☎ 92 00 72; www.tourisme -clervaux.lu; ☺ 9.45-11.45am & 2-6pm Jul-Aug, 9.45-11.45am & 1-5pm Sep-Oct, 2-5pm Mon-Fri Easter-Jun) is housed in a side turret of Clervaux's castle.

Sights

Clervaux's **castle** dates back to the 12th century, but it lost its fortified walls at the end of the 19th century and during battles in WWII it was razed. Today's gleaming white replica is famous for the **'Family of Man'** photography exhibition (☎ 92 96 57; adult/child €4.50/2.50; ☺ 10am-6pm Apr-Sep, Tue-Sun Mar & Oct-Dec) collated by Edward Steichen (1879–1973). Born in Luxembourg, Steichen was a babe when his parents moved to the USA. He compiled the exhibition of 500 B&W photos for New York's Museum of Modern Art in 1955 at the age of 76. Later it travelled the world before coming to rest in Clervaux in 1964, a gift from New York City. Now a Unesco World Heritage site, the exhibition contains images by 250 photographers from 68 countries. In Steichen's words, it was conceived as a 'mirror of the essential oneness of mankind throughout the world' and, whether you see it as an historic archive or social commentary, it's fabulous viewing.

The castle also contains the **Musée de la Bataille des Ardennes** (☎ 92 00 72; adult/child €2.50/1.25; ☺ 10am-6pm Apr-Sep, Tue-Sun Mar & Oct-Dec), another WWII museum.

Clervaux's other main sights are the Romanesque-style **church** (1910; ☺ 8am-6pm) sitting on the plateau immediately behind the castle, and the **Benedictine Abbey of St Maurice** (☎ 92 10 27), whose turrets pierce the forest skyline above town. It's accessible by a 1km track from the castle. The monks are known throughout Europe for their Gregorian chants – time your visit to listen to one of their **masses** (☺ 10.30am & 6pm Mon-Fri, 5pm Sat & Sun). There's also a permanent exhibition, **'The Monastic Life'** (☺ 9am-7pm), and a shop selling sacred art.

Little kids can let off steam at the old-fashioned **playground** (Rue de Parc) below Hôtel du Parc.

Sleeping & Eating

Camping Officiel (☎ 92 00 42; www.camping-clervaux.lu; 33 Rue Klatzewée; camp sites per adult/child/tent €5.30/2.50/5.50; ☺ Easter-Oct; ☒) About 200m from the town centre. It has plenty to keep kids happy – heated pool, ping pong and a playground.

Hôtel du Commerce (☎ 92 10 32; www.hotelducommerce.lu in Flemish, French, German & Lëtzebuergesch; 2 Rue de Marnach; s/d from €45/78; ☺ closed Dec–mid-Mar; ☒) Reliable, old-fashioned hotel with a no-fuss policy, situated immediately below the castle. Families are welcome, and there's a heated indoor swimming pool and a small garden out the back. Only the décor's off-putting – brown carpet and velveteen upholstery.

Hôtel International (☎ 92 93 91; www.interclervaux .lu; 10 Grand Rue; s/d from €56/82, ste €174; ☺ closed 24-25 Dec; ☒ ☒) Classy establishment in the heart of town aimed at those wanting to bliss out. The standard rooms have drab '70s décor; pay more for a plush four-poster bed and Jacuzzi. The restaurant offers a four-course

---

THE AUTHOR'S CHOICE

Hôtel-Restaurant du Parc (☎ 92 06 50; www.hotelduparc.lu; 2 Rue du Parc, Clervaux; s/d/tr €38/49/70; ☺ Mar-Dec) Full of character and perhaps the odd ghost, this old whitewashed mansion is one of Luxembourg's most atmospheric budget hotels. Sitting partway up a forested hill overlooking Clervaux, its seven rooms are fitted with a mix of modern and old, and some have town views. The hotel's restaurant – decked out with antiques, chandeliers, lounge chairs and old fireplaces – serves well-priced French/Luxembourg cuisine (mains €20). On warm days it's possible to dine on the sun terrace overlooking surrounding hillsides. A hidden gem.

---

menu terre-mer (€23; or mains €17 to €20) and the indoor pool is heated.

Café-Restaurant du Vieux Château (☎ 92 00 12; 4 Montée du Château; mains €13-16; ☺ Wed-Mon) Good spot for families wanting an outdoor break. Located well away from traffic, between the two gates of the castle, watch the kids picking daisies as you sip a Bofferding (or better still a Belgian Duvel).

Getting There & Away

Clervaux's train station is 800m from the town centre and there are no buses connecting the two. Regular trains connect with Luxembourg City (one hour, two hourly).

GUTLAND

The Gutland (literally 'Goodland') is a heavily farmed area immediately north of Luxembourg City. It encompasses the nondescript towns of Mersch and Ettelbrück, as well as vibrant Diekirch, best known for its excellent WWII museum. The country's main railway line passes through the region, providing easy access to the main towns. To explore side valleys, you'll need a vehicle.

VALLÉE DES SEPT CHÂTEAUX

This peaceful valley winds westward from Mersch along the Eisch River past the villages of Ansembourg and Septfontaines. As its name foretells, it's dotted with seven castles – either 'crumblies' or stately mansions – none of which are open to the public.

Should you decide to hang around overnight, there's a lovely **Auberge de Jeunesse** (☎ 30 70 37; www.youthhostels.lu; 2 Rue du Château; dm/s/ €17.50/29.50/45; ☒) in the village of Hollenfels. It's a stately cream-stone building located next to Hollenfels castle.

ETTELBRÜCK
pop 7500

WWII and entertainment are the reasons to visit Ettelbrück.

Vera Lynne's unmistakable voice floats through the air as you enter the **General Patton Museum** (☎ 81 03 22; www.patton.lu; 5 Rue Dr Klein; adult/child €2.50/1.25; ☺ 10am-5pm Jun–mid-Sep), five minutes' walk from Ettelbrück train station. This modern little museum is devoted to the audacious general of the US Third Army who played a large part in Luxembourg's WWII liberation. He reaped fame for his quote: 'No bastard ever won a war by dying for his country. He won it by making the other poor dumb bastard die for his'. Patton died following a car accident in Germany in December 1945. He's buried with his troops at the US Military Cemetery in Luxembourg City (see p274).

The town's **Centre des Arts Pluriels** (☎ 26 81 21 1; www.cape.lu in French; 1 Place Marie-Adélaïde) offers everything from opera, dance and theatre to magic, clowns and cabaret.

Ettelbrück is easily reached by train from Luxembourg City (30 minutes, half-hourly) or nearby Diekirch (10 minutes, half-hourly).

DIEKIRCH
pop 6000
If you're only here for the beer – sorry! Diekirch brewery, one of the Grand Duchy's main brewers, located opposite the train station, doesn't open to visiting beer buffs. So down your disappointment with a red label at any local café and contemplate what next – for a town this size, plenty is on offer. Diekirch boasts the country's best wartime museum and it's also great for renting a bike or canoe.

The **tourist office** (☎ 80 30 23; www.diekirch.lu; 3 Place de la Libération; ☺ 9am-noon & 2-5pm Mon-Fri, 2-4pm Sat Sep-Jun, 9am-5pm Mon-Fri, 10am-4pm Sat & Sun Jul-Aug) is a 10-minute walk from the train station, at the town's pedestrian core.

Sights & Activities
An excellent collection of wartime machinery, artefacts and photographs detailing WWII's Battle of the Ardennes (p245) and the liberation of Luxembourg by US troops is presented at the **Musée National d'Histoire Militaire** (☎ 80 89 08; www.nat-military-museum.lu; 10 Rue Bamertal; adult/child €5/3; ☺ 10am-6pm Apr-Nov, 2-6pm Dec-Mar), 200m north of the tourist office. It gives real feeling to the suffering of troops on both sides during the atrocious conditions of that winter in '44. In addition there are displays on Veianer Miliz, Luxembourg's resistance movement, which was based in caves and bunkers around the northern town of Vianden. There are also paintings, drawings and other memorabilia from Tambow, a Russian camp to which conscripted Luxembourgers were sent. The museum has English-language explanations throughout.

Diekirch's other main attraction is the **Musée des Mosaïques Romaines** (Place Guillaume; admission €1.30; ☺ 10am-noon & 2-6pm Easter-Oct). It houses Gallo-Roman relics, including 3rd-century mosaics

excavated from the Esplanade, one of the main roads encircling the town. The nearby turreted **Église St Laurent** (☺ 10am-noon & 2-6pm Easter-Oct), east of Place de la Libération, dates back in part to the 11th century and is worth a peek for its ancient tombs and crypt.

A great way to explore Diekirch and nearby towns or villages is to travel by bike. **Rent-a-Bike** (☎ 26 80 33 76; nordstad@cig.lu; 27 Rue Jean l'Aveugle; per half-/full day €10/15; ☺ 10am-5pm Apr-Oct), about 300m from the town centre on the road to Echternach, has a full complement of wheels. Nice, flat cycling paths follow the Sûre River all the way from Diekirch to Echternach (27km).

From April to September combine a bike tour with a **canoe trip** down the Sûre River to Echternach. Departure points vary depending on the time of year – either Diekirch (27km), Wallendorf (16km) or Dillingen (12km). Don't expect much adrenaline – the only thing resembling a rapid is near Wallendorf. The bike-canoe combo costs €25 per person. For full details contact **Outdoor Freizeit** (☎ 86 91 39; www.outdoorfreizeit; 10 Rue de la Sûre, Dillingen).

Sleeping & Eating
Camping de la Sûre (☎ 80 94 25; fax 80 27 86; 34 Route de Gilsdorf; camp sites per adult/child/tent €4.50/2.50/4.50; ☺ Apr-Sep) Leafy camping ground by the river and within a few minutes' walk from the town centre.

Hotel-Restaurant de la Gare (☎ 80 33 05; jamper@sl.lu; 73 Ave de la Gare; s/d €42/73) Family-run establishment opposite the train station that offers five renovated rooms and a restaurant (three-course menu €15 to €35) favoured by locals. Take to the terrace and try the homemade ham – it's the best around.

Also recommended:
B&B Weber-Posing (☎ 80 32 54; fax 80 06 54; 63 Rue Principale, Gilsdorf; s/d €22/44) Old-fashioned B&B, with squeaky floors and a small kitchen for guests to use. Located 2km west of central Diekirch.
La Fondue (☎ 80 49 92; 43 Grand Rue; mains €13-18, fondues €16-20; ☺ lunch & dinner) Simple eatery at the end of the pedestrianised main street.
Match (Rue Alexis Heck) Supermarket in the heart of town.

Getting There & Around
Diekirch's train and neighbouring bus stations are 1km west of the town's pedestrianised hub.

There are good train connections from here to nearby Ettelbrück (10 minutes, half-hourly), the nation's central rail junction, and on to Luxembourg City (40 minutes, half-hourly). The usual line-up of local buses head from Diekirch to outlying villages. For details on bike rental, see p289.

MÜLLERTHAL

Enter a world where the passage of time is visible at almost every turn, a landscape where deep gorges scoured by ancient streams through sandstone plateaus tell the tale of creation over the centuries. This is the Müllerthal, a pocket of land in Luxembourg's central east that leaves hiker's breathless. Not from sheer climbs or high peaks, but from a world that's removed from most realities, a place of delicate forests, narrow ravines, crystal creeks and strange rock formations. The Müllerthal is crisscrossed by well-marked hiking trails that are crowded on summer weekends but near deserted for the rest.

ECHTERNACH

pop 5100

As a Müllerthal base, nothing beats the poised but vibrant town of Echternach. Stay in a medieval tower or a brand-new hostel, spend the day hiking the mysterious forests or cycling the Sûre. Take the kids boating on an artificial lake or explore the basilica, Luxembourg's most important religious building. If you're into pageantry, time a visit for **St Willibrord Pageant** (opposite) on Whit Tuesday, when dancers take to the cobbled streets in a time-honoured religious festival to celebrate the town's founding father, St Willibrord, an Anglo-Saxon monk.

Though evidence of a Gallo-Roman settlement has been found (and can be visited, see right), Echternach pretty much rose around a 7th-century abbey founded by St Willibrord in 698. St Willibrord led the conversion to Christianity in parts of the Netherlands before settling in Echternach, which later became a centre for learning and art. When he died here in 739, his body was placed in the crypt of the abbey church where it remains today (see right).

The **tourist office** (☎ 72 02 30; www.echternach-tourist .lu; Parvis de la Basilique; ☺ 10am-12.30pm & 2-5pm Mon-Fri Sep-Easter, 10am-5.30pm Easter-Aug) is in a courtyard next to the basilica entrance. There's an **ATM** (Place du Marché) opposite the Ancien Palais de Justice. For internet access try **Café de la Poste** (2 Place du Marché; per hr €3; ☺ 10.30am-8.30pm Tue-Sun).

Sights & Activities

The town centre is based around the refined Place du Marché with its turreted **Ancien Palais de Justice**. This elegant former law court was built in 1520 (but is much restored) and features delicate statues dating from 1896. Biker fans should time a visit for any weekend in summer when motorcyclists en masse take to one of the terrace *cafés* on this square.

Little remains of Echternach's original abbey. The present-day version, built in the 18th century, is a huge complex that spreads out from near Place du Marché almost to the banks of the Sûre. It's home to the **Musée de l'Abbaye** (☎ 72 74 72; adult/child €3/1.50; ☺ 10am-noon & 2-6pm Easter-Jun & Sep-Oct, 10am-6pm Jul & Aug), which contains an engaging collection from Roman mosaics to illuminated medieval manuscripts. The focal point is the **basilica** (☺ 9.30am-6.30pm), built on the site of the original abbey church, gutted in 1016. The basilica was heavily restored in 1862, but suffered substantial damage during bombing in WWII's Battle of the Bulge (see boxed text, p245). Inside it's a dark and sombre affair, with few decorations aside from stained-glass windows and a chunk of crucifix with Christ's head that adorns the left-hand wall. The crypt is the only original section to survive the centuries and contains the highly venerated relics of St Willibrord, kept in a primitive stone coffin covered by an elaborate white marble canopy.

To explore Echternach's Roman era, head to **Villa Romaine** (☎ 26 72 09 74; 47 Rue des Romains; adult/child €3/1.50; ☺ 11am-6pm Tue-Sun Jul & Aug, 11am-1pm & 2-5pm Tue-Sun Easter-Jun & Sep-Oct), 1km from town (off Route de Luxembourg). It incorporates old Roman ruins, including a manor house excavated in 1975, plus virtual imaging depicting life in Roman days.

Marked **hiking trails** start from near the town's bus station. A board listing possibilities gives brief descriptions plus estimated times (from one to four hours). One of the best, 'B1' (2½ hours), winds up via Trooisknepchen and Wolfsschlucht, also known as the **Gorge du Loup**, a sheer-sided, moss-covered canyon flanked by dramatic sandstone formations. With stamina, continue hiking from there to the village of **Berdorf** (p292).

An enclosed **playground** behind the basilica near the riverside tennis courts is for families with kids. Alternatively try **swimming**, **boating** or **mini-golf** at the artificial lake, a few kilometres out of town (direction Rodenhal). **Bollig**

(Place du Marché; adult/child/family €6.50/4.50/17.50), a little tourist train, rolls around town hourly.

Echternach is well placed for **cyclists**, with flat riverside bike paths tracing the Sûre River all the way to Diekirch (27km), or south into the Moselle. For a change of culture en route, take a pit stop in Germany at one of the villages straddling the river – Bollendorf, for example, is good for Sunday's colourful flea market. It's also possible to ride from Echternach all the way to Luxembourg City. Rent wheels from **Motothek** (☎ 72 64 75; motothek@pt.lu; 17 Rue Ermesinde; half-/full day €10/15; ☑ 9am-noon & 1.30-6pm Tue-Sat), close to the bus station.

Festivals & Events

Those in Echternach on the Tuesday after Whitsunday can celebrate the **St Willibrord Pageant** (13 May 2008, 2 June 2009, 25 May 2010), famous far and wide for its Procession Dansante in which dancers with white handkerchiefs take to the streets as they've done for centuries. It's a 9am start so don't sleep in.

Sleeping & Eating

Camping Officiel (☎ 72 02 72; 5 Route de Diekirch; camp sites per adult/child/tent €4.80/2.80/5; ☑ Easter–mid-Oct; ☒) Draped along the hillside 200m from the bus station, this camping ground has tennis courts and a children's playground.

Auberge de Jeunesse (☎ 72 01 58; www.youthhostels.lu; Rue Grégoire Schouppe; dm/s/d €19.50/31.50/49; ☒ ☐ ☒) Brand-new hostel emphasising adventure, located next to the lake about 2km out of town. Sip a Mousel beer in the hip café while contemplating the hostel's star attraction, a 14m-high indoor *escalade*, or climbing wall (adult/concession €5/2.50, free if staying at the hostel; open 6pm to 10pm Tuesday, Wednesday and Friday). Alternatively, book a guided mountain-bike tour. Coming from Luxembourg City, take bus 110 (Luxembourg City–Echternach, 45 minutes, hourly) to the stop 'Nonnemillen/

Lac', from where it's a 1km walk (direction Rodenhof).

B&B Meyer-Ernzen (☎ 72 04 22; www.meyer-ernzen .lu; 1 Rodenhof; r per person €22-25) Great place for those with wheels (it's 3.5km south; direction Rodenhal). On a hill with a view towards the town and lake, this dairy farm has eight guestrooms in a separate building and accommodates overnighters or longer stays. Some rooms have well-equipped kitchenettes, making this a good family-holiday option.

Hôtel Le Petit Poête (☎ 72 00 72; www.lepetitpoete.lu; 13 Place du Marché; s/d/tr €40/59/84; ☑ mid-Jan–Nov) Pick of the cheapies. Its 15 rooms (some with a view of Place du Marché) are neat and spacious, with no-nonsense modest décor. The hotel's terrace restaurant is popular for a well-priced bite (ignore the traffic noise and fumes).

Hôtel Le Pavillon (☎ 72 98 09; diedling@pt.lu; 2 Rue de la Gare; s/d €55/70 Chic little corner hotel-restaurant with just 10 well-equipped rooms. The décor is decidedly old-fashioned – expect cream lampshades, brown carpet and beige wallpaper. The terrace restaurant (French cuisine; mains €16 to €23) is immensely popular.

Hôtel Puccini (☎ 72 03 06; www.puccini.lu; 21 Rue de la Gare; s/d €68/90, studio s/d/t €95/115/135) Modern comes to Echternach. The town's newest hotel-restaurant, located on the main pedestrianised street, has minimalist furnishings and subdued tones – greys, plums and black. Studios with small kitchenettes are handy if travelling with children. It's staffed by a friendly and enthusiastic young crew, and the restaurant (Mediterranean cuisine; mains €14 to €27) does vegetarian options.

Hostellerie de la Basilique (☎ 72 94 83; www.hotel -basilique.lu; 7 Place du Marché; s/d/tr €91/108/135; ☑ Easter–mid-Nov; ☒) Top address in town. Fourteen tidy rooms that don't suffer decoration overkill. It has a great location near the basilica entrance, with a popular terrace restaurant overlooking a fountain. The rooms are spacious, families

---

THE AUTHOR'S CHOICE

Fawlty Towers it ain't. Innovative it is. The Echternach tourist board has turned four of the town's eight remaining medieval **towers** (*tour* in French) into self-contained apartments for tourists. If your kids love running around shooting bows and arrows, this is the ultimate holiday house. Peer through narrow slits as you munch your morning croissant or go back in time by candlelight as you dine medieval style at the top of your tower. Prices cost €385 to €500 per week, depending on size and facilities offered. Tour 1 is the smallest (two to four people) and most basic – be prepared for outside toilet dashes here. Tour 5 (we know, there are only four towers!) is the largest (sleeps six) and most deluxe. Book via the tourist office (opposite).

with small children and babies are welcome, and bikes are available for free.

Giorgio (☎ 72 99 34; 4 Rue André Duchscher; mains €10-30; ☺ lunch & dinner, closed Tue Nov-Mar) Casual Italian restaurant that's always full. Choose between the outdoor terrace, the ground-floor section or the cavernous cellar.

Also recommended:

Caffé Venezia (☎ 72 01 69; 3 Rue de la Gare) Italian-gelato café.

Café de Philo'soff (☎ 72 00 19; 31 Rue de la Gare; ☺ Wed-Mon) Art-Nouveau showpiece with laidback music and a terrace out the back. Go for the good range of Belgian beers.

Match (off Place du Marché) Supermarket.

Getting There & Away

Echternach's bus station is a five-minute walk from Place du Marché – head straight along pedestrianised Rue de la Gare, the town's main shopping street. Only buses connect Echternach with Luxembourg City (45 minutes, hourly). From Echternach, buses head out to regional villages and towns.

AROUND ECHTERNACH
Schiessentüumpel

With a car and a good nose for direction, it's well worth finding the Schiessentüumpel bridge, about 12km southwest of Echternach. This much-photographed wooden and stone bridge arches over an attractive waterfall on the Ernz Noire, a babbling waterway that eventually joins the Sûre River. As always in this area, it's a great spot for walking. To get there, head out of Echternach on the N11 to Luxembourg City, then turn off to the village of Müllerthal. The bridge is in the middle of nowhere, on the road (CR121) between Müllerthal village and Breidweiler-Pont.

Berdorf
pop 950

Spread out high on a plateau, Berdorf is not picturesque, explaining why it's known only to hikers and diners. Just 5km west of Echternach, it's reached by beguiling footpaths that wind through rocky chasms and past waterfalls. Indeed, this is one of the Müllerthal's most delightful hiking spots – as usual, the **tourist office** (☎ 79 06 43; www.berdorf.lu; 7 An der Laach; ☺ 8am-noon & 1-5pm Mon-Fri) sells a local walking map.

With wheels, a good place to stay is **Le Bisdorff** (☎ 79 02 08; www.hotel-bisdorff.lu; 39 Rue Heisbich; s/d €87/100; ☺ Easter–mid-Nov; Ⓟ), set by a forest in the middle of nowhere about 2km from Berdorf (direction Kalkesbach). This hotel-restaurant is reputed to be one of Luxembourg's best countryside restaurants (mains €30 to €35; open dinner Wednesday to Friday, lunch and dinner Saturday and Sunday). Owner and chef Sylvie Bisdorff has written a book on Luxembourg recipes; she inherited some of her talent from her father, who was a chef for Grand Duke Jean. Go for the good-value *demi-pension* (half-board; per person €72) deal.

Beaufort
pop 1955

About 15km west of Echternach, Beaufort boasts a classic ruined **castle** (☎ 83 60 02; adult/child €3/1; ☺ 9am-6pm Apr-Oct), hidden in a wooded grove below the village and once the site of a Roman camp. It dates from the 12th century but was expanded in later centuries. Like many historic buildings in this part of Luxembourg, it was bombed during WWII's Battle of the Bulge (see boxed text, p245). It's all very atmospheric – wander with the sheep around the ruined remains.

From the castle, there's a 4km circular walk through the evocative Müllerthal forest – ask at either the castle or the **tourist office** (☎ 83 60 99 301; www.beaufort.lu in German; 87 Grand Rue; ☺ 8am-7pm Jul & Aug, 9am-noon & 2-5pm Mon-Sat, 9am-noon Sun Sep-Jun) for the brochure detailing the path. The tourist office also rents **bikes** (half-/full day €7.50/15).

Those resting weary limbs have various options. The big **Camping Plage** (☎ 83 60 99; www.campingplage.lu; 87 Grand Rue; camp sites per adult/child/tent €4.50/2.50/5.50, hikers' hut €43; ⓧ) is one of a handful of camping grounds in Luxembourg to stay open year-round, and even boasts hikers' huts (see p298). Next door is a big open-air heated **pool** (adult/child €3/1.50; ☺ May-Aug) plus an **ice-skating rink** (☺ Dec-Mar). Kids will love it.

The small, chalet-style **Auberge de Jeunesse** (☎ 83 60 75; www.youthhostels.lu; 6 Rue de l'Auberge; dm/s/d €17.50/29.5/45; ☺ Feb-Dec; ⓧ) is enjoyable.

The most pleasantly sited hotel is **Auberge Rustique** (☎ 83 60 86; www.aubergerustique.lu; 55 Rue du Château; s/d/tr €47/70/105), on the windy road down to the castle. It's your typical countryside Luxembourg hotel, with basic, affordable rooms and a pleasant sun terrace.

LAROCHETTE
pop 1850

Larochette is the Müllerthal's prettiest village. Secluded in the narrow valley of the Ernz

Blanche River, it's lorded over by a ruined castle and surrounded by wooded hills and sandstone plateaus. Just 26km north of Luxembourg City, it makes a delightful lunchtime or overnight stop, with a smattering of hotels and even a hostel.

The **tourist office** (☎ 83 76 76; www.larochette.lu; 4 Rue de Medernach; ⏰ 8am-noon & 2-6pm Mon-Fri) is in the town hall, next to the church on the main road.

Larochette's 12th-century **château** (☎ 83 74 97; Route de Mersch; adult/child €2/1; ⏰ 10am-6pm Easter-Oct) perches on a craggy outcrop overlooking town. In its time it must have been spectacular, well hidden within ancient forests, and appearing as if out of nowhere as you round a corner in the river valley. What's visible from street level is only the beginning of the ruin complex. Parts are slowly being restored, and it's possible to tour the site; to get there walk along the 'Mersch' road until you see the château signs.

The **Auberge des Jeunesse** (☎ 83 70 81; www.youth hostels.lu; 45 Osterbuer; dm/s/d €19.60/31.60/49.20; ⏰ Mar-Dec; ✗) is a pleasant, blue building, about 600m from the town centre.

Auberge Op der Bleech (☎ 87 80 58; www.opderbleech .lu; 4 Place Bleech; s/d €55/75; ⏰ closed 1-15 Sep), a peach-toned hotel on the main square, has spacious, minimalist rooms with a bandstand view. Children are welcome.

Hôtel Résidence (☎ 83 73 91; www.hotelresidence.lu; 14 Rue de Medernach; s/d from €65/75, d with castle view €85; ⏰ Mar-Nov) is a stately building slung along the road, with a long breakfast room to match. The room décor is heavy – steer clear if you're allergic to flowers. Request a front location for castle views (though from this angle, it's not spectacular).

Buses from Luxembourg City (one hour, hourly) connect to Larochette; alternatively there are regular services from Diekirch (20 minutes, hourly) and Echternach (40 minutes, two hourly).

MOSELLE VALLEY

Half an hour from Luxembourg City – not even time for the kids to start chorusing – and you'll arrive at one of Europe's smallest wine regions, the Moselle Valley. Drop in at a dozen towns and hamlets along the Route du Vin to taste test fruity whites. Remich is the best place to start.

CRUISING THE MOSELLE

View Luxembourg's steep vineyards and German wine-making villages during a Moselle River cruise. The MS *Roude Leiw* or the *Musel III*, both departing from Remich, offer one-hour trips (adult/child €6.50/4, daily Easter to October) upriver to Schwebsange and back, or longer voyages (adult/child from €12/6, three weekly May to September) downstream to Wormeldange, Grevenmacher or Wasserbillig. For more details, contact **Navitours** (☎ 75 84 89; www .navitours.lu in French & German).

Getting There & Around

Like much of rural Luxembourg, getting around the Moselle Valley region takes time if you don't have your own transport. From Luxembourg City, there are buses to Remich (30 minutes, two daily). From Remich, buses run via Ehnen to Grevenmacher (30 minutes, four daily). From Grevenmacher there are buses to Echternach (40 minutes, hourly). Trains from Luxembourg City stop at the northern town of Wasserbillig (35 minutes, half-hourly) only.

REMICH
pop 3000

Waterfront Remich, 23km southeast of the capital, is a popular weekend getaway. There's almost nothing to see – people come here to indulge in long, hearty lunches, wander the riverside promenade, check out a winery or two, and to stock up on cheap cigarettes and booze. One of the region's few **tourist offices** (☎ 23 69 84 88; Esplanade; ⏰ 10am-12.30pm & 1.30-6pm 15 Jun-15 Sep) is located in the bus station.

Start wine tasting at the main *cave* (cellar), **St Martin** (☎ 23 69 97 74; 53 Route de Stadtbredimus; adult/child €2.75/1.75; ⏰ 10am-noon & 1.30-6pm Apr-Oct), about 1.5km north of Remich's bus terminal. St Martin produces white and sparkling wines, the latter known as *crémant*, and offers tours delving into the *méthode traditionelle* used to process its sparkling wines. Like in champagne production, this traditionally involved turning each bottle by hand; guides at St Martin are adamant this age-old process is still carried out, though others in the industry claim all the large wineries now use machines. The tour winds through cool, damp tunnels hewn in the rock face and ends with a glass of bubbly. Bus 450 to Grevenmacher stops out the front.

On summer days cool off at the big open-air **swimming pool** (☎ 23 69 81 11), about 500m from the bus station on the road towards Schengen.

Auberge des Cygnes (☎ 23 69 88 52; hpcygnes@pt.lu; 11 Esplanade; s/d/tr €48/65/83; ☒ closed mid-Jan–mid-Feb) is the nicest of the cheap waterfront hotels. The busy reception-restaurant area contrasts with the calm, pastel-toned rooms. It's family run and family friendly, and has a highchair and cot. The restaurant does good woodfired pizzas.

Hôtel Saint Nicolas (☎ 26 66 3; www.saint-nicolas .lu in French; 31 Esplanade; s €77, d with/without river view €130/105, ste €150; ☒ ☐), on the waterfront on the northern edge of town, is a delightful mix'n'match of old world and ultramodern. The 40 rooms are contemporary and comfortable, and the enclosed French restaurant (vegetarian fare included; multicourse menu from €22 to €76) comes well recommended. Children are welcome.

AROUND REMICH

Antique wine presses announce the **Musée du Vin 'A Possen'** (☎ 23 69 73 53; 1 Rue Aloyse Sandt; adult/child €4.50/2; ☒ 2-7pm Tue-Sun May-Oct, 2-7pm Fri-Sun Nov-Apr), a block back from the riverfront in the hamlet of **Bech-Kleinmacher**, 2km south of Remich. This stone building, also known as 'A Possen', was once a local wine grower's home and now houses a tiny museum devoted to wine, folklore and nostalgia.

The town of **Mondorf-les-Bains**, 11km southwest of Remich, is Luxembourg's premier spa town, as well as a popular sporting and gambling centre. Warm waters bubble forth at **Le Domaine Thermal** (☎ 23 66 60; www.mondorf.lu; Ave des Bains), a 50-hectare relaxation complex, while **Casino 2000** (☎ 23 61 11; www.casino2000.lu; Rue Flammang) is for blowing your dough.

EHNEN
pop 470

Dozing next to a river bend, the picturesque hamlet of Ehnen is an essential stop for crustacean lovers. Here you'll find **Bamberg's** (☎ 76 00 22; bamberg@pt.lu; 131 Route du Vin; s/d €65/90; ☒ Wed-Mon), a distinguished little hotel-restaurant, generally considered to be one of the best places to eat (mains €20 to €26) on the Route du Vin. The blue European lobster is delicious.

The **Musée du Vin** (Wine Museum; ☎ 76 00 26; 115 Route du Vin; adult/child €3.50/1.50; ☒ 9.30-11.30am & 2-

5pm Tue-Sun Apr-Oct), signposted on the main road, houses a vast collection of old wine-making equipment (no English explanations).

Note the village houses with flood levels posted on their façades – the big one in 1947 reached 4m.

WORMELDANGE
pop 1300

Wormeldange's only attraction is the **Caves à Crémant Poll-Fabaire** (☎ 76 82 11; www.pollfabaire.lu; 115 Route du Vin; adult/child €2/1.25; ☒ 1-6pm Mon-Sat May-Oct). This huge salmon-coloured complex on the northern edge of the village makes one of the Grand Duchy's best *crémant* wines and offers tours and tastings.

Relais du Postillon (☎ 76 84 85; www.relaisdupostillon .lu in French; 113 Rue Principale; s/d €48/66; ☒), on the road parallel to Route du Vin, has pleasant if unexceptional rooms, and an atrium restaurant (serving pizza and pasta dishes). The owner happens to be the Duchy's most distinguished baker – he runs Schumacher, a *boulangerie/pâtisserie* (bakery/cake and pastry shop) next door, and is known in cake circles for his Gâteau de l'Europe and a few world records.

GREVENMACHER
pop 3900

Grevenmacher, 20km north of Remich, is the Route du Vin's largest town and the region's workaday capital. It has a **tourist office** (☎ 75 82 75; 10 Route du Vin; ☒ 8am-noon & 1-5pm Mon-Fri, 10am-1pm Sat Jul-Aug), but little in the way of accommodation. Internet access is available at **Kulturhuef** (☎ 26 74 64 1; 54 Route de Trèves; per hour €2; ☒ 2-6pm Tue-Sun), a new cultural centre. **Caves Bernard-Massard** (☎ 75 05 45 1; 8 Rue du Pont; adult/child €3/2; ☒ 9.30am-6pm Apr-Oct) is one of the region's largest sparkling-wine producers. Tours through this slick, fully mechanised operation end with a glass of its best bubbles.

A cold weather treat is the **Jardin des Papillons** (☎ 75 85 39; www.papillons.lu; Route de Trèves; adult/child €5.50/2.70; ☒ 9.30am-5pm Apr–mid-Oct), a hothouse filled with butterflies, insects, birds and plants from tropical climes. Don't bother in July and August when it's too hot and crowded.

Camping Route du Vin (☎ 75 02 34; www.grevenmacher.lu; Route du Vin; camp sites per adult/child/tent €3.80/2/4; ☒ Apr-Sep; ☒) is on the riverbank next to the Jardin des Papillons. It has tennis courts, a pool and playground.

THE SOUTHWEST

Luxembourg's southwest corner is low on most visitor itineraries. Though poetically known in tourist brochures as Le Pays des Terres Rouges (The Land of the Red Rocks), it's largely an industrial area – much of the Grand Duchy's former wealth came from here in the form of iron ore. Today money is being poured back in, with new entertainment venues and a whole new satellite suburb/business district, **Belval**, being whipped up on an abandoned industrial site to the west of Luxembourg's second largest city, Esch-sur-Alzette. Belval will also be home to many faculties of the new University of Luxembourg.

ESCH-SUR-ALZETTE
pop 27,000

There's an unmistakable buzz in Esch these days. Investment is huge, construction intense and the future bright for this regional hub, just 17km south of Luxembourg City. But it hasn't always been like this. Although there's mention of Esch-sur-Alzette right back in 773, the city basically began early last century when Italian immigrants arrived to work in the steel industry. The population flourished up until 1960 while jobs were easy to come by. But the industry's collapse saw Esch spiral dizzily downward, along with steel towns in nearby Belgium and France. While many of its neighbours are still a forlorn state of affairs, Esch has metamorphosed into a bustling regional centre, with a pedestrianised hub that offers terrace *cafés* and decent shops, including a designer boutique or two. There's a distinctly Italian feel to the place and even *gelateria* (ice-cream shops) dot Rue de l'Alzette, the city's main street.

The **tourist office** (☎ 54 16 37; www.esch-city.lu; 25 Rue Boltgen; ☯ 9am-5pm Mon-Sat May-Sep, 9am-5pm Mon-Fri Oct-Apr) is next to the town hall, a few minutes' walk from the train station. Note the Lëtzebuergesch inscription carved high up on the town hall's façade – *'Mir wëlle bleiwe wat mir sin'* (We want to remain what we are).

Internet access is available at **Click** (☎ 54 42 45 20 0; 97 Rue de l'Alzette; per hr €2; ☯ 9am-6pm Mon-Fri, 2-6pm Sat).

Sights & Activities

Without history or natural beauty on its side, Esch's attractions are limited. The main sight is the **Musée de la Résistance Nationale** (☎ 54 84 72; Place

de la Résistance; admission free; ☯ 3-6pm Thu, Sat & Sun). This resistance museum occupies the central pavilion of a large, very sombre memorial, dedicated to those killed in WWII. It stands sentinel-like at the end of Rue de l'Alzette. Very limited opening hours mean planning is essential.

Architecture is another draw, with the city noted for fine **houses** in both **Art Nouveau** (Nos 4, 61 & 96 Rue de l'Alzette) and **Art Deco** (55 Rue de l'Alzette & 14 Rue Zénon Bernard) styles. The former are not nearly as decorative as the gems in Brussels, but they're easily located and worth a look. Ask the tourist office for the architectural walk brochure (in English).

Escher Schwemm (☎ 26 53 13 53; Place des Sacrifiés; ☯ 11.30am-9.45pm Mon-Fri, 8am-5.45pm Sat, 8am-12.45pm Sun) is a heated indoor pool (with a small satellite outdoor section open in summer), boasting waterslides and a highly sought brasserie (see Club-5am Park, below). It's about 700m from the city centre.

Sleeping & Eating

Esch has no shortage of good places to sleep and eat.

Camping Gaalgebierg (☎ 54 10 69; www.gaalgebierg .lu; Galgenberg; camp sites per adult/child/tent €3.75/1.75/6; ☯ year-round) Pleasantly surrounded by woods, about 1km south of the train station. Kids will enjoy the large playground, and the deer next door.

Hôtel de la Poste (☎ 26 54 54 1; www.hotel-de-la-poste .lu in French; 107 Rue de l'Alzette; s/d Mon-Fri from €95/110, Sat & Sun €80/90; ✗) An Art Deco hotel, completely renovated in 2003 but still with touches of the original (1919) style. It's family friendly and has 20 neat rooms done out in soothing lemon tones. The fabulously friendly staff go out of their way to help.

Club-5am Park (☎ 26 17 57 75; Place des Sacrifiés; carpaccio €12-15, other mains €15-19; ☯ 10am-1am May–mid-Sep, closed Sun mid-Sep–Apr) Attached to the city's swimming pool and overlooking a leafy playground, this stylish modern brasserie serves the country's best carpaccio plus a host of other delicious Italian/French/vegetarian dishes. It's 700m north of the city centre.

Acacia (☎ 54 10 61; 10 Rue de la Libération; mains €25) Very good French cuisine is the mainstay of this restaurant, in the heart of Esch at the Hôtel Acacia.

Namur (☎ 54 17 78; 64 Rue de l'Alzette; ☯ 1-6pm Mon, 9am-6pm Tue-Sat) The place for salads, pastries and ice creams; dine in the big tearoom at the back.

AROUND THE GRAND DUCHY

Entertainment

Esch is entertainment central. The country's two biggest contemporary music venues are here; tickets for both can be bought at the tourist office.

Rockhal (☎ 24 55 51, tickets 24 55 55 55; www.rockhal .lu; 305 Blvd Charles de Gaulle) The newest is the red and black Rockhal, part of the new Belval urban development west of Esch. The closest train station is Belval Usines, one stop after Esch (direction Pétange).

Kulturfabrik (☎ 55 44 93 1; www.kulturfabrik.lu in French & German; 116 Rue de Luxembourg) This cultural centre is housed in an old abattoir, 1km north of the train station on the road to Luxembourg City. It sports a solid annual line-up of music, theatre and exhibitions. Music-wise it leans towards hip acts with an edge.

Getting There & Away

Esch and much of its surrounding region is easily explored by train from Luxembourg City – the line goes via Bettembourg to Esch (20 minutes, half-hourly) and then ambles on to Pétange (20 minutes, half-hourly).

AROUND ESCH-SUR-ALZETTE

Six kilometres southeast of Esch, **Rumelange** is worth a stop for its **Musée National des Mines** (☎ 56 56 88; www.mnm.lu; Rue de la Bruyère; adult/concession/child €8.50/7/5; ⏰ 2-6pm Thu-Sun Apr-Jun & Sep, Tue-Sun Jul & Aug, last departure 4.30pm) at Walert. This iron-ore museum occupies a disused mine shaft and

visitors are taken by train (20 minutes) 100m down to where old and new mining machinery and photos tell the industry's tale. Don yellow safety helmets for this 1½-hour adventure, and bring warm clothes.

Like Esch, the neighbouring town of **Dudelange** was heavily into steel, but it is now known for its neo-Gothic, vibrantly painted **church** (admission free; ⏰ 8am-6pm).

Travelling families should consider **Bettembourg** and the **Parc Merveilleux** (☎ 51 10 48; www .parc-merveilleux.lu in French & German; Route de Mondorf; adult/child €7/4; ⏰ 9.30am-6pm Apr–mid-Oct). This is Luxembourg's most popular family amusement park (though tiny in comparison to Belgium's), with a small zoo, mini-train and playground. It's been around for over half a century (the fairytale-theme houses look like they date from then) but there are also plenty of newer attractions. Old or new, little kids love it. From Bettembourg train station it's 1.5km (or take bus 304; four daily).

Camping families have **Camping Beetebourg** (☎ 51 36 46; www.sitb.lu; Parc Jacquinot, Bettembourg; camp sites per adult/child/tent €4/2/4; ⏰ mid-Apr–Sep), opposite Bettembourg train station.

Train spotters should head to **Fond-de-Gras** for a ride on either the steam-powered **Train 1900** (☎ 58 05 81; www.train1900.lu; adult/child €7/4; ⏰ Sun May-Sep) to Petange, or the narrow-gauge train **Minièresbunn** (☎ 50 47 07; adult/child €4/3; ⏰ Sun May-Sep) to Saulnes in France and back (via the border village of Lasauvage).

Directory

CONTENTS

Accommodation	297
Activities	300
Business Hours	303
Children	303
Climate Charts	305
Customs	305
Dangers & Annoyances	305
Discount Cards	305
Embassies & Consulates	306
Festivals & Events	307
Food	307
Gay & Lesbian Travellers	308
Holidays	308
Insurance	308
Internet Access	308
Legal Matters	309
Maps	309
Money	309
Photography & Video	310
Post	310
Shopping	310
Solo Travellers	310
Telephone & Fax	310
Time	311
Toilets	311
Tourist Information	311
Travellers with Disabilities	312
Visas	313
Women Travellers	313

ACCOMMODATION

Belgium and Luxembourg's accommodation scene ranges from riverside camping grounds to five-star hotels, with the whole spectrum in between. An interesting point about Belgium's scene is the rise in top-quality B&Bs – we've highlighted many throughout the guide.

Accommodation listings in this book are ordered from budget to midrange and then top end. Budget accommodation ranges from about €17 for a dorm bed to €60 for a double room, and includes camping grounds, hostels, some B&Bs and cheap hotels. In the midrange category there's a wealth of B&Bs and hotels with double rooms going for €60 to €140. Top-enders, once again B&Bs and hotels, start at €140. For more details on all these options, see the individual sections following.

Accommodation is usually heavily booked in the summer, so if you plan to visit from May to September it's wise to make reservations at least several weeks ahead. That said, the accommodation situation in Brussels is somewhat different to the rest of the Belgium due to the influx of Eurocrats and businesspeople on weekdays, and their mass evacuation at weekends and during the summer holiday months. Good deals can be found at these times. It's worth remembering that some hotels in other large cities – such as Antwerp and Luxembourg City – also offer weekend or summer discounts; for more details see p98. Weekend/weekday rates have been listed throughout this book.

In the event that you arrive without a booking, tourist offices will usually reserve accommodation for you (either for free or for a small fee); you simply pay a deposit that is deducted from your room rate.

Those into green tourism may want to investigate Luxembourg's Ecolabel initiative. This system gives hotels, camping grounds and long-term holiday dwellings a special Ecolabel logo if they comply with environmentally friendly management criteria (such as energy efficiency and waste disposal).

Accommodation in Belgium attracts 6% value-added tax (VAT) as well as a *stadsbelasting/taxe de séjour* (city tax) which varies from city to city but is usually no higher than 6%. In Luxembourg, 3% VAT is added. Prices for all accommodation mentioned in this guide includes the relevant taxes.

Something to keep an eye out for, particularly when travelling in rural areas in both countries, is hotels offering *demi-pension* (half board, ie breakfast and either lunch or dinner), *pension complète* (full board), and *weekend gastronomique* (accommodation plus breakfast and some meals which are usually four-course affairs). *Demi-pension,* in particular, can be an attractive option, allowing you to eat at a discounted rate at the hotel's restaurant, although you will have to settle for the menu of the day (you won't have a choice of à la carte options). On weekends in summer in extremely touristy places (such as Durbuy

---

PRACTICALITIES

■ Plug your hairdryer into a two round pin adaptor before plugging into the electricity supply (220V, 50Hz).

■ Keep up to date with *The Bulletin* (www.thebulletin.com), Belgium's invaluable English-language newsweekly (celebrated 40 years in 2006 and has some 50,000 international readers). The Luxembourg equivalent is *Luxembourg News 352*.

■ Leaf through *De Standaard* (Flemish), *Le Soir* (French) and *Grenzecho* (German) newspapers in Belgium, or *Lëtzebuerger Journal* in Luxembourg.

■ Tune into the Flemish radio stations Radio 1 (91.7 kHz FM; news, politics and current events) and Studio Brussel (100.6 kHz FM; light entertainment); French stations Action FM (106.9 kHz FM; commercial pop) and Musiq3 (91.2 kHz FM; classical music); and Radio Lëtzebuerg (RTL; 93.3 kHz FM; news, current affairs etc) and Den Neie Radio (DNR; 102.9 kHz FM; light entertainment) in Luxembourg. For international news check out the BBC World Service (648 kHz AM).

■ Switch on the box to watch the Flemish channels TV1 (news and sport), VTM (soaps and game shows) and Ketnet/Canvas (documentaries/foreign films), or the French channels La Une and La Deux1 (general news and sport) and ARTE (nonmainstream films and international documentaries). In Luxembourg RTL broadcasts nightly in Lëtzebuergesch.

■ Buy or watch DVDs set on Region 2, and videos on the PAL system.

■ Use the metric system for weights and measures. Decimals are indicated with commas and thousands with points (full stops).

---

in the Ardennes), some hotels rent rooms only on a *pension complète* basis.

If you happen to be travelling with a pet, midrange and top-end hotels often accept dogs and cats – expect to pay between €3 to €10 per night.

New laws in Belgium require visitors to show their passport when booking into accommodation.

B&Bs

B&Bs (*gastenkamers* in Flemish, *chambres d'hôtes* in French) have gained enormous ground in the last decade in Belgium. In Luxembourg, however, they're nonexistent in the capital and still light on the ground around the countryside.

B&Bs usually represent excellent value. Compared to a hotel room of the same price,

you'll get a spacious room full of character and individuality, breakfasts that are unfailingly feasts, and vibrant hosts that generally love what they're doing. At the top end, the quality is impeccable, with charming rooms and added extras such as a bottle of red wine or a bedtime chocolate.

Facilities and services, of course, vary with the price; cheaper B&Bs usually have shared bathroom and toilet facilities. Another point to consider is steps – many rooms in B&Bs are located on the 2nd floor of town houses. Elevators are nonexistent, so be prepared for lots of narrow staircases.

B&B prices start at single/double €35/45, rising to around €50/65 for midrange options and levelling out at €100 to €180 at the top end. Prices in Brussels tend to be a bit higher. Triples and family rooms are sometimes available and often don't cost all that much extra. Some B&Bs charge an extra €10 for stays of just one night; others offer discounts for stays of two or more nights. Some B&Bs in touristy areas will not accept one-night stays on weekends.

Camping, Caravan Parks & Hikers' Huts

Camping and caravanning facilities are plentiful and at their best in the Belgian and Luxembourg Ardennes, where the tranquil nature

---

BOOK ACCOMMODATION ONLINE

For more accommodation reviews and recommendations by Lonely Planet authors, check out the online booking service at www.lonelyplanet.com. You'll find the true, insider lowdown on the best places to stay. Reviews are thorough and independent. Best of all, you can book online.

of the countryside lends itself to outdoor living. That said, camping grounds are popular summer retreats for locals and are often sardined with permanent trailers. While space is always set aside for overnighters, don't expect too much solitude, serenity or communing with nature in the camp ground itself.

Rates vary, but on average you'll be looking at between €10 and €20 for two adults, a tent and car. Camping grounds in both countries may be rated under the Benelux (an abbreviation for Belgium, the Netherlands and Luxembourg) classification system, however this is a voluntary scheme and many grounds are not part of it. Under the system, camping grounds are awarded between one and five stars – the more stars, the higher level of comfort.

Hikers' huts (known as *trekkershutten* in Flanders and *wanderhütten* in Luxembourg) are situated around Flanders and in Luxembourg's Müllerthal and Ardennes regions. These small wooden cabins can sleep four people and have basic cooking facilities. In Belgium they're located in camping grounds along the Flanders Cycle Route (p301); in Luxembourg they're located within walking distance of each other (see Camping Plage, p292, and the boxed text on p286). The overnight price in Belgium is €32 per hut; in Luxembourg it's €43 for two persons (extra person €5; maximum four-night stay).

Useful websites:

Luxembourg National Tourist Office (www.visit luxembourg.lu) Publishes a free brochure listing all the country's camping grounds.

Trekkershutten (www.trekkershutten.nl in Dutch) Hikers' huts in Belgium, Luxembourg and the Netherlands.

Walloon camping (www.campingbelgique.be) Camping grounds in Wallonia.

Guesthouses

Self-contained guesthouses and apartments, where you can base yourself for a few days, a week or longer, are steadily gaining ground in both countries. Mostly they're rural retreats in the Ardennes (Chimay, p228) or Luxembourg (Schegdenhaff, p286), although excellent options can be found in towns such as Bruges (p133), Tongeren (p215) and Echternach (p291). For value for money, guesthouses are hard to beat, especially for groups of friends or families. And as a base for exploring a region, they're ideal.

In the countryside, guesthouses are known as *landelijke verblijven* in Flemish, or *gîtes*

ruraux in French. Often they're attached to farms – they might be old converted stables or milking sheds, or part of a farmhouse that has been refitted.

Guesthouse prices vary enormously and fluctuate depending on the season; the high season is July and August, plus other school holidays (p308). Expect prices to start at about €220 per week.

A few useful organisations:

Belsud (www.belsud.be) Arranges guesthouses in Brussels and Wallonia.

Gîtes de Wallonie (www.gitesdewallonie.be) Countryside retreats in Wallonia.

Luxembourg National Tourist Office (www.visitluxem bourg.lu) Publishes a good brochure entitled *Holiday Apartments Farm & Rural Holidays*.

Vlaamse Federatie voor Hoeve & Plattelandstoerisme (www.hoevetoerisme.be) Arranges guesthouses in Flanders.

Hostels & Gîtes d'Étapes

Belgium has a large number of hostels (*jeugdherbergen* in Flemish, *auberges de jeunesse* in French) affiliated with Hostelling International (HI). In some cities (such as Brussels and Bruges) there are also similarly priced private hostels. Luxembourg has a handful of HI-affiliated hostels. Some hostels in both countries close during winter.

Belgian HI hostels charge between €15 and €18 per night in a dorm, including breakfast and sheets. Many hostels also have single/double/family rooms from €29/42/50. For details on HI membership, see p306. There is no age limit for staying at HI hostels, though some private hostels cap it at 35 years.

In Luxembourg, the nightly dorm rate, including breakfast and sheets, is from €17.50 to €20.60, depending on facilities. Single/double rooms start at €29.50/45.

In the rural areas you'll occasionally come across *gîtes d'étapes*. These dwellings are predominantly for large groups, although individual travellers are welcome.

Hostel organisations:

Centrale des Auberges de Jeunesse Luxembourgeoises (Map p270; ☎ 26 27 66 40; www.youthhostels .lu; 2 Rue du Fort Olisy, L-1616 Luxembourg City) Luxembourg's hostel association.

Les Auberges de Jeunesse (Map pp72–3; ☎ 02 219 56 76; www.laj.be; Rue de la Sablonnière 28, B-1000 Brussels) Administers hostels in Wallonia.

Vlaamse Jeugdherbergcentrale (Map pp176–7; ☎ 03 232 72 18; www.jeugdherbergen.be in Flemish;

Van Stralenstraat 40, B-2060 Antwerp) Runs hostels in Flanders.

Hotels

Hotels use a Benelux classification system indicating that the hotel is licensed and follows set standards. Recognised hotels will have a small blue shield adorned with one to five stars displayed near the entrance. Stars are awarded for facilities (elevators, room service, dogs allowed etc), and don't necessarily reflect quality, location or price.

A room is a *kamer* in Flemish or a *chambre* in French. The cheapest hotels charge between €35 and €45 for a single room and from €50 to €60 for doubles. Bathroom facilities may be shared. Midrange hotel prices average €50 to €100 for singles and €60 to €140 for doubles. Top-end establishments start at €140. Check-in time in many top-end hotels is not before 2pm.

Some hotels in Belgium reduce their rates at weekends (see p98). Occasionally, you'll find hotels doing the opposite. In touristy villages in the Ardennes, hotels may either charge more on weekends or rent rooms on a half- or full-board basis only.

In Luxembourg, most hotels are in the midrange or top-end brackets. Like in Brussels, some hotels in Luxembourg City offer discounted accommodation on weekends and/or in July and August, to make up for the Eurocrat shortfall. Discounts are noted in the relevant reviews, and it's also worth checking hotel websites for last-minute deals.

Top-end hotels usually offer private parking – expect to pay from €10 to €20 for 24 hours.

ACTIVITIES

Cycling and hiking are the big two activities in both countries. From there the field widens – anything from kayaking or rock climbing in summer, to cross-country skiing or holing up in a billiard den in winter.

Cycling

BELGIUM

Cycling is one of Belgium's passions. On weekends it's the norm to see troupes of male cyclists of all ages whizzing around country lanes clad in fluorescent lycra gear or pulled up for a drink at their favourite wayside pub.

There are two cycling genres: in flat Flanders, bikes are a means of everyday travel and relaxation; while hilly Wallonia is favoured by mountain-bike (*terreinfiets* in Flemish,

VTT or *vélo tout-terrain* in French) enthusiasts. Wallonia also has RAVel paths (see the boxed text, opposite). Cycling is fine in most cities in Flanders but the major Walloon towns are much less bike friendly. Brussels is slowly accommodating cyclists, but in reality only adrenaline freaks would want to take on the city's potholes, cobblestones and taxi drivers.

In Flanders, many roads have dedicated cycle lanes and it's usual to see the whole family out for a day on just two bikes (kiddies' seats front and back). While Flanders is wonderfully flat, strong winds can make cycling a battle – as Murphy's law would have it, the wind always seems to come from ahead. Bikes are not allowed on motorways but they can be taken on trains (one-way/return €5/8 to anywhere in Belgium). Bike helmets are not a legal requirement and are generally ignored by adults (except competition cyclists). At night, it's illegal to cycle without a light (fines of €140). As in the Netherlands, the stolen bike racket flourishes in Flanders. Locals use two locks and chains to secure a bike, and even that's no guarantee it'll be there when you get back. Mopeds use bike paths, too – beware as they often speed past without warning.

Bikes can be hired from some train stations or from private operators. The going rate is about €6.50/9.50 per half-/full day, or €55 per week. Hiring from a train station is convenient, but you must also pay a deposit (€12 to €20 depending on the train station) and show your passport. Private operators, on the other hand, often don't ask for a deposit and have better-quality bikes. They can sometimes supply children seats, baskets and helmets, not to mention regional cycling maps and local advice. Two excellent bike outfits that can supply rental or secondhand bikes for the whole family are Fietsen Popelier (p130) in Bruges and Mobiel (see p160) in Kortrijk.

Many private rental outlets and participating train stations are mentioned in this guide, but for a full list of stations pick up the Belgian Railways' *Trein & Fiets/Train & Vélo* brochure from any large train station.

Depending on the length of time you plan to stay, buying a bike may be the way to go. Some bike-rental outfits sell new and secondhand bikes. A six-gear Oxford city bike, made in Belgium, costs around €440 new, but can be picked up (as a six-month-old ex-rental bike) for about €280. The cheapest used bikes go for about €100. Bikes will often be bought back by rental outfits provided they're in good nick. Most bike-rental shops also do repairs.

When mountain biking in the Ardennes, follow this code of rules: stay on marked tracks, don't litter or make fires, and respect the silence and inhabitants of the woods and fields. Good rental outfits are located in Rochefort (p238) and La Roche-en-Ardenne (p246).

Bicycles can travel on planes, and you can sometimes just check it in as baggage (confirm this with the airline in advance). You may have to fold the bike down and dismantle it as much as possible. Let much (but not all) of the air out of the tyres to prevent them from bursting in the low-pressure baggage hold.

LUXEMBOURG

Cycling is a popular pastime in Luxembourg but, due to hillier terrain, it's not a common means of day-to-day travel. Numbered bicycle paths, known as *pistes cyclables*, criss-cross the countryside and plenty of bike-rental outfits

ON YA BIKE IN BELGIUM & LUXEMBOURG

Cycling holidays are taking off in Belgium and Luxembourg. The countryside in both countries is riddled with well-marked cycling routes and if you hire a bike, bring your own or buy one cheap secondhand it's easy to either cycle from destination to destination, or to go from city to city by train, using the bike to explore once you're there. Alternatively, combine the two.

For those into a cycling holiday along easy flat paths, Flanders is the obvious draw. Get hold of the multilingual *Topogids Vlaanderen Fietsroute*. This book (€8.50) details the Flanders Cycle Route, a circular 800km route – half of which is along traffic-free paths – that takes in many of Flanders' most picturesque villages and historic towns. The entire route is marked in both directions by white signposts with green symbols. The book has 61 detailed route maps (scale 1:50,000), as well as accommodation options such as hikers' huts (p298) where cyclists are also welcome to stay.

If 800km is too daunting, shorter circuits are also possible by taking one of the LF Cycle Routes – such as the LF2 Stedenroute – that divides the Flanders Cycle Route into four smaller loops. For those who prefer cycling without luggage, all-inclusive package holidays can be organised via Toerisme Vlaanderen (p311). These packages generally last four to five days, and spotlight one part of the Flanders Cycle Route.

Those going it alone can get information on bike-friendly accommodation options from Tourisme Vlaanderen (www.vlaanderen-vakantieland.be/fietsvriendelijk). Their brochure *Accommodation at the Belgian Coast* lists places that are no more than 5km from a cycle route and provide a secure bike shed.

It's not only Flanders that offers flat cycling. Wallonia has RAVel (www.ravel.wallonie.be), a network of pathways – canal or river towpaths, or old tram or railway tracks (rebuilt with hard surfaces) – that give a safe, motorist-free environment to slow movers such as cyclists, hikers, skaters or people with reduced mobility. The longest, RAVel 1, crosses Wallonia for 330km from east to west, starting at Lanaye near the Dutch border and finishing at Houplines on the French border. A fifth RAVel track is planned and will join Verviers in the north to Virton in Wallonia's south. To try out a section of a RAVel track, try the old train line at Rochefort (p238).

Although Luxembourg usually conjures up images of hilly terrain, cycling here can also be flat, easy and enjoyable. Many fine *pistes cyclables* (bicycle paths), all named and numbered, criss-cross the countryside and while you'll need good muscles for many, some are leisurely meanders. PC3, for example, winds right along the Moselle and Sûre Rivers – Echternach–Diekirch is a particularly nice stretch of this path (and there are now bike-hire outlets in both towns), as is Remich–Grevenmacher.

The excellent French, German and English guide *40 Cycle Routes*, published by Éditions Guy Binsfield, is well worth buying if you intend exploring Luxembourg on two wheels. It describes 40 specially selected cycle tours throughout the country and gives good topographical maps of each route plus track descriptions. It's sold in bookshops and newsagents around the country.

Depending on your level of fitness, the terrain and the wind factor, adult cyclists average about 15km per hour. For more on cycling possibilities, see p17. For listings of bike-rental outfits, see individual destinations. Also take a look at www.cycling-belgium.be and www.fietsen-wandelen .be (in Flemish).

have sprung up in recent years. Try those in Luxembourg City (p274), Echternach (p291) or Diekirch (p289). Bikes can be taken on trains for €1.50, and helmets are not compulsory. For more on cycling in Luxembourg, see boxed text, p301.

Hiking

As with cycling, both countries are big on hiking.

In Belgium, hikers have the choice of easy, flat terrain in Flanders or the more inspiring hills of the Ardennes in Wallonia. Popular hikes in Flanders generally follow countryside bike paths (but make sure you give way to cyclists if walking on designated cycle paths). For a bed for the night, check out Flanders' hikers' huts (p298).

Serious hikers should head to the Ardennes – either in southeast Belgium or northern Luxembourg – as well as Luxembourg's Müllerthal region. These beautiful areas are dotted with wooded tracks that wind through largely coniferous forests and ford streams and rivers. Needless to say, in winter you'll have the tracks to yourself – cold, wet weather between November and March sees few locals venturing along muddy paths. Come April, snowdrops pop their heads up through thick layers of fallen leaves, and townsfolk yearning for spring and a touch of the outdoors start heading for the hills. In July and August it's high season and, during fine weekends at this time of the year, tracks can get crowded. Various *sentiers de grande randonnée* (long-distance footpaths, simply known as GR tracks) cross Belgium and there's also the 160km-long 'Transardennaise' footpath which goes from La Roche to Bouillon.

The best places for hiking are the Hautes Fagnes (p259), Bouillon (p241), La Roche-en-Ardenne (p246) and Rochefort (p238) in Belgium, or Echternach (p290), Berdorf (p292), Beaufort (p292) and Vianden (p283) in Luxembourg. Echternach, the main town in Luxembourg's Müllerthal region, is superb for hiking with paths weaving up, down and around gorgeous sandstone plateaus hidden deep within the forests. In this region, too, are overnight hikers' huts (p298).

Local tourist offices have copious information about hiking paths and they also sell maps of paths in their area. The biggest publisher of hiking maps is the Institut Géographique National (IGN), which puts out topographical maps covering all of Belgium, as well as specialist hiking maps.

In Luxembourg, consider buying the excellent multilingual *182x Luxembourg* published by Éditions Guy Binsfield. It describes 182 of the country's most charming hikes ranging from 2km to 17km. All are signposted and most can easily be covered in an afternoon. It's readily available in bookshops throughout the Grand Duchy.

On the internet, check www.walking.lu and www.europaventure.be.

Billiards

Every town and village worth its weight in Belgium has a billiards *café* (bar/pub) where elderly gents congregate for a game and a gossip. Billiards (*biljart* in Flemish, *billard* in French) differs from snooker or pool in that only three balls are used and the table has no holes – the aim is not to pot the balls but to use one ball to hit the other two. Some billiards *cafés* have snooker and pool tables, too. The country's best-known billiards den is Mister 100 (p201) in Lier. It was set up by Raymond Ceulemans who won the world billiards championships 17 times since 1962 and is known as Mister 100% because he never misses a shot.

Boating

Despite its many rivers and canals, boating in Belgium is nowhere near as popular as it is in the neighbouring Netherlands. In summer, the North Sea between Knokke and De Panne is sprinkled with catamarans and sailing boats; inquire at tourist offices at any of the coastal resorts for operators hiring boats out for a few hours or a day.

Luxembourg is also not a boating nation and the only option is a cruise along the Moselle River (p293).

Canoeing & Kayaking

Belgium's Ardennes region is the place to ride rivers. Canoes and kayaks can be hired from several towns including Dinant (for the Lesse River; p236), Bouillon (Semois River; p242) and La Roche-en-Ardenne (Ourthe River; p246). All three rivers, particularly the Lesse, attract hoards of Flemish and Dutch holidaymakers every summer – you won't be alone on the water here. The Lesse is the 'wildest' of the trio, but don't expect rapids of any magnitude – conditions sometimes are so sedate (and water levels so low) that the rivers are closed to kayakers.

In Luxembourg, head to Diekirch (p289) for canoeing.

Chess
Belgian men – both young and old – are the ones huddled deep in concentration over a chessboard in smoky *cafés* around the country. Many *cafés* have chess sets available for clients – the country's best-known chess den is Le Greenwich (p106).

Golf
Despite the relative lack of space in Belgium, golf is a fashionable and increasingly popular activity. Courses are dotted around the country, with a heavy concentration around the green periphery of Brussels (p91). The main golfing organisation is the **Royal Belgian Golf Federation** (www.golf.be).

Horse Riding
For details on horse riding in the Ardennes, see the boxed text on p246.

Rock Climbing
The most popular area for rock climbers in Belgium is along the Meuse River in the vicinity of Namur and Dinant. It was here, near Marche-les-Dames, that King Albert I died after a fall in 1934. Belgium's escarpments are generally high-quality limestone, while Luxembourg has hard sandstone cliffs. For more details you may be able to pick up *Selected Rock Climbs in Belgium & Luxembourg* by Chris Craggs from bookshops in Brussels, or ask at local tourist offices.

Skiing
The Ardennes is Belgium's and Luxembourg's winter playground, albeit a very modest one. Cross-country skiing is all that's offered – the slopes are too short for alpine skiing. Even cross-country skiing is struck off the list some years when snowfall is too light (or almost nonexistent as in recent times). Given these odds, you can safely bet that no-one comes to Belgium or Luxembourg specifically to ski.

BUSINESS HOURS
Restaurants generally open for lunch from 11.30am or noon until 2pm or 3pm. Dinner starts at about 6.30pm, and goes to 10pm or 11pm. Brasseries have more fluid hours, usually opening by 11am and staying open until midnight or 1am.

Defining business hours for bars and *cafés* is nigh on impossible. There are absolutely no regulations governing trading hours for these establishments – they open when they want and close when the last barfly drops. Most *cafés* are open by 10am or 11am, and some will still be going at 5am.

In general, shops in both countries are open from 9am until noon or 12.30pm, and again from 2pm to 6pm, Monday to Saturday. Many shops in major tourist destinations, such as Brussels, Bruges, Antwerp and Luxembourg City, don't close for lunch, and many also open on Sunday. The occasional convenience shop opens 24 hours – look for signs indicating *nachtwinkel* or *magasin de nuit*.

Banks open from 8.30am or 9am and close between 3.30pm and 5pm Monday to Friday. Some close for an hour at lunch, and many also open Saturday mornings.

Post offices generally operate from 9am to 5pm Monday to Friday and until noon Saturday. Smaller branches close for lunch and larger ones stay open until 6pm.

Throughout this guide, we've provided opening hours for sights and activities. For other businesses, like restaurants and shops, we've listed hours only when they differ from the norm.

CHILDREN
Kids are adored in Belgium and Luxembourg, and both countries are extremely child-friendly when it comes to almost all aspects of travelling with children (see p18 for suggestions).

Both countries can easily be explored with children in tow but it will require planning and effort. For further general information, see Lonely Planet's *Travel with Children*.

Practicalities
The only hole in the system in both countries is the scarcity of nappy-changing facilities – you'll soon get the hang of wrestling in the backseat of a car. Belgium's national chain of hamburger restaurants, Quick, generally have baby-change tables or a foam mat tucked away in a corner of the female toilets. They're not much chop but better than nothing during those tricky moments. Expect to pay €0.50 for this service. Unlike in the UK, chain shops such as Prémaman don't offer change facilities. Breastfeeding in public is fine, though it's not commonly seen (Belgians generally bottle feed from an early age).

Baby cots are readily available in many B&Bs, hotels and even some hostels, but you should reserve in advance as many places stock only one cot. Accommodation options which welcome babies and children, and which have facilities for them, have been noted throughout the guide. Cots are often free, but at the most you'll pay €15 per night. If you're travelling by car, it's easier to bring a portacot.

There's no fast rule about pricing for older children in B&Bs and hotels. Many places offer free accommodation for children under two or three years, others raise the age to seven or even 12. Some hotels charge €15 for an extra bed for a child, others charge a flat fee of 50% extra. Many hostels have rooms with four beds, making family travel economical.

If you're travelling with kids small enough to be carried in a backpack or baby-sling, this is the way to go. Strollers certainly have their place, but they're a nuisance when negotiating access to old buildings, shoddy pavements and endless flights of stairs. The locals commonly take strollers on buses, trams and trains (avoiding peak hour).

Also remember that in cities such as Bruges there are a lot of canals and open water – beware no-one takes an unexpected plunge.

A law introduced in 2006 means children under 1.35m must travel in a child's safety seat in cars. Most car-rental firms in Belgium and Luxembourg have safety seats for hire (Avis charges a flat fee of €30; at Budget it's €10 per week), but it's essential to book them two or three days in advance. The law means taxis too should provide a seat if you book in advance.

Take note that train travel in Belgium is free for under 12s providing they're accompanied by an adult and the journey starts after 9am.

Arranging baby-sitting in Belgium is possible but it's not easy, except in Brussels. Sitters can be arranged through **Gezinsbond** (www.gezinsbond .be), a family-oriented organisation with centres throughout Flanders. They charge €2.50/3 per hour in the day/evening for baby-sitters, or €15 for overnight service. The catch for travellers is you must be an organisation member to use the baby-sitting service (annual membership costs €30) and, for security reasons, baby-sitters may not be willing to come to your hotel. Baby-sitting agencies have been mentioned in the larger cities throughout this book.

Those heading to Luxembourg may want to pick up the new *Family Guide* by Vivianne Bumb. It includes 600 activities, trips and contacts and is well researched and beautifully illustrated. Note that it's impossible to find a baby-sitter in Luxembourg unless you're staying at a top-end hotel that provides that service.

For information on dining with kids, see p57.

Sights & Activities

Antwerp (p186), Bruges (p131) and Brussels (p93) have plenty to offer kids. Luxembourg City (see p276) does too although a day or two is about all you'd need here. Ostend is the most accessible resort on the Belgian coast – see p141 for details on its beach. Close to the coastal resort of De Panne is Belgium's most popular children's theme park, Plopsaland (p148). Near Mechelen there's the science-oriented Technopolis (p204) as well as Planckendael zoo (p205). In a wooded area close to Hasselt is an open-air museum, Bokrijk (p212), plus the country's largest playground. Schedule a whole day for these, as kids love both. In Hasselt there's the new Plopsa Indoor (p211). In the Ardennes, small towns such as Rochefort (p238) offer cycling and ancient caves to explore, Bouillon (p241) has a creepy castle and kayaking, and at La Roche-en-Ardenne (p245) you can cycle, kayak, hike or horse ride. All kids get right into the Euro Space Center (p240).

There's nothing like a ride in the country against a stiff North Sea wind to give kids a good night's sleep. Adult bicycles are readily available for hire in Belgium but if you want to plop young kids on a bike too, you'll need prior planning. Bruges (p130), Kortrijk (p160) and Luxembourg City (p274) all have excellent rental agencies offering both child bikes and baby/toddler seats. The latter are fitted to the front and/or rear of an adult bike and are ideal for getting around when kids are too young to saddle up themselves. You'll see this setup everywhere in Flanders: mum, dad and two or even three kids out for a half-day on just two bikes. Toddlers love travelling this way, although you'll have to limit journey lengths to suit them. An option for older children (four or five years) is the so-called 'third-wheel'. This is an extra wheel, complete with seat, pedals and handle bar, that is screwed onto the back of the adult bike and trails along behind. This system takes getting use to – by both adult and child – and you'll find some kids love it while others feel insecure. For more general information on cycling, see p300.

CLIMATE CHARTS

Belgium and Luxembourg share a generally mild, maritime climate characterised by many days of grey and/or rainy weather. For more on local weather conditions and suggestions on when to go, see p12.

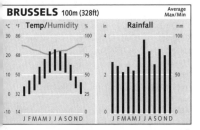

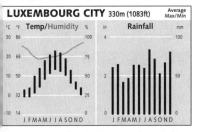

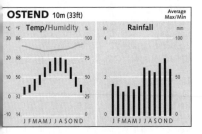

CUSTOMS

Duty-free goods are no longer sold to those travelling from one EU country to another. For goods purchased in airports or on ferries *outside* the EU, the usual allowances apply for tobacco (200 cigarettes, 50 cigars or 250g of loose tobacco), alcohol (1L of spirits or 2L of liquor with less than 22% alcohol by volume; 2L of wine) and perfume (50g of perfume and 0.25L of eau de toilette).

Do not confuse these with *duty-paid* items (including alcohol and tobacco) bought at normal shops and supermarkets in another EU country and brought into Belgium or Lux-embourg, where certain goods might be more expensive. The allowances for these goods are far more generous: 800 cigarettes, 200 cigars or 1kg of loose tobacco; 10L of spirits (more than 22% alcohol by volume), 20L of fortified wine or apéritif, 90L of wine or 110L of beer, and unlimited quantities of perfume.

DANGERS & ANNOYANCES

Both countries are, in general, very safe. The only danger you're likely to confront is a big night out on Belgian beer. That said, Belgians were shocked in 2006 by two separate murders in broad daylight in busy public places in the country's main cities (see p21 and p33). These events have put personal security back on the public agenda.

While the rate of violent crime is low compared with many European countries, petty theft does occur, more so in large cities. Favoured haunts for pickpockets in Brussels include the Grand Place, the narrow streets around Ilôt Sacré, Rue Neuve, and the markets at Gare du Midi and Place du Jeu-de-Balle. In Luxembourg, keep your hands on your valuables around the train station area.

In January 2007, restaurants in Belgium – but not Luxembourg – became smoke-free. But unlike in a growing number of European countries, the new law didn't extend to *cafés* and pubs. Although *cafés* are required by law to have adequate ventilation, in reality few do. Even fewer have sections for *niet rokers/ non-fumeurs* (nonsmokers). If you're used to socialising in a smoke-free environment, you'll find both countries challenging.

And lastly there's the subject of dog mess. Belgians' love of dogs unfortunately manifests itself in footpaths dotted with doggie-doos. Pictograms stencilled onto pavements ordering dogs 'not to squat here' have made little difference, and rare is the Belgian who follows his or her hairy companion and faithfully scoops up after it. A few years back, Brussels introduced hefty fines for failing to do just that, but they seem to have made little difference. A poll in 2005 showed dog mess on the street was the one thing that most irritated most Belgians.

DISCOUNT CARDS

There is no national museum card in Belgium, but the Grand Duchy has the Luxembourg Card, which offers good value for those really keen on exploring (for details, see p271).

Many individual cities offer discounted passes to a variety of sights – these have been detailed throughout the guide. Museums in both countries offer concession prices for children, students and seniors.

Senior Cards

Seniors over 65 (including visitors) pay only €4 for a return 2nd-class train trip anywhere in Belgium (not on weekends from mid-May to mid-September). Most museums and other attractions offer discounts for those aged over 65 – there's no standard rule so check tariffs to see if you're eligible.

Student & Youth Cards

To stay at the hostels run by Vlaamse Jeugdherbergcentrale (in Flanders), Les Auberges de Jeunesse (in Wallonia) and Centrale des Auberges de Jeunesse Luxembourgeoises (in Luxembourg) you must be a member of an organisation affiliated to Hostelling International (HI). If you don't have an HI card you'll pay €3 extra per night for up to six nights, after which an International Guest Card, valid for one year, is issued.

The International Student Identity Card (ISIC) provides discounts on admission to many museums and sights and on train fares.

EMBASSIES & CONSULATES
Belgium Embassies & Consulates

For up-to-date visa information, check Belgium's Ministry of Foreign Affairs website at www.diplomatie.be.

Diplomatic representation abroad:

Australia (☎ 02-6273 2501; fax 02-6273 3392; 19 Arkana St, Yarralumla, ACT 2600)

Canada (☎ 613-236 7267; fax 613-236 7882; Constitution Sq, 360 Albert St, Suite 820, Ottawa ON K1R 7X7)

France (☎ 01 44 09 39 39; fax 01 47 54 07 64; rue de Tilsitt 9, Paris F-75840 Cedex 17)

Germany (☎ 49-3020 6420; fax 49-3020 642 200; Jägerstrasse 52-53, Berlin D-10117)

Ireland (☎ 01-205 7100; fax 01-283 9403; 2 Shrewsbury Rd, Ballsbridge, Dublin 4)

Luxembourg (☎ 25 43 251; fax 45 42 82; 4 Rue des Girondins, L-1626 Luxembourg City)

Netherlands (☎ 070-312 34 56; fax 070-364 55 79; Alexanderveld 97, NL-2585 DB The Hague)

New Zealand (☎ 09-575 6202; ismackenzie@xtra.co.nz; 15A Rarangi Rd, St Heliers, Auckland)

UK (☎ 020-7470 3700; fax 020-7470 3795; 103-105 Eaton Sq, London SW1W 9AB)

USA (☎ 202-333 6900; fax 202-333 5457; 3330 Garfield St, NW, Washington, DC 20008)

Luxembourg Embassies & Consulates

In countries where there is no representative, contact the nearest Belgian or Dutch diplomatic missions. Visa information can be obtained online at www.mae.lu.

Diplomatic missions abroad:

Belgium (☎ 02 735 57 00; fax 02 737 57 10; Ave de Cortenbergh 75, B-1000 Brussels)

France (☎ 01 45 55 13 37; fax 01 45 51 72 29; 33 Ave Rapp, Paris F-75007)

Germany (☎ 030-26 39 570; fax 030-26 39 5727; Klingelhöferstrasse 7, Berlin D-10785)

Netherlands (☎ 070-360 75 16; fax 070-346 2000; Nassaulaan 8, NL-2514 JS The Hague)

UK (☎ 020-7235 6961; fax 020-7235 9734; 27 Wilton Crescent, London SW1X 8SD)

USA (☎ 202-265 4171; fax 202-328 8270; 2200 Massachusetts Ave NW, Washington, DC 20008)

Embassies & Consulates in Belgium

The following diplomatic missions are all embassies and are located in or around Brussels.

Australia (Map pp72-3; ☎ 02 286 05 00; fax 02 230 68 02; Rue Guimard 6, B-1040 Brussels)

Canada (Map pp70-1; ☎ 02 741 06 11; fax 02 741 06 43; Ave de Tervuren 2, B-1040 Brussels)

France (Map pp72-3; ☎ 02 548 87 11; fax 02 513 68 71; Rue Ducale 65, B-1000 Brussels)

Germany (Map p86; ☎ 02 787 18 00; fax 02 787 28 00; Rue Jacques de Lalaing 8-14, B-1040 Brussels)

Ireland (Map p86; ☎ 02 235 66 76; fax 02 235 66 71; Rue Wiertz 50, B-1050 Brussels)

Luxembourg (Map p86; ☎ 02 735 57 00; fax 02 737 57 10; Ave de Cortenbergh 75, B-1000 Brussels)

Netherlands (Map pp70-1; ☎ 02 679 17 11; fax 02 679 17 75; Ave Herrmann-Debroux 48, B-1160 Brussels)

New Zealand (Map pp76-7; ☎ 02 512 10 40; fax 02 513 48 56; 7th fl, Sq de Meeus 1, B-1100 Brussels)

UK (Map p86; ☎ 02 287 62 11; fax 02 287 63 55; Rue d'Arlon 85, B-1040 Brussels)

USA (Map pp72-3; ☎ 02 508 21 11; fax 02 511 27 25; Blvd du Régent 27, B-1000 Brussels)

Embassies & Consulates in Luxembourg

The nearest Australian, Canadian and New Zealand embassies are in Belgium. The following foreign embassies are in Luxembourg City:

Belgium (Map p270; ☎ 25 43 251; fax 45 42 82; 4 Rue des Girondins, L-1626 Luxembourg City)

France (Map p270; ☎ 45 72 71 1; 8 Blvd Joseph II, L-1840 Luxembourg City)

Germany (Map p270; ☎ 45 34 45 1; 20-22 Ave Émile Reuter, L-2420 Luxembourg City)

Ireland (☎ 45 06 10; 28 Route d'Arlon, L-1140 Luxembourg City)

Netherlands (Map p270; ☎ 22 75 70; 6 Rue Ste Zithe, L-2763 Luxembourg City)

UK (Map p270; ☎ 22 98 64; 14 Blvd Joseph II, L-1840 Luxembourg City)

USA (Map p270; ☎ 46 01 23; 22 Blvd Emmanuel Servais, L-2535 Luxembourg City)

FESTIVALS & EVENTS

Both countries are big on festivals and celebrations. Throughout the year there are jazz marathons, religious processions, local fairs, film festivals and classical music extravaganzas, though the lion's share of events takes place over summer.

The intimacy and originality of some of Belgium's festivals is one of the country's best-kept secrets. Many festivals have religious roots but have grown into unique events. The Heilig-Bloedprocessie (p132) in Bruges in May, Ommegang (p96) in Brussels in late June/early July and the seven-yearly Kroningsfeesten (p215) in Tongeren are three of the most famous religion-inspired events. Carnival (p223) is a big do in many towns and villages in both countries – people shake off the winter blues with outrageous celebrations ranging from balls to masked parades, with lots of drinking. Other quirky events include the Kattenfestival (Festival of the Cat, p152) in Ypres, the Penitents' Procession (p149) in Veurne, La Doudou (p222) in Mons, and the Procession of the Giants (p222) in Ath.

For a complete list of annual events in the Grand Duchy, look up the Luxembourg National Tourist Office's website (www.visitluxem bourg.lu).

The following list covers national events in both countries; local festivals are listed in the relevant town sections earlier in this book.

February
Carnival Celebrated throughout Belgium and Luxembourg, but the most renowned festivities take place in the Walloon towns of Binche, Malmédy and Stavelot. For more information, see p223.

Buergsonndeg Luxembourg's Bonfire Day celebration started in pagan times and is held on the first Sunday after carnival. Bonfires in the shape of a cross are lit on hillsides all over the Grand Duchy and people – young and old – gather to eat, drink and socialise.

April
Festival van Vlaanderen (www.festival.be) The Festival of Flanders is an umbrella organisation for a host of festivals that, combined, add up to Belgium's biggest event. Top classical and international music performances, dance, world music and theatre are held from April to October in churches, abbeys, town halls and other historical locations throughout Flanders, including Brussels. Most of the events take place between July and September.

Octave One of Luxembourg's biggest events, this pilgrimage dates back to the 17th century and is held from the 3rd to the 5th Sunday after Easter. People from all around the Grand Duchy come to the capital to worship the Lady Comforter of the Afflicted, a small statue of the Virgin. On the 5th Sunday, the statue is carried around the city in a much-honoured, solemn procession that includes the Grand Ducal family and government officials. If you're driving around during these two weeks take note, pilgrims have the right of way.

June
Luxembourg National Day This is the Grand Duchy's biggest event – a celebration of the birth of the Grand Duke (though it doesn't actually fall on a Grand Ducal birthday). Fireworks from Pont Adolphe in Luxembourg City kick it off on the evening of 22 June. Later there's dancing on Place d'Armes followed by an all-night party, with cafés and bars around town open 'til dawn. On 23 June, a military parade winds through the streets of the capital and festivities are held around the country.

Festival of Wallonia (www.festivaldewallonie.be in French) Young Belgian musicians perform classical concerts throughout Brussels and Wallonia from June until October.

July
Belgium National Day Celebrations on 21 July change little from one year to the next. A modest military procession in Parc de Bruxelles, opposite Brussels' royal palace, is followed by evening fireworks.

September
Open Monumentendag/Journées du Patrimoine
On selected weekends in September, Belgium opens a handful of protected monuments to the public in what are known as Heritage Days. Different buildings are selected each year and, if recent years are anything to go by, the masses are impressed. These events usually fall on the second weekend in September each year for monuments in the countryside and the following weekend for those in Brussels.

FOOD

Throughout this guide, restaurants and other eateries have been ordered by price, from budget options (roughly €5 to €15 for a main course) through midrange (€15 to €25) and up to top end (€25 and above). See p52 for details on what to expect.

GAY & LESBIAN TRAVELLERS

Belgium is a world leader in equal rights for gays and lesbians. Same-sex couples have been able to wed legally in Belgium since 2003 when laws were passed overwhelmingly through parliament, and they now have the same rights enjoyed by heterosexuals, including inheritance and adoption. Laws governing the latter narrowly passed through the Senate in 2006, making Belgium the third EU member state (following Spain and Sweden) to grant homosexual couples adoption rights. In 2005, parliament voted to make Belgium the second country after Canada to celebrate national anti-homophobia day on May 17.

Attitudes to homosexuality are pretty laid-back in both Belgium and Luxembourg, and the age of consent in both countries is 16.

For details on gay and lesbian organisations and festivals, see boxed texts under Brussels (p97), Antwerp (p188), Ghent (p165) and Luxembourg City (p276).

HOLIDAYS
Public Holidays

New Year's Day 1 January
Easter Monday March/April
Labour Day 1 May
Ascension Day 40th day after Easter
Whit Monday 7th Monday after Easter
Luxembourg National Day 23 June (Luxembourg only)
Festival of the Flemish Community 11 July (Flanders only)
Belgium National Day 21 July (Belgium only)
Assumption Day 15 August
Walloon Community 27 September (Wallonia only)
All Saints' Day 1 November
Armistice Day 11 November (Belgium only)
Christmas Day 25 December

School Holidays

Belgium July and August; one week in November; two weeks at Christmas; one week around Carnival; two weeks at Easter; one week in May.
Luxembourg Mid-July to mid-September; first week in November; two weeks around Christmas; one week at Carnival; two weeks at Easter; one week at Ascension.

INSURANCE

A travel-insurance policy to cover theft, loss and medical problems is a good idea. Worldwide travel insurance is available at www

.lonelyplanet.com/travel_services. You can buy, extend and claim online anytime – even if you're already on the road.

Also see p326 for health insurance.

INTERNET ACCESS

The internet is a rich resource for travellers. You can research your trip, hunt down bargain air fares, book hotels, check weather conditions or chat with locals and other travellers about the best places to visit.

Most travellers make use of internet cafés and free web-based email such as **Yahoo** (www.yahoo.com), **Hotmail** (www.hotmail.com) or **Gmail** (www.gmail.com). You'll need to carry three vital pieces of information with you so you can access your internet account: your incoming (POP or IMAP) mail server name, your account name and your password. Your ISP or network supervisor should provide you with these. Armed with this information, you should be able to access your internet account from any internet-connected machine in the world, provided it runs some kind of email software (remember that Netscape and Internet Explorer both have mail modules). Most ISPs will also enable you to receive your emails through their website, which only requires you to remember your account name and password. It's a good idea to become familiar with the process for doing this before you leave home.

Internet cafés are plentiful in major cities around Belgium, as well as in Luxembourg City, but don't expect too much away from main centres. Prices vary from €0.50 to €1.50 for 15 minutes, or €1 to €5 per hour. You'll also find public internet access in some libraries, hostels, hotels and tourist offices. To find out where you can log on, check the Information section in the individual cities and towns in this guide. In the listings, accommodation options offering internet access for guests are marked with a computer/internet symbol.

If you're travelling with a notebook or hand-held computer, be aware that your modem may not work once you leave your home country. The safest option is to buy a reputable 'global' modem before you leave home, or buy a local PC-card modem if you're spending an extended time in any one country. For more information on travelling with a portable computer, see www.teleadapt.com.

See p14 for useful websites for planning your trip or to use while on the road.

LEGAL MATTERS

Police in both countries usually treat tourists with respect and many officers, particularly in Flanders and in Luxembourg, speak English fluently. In both countries you are legally required to carry either a passport or national identity card at all times. A photocopy should suffice if you don't want to carry your passport for security reasons. Should you be arrested for any reason, you have the right to ask for your consul to be immediately notified.

In Luxembourg, you can seek free legal advice at the **Service d'Accueil et d'Information Juridique** (☎ 22 18 46; Côte d'Eich) in Luxembourg City.

MAPS

Good maps are easy to come by once you're in Belgium or Luxembourg, but you might want to buy one beforehand to plan and track your route. The maps in this book will help you get an idea of where you might want to go and will be a useful first reference when arriving in a city. Once there, most tourist offices have decent, if basic, free maps. Proper road maps are essential for driving or cycling.

Michelin's fold-out Belgium/Luxembourg map (No 716, scale: 1:350,000) includes a town index and enlargements of Brussels, Antwerp and Liège. In Luxembourg, Geoline does a booklet of maps covering Luxembourg City and other main towns.

For hiking and off-road cycling, one of the best map resources is the topographical series published by Belgium's Institut Géographique National. They cover the whole country in scales ranging from 1:10,000 to 1:50,000. Many of these maps are available in major bookshops and local tourist offices. The latter also stock other maps and route descriptions relevant to their area, and are usually the best place to get the lowdown on the local walking/hiking scene.

Online maps are available at www.derouck geomatics.com (in Flemish and French only).

MONEY

Belgium and Luxembourg are still largely cash-based societies. Locals generally use cash for small purchases so you can't avoid having at least some cash in your pocket. Major credit cards are widely accepted at top and midrange hotels and restaurants, and in many shops and petrol stations.

Belgium and Luxembourg both use the euro, which has the same value in all eurozone countries. There are seven euro notes (five, 10, 20, 50, 100, 200 and 500 euros) and eight euro coins (one, two, five, 10, 20 and 50 cents, and one and two euros). One side is standard to all euro coins and the other bears a national emblem of participating countries.

Prices quoted in this book are in euros (€), unless otherwise stated. For exchange rates, see the inside front cover. For information on local costs, see p13.

Moneychangers

Banks are the best place to change money, charging only a small commission on cash or travellers cheques. Out of hours, there are less generous exchange bureaus. Banks in both countries generally open from 8.30am or 9am to between 3.30pm and 5pm Monday to Friday, and also Saturday mornings. In smaller places, they may close for an hour at lunch.

Outside banking hours, there are exchange bureaus (*wisselkantoren* in Flemish, *bureaux d'échange* in French) at airports or train stations. These mostly have lower rates and higher fees than banks.

Automated teller machines (ATMs) are not widespread around the countryside, but are well populated in city centres and at the main international airports (Brussels National and Luxembourg Airport). They generally accept MasterCard (called EuroCard in Belgium and Luxembourg) and Visa.

Tipping

Tipping is not obligatory as service and VAT are included in hotel and restaurant prices. Cinema and theatre attendants generally expect a €1 tip, and in public toilets you'll be given a foul look or be reprimanded if you attempt to leave without tipping the

---

OF AGE

The legal ages in Belgium and Luxembourg:

- drinking alcohol – 16 in Belgium, 17 in Luxembourg
- driving – 18
- marriage – 18
- sexual intercourse – 16 (both heterosexual and homosexual)
- voting – 18

310 DIRECTORY •• Photography & Video · lonelyplanet.com

DIRECTORY

attendant (€0.30 to €0.50); this goes for both men and women.

PHOTOGRAPHY & VIDEO

The time of year will dictate, to a degree, what film to take or buy locally. Winter's dull and often overcast conditions mean photographers should bring higher-speed film (eg 200 ISO). With summer's (hopefully) blue sunny skies, slower film is the answer (100 ISO).

If using a digital camera, check that you have enough memory to store your snaps – 256MB will probably be enough. If you do run out of memory space your best bet is to burn your photos onto a CD. Increasing numbers of photo labs now offer this service.

Lonely Planet's *Travel Photography*, by Richard I'Anson, is a helpful guide to taking the pictures you've always wanted.

If you're taking along your video camera, make sure you have the necessary charger, plugs and transformer.

POST

Post offices in both countries are generally open from 9am to 5pm weekdays and 9am to noon Saturday.

In Belgium, mail can be sent either *prior* (priority) or *nonprior* (nonpriority) but, given the delays experienced with priority mail, don't even consider sending things nonpriority. Letters under 50g to European countries cost €0.60 and €0.65 to non-European countries.

In Luxembourg, letters (under 20g) cost €0.70 to send to EU countries and €0.90 to non-EU countries.

From both countries, letters average a week to 10 days to reach places outside Europe, two to three days inside the continent.

In addresses, the street number follows the street name in Flanders. In Luxembourg, the number is always placed first. In Wallonia, it's a mix of the two. In both countries, a four-digit postal code is given in front of the city or town name (B-1000 Brussels, for example). The 'B' attached to the postal code stands for the country, ie Belgium). The abbreviation for PO Box is 'PB' *(postbus)* or 'BP' *(boîte postale);* '*bus*' or '*bte*' *(boîte)* in an address stands for 'box number'.

Poste restante attracts a €0.40 fee and you may need to show your passport. Some useful poste restante addresses:

Antwerp (Poste Restante, Hoofdpostkantoor, Groenplaats, B-2000 Antwerp)

Bruges (Poste Restante, Hoofdpostkantoor, Markt 5, B-8000 Bruges)

Brussels (Poste Restante, Bureau de Poste Central, Blvd Anspach 1, B-1000 Brussels)

Ghent (Poste Restante, Hoofdpostkantoor, Lange Kruisstraat 55, B-9000 Ghent)

Luxembourg City (Poste Restante, Luxembourg-Centre Bureau de Post, L-1118 Luxembourg 2)

Namur (Poste Restante, Bureau de Poste Namur 1, Blvd E Mélot 25, B-5000 Namur)

SHOPPING

Belgium's specialities are chocolate (p54), beer (p45) and lace (p138). Antwerp, and to an increasing extent Brussels, is also famous for its avant-garde designer fashions (see boxed texts, p197 and p114) and for diamonds (p183). Antiques are popular buys in Brussels (p113), as well as in the Flemish town of Tongeren (p214). It's worth remembering that with expensive purchases like diamonds or antiques you can claim the 21% VAT back if you live outside the EU.

Markets are part of life for many people in Belgium. Vendors selling food, clothing and miscellaneous goods set up on a weekly basis in most Belgian towns, and the young and elderly with trolleys in tow jostle to see what's on offer. Two of the best such markets are Brussels' Gare du Midi market (p115) and Antwerp's Vogelmarkt (p192). Weekly food markets are listed in the Eating section in major cities and towns.

Bric-a-brac *(curiosa/brocante)* markets are also very popular – don't miss Brussels' Place du Jeu-de-Balle flea market (p115) or the centuries' old Vrijdagmarkt (p198) in Antwerp. Bargaining is not customary, though it's worth trying at flea markets.

SOLO TRAVELLERS

Dangers are few when travelling solo through Belgium and Luxembourg, but women still need to take extra precautions (p313). Be aware that accommodation places can charge higher single supplement fees, and you may not be seated at the best table in restaurants as a lone diner. Hitchhiking is risky and not recommended at all, particularly for single travellers.

TELEPHONE & FAX
Belgium

Belgium's international country code is ☎ 32. To telephone abroad, dial the international access code ☎ 00. For an international operator, call ☎ 1324.

Belgium has a single telephone zone for the entire country. This means it costs the same to make a telephone call within Brussels as to call, for example, from Brussels to Bruges. Area codes are incorporated into phone numbers. This means you must dial the area code as well as the telephone number, even when dialling from the relevant area.

Phone calls are metered. Telephone numbers prefixed with 0900 or 070 are pay-per-minute numbers (€0.17 to €0.45 per minute). Numbers prefixed with 0800 are toll-free calls. Those prefixed with 0472 to 0479, 0482 to 0489 and 0492 to 0499 are mobile numbers. Note also that a call to an English-speaking directory assistance operator (☎ 1405) costs a mighty €3.

You can ring abroad from almost any phone box in Belgium or Luxembourg. Public telephones accepting stored-value phonecards (available from post offices, telephone centres, newsstands and retail outlets) are the norm.

Mobile phones are the trend worldwide and travellers can rent (or purchase) phones with international capabilities. Belgium and Luxembourg use the GSM 900/1800 network, covering Europe, Australia and New Zealand. It's not generally compatible with North America. If you have a GSM phone, check with your service provider about using it in Belgium and Luxembourg.

Belgium's main mobile networks are Proximus, operated by Belgacom, Mobistar and Base. Mobiles can be rented from **Locaphone** (☎ 02 652 14 14) in the arrivals hall at Brussels National Airport. Prices start at €7 per day for the first five days, then drop to €2.50 per day (not including 21% VAT). Payment is by credit card only, and there's a one-off insurance payment of €9.50. Note that it's illegal to use mobile phones while driving a vehicle in Belgium.

The Yellow Pages, in major cities in Belgium, has a handy English-language index.

Faxes can be sent and received from some post offices or private shops. Expect to pay around €3 for one page to the UK, or €4.70 to the USA or Australia.

Luxembourg

Luxembourg's international country code is ☎ 352. To telephone abroad, the international access code is ☎ 00. Call ☎ 12410 for an international operator. Collect calls can be made by dialling ☎ 80 02 00. For directory inquiries call ☎ 016/017.

Local telephone calls are time based. International phone calls can be made using phonecards. Numbers prefixed with 0800 are toll-free numbers.

Mobile-phone users will find that Luxembourg, like Belgium, works on GSM 900/1800 (for more details, see left).

Post offices are the best places to send and receive faxes. The cost is €3.95 for one page to the UK or USA; to Australia it costs €4.95.

TIME

Both countries run on Central European Time. See the World Time Zones map (pp350–1) for time zones.

Daylight-saving time comes into effect on the last Sunday in March, when clocks are moved forward one hour. On the last Sunday in October, they're turned back an hour. The 24-hour clock is used.

TOILETS

Public toilets in Belgium and Luxembourg are few and far between, which is why most people use the facilities in pubs and cafés. A €0.30 fee (occasionally as high as €0.50) is charged in almost all public toilets, as well as in the toilets in some bars, cafés and fast-food restaurants. It's an honour system of sorts – drop the coins in the china dish on the table or expect the woman running the show to come after you if you don't cough up.

TOURIST INFORMATION

Both countries are dotted with tourist offices. In Flemish they're signposted as *dienst voor toerisme* or *toeristische dienst*, and in Wallonia and Luxembourg you'll see signs for *syndicat d'initiative* or *office de tourisme*. Staff are generally friendly and efficient, and will book accommodation and arrange guided tours.

As is the case with many things in Belgium, there are two separate organisations promoting tourism: **Toerisme Vlaanderen** (www.visit flanders.com) covers Flanders and **Office de Promotion du Tourisme** (OPT; www.belgique-tourisme.net) Wallonia. Both organisations publish vast numbers of free glossy, detailed brochures on their individual regions, as well as a range of national booklets covering topics such as hotels, camping, rural holidays and the useful annual *Guide to Tourist Attractions and Museums in Belgium*.

In Brussels, both organisations come under the umbrella title of the Belgian Tourist Information Centre (p68). The Luxembourg National Tourist Office (p271) is located inside the train station in Luxembourg City. The postal address is BP 1001, L-1010 Luxembourg.

Belgian Tourist Offices Abroad

Australia, Ireland, Luxembourg and New Zealand do not have a Belgian tourist office – inquiries should be addressed to the Belgian Tourist Information Centre (see previous).

Otherwise, Belgium has tourist offices in the following countries (some countries have separate offices for Flanders and Wallonia):

Canada (Office du Tourisme Wallonie-Bruxelles; ☎ 418-692 49 39; www.belgique-tourisme.qc.ca; 43 Rue de Buade, Quebec, Quebec G1R 4A2)

France Flanders (Tourisme Belgique – Flandre et Bruxelles; ☎ 01 56 89 14 42; www.tourismebelgique.com; 6 rue Euler, F-75008 Paris); Wallonia (Office Belge du Tourisme Wallonie-Bruxelles; ☏ 01 53 85 05 20; www.belgique-tourisme.be; Blvd St-Germain 274, F-75007 Paris)

Germany (Belgisches Haus; ☎ 0221-27 75 90; www.belgien-tourismus.de; Cäcilienstrasse 46, D-50667 Köln)

Netherlands Flanders (Toerisme Vlaanderen-Brussel; ☎ 070-416 81 10; www.toerismevlaanderen.nl; Koninginnegracht 86, NL-2514 AJ The Hague); Wallonia (Belgisch Verkeersbureau Wallonië & Brussel; ☎ 023-534 44 34; www.belgie-toerisme.be; Postbus 2324, NL-2002 CH Haarlem)

UK Flanders (Tourism Flanders-Brussels; ☎ 020-730 777 38; www.visitflanders.co.uk; 1a Cavendish Sq, London W1G 0LD); Wallonia (Belgian Tourist Office Brussels-Wallonia; ☎ 020-7531 0390; www.belgiumtheplaceto.be; 217 Marsh Wall, London E14 9FJ) To order brochures call ☎ 0800-95 45 245.

USA (Belgian Tourist Office; ☎ 0212-758 8130; www.visitbelgium.com; 220 East 42nd St, Suite 3402, New York, NY 10017)

Luxembourg Tourist Offices Abroad

The Luxembourg National Tourist Office has offices in the following countries:

UK (☎ 020-7434 2800; www.luxembourg.co.uk; 122 Regent St, London W1B 5SA)

USA (☎ 212-935 88 88; www.visitluxembourg.com; 17 Beekman Place, New York, NY 10022)

TRAVELLERS WITH DISABILITIES

Neither Belgium nor Luxembourg are terribly accessible countries for travellers with a mobility problem. Both have buildings that are centuries old and although efforts are being made to consider the needs of travellers with disabilities when renovating buildings, this is no small task. Some government buildings, museums, hotels, restaurants, *cafés* and arts venues have lifts and/or ramps, but the majority don't. According to Cléon Angelo, spokesperson from the National Association for Handicapped People's Housing (ANLH), only half of new public buildings in Brussels comply with a 2000 law that obliges architects to ensure buildings, including hotels and shops, are built in a 'disabled-friendly' way.

Out on the street, things aren't much better. Wheelchair users will be up against uneven cobblestones, rough pavements and steep kerbs. To access metro or train stations, there's usually a seemingly unending flight of steps or escalators. When travelling by train, wheelchair users must give an hour's notice. Ten of Brussels' 68 metro stations have lifts for travellers with disabilities, but only three are central – Gare Centrale, Maelbeek and De Brouckère (two other stations, Gare du Midi and Porte de Namur should also have lifts by the time you read this). According to the city's public transport organisation, Société des Transports Intercommunaux de Bruxelles (STIB), 18 metro stations will have lifts by early 2008.

De Lijn, the company running buses throughout Flanders, plans to make all its buses accessible to wheelchair users by 2010.

In all cities and many big towns you'll find hotels (in the midrange or top-end price range) that can accommodate travellers in wheelchairs – the ones in this guide are noted with a wheelchair icon. Many official HI hostels in Belgium also have suitable rooms (such as in Brussels, Antwerp, Bruges, Namur, Tongeren and Tournai).

In Luxembourg, the tourist office produces an annual brochure, *Holiday Apartments Farm & Rural Holidays*, which flags accommodation accessible to people with reduced mobility, as well as fully accessible options (though in reality there is little on offer for either).

Attempts have been made to assist the visually impaired, such as Braille plaques at the entrance to some metro stations in Brussels and a model of the belfry in Bruges with explanatory notes in Braille (it's located on the Markt).

Some useful organisations:

Accessible Travel Info Point (Map p74; ☎ 070 23 30 50; www.accessinfo.be; Rue du Marché aux Herbes 61, Brussels) Information for Flanders.

Adapth (Association pour le développement et la propagation d'aides techniques pour personnes handicapées; ☎ 43 95 58 1; www.adapth.lu in French) Keeps a comprehensive database relating to disability issues in Luxembourg.

British Royal Association for Disability and Rehabilitation (RADAR; ☎ 020-7250 3222; www.radar.org.uk; 12 City Forum, 250 City Rd, London EC1V 8AF, UK)

Info-Handicap (☎ 36 64 66 1; www.welcome.lu; 65 Ave de la Gare, Luxembourg City) Luxembourg organisation which publishes *Guide du Handicap,* listing services and organisations.

Mobility International (☎ 541-343 1284; www.miusa.org) In the USA.

National Information & Awareness Network (Nican; ☎ 02-6241 1220; www.nican.com.au) In Australia.

Taxi Hendriks (☎ 02 752 98 00; fax 02 752 98 01) Brussels' taxi company specialising in minibus services for disabled people – book a few days in advance.

VISAS

There are no entry requirements or restrictions on EU nationals visiting Belgium and Luxembourg. Citizens of Australia, Canada, Israel, Japan, New Zealand and the USA do not need visas to visit the country as tourists for up to three months. Except for people from a few other European countries (such as Switzerland and Norway), everyone else must have a visa. Three-month tourist visas are issued by Belgian or Luxembourg embassies or consulates. They can take a while to be processed, so leave enough time before departure to apply. Fees vary depending on your nationality. For more on up-to-date visa information, check www.lonelyplanet.com.

Visa information can be obtained from Belgium's Ministry of Foreign Affairs website, www.diplomatie.be. For Luxembourg, check www.mae.lu.

WOMEN TRAVELLERS

Belgium's strong Catholic background has kept women's issues firmly on the back burner, which explains the huge difference between Belgium and its neighbour the very progressive Netherlands. It wasn't until 1990 that abortion was legalised in Belgium, and even then it caused a national drama (see boxed text, p27). Only in 1991 was succession to the Belgian throne opened to women.

Women should encounter few problems while travelling in either Belgium or Luxembourg. Brussels is small by capital-city standards but violent crime is on the increase, so it's advisable not to wander alone late at night or to arrive late at the Gare du Midi or Gare du Nord. The northern end of Blvd Adolphe Max (close to Place Rogier) is lined with striptease joints and peep shows. The metro is relatively safe at all times.

In Luxembourg City, the area around the train station – particularly Rue Joseph Junck – is pretty seedy.

Useful organisations for women:

Amazone (Map pp72-3; ☎ 02 229 38 00; www.amazone.be; Rue du Méridien 10, Brussels) A centre housing a variety of women's organisations that was set up in the mid-1990s. From a traveller's point of view, it's not the sort of place you can just drop in to find out what's happening on the women's scene in Belgium. However, it's possible to pick up information and potentially make contacts at the centre's restaurant (open noon to 2pm Monday to Friday).

Helpline (☎ 02 648 40 14) Twenty-four-hour helpline based in Brussels.

SOS Viol (☎ 02 534 36 36) Rape crisis line in Brussels.

Waisse Rank (☎ 40 20 40) Women's crisis organisation in Luxembourg City.

Transport

CONTENTS

Getting There & Away	**314**
Entering the Country	314
Air	314
Land	316
Sea	319
Getting Around	**319**
Air	319
Bicycle	319
Boat	319
Bus	319
Car & Motorcycle	320
Hitching	323
Local Transport	323
Train	324

This chapter gives the nuts and bolts about getting to Belgium and Luxembourg, as well as information related to getting around the two countries once you're there. Flights, tours and rail tickets can be booked online at www.lonelyplanet.com/travel_services.

GETTING THERE & AWAY

ENTERING THE COUNTRY

Entering both countries is straightforward, no matter what form of transport you choose to get there.

Passport

To enter Belgium and Luxembourg you need a valid passport or, for EU nationals, travel

THINGS CHANGE...

The information in this chapter is particularly vulnerable to change. Check directly with the airline or a travel agent to make sure you understand how a fare (and ticket you may buy) works and be aware of the security requirements for international travel. Shop carefully. The details given in this chapter should be regarded as pointers and are not a substitute for your own careful, up-to-date research.

documents (ie ID card or passport). By law, everyone in Belgium, including tourists, must carry some sort of ID on them at all times. For foreign visitors, this means your passport.

AIR
Airports in Belgium & Luxembourg

Antwerp (ANR; ☎ 03 285 65 00; www.antwerpairport.be) Near Antwerp (p198); services a modest number of flights to/from London.

Brussels National Airport (BRU; ☎ 0900 70 000; www.brusselsairport.be) Belgium's main international airport (see p115).

Charleroi (CRL; www.charleroi-airport.com) About 55km south of Brussels at Charleroi (p227).

Liège (LGG; ☎ 04 234 84 11; www.liegeairport.com) Located at the city's former military base, Bierset.

Luxembourg airport (LUX; ☎ 24 64 1; www.lux-airport.lu) Luxembourg's only international airport, also known as Aéroport de Luxembourg, 6km east of the capital. A big new glass terminal, under construction next to the original building, is expected to be finished by the end of 2007.

Airlines
BELGIUM

Belgium's main international carrier is Brussels Airlines, recently renamed following a merger between SN Brussels Airlines and Virgin Express. The only other Belgian airline is VLM Airlines, with flights from Brussels National and Antwerp airport to London City.

Check the following websites for cheap airlines flying into Belgium: www.wizzair.com, www.welcomeair.com, www.skyeurope.com, www.condor.com and www.aerarann.com.

Airlines (*luchtvaartmaatschappijen* in Flemish, *lignes aériennes* in French) flying into Belgium include the following (with Belgian phone numbers):

Aer Lingus (EI; ☎ 02 548 98 48; www.aerlingus.com)
Air Canada (AC; ☎ 02 627 40 88; www.aircanada.ca)
Air France (AF; ☎ 02 526 12 70; www.airfrance.com)
Air New Zealand (NZ; ☎ 03 202 13 55; www.airnewzealand.com)
Alitalia (AZ; ☎ 02 551 11 22; www.alitalia.be)
American Airlines (AA; ☎ 02 711 99 69; www.aa.com)
British Airways (BA; ☎ 02 717 32 17; www.britishairways.com)
Brussels Airlines (SN; ☎ 070 35 11 11; www.brusselsairlines.com)

CLIMATE CHANGE & TRAVEL

Climate change is a serious threat to the ecosystems that humans rely upon, and air travel is the fastest-growing contributor to the problem. Lonely Planet regards travel, overall, as a global benefit, but believes we all have a responsibility to limit our personal impact on global warming.

Flying and Climate Change

Pretty much every form of motor transport generates CO_2 (the main cause of human-induced climate change) but planes are far and away the worst offenders, not just because of the sheer distances they allow us to travel, but because they release greenhouse gases high into the atmosphere. The statistics are frightening: two people taking a return flight between Europe and the US will contribute as much to climate change as an average household's gas and electricity consumption over a whole year.

Carbon Offset Schemes

Climatecare.org and other websites use 'carbon calculators' that allow travellers to offset the greenhouse gases they are responsible for with contributions to energy-saving projects and other climate-friendly initiatives in the developing world – including projects in India, Honduras, Kazakhstan and Uganda.

Lonely Planet, together with Rough Guides and other concerned partners in the travel industry, supports the carbon offset scheme run by climatecare.org. Lonely Planet offsets all of its staff and author travel.

For more information check out our website: www.lonelyplanet.com.

Continental Airlines (CO; ☎ 02 643 39 39; www.continental.com)

Japan Airlines (JL; ☎ 02 745 44 00; www.jal.co.jp)

KLM (KL; ☎ 070 22 27 47; www.klm.be)

Lufthansa (LH; ☎ 070 35 30 30; www.lufthansa.be)

Ryanair (FR; ☎ 0902 88 007; www.ryanair.com)

United Airlines (UA; ☎ 02 713 36 00; www.unitedairlines.be)

VLM Airlines (VG; ☎ 03 287 80 80; www.flyvlm.com)

LUXEMBOURG

The national carrier, Luxair, flies to European destinations including London, Paris and Frankfurt. The airline's four decades of accident-free flying came to an end in 2002 when one of its planes crashed while landing at Luxembourg airport, killing 15 people.

Budget airline, Ryanair, flies to Frankfurt-Hahn in Germany from where there's a bus connection (www.easybycoach.com; one way €17; 1¾ hours; 10 per day) to Luxembourg City.

Airlines flying into Luxembourg include the following:

Air France (AF; ☎ 27 30 20 06; www.airfrance.lu)

British Airways (BA; ☎ 43 86 47; www.britishairways.com)

Czech Airlines (OK; ☎ Belgium 32 2 217 17 92; www.czechairlines.com)

KLM City Hopper (KL; ☎ The Netherlands 31 20 4 747 747; www.klm.com)

Lufthansa (LH; ☎ 47 98 50 50; www.lufthansa.com)

Luxair (LG; ☎ 24 56 42 42, arrival & departure information 24 56 50 50; www.luxair.lu)

SAS Scandinavian Airlines (SK; ☎ Belgium 32 2 643 6900; www.flysas.com)

Swiss International Air Lines (LX; ☎ Switzerland 41 61 582 36 56)

TAP Portugal (TP; ☎ 47 98 21 33; www.flytap.be)

VLM Airlines (VG; ☎ 49 33 95; www.flyvlm.com)

Tickets

The airline industry and the way travellers book tickets has changed dramatically in recent years. Once you'd automatically go to a travel agent rather than direct to an airline for a bargain fare, but that's no longer the case. The growing number of 'no-frills' carriers operating in the US and northwest Europe, which mostly sell direct to travellers, is responsible for the change. One such airline flying into Belgium is Ryanair. Unlike the 'full-service' airlines, no-frills carriers often make one-way tickets available at around half the return fare, meaning it's easy to put together a return ticket when you fly into one place but leave from another.

The internet has also changed ticketing. Many airlines, full-service and no-frills, offer some excellent fares to web users. They may sell seats by auction or simply cut prices to reflect the reduced cost of electronic selling. Many travel agents around the world also have websites, which can make the internet a quick and easy way to compare prices.

Online Booking Agencies

Air Brokers International (www.airbrokers.com) USA.
Cheap Tickets (www.cheaptickets.com) USA.
Ebookers (www.ebookers.com) UK, Continental Europe.
Expedia (www.expedia.ca, www.expedia.com) Canada, USA, UK, France, the Netherlands.
House of Travel (www.houseoftravel.co.nz) New Zealand.
JustFares (www.justfares.com) USA.
My Travel (www.mytravel.com) UK.
Orbitz (www.orbitz.com) USA.
Travel (www.travel.com.au) Australia.
Travelocity (www.travelocity.ca) Canada.
Webjet (www.webjet.com.au) Australia.

Australia & New Zealand

Flights to Belgium or Luxembourg from this side of the world require first going to London, Paris or Frankfurt and changing there to a Brussels or Luxembourg flight.

The following are well-known agents for competitive fares:

Flight Centre Australia (☎ 131 600; www.flightcentre.com .au); New Zealand (☎ 0800 24 35 44; www.flightcentre.co.nz)
STA Travel Australia (☎ 03-9207 5900; www.statravel.com .au); New Zealand (☎ 0800 474 400; www.statravel.co.nz)

Continental Europe

As the Thalys fast train network linking Belgium with France, the Netherlands and Germany steadily expands, less and less people travel between Belgium and its neighbouring countries by plane. It's almost as quick to go by train.

To Luxembourg, there are daily flights from Paris (one hour), Amsterdam (1¼ hours) and Frankfurt (50 minutes).

A few recommended travel agents include the following:

JustTravel (☎ 089 747 3330; www.justtravel.de) Germany.
NBBS Reizen (☎ 0900 10 20 300; www.nbbs.nl in Dutch) The Netherlands.
Nouvelles Frontières (☎ 0825 000 747; www .nouvelles-frontieres.fr) France.

UK & Ireland

There isn't really a low or high season for flights to Belgium or Luxembourg: prices depend more on special offers and availability of seats. Special offers usually involve booking in advance and being away a minimum number of nights or staying over a Saturday night.

The flight time from London to Brussels is one hour and 10 minutes. To compare the difference between flying from London to Brussels National Airport, or travelling by Eurostar train service, see boxed text, (p319). A London–Antwerp flight also takes about an hour, but as there is no competition on this route and few flights it's not an interesting option. The only airline servicing the route is the small Flemish company VLM Airlines. London to Luxembourg City also takes about an hour.

From the UK, no-frills airline Ryanair flies out of Glasgow-Prestwick to Charleroi airport (about 55km south of Brussels).

From Ireland, Aer Lingus has Dublin–Brussels flights, while Ryanair offers flights from Dublin and Shannon to Charleroi airport.

Competitive travel agencies include the following:

Flightbookers (☎ 0800 082 3000; www.ebookers.com)
STA Travel (☎ 0871 230 0040; www.statravel.co.uk)
Trailfinders (☎ 0845 058 5858; www.trailfinders.co.uk)

USA & Canada

There are few direct flights from the US or Canada to Belgium and none at all to Luxembourg; in most cases you'll have to travel via London. Travel time from New York is approximately eight hours.

Competitive travel agencies include the following:

Council on International Educational Exchange (☎ 1-800-40-STUDY; www.ciee.org) America's largest student travel organisation.
STA Travel (☎ 800 781 4040; www.statravel.com) Has offices around America.
Travel CUTS (☎ 800 667 2887; www.travelcuts.com) Canada's national student travel agency.

LAND
Car & Motorcycle

The main motorways into Belgium are the E19 from the Netherlands, the E40 from Germany, the E411 from Luxembourg and the E17 and E19 from France. Into Luxembourg, the main roads are the E411 from Belgium, the A4 and the E25 from France, and the E44 from Germany. If travelling from any of these countries, fill up in Luxembourg – fuel prices here are among the lowest in Western Europe. There are no controls at border crossings into Belgium

EUROLINES

Eurolines (☎ Brussels 02 271 13 50; Luxembourg 26 29 80; Amsterdam 020-560 8788; Frankfurt 069-790 350; London 1582 404 511; Paris 0892 89 90 91; www.eurolines.com) is a consortium of coach operators with offices all over Europe. Belgium and Luxembourg are well connected to the UK, the rest of Continental Europe, Scandinavia and North Africa by Eurolines buses.

Eurolines' coaches are fairly comfortable, with reclining seats, air-conditioning and on-board toilets. They stop frequently for meals.

Discounts depend on the route, but children aged between four and 12 typically get 30% to 40% off, while seniors and those aged under 26 get a 10% to 20% discount on some routes. It's a good idea to book at least several days ahead in summer.

Real coach junkies can investigate a Eurolines Pass, which gives unlimited travel between 35 European cities for a set period of 15 or 30 days.

and Luxembourg. Plans are afoot to introduce a €60 motorway toll when entering Belgium.

France

BUS

The only bus company operating between France and Belgium or Luxembourg is **Eurolines** (☎ 0892 89 90 91; www.eurolines.fr). Buses depart daily from Paris to Brussels (one way €25, 3¾ hours, nine daily), Antwerp (€25, 4¾ hours, one daily), Mons (€22, 2¾ hours, two daily) and Liège (€25, 4¾ hours, one daily). There are also less frequent services to Ghent (€20, three hours, one daily), Kortrijk (€20, 2¾ hours, one daily), Leuven (€23, five hours, one daily) and Luxembourg City (€27, 5½ hours, two weekly). For more on Eurolines, see above.

TRAIN

France's national rail network is operated by the **Société Nationale des Chemins de Fer Français** (SNCF; ☎ 0890 36 10 10; www.sncf.com).

Thalys fast trains (p318) efficiently link Paris' Gare du Nord station with Brussels' Gare du Midi (one way €74.50, 1½ hours, hourly). There are also services to Antwerp (€83.30, 2¼ hours, seven per day) as well as Bruges (€88.70, 2½ hours, one per day) and Liège (€92.30, 2½ hours, seven per day).

To Luxembourg, SNCF trains depart five times daily from Paris-Est station to Luxembourg City (€47, four hours, six daily). The high-speed TGV is expected to start operating between Luxembourg City and Paris in 2007 or 2008.

Germany

BUS

The main company is **Deutsche Touring/Eurolines** (☎ Frankfurt 069 790 350; www.deutsche-touring.com),

which has buses departing daily from several German cities, including Aachen, Frankfurt and Cologne, to a limited number of destinations in Belgium. As an example, there are buses from Frankfurt to Brussels (one way €34, 5¼ hours, one daily) and Liège (€34, 5¼ hours, one daily). For more on Eurolines, see above.

There's a bus connection (see www.easyby coach.com) from Frankfurt-Hahn to Luxembourg City (one way €17, 1¾ hours, 10 daily).

TRAIN

Thalys trains (p318) link Cologne with Liège (one way €25) and Brussels (€40, 2¼ hours, six daily). Regular Thalys fares are more expensive than ordinary **Deutsche Bahn** (DB; ☎ 01805-99 66 33; www.bahn.de) train fares; however, the Thalys discounted return tickets usually work out cheaper than DB fares.

To Luxembourg City, DB trains run from Cologne (€43, 3½ hours, hourly) and Frankfurt (€52, four hours, hourly).

Netherlands

BUS

Eurolines (☎ 020-560 8788; www.eurolines.nl) operates daily buses between the Netherlands and Belgium or Luxembourg. From Amsterdam buses run to Antwerp (one way €18, 2½ hours, six daily), Brussels (€18, 3½ hours, six daily), Bruges (€18, 4¾ hours, three daily) and Luxembourg City (€22, 8½ hours, one daily). For more on Eurolines, see above.

TRAIN

The Netherlands' train network is run by **Nederlands Spoorwegen** (NS; ☎ 0900 20 21 163; www.ns.nl).

Thalys trains (see p318) link Amsterdam, The Hague and Rotterdam with a handful of cities in Belgium. From Amsterdam, there are

TRANSPORT

THALYS

Thalys (www.thalys.com; ☎ Belgium 070 66 77 88; France 0892 35 35 36; Germany 01805 215 000; Netherlands 0900 9296) fast trains are a service provided jointly by the Belgian, Dutch, French and German railways. They link various cities in Belgium with destinations in the Netherlands, Germany and France. Belgian Railways has phased out many of its trains on these routes, as more and more people opt for the fast trains. Some routes are still being upgraded to accommodate the Thalys (Antwerp train station has been undergoing massive construction works for the last few years), but all the tracks are expected to be upgraded to high-speed lines by mid-2007. In Brussels, Thalys trains depart only from Gare du Midi.

Several types of Thalys tickets are available. The most expensive 1st- and 2nd-class fares are for fully flexible, refundable Librys tickets. Cheaper nonflexible return fares, known as Smilys, are also available. Discounted adult fares are also offered on weekends and for trips booked well in advance. Travellers aged 12 to 26 get a 50% discount and seniors a 30% reduction on standard fares.

All the fares mentioned in the country sections are one-way Librys tickets.

Thalys trains to Antwerp (€37, two hours, five daily) and Brussels (€44, 2¾ hours, five daily).

UK

BUS

With the increase in availability of low air fares, buses no longer offer the cheapest public transport to and around Europe. But if you prefer to stay on the ground, buses are a good deal.

From London's Victoria coach station, **Eurolines** (p317) runs buses to Brussels (one way/return €41/69, eight hours, six daily) and various other cities in Belgium, including Antwerp (€41/69, 8½ hours, two daily), Liège (€41/69, nine hours, two daily) and Luxembourg City (one way €50, 11½ hours, five per week). Prices in high season are €5 to €10 higher. Bookings can be made through Eurolines or any **National Express** (www.nationalexpress.com) office.

An alternative to Eurolines is **Busabout** (☎ 020-7950 1661; www.busabout.com). This UK-based company is aimed at younger travellers, but has no upper age limit. It runs coaches along interlocking European circuits, known as the Northern, Southern and Western Loops. The Northern Loop passes through Belgium, stopping in Bruges en route from Paris to Amsterdam (May to October only). Prices start with a one-loop pass for €455.

CAR & MOTORCYCLE

For details on taking a car or motorcycle through the Eurotunnel, see right. For information on car-ferry services, see opposite.

TRAIN

The Channel Tunnel allows for a land link between Britain and France. The high-speed

Eurostar (☎ London 08705 186 186; Brussels 02 528 28 28; www.eurostar.com) passenger train service uses the Channel Tunnel to connect London–Paris or London–Brussels. Ten trains per day Monday to Friday, and seven per day on weekends make the journey from London to Brussels' Gare du Midi. Fares include travel on to any train station in Belgium (for example, you can choose to stop in Brussels or immediately continue on to say Bruges or Ghent at no extra cost).

A wide variety of fares is available. The regular 2nd-class fare (known as Standard) is UK£149/298 one way/return. The equivalent fare in 1st class (meal included) is UK£205/400. These tickets are fully refundable and you can make changes to the date and time of travel.

Other tickets may not be as flexible and usually have conditions attached. A fully-flexible Leisure Select ticket (return only) costs UK£329 and requires that you stay away a Saturday night. The weekend-day-return Leisure Select costs from UK£105. In addition, there are often special deals.

Youth tickets (one way/return UK£40/59) are available to those aged under 26; children's fares (from four to 11 years) are UK£25/50 in 2nd class and UK£50/100 in 1st.

Eurostar tickets are sold at main-line railway stations in the UK.

The **Eurotunnel** (☎ UK 08705 35 35 35; Belgium 070 22 32 10; France 03 21 00 61 00; www.eurotunnel.com) vehicle service travels between terminals in Folkestone and Coquelles (5km southwest of Calais in France). Trains carry cars, motorcycles and bicycles with their passengers/riders. Trains run 24 hours, every day of the year, with four departures per hour in peak times. During the 35-minute crossing, passengers can sit in

TRAIN OR PLANE FROM THE UK?

For quick, hassle-free travel from London to Brussels (and on to cities such as Bruges or Antwerp), Eurostar train is the way to go. From mid-November 2007, the journey time from London to Brussels' Gare du Midi will be slashed from two hours and 20 minutes to one hour and 50 minutes, making this the most efficient and relaxing way to travel to Belgium. The reduction in travel time is due to the expected completion of a high-speed link between the Channel Tunnel and London, as well as Eurostar moving its services from London's Waterloo station to St Pancras station.

In comparison, a flight from London to Brussels takes between 60 and 75 minutes, on top of which is time getting to and from the airports, check-in and waiting for luggage. Also, keep in mind if you're flying with a low-cost airline that you may leave and/or arrive at secondary airports (such as Belgium's Charleroi, 55km south of Brussels), thus further increasing the overall journey time.

For more details on Eurostar, see opposite.

their cars or walk around the air-conditioned, soundproofed rail carriage. The entire process, including loading and unloading, takes about an hour.

Fares vary enormously depending on the time of year, the day of the week and the time of day. A return fare for a car (driver and all passengers included) starts at UK£160 but prices can increase substantially in peak periods. Special promotional fares, such as Short-Day Saver and Five-Day FlexiPlus, are worth investigating.

The fare for a motorcycle (with riders) starts at UK£22 for a same-day return and UK£38 for longer stays. Bicycles (with rider) cost UK£15 return but can be taken on limited services only.

SEA

Three car-ferry services exist between Belgium and the UK. Fares and schedules vary widely according to seasonal demand.

The following are the operators:

P&O (☎ Belgium 02 710 64 44; UK 0870-520 2020; www.poferries.com) Sails overnight from Zeebrugge in Belgium to Hull in the UK (14 hours) and charges from €162/245 one way/return for two passengers, a car and cabin.

Superfast Ferries (☎ Belgium 050 25 22 52; UK 0870-234 0870; www.superfast.com) Ultramodern ferry sails overnight three times per week between Zeebrugge in Belgium and Rosyth in Scotland (18 hours). Fares start at €92/165 one way/return for a car. Adult passengers pay from €60 one way.

TransEuropa Ferries (☎ Belgium 059 34 02 60; UK 01843-595 522; www.transeuropaferries.com) Ferries sail three times daily from Ostend to Ramsgate in the UK (four hours). Fares start at €60/120 one way/return for a car (passengers included).

GETTING AROUND

AIR

Belgium is so small that there are very few internal flights: Brussels–Antwerp is the only connection and it's rarely used as it's quicker and much cheaper to go by train. Luxembourg is even smaller and has no domestic services.

BICYCLE

Belgium and Luxembourg are fab destinations to explore by bike. Bikes can easily be hired or bought. For a complete rundown on cycling in both countries, see p300. Also see the cycling itinerary, p17.

BOAT

Getting around by boat is not big in Belgium, but there are possibilities. Try the following companies:

easyCruise Two (☎ UK 01895-651 191; www.easycruise .com) This 52-cabin ship cruises along the rivers and canals of Belgium and the Netherlands, stopping in Antwerp, Brussels, Rotterdam and Amsterdam. You must spend a minimum of two nights on board. A four/two-bunk cabin costs £35/45 per person per night, a twin cabin starts at £58.

Hoseasons Holidays Abroad (☎ UK 01502-502 588; www.hoseasons.co.uk) UK travel company arranging one- or two-week cruises around the fields of Flanders starting from Nieuwpoort and taking in towns along the way such as Veurne, Ypres, Bruges, Kortrijk and Ghent. Prices range from £550 to £825 per week (for two adults and a child) for the cheapest boat. Prices are seasonal, with July to August being the most expensive time.

BUS

Buses tend to be a secondary means of getting around in Belgium as the rail network is so efficient and widespread. The exception to this rule is the Ardennes. Here train lines run to some bigger settlements but many smaller places are connected only by bus. Without a vehicle, you'll find relatively short distances can involve long waits as bus routes are often sparsely serviced.

In Luxembourg, buses are a vital element of the country's public transport network.

The various companies:

De Lijn (☎ 070 220 200; www.delijn.be in Flemish) Flanders' public transport company, operating buses, trams and, in some cities, a *premetro* (trams that run underground for part of their journey).

Société des Transports Intercommunaux de Bruxelles (STIB; ☎ 0900 10 310; www.stib.irisnet.be in French & Flemish) Operates buses, trams, the metro and *premetro* in and around Brussels and Brabant-Wallon province.

Société Nationale des Chemins de Fer Luxembourgeois (CFL; ☎ 24 89 24 89; www.cfl.lu) Operates all buses and trains in Luxembourg.

Transport en Commun (TEC; ☎ 081 32 17 11; www .infotec.be) Buses in Wallonia.

Costs & Services

BELGIUM

The Ardennes is the only place you're quite likely to get around by bus, and if you intend to do a bit of travelling on local TEC buses, consider buying a 'Cartes Inter' available from bus drivers or a TEC office. You control how much money you credit this card with (minimum €6) and using it works out considerably cheaper than buying a string of single tickets (€1.30) or purchasing a book of 10 tickets (€6.50).

Keep in mind that TEC services to many destinations are more frequent on weekdays during the school term; however, to some touristy places, services improve marginally during school vacations and on weekends. When reading TEC timetables, 'EC' means the bus operates on *les jours d'école* (school days) and 'VAC' means services run during *vacances scolaires* (school holidays).

If using De Lijn buses in Flanders, remember that tickets are slightly cheaper when bought before travelling, either from a De Lijn information/ticket kiosk, or from a supermarket or newsagency.

LUXEMBOURG

The fare system, valid for both bus and train travel, is simple: €2.25/1.50 in 1st-/2nd-class

for a 'short' trip of about 10km or less (this ticket is valid for one hour) or €7.50/5 for a 1st-/2nd-class unlimited day ticket (known as a *billet réseau*). The latter is good for travelling on buses and trains anywhere in the country and is valid from the first time you use it until 8am the next day.

Many visitors opt for the Luxembourg Card (p271), which gives free bus and train travel plus discounted admissions to various sights. Another possibility available is the Benelux Tourrail pass (p325).

Unfortunately the comprehensive bus network is not always matched by abundant services. Buses in some villages are geared mainly to meeting the needs of school kids and commuters, thus some towns and villages will have only a couple of bus services per day. Services on Sundays are scant to nonexistent.

CAR & MOTORCYCLE

Belgium's motorway system is excellent with, in general, an easy flow of traffic from one side of the country to the other. There are exceptions of course: peak-hour traffic grinds to a halt on the ring roads around Brussels and Antwerp, and the E40 to the coast is usually crammed on fine weekends in summer. There's also a downside to driving in Belgium – see boxed text, (p323).

Driving in Luxembourg is more relaxed – drivers here are simply much less pugnacious and the country is not so congested. Motor-

---

ALTERNATIVE PLACE NAMES

The following is but a few of the towns you'll come across in Belgium that have different names in Flemish and French.

Flemish	French
Antwerpen	Anvers
Bergen	Mons
Brugge	Bruges
Brussel	Bruxelles
Doornik	Tournai
Ieper	Ypres
Kortrijk	Courtrai
Leuven	Louvain
Mechelen	Malines
Namen	Namur
Nijvel	Nivelles
Veurne	Furnes

ways are mainly confined to the south, though a new motorway connecting Luxembourg City with the country's north is progressively being built.

On the road in Belgium, place names can cause considerable confusion due to the different spellings used in Flanders and Wallonia. This isn't a problem in and around Brussels where most signs are bilingual; however, once you get into the countryside, where signs are in either Flemish or French, you'll have to be familiar with both versions of a town's name. All this becomes pertinent when the sign to 'Bergen' (in Flanders) suddenly disappears, to be replaced by a pointer to 'Mons' (in Wallonia). To help keep your sanity while on the road, refer to the list of the various Belgian place names (see opposite).

Automobile Associations

Automobile Club de Luxembourg (☎ 45 00 45 1; www.acl.lu in French & German; 54 Route de Longwy, L-8007 Bertrange) Luxembourg's only motoring club.
Touring Club de Belgique (Map pp72-3; ☎ 02 233 22 11; www.touring.be in Flemish & French; Rue de la Loi 44, B-1040 Brussels) Belgium's biggest motoring club,

offering a 24-hour Touring Secours breakdown service (☎ 070 344 777). It's a free service for members and foreign visitors who are members of their own country's automobile club; nonmembers will be looking at a call-out fee of €100.

Bring Your Own Vehicle

If you're driving your own car into Belgium and Luxembourg, in addition to your passport and driving licence, you must carry vehicle registration (proof of ownership) and insurance documents (see p322). All cars should also carry a first-aid kit, warning triangle and fire extinguisher.

Driving Licence

Visitors from non-EU countries officially need an International Driving Permit (IDP) to drive in Belgium or Luxembourg; however, police will generally tolerate a valid licence from your home country. If you plan to hire a car or motorcycle, it can make life easier to have an IDP. They are issued by your local motoring association – you'll need a passport, photo and valid licence. IDPs are usually inexpensive and valid for one year.

TRANSPORT

ROAD DISTANCES (KM)

	Antwerp	Bouillon	Bruges	Brussels	Ghent	Hasselt	Kortrijk	La Roche	Liège	Luxembourg City	Mechelen	Mons	Namur	Ostend	Tournai
Bouillon	202														
Bruges	113	270													
Brussels	47	155	115												
Ghent	58	115	55	60											
Hasselt	75	160	188	80	133										
Kortrijk	106	240	44	92	48	172									
La Roche	175	67	243	113	188	110	213								
Liège	115	105	205	90	173	40	182	70							
Luxembourg City	262	107	330	200	275	200	300	108	140						
Mechelen	24	180	123	25	68	81	116	138	110	225					
Mons	112	170	114	65	92	145	70	143	140	230	88				
Namur	112	90	180	65	125	70	150	63	60	150	90	80			
Ostend	138	295	25	140	80	220	59	253	230	355	148	129	205		
Tournai	131	215	69	75	73	155	25	188	185	275	141	45	125	84	
Ypres	134	268	57	120	76	200	28	241	210	328	144	98	178	45	53

TRANSPORT

Fuel & Spare Parts

In Belgium, fuel prices per litre are about €1.40 for unleaded and €1.10 for diesel.

Luxembourg's fuel prices are among the lowest in Western Europe: unleaded costs €1.15 per litre and diesel is €0.90. Residents of neighbouring countries regularly fill up here, and the prices are reflected in the number of huge petrol stations lining the road at every border town.

Repairs and spare parts are easy to come by in both countries.

Hire
CAR

Renting a car for inner-city travel is madness, but having your own wheels certainly makes it easy to mosey around the countryside. If you intend to do so, organise the rental before you leave home – it's usually much cheaper. If that doesn't suit, avoid renting a car from an airport or train station in Belgium as tariffs are 15% higher.

Rental prices include insurance and VAT, and most companies offer unlimited kilometres. Foreign drivers will need to show their passport or ID card as well as their driving licence, and most car-hire companies prefer that you have a credit card (some won't even look at you without one). Most companies require drivers to be aged 23 or over and to have been driving for at least one year.

If you plan to spend a good deal of time in Belgium and Luxembourg and even other European countries it's well worth investigating car-leasing programmes such as those offered by Peugeot or Renault (see right). These allow you to drive in many countries in Western and Central Europe; all you need is a credit card, passport and driving licence valid in the countries in which you'll be driving. Payment must be made in advance and the minimum age is 18. All of the cars in these programmes are brand new; prices include unlimited kilometres and comprehensive insurance, and prices are much cheaper than for normal rental cars, especially if you want a car for an extended period (ie more than 17 days). Cars can be picked up and dropped off in many European cities, including Brussels; however, you'll have to pay an added fee if you don't start your journey in France where these programmes originate. Allow at least three weeks for the paperwork. Many travel agents have details and brochures.

Rental/leasing companies include the following:

Avis (☎ Belgium 02 537 12 80; Luxembourg 48 95 95; www.avis.com)

Budget (☎ Belgium 02 646 51 30; Luxembourg 44 19 38; www.budget.com)

Hertz (☎ Belgium 02 513 28 86; Luxembourg 43 46 45; www.hertz.be)

Peugeot (☎ France 0825 120 120; www.peugeot.com)

Renault Eurodrive (☎ France 01 40 40 32 32; www.eurodrive.renault.com)

MOTORCYCLE

Motorcycles are only available for hire in Brussels (see p115).

Insurance

Motor-vehicle insurance with at least third-party cover is compulsory throughout the EU. Your home policy may or may not be extendable to Belgium and Luxembourg; it's a good idea to get a Green Card from your home insurer before you leave home. This confirms that you have the correct coverage.

If you're hiring a car in either country, rental companies will provide insurance as a standard part of the rental package.

Road Hazards

Most Belgian cities are congested and full of one-way streets, making driving frustrating and time-consuming. Trams have priority, and be aware of passengers disembarking onto the street. Also, be conscious of cyclists. Although cyclists often have separate bike lanes, the chances of a collision increase at intersections when vehicles are turning right and drivers fail to notice that a cyclist has come alongside the car on the cycle path to their right.

Road Rules

Road rules are generally easy to understand, although the give way to the right law takes a lot of getting used to (see boxed text, opposite). Standard international signs are in use. Both countries have good motorways – they're free in Luxembourg but a €60 motorway toll may be introduced in Belgium from 2008 or 2009. Driving is on the right, and the speed limit is 50km/h in built-up areas, 90km/h outside urban centres and 120km/h on motorways (130km/h in Luxembourg). Seat belts are compulsory in the front and rear. In Belgium the blood-alcohol limit is 0.05%, which means two strong beers and you're over the limit.

TRANSPORT

BELGIAN DRIVERS

'Aggressive' is the word generally used to describe Belgian drivers, and many foreigners who take to the roads here find it apt. Whether cruising on a sleek highway or bouncing over potholed inner-city streets, drivers have a reputation for being fast, impatient and at times abusive (though rarely incited to road rage). Anyone idling at 120km/h in the fast lane of a motorway will be flashed from behind by speed demons doing 160km/h. Belgium has the most dense road network in Europe and, considering the way people drive here, you'd think they were pressed to test-drive every inch of it.

One peculiarity that ensures adrenaline-pumped journeys is the *voorrang van rechts/priorité à droite* (give way to the right) law, which operates in both Belgium and Luxembourg. Thanks to this rule, cars darting out from side streets sometimes have right of way over vehicles on the main road (but not always – signs with an orange diamond surrounded by white mean the main road has priority). Recent figures show that 250 people die each year due to this rule. In 2006, Belgium's Mobility Minister, Renaat Landuyt, said the government may consider scrapping the system as it is 'not always logical'.

Although required to by law, Belgian drivers rarely stop at pedestrian crossings (it halts the flow of traffic!). If you decide to stop, make sure you're not being tailgated and that the vehicle behind you has plenty of time to stop as well. Obviously, pedestrians must also take care at crossings. No matter how steely your glare, drivers generally will not stop – only suicide-seekers step out in front of oncoming traffic.

Statistically, Belgium has double the rate of road fatalities of most of its neighbouring countries (France is the exception). Compared to zealous nations such as Australia, speed checks and Breathalyser tests are almost nonevents. To make it worse, you'd be horrified by the number of Belgians who think they've every right to drive when sozzled. The government implemented hefty fines for speeding and drink-driving in 2002 in a bid to halve road fatalities by 2010. Since then, numbers have been reduced but at a rate lower than the European average. So another crackdown came into effect in 2006, with new laws aimed to reduce accidents and bring the country's safety improvements up to the level of neighbouring countries. Only time will tell whether the harsher fines and increased use of permanent speed cameras has the desired effect on drivers.

And if you think all this is a bit exaggerated, have a read of Pisa Test's recent study of 3000 European drivers in which the Belgians came out as the worst drivers in Europe. Just 48% are capable of passing their driving test, according to the study, compared to the average success rate of 54%. Or for something less dry, pick up Harry Pearson's *A Tall Man in a Low Land*. Anecdote after anecdote attests to Belgium's reputation for having Europe's worst drivers and Pearson's descriptions of 'swashbuckling driving methods' and an 'apparent delusion that the brake pedal is actually a spare clutch' are spot on.

In Luxembourg, the limit is 0.08%, though with debate raging within the government it's widely expected that it will soon drop to 0.05%. Luxembourg is one of only three Western European countries (including Ireland and the UK) to have retained this high limit.

HITCHING

Hitching is never entirely safe in any country in the world, and we don't recommend it. Travellers who decide to hitch should understand that they are taking a small but potentially serious risk. People who do choose to hitch will be safer if they travel in pairs and let someone know where they are planning to go. It's illegal to hitch on motorways in Belgium and Luxembourg.

TaxiStop (p69) is an agency that will match long-distance travellers with drivers headed for the same destination for a reasonable fee.

A similar agency in Luxembourg is **Luxstop** (www.luxstop.8m.com) but it arranges travel only via its website. The basic charge is €0.05 per kilometre, which means you'll be looking at about €9 to Brussels and €25 to London.

LOCAL TRANSPORT

The major cities in both countries have efficient and reliable bus networks. Trams are also used in some Belgian cities, and Brussels and Antwerp also have metro systems and a *premetro* (trams that run underground for part of their journey). Public transport services generally run until about 11pm or midnight in major cities, or until 9pm or 10pm in towns.

Taxis are metered and expensive – you'll find them waiting outside train stations and close to major city hubs.

TRAIN

Trains are the best way to get around in Belgium. Belgium built continental Europe's first railway line (between Brussels and Mechelen) in the 1830s and has since developed an extremely dense network. Trains are run by the **Belgische Spoorwegen/Société National des Chemins de Fer Belges** (Belgian Railways; ☎ 02 528 28 28; www.b-rail.be), whose logo is a 'B' in an oval. Major train stations have information offices, open until about 7pm (later in large cities).

There are four levels of service: InterCity (IC) trains (which are the fastest), Inter-Regional (IR), local (L) and peak-hour (P) commuter trains (the latter stop at specific stations only). Depending on the line, there will be an IC and an IR train every half-hour or hour. For a comprehensive list of destinations serviced from Brussels, complete with fares, journey time and frequency, see p115.

frequency, see p115.

DISCOUNTED DAY TRIPS

If you intend to do much sightseeing around Belgium, investigate the discounted day-trip tickets offered by Belgian Railways. Known as B-Excursions (in French) or B-Dagtrips (in Flemish), these packages include a return 2nd-class ticket plus selected admission fees and a range of incentives such as a complimentary drink in a local *café* (pub/bar). The price is less than a normal return train ticket plus admission and almost always represents excellent value. The free booklet *B-Excursions/ B-Dagtrips* is available from most railway stations but it's in French and Flemish only; ask staff at information offices or ticket windows to explain the details.

Luxembourg's rather sparse rail network radiates out from Luxembourg City, the principal hub. Trains in Luxembourg work largely in partnership with buses – both are operated by the same company and have the same fare system (see p320). The main north–south train line slices straight through the middle

of the country, with a couple of side shoots branching off. From Luxembourg City, lines run east into Germany, south into France and west and north to Belgium.

Trains have 1st- and 2nd-class compartments; both are completely nonsmoking.

Costs

Second-class tickets are 50% cheaper than 1st-class tickets. At weekends, return tickets to anywhere within Belgium are 50% cheaper than on weekdays. Children under 12 travel for free when accompanied by an adult, provided the journey starts after 9am. Seniors over 65 (including visitors) pay only €4 for a return 2nd-class trip anywhere in Belgium (except on weekends from mid-May to mid-September). For discounted day-excursion packages, see boxed text, opposite.

Train Passes

Benelux Tourrail Allows five days' travel within one month in Belgium, Luxembourg and the Netherlands, and costs €195/130 in 1st/2nd class (under 26 is €90, 2nd class only). It can be purchased in Belgium or Luxembourg but not in the Netherlands (though it's valid for use there).

Go Pass Provides 10 one-way trips anywhere in Belgium for people under 26 (€45, 2nd class only).

Rail Pass Gives 10 one-way trips anywhere in Belgium. Valid for one year and costs €104/68 in 1st/2nd class.

TRANSPORT

Health

CONTENTS

Before You Go 326
Insurance 326
Recommended Vaccinations 326
Online Resources 326
Further Reading 326
In Transit 327
Deep Vein Thrombosis (DVT) 327
Jet Lag & Motion Sickness 327
In Belgium & Luxembourg 327
Availability & Cost of Health Care 327
Environmental Hazards 327
Travelling with Children 328
Women's Health 328
Sexual Health 328

Travel health depends on your predeparture preparations, your day-to-day health care while travelling and how you handle any medical problems that may develop during your trip. Health-care standards in both Belgium and Luxembourg are excellent.

BEFORE YOU GO

Prevention is the key to staying healthy while abroad. A little planning before you depart, particularly for preexisting illnesses, will save you trouble later. For instance, see your dentist before a long trip, carry a spare pair of contact lenses and glasses, and take your optical prescription with you. Bring medications in their original, clearly labelled, containers. A signed and dated letter from your physician describing any medical conditions you have and the medications you are using, including generic names, is also a good idea. If carrying syringes or needles, be sure to have a physician's letter documenting their medical necessity.

INSURANCE

If you're an EU citizen, an E111 form, available from health centres or, in the UK, post offices, covers you for most medical care. An E111 will not cover you for nonemergencies or emergency repatriation home. Citizens from other countries should find out if there is a reciprocal arrangement for free medical care between their country and Belgium and/or Luxembourg. If you do need health insurance, make sure you get a policy that covers you for the worst possible scenario, such as an accident requiring an emergency flight home. Find out in advance if your insurance plan will make payments directly to providers or reimburse you later for overseas health expenditures.

RECOMMENDED VACCINATIONS

The World Health Organization (WHO) recommends that all travellers should be vaccinated against diphtheria, tetanus, measles, mumps, rubella and polio, as well as hepatitis B, regardless of their destination. Since most vaccines don't produce immunity until at least two weeks after they're given, visit a physician at least six weeks before departure.

ONLINE RESOURCES

The WHO's publication *International Travel and Health* is revised annually and is available online at www.who.int/ith/. Other useful websites include:

Age Concern (www.ageconcern.org.uk) Advice on travel for the elderly.
Fit For Travel (www.fitfortravel.scot.nhs.uk) General travel advice for the layperson.
Marie Stopes International (www.mariestopes.org.uk) Information on women's health and contraception.
MD Travel Health (www.mdtravelhealth.com) Travel-health recommendations for every country; updated daily.

It's usually a good idea to consult your government's travel health website before departure, if one is available:
Australia (www.dfat.gov.au/travel/)
Canada (www.travelhealth.gc.ca)
UK (www.doh.gov.uk/traveladvice/)
USA (www.cdc.gov/travel/)

FURTHER READING

Health Advice for Travellers (currently called the 'T6' leaflet) is an annually updated leaflet by the Department of Health in the UK, available free from post offices. It contains some general information, details of legally required and recommended vaccines for different ountries, reciprocal health agreements and n E111 application form. Lonely Planet's *Travel with Children* includes advice on travel health for younger children. Other recommended references include *Traveller's Health* by Dr Richard Dawood (Oxford University Press) and *The Traveller's Good Health Guide* by Ted Lankester (Sheldon Press).

IN TRANSIT

DEEP VEIN THROMBOSIS (DVT)

Blood clots may form in the legs (deep vein thrombosis or DVT) during plane flights, chiefly because of prolonged immobility. The longer the flight, the greater the risk. The chief symptom of DVT is swelling or pain in the foot, ankle or calf – usually but not always – on just one side. When a blood clot travels to the lungs, it may cause chest pain and breathing difficulties. Travellers with any of these symptoms should seek medical attention immediately.

To prevent the development of DVT on long flights, you should walk about the cabin, contract the leg muscles while sitting, drink plenty of fluids, and avoid alcohol and tobacco.

JET LAG & MOTION SICKNESS

To avoid jet lag, which is common when crossing more than five time zones, try drinking plenty of nonalcoholic fluids and eating light meals. Upon arrival, get exposure to natural sunlight and readjust your schedule (for meals, sleep and so on) as soon as possible.

Antihistamines, such as dimenhydrinate (Dramamine) and meclizine (Antivert, Bonine), are usually the first choice for treating motion sickness. A herbal alternative is ginger.

IN BELGIUM & LUXEMBOURG

AVAILABILITY & COST OF HEALTH CARE

Good health care is readily available. For minor self-limiting illnesses pharmacists can give valuable advice and sell over-the-counter medication. They can also advise when more specialised help is required and point you in the right direction. The standard of dental care in both countries is usually good; however, it is sensible to have a dental check-up before a long trip.

Hotels and tourist offices will be able to assist you in finding a hospital (*ziekenhuis/hôpital* in Flemish/French) with an English-speaking doctor.

Apotheek/pharmacie (pharmacies) in both countries usually sport a green cross or the symbol of Aesculapius (the Roman god of medicine or healing) and are open from about 8.30am to 7pm Monday to Friday, as well as Saturday mornings. In cities and major towns, pharmacies work on a weekend and late-night roster: in Belgium look for the notice displayed in the pharmacy windows listing which are on duty that weekend or night; in Luxembourg on-duty pharmacies are listed in local newspapers.

ENVIRONMENTAL HAZARDS
Insect Bites & Stings

Mosquitoes are found in most parts of Europe, and while they may not carry malaria, they can cause irritation and infected bites. Use a DEET-based insect repellent.

Bees and wasps only cause real problems to those with a severe allergy (anaphylaxis.) If you have a severe allergy to bee or wasp stings, carry an 'epipen' or similar adrenaline injection.

Bed bugs lead to very itchy, lumpy bites. Spraying the mattress with crawling-insect killer after changing bedding will get rid of them.

Scabies are tiny mites that live in the skin, particularly between the fingers. They cause an intensely itchy rash. Scabies is easily treated with lotion from a pharmacy; other members of the household also need treating to avoid spreading scabies between asymptomatic carriers.

Tickborne encephalitis is spread by tick bites and it's possible to contract it in the Ardennes. It is a serious infection of the brain and vaccination is advised for those in risk areas who are unable to avoid tick bites (such as campers, forestry workers and hikers/ramblers). Two doses of vaccine will give a year's protection, three doses up to three years.

Snake Bites

Avoid getting bitten in the first place: do not walk barefoot or stick your hand into holes or cracks. Half of those bitten by venomous snakes are not actually injected with poison (envenomed). If bitten by a snake, do not panic. Immobilise the bitten limb with a splint (eg a stick) and apply a bandage over the site. Make sure you apply firm pressure, similar to a bandage over a sprain. Do not apply a tourniquet, or cut or suck the bite. Get the

HEALTH

victim to the nearest medical facility as soon as possible.

TRAVELLING WITH CHILDREN

All travellers with children should know how to treat minor ailments and when to seek medical treatment. Make sure children are up to date with routine vaccinations, and discuss possible travel vaccines well before departure as some vaccines are not suitable for children under one year old.

Remember to avoid contaminated food and water. If your child is vomiting or has diarrhoea, lost fluid and salts must be replaced. It may be helpful to take rehydration powders for reconstituting with boiled water.

Children should be encouraged to avoid and mistrust any dogs or other mammals because of the risk of rabies and other diseases. Any bite, scratch or lick from a warm-blooded, furry animal should be thoroughly cleaned immediately. If there is any possibility that the animal is infected with rabies, immediate medical assistance should be sought.

WOMEN'S HEALTH

Emotional stress, exhaustion and travelling through different time zones can all contribute to an upset in the menstrual pattern. If using oral contraceptives, remember diarrhoea, vomiting and some antibiotics can stop the pill from working and lead to the risk of pregnancy – remember to take condoms with you just in case. Time zones, gastrointestinal upsets and antibiotics do not affect injectable contraception.

Travelling during pregnancy is usually possible but there are important things to consider. Always seek a medical check-up before planning your trip. The most risk times for travel are during the first 12 week of pregnancy and after 30 weeks. Antenata facilities vary greatly between countries an you should think carefully before travelling to a country with poor medical facilities, or where there are major cultural and language differences from home. Illness during pregnancy can be more severe, so take special care to avoid contaminated food and water and insect and animal bites. A general rule is to only use vaccines, as with other medications, if the risk of infection is substantial. Remember that the baby could be at serious risk if you were to contract infections such as typhoid or hepatitis. Some vaccines are best avoided, for example those that contain live organisms; however, there is very little evidence that damage has been caused to an unborn child when vaccines have been given to a woman very early in pregnancy or before the pregnancy was suspected. Take written records of your pregnancy with you. Ensure your insurance policy covers pregnancy delivery and postnatal care, but remember insurance policies are only as good as the facilities available. Always consult your doctor before you travel.

SEXUAL HEALTH

Emergency contraception is most effective if taken within 24 hours after unprotected sex. The **International Planned Parent Federation** (www.ippf.org) can advise about the availability of contraception in different countries.

When buying condoms, look for a European CE mark, which means it has been rigorously tested. Keep condoms in a cool, dry place or they may crack and perish.

Language

CONTENTS

What Lingo Where?	329
Flemish	**330**
Pronunciation	330
Accommodation	330
Conversation & Essentials	331
Directions	331
Health	331
Emergencies – Flemish	332
Language Difficulties	332
Numbers	332
Shopping & Services	332
Time & Dates	333
Transport	333
French	**333**
Pronunciation	333
Be Polite!	334
Gender	334
Accommodation	334
Conversation & Essentials	334
Directions	334
Health	335
Emergencies – French	335
Language Difficulties	335
Numbers	335
Shopping & Services	336
Time & Dates	336
Transport	336

WHAT LINGO WHERE?
Belgium
Belgium's three main languages are Flemish, French and German. Flemish speakers occupy Flanders, the northern half of the country, and French speakers live in Wallonia in the south. The small German-speaking region, known as the Eastern Cantons, is in the east, based around the towns of Eupen and St Vith. Brussels is officially bilingual though French has long been the city's dominant language.

Flemish, or *Vlaams* as it's known by most Belgians, is a form of Dutch; some Belgians do in fact prefer to call the language Dutch, or *Nederlands* as it's correctly known.

For details on the underlying tensions between the Flemish- and French-speaking communities in Belgium, see The Linguistic Divide, p31.

If you spend any time travelling around Belgium you'll have to get used to switching between Flemish and French. If you're unsure of which language group someone comes from, it's probably best to stick to English until you've sussed it out – some Flemish take exception to being greeted in French and, vice versa, Walloons may also feel insulted if addressed in Flemish.

In Brussels, tourists can get by with English most of the time. In Flanders you'll have few problems using English – many Flemish speak English fluently and are very accommodating when it comes to speaking to foreigners. In Wallonia far fewer people speak English and once you get away from major cities or tourist centres you'll need French to get by. The people in the Eastern Cantons tend to be fluent in both German and French and also have a smattering of English.

Belgium's linguistic divide may cause some confusion, particularly when crossing between Flanders and Wallonia. For example, when driving from Antwerp, the sign you're following to Bergen (the Flemish name) will disappear and Mons (French) will appear – you'll need to know both the Flemish and French names for a city in order to keep up with road signs. The same goes for reading timetables and signboards at train stations. With the exception of Brussels, these are written in the local language only, hence you may start your journey scanning a timetable to 'Courtrai' and end up needing to look out for a station sign displayed 'Kortrijk'. For a list of alternative placenames, see p320.

Luxembourg
Like Belgium, Luxembourg also has three official languages: French, German and Lëtzebuergesch. Unlike in Belgium, these languages live together harmoniously. Most Luxembourgers are fluent in all three as well as in English, which is widely spoken in the capital and by younger people around the countryside.

Lëtzebuergesch is most closely related to German and was proclaimed as the national tongue in 1984. Luxembourgers speak Lëtze-buergesch to each other but generally switch to French when talking to foreigners.

The Grand Duke and government min-isters address the nation in Lëtzebuergesch and debates in parliament are usually car-ried out in the national tongue; however, French is the official language of govern-ment announcements, laws, legislation and the judiciary. Street names and road signs tend to be in French and Lëtzebuergesch and the press is predominantly German and French.

A couple of Lëtzebuergesch words often overheard are *moien* (good morning/hello), *äddi* (goodbye) and *wann ech gelifft* (please). Like French speakers, Luxembourgers say *merci* for 'thank you'. A phrase that might come in useful is *schwatzt dir Englesch?* (pronounced 'schwetz dear anglish'), which means 'Do you speak English?'.

FLEMISH

Flemish nouns come in one of three gen-ders: masculine, feminine (both with *de* for 'the') and neuter (with *het* for 'the'). Where English uses 'a' or 'an', Flemish uses *een*, regardless of gender.

There's also a polite and an informal ver-sion of the English 'you'. The polite form is *u* (pronounced with the lips both pursed and rounded), the informal is *je*. As a general rule, people who are older than you should be addressed as *u*.

For useful information on food and dining out, including Flemish words and phrases, see p58. For more extensive coverage of Dutch/Flemish than we have space for here, pick up a copy of Lonely Planet's *Dutch Phrasebook*.

PRONUNCIATION

The following lists describe the letters used in our guides to pronunciation, not the ac-tual letters of the Flemish alphabet (which wouldn't include the symbol ə or the letter combinations **ow** or **əy**, for example).

Vowels
a	as the 'u' in 'run'
e	as in 'bet'
i	as in 'hit'
o	as in 'pot'

u	pronounced with pursed, rounded lips, as in the French *tu*
ə	a neutral vowel, as the 'a' in 'ago'
aa	as the 'a' in 'father'
ee	as in 'eel'
oa	as in 'boat'
oo	as in 'zoo'
ow	as in 'cow'
ay	as in 'say'
əy	similar to the sound of 'er-y' in 'her year' (with no 'r' sound) or, if you're familiar with it, as the 'eui' in the French *fauteuil*
eu	similar the 'er' in 'her', but with no 'r' sound

Consonants
Most consonants in the pronunciation guides are similar to their English counter-parts (**b**, **d**, **f**, **g**, **h**, **k**, **l**, **m**, **n**, **p**, **s**, **t**, **v**, **w**, **z**). A few trickier sounds are listed below:

ch	as in 'chip'
g	as in 'go'
kh	as the 'ch' in the Scottish *loch*; it's like a hiss produced between the tongue and the back 'roof' of the mouth
ng	as in 'ring'
r	trilled, either with the tongue forward or held back restricting the flow of air in the throat
y	as in 'yes'
zh	as the 's' in 'pleasure'

ACCOMMODATION
I'm looking for	*Ik ben op zoek*	ik ben op zook
a ...	*naar een ...*	naar ən ...
camping ground	*camping*	kem·ping
guesthouse	*pension*	pen·syon
hotel	*hotel*	ho·tel
youth hostel	*jeugdherberg*	yeukht·her·berkh

Do you have any rooms available?
Heeft u een kamer vrij?
hayft u ən kaa·mər vray

I'd like (a) ...	*Ik wil graag een ...*	ik wil khraakh ən ...
bed	*bed*	bet
single room	*eenpersoons-kamer*	ayn·pər·soans·kaa·mər
double room	*tweepersoons-kamer*	tway·pər·soans·kaa·mər
room with two beds	*kamer met twee bedden*	kaa·mər met tway be·dən
room with a bathroom	*kamer met badkamer*	kaa·mər met bat·kaa·mər

to share a dorm	bed op een slaapzaal	bet op ən slaap·zaal
ow much is it ...?	Hoeveel is het ...?	hoo·vayl is hət ...?
per night	per nacht	pər nakht
per person	per persoon	pər per·soan

May I see the room?
Mag ik de kamer zien?   makh ik də kaa·mər zeen
Where is the bathroom?
Waar is de badkamer?   waar is də bat·kaa·mər

CONVERSATION & ESSENTIALS
Hello.
Dag/Hallo.   dakh/ha·loa
Goodbye.
Dag.   dakh
Yes.
Ja.   yaa
No.
Nee.   nay
Please.
Alstublieft. (pol)   als·tu·bleeft
Alsjeblieft. (inf)   a·shə·bleeft
Thank you (very much).
Dank u (wel). (pol)   dangk u (wel)
Dank je (wel). (inf)   dangk yə (wel)
Thanks.
Bedankt. (pol or inf)   bə·dangt
That's fine./You're welcome.
Graag gedaan.   khraakh khə·daan
Excuse me.
Pardon.   par·don
or Excuseer mij.   eks·ku·zayr may
I'm sorry.
Sorry/Excuses.   so·ree/eks·ku·zəs
How are you?
Hoe gaat het met u/jou? (pol/inf)   hoo khaat hət met u/yow
I'm fine, thanks.
Goed, bedankt.   khoot, bə·dangt
See you soon.
Tot ziens.   tot zeens
What's your name?
Hoe heet u? (pol)   hoo hayt u
Hoe heet je? (inf)   hoo hayt yə
My name is ...
Ik heet ...   ik hayt ...
Where are you from?
Waar komt u vandaan? (pol)   waar komt u van·daan
Waar kom je vandaan? (inf)   waar kom yə van·daan
I'm from ...
Ik kom uit ...   ik kom əyt ...

DIRECTIONS
Where is ...?
Waar is ...?   waar is ...
Can you show me (on the map)?
Kunt u het mij tonen (op de kaart)?   kunt u hət may toa·nən (op də kaart)
Could you write the address, please?
Kunt u het adres opschrijven alstublieft?   kunt u hət a·dres op·skhray·vən als·tu·bleeft
(Go) straight ahead.
(Ga) rechtdoor.   (khaa) rekht·doar
(Turn) left.
(Ga) naar links.   (khaa) naar lings
(Turn) right.
(Ga) naar rechts.   (khaa) naar rekhs
at the corner
op de hoek   op də hook
at the traffic lights
bij de verkeerslichten   bay də vər·kayrs·likh·tən
What street/road is this?
Welke straat/weg is dit?   wel·kə straat/wekh is dit?

SIGNS – FLEMISH	
Ingang	Entrance
Uitgang	Exit
Informatie/Inlichtingen	Information
Open	Open
Gesloten	Closed
Verboden/Niet Toegelaten	Prohibited
Kamers Vrij	Rooms Available
Vol	Full/No Vacancies
Politiebureau	Police Station
WC's/Toiletten	Toilets
Heren	Men
Dames	Women

behind	achter	akh·tər
in front of	voor	voar
far (from)	ver (van)	ver (van)
near (to)	dichtbij	dikht·bay
opposite	tegenover	tay·khən·oa·vər

HEALTH
I need a doctor.	Ik heb een dokter nodig.	ik hep ən dok·tər noa·dikh
Where is the hospital?	Waar is het ziekenhuis?	waar is hət zee·kən·həys
I'm ill.	Ik ben ziek.	ik ben zeek
I'm ...	Ik ben ...	ik ben ...
asthmatic	asthmatisch	ast·maa·tis
diabetic	suikerziek	say·kər·zeek

LANGUAGE

EMERGENCIES – FLEMISH

Help!
 Help! help
There's been an accident.
 Er is een ongeluk ər is ən on·khə·luk
 gebeurd. khə·beurt
I'm lost.
 Ik ben de weg kwijt. ik ben də wekh kwayt
Go away!
 Ga weg! kha wekh

Call ...!	Haal ...	haal ...
a doctor	een doktor	ən dok·tər
the police	de politie	də po·leet·see

I'm allergic	Ik ben allergisch	ik ben a·ler·khis
to ...	voor...	voar ...
antibiotics	antibiotica	an·tee·bee·o·tee·ka
nuts	noten	noa·tən
penicillin	penicilline	pay·nee·see·lee·nə

antiseptic	ontsmettings-middel	ont·sme·tings·mi·dəl
aspirin	aspirine	as·pee·ree·nə
condoms	condooms	kon·doams
contraceptive	anticonceptie-middel	an·tee·kon·sep·see·mi·dəl
diarrhoea	diarree	dee·a·ray
nausea	misselijkheid	mi·sə·lək·hayt
sunscreen	zonnebrandolie	zo·nə·brant·oa·lee
tampons	tampons	tam·pons

LANGUAGE DIFFICULTIES

Do you speak English?
 Spreekt u Engels? spraykt u eng·əls
How do you say ... in Dutch?
 Hoe zeg je ... hoo zekh yə ...
 in het Nederlands? in hət nay·dər·lants
I (don't) understand.
 Ik begrijp het (niet). ik bə·khrayp hət (neet)

NUMBERS

0	nul	nul
1	één	ayn
2	twee	tway
3	drie	dree
4	vier	veer
5	vijf	vayf
6	zes	zes
7	zeven	zay·vən
8	acht	akht
9	negen	nay·khən
10	tien	teen
11	elf	elf
12	twaalf	twaalf
13	dertien	der·teen
14	veertien	vayr·teen
15	vijftien	vayf·teen
16	zestien	zes·teen
17	zeventien	zay·vən·teen
18	achttien	akh·teen
19	negentien	nay·khən·teen
20	twintig	twin·təkh
21	eenentwintig	ayn·en·twin·təkh
22	tweeëntwintig	tway·en·twin·təkh
30	dertig	der·təkh
40	veertig	vayr·təkh
50	vijftig	vayf·təkh
60	zestig	zes·təkh
70	zeventig	zay·vən·təkh
80	tachtig	takh·təkh
90	negentig	nay·khən·təkh
100	honderd	hon·dərt
1000	duizend	dəy·zənt
2000	tweeduizend	twee·dəy·zənt

SHOPPING & SERVICES

I'd like to buy ...
 Ik wil graag ... kopen. ik wil khraakh ... koa·pən
How much is it?
 Hoeveel is het? hoo·vayl is hət?
May I look at it?
 Mag ik het zien? makh ik hət zeen
I don't like it.
 Ik vind het niet leuk. ik vint hət neet leuk

Do you accept ...?	Accepteert u ...	ak·sep·tayrt u ...
credit cards	kredietkaarten	kray·deet·kaar·tən
travellers cheques	reischeques	rays·sheks

more	meer	mayr
less	minder	min·dər
smaller	kleiner	klay·nər
bigger	groter	khroa·tər

I'm looking for ...	Ik ben op zoek naar ...	ik ben op zook naar ...
the bank	de bank	də bangk
a bookshop	een boekenwinkel	ən boo·kən·win·kəl
the chemist/ pharmacy	de drogist/ apotheek	də dro·khist/ a·po·tayk
a laundry	een wasserette	ən wa·sə·re·tə
the market	de markt	də markt
the post office	het postkantoor	hət post·kan·toar

a public toilet	een openbaar	ən oa·pən·baar
	toilet	twa·let
a supermarket	een supermarkt	ən su·pər·mart
the tourist office	de VVV	də vay·vay·vay

What time does it open/close?

| Hoe laat opent/ sluit het? | hoo laat oa·pənt/ sløyt hət |

TIME & DATES

What time is it?

| Hoe laat is het? | hoo laat is hət |

It's (8 o'clock).

| Het is (acht uur). | hət is (akht ur) |

in the morning	's morgens	smor·ghəns
in the afternoon	's middags	smi·dakhs
in the evening	's avonds	saa·vonts
When?	Wanneer?	wa·nayr
today	vandaag	van·daakh
tomorrow	morgen	mor·khən
yesterday	gisteren	khis·tə·rən

Monday	maandag	maan·dakh
Tuesday	dinsdag	dins·dakh
Wednesday	woensdag	woons·dakh
Thursday	donderdag	don·dər·dakh
Friday	vrijdag	vray·dakh
Saturday	zaterdag	zaa·tər·dakh
Sunday	zondag	zon·dakh

January	januari	ya·nu·aa·ree
February	februari	fay·bru·aa·ree
March	maart	maart
April	april	a·pril
May	mei	may
June	juni	yu·nee
July	juli	yu·lee
August	augustus	ow·gus·tus
September	september	sep·tem·bər
October	oktober	ok·to·bər
November	november	no·vem·bər
December	december	day·sem·bər

TRANSPORT

What time does the ... leave?

| Hoe laat vertrekt ...? | hoo laat vər·trekt ... |

What time does the ... arrive?

| Hoe laat komt ... aan? | hoo laat komt ... aan |

boat	de boot	də boat
bus	de bus	də bus
plane	het vliegtuig	hət fleekh·təykh
train	de trein	də trayn

Where is ...?	Waar is ...?	waar is ...
the airport	de luchthaven	də lukht·haa·vən
the bus stop	de bushalte	də bus·hal·tə
the train station	het (trein)-station	hət (trayn) sta·syon
the tram stop	de tramhalte	də trem·hal·tə

I'd like ... ticket.	Ik wil graag ...	ik wil khraakh ...
a one-way	een enkele reis	ən eng·kə·lə rays
a return	een retourticket	ən rə·toor·ti·ket
a 1st-class	eerste klas	ayr·stə klas
a 2nd-class	tweede klas	tway·də klas

the first	de eerste	də ayr·stə
the last	de laatste	də laat·stə
platform number	spoor/perron nummer	spoar/pe·ron nu·mər
ticket office	loket	loa·ket
timetable	dienstregeling	deenst·ray·khə·ling

I'd like to hire a/an ...	Ik wil graag een ... huren.	ik wil khraakh ən ... hu·rən
bicycle	fiets	feets
car	auto	ow·to
motorbike	motorfiets	mo·tər·feets

FRENCH

For useful information on food and dining out, including French words and phrases, see p59. For more extensive coverage of French than we have space for here, get a copy of Lonely Planet's *French Phrasebook*.

PRONUNCIATION

Most letters in French are pronounced more or less the same as their English counterparts, and the pronunciation guides we include should help you get your tongue around the trickier aspects of the language.

j	as the 's' in 'leisure', eg *jour* (day)
c	before **e** and **i**, as the 's' in 'sit'; before **a**, **o** and **u** it's pronounced as English 'k'. When undescored with a 'cedilla' (**ç**) it's always pronounced as the 's' in 'sit'.
r	pronounced from the back of the throat while constricting the muscles to restrict the flow of air
n, m	where a syllable ends in a single **n** or **m**, these letters are not pronounced, but the vowel preceding them is given a nasal pronunciation

LANGUAGE

BE POLITE!

An important distinction is made in French between *tu* and *vous*, which both mean 'you'; *tu* is only used when addressing people you know well, children or animals. If you are addressing an adult who isn't a personal friend, *vous* should be used unless the person invites you to use *tu*. In general, younger people insist less on this distinction between polite and informal, and you will find that in many cases they use *tu* from the beginning of an acquaintance.

GENDER

All nouns in French are either masculine or feminine and adjectives reflect the gender of the noun they modify. The feminine form of many nouns and adjectives is indicated by a silent **e** added to the masculine form, as in *ami* and *amie* (the masculine and feminine for 'friend').

In the following phrases both masculine and feminine forms have been indicated where necessary. The masculine form comes first and is separated from the feminine by a slash. The gender of a noun is often indicated by a preceding article: 'the/a/some', *le/un/du* (m), *la/une/de la* (f); or one of the possessive adjectives, 'my/your/his/her', *mon/ton/son* (m), *ma/ta/sa* (f). With French, unlike English, the possessive adjective agrees in number and gender with the thing in question: 'his/her mother', *sa mère*.

ACCOMMODATION

I'm looking for a ...	Je cherche ...	zher shersh ...
campground	un camping	un kom·peeng
guesthouse	une pension (de famille)	ewn pon·syon (der fa·mee·ler)
hotel	un hôtel	un o·tel
youth hostel	une auberge de jeunesse	ewn o·berzh der zher·nes

Could you write it down, please?
Est-ce que vous pourriez l'écrire, s'il vous plaît?
e·sker voo poo·ryay lay·kreer seel voo play
Do you have any rooms available?
Est-ce que vous avez des chambres libres?
e·sker voo·za·vay day shom·brer lee·brer

I'd like (a) ...	Je voudrais ...	zher voo·dray ...
single room	une chambre à un lit	ewn shom·brer a un lee

double-bed room	une chambre avec un grand lit	ewn shom·brer a·vek un gron lee
twin room with two beds	une chambre avec des lits jumeaux	ewn shom·brer a·vek day lee zhew·mo
room with a bathroom	une chambre avec une salle de bains	ewn shom·brer a·vek ewn sal der bun
to share a dorm	coucher dans un dortoir	koo·sher don zun dor·twa

How much is it ...?	Quel est le prix ...?	kel e ler pree ...
per night	par nuit	par nwee
per person	par personne	par per·son

May I see it?
Est-ce que je peux voir la chambre?   es·ker zher per vwa la shom·brer
Where is the bathroom?
Où est la salle de bains?   oo e la sal der bun

CONVERSATION & ESSENTIALS

Hello.	Bonjour.	bon·zhoor
Goodbye.	Au revoir.	o·rer·vwa
Yes.	Oui.	wee
No.	Non.	no
Please.	S'il vous plaît.	seel voo play
Thank you.	Merci.	mair·see
You're welcome.	Je vous en prie.	zher voo·zon pree
	De rien. (inf)	der ree·en
Excuse me.	Excusez-moi.	ek·skew·zay·mwa
Sorry. (forgive me)	Pardon.	par·don

What's your name?
Comment vous appelez-vous? (pol)   ko·mon voo·za·pay·lay voo
Comment tu t'appelles? (inf)   ko·mon tew ta·pel
My name is ...
Je m'appelle ...   zher ma·pel ...
Where are you from?
De quel pays êtes-vous?   der kel pay·ee et·voo
De quel pays es-tu? (inf)   der kel pay·ee e·tew
I'm from ...
Je viens de ...   zher vyen der ...

DIRECTIONS

Where is ...?
Où est ...?   oo e ...
Can you show me (on the map)?
Pouvez-vous m'indiquer (sur la carte)?   poo·vay·voo mun·dee·kay (sewr la kart)
Go straight ahead.
Continuez tout droit.   kon·teen·way too drwa

Entrée	Entrance
Sortie	Exit
Renseignements	Information
Ouvert	Open
Fermé	Closed
Interdit	Prohibited
Chambres Libres	Rooms Available
Complet	Full/No Vacancies
(Commissariat de) Police	Police Station
Toilettes/WC	Toilets
Hommes	Men
Femmes	Women

Turn left.
Tournez à gauche.   toor·nay a gosh
Turn right.
Tournez à droite.   toor·nay a drwa
at the corner
au coin   o kwun
at the traffic lights
aux feux   o fer

behind	*derrière*	dair·ryair
in front of	*devant*	der·von
far (from)	*loin (de)*	lwun (der)
near (to)	*près (de)*	pray (der)
opposite	*en face de*	on fas der

HEALTH

I need a doctor.	*J'ai besoin d'un médecin.*	zhay ber·zwun dun mayd·sun
Where is the hospital?	*Où est l'hopital?*	oo e lo·pee·tal

I'm ...	*Je suis ...*	zher swee ...
asthmatic	*asthmatique*	(z)as·ma·teek
diabetic	*diabétique*	dee·a·bay·teek
epileptic	*épileptique*	(z)ay·pee·lep·teek
ill	*malade*	ma·lad

I'm allergic to ...	*Je suis allergique ...*	zher swee za·lair·zheek ...
antibiotics	*aux antibiotiques*	o zon·tee·byo·teek
nuts	*aux noix*	o nwa
peanuts	*aux cacahuètes*	o ka·ka·wet
penicillin	*à la pénicilline*	a la pay·nee·see·leen

antiseptic	*l'antiseptique*	lon·tee·sep·teek
aspirin	*l'aspirine*	las·pee·reen
condoms	*des préservatifs*	day pray·zair·va·teef

EMERGENCIES – FRENCH

Help!
Au secours!   o skoor
There's been an accident!
Il y a eu un accident!   eel ya ew un ak·see·don
I'm lost.
Je me suis égaré/e. (m/f)   zhe me swee·zay·ga·ray
Leave me alone!
Fichez-moi la paix!   fee·shay·mwa la pay

Call ...!	*Appelez ...!*	a·play ...
a doctor	*un médecin*	un mayd·sun
the police	*la police*	la po·lees

contraceptive	*le contraceptif*	ler kon·tra·sep·teef
diarrhoea	*la diarrhée*	la dya·ray
nausea	*la nausée*	la no·zay
sunblock cream	*la crème solaire*	la krem so·lair
tampons	*des tampons hygiéniques*	day tom·pon ee·zhen·eek

LANGUAGE DIFFICULTIES

Do you speak English?
Parlez-vous anglais?   par·lay·voo ong·lay
How do you say ... in French?
Comment est-ce qu'on dit ... en français?   ko·mon es·kon dee ... on fron·say
I understand.
Je comprends.   zher kom·pron
I don't understand.
Je ne comprends pas.   zher ner kom·pron pa

NUMBERS

0	*zero*	zay·ro
1	*un*	un
2	*deux*	der
3	*trois*	trwa
4	*quatre*	ka·trer
5	*cinq*	sungk
6	*six*	sees
7	*sept*	set
8	*huit*	weet
9	*neuf*	nerf
10	*dix*	dees
11	*onze*	onz
12	*douze*	dooz
13	*treize*	trez
14	*quatorze*	ka·torz
15	*quinze*	kunz
16	*seize*	sez
17	*dix-sept*	dee·set
18	*dix-huit*	dee·zweet
19	*dix-neuf*	deez·nerf

20	vingt	vung
21	vingt et un	vung tay un
22	vingt-deux	vung-der
30	trente	tront
40	quarante	ka-ront
50	cinquante	sung-kont
60	soixante	swa-sont
70	soixante-dix	swa-son-dees
80	quatre-vingts	ka-trer-vung
90	quatre-vingt-dix	ka-trer-vung-dees
100	cent	son
1000	mille	meel

SHOPPING & SERVICES

I'd like to buy ...
Je voudrais acheter ...   zher voo-dray ash-tay ...
How much is it?
C'est combien?   say kom-byun
May I look at it?
Est-ce que je peux le voir? es-ker zher per ler vwar
I don't like it.
Cela ne me plaît pas.   ser-la ner mer play pa

Can I pay by ...?	Est-ce que je peux payer avec ...?	es-ker zher per pay-yay a-vek ...
credit card	ma carte de crédit	ma kart der kray-dee
travellers cheques	des chèques de voyage	day shek der vwa-yazh

more	plus	plew
less	moins	mwa
bigger	plus grand	plew gron
smaller	plus petit	plew per-tee

I'm looking for ...	Je cherche ...	zhe shersh ...
a bank	une banque	ewn bonk
the hospital	l'hôpital	lo-pee-tal
the market	le marché	ler mar-shay
the police	la police	la po-lees
the post office	le bureau de poste	ler bew-ro der post
a public phone	une cabine téléphonique	ewn ka-been tay-lay-fo-neek
a public toilet	les toilettes	lay twa-let
the tourist office	l'office de tourisme	lo-fees der too-rees-mer

TIME & DATES

What time is it? *Quelle heure est-il?* kel er e til
It's (8) o'clock. *Il est (huit) heures.* il e (weet) er
It's half past ... *Il est (...) heures et demie.* il e (...) er e day-mee
in the morning *du matin* dew ma-tun
in the afternoon *de l'après-midi* der la-pray-mee-dee

in the evening	du soir	dew swar
today	aujourd'hui	o-zhoor-dwee
tomorrow	demain	der-mun
yesterday	hier	yair

Monday	lundi	lun-dee
Tuesday	mardi	mar-dee
Wednesday	mercredi	mair-krer-dee
Thursday	jeudi	zher-dee
Friday	vendredi	von-drer-dee
Saturday	samedi	sam-dee
Sunday	dimanche	dee-monsh

January	janvier	zhon-vyay
February	février	fayv-ryay
March	mars	mars
April	avril	a-vreel
May	mai	may
June	juin	zhwun
July	juillet	zhwee-yay
August	août	oot
September	septembre	sep-tom-brer
October	octobre	ok-to-brer
November	novembre	no-vom-brer
December	décembre	day-som-brer

TRANSPORT

What time does ... leave/arrive?	À quelle heure part/arrive ...?	a kel er par/a-reev ...
boat	le bateau	ler ba-to
bus	le bus	ler bews
plane	l'avion	la-vyon
train	le train	ler trun

I'd like a ... ticket.	Je voudrais un billet ...	zher voo-dray un bee-yay ...
one-way	simple	sum-pler
return	aller et retour	a-lay ay rer-toor
1st class	de première classe	der prem-yair klas
2nd class	de deuxième classe	der der-zyem klas

the first	le premier (m) la première (f)	ler prer-myay la prer-myair
the last	le dernier (m) la dernière (f)	ler dair-nyay la dair-nyair
platform number	le numéro de quai	ler new-may-ro der kay
ticket office	le guichet	ler gee-shay
timetable	l'horaire	lo-rair
train station	la gare	la gar

I'd like to hire a/an...	Je voudrais louer ...	zher voo-dray loo-way ...
car	une voiture	ewn vwa-tewr
motorbike	une moto	ewn mo-to
bicycle	un vélo	un vay-lo

LANGUAGE

Glossary

See p59 for a list of culinary terms. Fl after a term signifies Flemish, Fr French.

abdij/abbaye (Fl/Fr) – abbey
apotheek (Fl) – pharmacy
ARAU (Fr) – Atelier de Recherche et d'Action Urbaine (Urban Research & Action Group)
auberge de jeunesse (Fr) – youth hostel

bakker/bakkerij (Fl) – baker/bakery
barouches (Fr) – horse-drawn carriages
begijn/béguine (Fl/Fr) – Beguine; member of a Catholic order of women
begijnhof/béguinage (Fl/Fr) – community of *begijnen/ béguines*; cluster of cottages, often around a central garden
beiaard (Fl) – carillon
Belasting Toegevoegde Waarde (BTW) (Fl) – value-added tax, VAT
Belgische Spoorwegen (Fl) – Belgian National Railways
Benelux – the common abbreviation for Belgium, the Netherlands and Luxembourg
benzine met lood (Fl) – leaded petrol, Super
benzine zonder lood (Fl) – unleaded petrol
betalend parkeren (Fl) – paid street parking
biljart/billard (Fl/Fr) – billiards
billet (Fr) – ticket
boulangerie (Fr) – bakery
BP (boîte postale) (Fr) – post office box
brasserie (Fr) – brewery; café/restaurant serving food all day
brocante (Fr) – bric-a-brac
brouwerij (Fl) – brewery
brown café – small, old-fashioned pub, noted for the interior
bruine kroeg (Fl) – *brown café*
Brusselaar (Fl) – inhabitant of Brussels
Bruxellois (Fr) – inhabitant of Brussels and the name of the city's old dialect
bureau d'échange (Fr) – foreign-exchange bureau

café – pub, bar
carte (Fr) – menu
centrum (Fl) – centre
chambre (Fr) – room
chambre d'hôte (Fr) – B&B/guesthouse
château (Fr) – castle
chocolatier (Fr) – chocolate-maker
commune (Fr) – municipality
confiserie (Fr) – chocolate and sweet shop
curiosa (Fl) – bric-a-brac

dagmenu (Fl) – fixed-price, multicourse meal of the day
dagschotel (Fl) – dish of the day
demi-pension (Fr) – half-board, ie breakfast and either lunch or dinner
dentelle (Fr) – lace
dienst voor toerisme (Fl) – tourist office

Ecolabel – Luxembourg's system of classification for hotels, camping grounds, long-term holiday accommodation etc that comply with environmentally friendly management criteria
eetcafé/eetkroeg (Fl) – *café* serving food
église (Fr) – church
entrée (Fr) – entry
essence avec plomb (Fr) – leaded petrol, Super
essence sans plomb (Fr) – unleaded petrol
estaminet (Fr) – tavern
étang (Fr) – pond
EU – European Union
Eurocrat – administrative official at the headquarters of the EU
Europese Instellingen (Fl) – EU Institutions

fiets (Fl) – bicycle
fietspad (Fl) – bicycle lane
frieten/frites (Fl/Fr) – chips or fries
frituur/friture (Fl/Fr) – chip shop

galerij/galerie (Fl/Fr) – covered shopping centre/arcade
gare (Fr) – train station
gastenkamer (Fl) – B&B/guesthouse
gaufres (Fr) – waffles
gebak (Fl) – cakes and pastries
gemeente (Fl) – municipality
gemeentehuis (Fl) – town hall
genièvre (Fr) – gin
gezellig (Fl) – cosy, convivial atmosphere
gîtes d'étapes (Fr) – group accommodation (individuals also welcome) set in the countryside
gîtes ruraux (Fr) – countryside guesthouses
glacier (Fr) – ice-cream shop
godshuis (Fl) – almshouse
grand café (Fr) – Opulent *café* usually built around the turn of the 19th century
gratis/gratuit (Fl/Fr) – free
grotte (Fr) – cave
gyros – stuffed pitta bread

hallen/halles (Fl/Fr) – covered market
herberg (Fl) – old-style pub
hof (Fl) – garden

hôpital (Fr) – hospital
hôtel de ville (Fr) – town hall

ingang (Fl) – entry
Institutions Européennes (Fr) – EU Institutions
ISIC – International Student Identity Card

jardin (Fr) – garden
jenever (Fl) – gin
jeugdherberg (Fl) – youth hostel

kaartje (Fl) – ticket
kamer (Fl) – room
kant (Fl) – lace
kasteel (Fl) – castle
kerk (Fl) – church

laverie (Fr) – laundrette
landelijke verblijven (Fl) – countryside guesthouses
loodvrije benzine (Fl) – unleaded petrol

magasin de nuit (Fr) – 24-hour shop
marché aux puces (Fr) – flea market
markt/marché (Fl/Fr) – market
menu (Fl & Fr) – fixed-price meal with two or more courses
menu du jour (Fr) – fixed-price, multicourse meal of the day
molen (Fl) – windmill
Mosan (Fr) – art from the Meuse River valley
moules-frites (Fr) – mussels and chips
musée (Fr) – museum

nachtwinkel (Fl) – 24-hour shop
niet rokers/non fumeurs (Fl/Fr) – nonsmoking
non-prioritaire (Fr) – nonpriority mail

office de tourisme (Fr) – tourist office
ondertitels (Fl) – subtitles
oude stad (Fl) – old town or city
OV (originele versie) (Fl) – a nondubbed film, shown in its original language

patinage à glace (Fr) – ice skating
pâtisserie (Fr) – cakes and pastries; shop selling them
pékèt (Fr) – a type of gin
pension complète (Fr) – full board
pharmacie (Fr) – pharmacy
piste cyclable (Fr) – bicycle lane
pitas (Fr) – stuffed pitta bread
place (Fr) – square
plat du jour (Fr) – dish of the day
plein (Fl) – square
poort/porte (Fl/Fr) – gate in city wall
pralines (Fr) – filled chocolates
premetro (Fl & Fr) – trams (found in Brussels and Antwerp) that go underground for part of their journey

prioritaire (Fr) – priority mail
priorité à droite (Fr) – priority-to-the-right traffic rule

RACB (Fr) – Royal Automobile Club de Belgique
rommelmarkt (Fl) – flea market
rond punt/rond point (Fl/Fr) – roundabout
routier (Fr) – trucker (also truckers' restaurant)

sentiers de grande randonnée (Fr) – long-distance footpaths, known simply as GR tracks across Belgium
slijterij (Fl) – shop selling strong alcohol
Société National des Chemins de Fer Belges (Fr) – Belgian National Railways
sortie (Fr) – exit
sous-titres (Fr) – subtitles
spijskaart (Fl) – menu
stadhuis (Fl) – town hall
stadsbelasting (Fl) – city tax
stationnement payant (Fr) – paid parking
STIB (Fr) – Société des Transports Intercommunaux de Bruxelles (Brussels Public Transport Company)
syndicat d'initiative (Fr) – tourist office

taxe de séjour (Fr) – visitors tax
Taxe sur la Valeur Ajoutée (TVA) (Fr) – value-added tax, VAT
teleboetiek/téléboutique (Fl/Fr) – telecommunications shop where you can send faxes
téléférique (Fr) – cable car
terreinfiets (Fl) – mountain bike
TIB – Tourist Information Brussels
toeristische dienst (Fl) – tourist office
toneel/théâtre (Fl/Fr) – theatre
toren/tour (Fl/Fr) – tower
treinstation (Fl) – train station
trekkershut (Fl) – hikers' hut
tuin (Fl) – garden

uitgang (Fl) – exit
ULB (Fr) – Université Libre de Bruxelles

vélo (Fr) – bicycle
vélo tout-terrain (VTT) (Fr) – mountain bike
vieille ville (Fr) – old town or city
vijver (Fl) – pond
VO (version originale) (Fr) – nondubbed film
voorrang van rechts (Fl) – priority-to-the-right traffic rule
vrachtwagenbestuurder (Fl) – trucker

wassalon (Fl) – laundrette
weekend gastronomique (Fr) – accommodation plus breakfast and some meals
wisselkantoor (Fl) – foreign-exchange bureau

ziekenhuis (Fl) – hospital

Behind the Scenes

THIS BOOK

This 3rd edition of *Belgium & Luxembourg* was researched and written by Leanne Logan and Geert Cole who also wrote the first two editions. The Health chapter was adapted from material written by Dr Caroline Evans. This guidebook was commissioned in Lonely Planet's London office, and produced by the following:

Commissioning Editors Judith Bamber, Fayette Fox, Tashi Wheeler, Meg Worby

Coordinating Editors Barbara Delissen, Susan Paterson

Coordinating Cartographer Anita Banh

Coordinating Layout Designer Jacqui Saunders

Managing Editor Imogen Bannister

Managing Cartographer Mark Griffiths

Assisting Editors Joanne Newell, Rosie Nicholson, Kristin Odijk, Phillip Tang

Cover Designer Jane Hart

Project Managers Craig Kilburn, Sarah Sloane

Language Content Coordinator Quentin Frayne

Thanks to Sally Darmody, Stefanie Di Trocchio, Katie Lynch, Brooke Lyons, Trent Paton

THANKS
LEANNE LOGAN & GEERT COLE

Round Three Belgium & Luxembourg – and what a trip it was. We'll never forget the look on Eleonor's face as she braved Plopsaland's terrifying SuperSplash, or on Gwynevere's after sipping her first Trappist beer.

As always, there's a host of Belgians and Luxembourgers we'd like to thank for their enthusiastic help. To start with, a big *merci* to Jean-Claude

Conter from the Luxembourg National Tourist Office. In Brussels, thanks to Catherine Langue at the Office Promotion de Tourisme, Anousjka Schmidt at Brussels International, and Tama d'Haen and Els Maes at Toerisme Vlaanderen (and congratulations on little boy, Seppe). *Bedankt* also to effervescent Anne De Meerleer at In&Uit Brugge, to Tamara De Vliegher at Dienst Toerisme Gent, Stephane Nijssen at Toerisme Tongeren and Zygmund Krzywania at Toerisme Hasselt.

To Brigid Grauman and Kathleen Cagney from *The Bulletin,* Belgium's excellent English-language newsweekly, a huge thank-you for access to your archives.

Thanks to the many locals who answered numerous questions and made us welcome. Thanks also to those readers who provided insights, opinions and criticisms, and to the travellers we met on the road for their many suggestions.

Heartfelt thanks must also go to the best baby-sitting teams on both sides of the globe: Roos and Bert Cole, Barbara and Nev Logan, and June Logan and Bernie Waldon. What can we say except we couldn't have done it without you.

To Eleonor and Gwynevere, our fabulous daughters, thanks for your hard work checking restaurants, B&Bs and museums for their child-friendly factor, and most of all for being naturals when it comes to life on the road. To our long-standing travel mates, Sixy and Bluey, thanks for keeping the girls company.

At Lonely Planet, we're grateful to Sam Trafford, Meg Worby, Tashi Wheeler, Judith Bamber and Fayette Fox for steering the way and giving

---

THE LONELY PLANET STORY

The story begins with a classic travel adventure: Tony and Maureen Wheeler's 1972 journey across Europe and Asia to Australia. There was no useful information about the overland trail then, so Tony and Maureen published the first Lonely Planet guidebook to meet a growing need.

From a kitchen table, Lonely Planet has grown to become the largest independent travel publisher in the world, with offices in Melbourne (Australia), Oakland (USA) and London (UK). Today Lonely Planet guidebooks cover the globe. There is an ever-growing list of books and information in a variety of media. Some things haven't changed. The main aim is still to make it possible for adventurous travellers to get out there – to explore and better understand the world.

At Lonely Planet we believe travellers can make a positive contribution to the countries they visit – if they respect their host communities and spend their money wisely. Every year 5% of company profit is donated to charities around the world.

SEND US YOUR FEEDBACK

We love to hear from travellers – your comments keep us on our toes and help make our books better. Our well-travelled team reads every word on what you loved or loathed about this book. Although we cannot reply individually to postal submissions, we always guarantee that your feedback goes straight to the appropriate authors, in time for the next edition. Each person who sends us information is thanked in the next edition – and the most useful submissions are rewarded with a free book. See the Behind the Scenes section.

To send us your updates – and find out about Lonely Planet events, newsletters and travel news – visit our award-winning website: **www.lonelyplanet.com/contact**.

Note: we may edit, reproduce and incorporate your comments in Lonely Planet products such as guidebooks, websites and digital products, so let us know if you don't want your comments reproduced or your name acknowledged. For a copy of our privacy policy, go to www.lonelyplanet .com/privacy.

us yet another opportunity to add to our beer/chocolate tally. Thanks too to Barbara Delissen for enthusiastically coordinating the editing, and Mark Griffiths and Anita Banh for expert handling of the maps. And lastly but never least, *bedankt* to all those other LPers who were involved in the production of this book.

OUR READERS

Many thanks to the travellers who used the last edition and wrote to us with helpful hints, useful advice and interesting anecdotes:

Kristof Agache, Flemming Andersen, Hugh Annand, Achim Armbruster, Richard Barker, Alan Behn, Ivana Bezecna, Alain Boeyden, Matt Colonell, Rita Colonell, Filip De Haes, Annemie Deruytter, Anke Dijkstra, Andrew Estroff, Liz Evans, Catherine Gaspard, Paula Griswold, Mike Grote, Saji Haratani, Frederik Helbo, Arnaud Hesselink, Katrin Huber, Yuen Ineson, Rob Jones, Anne Julh, Jason Kaufman, Maria Kekki, Maureen Kelly, Lis Maurer, Rob Mcclure, JS McLintock, Heather Monell, Anthony Oldfield, Clairie Papazoglou, Fabrizio Picca, Lizzy Pike, Silvia Roth, Ian Sandison, Marjory Sandison, Ron Shaw, Daniel Sher, Noa Sher, Natashya Sherbot, Bob Simpson, MD Smith, Mara Soplantila, Russ Speiser, Pamela Stokes, Aesen Thambiran, Gail & Helen Thomas, Jeroen van Dyck, Randy van Mingeroet, Camille van Wessem, Brecht Vergult, Jean-Marc Vierset, Tory Waterman, B Weston, Edwin Wolff, Rainer Zorn

ACKNOWLEDGMENTS

Many thanks to the following for the use of their content:

Brussels Transit Map ©STIB/MIVB 2006

Index

A
Aarlen 244
Abbaye de Villers 225-6
abbey beers 50
abortion 27
accommodation 297-300, *see
also individual locations*
Achel 47
activities 300-3, *see also* cycling,
    hiking, kayaking, swimming
    billiards 90, 302
    bird watching 42
    boating 302
    bowling 90
    canoeing 289, 302-3
    chess 90, 303
    cross-country skiing 255, 303
    golf 91, 303
    horse riding 246, 303
    ice skating 91, 256, 292
    rock climbing 303
    squash 91
    tennis 32, 91
    whitewater rafting 258
Adoration of the Mystic Lamb 161, 6
air travel
    to/from Belgium & Luxembourg
        314-16
    within Belgium & Luxembourg
        319
airlines 314-15
airports 314
Albert I 26, 91, 147, 148
Albert II 27-8, 91
almshouses 130, 164
animals 42
Antwerp 171-99, **174-7**, 6
    accommodation 187-90
    attractions 179-85
    drinking 193
    emergency services 175
    entertainment 193-5
    festivals 51, 187
    food 190-2
    internet access 175
    markets 198
    shopping 195-8
    tourist offices 179
    tours 187
    travel to/from 198

    travel within 198-200
    walking tour 185-6
Antwerp port 199
Antwerp Six 197
Apollinaire, Guillaume 257
Aquatopia 186
architecture 13, 36-8
Ardennes
    Belgium 229-64, **230**
    Luxembourg 283-8
Arlon 244
Arsdorf 286
Art Deco 88, 89, 183, 186, 295
Art Nouveau 37, 7
    Antwerp 184, 185
    Brussels 81, 82, 83, 87, 92-3,
        95
    Esch-sur-Alzette 295
    Tournai 219
arts 34-40, *see also* music
    architecture 13, 36-8
    cinema 38-9, 251
    dance 40, 109, 226
    internet resources 39, 40
    literature 14, 38
    painting 13, 34-6
    theatre 40
Ath 222
ATMs 309
Atomium 89, 7

B
B&Bs 298
baby-sitting 94, 132, 304
Bastogne 244-5
bathrooms 311
Battle of the Ardennes 244, 245, 246,
    287, 292
Battle of the Bulge, *see* Battle of the
    Ardennes
Battle of the Golden Spurs 159
Battle of Waterloo 224, 225
Baudouin I 27, 91
beaches
    Blankenberge 145-6
    De Haan 145
    Knokke-Heist 146
    Nieuwpoort 147
    Ostend 141-2
    Zeebrugge 145-6

Beaufort 292
Bech-Kleinmacher 294
beer 45-51, 53, **46**, 5, *see also*
    breweries
    books 45, 49
    cafés 50
    festivals 51, 97, 187
    history 45
    internet resources 45, 47, 50
    museums 49, 79, 90
    shops 51, 113, 138, 196
beffroi, *see* belfries
begijnhoven 129
    Bruges 128
    Diest 209
    Kortrijk 157
    Leuven 206
    Lier 200
    Tongeren 214
béguinages, *see* begijnhoven
belforts, *see* belfries
belfries
    Bruges 124
    Ghent 163
    Kortrijk 157
    Lier 200
    Mons 221
    Tournai 219
    Veurne 149
    Vianden 283
    Ypres 151-2
Belval 295
Berdorf 292
Bergen 221-2
Bettembourg 296
bike rental
    Antwerp 187, 198
    Beaufort 292
    Bruges 130
    Brussels 116
    Diekirch 289
    Dinant 237
    Echternach 291
    Ghent 169
    Hasselt 212
    Kortrijk 160
    La Roche-en-Ardenne 246
    Leuven 208
    Liège 254
    Mechelen 204

bike rental *continued*
　　Namur 235
　　Rochefort 238
　　Rochehaut 243
　　Ruttermolen 216
　　Spa 255
bike tours 187
billiards 90, 302
Binche 222, 223
bird watching 42
bistros 55
Blankenberge 145-6
boat tours
　　Antwerp 187
　　Dinant 235, 236
　　Lier 200
　　Namur 235
boat travel
　　to/from Belgium & Luxembourg
　　　144, 319
　　within Belgium & Luxembourg 319
boating 302
Bock 275
Bock Casemates 273
Bokrijk Openluchtmuseum 212-13
Bonaparte, Napoleon 224, 225
books 326-7
　　animals 42
　　arts 35
　　beer 45, 49
　　festivals 240
　　food 52
　　history 24, 26
Bosch, Hieronymus 35
Botrange Nature Centre 260
Botte de Hainaut 227-8
Boudewijn I 27, 91
Boudewijn Seapark 131
Bouillon 241-3
Bouillon, Godefroid de 82, 242
bowling 90
Brabo, Silvius 180
brasseries 55, 56
breakfast 52
Brel, Jacques 80
Breugel the Elder, Pieter 35, 82, 84, 182
Breughel, Jan 84
Breughel the Younger, Pieter 84
breweries 47-51
　　Abbaye de St Rémy 48, 238
　　Abbaye Notre Dame 48

000 Map pages
000 Photograph pages

Abbaye Notre Dame de Scourmont
　　48, 228
Abbaye Notre Dame d'Orval 243-4
Abdij St Sixtus 47, 150
Brasserie à Vapeur 51
Brasserie Dubuisson 51
Brouwerij De Halve Maan 128
Brouwerij Het Anker 204
Cantillon Brewery 49, 90
De Achelse Kluis 47
De Dolle Brouwers 50
De Halve Maan 49
Domus 208
La Ferme au Chêne 249
museums 79, 90
Westmalle 47
Bruges 120-39, **123**, **126**, 4, 7
　　accommodation 133-5
　　activities 130
　　attractions 122-30
　　drinking 137
　　emergency services 122
　　entertainment 137-8
　　festivals 132
　　food 135-7
　　internet access 122
　　shopping 138
　　tourist offices 122
　　travel to/from 138-9
　　travel within 139
　　walking tour 130-1
Bruparck 94
Brussels 30, 65-118, **70-8**, **86**, 5,
　　6, 7
　　accommodation 97-101
　　activities 90-2
　　Anderlecht 67, 90, 106
　　Art Nouveau 81, 82, 83, 87, 92-3
　　Atomium 89, 7
　　dialect 83
　　drinking 106-7
　　emergency services 67
　　entertainment 107-12
　　EU district 67, 85-7, 104-5, 107
　　festivals 95-7
　　food 101-6
　　gay & lesbian travellers 97
　　Ilôt Sacré 66
　　internet access 67
　　Ixelles 67, 87, 105, 107
　　Jette 67, 89-90
　　Koekelberg 67, 89-90
　　Laeken 67, 88-9
　　Lower Town 66
　　markets 115

Marolles 66, 82, 83, 103-4, 107
Matonge 67
Molenbeek 67, 89-90, 106
parks 84, 86-7, 88, 89, 94, 95
Sablon 104
St Géry 66, 81-2, 102-3, 106-7
St Gilles 67, 87, 107
St Josse 67, 88, 105-6
Ste Catherine 66, 81-2, 102-3, 106-7
Schaerbeek 67, 88, 107
shopping 112-15
tourist offices 68-9
tours 95
travel to/from 115-16
travel within 116-17
Uccle 67, 88
Upper Town 67, 107
walking tour 92-3, **92**
bus tours
　　Antwerp 187
　　Bruges 132
　　Brussels 95
　　Damme 140
　　Luxembourg City 276
bus travel
　　to/from Belgium & Luxembourg
　　　317-18
　　within Belgium & Luxembourg
　　　319-20
business hours 303

C
cafés 56
　　beer 50
　　Brussels' best 107
　　jenever 55
camping 298-9
canal tours
　　Bruges 132
　　Ghent 165
canoeing, *see also* kayaking
　　Belgium 302-3
　　Diekirch 289
　　Luxembourg 303
Cantons de l'Est 262-4
car hire 322
car travel 316-17, 319, 320-3, **321**
caravan parks 298-9
carnival 222, 223, 259
casemates 273
castles
　　Antwerp 185
　　Beaufort 292
　　Bouillon 241-2
　　Brussels 117

Château de Bourscheid 286
Clervaux 287
Ghent 163
Kasteel Beauvoorde 150
La Roche-en-Ardenne 246
Luxembourg City 275
Petite Somme 249
Rochefort 238
Vallée des Sept Châteaux 288
Vianden 283
Wiltz 286-7
caves
Cavernes de l'Abîme 227
Grotte de Lorette 238
Grottes de Han 239
Grottes de Hotton 248
Grottes de Neptune 227
Caves à Crémant Poll-Fabaire winery 294
Caves Bernard-Massard winery 294
cell phones 311
cemeteries 152, 154, 155, 274
Charleroi 226-7
Charleroi/Danses 226
Château Comtal 238
Château de Bouillon 241-2
Château de Bourscheid 286
chess 90, 303
children, travel with 303-4
    Antwerp 186-7
    baby-sitting 94, 132, 304
    Bruges 131-2
    Brussels 93-4
    Euro Space Center 240
    food 57
    health 328
    Het Land van Ooit 214
    itineraries 18
    La Grange aux Papillons 228
    Luxembourg City 276
    Parc Attractif Reine Fabiola 233
    Parc Merveilleux 296
    Park Bellewaerde 156
    Planckendael 205
    playgrounds 88, 94, 117, 187, 209,
        210, 213, 214-15, 238-9, 240,
        276, 285, 288, 290, 296
    Plopsa Coo 258
    Plopsa Indoor 211
    Plopsaland 148
    Technopolis 204-5
Chimay 48, 228
chocolate 52, 53, 54, 80
    museums 80, 125, 263
    shops 113, 138, 196

cinema 38-9, 251
    festivals 39, 96, 132, 165
Clervaux 287-8
climate 12, 41, 305
coast 145-9
coffee 53
comic strips 39
    murals 81, 82
    museum 81
    shops 114, 169
Congo 26, 96
consulates 306-7
Coo 258
costs 13-14
Couvin 227-8
cross-country skiing 255, 303
Cuesmes 222
culture 29-40
customs regulations 305
cycling 30-4, 319, see also bike rental
    Antwerp 187
    Belgium 300-1
    Bruges 130, 131, 132
    Brussels 95
    Coo 258
    Diekirch 289
    Dinant 237
    Echternach 291
    La Roche-en-Ardenne 246
    Luxembourg 301-2
    Luxembourg City 274
    Rochefort 238
    tours 132
    Vianden 283
    Western Flanders 17
    Ypres 152

D
Damme 139-40
dance 40, 109, 226
Dardenne brothers 38, 251
David, Gerard 125
De Haan 145
De Panne 148-9
De Westhoek Vlaams Natuurreservaat
    43, 148
Delvaux, Paul 148
diamonds 128, 182, 183, 187, 198
Diekirch 289-90
Diest 209-10
Diksmuide 150
Dinant 236-7
dinner 52
disabilities, travellers with 312-13
discounts 68, 98, 124, 161, 305-6, 324

dog poo 305
d'Oignies, Hugo 233
Domaine de Chevetogne 240
Doornik 218-21
Dranouter 156
drinks 45-51, 53, see also beer,
    breweries, wineries, jenever
driving licence 321
Dudelange 296
Durbuy 248-9
Dutroux, Marc 21
Duvel 49
DVDs 298

E
Earth Explorer 142
Eastern Cantons 30, 262
Echternach 290-2
Ehnen 294
electricity 298
embassies 306-7
emergency services, see inside front
    cover
Ensor, James 142
environmental issues 43-4
Esch-sur-Alzette 295-6
Esch-sur-Sûre 285-6
Ettelbrück 288-9
Eupen 262-4
Euro Space Center 240
Eurolines 317
Eurotunnel 318
euthanasia 21
events, see festivals
exchange rates, see inside front cover

F
fashion 114, 197
    museums 179, 211
    shops 114-15, 138, 169, 196-8
fax services 311
festivals 13, 34, 307
    Antwerp 187
    Ath 222
    Binche 223
    Bruges 132
    Brussels 95-7
    Dranouter 156
    Echternach 291
    film 39, 96, 132, 165
    food 53-5
    Ghent 165-6
    Hasselt 211
    Leuven 207
    Luxembourg City 276

festivals *continued*
Malmédy 223
Mechelen 203
Mons 222
Namur 233
Ostend 143
Redu 240
St Hubert 241
Spa 256
Stavelot 223, 257
Tongeren 215
Tournai 220
Veurne 149
Wiltz 287
Ypres 152
Flanders 30, 119-216, **121**, **172**
Flemish Primitives 125
Fond-de-Gras 296
food 52-64, 307-8, 5, *see also* chocolate
books 52
customs 57
festivals 53-5
internet resources 52, 53
Luxembourg 267
sirop de Liège 262
vegetarian travellers 53
football 32
Forêt de Soignes 117
Formula One 256, 257
Fort Breendonk 205
Frahan-sur-Semois 243

G
gay & lesbian travellers 308
Antwerp 188
Brussels 97
Ghent 165
Luxembourg City 276
genièvre, see jenever
geography
Belgium 41-2
Luxembourg 266
Gezelle, Guido 129
Ghent 160-9, **162-3**, 6
accommodation 165-6
attractions 161
drinking 167-8
entertainment 168-9
festivals 165-6
food 166-7
internet access 161

shopping 169
tourist offices 161
travel to/from 169
travel within 169
walking tour 164-5
gîtes d'étapes 299
golden ales 49-50
golf 91, 303
government 27
Grand Place 69-79, 101-2, 106
Gravensteen 163
Grevenmacher 294
Groeningemuseum 125-7
guesthouses 299
Gutland 288-90

H
Haan 145
Halve Maan 209-10
Han-sur-Lesse 239-40
Hare Krishna 249
Hasselt 210-12
Hautes Fagnes 259-61, 8
Hautes Fagnes-Eifel Nature Park 260
health 326-8
health resorts 255
Heilig-Bloedbasiliek 124, 7
Henri, Grand Duke 273
Hergé 39
Herzogenhügel 260
Het Land van Ooit 214
Het Zwin 42, 146-7
Heysel stadium 32
hikers' huts 299
hiking
accommodation 299
Belgium 302
Berdorf 292
Bouillon 242
Echternach 290
Hautes Fagnes 260
Het Zwin 147
La Roche-en-Ardenne 246
Luxembourg 302
Malmédy 259
Meerdaalwoud 209
Rochefort 238
Schiessentümpel 292
Stavelot 257
Vianden 283
Ypres 152
Hill 60 156
history
beer 45
Belgium 22-8, 96, 159

books 24, 26
independence 25-6, 110
internet resources 22
Luxembourg 266, 269
museums 157
WWI 26
hitching 323
Hitler, Adolf 227
Hoegaarden 49
holidays 308
Holocaust 203
horse riding 246, 303
horse-drawn carriages
Antwerp 187
Bokrijk Openluchtmuseum 213
Bruges 132
Brussels 95
Horta, Victor 37, 81, 87, 88, 92, 93, 110, 219
hostels 299-300
hotels 300
Hugo, Victor 283
Huis van Alijn, 164
hunting 42, 241

I
ice-skating 91, 256, 292
identification 309, 314
immigration 32-3
insurance
car 322
travel 308
health 326
internet access 308
internet resources
accommodation 298
air tickets 316
arts 39, 40
beer 45, 47, 50
Belgium 27
climate 41
environment 42
food 52, 53
health 326
history 22
Luxembourg 266, 267
politics 28
royal family 25
travel 14
weather 41
itineraries 11, 15-18
Antwerp 173, 185-6
Bruges 130-1
Brussels 68, 92-3
Ghent 164-5

000 Map pages
000 Photograph pages

Luxembourg City 271, 275-6
Ypres Salient 154-6

J
jenever 53, 55
cafés 55, 168, 193, 253-4
festival 211
museum 211
shops 138, 196
Jews 203

K
Kalmthoutse Heide Nature Reserve 43
Kasteel Beauvoorde 150
kayaking, *see also* canoeing
Belgium 302-3
Bouillon 242
Coo 258
Dinant 236-7
La Roche-en-Ardenne 246
Kessel-Lo 209
Kirchberg Plateau 273
Knokke-Heist 146
Koksijde 147-8
Koninklijk Museum voor Schone Kunsten 182-3
Kortrijk 157-60
Kusttram 145

L
La Doudou 222
La Ducasse 222
La Roche-en-Ardenne 245-8
Lac de la Haute Sûre 286
Lac de Warfaaz 255
lace 138
courses 138
museums 79-80, 129, 158
shops 115, 138
lambic beers 49
Land van Ooit 214
language 31, 329-36, **31**, *see also
inside front cover*
Bruxellois 83
food 58-64
linguistic divide 31, 208
Luxembourg 266
place names 320
street names 69
Larochette 292-3
legal matters 309
Léopold I 26, 91, 148
Léopold II 26, 37, 91, 96
Léopold III 26-7, 91
Les Jardins d'Annevoie 235

lesbian travellers, *see* gay & lesbian travellers
Leuven 205-9, **206**
Liège 249-54, **250**
accommodation 252-3
attractions 251-2
drinking 253-4
entertainment 254
food 253
travel to/from 254
travel within 254
Lier 199-201
Lillo 199
linguistic divide 31, 208
literature 14, 38
lunch 52
Luxembourg **284**
Luxembourg City 268-81, **270**, **272**
accommodation 276-7
attractions 271-4
drinking 279
entertainment 279-80
festivals 276
food 278-9
internet access 269
shopping 280-1
tourist offices 271
travel to/from 281
travel within 281
walking tour 275-6

M
Maboge 246
Magritte, René 83, 89, 90
Maison Cauchie 93, **7**
Malmédy 223, 258-9
Manneken Pis 80
maps 309
markets 310
Antwerp 192, 198
Brussels 115
Ghent 169
Liège 251
Luxembourg City 279
Malmédy 259
Spa 255
Tongeren 214
measures 298, *see also inside front cover*
Mechelen 201-4, **202**
Meerdaalwoud 209
Memling, Hans 125, 131
Merckx, Eddy 30
metric conversions, *see inside front cover*
Meunier, Constantin 87

military cemeteries 152, 154, 155, 274
mobile phones 311
Mondorf-les-Bains 294
money 13-14, 309-10
discounts 305-6
Mons 221-2
Mosan art 233, 251
Moselle Valley 293-4
motorcycle hire 322
motorcycle travel 316-17, 319, 320-3, **321**
Müllerthal 290-3
multiculturalism 32-3, 266
murals 81, 82, 211, **6**
Musée Bruxellois de la Gueuze 49, 90
museums, *see also individual museums*
Apollinaire, Guillaume 257
art 83-4, 86, 87-8, 125-8, 142, 158, 163-4, 169, 182-3, 185, 200, 219, 221, 226, 232, 251, 252, 261, 273-4
Battle of Waterloo 224
Bonaparte, Napoleon 224
Bouillon, Godefroid de 242
Brel, Jacques 80
Breugel the Elder, Pieter 82
carnival 222, 259
comic strips 81
Delvaux, Paul 148
diamonds 128, 182
drinks 49, 79, 90, 156, 211, 294
Ensor, James 142
fashion 179, 211
folklore 129, 220, 221, 251, 261, 287
food 80, 125, 149, 246, 263
Gezelle, Guido 129
history 79, 84, 86-7, 94, 157, 184, 202, 211, 212-13, 214, 244, 257, 262, 271-3, 283, 289, 290
Horta, Victor 87
Hugo, Victor 283
lace 79-80, 129, 158
Magritte, René 89
Meunier, Constantin 87
music 80, 83, 156, 180
Patton, General George S 288-9
religion 124, 206, 209
Rockox, Nicolaas 180
Rops, Félicien 233-63
Rubens, Pieter Paul 181
Van Gogh, Vincent 222
Wiertz, Antoine 86
WWI 152, 155-6
WWII 143, 202, 227, 244, 246-7, 274, 287, 288-9

music 39-40
festivals 95, 96, 132, 156, 165,
187, 207, 276, 287, 307
Gregorian chants 288
museums 80, 83, 156, 180
saxophone 236

N
Nadrin 246
Namur 231-5, **232**
Nationaal Park Hoge Kempen 42
national parks & nature reserves 42-3
De Westhoek Vlaams
Natuurreservaat 43, 148
Hautes Fagnes Nature Reserve 260
Hautes Fagnes-Eifel Nature Park 260
Het Zwin 42, 146-7
Kalmthoutse Heide Nature
Reserve 43
Nationaal Park Hoge Kempen 42
Parc et Réserve Naturelle de
Furfooz 237
Zwin-Polder 42, 147
Nationale Plantentuin van België
117-18
NATO 27
nature reserves, see national parks &
nature reserves
Neuhaus 54
newspapers 33, 298
nicknames 215
Nieuwpoort 147
Nijvel 223-4
Nivelles 223-4

O
Octave 307
Onze Lieve Vrouwekathedraal 179
Oostduinkerke 147-8, **8**
Oostkantons 262-4
opening hours 303
Orval 48, 243-4
Ostend 140-5, **141**
Ostkantons 262-4
oud bruin beers 50
Oudenaarde 160

P
paardevissers 147, **8**
painting 13, 34-6
books 35

palaces 85
Panamarenko 36
Panne 148-9
Parc à Gibier 247
Parc d'Aventures 285
Parc et Réserve Naturelle de Furfooz 237
Parc Merveilleux 296
Parc Naturel de la Haute Sûre 286
Park Bellewaerde 156
passport 314
Patton, General George S 274, 288-9
pédalo hire 255
perfume 232
Petite Somme 249
Pétrusse Casemates 273
Philippe, Crown Prince 21, 91
photography 310
pilgrimage 210
Planckendael 205
planning 12-14
plants 42
playgrounds 88, 94, 117, 187, 209,
210, 213, 214, 238-9, 240, 276,
285, 288, 290, 296
Plopsa Coo 258
Plopsa Indoor 211
Plopsaland 148
politics
Belgium 21, 28, 33
internet resources 28
Luxembourg 266
Poperinge 156-7
population
Belgium 30
Luxembourg 266
postal services 310
Provinciaal Recreatiedomein
Kessel-Lo 209
Provinciedomein Halve Maan 209-10

R
racism 33
Radhadesh 249
radio 298
Redu 240
religion
Belgium 34
Luxembourg 266
museums 124, 206, 209
Remich 293-4
restaurants 55
Rochefort 48, 238-9
Rochehaut 243
rock climbing 303
Rockox, Nicolaas 180

Roma 203
Rops, Félicien 233
royal families
Belgium 21, 25, 26, 91
Luxembourg 273
royal palaces 84, 273
RSC Anderlecht 111
Rubens, Pieter Paul 35, 179, 181
Rubenshuis 181, **6**
Rumelange 296
Ruttermolen 215

S
safe travel 305
hitching 323
road hazards 322, 323
St Baafskathedraal 161-3, **6**
St Carolus-Borromeuskerk 180
St Hubert 240-1
St Idesbald 147-8
St Martens-Latem 169
St Martin winery 293
St Willibrord 290
Sax, Antoine-Joseph 236
saxophone 236
Scherpenheuvel 210
Schiessentüumpel 292
senior travellers 306
separatism 21, 29, 31
shopping 310
Antwerp 195-8
beer 51, 113, 138, 196
Bruges 138
Brussels 112-15
chocolate 113, 138, 196
comic strips 114, 169
fashion 114-15, 138, 169,
196-8
Ghent 169
jenever 138
lace 115, 138
Leuven 208
Luxembourg City 280-1
shopping galleries 112
Simenon, Georges 252, 253
sirop de Liège 262
skiing 255, 303
smoking 57, 305
soccer 32
Spa 254-7
sports
cycling 30
football 32
Formula One 256, 257
tennis 32

squash 91
Stavelot 223, 257-8
Steen 185
Steichen, Edward 287
Straffe Hendrik Blonde 49
surrealism 35
swimming 91-2, 94, 210, 238, 242, 255, 290, 292, 294, 295

T
tax 297
Tchantchès 252
tearooms 55
Technopolis 204-5
telephone services 310-11
tennis 32, 91
Thalys 318
theatre 40
theft 305
theme parks
    Aquatopia 186
    Boudewijn Seapark 131
    Bruparck 94
    Earth Explorer 142
    Het Land van Ooit 214
    Parc Merveilleux 296
    Park Bellewaerde 156
    Plopsa Coo 258
    Plopsa Indoor 211
    Plopsaland 148
    Walibi & Aqualibi 94
tick bites 327
time 311
Tintin 39, 115, 138
tipping 309-10
toilets 311
Tongeren 213-16, **214**
tourist information 311-12
Tournai 218-21, **219**
tours
    bike 187
    boat 187, 200, 235, 236
    bus 95, 132, 140, 187, 276
    canal 132, 165
    horse-drawn carriages 95, 132, 187, 213

toy-train 276
    walking 95, 130-1, 164-5, 185-6, 275-6
train travel 318, **324**
    to/from Belgium & Luxembourg 317-19
    within Belgium 324-5
Trappist beers 46-8
travel to/from Belgium & Luxembourg 314-19
travel within Belgium & Luxembourg 319-25
treasury 232
TV 33, 298

U
Unesco World Heritage sites 18, 36, 129
    Belfort 124
    Clervaux castle 287
    Groot Begijnhof 206
    La Ducasse 222

V
vacations 308
vaccinations 326
Vallée des Sept Châteaux 288
Van Beirendonck, Walter 197, 198
Van Damme, Jean-Claude 38
Van der Weyden, Rogier 125
Van Dyck, Antoon 35
Van Eyck, Jan 125, 161, 6
Van Gogh, Vincent 222
vegetarian travellers 53, 56-7
Verviers 261-2
Veurne 149-50
Vianden 283-5, 8
video cameras 310
video systems 298
Villers-la-Ville 225-6
visas 313, *see also* passports
Vlaams *rood* beers 50

W
Walibi & Aqualibi 94
walking, *see* hiking

walking tours
    Antwerp 185-6
    Bruges 130-1
    Brussels 95
    Ghent 164-5
    Luxembourg City 275-6
Wallonia 30, 217-64, **218**, **232**
war cemeteries 152, 154, 155, 274
Waterloo 224-5
weather 12, 41, 305
weights 298, *see also inside front cover*
Wellington, Duke of 224, 225
Westhoek Vlaams Natuurreservaat 43, 148
Westmalle 47
Westvleteren 47, 150
white beers 48-9
White March 21
whitewater rafting 258
Wiertz, Antoine 86
Wiltz 286-7
wineries 293, 294
women travellers 313
women's health 328
Wormeldange 294
Wulveringem 150
WWI 26, 147, 148, 150-1, 152, 153-6, 266
    museums 152, 155-6
WWII 148, 202, 203, 205, 266, 274, 288, 292
    American Memorial 244, 259
    German Headquarters 227
    museums 143, 202, 227, 244, 246-7, 274, 287, 288-9

Y
Ypres 150-3, **151**
Ypres Salient 153-6, **155**

Z
Zeebrugge 145-6
Zoutleeuw 216
Zwin 42, 146-7
Zwin-Polder 42, 147

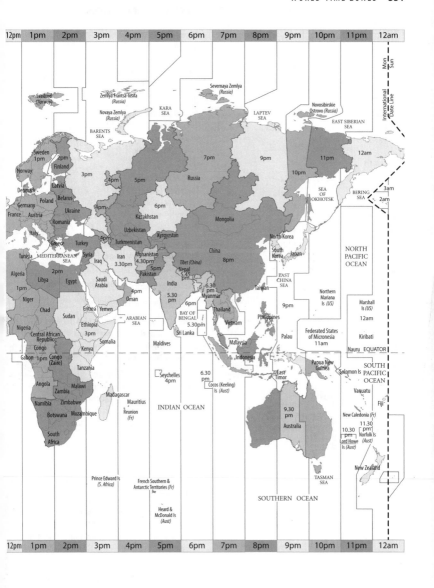

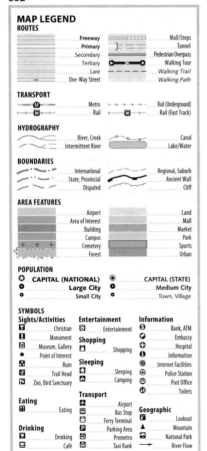

MAP LEGEND

ROUTES

Freeway	Mall/Steps
Primary	Tunnel
Secondary	Pedestrian Overpass
Tertiary	Walking Tour
Lane	Walking Trail
One-Way Street	Walking Path

TRANSPORT

Metro	Rail (Underground)
Rail	Rail (Fast Track)

HYDROGRAPHY

River, Creek	Canal
Intermittent River	Lake/Water

BOUNDARIES

International	Regional, Suburb
State, Provincial	Ancient Wall
Disputed	Cliff

AREA FEATURES

Airport	Land
Area of Interest	Mall
Building	Market
Campus	Park
Cemetery	Sports
Forest	Urban

POPULATION

CAPITAL (NATIONAL)	CAPITAL (STATE)
Large City	Medium City
Small City	Town, Village

SYMBOLS

Sights/Activities
Christian
Monument
Museum, Gallery
Point of Interest
Ruin
Trail Head
Zoo, Bird Sanctuary

Eating
Eating

Drinking
Drinking
Café

Entertainment
Entertainment

Shopping
Shopping

Sleeping
Sleeping
Camping

Transport
Airport
Bus Stop
Ferry Terminal
Parking Area
Premetro
Taxi Rank

Information
Bank, ATM
Embassy
Hospital
Information
Internet Facilities
Police Station
Post Office
Toilets

Geographic
Lookout
Mountain
National Park
River Flow

LONELY PLANET OFFICES

Australia
Head Office
Locked Bag 1, Footscray, Victoria 3011
☎ 03 8379 8000, fax 03 8379 8111
talk2us@lonelyplanet.com.au

USA
150 Linden St, Oakland, CA 94607
☎ 510 893 8555, toll free 800 275 8555
fax 510 893 8572
info@lonelyplanet.com

UK
72-82 Rosebery Ave,
Clerkenwell, London EC1R 4RW
☎ 020 7841 9000, fax 020 7841 9001
go@lonelyplanet.co.uk

Published by Lonely Planet Publications Pty Ltd
ABN 36 005 607 983

© Lonely Planet Publications Pty Ltd 2007

© photographers as indicated 2007

Cover photograph: Galler pralines, or filled chocolates, in Brussels, Leanne Logan/Lonely Planet Images. Many of the images in this guide are available for licensing from Lonely Planet Images: www .lonelyplanetimages.com.

Printed through Colorcraft Ltd, Hong Kong.
Printed in China